KT-199-268

JOWETT

by the same author

★

OXFORD APOSTLES

1. Marble bust by H. R. Hope Pinker
(*Balliol*)

JOWETT

a portrait with background

by

GEOFFREY FABER

Fellow of All Souls College

FABER & FABER LIMITED
24 Russell Square
London

First published in mcmlvii
by Faber and Faber Limited
24 Russell Square London W.C.1
Printed in Great Britain by
R. MacLehose and Company Limited
The University Press Glasgow
All rights reserved

© *Geoffrey Cust Faber*
1957

'*You laugh at my pope Jowett, but really I know of nobody so clever.*'

James Lonsdale to his mother, 1842

(Here's the town-gate reached: there's the market-place
Gaping before us.)
Yea, this in him was the peculiar grace
(Hearten our chorus!)
That before living he'd learn how to live—
No end to learning:
Earn the means first.—God surely will contrive
Use of our earning.

Browning: *The Grammarian's Funeral*

'*But we want to know his faults—that is probably the most interesting part of him.*'

Jowett to Lady Tavistock, 1885

To

FRANK VIGOR MORLEY

Contents

Illustrations

Of the fourteen illustrations nine are reproduced with the kind consent of the Master and Fellows of Balliol College; number 2 from the copy in Balliol Library. Number 13 is reproduced by courtesy of the Oxford City Council. All these subjects have been specially photographed by Messrs. Thomson-Photos of Oxford. Particular thanks are due to their photographer for his care and skill; and to Mr. Quinn for making the necessary arrangements, and for providing most of the information, upon which the notes (below) are based. The other four illustrations are reproduced by courtesy of the National Portrait Gallery and *Hulton Picture Library*.

NOTES ON SOME OF THE ILLUSTRATIONS

1. The Balliol bust belonged to the late Sir David Kelly and was bought by Balliol in 1955. Sir David was a Magdalen man, born in 1891. He was educated at St. Paul's, but this hardly explains his ownership of the bust. It had stood in his garden and is a little discoloured. A bust, which is almost certainly this one, was exhibited in the Royal Academy in 1892. There is a replica (how exact I cannot say) in the entrance hall of the Oxford Examination Schools dated 1896; Balliol also has a small plaster cast inscribed 'H. R. Hope Pinker sculpt. 1893'. Pinker was born 1849, died 1927. The bust is a realistic and convincing likeness of a man still in full vigour. I guess that the original (whether the Balliol or the Schools bust) was done *circa* 1880; but that is a mere guess.

2. This was a newspaper drawing from a photograph taken by Jowett's butler, Perroud, who succeeded Knight. (For the *Westminster Extra* see below, 435.)

5. Reproduced in the *Life and Letters*. Re-photographed for the present volume.

6. No likeness of the young Morier seems to exist. Balliol has one or two photographs of him, but they are not to be compared with this superb photograph.

7. and 8. These are intensified photographs of two *cartes de visite* in a Balliol album, which seemed faded beyond all hope of reproduction. They exhibit remarkable skill on the part of the Oxford photographer. The first was an amateur photograph of Jowett's father, taken in France by William Wilberforce, the Bishop of Oxford's brother. It must, therefore, be dated not later than 1856, when Jowett's parents had returned from France to England. (It was sent to Abbott by Sidney Irwin.) The second was a professional photograph of Jowett, taken in Oxford by Hills and Saunders. Mr. Quinn thinks 'perhaps about 1860?' I agree.

9. The nearest I can get to the Florence Nightingale of 1862.

10. Reproduced as a frontispiece to the *Letters*. The engraving there used, though made by Walker and Boutall, has a steely quality which misrepresents the soft tones of Laugée's drawing. The photograph here reproduced is made from the original drawing, which belonged to the late Professor A. V. Dicey and was presented to Balliol by Mrs. Dicey in 1922.

11. Also reproduced in the *Life and Letters*.

12. The date 1889, painted by the artist, is misleading. Jowett sat to Watts between '77 and '79 (*L. & L.* ii, 109). The conception of the portrait obviously belongs to that stage of his life, not to a date only four years before his death. Whether Watts dated it 1889 by mistake for 1879, or whether the portrait was laid aside unfinished for ten years, is a question to which I do not know the answer.

13. This very amusing picture was taken in 1892 by Henry W. Taunt, an Oxford photographer, outside the Master's lodge. (A print, from which the President of Trinity had been obliterated, not without damage to the figure of Jowett, was given to me by a friend a few years ago.) Taunt aimed to write a book about 'The Master: Reminiscences of Jowett and Balliol College'. The MS of this unpublished book (Oxford City Library) contains the following lively passage:

For many years the late Master would never be photographed. One day (July 19th '92) seeing him and Sir Henry Acland engaged in conversation with the President of Trinity at his own door we quietly levelled a camera at them and shouted to attract their attention. The result was the above snap shot. Sir Henry Acland on the right [*sic*] seems very amused at the idea. The Master in the centre has a mixed expression of surprise and perhaps a little annoyance at being interrupted. The President of Trinity turned his head at the moment of exposure to see what was proceeding and thus unfortunately has a double expression which somewhat mars the completeness of the picture but the result as a whole is characteristic.

The President of Trinity was H. G. Woods.

Preface and Acknowledgments

Two debts greatly over-ride my many others.

The first is to Balliol, for allowing me to examine Jowettiana belonging to the college at leisure in my own house. I wish that I could dare to indicate my gratitude for this generous loan by dedicating my book to the Master and Fellows of Balliol; but I have deliberately refrained from asking permission to do so. Such a dedication would seem not only to imply their collective approval of what I have written, but to suggest that this book has been, in some degree, officially inspired. Much as I owe to the help and criticisms of individual Balliol friends, and to the material freely lent me, it was I who chose to write about Jowett, not Balliol who asked me to do so. Not the slightest attempt has been made to influence either the manner or the matter of my book.

My second debt is to a man dead for nearly fifty years — Lewis Campbell, who wrote the first volume of *The Life and Letters of Benjamin Jowett*, published in 1897. In Appendix I on 'Abbott and Campbell' I have described the circumstances which governed the composition of the official biography and resulted in Campbell's subordination to his junior co-biographer Abbott. My overall debt to the two volumes of the *Life and Letters* and to the supplementary volume of *Letters* (1899) is very great. It is larger to Campbell than to Abbott. But it is not this debt to the published biography, or to Campbell's part in it, that I seek to acknowledge here. What I have specially to acknowledge is the evidence which Campbell was obliged to leave behind him unused in what I have rather grandiloquently called the 'Jowett Papers'.

The Jowettiana lent to me by Balliol comprised the Nightingale Letters as well as the Jowett Papers.

With Jowett's letters to Florence Nightingale neither Campbell nor Abbott had anything to do, except that she sent them extracts, copied out by herself in pencil, which she allowed — indeed wished — them to publish, on condition that her name was not disclosed. The letters themselves and the copyright in them passed eventually into the ownership of Balliol. Sir Edward Cook had access to them, while he was writing his *Life of Florence Nightingale* (1914). That book contains an admirable account of Jowett's letters, limited (rather unfortunately) by the design of exhibiting 'the influence of his character upon hers'. Sufficient light, Cook thought, had been thrown upon Jowett's own views by the extracts published in the *Life and Letters*, though the reader had not been told 'the name of the recipient'. By Cook's advice a few of Jowett's letters were withheld from those given to Balliol and were later deposited in the British Museum with other Nightingale papers. The rest were bound up in eight volumes; and these were the volumes loaned to me by Balliol.

A complete edition of this extraordinary correspondence, between a man and a woman of equal but different genius, covering a period of more than thirty years, is being edited for publication by Mr. J. N. Bryson, Fellow and Librarian of Balliol. Miss Nightingale's part in the correspondence will be represented in Mr. Bryson's edition by a few of her later letters recently found at Balliol, and by the epitomes she herself sometimes made of letters which she particularly wished to remember.

Concerning the Jowett Papers there is not a great deal which I need add to the brief account given in Appendix II. They came to me in a number of boxes (six of Jowett's deed-boxes and a large wooden box). The contents of the boxes were not systematically arranged; and there was no accompanying guide or list. It was not an easy or quick matter to discover what was of new value and what was not. I formed the opinion that Abbott probably put the papers back, not much caring what went where, in the belief that the job had been done once and for all and that nobody would ever again think it worth while to go through the amorphous mass of used or discarded material. The fact that most, perhaps all, of Campbell's 'stuff' was found in the boxes, but little or nothing of Abbott's, seems to support this inference. For example, the whole series of Campbell's letters to his co-biographer is there; but not Abbott's replies. Before I returned the boxes to Balliol I arranged and listed their contents as well as I could. The rough guide to 'the general disposition of the Jowett Papers', which I then made out, is reproduced on pages 440–1. I used an additional old brown tin box of my own, in order to house the Nightingale Letters. These are not part of the Jowett Papers and had been separately delivered to me. I put the series of small 'personal notebooks' into the same box.

This rough list gives some idea of the very miscellaneous character of the papers. It does not, perhaps, quite convey the apparent absence of fresh biographical material, which seemed at first sight to be almost complete. Even the private notebooks looked to have been so thoroughly gutted that they had nothing more to offer. This was not quite the fact. Two notebooks in particular (those of 1841 and 1867) yielded new evidence of great interest. Other real *trouvailles* turned up in the slow process of sorting the contents of the boxes. These will make their appearances in the following pages. Most important of them all is Campbell's 'M.E.' notebook, which I have reproduced *verbatim* in Chapter XIII. But for this notebook nothing would now be known of Jowett's one approach to marriage or of 'M.E.''s sudden eclipse by 'F.N.' The complex emotional storm which overtook him in his middle forties, still difficult to describe and understand, would otherwise remain almost impenetrably obscure. If this were all that Campbell had left behind him, it would be enough to justify him. It is very far from being all; but, having tried to indicate in a general way what I owe to Campbell, I must leave the rest of my debt to discover itself.

There are two particular matters to which I ought briefly to draw the reader's attention. The first of these is the impossibility of exact reference to documents in the Jowett Papers. I cannot use — at any rate I have not tried to use — my own makeshift and amateurish lists as bases of reference. Nor do I wish to burden my book with unintelligible symbols. Where it has seemed necessary to support a statement made in the text, and derived from the Jowett Papers, I have cited the 'Jowett Papers' (or *J.P.*), usually with some indication of the nature of the document, such as the name of the writer or the date of a letter.

The other matter is the form in which I became acquainted with Jowett's letters to his mother and sister and his young cousin Sidney Irwin — letters of which I have made some considerable use. What I saw were copies. The originals have recently been found; too late for me to inspect them. Of the five letters I have used only two.

In the field of copyright I am grateful to Viscountess Milner and to Mr. Philip Gell for permission to reproduce the two letters in the first section of Chapter XVII. I have to thank my friend Sir Llewellyn Woodward and his publishers, the Clarendon Press, for permission to reproduce (on page 192) a passage from his book *The Age of Reform*. Dr. Joan Evans has most generously allowed me to make free use of *Time and Chance* in the section of Chapter XVIII called 'Tradescant's Ark'. She has placed me further in her debt by a number of valuable comments.

I wish particularly to thank several readers who have given me unstinted help and criticism. Mr. Cyril Bailey, *doyen* of Balliol, must allow me to confess how much I have profited by his kindly and incisive comments twelve years ago on the first, prolix draft of nearly half my book.

Next, I owe more than I can briefly explain to the private friend (like myself, not a Balliol man) whose encouragement led me to begin, and whose constant girding and goading compelled me to finish an effort I have often been on the brink of abandoning, as beyond my powers. This is the friend to whom it is dedicated, Mr. Frank Morley. Except for Mr. Cyril Bailey he is the only person who read the first over-long draft of the opening chapters. He has also read the penultimate draft of the whole MS and the paged proofs. It is worth saying that Mr. Morley is an American-born citizen, a Rhodes Scholar of New College, and a mathematician as well as a man of letters; for this indicates the universality of Jowett's claim upon the interest of sensible men everywhere.

To three other friends, who have read through the penultimate draft, I owe a similar debt for encouragement and shrewd comment. One of these is a Balliol man — Mr. John Bryson. I cannot sufficiently thank him for the expert help he has given me at many points of difficulty. The other two are my own editorial colleagues — Mr. Alan Pringle and Mr. Charles Monteith — who have both given me invaluable advice and have (to my surprise) refused to let me make more than a few minor cuts in a book which I felt sure they would think far too long.

I am deeply in debt to Dr. Richard Hunt of Balliol, who has rescued me at the eleventh hour from some errors of fact and inference, especially concerning Scott's election to the Mastership in 1854 and Jowett's failure to acquire freedom to marry. If only I had known Dr. Hunt earlier!

I am also greatly in debt to Mr. John Sparrow, Warden of All Souls. His unfailing interest and sympathy have helped me to stay the course. It was he who introduced me to Atlay's *Victorian Chancellors* and reminded me of Benson's *Walter Pater*—two books which have contributed not a little to mine. He has read my proofs and prevented me from several lapses and inaccuracies.

Not the least helpful of my counsellors has been Mr. V. Quinn, Assistant Librarian at Balliol. His courtesy to a stranger within his gates has been such that the stranger will never forget it. I hope that the spirit of Jowett revisits the Library and looks over Mr. Quinn's shoulder. If so, it is quickened by the sight of a very beautiful script.

I am grateful to Mrs. David Bland for compiling an index so full and accurate that the author himself has used it repeatedly. Last of all I must try to suggest, since I can never fully say, what I owe to my secretary, Miss Ash, who has typed and retyped the whole of my MS (many parts of it more than twice). Without her unfailing skill it could not have reached a form fit either for printer or reader.

GEOFFREY FABER

Minsted, *Easter*, 1957

CHAPTER I

Introductory

1. THE BARE BONES

On 15th April 1817 a Mrs. Jowett of Peckham, whose husband was in business with his father as a furrier, gave birth to her second son. The boy was named Benjamin after his father and his father's father. Born within three years of his parents' marriage he was the third child in a family of nine, of whom only two — Benjamin and his elder sister Emily — were to outlive either parent. The family business, founded by his great-grandfather Henry Jowett, had passed from prosperity into decline. Within ten years it would be extinct; the father's incompetence would isolate the boy from his home and breed in his mind lasting contempt for worldly failure.

On 1st October 1893 the moon shone through the windows of Headley Park, Hampshire,[1] upon the 'beautiful marble face and the shining white hair' of the dead Master of Balliol. Not only to those who stood by the moonlit bed, but to many others in many walks of life, it seemed that a sustaining force had been withdrawn that night from their lives. Inheriting the stigma of trade without its compensating advantages, hampered by poverty and unhelped by influence, cradled in a narrow evangelicalism and separated by temperament and physique from the intimacies and habits of ordinary men, the suburban baby had lived to become one of the key-figures of Victorian England, the mentor-in-chief of its golden age.

Nothing of serious value has been written about Jowett since Campbell's and Abbott's biography was published in 1897. The significance of his career and the character of his achievement have been generally forgotten. To an increasing number of educated people his name means nothing, unless it reminds them of the celebrated quatrain which, when it was first printed, ran thus:

> First come I. My name is J—w—tt.
> There's no knowledge, but I know it.

[1] He had gone there to stay with one of his favourite ex-pupils, Sir Robert Wright, a Judge of the Queen's Bench. The house is now (1956) a Polish hostel.

I am Master of this College.
What I don't know, isn't knowledge.[1]

Yet Jowett was one of the greater Victorians. I have called him a key-figure. He was more than that; but the phrase goes deep enough to provoke the question, why no resurrectionist has tried to lift him out of his tomb. One answer stands out above others. When Jowett died, his Mastership of Balliol had lasted for almost a quarter century; it overhung his earlier achievement as a tutor of genius. He was an old man, head of a famous, if small, society. There was not very much more, so it seemed, to be said about that, than had been already said in the *Life and Letters*. The awakening tide of twentieth-century interest in the Victorian age passed him by, almost as if he were an awkwardly large specimen of a fossil better studied from smaller and more amusing examples.

It is a pity that Lytton Strachey did not include Jowett among his *Eminent Victorians*.[2] To his portrait of the 'puzzled' Dr. Arnold he might so easily have added a complementary portrait of an un-puzzled Professor Jowett. He would, then, have seemed to cover the whole higher educational scene in the period he sought to illustrate. Had he done so, he would have destroyed one legend by inventing another. But at least he would have kept the memory of Jowett alive; and other explorers of the nineteenth century, more concerned to discover its virtues than to satirize its foibles, would have taken up the challenge. The difficulty, which first confronts the modern would-be biographer of Jowett, is that he must begin by telling his readers who Jowett was and what he did.

Nothing is easier than to lay out the bare bones. Benjamin Jowett was born at Peckham in 1817. He was a day-boy at St. Paul's for seven years, living alone in lodgings all this time. He won an open scholarship at Balliol, and was elected a fellow while still an undergraduate. When he was twenty-five he was appointed one of the three Balliol tutors by the 'Old Master', Dr. Jenkyns. His tutorship lasted until he became Master himself in 1870. He was then fifty-three. He died unmarried in 1893, at the age of seventy-six.

---

[1] From *The Masque of B-ll--l*, a set of witty verses upon a number of Balliol personalities, printed and circulated by a group of undergraduates in 1881. Mr. Cyril Bailey's letter in *The Times* of 30th August 1954 settles the printed version; but the jingle had been floating around from mouth to mouth for some little time and was probably tailored for the Broadsheet. As I first heard it, it ran thus:

> *I am the great Professor Jowett.*
> *What there is to know, I know it.*
> *I am the Master of Balliol College,*
> *And what I don't know isn't knowledge.*

[2] Jowett has a couple of mocking pages in the essay on Florence Nightingale. See below, 308–9.

His professional life falls, therefore, into two periods: twenty-eight years as tutor, twenty-three as Master.

The first (and the more interesting) of these two periods was broken by a decade of severe frustration. In 1854, when the Old Master died, Jowett was bitterly disappointed in his expectation of being elected Master; and for the next ten or eleven years he and his friends were in an unhappy minority at Balliol. The tide turned finally in his favour in 1865. But in 1855 he was appointed by Lord Palmerston to the Regius Professorship of Greek. This seemed at first to be a consolation for his disappointment in Balliol. In fact, it involved him in a long and humiliating persecution for his 'heretical' opinions. This tide also ran against him for ten years, until Christ Church at last raised his professorial stipend of £40 a year to £500.

Flesh will be put on these bones in later chapters. Here, as to the causes of the persecution, it need be said only that they were theological. Jowett had, of course, taken orders soon after his appointment as a tutor. At that date it was a statutory requirement that fellows of colleges must normally be ordained within a few years of their election.[1] Jowett had no desire to avoid this obligation for himself, though he was entirely at one with the removal of it for others. He took his clerical profession seriously. Theology was his first, perhaps his abiding love. His theological views, however, underwent a long process of change. When he went up to Balliol he was an evangelical — like most of his generation. Unlike many of them, he resisted the extraordinary pull of the 'Oxford Movement'. His own mind, turning away from the evangelical party then dominant in the Church, embraced 'liberalism'. That was a 'heresy', equally detested by the mutually opposed 'high' and 'low' wings of the Anglican church militant.

To this twofold hatred, this alliance of enemies united by a common desire to exclude private judgment from Anglican theology, Jowett had, perhaps rather naively and prematurely, exposed himself by two published essays. The first of these was an essay on the doctrine of the Atonement, in his commentary upon the Epistles of St. Paul (1855). The second was an essay on the interpretation of Scripture, which he contributed to the notorious symposium *Essays and Reviews* (1860). More will be said, later on, about these two essays and about the circumstances and consequences of their publication. They are mentioned here, only in order to make this quick sketch of his career intelligible.

More will be said, too, about the movement of Jowett's mind in the

[1] This was finally abolished at Oxford by the Executive Commissioners of 1854.

field of theology. A systematic account of this is impossible, since after 1860 he published no theological writings. In 1870 he wrote that he was glad to have held his tongue 'because he began to see things more clearly'. His final position was certainly 'modernist'; as certainly, it was not that of atheism or mere agnosticism. It always rested upon a simple and genuine piety.

His main life-work lay with pupils and friends and with Balliol and Oxford. These constituted his *monumentum aere perennius*. But he left another monument of lasting value in the great translation and interpretation of Plato, which occupied him for a long part of his life.

By education Jowett was a classical scholar. He was not, and never seriously wished to be, a philologer or a highly specialized and exact scholar of either the old or the modern pattern. Scholarship, for him, was a method of bringing the past to bear on the present, of enlarging and not of contracting the field of thought. The quotation from *The Grammarian's Funeral*, which I have put after the title-page of this volume, is, therefore, not wholly apt. But it does indicate the essential truth about Jowett. He had to 'learn how to live', and he learned a part of that lesson through his study of the great Greeks.

By temperament and inclination he was a philosopher. It was his influence which transformed the final classical examination at Oxford, called 'Greats', into an examination which came to cover modern as well as ancient philosophy. He was the first man in Oxford to master the new, exciting, bafflingly difficult system of Hegel; possibly even the first Englishman. But he was never a philosopher of the closet. He was a thinker after Plato's kind, seeking to share with others what he had found for himself and to use it for the practical ends of society.

These ends he served through his pupils and his friends, and not by any attempt to play the part of public sage. His influence upon English higher administration in the later decades of the nineteenth century, and by natural consequence in the opening decades of the twentieth century, was very great indeed: much greater than has been generally understood, since it was an indirect influence, discoverable only by studying the life-stories of the men to whom he communicated it through his gospel of hard and unselfish work.

I do not know that Jowett ever accepted any political label. He was not a Conservative, and not a Radical; not a Tory, and not a Whig. I doubt if he would have consented even to the political epithet of Liberal. He was, of course, a reformist — owning his kind of intelligence, he could not have been otherwise in the church-ridden Oxford of the early middle nineteenth century. He was a leader of the reforming party in the Univer-

sity, and one of the men to whom the reforms made by the Executive
Commissioners of 1854 were due. This naturally made him an object of
hatred or suspicion to those who disliked and resisted reform. Here,
again, the story is far more complex than it is possible to explain in a few
sentences. There was a vital difference between Jowett's ideas of reform
and those of Mr. Gladstone; and between his ideas of the functions of a
University and those which have since prevailed. But these are matters
for later discussion.

2. BACK-DROP

Fully to understand the nature of the ascendancy, which Jowett came
to exercise, would be to understand not only Jowett himself and his
Oxford environment but the greater part of nineteenth-century England.
We still stand too near his century to be capable of knowing it objec-
tively. Its controversies are not yet approachable in an impartial spirit.
They are the parents of our own perplexities. Even if they seem to us to
be dead, we are seldom able to play fairly with their ghosts. This is especially true of those religious disputes in which Jowett figured either, in
Carlyle's violent metaphor, as the deserting sentinel who deserves to be
shot or, to borrow his own hopeful description of Dean Stanley, as a
leader of those engaged in 'the great work of placing religion on a rational
basis'. Modern churchmen are seldom to be trusted upon these recent
battlefields; they are too anxious to have it thought that the war was a
war about nothing. The rest of us are in no better case; we are too anxious
for our own doubts or disbelief.

These are not reasons for avoiding the attempt to understand the world
into which our grandfathers or great-grandfathers were born. But they
are danger-signals which explorers of an age so near, yet so remote, are
rash to ignore. Schooling themselves to suspect their own prejudices,
they can begin to make some small use of the advantage gained from the
passage of time. Perspective still rules their view of the nineteenth century; but it is the perspective of a landscape seen now from a moderate
height. The way taken through the country by such a man as Jowett has
much to tell them both of the hazards which determined the traveller's
route and of the traveller himself. Far better than contemporaries, such
as Sir Leslie Stephen, they can guess the ultimate purpose and sympathize with the changing direction of the seventy-six years long
journey.

If the fortune of the Peckham baby was unpredictable, so were the fortunes of the infant century. The lassitude which followed the long effort of the Napoleonic wars exhibited itself in the extraordinary decline of English letters. The initial wave of rebellion against the Augustans had spent its force before Jowett was born. Coleridge was a tame lion at Highgate, Wordsworth on his dignity at Rydal Mount. The second and the eagerer wave died, with Keats and Shelley and Byron, before the 'twenties were half through. Except for the tail end of the Waverley Novels and a faint gleam or two from Grasmere, the succeeding decade — from, say, 1825 to 1835 — was all but barren. The third and fourth volumes of Landor's *Imaginary Conversations*, the earlier and least readable of Disraeli's novels, a little Peacock, a lot of Leigh Hunt, the first shallow 'best-sellers' of Bulwer-Lytton, the poetry of Felicia Hemans, a few good things by Hood, a *jeu d'esprit* from De Quincey, and Keble's *Christian Year* — such were the best remembered productions of Jowett's school-days. They were not prophetic of things to come.

In 1830, it is true, when Jowett was thirteen, a young man of twenty-one, with an undergraduate's reputation at Cambridge, published *Poems chiefly Lyrical*, and in 1832 a second volume of *Poems*. Later on the famous poet and the Balliol tutor were to become fast friends. But even 'The Lotus-Eaters'— a poem of which Jowett can surely never have approved — failed to make the name of Tennyson known. In 1833 another young man of twenty-one, with no reputation at all, made an even less successful bid for fame with *Pauline*, repeated in 1835 with *Paracelsus*. Browning, also, was to be one of Jowett's friends: it was of him that Jowett once said, 'I had no idea that there was a perfectly sensible poet in the world.' Another new and powerful voice was heard in 1833, when *Sartor Resartus* upset the digestions of a few omnivorous readers. Carlyle, whom Jowett at once admired and detested, was the first of these three newcomers to make a popular reputation with his *History of the French Revolution*. Tennyson had five years more to wait for the beginning of his reign, Browning much longer. But the day of the little men was passing before the 'thirties were out. Dickens was in full swing by 1840; and the sequence of Victorian giants unrolled itself thenceforward in a crescendo of confident genius.

Whatever future an intelligent and sensitive critic might have anticipated for English literature in 1817, it could not possibly have borne any resemblance to the event. If there was a factor common to most of the great Victorians, it was an optimistic faith in progress as opposed to revolution. In 1817 there was no visible ground for optimism of this kind. The year of Jowett's birth found England enfeebled by her victory over Napoleon and threatened with civil disaster. Spiritually and mentally and economically the country presented an appearance of empty exhaustion. The Church and the Universities, upon which the hand of the Church was closed with a death-like grip, were still for the most part living in an eighteeenth-century dream. The fashionable world revolved about a fancy-dress court. Authority, whether of high or of low degree, was more often animated — so far as it was animated at all — by a sense of privilege than by a sense of responsibility.

Unemployment, hunger, mass pauperization, riots repressed by panic-stricken legislators — everything seemed to forebode either the collapse of the old aristocratic order or its transformation into a desperate tyranny. The peasantry and yeomanry, the ballast which for centuries had stabilized the ship of state, were all but down and out. An appalling collapse of prices, threatening the newfound wealth of landowners, drove them into the disastrous folly of the Corn Laws. The first phase of the industrial revolution had completed the evil consequences of the agricultural revolution and established conditions of life among the working classes, of which we read to-day with incredulous horror. In spite of Robert Owen and his model New Lanark Mills these frightful sores were left to fester until a third of the century had gone by. The landed aristocracy, many of whose members had tasted the sweetness of mining royalties, were united with the mill-owners in believing that these things must be. Yet it was an aristocrat, the seventh Earl of Shaftesbury, who was to do more than any other man to right the colossal wrong. The fact is significant of a power of moral and mental recuperation in the privileged classes of English society which was to save not only the old aristocratic order but England itself from seemingly inevitable and irretrievable disaster.

In 1817, however, two years before the crowning stupidity of Peterloo, there was no sign of that recovery; there was only fear, and war against freedom of speech, and the suspension of Habeas Corpus. Cobbett, escaping at the end of March from London to Liverpool on his way to America, just at the time when Isabella Jowett knew that she was again pregnant, left a vivid record of the contrasts which his journey afforded. As he rode through Warwickshire,

every object seemed to say: here are resources! here is wealth! Here are all the means of national power, and of individual plenty and happiness! And yet, at the end of those ten beautiful miles, we entered that city of Coventry, which, out of twenty thousand inhabitants, contained at that very moment upwards of eight thousand miserable paupers. As we passed onwards through Staffordshire and Cheshire all the same signs of wealth and of the sources of power, on the surface of the earth struck us by day; and, by night, those more sublime signs, which issued from the furnaces on the hills. . . . Every object seemed to pronounce an eulogism on the industry, skill, and perseverance of the people. And why, then, were those people in a state of such misery and degradation?

It would have been difficult indeed, at that date and for many years afterwards, to forecast the coming English golden age of wealth and genius.

It would have been more than difficult to foresee the expansion of intellectual forces which were to give to the United Kingdom, during the coming century, its peculiar place in the history of world civilization. It would be a mistake to think of this unforeseeable expansion as merely an expansion of scientific or industrial knowledge, leading to a new understanding and mastery of matter. This was but one aspect of the coming intellectual ferment — the ferment of which Jowett, lacking even the rudiments of scientific knowledge, was to be one of the ablest and awarest promoters.

3. THE CLAIM TO GREATNESS

The proverb says that the boy is the father of the man. To the biographer it often seems that the truth is the other way round; that the man-to-be somehow determines the pattern of his own boyhood.

In retrospect the life of Jowett, like the life of any man who has successfully pursued a steady aim, wears the look of a pre-arranged affair. The contrast between the circumstances of his birth and those of his death suggests that this must be an illusion. But it is so powerful an illusion that the sense of newness, of an unknown future round the bend of the road, is more than usually difficult to recapture.

Perhaps that is because we are easily hypnotized by legend, and because we are apt to measure adventure in terms of dramatic action. It is in the life of the explorer, not the teacher or the student, that the wind of time seems to blow most freshly. Our nomad instincts revel more in change of scene than in change of mind. If we bring ourselves to think of intellectual and spiritual adventure as more truly exciting than battle, murder and sudden death, we still would have it rapid and theatrical, a great revolution of the mind accomplished, like Cardinal Newman's, in a short space of time and attended by appropriate portents. Or we would have it transposed into the key of romance, and its hero set voyaging on strange seas of thought alone.

The legendary Jowett appears to contradict these cravings; but the legend is both more and less than the truth about him. It is not, in fact, difficult to dramatize his life. Much can be made — and must be made

— of the storm which followed *Essays and Reviews;* of his ten years in the wilderness; of the movement of his mind from the naive fundamentalism of childhood to the Socratic conformity of his old age. It would not even be difficult to construct the picture of a self-tormented neurasthenic, paying by an ever-unresolved inner conflict the price of repression and of compromise between intellectual honesty and worldly success.

Such a picture might attract some attention. And truth requires that the evidence, which could be used to give it a look of plausibility, must not be suppressed. Jowett's weaknesses and faults were real; and they have to be taken seriously into any account of him which seeks to depict the real man. They were elements in his unique personality. But, while it would be fraudulent to ignore them, it would be much more fraudulent to overstress them, or to refrain from the attempt to understand how they were related to the qualities which made him an outstanding figure in his own time. The picture to be drawn is that of a serene man, not a neurasthenic; of a stable, not a double-minded man.

Was he, then, no more than a rather oddly constituted man, who achieved a limited, if memorable distinction? Or is he to be considered a 'great' man — a man genuinely great in the critical eye of posterity, and not simply by virtue of his performance in an age which bestowed that epithet rather too easily?

To those who fell, at an impressionable time of life, under the influence or authority of the ageing Master of Balliol it seemed inevitable that he should be what he was and where he was and inconceivable that he should ever have been anything or anywhere else. It was an age of 'great' men. The 'Jowler' was a given fact, as needless of explanation as the Great Western Railway, which took so many of his young men to their London careers. Given them, too, was the whole of that mature, wealthy, powerful, Victorian England, in whose service they were to find their abundant opportunities.

Behind the railway system itself, in the time of Jowett's final ascendancy already 'the permanent way', lay a tangled, an almost fortuitous history of invention and speculation. The young men remembered little or nothing of that. Beneath the domestic solidities and the imperial magnificence, buried only by the deposits of a generation or two, lay the records of an anxious and unsettled time. Not that the second half of the nineteenth century lacked its own troubles. The Crimean War, the Indian Mutiny, Majuba and Phoenix Park and Khartoum punctuated the new imperial chapter. But these grim events served only to heighten the sense of world-wide responsibility which took possession of the young men's minds and, through one of Jowett's most realistically thoughtful pupils, Alfred Milner, gave impetus to a new philosophy of empire. This sense of responsibility sprang from a general conviction that in England, more than anywhere else in the world, the great problems had all been resolved or were well on the way to being resolved — in particular the problem of serving both God and Mammon. Clough's *Latest Decalogue* with its 'Thou shalt have one God only; who would be at the expense of two?' seemed to be — and perhaps in fact was — only a cynical-feeble reaction from the strong and dominant mood of this new English age which, even in its most painful doubts, thought of itself as 'in a very special sense, an age of transition — an exceptional age'.[1]

The visible personality of Jowett, so assured and fearless, so uncompromising in compromise, fitted perfectly into this society, as it developed its unique conception of an oligarchically controlled transition from oligarchy to democracy. Turning in it, he turned like a key in a well-oiled lock. Yet the lock had not always obeyed the key; and the key was a home-made, even a self-made, article. Behind the Master's high-pitched *brusqueries*, which the young men took rather less respectfully as he grew older, lay a personal history of which they knew absolutely nothing at all. They did not know how or where he had started. They did not know what manner of man he really was, or seemed to himself to be. If they could have read his private notebooks they would have been very much surprised — even, perhaps, shocked — to discover that his ascendancy was not automatic, but achieved by deliberate aim and maintained be perpetual effort. 'To arrange my life' ran a typical note written on his fifty-ninth birthday 'in the best possible way, that I may be able to arrange other people's.'

Such constant, conscious planning to make the best use of his powers may seem to suggest an inner insecurity, which the assurance of the outer man belied. But no rational man can exist without inner conflict; the question is not so much how to resolve as how to localize and contain it. His notebooks prove that Jowett admitted part, at least, of the war between his members to his conscious mind; and that he paid not infrequent visits to the seat of war. What he saw there often disquieted him, but he neither shut his eyes to it nor allowed it to infect his overriding purpose — the deliberate improvement of mind and character in himself and in others. 'Some passing vanity or semi-sensuality is constantly interrupting me in prayer, or in any other serious thought', he notes, at the age of sixty-six; and a few weeks later: 'Any thought about self, sometimes thoughts of evil, day-dreams, love fancies, easily find an abode in the mind.' The context shows that he was writing of his own

---

[1] Jowett to the Rev. E. A. W. Seymour in 1888.

mind. But, on balance, he was satisfied with the way the battle went. 'I eat or drink too much, and do not retain thorough self-command or self-respect. Yet upon the whole I certainly make progress.'

In the series of private, confessional, notes[1] from which these sentences are quoted he regrets his own failure to attain to real greatness. Though he does not say so, the greatness of which he is thinking is evidently greatness in the field of learning or literature. 'My own experience of life suggests such enormous waste. Had I been taught well in my youth, had I had guidance, had I not wasted my memory, had I had any noble ideal better than success in life, I seem as if I might have attained to real greatness.' He consoles himself with the reflection that, if he has missed the best that might have been, he has also missed the worst. 'I have' he records simply 'a great position.' And three days later he adds, with the unashamed naivety of true self-judgment: 'I find that a new position, e.g. the headship of a College, or the Vice-Chancellorship, does really change the character a good deal.'

The lament over his 'wasted memory' is a very curious, a very revealing self-accusation. Talking once with Florence Nightingale, he said that he had no memory, that every time he returned to a subject he had to begin it all over again; and saying this he suddenly burst into tears.[2] It was the scholar's abnormal memory that he yearned for — the inability to forget anything once observed. Some say that a memory of this kind is not a good, but a bad memory; that memory is a mechanism of forgetting as well as of remembering; that the mind needs to dismiss from conscious recollection facts which would otherwise accumulate and clog its higher powers. That may perhaps be true; but it is an imperfection of the human mind that it should be true. Jowett's own mind had made the best it could of this imperfection. To ordinary people it seemed that he had an exceptionally good memory. He knew better. Grasping as he did at the unattainable ideal of intellectual perfection, he was painfully aware of this particular failure. There were times, nevertheless, when he took — or affected to take — a commonsense view of it, saying that 'the memory of the man who could repeat a book of *Paradise Lost*, after once reading it over, was simply a disease'.

Meditating the Life of Christ, which he intended to be the work of his old age, he asked himself: 'Could I write as well as Renan?' To Sir Leslie Stephen the answer was all too clear.[3] And certainly Jowett's writing

[1] See below, 406 *foll.* where a fuller account of them is given.
[2] From an unpublished note by Lewis Campbell of an interview with Miss Nightingale. (*J.P.*)
[3] *Studies of a Biographer*, ii, 132. Stephen misquotes the question as: 'Can I write like Renan?'

does not achieve the indefinable glow of genius. It is clear, persuasive, balanced, resourceful; it has all the weight of his remarkable intellect behind it; occasionally it rises to rhetorical beauty. But except in letters to intimate friends, written without a thought of publication and often sparkling with felicitous phrases, it lacks the peculiar quality which makes almost every sentence that Newman wrote live in the reader's mind, even if one rejects its intended meaning. 'Better teaching' and a more highly organized memory might have made Jowett's prose unreadable. But 'real greatness' is by no means reserved for artists and men of letters. If the expression means anything, it must apply to any signal achievement in which quality of mind or character, rather than luck, has been the prime factor.

What, then, if Jowett is to be considered as a great man, was this signal achievement? He made no important discoveries; he did little to enlarge the horizon of knowledge; he provided no firm or lasting reconciliation between religion, philosophy and science. His chief concrete memorials are Balliol and his translation of Plato, with its attendant analyses and essays. The Plato is a magnificent effort of interpretation. The facts that it is not a work of narrowly impeccable scholarship, and that the interpretation is sometimes dictated by moral ideas unknown to Plato, do not seriously diminish its value.[1] But it would be difficult to base a claim to greatness upon a translation which has no pretence to originality, even though it was used as an indirect means of saying important things which could not be said directly.

Balliol is another matter. There can be no question of the debt which nineteenth-century Balliol owed to Jowett. Nor can it be doubted that twentieth-century Balliol derived from Jowett's Balliol. But the nature of the debt was not so simple as it seems. Jowett made Balliol 'count', and Balliol continued to count — but not quite in the same way; becoming concerned for the cure of a sick society, rather than for the improvement of a healthy social order. If, then, the stimulus which she received from Jowett remained operative, it must have been no mere impulse towards worldly success, nor the communication of any fixed moral or intellectual system; it must rather have been the infusion of a living principle.

One might define that principle as an active faith in the supremacy of right reason, but the definition itself needs to be further defined. 'Faith', in that this is an attitude of mind which reason by itself can never com-

[1] I think it was Professor Conington who said that, however people might criticize any of Jowett's renderings, Jowett always had a good case. For an illustration of the way in which Jowett sometimes distorted Plato see below, 98 *foll.*

pletely justify and has often treacherously attacked. 'Active', in that the mind possessing such a faith never ceases to move, and must of necessity pass from one position to another, as its powers expand by exercise and the challenge of the outer world alters. 'Right reason', in that reason is not a faculty to be isolated from the basic affections and aspirations of human nature. As Newman put it: 'the whole man moves.' To have lived by such a rule and to have imparted it to others, is certainly one mark of greatness.

'Greatness' is a loose and relative term. We know, in a rough way, what we mean by it; but when we try to explain what we mean we are quickly bogged down and have to cast about for hard evidence to catch hold of. That is why those who are remembered as great men are, for the most part, either men whose actions or theories or inventions plainly changed the course of history, or writers or artists whose *œuvre* is part of our inheritance — poets, painters, sculptors, architects, musicians, historians, philosophers *et hoc genus omne*. The world's judgment of the lower places in the scale of 'greatness' varies almost wildly from generation to generation. Once famous names are dismissed and then, perhaps, after a lapse of time reinstated. Forgotten names are substituted and then, after a time, again crossed off. Only a very few are free. Almost all abide our question.

There are other criteria of 'greatness' than those ordinarily used. A man can be accounted great, even if he has not directly changed the course of history or written poems or painted pictures or composed music or designed buildings or constructed a system of philosophy or unravelled the secrets of matter. Jowett deserves the title more than many of those to whom it has been accorded. But neither his Plato nor his Balliol will seem, for most people, good enough evidence to support the claim. If it were possible to trace in detail the influence which he exerted upon his own time through his pupils and friends, the claim might be convincingly established upon that single level. Such a task would be laborious to perform and the report of it laborious to read. Let it be assumed, however, that Jowett did so influence the life of his time, and that the title of great man might be allowed to him simply on that ground. It would, nevertheless, be the wrong ground. The claim that Jowett should be considered as a great man rests, finally, not upon his external achievements (great as they were) but upon the quality of the man himself.

In making this claim it is necessary to beware of over-statement. The claim, so far as I have formulated it, rests upon Jowett's use of a 'living principle' defined as 'an active faith in the supremacy of right reason'.

But there were some large deficiencies in his use of reason and in his understanding of the world. He knew nothing of, and for most of his life cared nothing for, science.[1] His 'discursions into ethics'— Leslie Stephen almost, but not quite, justly observed — 'do not even suggest any new solution of the old difficulties.' The moral code of the day — in spite of his occasional, private and daring, speculations to the contrary — tended to wear, for him, the aspect of an established and absolute system, developed (as he wrote in one of his notebooks) 'out of the feelings of the sexes' but no longer dependent upon them, having 'gained another and more universal standing ground'.[2] It is sometimes difficult not to think, again with Leslie Stephen, that his treatment of Christianity emptied out the baby with the bath. It is sometimes equally difficult not to think that his hatred of failure drove him into putting too high a value upon success.

These criticisms do not invalidate the claim to greatness which closer study of his life supports. Some of them are dissipated by that closer knowledge. Jowett was a man of his time. The key had to turn in the lock. He is not to be judged as a *savant*, whose work is done in the privacy of his own room and submitted to an academic or posthumous jury. He is to be judged, rather, as a man doing a job under conditions he could not alter. He had to do his best with an endless series of adolescents, in a still strongly oligarchical society governed by inescapable if often unwritten laws. He came of pious farming and business stock. He was born into an arranged and ordered community; into a class which hung suspended from its superiors. As he grew up, he embraced the ideals of reform, social and academic and religious. But, for him, reform must be a process from within, not an imposition from above; and the idea of violent revolution from below held no promise of anything but further violence.

Jowett was never a man to take a sudden jump. His development was continuous and always in relation to his given *milieu*. A man of his temperament — that is to say, a man who at every stage of his life has done his utmost to reconcile what he already has with what is being given to him — can never jettison all his mental possessions. He will throw overboard only the little that he must. Jowett could no more have been an infidel than he could have been a revolutionary. However far from orthodoxy he might find himself obliged to travel, Christianity remained the one religion open to him. And he was a fundamentally religious man. Moreover, he was a believing man. He believed in God: in a divine governor of the world, in a divine companion of mankind, in a divine originator and sustainer of all known and unknown values. This

---

[1] See below, 81.   [2] See below, 142 *foll.*

God was never reduced, in his mind, to a formless 'something, not ourselves, which makes for righteousness'. Nor did he doubt the reality of that City of God, to the freedom of which he sought all his life to be admitted. These are simple beliefs, and their simplicity is their strength.

Citizen of the unseen world though he would be, Jowett was so fully a citizen of this world, that he has often been accused of inconsistency and insincerity. The charge misses the simplicity of his position. The more strongly you believe in an unseen world, the more reason you have for taking the seen world seriously. The main conditions of human life have been willed by God; the institutions which men have contrived for their better living together, shaped by these conditions, have at least the value of a tried human solution to a divinely appointed problem. To turn your back upon the things of this world is not, on this view, a mark of true religion. It is better to do your duty in that state of life into which it shall please God to call you. Cranmer's formula has been accused of reflecting a satisfaction with the social order which has nothing to do with religion. Jowett was the last man to prevent ability from finding its proper level. But to the doctrine that religion requires every man to do his job as well as it can possibly be done he gave his absolute assent. Nor did he think it the sign of a religious man to despise or refuse power, whether earned or inherited.

There was no inconsistency or insincerity in this attitude of mind. But there was, certainly, a strong personal reason for Jowett's superb worldliness. He had seen incompetence and failure at close quarters in his own family, and he knew and abhorred the waste and the pain for which they are responsible. He had had his own way to make in the world; and, having made it, he was concerned to see that the young men under his charge should make the most of their opportunities.

It is easy to make fun of his passion for the arrangement of other people's lives. Yet, after all, this was his job, his professional business, a business which he pursued with extraordinary zest and success. It is easier still to sneer at the worldliness of the objectives which he was sometimes supposed to set before his young men. If to aim at high position and to train oneself for the discharge of high duties are worldly purposes, then 'worldly' is not a dishonourable epithet. And apart from his understanding of the need which society has for the man of dignity and talent, the leader of lesser men, Jowett — like Samuel Butler and Bernard Shaw — knew that worldly success has a moral value of its own. It may be hard for a rich man to enter into the kingdom of heaven. But we have it on the same authority that admission is not to be bought with a talent buried in a napkin.

During his lonely boyhood and adolescence this particular lesson etched itself, with the firmest lines, deeply into Jowett's character. Such a lesson cannot be learned by those who are congenitally incapable of profiting by it. The invisible godmother at Jowett's christening had seen to it that the child should make his mark in the world, and should profit by his very handicaps. She was, indeed, free with her gifts. To the capacity for success she added a resolute will, a disposition fearless and serene, and a physical constitution weak enough to remind him of mortality yet strong enough to serve the purposes of an untiring brain. To continue the list of his qualities would seem to reduce a unique individual to a bundle of abstract attributes. Nothing in the memory of Jowett's friends and enemies was so plain and so hard to describe as the unforgettable personality which used and was not contained in its equipment.[1] Yet among his more subtle endowments is to be distinguished one whose nature has already been suggested and which, more than any other, gave to his career its peculiar significance. This was a power of continuous growth, of unhurried intellectual development, which proceeded not by fits and starts and acts of rebellion, but by a kind of mental metabolism, accepting and assimilating and transforming the old and the new.

The very circumstances, which helped him as a boy to take the first steps towards intellectual freedom, accentuated his inborn differences from common men. His physical inheritance was markedly abnormal. As a boy he looked like a girl; as an old man he looked and spoke something like a eunuch. With this lack of physical masculinity, for which some inherited glandular disequilibrium was responsible,[2] went a shyness which cost all his power of will to conquer. Conquer it he did, to the extent of never letting it prevent him from doing what he willed to do. But in that range of life which is not subject to will it remained his master and prevented him from rooting himself in ordinary soil.

He never learned to play, to make love, to break down the barriers of reserve in himself or in others. He never sowed any wild oats or kicked over the traces. Fearlessly as he used his mind upon religious dogma, metaphysical systems, educational questions and national affairs, he was apt to be less courageous in face of orthodox moral assumptions. He was not the first or the last teacher to refuse this most difficult and dangerous of fences. But the refusal was mainly unconscious. It was perhaps determined by the fact that the fence was a protection for his own unalterable deficiencies.

[1] 'He was a man, not a set of opinions', said one of his biographers' correspondents in a letter which I read long after penning the above sentence. (*J.P.*)
[2] It was a recurring character in his family. See below, 53.

It might be thought that a character so strongly and strangely tempered must pursue its ends in isolation. Yet few men have ever had so many or so devoted friends, both men and women. If there was something in him which prevented passion as the world understands it, the current of his emotional life ran, for the greater part of its course, calmly broad and full. And since to this inexhaustible sympathy, always as critical as it was affectionate, he added humour, humour of the kind which springs from the apprehension of human possibilities as well as of human shortcomings, he fell very seldom into the pit of moral snobbery which engulfed so many of his contemporaries.

It was the characteristic assumption of the Victorians that the inward and the outer self were, or must be supposed to be, in perfect harmony. If they were not, then the man must be a conscious hypocrite, a Pecksniff. The great Victorians themselves were at once the victims and the beneficiaries of this heroic illusion. They lived in, and by and large up to, their public characters and positions. What they lost in self-knowledge they gained in objective achievement. And the universality of the illusion provided a medium for the development of friendships, which could be warm without becoming embarrassingly intimate.

Friendship with Jowett was a strenuous undertaking. The Victorians, with their perpetual anxiety to improve their characters, prized it the more on that account. But they would not have submitted so willingly to his exacting companionship if, in spite of his awkward reserves and silences, he had not possessed that mysterious quality called charm. The charm did not work on everybody; for it was related to an ambiguity of sex, which helped some of his enemies to dislike him. But the unconscious changeling in him drew the unconscious sympathy of his friends. Whenever they spoke or wrote about him, an undercurrent of protective tenderness ran beneath the words of reserve. And when, in his early years as a tutor, his best pupils earned the half-mocking name of 'Jowett-worshippers', they were, without knowing it, answering to an appeal which he was also unaware of making.

Sitting down to be photographed in characteristic attitude, knees well apart, hands resting upon his thighs with the fingers spread out, squarely facing the camera, head upright, eyes unwavering, his expression that of a man who is ready for anything that may happen and will judge it calmly, and not without humour, upon its merits, Jowett wears a look of unshakable fortitude and independence.[1] The camera reported the truth. This was the most important part of him — this was what he had made

---

[1] This describes a lost photograph by Perroud, Jowett's butler; a drawing of it was reproduced in the *Westminster Extra* (see below, 435).

of himself — this was his conscious personality, no mask or shell beneath which another Jowett, unknown to his friends, cowered from the external world. This *was* the real, thinking, purposing man. Yet there was in him, as in all of us, a limbo of unused or discarded characters seeking their means of life; and among the more vigorous of these was that unsatisfied and lonely changeling, who could still faintly trouble the old man's serene mind with erotic imaginations, and whose desire for love was only to be consoled by friends and ever more and more friends. Consoled, but never assuaged; for, as he once said, 'people go on expecting more from friendship than it can ever give.'

The real Jowett may, perhaps, have never understood why he was in such special need of friends. He knew, at least, that he wanted them. Every now and then he would fill pages of his notebooks with mere lists of their names. He had the pride of a collector in their number and quality; and he treated each one as a collector treats a special piece. He sought to make his friend show to the best advantage. And as the best collectors do — but only the best — he lavished trouble upon his collection, not because it was *his* collection, but because all the pieces in it were genuine. When Florence Nightingale was told that he was lying unconscious in his last illness, she said: 'I have no doubt that he is passing in review a procession of all his friends.'[1]

Yet perhaps he did consciously understand something of what the possession of so many friends meant to him. They were his channels of communication with the world of action, the world of full-blooded masculinity, as well as his means of influencing action. Not that he was a wire-puller. There were no wires in his world. If he pulled at all, he pulled at a rope; and the bell pealed with gentlemanly candour. His purposes were pursued without the tortuous discretion which his enemies attributed to him.[2]

His part in the manufacture of that 'criminal' book *Essays and Reviews* illustrates how little he cared — at least until he had been taught otherwise — to measure opposition. In academic business he is said to have given too little thought, rather than too much, to diplomatic preparation of the ground. Often, in consequence, he failed to bring off a cherished scheme. It was then that he was seen at his best; accepting defeat without rancour, without a shrug of the shoulders, and turning with equanimity and undiminished energy to the pursuit of other plans. Was not that, in itself, a mark of greatness?

[1] From an unpublished letter of Lewis Campbell to Evelyn Abbott. (*J.P.*)
[2] See below, 394 *foll.*

From a special sitting to Mr. Perroud.

2. 'Sitting down to be photographed'
A drawing in *Westminster Extra No.* 4

4. DECLINE AND FALL OF A REPUTATION

A Third Programme feature, in September 1954, called 'A Criminal Production', reproduced the extraordinary public agitation over *Essays and Reviews*, to which Jowett contributed his famous essay on the Interpretation of Scripture.[1] In the broadcast the utterances of the various people concerned were distinguished by the voices of different actors. The impersonator of Jowett imitated the prim diction of a desiccated old man. But in 1860, when *Essays and Reviews* was published, Jowett was only forty-two and still the captivator of ardent and intelligent youth.

This curious mistake illustrated something other than the general tendency to remember dead men as if they had always been old men — for that is a tendency which dramatic reconstructions nowadays delight in correcting. It illustrated the peculiar eclipse of the young and young-middle-aged Jowett, even of the still relatively young Master of Balliol, by the old man that he eventually became.

Even so early as 1860 (or thereabouts) Jowett was attracting hostility as well as partisanship. It was already beginning to be said against him that he paid too much deference to genius and to success. To quote Campbell:[2]

The former imputation was more rife in earlier years, the latter afterwards, when his own position was now assured. Both really turned on one peculiarity: that in judging of persons and in determining his own relation to them, he never separated their individual characteristics from the thought of what they might effect. This was equally his way of regarding his own life and the lives of others.

Success, after his death, came to hang like a motionless cloud round the top of Mount Jowett, obscuring the peak of his achievement from view. People instinctively admire and also instinctively distrust success. When it is threatened, they rally to defend it; when it is triumphant, they unite in suspecting it. By many outside and even by some inside Balliol it began to be imagined that worldly distinction was all that had counted with the Master, as the ranks of higher civil servants, parliamentarians, statesmen and proconsuls became more and more infiltrated by Balliol men.

It came to be supposed that he must have discovered a trick of landing his young men at this or that starting point, where they would find themselves treated with some peculiar favour which he had managed to procure for them by some more or less backstairs ingenuity. Notions of this

---

[1] See below, 229 *foll*. and 244-5. [2] *L. & L.*, i, 328.

sort, however intrinsically absurd, have a way of propagating themselves without contradiction and of creating indifference towards the person about whom they are entertained. 'That bogus old man!' was the slick verdict of a clever young man in the early nineteen-thirties, delivered with a contemptuous shrug of the shoulder.

The growth of this false idea in Oxford at large was accompanied by the posthumous development, inside Balliol itself, of a reaction which had already begun before Jowett died.

Even at the time of his election to the Mastership in 1870 there were anticipations of trouble ahead in the mind of at least one ardent supporter. 'We shall have' wrote the philosopher T. H. Green, his former pupil and his close friend, 'a *régime* of strong "personal government", and in many respects shall be the better for it. But "constitutional opposition" is desirable, and I don't feel much energy or inclination for it.'[1] In the later years of Jowett's reign 'signs of restiveness' appeared among the younger fellows, though 'the respect and deference with which he was regarded were as great as ever'.[2] There was, in fact, an opposition party strong enough, when the great old man died, to determine the election of his successor.

It had looked as if the mantle must fall upon Strachan-Davidson, Jowett's loyal vicegerent, 'a figure without whom it seemed hardly possible that Balliol could exist.' Instead, Edward Caird was recalled from his long tenure of the chair of Moral Philosophy at Glasgow.

The election of Caird to succeed Jowett was significant of a new spirit in Balliol and abroad in the country. It was not due to mere reaction against 'personal government'. Jowett had been a leader of the early reforming movement in Oxford. He had never been a 'radical'; he believed in the virtue of an aristocratically framed society, though not in its exclusive character; and his main social purpose can be truly represented as teaching that privilege, whether inherited or acquired, means responsibility, and that responsibility means hard work. But, as Mackail says, 'the reformers of the 'sixties were insensibly becoming the Conservatives of the 'eighties, and beginning to be alarmed at the results of their own past action.'

Caird, by contrast, was 'a radical . . . not only in politics, but in religion and philosophy'.[3] In electing him Balliol set the pattern of her future for many years to come — a pattern fundamentally different from

---

[1] R. L. Nettleship, *Thomas Hill Green*, 163.
[2] J. W. Mackail, *James Leigh Strachan-Davidson*, 52.
[3] *D.N.B.* (unsigned article).

that which Jowett had devised and almost, it seemed, laid down in per-
petuity.

Caird resigned from ill health in 1907. Strachan-Davidson, now sixty-
three and also in poor health, was elected to the Mastership without (it is
said) any opposing voice. The new election implied nothing like a return
to the Jowett tradition. After a short, quiet, nine years' reign, Strachan-
Davidson was followed in 1916 by the dynamic A. L. Smith.

'A.L.' had been one of Jowett's most trusted and most ruthlessly ex-
ploited tutors. He resembled Jowett in his immense capacity for work and
his interest in social problems. In almost every other particular he was
the very antithesis of Jowett — virile, unconventional, a devotee of
violent exercise, the father of a large family, anything but the serene,
sexless, platonic ruler. And the social problems uppermost in his time
and consciousness were utterly different from those to which Jowett had
applied his mind. His dominant social passion, for some years before he
became Master, was the education of the proletariat. In this he was,
indeed, developing Jowett's own interest in the admission of intelligent
working-class boys to an Oxford or University education. But that was
one of the things belonging to Jowett which had been more than half
forgotten; and 'A.L.' gave it a stress and turn, which Jowett would have
certainly thought excessive.

The new Master's reign was brief — 1916 to 1924. For the first three
of these eight years Balliol was a training school for military cadets
rather than a college of undergraduates. During the last five the Master
was sickening towards his death. But it was he, even more decisively
than Caird, who turned the mind of the college away from Jowett's ideal
of a dedicated *élite* to the ideal of an educated, industrial, democracy.[1]

It may be that there is no ultimate incompatibility between the one
ideal and the other, and that the hope of the future lies in their reconciliation. But even the greatest and ablest men must take the colouring of their
times, and achieve little or nothing unless they do so. Jowett went as far,
perhaps, as a man of his time and kind could, in the attempt to reconcile
what was given and what might be. But his view was soon treated by
many in his own college as an old-fashioned view which had served the
purposes of education for a while and must be replaced by another.

In some such way as this must the outsider, to whom Jowett is more
important than Balliol, seek to understand the admixture of indifference
and piety with which Balliol came to regard her greatest son. There was
first a natural reaction against an overpowering legend; and this was very

[1] A different, and much more lighthearted, picture of Balliol in the years just
before 1914 has recently been drawn by Sir L. E. Jones in *An Edwardian Youth*.

quickly followed by the development of a new purpose, apparently incompatible with the old.

Even so soon as 1899, when Jowett had been only six years dead, a significant note of coolness is apparent in the appreciation of him which H. W. C. Davis made in the last chapter of his brilliant monograph on *Balliol College*. Jowett, there, is naturally remembered as Master rather than tutor — though Davis says some very excellent things about the young Jowett and his 'almost preternatural sagacity', the bill is topped by the old man, whose supremacy in Balliol had not been in question for a quarter of a century before young Davis set eyes on him in 1891. 'His ideal' says Davis, writing of 1864 (six years before Jowett became Master) 'was now thoroughly formed, and so, too, was the method through which he thought it could be realized.' But once he had become Master 'it was no longer his part to show how the work should be done, any more than it is the duty of a general to drill the rank and file'. He had created a 'machine' which 'continued to work with unabated vigour'. An efficient machine, Davis is at pains to insist. But the choice of metaphor contains an evidently hostile criticism derived from older men. And even of Jowett's own method as a tutor Davis, after setting out somewhat lamely to justify it against the old and ridiculous charge that it was too 'negative', concludes that 'the work of a tutor in that age was much more to clarify ideas than to impart them'.

Who now, in the west, except a confessed ideological partisan, would dare to think or to say that it is not the supreme business of an educator to 'clarify' the ideas which swarm, unbidden by him, in the mind of every intelligent youth, rather than to 'impart' his own? Davis, with the assurance of his twenty-five years and of the generation to which he belonged, had no doubt that it is a tutor's business to influence, and even to change, the direction of his pupils' thoughts; and that Jowett had failed in this respect.

The general direction of Balliol during the fifty years or so after Jowett's death seems, then, to have been different from, and in many ways deliberately opposed to, that which the college followed under his guidance. Moreover, the gospel of work was being re-interpreted in a way which he would not have approved. Mackail says of the situation in Balliol at the time of his death, that several of the fellows 'wished more leisure for the pursuit of their own studies and researches, less concentration on preparing their pupils for the Schools, a pursuit of knowledge more for its own sake and less for ulterior ends, however valuable'. This new aim, or this revival of a mediaeval aim, did not originate in Balliol — who can say where or when or how it originated?

It was strong in the air of the west a long time before Jowett died. He never concealed his own view that education, not research, was the first and the final function of a tutor. Research, he seems to have thought, was more often than not a self-indulgence, an agreeable escape from more urgent, if more tedious, duties. If it was other than that for some exceptional teachers, if a room in a tower was essential to them, then they should make the kind of sacrifice in order to work in it and return to it that he himself made throughout his life. It was wrong to use public money to make their choice easy. If teaching was their function they must put their pupils first and do their research in their spare time.[1]

This did not mean that he was never himself tempted (like Cardinal Newman) to pursue the life of the pure scholar. 'If I had not hampered myself with these ties,' he once said to Campbell 'I should be all over Europe, collating MSS.'[2] The 'ties' were human ties, between the teacher and his pupils, imposing upon the teacher an absolute duty which could not be reconciled (so it seemed to him) with a devotion to what he often called 'useless learning'.[3]

This attitude towards research had been breeding opposition and resentment in Balliol long before he died. Since his death it has been defeated everywhere in the western world by the modern view of research as the final academic aim. A hundred years of University reform in England have resulted in this complete reversal of the view strongly held by the man in Oxford who did more than anybody else to get the engine of reform started.

So the star of Jowett declined and fell, alike in Balliol and in Oxford and in the larger society he had done so much to fashion.

[1] L. & L., ii, 125. 'He had no sympathy with the organized endowment of research.'

[2] ibid., i, 327; where another revealing remark is reproduced: 'If I had gone abroad —— would have done nothing, at the most critical moment of his life.'

[3] ibid., ii, 132–3. 'There was nothing of which he spoke with so much bitterness as useless learning.'

CHAPTER II

Family Album[1]

1. 'MELCHIZEDEC'

'Without father, without mother, without descent' Jowett's young contemporaries said of him at Balliol. The nickname of Melchizedec stuck to him for many years. As late as 1856, when Jowett was in his fortieth year, Arthur Stanley described how he had just been to St. Germain's 'and saw — the parents of Melchizedec! a truly antique and venerable pair, each bearing a slight resemblance to the son, each with some of the qualities in him concentrated'. Six years earlier F. T. Palgrave, one of Jowett's very earliest pupils, had also been allowed behind the curtain. He called on Jowett's parents, who were then living in Paris, and was not quite so favourably impressed as Stanley. He remembered Mr. Jowett for 'the manner, more easily recognized than defined, of one who had not been successful in his profession' and Mrs. Jowett as 'a pale, white, graciously dignified lady' whose voice, features and bearing 'wore the air of a long, perfect, uncomplaining resignation'.

When the Master of Balliol died half a century later, full of years and honour, his biographers were confronted with the difficult task of reconstructing his family history. By patient and enthusiastic research Lewis Campbell uncovered the main story. He had some of Jowett's own letters to help him. But nearly all the letters Jowett had ever received, including letters written by members of his family, had been destroyed. How this came about was described by his confidential housekeeper Miss Martha Knight, in an unpublished letter written to Lady Airlie after his death.

He often spoke to me about his mother and brothers and sisters, but seldom mentioned his father. Some years ago he was talking about his letters, and was regretting that he had kept them all his life, especially because so many of them had been written by his family, all of whom were then dead, with the exception of one sister, Emily. He asked me if I would undertake a rather difficult task — to devote a portion of each day, or a few hours a week, to going through his oldest letters, dating from the time of his coming up to Oxford, and to withdraw from them all those relating to

[1] The information used in this and the following chapter was collected by Campbell, but little of it has been published. The governing reference, where reference is absent, is *J.P.* The 'family outlines' in Appendix III may be helpful.

his family affairs. This I did, and he seemed glad to think that he could make away with them at any time, if he chose to do so. While seeking those he named, I came across many *very* private letters, written in the deepest confidence to the Master, by his friends, in times of great sorrow, and it troubled me that they should *still* exist. I spoke to him about this, and to my relief he wrote a little note addressed to me, authorizing me to 'burn' all his letters in the event of his death. This wish was afterwards confirmed in his Will, and I was thankful to be permitted by his executors to destroy them all myself before leaving Balliol, a few months after his death.

According to Miss Knight, Jowett's own original concern was the isolation of his family letters, so that 'he could make away with them at any time'. It was Miss Knight's idea that all the other letters should be burned. He was no longer able to go through them himself and to decide which should be kept and which ought to be destroyed. As old bachelors are too apt to do, he followed the advice of a confidential servant and forgot the existence of friends who would know better what to keep and what to destroy.

That is easy to understand. It is less easy to understand why he was so specially anxious to obliterate his family history. The more a man seeks to hide this kind of matter, the more it becomes something to be discovered. But his attitude towards his family was pathological. He did his duty; he hated the existence of the duty. He rarely spoke or wrote about his family or childhood. The unwanted memories could not be quite dismissed. They were irrelevant; they were cumulatively painful; yet they were all the inheritance he had of the intimacies belonging to family life.

Writing to Lady Airlie in 1880, when his sister Emily had had a stroke, he said sadly:

As you say, calamities of this sort bring back many recollections. There were once nine of us and now there are only two. Two of the sisters died of consumption more than forty years ago; two brothers, who went into the Indian Army, more than twenty years ago. They had all passed away before I knew Airlie[1] or you. I have the pleasantest recollection of them. They were all intelligent and had a very uncommon disinterestedness and unselfishness.

To Florence Nightingale, after his mother's death in 1869, he wrote, with an unusual and pathetic accent of tenderness. 'I have her face following me as she looked when she was alive. It was the pleasantest face, when she was laid to rest, and the youngest for her age that I ever saw.'

---

[1] This was the 7th Earl of Airlie, who died in the following year. Lady Airlie was a cousin of Arthur Stanley; that was probably the cause of Jowett's intimacy with her and her husband. The letter is given by Abbott (*L. & L.*, ii, 196) without the name of the recipient or of her husband.

There was a mixture of reasons for his desire to bury this past — reasons not, perhaps, ever wholly admitted to his conscious mind. The history of his immediate family circle was a very sad one. His own boyhood had been bare and solitary. His odd reluctance had, however, deeper roots than these. Essentially he was a chip of the old God-fearing block; but a chip which had insisted upon having a mind of its own. For the sake of his own intellectual freedom and integrity he had been obliged to separate himself from his inherited background. His relations spoke of him in his early manhood as 'poor Ben', as they might have spoken of a dead man. After his death an elderly first cousin on his mother's side, a Miss Langhorne who ran a school with her brother at Brighton, was at pains to tell Professor Campbell that, while she admired Dr. Jowett's private character, 'with his teaching, and the influences he exercised on the minds of others on one great *vital* Truth, I have no sympathy: it has always been a grief to me.' She consoled herself with the belief that

in his *seeming extremity* two years since [i.e. his illness in 1891] he shewed that the heart, not the intellect, asserted its need, and was listened to. I believe this is the case with many, and that, as in a palimpsest, deep below all the writing of doubt and 'criticism' is the Writing of God and shall remain there. Times come in our lives when the Soul must reach it.

Miss Langhorne added a valuable postscript: 'I much wish to add that in his home life Dr. Jowett had the inestimable advantage of decidedly evangelical teaching and influence.' The postscript goes to the root of the matter, as the old lady's firm cursive script would lead one to expect. The 'inestimable advantage' *had* formed his moral character and *had* given a deeply religious cast to his temper. But it had violated his intellectual innocence. He paid honour to the spiritual force which generated the evangelical movement a century before his own time; but he could never forgive its betrayal of reason.

This is a farm-house in which I am writing: it is full of religious books of the worst and most unmeaning kind; the *Arminian Skeleton*, etc. . . . Half the books that are published are religious books. And what trash this religious literature is! Either formalisms or sentimentalisms about the atonement, or denunciations of rational religion, or prophecies of the end of the world, explanations of the Man of Sin, the little Horn, and the number of the Beast — even these last are no inconsiderable part of English literature.

Deeper even than this adult distaste for the stupidities in which he had been reared lay shame for his father's failure to support his family. When his stipend as Professor of Greek was at last raised from £40 to £500 a year, he wrote to Stanley: 'I am obliged always to deduct about £400 a year from my income (this is a matter which I never mention and do not you mention; it has continued nearly twenty-five years — I never like to speak or to think of it).' A son, who does not like even to think of the support he is able to give his father and mother, stands in a peculiar relation to them. It was not that he hated parting with the money, for he was a generous giver. What he hated was failure, the failure which springs from incompetence and ruins the lives of others. His father's failure was of this kind. Even his mother was included in this condemnation, gently though he expressed it in a note written after his sister Emily's death:

She [Emily] was a saint in private life who never thought of herself. All her days were devoted to my father and mother, and she made life possible and easy for them. For though intelligent and educated people, they were unable to take care of themselves.[1]

Apart from his own father, brothers and sisters, the other members of the Jowett clan might never have existed, so far as the Master of Balliol was consciously concerned. He was partly brought up as a boy by his father's two unmarried sisters, Elizabeth and Irene, but we hear nothing more of them. He had two Jowett uncles, Josiah and Henry. Josiah emigrated to Australia and a letter of Josiah's father (the Master's grandfather) in 1837 recorded that he was apparently 'in a thriving way'. Concerning Henry the silence is complete.

If there were no first cousins on his father's side, or no first cousins nearer than Australia, there were quantities of second cousins, and of first cousins once removed. They knew of the Balliol prodigy, for they spoke of him as 'poor Ben'. But the clan was already splitting, as no doubt it had split again and again in the forgotten past. This time, the split ran up the whole of the prolific branch, to which the Master of Balliol belonged. By the end of the century all its sub-branches were dead and the branch itself died with them.

2. THE PATRIARCH

The Jowetts were a Yorkshire family of yeoman farming stock. Their general history seems to have been like that of many another northern English clan. With the development of the export trade in woollen cloth, the more enterprising farmers found it good business to deal in wool. From the trade of a wool-stapler to that of a tanner or a skinner, and then to that of a furrier or a hatter, was a frequent transition. The new class of tradesmen, which came in this way into being, was vigorous and intelli-

[1] *L. & L.*, ii, 237.

gent. Prosperity made clergymen and scholars of their younger sons; their descendants pushed their way into the forefront of the professions and sometimes, with the aid of a shrewd marriage or two, into the ranks of the landed gentry and even the nobility.

Jowett's ancestors emerged as tradesmen of this type, at Manningham near Bradford, before the end of the seventeenth century. One of them, named Henry, migrated about the end of the century to London and there set up in business. Probably he was a younger son, for his brother Benjamin stayed in business in York. Benjamin's son was a flax-dresser and became sheriff of York in 1784, while Henry's son built up his own, new, business in London as a skinner or furrier.

The two branches of the family, thus separated, were reunited some eighty years later when Benjamin's grand-daughter Anne married Henry's grandson Benjamin, and so became the Master of Balliol's grandmother.

The marriage of these two second cousins had a curious material consequence for the Master. It made him, all of a sudden, a landed gentleman. The chain of events is worth a paragraph. Anne's mother was the great-granddaughter of a certain William Bilton, the owner of a small estate in Yorkshire, partly freehold and partly copyhold, called Hirst Grove: 'a place nicely secluded from the world, yet warm and comfortable and fair fields and winds.' This pleasant property descended through four generations to a Mr. Bilton Josephus Wilson, who died in 1866. When Mr. Wilson was nearing ninety he made a will, by which the freehold part of the estate, after the life interest of a Mrs. Moorhouse, was left to 'Benjamin Jowett, father of the Rev. Benjamin Jowett, a Professor of Greek in the University of Oxford', and, after the death of the first-named Benjamin, then to the said Benjamin his son. In 1870, a month after his election to the Mastership of Balliol, Jowett thus suddenly became a freehold landed proprietor through the will of a very old gentleman whom he had never met and possibly never even heard of. He was, also, one of the heirs-at-law to the copyholds; eventually he bought out his co-heirs and sold the copyhold land for £5,505. 'The Freehold' noted Bishop Stubbs, from whose letters to Evelyn Abbott this information derives, 'was probably a good deal more, but I have no data.' If it is asked how Stubbs came into the matter, the answer is that he had a passion for genealogy, and that the original William Bilton, who was one of Jowett's ancestors six generations back, was the great-nephew of an Alice Bilton, who married a still remoter ancestor of the Bishop.[1]

[1] There is a brief reference to all this in the *Life and Letters*; but most of it comes from Stubbs's unpublished letter. (*J.P.*)

The Henry Jowett who migrated to London about 1700 had a son of the same name. This son died in 1801 — only sixteen years before the birth of his famous great-grandson. A man of magnificent patriarchal type, and the ancestor of innumerable Jowetts, he must be drawn full-size, if with few strokes.

Born in London in 1719, he was brought up by an aunt at Whitby. After a wilful 'voyage to Petersburg', he was apprenticed by his father to a London hat-maker, attended the early sermons of George Whitefield, and experienced religion. He married before he was twenty-three, and most of his children died in infancy. But there were five children left, when he removed from London to Leeds in 1757. The move was, no doubt, made for business reasons. His business was that of a skinner or furrier. It was, presumably, that which had been established by his father and which finally fell to pieces under his grandson's ineffective management. At Leeds he became a close friend of the celebrated evangelical surgeon, William Hey; and also of Henry Venn, the equally celebrated disciple of John Wesley. His wife died in 1771. After her death he came back to London, married an excellent widow whose 'conduct in the family was such as to gain their esteem', and eventually settled in Camberwell Green where he spent the last twenty-one years of his life. One of his granddaughters, a Mrs. Elizabeth Pratt, wrote a fascinating account of him.

In the government of his family my grandfather was thought to be strict; his children greatly reverenced him, yet it must be confessed that they often felt a degree of awe in his presence, which made them in their boyish days rather shrink from his company. His family worship too was somewhat calculated to exhibit religion in an austere light. He usually read in the evening a whole chapter with Matthew Henry's commentary, which occupied so much time that the children and servants got sleepy and tired. If the boys showed symptoms of drowsiness, they were required to stand up, and their father would ask their opinion of a sentiment or put some question which required them to have attended to the reading in order to answer it. . . . I shall never forget his patriarchal benediction which he pronounced on me and Mr. Pratt when we went to take leave of him. He was sitting by the fireside in his dressing gown with his night cap and a large cocked hat on his head, and before we left him he raised himself on his feet, feeble and tottering as he was, and with a most graceful air took his hat off and prayed that the blessing of God the Father, God the Son, and God the Holy Ghost might rest upon us. He did this with much emotion, and I could have imagined that it was the patriarch Jacob blessing his posterity.[1]

Henry left behind him 'a very striking dedication of himself to God', according to the formula given in Doddridge's *Rise and Progress of*

---

[1] *L. & L.*, i, 5 to 6. The original narrative, preserved in the Jowett Papers, is unfortunately much too long to reproduce.

Religion in the Soul. He was always addressed by his grown-up sons as 'Dear and honoured Sir'. His own letters 'expressed in the peculiar dialect of Methodism' showed that he had his wits fully about him. In *The Life and Correspondence of Henry Venn* there is a pleasing pendant to Mrs. Pratt's description. 'The sight of your venerable father,' wrote Mr. Venn to one of the Patriarch's sons 'so unexpected, revived and rejoiced my heart. An old disciple who has always walked uprightly, and been a credit to his profession, is one of the finest sights upon earth. . . . I could not help looking on your dear father as on the verge of a glorious eternity.' Beside the warmth of this testimonial, not the less genuine because the verge of eternity was still twenty-one years away, the following sentence from Pearson's *Life of Hey* has a prosaic, but confirmatory, ring. 'Mr. Jowett, senior, was not less remarkable for the soundness of his understanding, than for his steady and ardent attachment to the cause of religion.'

With the exception of a first cousin of his father's named William, who died unmarried, and a second cousin, Surgeon-Major Thomas Joseph Jowett, the Master of Balliol was said to have been the last surviving male member of the family founded by his great-grandfather. It is not easy to understand how it came about that, after three prolific generations, the vigorous patriarchal stock died away so completely.

3. THE OTHER PROFESSOR

The 'Other Professor' was Jowett's great-uncle Joseph, the patriarch's second son, Regius Professor of Civil Law in the University of Cambridge from 1782 to 1813.

He, too, needs to be drawn life-size. It is not often that great-uncles present themselves as laughable caricatures of famous great-nephews. That is Joseph's possibly unique fate. It is hard on his ghost that it should have to stand comparison with that of the Master of Balliol; for he was a well-meaning little man. But the comparison cannot be avoided.

Joseph was born in 1752. He was educated at Leeds, and was admitted as a sizar of Trinity College, Cambridge, at the age of seventeen. Four years later he migrated to Trinity hall, having been recommended by his tutor, the Rev. Dr. Postlethwaite, to Dr. Postlethwaite's intimate evangelical friend, Dr. Halifax, as a likely young man. Dr. Halifax was the Regius Professor of Civil Law. He appears to have had in his pocket not only the certainty of a bishopric for himself but the power of dictating who should succeed him first as a fellow of Trinity hall and subsequently as Regius Professor.

All befell according to plan, after the patriarch had been brought round to give his reluctant consent. 'The present plan' he said 'was quite contrary to all his views and wishes. He had set his heart on his son's becoming a useful, active minister in the church, and not that he should be buried in pursuits of literature.' In a couple of years Joseph succeeded to Halifax's fellowship and prepared himself, by taking the degree of a Doctor of Laws, to succeed also to Halifax's professorship when Halifax became Bishop of Gloucester. No difficulties occurred in the issue of His Majesty's patent, and in 1781, at the age of twenty-nine, Dr. Joseph Jowett became Regius Professor of Civil Law.

Joseph was pious and sentimental. He was given to masculine friendships. He had an exquisite falsetto voice. He was an ardent evangelical. He had no influence other than his personal charm; and he had no serious intellectual qualifications. His attainments were not rated highly in Cambridge. A later Master of Trinity hall wrote dryly to the Master of Balliol's biographers:

Professor Jowett, it seems, published some *Lectures on Civil Law* in 1795, but his memory is mainly preserved by some verses written on him by Wrangham. The Professor was not a man of mark, and but for these lines would be unknown.

As remembered in Trinity hall the verses ran thus:

> *A little garden little Jowett made*
> *And fenced it with a little palisade.*
> *If you would know the little wit of Jowett,*
> *This little garden doth a little show it.*[1]

The garden filled up a small irregular space between the college wall and the street. There, in the phraseology of his admiring obituarist, he 'amused both himself and the public by a pretty little fairy garden, with

---

[1] There are almost as many variants of this quatrain as of the more familiar quatrain about the Master of Balliol. They turn mostly upon the substitution of 'taste' for 'wit'. In the *Biographia Leodiensis* the verses were assigned not to Wrangham (later Archdeacon Wrangham), who was an undergraduate at Trinity hall in Joseph Jowett's time, but to Dr. Mansel, the Master of Trinity. J. W. Clark in the *D.N.B.* adds the following lopsided couplet between the opening and closing couplets:

> *But when this little garden made a little talk*
> *He changed it to a little gravel-walk.*

Clark, who takes a sympathetic view of Joseph Jowett, thinks that Wrangham was the author and that the lampoon was inspired by personal malice—Joseph having successfully opposed Wrangham's candidature for a fellowship of Trinity hall.

narrow gravel walks, besprinkled with shells and pellucid pebbles, the whole being enclosed by a delicate Chinese railing.'

If not a man of serious academic distinction (though he is said to have been a sound Latinist) the fat little alto-voiced professor shone like a cherub among his evangelical friends. 'Perfectly orthodox in his religious sentiments, extraordinarily well acquainted with the severe parts of Holy Writ, he was an inestimable friend to the Established Church.' Nor was his influence 'confined to speculations in the closet. . . . How often has the modest, diffident youth, when derided by his companions for being over-religious, silenced their profane reproaches by appealing to the example of Dr. Jowett!'

Nothing could have been more admirable than the management of his private life:

Notwithstanding his great attainments, and his numerous occupations, the professor was rarely observed to be pressed for time. Exact and regular in his arrangements, temperate and even abstemious in his indulgences, he found the twenty-four hours sufficient for every necessary or desirable purpose of life. . . . His temper was naturally cheerful and lively; and his passions were at all times obedient to a systematic discipline. His own internal resources were so abundant, that his spirits were rarely known to flag; he was not only an example of a person of excellent health, but of one who himself possessed many of the very best preservatives of good health — viz. a natural serenity of mind, supported and improved by a good conscience, and a steady hope and prospect of eternal happiness; and these superior principles by no means excluded from the mind of Dr. Jowett an extraordinary relish for many innocent and rational enjoyments of an inferior value. Often he regaled his senses in admiring the beauties of nature, but oftener refreshed his intellectual faculties by perusing the best compositions both in prose and verse. He was passionately fond of music, and a warm admirer of the finest productions of the great masters in painting and architecture.

After the Bible and the Cambridge Auxiliary Bible Society the professor's chief enthusiasms were music and Dean Milner. He sang alto (and sang very well) and played the violin, and promoted musical parties and concerts. Two evenings in every week were spent alone with his contemporary, Isaac Milner, the first Professor of Natural Philosophy at Cambridge, President of Queens' College and Dean of Carlisle. And Milner, after his friend's sudden death in 1813, lamented with a pen as heavy as his heart that, after the first effusions of grief and surprise had subsided into a more sedate and pensive state of the affections, no individual would experience more substantial causes for painful and melancholy reflection than himself.

A notable feature of the professor's life was a benevolent interest in young men. 'How often' exclaimed his obituarist 'have both young graduates and undergraduates, of a pious turn of mind, been kindly taken by the hand, and directed and supported in their Christian course by the same judicious and excellent person!' An especial favourite was his nephew Joe, his elder brother John's son, who shared his passion for music. It was said in the family 'that the Doctor acted injudiciously in leading his nephew to give more time to musical parties than was compatible with studious habits. (Dr. Jowett was a bachelor.)'[1]

The similarities between Professor Jowett of Cambridge and Professor Jowett of Oxford are almost too obvious. Each had the same falsetto voice, the same puny physique running into plumpness, the same celibate habit, the same constancy in friendship, the same liking for young men, the same serenity of temperament, the same calmness in the face of opposition. But these similarities are the superficial cover for profound differences. The great-uncle was a man of closed and commonplace mind, the great-nephew a man of expanding and exceptional mind; the one orthodox, the other unorthodox; the one ridiculous, the other formidable; the one presented with the easiest of passages through life, the other confronted with successive hard and bitter tests of his quality; the one flatteringly mirrored in a society of religious sentimentalists, the other steering his difficult course between credulity and scepticism, a moving target for the extremists on either flank.

4. 'THE CHRISTIAN FAMILY'

Joseph's portrait has been exhibited by itself. But he was the second, not the first, of the patriarch's four sons. The eldest son was John, who joined his father in the family business. The third son was Benjamin, the Master of Balliol's grandfather, who also went into the firm. The fourth was Henry, who — like his brother Joseph — was designed by his father for a clerical career and sent to Cambridge. All these three sons married and had numerous children. There was one daughter, Sarah, who died unmarried.

Except for anybody with a relish for family history, it would be tedious to follow in detail the fortunes of the two prolific branches of the Jowett family founded by John and Henry. Both branches died out — or, at any rate, vanished from sight — in the third generation. The third and equally prolific branch, founded by Benjamin, died with the Master of Balliol. It is essential, nevertheless, to take more than a mere passing glance at the pages of the Jowett family album. For the background of failure,

[1] From an unpublished letter written in 1878 by his great-niece Isabella Hudson. (*J.P.*)

which was so powerful a determinant in Jowett's character and career, was not provided only by his father's failure, though that touched him most closely. It was provided by the entire failure of a once numerous and prosperous and confident clan. And, as we turn over the leaves of the album, we begin to perceive why the young Balliol tutor revolted so strongly against the shallow quasi-religious optimism which ran in his family. We have already seen, in his great-uncle Joseph, that his physical inheritance belonged to a recurring and abnormal pattern. His mental inheritance more than made good the physical inheritance. But the family history strongly suggests that another fatal and connected weakness was introduced into the vigorous patriarchal stock — possibly by the patriarch's first wife, Sarah Woodman, ancestress of the whole clan. This weakness defies exact description. It showed itself in the repeated inability or unwillingness of the patriarch's descendants to face unpleasant facts and to master reverses; and, finally, in the death of the whole prolific tree. Jowett's singular strength of will and clarity of mind enabled him to defeat it, so far as it threatened his individual career; though traces of it seem, now and again, to be discernible, as in his recurring bouts of depression and in the childish withdrawal to his tent after his disappointment over the Mastership in 1854. But he could not save the tree.

The first of the leaves to be turned records a meeting of Christian Latrobe, at the house of 'the Rev. Mr. Gambier', with the Master of Balliol's great-uncles, John and Henry Jowett, in 1790; and Latrobe's subsequent admission to the intimacy of John's household, which was then the central sun of the Jowett system.[1]

Latrobe was the English-born son of a Moravian missionary. He had been educated abroad at a Moravian college, came back to England in 1784 and was ordained as a Moravian minister. He 'laboured at home with great zeal'. But the common interest which brought him and John and Henry Jowett into quick sympathy was not theology. It was music. Latrobe is remembered, still, as a minor composer 'of no little excellence'; and he had, of course, easy command of the harpsichord.

When John and his youngest brother walked over from John's house at Newington Butts they supposed that they were merely paying an evening call upon Mr. Gambier. But Mr. Gambier had Latrobe as his guest. The arrival of two 'grave looking gentlemen' seems to have been at first a little unwelcome. The encounter began rather stiffly. It warmed up into an argument about the virtues of Handel, which did not end till

---

[1] A short account of this meeting is given in the *Life and Letters*, i, 11, abbreviated from the long description of it in Latrobe's *Letters to my Children*.

one in the morning, and was resumed at six. 'We could hardly part at nine.' After this Latrobe became a fast friend of John Jowett's family circle and a convert to their Handelian views. 'They had made *Home* the most pleasant place on earth'; distinguished by the decorous behaviour of John's children and by the astonishing fact that it contained 'a choir of vocal performers, the most perfect of its kind!' John's two daughters sang the treble, Professor Joseph the alto, John and his brother Henry the tenor parts. John's eldest son, another Henry, sang bass. This family choir rendered 'all Handel's oratorios, or rather select portions of them, with great precision'. Latrobe accompanied them at the harpsichord. He thought as highly of their singing as of their Christian graces. 'All their voices were good — but Eliza's treble, and Dr. Jowett's alto were, I may truly say, the sweetest and richest of their kind *I* have ever heard.'

At the time of his first meeting with Latrobe, John Jowett was a prosperous merchant in partnership with his brother Benjamin (the Master of Balliol's grandfather) in Red Lion Court, Bermondsey. The firm is said to have dealt in furs supplied by the Hudson's Bay Company. Family tradition had it that they were in the 'beaver-trade'. It is a probable guess that the business had been founded by John's father, the patriarch, on the connections which he had formed as a young man during his apprenticeship to a hat-manufacturer. Its headquarters seem to have been transferred from London to Leeds, when the patriarch went back to Leeds in 1757; for it was there that John, after the beginnings of an education in London, 'was brought up to his father's business, that of a skinner.' When his father returned to London, John stayed behind. For a few years there were, perhaps, two offices — one in London and one in Leeds. About 1780, when his father retired from business, John came to London, presumably to take over from his father in partnership with his brother Benjamin. A business connection with Leeds was maintained by regular visits. This is implied by a letter from the patriarch to one of his sons in 1782, in which he says: 'Your brother John goes the north journey.'

John was a chip off the old block. Like his father, he suffered conversion. When he lived in the north, he was an eager disciple of his father's friend Henry Venn, the Vicar of Huddersfield, and a close companion of the pious surgeon, William Hey. He walked frequently with Hey to Huddersfield, was encouraged by Hey to play the organ, was introduced by Hey to the writings of Locke and Butler, and married Hey's sister-in-law. Hey's verbose biographer says this of him:

Although Mr. John Jowett had not been educated for any of the learned professions, yet he was well informed in many departments of knowledge, and had directed his studies more especially to moral and theological subjects. He possessed a sound and penetrating observation, his elocution was fluent, perspicacious, and agreeable; and he would carry on his discussions, upon the subjects he had considered, with an acuteness that tended to the eliciting of truth, and a vivacity tempered with good humour, which was always interesting.

Later, in London, John became an intimate disciple of John Newton, the incumbent of St. Mary Woolnoth and friend of Cowper. He was an influential lay evangelical and was active in the foundation of the Church Missionary Society.

But John lacked the patriarchal mark of long life. When the century died he died with it, at the age of fifty-six, a year before his father. Their deaths marked the end of the Jowett golden age. 'The family' wrote Latrobe 'gradually dispersed, and its members now occupy different stations in life, preserving however, that character generally, which still entitles them to the appellation of the *Christian* family.'

On John's death his brother Benjamin succeeded to the management of the family business. John's own eldest son Henry had naturally been brought up with the prospect of following his father and his uncle; he was a partner with his uncle Benjamin and his cousin Benjamin (the Master of Balliol's grandfather and father) until the firm collapsed in 1825. What became of him after that the record does not say; or whether he was a married or unmarried man. He had four younger brothers. John, nearest in age to himself, studied medicine with his 'uncle Hey', took orders and died unmarried. The next brother, Joshua, set up as an ironmonger in Liverpool; having failed there, he came back to London where he 'gave musical parties', and was again unsuccessful in business. He married twice and had a number of children. If it is true that there were only two surviving descendants of the patriarch bearing the name of Jowett, at the time of the Master of Balliol's death, then Joshua's branch (and Henry's, if he started one) had completely died off.

The two younger brothers fared better. Joseph — John's fourth son — went up to Cambridge soon after his father's death. He was the Joe who was thought by the family to give more time than he should to his uncle Joseph's musical parties. But Joe did well for himself. He married money and acquired the Lincolnshire living of Silk Willoughby. His health was weak, and he passed most of his life in the south of England, writing hymn-tunes and sermons, and doing editorial work for the C.M.S. Five of his six children died of consumption. The one survivor was the Surgeon-Major Jowett (of the Indian Army) who outlived the Master of Balliol.

John's youngest son, William, also went to Cambridge. Coached by his mathematical uncle Henry, Rector of Little Dunham, he was placed twelfth wrangler and became a fellow of St. John's. He married young, and spent several years travelling in the Levant for the C.M.S., before he became clerical secretary to the Society in London. For a few years before his death in 1855 he was Rector of St. John's Clapham — the living formerly held by his uncle Henry's friend, John Venn. All his children died of consumption. William was a prolific writer. He translated the fourth Gospel into Italian and Maltese, and published many sermons, some verse and a book called *Christian Researches in the Mediterranean*.

Besides the five sons of John Jowett there were two daughters. One, Elizabeth, married the Rev. Josiah Pratt; it was she who wrote the memorable description of her grandfather, the patriarch. The other, Hannah, married 'a Mr. Hudson of the Haymarket, a chemist and druggist, purveyor of Extract of Sarsaparilla, by which he made a very considerable fortune'. Both the Pratts and the Hudsons had children, whose descendants may well be alive and prosperous. It was only upon the male line that the curse of final sterility was said to have fallen.

So much for the senior of the branches founded by the patriarch's three married sons. The second branch, founded by Benjamin, died out with his grandson. That story needs to be told separately; its sad, slow ending is a recurrent theme in Jowett's family life. There remains the third branch, founded by the youngest son, Henry — one of the two grave-looking gentlemen who made Latrobe's acquaintance at Mr. Gambier's house.

Like his brother Joseph, the little professor, Henry was sent by the patriarch to Cambridge. In his fourth year he was ranked as 6th senior optime. Soon afterwards he was made a fellow of his college, Magdalene. It seemed as if the patriarch's desire to see his four sons pulling their active weight alternately in his business and in the ministry was to be again frustrated. Henry spent twelve years at Cambridge as a tutor and lecturer in mathematics. During this time he became intimate with Charles Simeon, the evangelical fellow of King's. He was already a friend of John Venn who was three years his junior, the son of his father's friend Henry Venn. The call of nature, rather than the call of God, at last obliged him to give up his academical career. Two years after his meeting with Latrobe he married, and became Rector of Little Dunham in Norfolk in succession to John Venn. At Little Dunham he augmented his stipend by taking pupils.

The retiring Rector stayed on at Little Dunham for a few months side by side with the new Rector. John Venn had a strong 'turn for forming societies'. As an undergraduate he had planted several about Cambridge; he was to be one of the principal founders of the Church Missionary Society; and he had just started 'a Clerical Society, among a few zealous but distantly scattered clergy, who were to meet twice a year at Little Dunham'. On hearing of this his father wrote to him ecstatically:

What am I that I should ever live to see my prayers for a beloved son, a Gospel minister, now more than ever answered. *Usefulness is all, in Christians*. . . . I could not help clapping my hands, and singing Hallelujah. . . . Your proposal of meeting twice a year is from above.

The old man's excitement seems excessive. It expressed the febrile tone of the religious world in which the 'Christian family' was shaped. But the emphatic phrase *usefulness is all* deserves to be noticed. For this was the active, healthy principle, which Jowett's stronger and cooler brain isolated from the slops of evangelical sentiment.

Henry stayed at Little Dunham until his death at the age of 74 in 1830. The tradition of the parish, sixty years later, had it that he was a mild and simple man 'much beloved'; and stories were still current of the pranks played by his pupils, who took advantage of these characteristics. Some of these pupils became men of distinction — such as Sir James Stephen, the Colonial under-secretary nicknamed 'Mr. Over-Secretary Stephen'; and Charles Grant, afterwards Lord Glenelg, who was Colonial secretary under Melbourne. There were eight children — six sons and two daughters. Writing to his sister Sarah in 1806 the Rector told her:

You would have been much entertained this afternoon to hear Henry and Edward sing in grand chorus 'There was a jolly miller etc.', and I think it won't be long ere we shall again have a musical family, and be able as formerly . . . with united voices to sing the praises of God.

Alas! The Christian musical family was beyond resurrection. Henry's eldest son married 'a woman of humble origin' and he and his descendants (if any) sank out of sight. Three other sons died young. Another married, and also passed out of the family view. There was a fifth son, William, about whom his father wrote humorously to his sister Sarah in 1806:

We have a very respectable young gentleman here, who seems to be unaccountably forgotten at Newington. If any person should happen to enquire after Mr. W. Jowett, I am happy to say that he is well and braves neglect as well as I think he ought.

Our next and only other glimpse of Mr. W. Jowett is at Brighton in 1894, after the Master of Balliol's death, as an old bachelor getting on for ninety, being pumped for information about his distinguished cousin's history. The lady engaged in this task met with no success.[1] She wrote to Campbell:

> I have not been able to get much information from Mr. Jowett; he knew very little of his cousin, and he so quickly gets confused. If Aunt Charlotte had been still alive we could have found out a great deal from her, as she was up in all the family history. I remember her telling me that the Master was brought up by two aunts, and that he was always a very genteel little child. The only information we can really get from Mr. Jowett is that the Master was always spoken of as 'poor Ben'.

5. THE TRIBE OF BENJAMIN

The patriarch called his third son Benjamin. Luckily there are only three Benjamin Jowetts who need to be remembered: the patriarch's son Benjamin I; his grandson Benjamin II; and his great-grandson 'little Benjamin their ruler', as men outside Balliol sometimes irreverently described the Master of Balliol.

Benjamin I was born in 1754 and died in 1837, when his grandson Benjamin was nineteen. He was educated at Leeds Grammar school. On leaving school he was put to his father's business, in accordance with his father's determination to dedicate his sons alternately to business and religion. When his father retired, he was already a partner with his eldest brother John. In 1785 he married Anne Jowett, his second cousin.[2] They lived in Camberwell, within easy reach of his father's house, of the warehouse in Bermondsey, and of brother John's establishment in Newington Butts, in that part of suburban London where the name of Jowett had become known and respected. There Anne bore him five children.

This was the golden age of the Jowett clan, while the patriarch watched the multiplication of his seed. The first disaster befell in 1799, when 'Nancy' — as the old man called Anne — died under her sixth confinement. Next year died brother John, and the year after that the patriarch himself. To the survivors it must have seemed — and truly — that the earth had been shaken.

With John's guiding hand removed the business, under Benjamin I, entered a swift decline. John's eldest son, Henry, had been taken into partnership. So, too, was Benjamin's eldest son, Benjamin II, almost before he was out of his 'teens. The style of the firm was altered to Benjamin Jowett and Sons.

A year or two after his wife's death Benjamin I married again — a

---

[1] Mary Whiting, niece of a Dr. Whiting, who had married William's sister Charlotte. She was put on to the job by the indefatigable Campbell. (*J.P.*)
[2] See above, 48.

lady named, curiously enough, Sarah Ann Jowitt, by whom he had two daughters. Before long he was running into financial difficulties and borrowing money from his good-natured younger brother Henry of Little Dunham. In 1815 the debt was still owing: 'I forgot that he had not yet received my father's legacy. I shall wait patiently' wrote Henry to Sarah. This was fourteen years after the patriarch's death; the widow would have had a life-interest in the estate.

In 1823, when his eldest grandson was six years old, Benjamin I, now nearing seventy, suddenly abandoned the dying business in Bermondsey to the charge of his son and his nephew and migrated to Liverpool, where his two younger sons Josiah and Henry had taken a shop of some kind, and his nephew Joshua had set up as an ironmonger. There he was visited, in the same year, by his brother Henry of Little Dunham, who wrote to Sarah expressing relief at an appearance of prosperity which he had evidently not at all expected. 'The sons have a very handsome shop in one of the principal streets.'

Meanwhile in Bermondsey Benjamin II and his cousin Henry were failing to stave off disaster. It was the second Benjamin's unhappy destiny to decline from failure to failure, and there can be little doubt that this destiny was largely of his own making. But it is impossible not to perceive an equal weakness in his father, whose first duty it was to preserve the business of which he had inherited the major direction, and which had nourished himself and his brothers and sister. His migration to Liverpool was the pursuit of a mirage. The 'handsome shop' failed; his sons (or at any rate one of them) emigrated to Australia. His nephew Joshua also failed. The old man himself remained — apparently without moral or material discomfort — in Liverpool until he died in 1837, at the age of eighty-two.

By that date the Bermondsey business was long defunct, and his eldest son had become a poverty-stricken hack-writer. By what means his own *ménage* in Liverpool was maintained, and on what level, the family records do not say. It is a probable guess that he lived off his second wife. But out of the tantalizing fog emerges at least one remarkable fact. Benjamin I simply ignored the slings and arrows of fortune. He retained to the very end of his life the serenest confidence in a long departed dream. 'I would recommend to your young folks' he wrote just before his death to one of his relatives 'to encourage music in a moderate degree, it is a great assistance to sacred words, and helps to keep a family alive.' This optimistic self-deceit was inherited by his son Benjamin; his grandson inherited the serenity and the optimism, but not the self-deceit. He inherited also the love of music.

But music had sadly failed to keep the Christian family alive. Perhaps it had occupied too much of the time which ought to have been given to mundane affairs. Old Benjamin seems to have been half aware of this, when he counselled the younger folks to be 'moderate' in their musical pleasures. But even this advice was long out-of-date. It was forty-seven years since Latrobe had made the acquaintance of the 'Christian family'; and the family was now fallen into pieces which would never come together again. Evidences of this disunity were present in the old man's mind, as he wrote; but not its causes. 'It is now several years since I heard of Edward and Henry; in what way they are settled and how they live, if I could hear anything well of them it would afford me much pleasure.' Edward and Henry were two of his younger brother Henry's children.

In the correspondence of the eldest Benjamin and his brothers, and of their father the patriarch, nothing is more marked than the strong sense of solidarity which then prevailed in the family. They visited each other frequently, they entertained their nephews and nieces, they followed the fortunes of each other's children. It is curious and sad to observe how quickly in the succeeding generation of these same nephews and nieces, even in the lifetimes of their fathers, this solidarity vanished. The collapse of the family business was certainly a main cause of the dispersion; another was, perhaps, that centrifugal tendency which characterizes so much of English family life. Whatever the reason for the fact, the fact itself needs to be noticed, because it brought about that singular detachment from his family background, which was necessary for the development of the last Benjamin Jowett.

CHAPTER III

The Parents of Melchizedec

1. ISABELLA LANGHORNE

The high-pitched voice, the celibate habit, the seriousness of aim, the serenity of temperament — these were characters which came to Jowett from his father's family. It must have been through his mother that he derived qualities of which there is no trace in his Jowett ancestry — the patient tenacity of purpose, the adventurous width and poise of mind, the unselfconscious power of leadership. Nor is there any evidence, in the Christian family album, that its members possessed either wit or a sense of humour. Jowett's wit tended to be sharp; his sense of humour a little wry. But there is abundant evidence of both wit and humour in his published letters, especially in his letters to Arthur Stanley.[1] The stories of his wit are legion.

His mother's maiden name was Isabella Langhorne. The Langhorne tree had never borne fruit like Jowett before. And it cannot be said that Jowett, like so many great men, owed his greatness to his mother. Yet there were a forceful and adventurous strain and a touch of uncommon distinction in her ancestry. The Langhorne clan, with its traditional coat of arms (three hunting horns) cherished historical and genealogical memories of a kind wholly unknown to the Jowetts. They liked to think that they carried in their veins the blood of Andrew, King of Hungary. They claimed that the first of their name was Huntsman to William the Conqueror. A Major Langhorne had defended Ludlow Castle against Oliver Cromwell. A Richard Langhorne had been a victim of Titus Oates. A Sir William Langhorne was governor of Madras late in the eighteenth century.

For the Kirkby Stephen branch of the family (from which Isabella was descended) these were remote connections. But of one distinguished collateral (not direct) ancestor they boasted with certainty. This was John Langhorne, Rector of Blagdon, the poet and translator of *Plutarch*

---

[1] For a very good example of both see the humorous account of his experiences at Cuddesdon, as a candidate for ordination, in a letter to Stanley, *L. & L.*, i, 120–2.

who died in 1779; described by Saintsbury as an excellent specimen of a
not excellent poet, owning 'at least sometimes a melancholy clangour of
verse too rare in his century'.

The poet's family belonged to a younger branch of the Westmorland
Langhornes. His father was a village parson and schoolmaster. While the
first Henry Jowett (the Master of Balliol's great-great-grandfather) was
establishing himself as a skinner in London, the Rev. Joseph Langhorne
(also the Master's great-great-grandfather) was preaching and teaching
in the little village of Winton beneath the fells. John Langhorne was
one of two sons. Jowett's Langhorne descent did not go through John,
but through a brother of John's. While the second Henry Jowett (the
patriarch) was consolidating his father's business, a nephew of John
Langhorne, named Joseph like his grandfather, seems to have broken
away from the traditions of his family and sought his fortune in trade, as
a Lancashire cotton merchant, and to have done well enough to retire
from business early in middle age.[1] After his retirement he settled in the
south, near Camberwell, where his daughter Isabella met and married
the Master of Balliol's father in 1814.

Isabella was the youngest daughter in a family of five. Her elder
brother, Henry, set up as a banker in Bucklersbury. The bank failed,
like so many other small banks — among them the bank in which
Cardinal Newman's father was a partner — in the financial crisis which
followed the Anglo-American war of 1812 to 1816. Undismayed, Henry
started again as an insurance broker and succeeded in rearing fifteen sons
and daughters. Many of the sons emigrated to Australia. Youngest of this
large family was the Miss Langhorne already mentioned[2] who assisted
one of her brothers to run a school at Brighton.

Not the slightest trace remains of any intimacy between the Master
of Balliol and this huge batch of first cousins on his mother's side. This
is the more remarkable because, as a little boy, he used to stay with them
at Mitcham (where Henry Langhorne then lived) and do lessons with
their tutor. 'I have heard my brothers say' recalled Miss Langhorne
'that they had no chance against him with their Greek lessons.' Perhaps
that was part of the reason for the failure of contact. But his sister Emily
'was as a sister' to Miss Langhorne.

Isabella's father was already dead (he was said to have died 'young')

---

[1] This account follows Jowett's recollections of what his mother had told him.
(*L. & L.*, i, 14.) But who was the cotton-merchant's father? Was he John's elder
brother William, who was also something of a poet and co-operated with John in
the translation of Plutarch? I have assumed so in constructing the outline
pedigree for Appendix III; but this is mere assumption. The Curate of Winton
may have had another son, who was Jowett's actual great-grandfather.
[2] See above, 46.

when her brother Henry started his bank, but her mother and her mother's three sisters were living with Henry at the time of her marriage. Besides Henry, who was then a man of about thirty-five, there was a younger brother named Thomas. Thomas is a man of mystery; an Australian nephew, George Langhorne, who was keenly interested in the history of his family, had 'never seen or heard of him'. There were also two twin sisters, Jane and Frances. These two Langhorne aunts mattered in young Ben's life, as his Jowett relations did not.

Frances married a Rev. William Smith, who died in 1823. After her elderly husband's death Mrs. Smith went to live in Bath. She had no children of her own, and her house became later on a haven of refuge for Isabella.

Jane 'pretty and charming' was married some years before Isabella, to a Mr. J. B. Courthope, a wholesale stationer off Lombard Street, with a substantial house at Blackheath. The unhappy fate which dogged so many of Jowett's relatives lay in wait for Jane and her husband. Mr. Courthope's business went downhill. The family moved out of the substantial house into a smaller one. The children died one after another — no doubt from the 'consumption' which was then the scourge of so many households. The last to go was Sidney, Jowett's own equal in age.[1] He died soon after his father and mother in 1845, and the young Balliol tutor sat by his cousin's bedside.

Only the youngest daughter Elizabeth survived. She and her brothers and sisters — aunt Jane Courthope's children — had always meant more to Jowett than his uncle Henry Langhorne's children, and far more than any of his own Jowett cousins. Elizabeth married a Colonel Irwin, at one time Commandant of the troops at the Swan River settlement in western Australia. The Colonel died about 1859,[2] when Jowett was in his early forties, leaving a widow and five children and little else. Miss Langhorne, severely as she disapproved of the Master's religious opinions, laid it to his credit that after the Colonel's death 'Dr. Jowett had been like a Father to Sidney and the others who were quite young, watching them through Wellington College and Oxford'.

Miss Langhorne was a just and accurate old lady. 'Watching' was the word. Five unpublished letters remain, which Jowett wrote to Sidney. Two of these exhibit his solicitude in a peculiarly interesting way. They reveal a paternal — at any rate, an avuncular — aspect of Jowett which would otherwise be unknown, and brighten the blank picture of his

[1] Not to be confused with Sidney Irwin, Jowett's young second cousin, who is about to come into the story.
[2] According to another account, 'in the Crimean War.'

family life. They throw, incidentally, a revealing light upon his own character.[1]

The first was written in 1860, when Sidney had just gone to Wellington, and at a time when Jowett was in the middle of his own distressful decade (1855 to 1865). It is an attempt to put the fatherless boy on guard against schoolboy immorality. It opens with a characteristic, interrogatory, gambit 'Shall I give you one warning?' and continues:

I need not warn you about lying or falsehood. But there is another matter about which I ought to warn you because you have been brought up at home and are therefore happily innocent about it. It is one of the great trials of life at school. Boys about your age or a little older are sometimes very vicious and indecent both in word and also sometimes in action; indeed, it happens occasionally that there are one or two boys in a school horribly wicked about these things. Now if you come across anything of this sort take no part in it. Shut your ears to it, never allow an indecent word to pass your lips and don't laugh at indecent jests — don't sermonize to the boys about it but tell them it is beastliness and when you are strong enough give a boy a cuff in the eye who uses such language. Make it unmistakeable that you think it unmanly and filthy, and may God keep you pure from it as you are now. . . . (Perhaps there is no such thing in your school as I have described: if it creeps in set yourself decidedly against it.)

The second letter is no less interesting. It was written when Sidney had been at Wellington for a year.

Shall I give you some good advice? It is only this — to make yourself a good cricketer, football player etc., and not to sit 'sapping' too much while other boys are at play. It does not answer in the long run. You want to improve your mind as well as to do a certain number of lines, sums, etc. But you cannot do this unless you improve your health. The boys are not far wrong in respecting a boy who is 'good at games' and I would advise you to try and gain their respect in this way as well as in books. As to your work you should always do everything as well as you can. Write out your exercises neatly, say repetitions without missing a word, because that gets the habit of memory and accuracy. But don't try to do too much and don't lounge over your work. The real effort is to do well without spending a long time at your books.

Admirable, and crafty, advice to a studious boy! He might so easily have tried to make it acceptable by pinning it to himself. 'When I was a boy of your age' he might have written, with persuasive candour, 'I spent far too much time over my books, and indeed I fear that I am still guilty of doing so. It would have been better for me, and would have helped me much later on, if I had ever learned how to handle a cricket bat or to kick a football.' But, if he had so written, Sidney might well

---

[1] The letters come, of course, from the Jowett Papers. More use of the first of the two letters quoted here is made below at 84 foll.

have thought that what had been good enough for Cousin Benjamin was good enough for him. Moreover, though Jowett had already learned to regret that he had never shared the ordinary pleasures of boyhood, he knew well that he owed his success in life to 'sapping'. His advice to Sidney must, therefore, be adjusted to Sidney's circumstances and talents; the slightest element of self-confession must be excluded. The prescription was followed. Sidney became a schoolmaster at Clifton, whom his pupils remembered long after his death with affection and gratitude.

For all Jowett's kindness to his young Irwin cousins, there was a curious note of deliberate aloofness in his relations with them. The financial help, which he gave generously to the two boys, was always expressed as a loan, never (until towards the end of his life) as a gift; though, as he told his mother, they were loans he did not expect to be repaid. Guy Irwin, writing gratefully to him from India, addressed him not as 'Dear Cousin Benjamin' but as 'Dear Mr. Jowett' and was evidently in dread that he would be unable to discharge his debt. The terms of Jowett's Will show that these 'loans' were forgiven later on, when they had served the purpose of stimulating the fatherless boys to achieve independence. Perhaps they served, also, another purpose of which Jowett was not fully conscious, enabling him to pretend to himself that his motives had been dictated by a sense of duty rather than by natural affection.

In his Will he left £1,500 each to Sidney and Sidney's sister Harriett. His plate went to a cousin, Mrs. Stevens of Clifton, who was probably another member of the Irwin family; for Mrs. Irwin had settled at Clifton, where Sidney had become a master at the college. It was in the Irwins' house at Clifton that Emily Jowett passed the last years of her life. Guy Irwin was not named in the Will; but the omission meant only that he had been equally assisted in other ways. Both he and Sidney followed the Master's coffin.

2. BENJAMIN AND ISABELLA

When Isabella Langhorne was married to Benjamin Jowett on 22nd September 1814, her only male relative to sign the register was her brother-in-law John Courthope. The Jowetts were there in reasonable force. The bride's father was dead. The absence of her brother Henry, to whom she had always been 'devotedly attached', is noticeable. Perhaps Henry had his doubts of the bridegroom's staying power; perhaps there was already reason to suspect the stability of the Jowett business —

such reason as a local banker would be in a position to learn. If he showed disapproval of his sister's marriage by not attending the ceremony he did not carry it further. There was no estrangement. Yet there is a faint hint, an echo caught from the past, of patronage towards the Jowetts in Miss Langhorne's description, written eighty years later, of the Master of Balliol's mother as 'gentle sweet highly educated and superior in every way'. It was almost as much as to say that she was too good for the man she had married.

She was at once too good for him and not good enough. A woman with more force of character would not have merited her son's verdict 'unable to take care of herself'; would not have fallen back, as she did, upon her sister's charity; would have struggled to supply her husband's deficiencies and to keep the family together under one roof. Isabella was not cast in that heroic mould. She was sweet, she was pretty, she was gentle and uncomplaining; as an old lady 'her alabaster complexion, touched with shell-pink, was often suffused with a girlish blush at some casual surprise'; she was a favourite with children; she made 'a beautiful picture of refined old age'. Nevertheless, it was she who contrived to start her eldest son on his astonishing career.

Her husband was an attractive, virtuous and confident young man who never grew up or learned his way about the world of fact. He had high principles and great powers of self-belief. His son described him as 'one of the most innocent of men'. The same innocence belonged to his uncles Joseph and Henry. They had been allowed to follow their scholastic bents; he, like his father, had been put to a declining trade for which he had neither capacity nor inclination. Yet he never realized his own incapacity; nor did his innocence prevent him from always entertaining extremely decided opinions upon all subjects. He was tall, with 'a large face and head' and a profusion of long hair, which turned white in middle age and would have given him an impressive appearance, if it had not been for the indelible mark of worldly failure.

His mother 'Nancy' died when he was not yet eleven. Arrangements were made at once for the older children to be sent away to various schools. Benjamin was sent to 'Mr. Robinson's' at Leicester. This was in 1799, just before the break-up of the Jowett golden age. There can be little doubt that his upbringing suffered severely from this general family upheaval, from his mother's death and his father's subsequent remarriage. But we hear no more of him till his marriage to Isabella in 1814; he was then twenty-six and a fully-fledged 'furrier'.

The newly married couple set up house in Peckham. Their relations were all round them — the Courthopes at Blackheath, the John Jowetts at Newington, the elder Benjamin at Camberwell, the Langhornes only a few miles off at Mitcham.

Children came thick and fast — nine in twelve years. First Isabella, who died in infancy; then Emily, followed by Benjamin — the only two who were to outlive their parents. After Benjamin came Frank, who died when he was four years old. When Isabella removed to Bath in 1829, leaving her husband and her eldest son in London, she had with her Emily and five younger children. Of these Agnes and Ellen died in their 'teens; two sons, Alfred and William, entered the Indian army and died in India (in 1858 and 1850); a fourth son, Frederick, who 'never was himself', died in the same year as William.

It cannot have been long before Isabella began to know that her married life was not to be a bed of roses. Her adored brother Henry's failure as a banker had already warned her that business could go wrong. It is only too easy to picture the progress of disillusionment, as her husband's confident and opinionated manner failed to conceal the downward drift of his fortunes, and as she observed him giving to books time that he ought to have been spending on business. Little by little the two innocents drew apart; and their companionship gradually became, for Isabella, a painful farce. The pathetic story is revealed in a letter which she wrote in 1851 to her son Alfred:[1]

I have now no pecuniary cares, and Papa is, I must say, very kind and attentive to me. . . . The thing which pains me is to see that the Psalmody Versification has now become a complete monomania and occupies his time from morning till evening. This would be nothing to a stranger, but 22 years I have seen it,[2] and I will not say that it does not recall many painful reminiscences. But I sit in my own room, and feel it is a duty to bear with it, especially in his old age. I could not interfere with a harmless, if not useful, employment which gave him pleasure.

It is not easy to piece together the broken picture of Benjamin's childhood. 'He, who all his life was the friend of children' says Campbell 'must have had a happy childhood; but few traces of it can be recovered now.' It would have been a strange childhood, if it had contained no happy passages; and Campbell relates that 'he was seen by some who long remembered it' as a bright and merry child running about on Blackheath Common. His natural zest in quick movement was a conspicuous trait in the first half of his life. Campbell, vividly recalling him as he was

[1] *J.P.* Only one of Isabella's letters to Alfred is reproduced in the *Life and Letters* (i, 221). This was written in April 1851, soon after his arrival in India. She refers to her 'next' letter as one that Emily 'says I must send'. The reference is probably to the letter here quoted.
[2] The dating is oddly exact; it seems to suggest that the 'psalmody versification' began to trouble Isabella about 1829. This was the year when she went to live with her sister at Bath.

in his early thirties, wrote that 'those who knew him only in the late years, would have been surprised to see his slight figure racing about the Balliol quadrangle, or to hear him, as he often did, hum or whistle, as he came back to his room, some broken phrase of a familiar melody'.

Whatever happinesses entered into Jowett's childhood must have been largely of his own making. His father's religious views were strongly and narrowly evangelical; they were enforced upon all his children with a rigidity from which Emily and Benjamin escaped in later years — she into romanism, he into liberalism. His delicate mother's preoccupation with his sickly younger brother Frank and the two consumptive girls, as well as her successive confinements, must have robbed him of her care, though not of her love. Henry Langhorne and his wife strongly disapproved of the 'intellectual pressure' put upon Emily and Benjamin. Both children responded, almost too easily, to that pressure. Benjamin would be made to stand on the table after dinner and recite poetry — no doubt the poetry of Cowper. 'I was brought up on Cowper' he is reported to have said some fifty years later to a chance acquaintance, with whom he exchanged quotations for the best part of an hour without exhausting his or her repertoire.[1] His parents told Arthur Stanley 'how deeply historical he then was, studying Rollin's *Ancient History*, well versed in Assyrian dynasties, standing long in silent contemplation of a "Stream of Time" suspended in his little bedroom'. He and Emily, as children, shared the same precocious tastes. While she played Beethoven on the piano, he would listen and criticize; and the two would shut themselves up for hours in a room, in order to read together. And when visits were paid to their Courthope cousins 'sometimes, when the other children were at play, young Benjamin would be stretched upon the hearthrug with Pope's *Homer*'.[2]

The education which the boy picked up before he was twelve was partly the result of this spontaneous browsing, partly administered by an unconnected succession of casual teachers. At one time he lived with his Jowett aunts; this must have been before he was six years old, when his grandfather migrated to Liverpool. At another, later, time he had lessons from his father. It would be later still that he went to live with his Langhorne cousins at Mitcham, in order to share the teaching of their tutor, Mr. Richardson. The Langhorne boys 'had no chance against him with their Greek Lessons'.

A serious childhood is not necessarily an unhappy childhood. But Jowett's childhood was one in which there was little play or settled home life; especially as a preparation for the unnatural loneliness which was to

[1] *L. & L.*, i, 31. [2] *ibid.*, i, 30.

follow. He knew, afterwards, what he had missed. 'I was never taught how to play at cards, or even at billiards' he confessed half-humorously to a friend, when he was in his middle forties, 'and it seems too late to repair the error now. Do you think I could learn to waltz?' He was right, perhaps, to put the blame on others; though, if a boy wishes to play, he can surely do so without being 'taught'. The wish came too late.

Mrs. J. A. Symonds wrote about this to Abbott, after reading the *Life and Letters*:

It is impossible not to wonder a little how far *more play* and less gravity in childhood might have modified our dear Master's character. The play, or at least a kindly sympathy in it, seemed to come into him more and more quite late in his many-sided life out of his kindliness to young people.

A charming illustration of that late development is given in an unpublished letter written by Lord Westbury's daughter, Augusta Nash.

I have a lively recollection of a race to which he challenged me one Sunday afternoon when we were walking in the Park at Hinton, a challenge I accepted on condition that the further side of a five-barred gate should be the finish for both competitors. I was the winner, but he complied with the condition and clambered over the gate with a fair amount of agility. He was quite hilarious over it all. I shall never forget the funny appearance he presented as he ran along with the swallow tails of his coat flying up in the air and a benevolent smile on his face! When we joined the rest of the party round the tea-table and I remarked quietly that the Master and I had had a race, he greatly enjoyed the incredulity with which the announcement was received.

During the years of his childhood the Bermondsey business was fast dying. Grandfather Benjamin had deserted the ship when the boy was five years old. Two years later the partnership came to an end, and 'Benjamin Jowett Junior, Furrier' transferred what business still remained to his brother-in-law's (John Courthope's) office off Lombard Street. Nominally, he continued to trade from this address for another ten years; but the business done must have been negligible, for in 1826 he joined a mushroom firm of printers, 'Mills Jowett and Mills' of Bolt Court, Fleet Street. The firm had its chances, for its imprint appeared on the 1826 volume of *The Lancet*. But the new undertaking was no more successful than the old. It ceased to exist as the youngest Benjamin's school-days came to a close.

It is easy to understand the fatal attraction of printing for the literary-minded furrier; and easy to imagine the roseate optimism with which he entered upon his new venture. Certainly optimism was necessary, for there were already six children to feed and clothe and a seventh was about to arrive. The most serious problem was that of Ben's education. The boy was rising nine, and obviously a very clever child. The problem was solved, for the time being, by the lessons which he shared with his cousins at Mitcham. No doubt it was Isabella who contrived this arrangement; and no doubt it was Isabella who procured through her sister Jane's husband, John Courthope, the wholesale stationer, a nomination to St. Paul's school in the summer of 1829, when the boy was twelve years old; just as it was Isabella who planned, later on, his candidature for a scholarship at Balliol.

In the year of the nomination to St. Paul's, when the printing venture was some three years old, the affairs of Benjamin and Isabella reached a crisis. Isabella accepted an invitation from her widowed sister, Frances Smith, to make a home with her at Bath. Accident or an effort of desperation had provided for her eldest boy's education; and 'poor Ben' was left behind in London, terms and vacations alike, under the eye of his father. The rest of the family — that is to say, Isabella with her boys Alfred and William and the mentally deficient baby Frederick, and her three daughters, the precocious Emily and the consumptive Ellen and Agnes, — withdrew to Bath. There she remained for the next twelve years; while her husband, just turned forty, relieved of the cares of his family and already sitting loose to his new profession of printer, looked about for quasi-literary employment. 'He aspired' says his son's biographer 'to be a publisher's reader, and sought opportunities for dabbling in journalism, especially on questions of philanthropy.'

By one of those obscure compensations which almost compel belief in providence, Mr. Jowett's inability to earn a living was the indirect cause of his son's great career.

The first Factory Act of 1833, like its successors, was the consequence not so much of pressure from below as of research and persuasion by men of wealth and standing. Wood of Bradford, a brother-in-law of Gathorne-Hardy later Lord Cranbrook, and a friend of Lord Shaftesbury, was one of these. Wood, wrote Cranbrook more than half a century afterwards, 'was one of those who did good by stealth and left others to get much of the credit of his own work. He was deeply interested in the Factory question and in his quiet way furthered the success of the measures connected with it far more than those who took a more public part.'[1] Somehow the ex-furrier, printer and would-be litterateur, became one of Wood's, and later on one of Shaftesbury's 'writers'. He did that kind of work well. Lord Shaftesbury, in his diary, called him 'matchless'. There was not much money to be had from employment of this kind. But Wood's philanthropy was of a practical sort. Jowett was 'a poor man in whom he became interested', and his interest extended to

[1] From an unpublished letter, dated 13th October 1893. (*J.P.*)

his employee's family. He 'helped materially in the education' of the boy at St. Paul's — help which the Balliol tutor, according to Lord Cranbrook's belief, afterwards insisted on repaying — and Mrs. Wood corresponded kindly with Mrs. Jowett at Bath. It was the acquaintance of Isabella with the wife of her husband's benefactor which eventually sent Benjamin to Balliol.

So, for many years, Benjamin II eked out a scanty income, devilling for Wood and Shaftesbury, occasionally ghosting for unprofessional authors, his mind increasingly possessed by the grand vision of a new metrical version of the psalms, while his wife and his children lived on charity and his eldest son learned to regard him and his opinions with a feeling as near to contempt as a naturally affectionate and dutiful son could allow himself to entertain.

CHAPTER IV

Adolescence

1. ISOLATION AND SUCCESS

Jowett seldom — if ever — mentioned his school days, except to disparage the education he had received. This was unfair; for he owed his whole career to the Balliol scholarship which the teaching at St. Paul's enabled him to win.

The broad circumstances of his life from his twelfth to his nineteenth year are not in doubt. They were extraordinary. But the detailed record is meagre. There are no family or other letters; no autobiographical data. It is as if he deliberately screened this part of his life from view. And undoubtedly this was what, in fact, he sought to do — not because he had anything to be ashamed of for himself, but because he was ashamed for his father and because his school life was associated in his mind with the separation from his mother and brothers and sisters, which his father's incompetence brought about. It is possible that there was a further reason; this will be discussed in the next chapter.

It was in June 1829 that the eleven year old boy went to St. Paul's school, which then still stood under the shadow of Wren's cathedral church. He was a day-boy — there were no boarders at that date. The school-hours were from 7 or 8 to 11 or 12 in the mornings, and from 2 to 4 in three afternoons of the week. He had no home to go back to from school. He lodged by himself, within walking distance, somewhere in the City Road.

Mr. Jowett seems to have lived over the printing works in Bolt Court until his business was moved in 1834 to Johnson's Court before its third move and final demise. Sometimes Benjamin went to see his father in Bolt Court — an earnest fragile child, in a green sateen suit, exploring the tangle of courts and alleys in which Dr. Johnson's ghost was less than fifty years old. William Cobbett, not yet a ghost, one day opened the door to the boy and a couple of his school-fellows, sporting a tricolour ribbon in his buttonhole. Sometimes Benjamin was taken to the Cheshire Cheese by his father and put through an embarrassingly public examination while he ate his mid-day dinner.

73

He was an exile from home in holiday as well as in term time. His father paid occasional visits to Bath, but there was either no money for Benjamin to make the journey regularly or no room for him in his aunt's house. It is not credible that he spent his holidays, as a young boy, alone in the City Road lodgings. It appears that he stayed with his Courthope cousins at Blackheath, or with his Langhorne cousins at Clapham; and that Emily was sometimes asked up from Bath to be with her brother. Campbell speaks of 'the holidays passed with his sister at Blackheath or Clapham'.

This solitary way of life threw him upon his own internal resources. Other boys of his age have often found themselves alone in the world and made successes of their lives. But the self-made man, who has been compelled in childhood to stand upon his own feet, has usually been a man of action or business, not a scholar or a philosopher; or, if he has become a scholar in the end, he has had to begin by earning his living — like Schliemann, the excavator of Troy — and to educate himself in his spare time. Jowett's case must be almost unique. So far as his intellectual education was concerned, he had all the essential advantages, though he himself seems to have afterwards thought otherwise. The school which had educated Milton and Halley, Pepys and Marlborough and many another famous man, could meet his intellectual needs. Outside this part of education it could, in those days, do little or nothing. Out of school, young Ben was alone, from the age of eleven upwards.

All the accounts of him as a schoolboy tell the same story. A pretty-looking, gentle, delicate boy, with a round smooth face and very bright eyes, who kept himself to himself and to his books. The other boys called him Miss Jowett. They also called him, as time went on, 'a very nice fellow'. When a bigger boy 'of inferior capacity' tried to bully him, Ben's schoolfellows came to his defence and gave his tormentor a thrashing. It was their instinctive acknowledgment of his uncommon clay; the same impulse as that which later on drew his Balliol pupils together. He does not seem to have made a particular friend of any school-fellow, or to have tried to exercise any moral influence, as boys of his serious kind often do. That may have been because he had not yet learned to master his extreme shyness; and because his energy was being absorbed by the rapid growth of his mind. But he was far from regarding himself, like many diffident and precocious boys, either as the one reality in a world of shadows or as a shadow in a world of uncomprehended realities. Young and solitary as he was, he had a sharp understanding of the society to which he belonged and a most unusual sense of the duties owed by one of its members to another.

A story told to Strachan-Davidson very many years later by Henry Coxe, Bodley's librarian, illustrates the early development of this life-long characteristic. Coxe himself was a Westminster boy, six years older than Jowett; but he had a younger brother at St. Paul's. One night at 2 a.m. the Coxe household in St. John's Wood was roused by a peal of the front door bell. A small boy stood on the doorstep. The younger Coxe had been absent from school for two days; and one of his school-fellows had walked through London in the small hours to warn him that he was in danger of losing his place at the school unless he showed up that day.[1]

In his last year or two at St. Paul's Jowett spent most of his time work-ing in the school library, along with one or two other senior boys, and was not much seen by the lesser fry. Now and again these Olympians had to go down from their remote heights in order to fetch books from their lockers. This meant a passage through a lower form. Whenever this happened they were coaxed to 'give a con' (i.e. a construe). It was remembered of Jowett that he 'was always too good-natured to refuse'.

From the start he was seen to be an exceptionally promising boy. He went at once into the sixth of the eight forms — numbered, in the usual way, from bottom to top. Very soon he was in the 'eighth', and before the end of his time he was head boy of the school. At the beginning his class-mates used to 'put him up to say curious things to old Sleath [the High Master] which would certainly not lead that scholastic divine to predicate anything like what was the real future of his simple-minded pupil'. But Sleath took his measure soon enough. Only a purblind teacher — and Sleath was anything but blind — could fail to be struck by the fine and scrupulous intelligence which informed the innocent face and the piping treble voice.

By 1835, when Jowett was eighteen, Sleath knew him for 'the best Latin scholar' he had ever turned out. It was unthinkable that a boy so gifted should not go either to Oxford or to Cambridge. There was a school exhibition worth £100 a year, tenable at Trinity college in Cam-bridge for five years, which was usually given to the head boy. But to qualify for this, or for any of the minor exhibitions tenable at either University, a boy must be on the 'foundation' — that was, he must have entered the school before he was ten.

Mrs. Jowett turned, now, for advice to Mrs. Wood, and Mrs. Wood wrote to a Mr. Walker, a Bradford acquaintance, and Mr. Walker wrote to his brother, who was a young tutor at Brasenose. It was explained that a scholarship 'or some extraneous help' was necessary to enable the boy (whose Christian name alone was given) to go to the University. Did Mr.

[1] *L. & L.*, i, 35. For the detail, not there given, *J.P.*

Walker's brother know of any opening at Oxford? Fifty-eight years later, a week after the Master of Balliol's death, the Rev. J. Walker wrote to the Principal of Brasenose:

My reply was that there were not many open scholarships at Oxford at that time, but I remembered that it was near the time of Exam^n for the Balliol Schol^{ps}, & that the said Benjamin —, if he was thought clever enough, might try for one of them. I heard no more & thought no more of the matter, & not knowing the surname I never knew whether he stood and was elected or not. Well, *30* or *40* years after this, when the name of the Master of B. became more known to the world, & to myself, I considered the matter, & felt sure that as the time & Christian name agreed & other circumstances were in harmony, the said Benjamin — was no other than the (in future) Master of Balliol.[1]

St. Paul's had not previously attempted to carry off what had recently come to be the blue riband of Oxford scholarships. But Sleath had confidence in his fledgling; and Jowett took his flight by coach to Oxford in November 1835. Absurdly young he looked, innocent and inexperienced, to be pitted against the champions assembling in Balliol hall, many of them already undergraduates of standing. The adventure seemed, even, rather ridiculous; and two of his more sophisticated Pauline contemporaries — Barham, son of the author of the *Ingoldsby Legends*, and Pollock, one of the Chief Baron's sons — amused themselves by inventing conversation between 'the boy Jowett', as they affected to call him, and the guard of the coach.

We have a glimpse of 'the boy Jowett' being met by an undergraduate named John Turner, who lived at Bath and whose parents knew Isabella Jowett and his sister. So little was Ben known in Bath by his mother's friends, that Turner was told to recognize him by the colour of his tie. He stayed with Turner during the examination, together with a boy from Winchester named Trower. As their host was a Wykehamist, it was natural that he should say to his guests: 'You are the two I should like to be elected.' So it was. Of the thirty odd candidates Jowett took the first place, and Trower the second. On the evening of the election some of the senior Balliol scholars inspected the new recruits. One of them, Henry Holden, a scholar of three years' standing, remembered introducing himself 'to the slightly built, curly-headed lad, who seemed the last candidate likely to gain' the prize.

All that Jowett himself left on record of this determining day occurs, characteristically, not as a passage of autobiography but in the preface to a memoir of Robert Lowe, first Viscount Sherbrooke, barrister and liberal politician, which he wrote after Sherbrooke's death in 1892.

[1] From an unpublished letter in the *Jowett Papers*.

The first time that I saw him [Lowe] was on the evening of the 26th of November, 1835. The date is fixed on my mind because I had just been elected to a Balliol Scholarship, an event which, as the Home Secretary, Mr. Asquith, has recently told us, was the greatest joy of his life, and, I may add, of mine. Immediately after the announcement I was hurried off to the Union, which at that time was held at Wyatt's Room in the High Street. We were promised a great passage of arms between two heroes of debate.

One of those heroes was Bob Lowe, then an undergraduate at University college, to whom Jowett owed, thirty-five years later, the Mastership of Balliol.[1]

Next morning Jowett figured for a moment in one of those absurd little scenes which refuse to be forgotten. Along with two or three other youngsters he was waiting in the Master of Balliol's drawing-room before his matriculation. The Master, Dr. Jenkyns, had not appeared.

Jowett, who was attired in his new Scholar's gown, was struck with his own appearance, as he stood before the pierglass; and in order to heighten the effect, he put on his trencher cap, that he might have the *tout ensemble* complete. While he was so engaged, we heard a voice behind us, in the very peculiar tones, with which all Balliol men were familiar: 'Do my eyes deceive me, or is there a gentleman in my drawing-room with his hat on?' Jowett removed the cap, turned round and apologized most humbly, assuring the Master that he had not intended the smallest offence, but had simply forgotten where he was. 'Well, Sir,' returned Dr. Jenkyns 'we will *hope* it was so. But I fear this is a very bad beginning!' I told this story [continued the narrator, H. C. Adams] to Dr. Scott, Dr. Jenkyns's successor, and remarked how hard it was on a lad of 18. Scott assented, but added drily: 'But I expect he paid Jenkyns out for it very fully!'[2]

We have to imagine how Ben communicated the news of his success to his family, and how it was received. At St. Paul's it made a great stir. Nearly sixty years later one of his class-mates (Alford, Bishop of Victoria) recalled how, after Jowett's return to school, 'We boys held up our heads an inch or two higher than we did before, and it was a sight worth beholding to gaze on the beaming countenance of our dear old High Master, Dr. Sleath.'

The ten months before Jowett could take up his scholarship were not free from anxiety. The most frugal-tempered youth could not hope — even in 1835 — to exist at Oxford on £30 a year. St. Paul's, bound by antiquated rules, could do nothing to help him. In July, however, the Mercers' Company elected him to an exhibition and made him a small

---

[1] See below, 349 *foll.*

[2] This account is taken from an unpublished letter of Adams, written in 1894. (*J.P.*) It seems more likely to be accurate than the parallel version by Escott, which is used in *L. & L* (i, 39), though Escott adds a plainly authentic further observation from Jenkyns: 'I suppose it was the novelty of the bauble!' Scott's comment reflected his own discomfort after he had defeated Jowett in his election as Master in 1854. See below, 206 *foll.*

additional grant. The combined total is said to have been small enough. A further sum of 100 guineas, also provided by the Mercers as a fee for cataloguing the St. Paul's school library, was not paid to him until 1837.

The young scholar's industry and serenity suffered no diminution. He let himself go a little in a debating society which met in the neighbourhood of St. Paul's Churchyard. One may guess that, conscious of a great forward step taken and of a destiny, certain though undefined, to which he would not prove unequal, he felt a new freedom in the surroundings familiarized to him during six enormous years. It was then, perhaps — or so I like to imagine — that he consummated his love of St. Paul's Cathedral. Wren, for him, was the architect of architects; and St. Paul's was the church in which, as a schoolboy, he had once heard Sydney Smith preach, a man who seemed to him to combine wit and humour with serious understanding as no other Englishman, save Swift, had ever done.[1]

He spent Christmas in his City Road lodgings, where he was visited by Holden, the Balliol scholar whom he had already met at Oxford. They 'worked together frequently during the winter vacation'.

The scholar-elect figured prominently in the 'Apposition Day' (Founder's Day) ceremonies at St. Paul's in May; delivering a Greek speech, reciting with effective 'gesticulation' his two prize compositions in Latin Hexameters and Greek Iambics, and — mirabile dictu — creating 'much laughter even amongst that portion of the audience customarily presumed to be ignorant of the learned languages' by a brilliantly comic rendering of Dionysus in a scene from The Frogs of Aristophanes.[2]

In the high summer and early autumn of 1836 — the year before Queen Victoria's accession, the year of the Lyra Apostolica, of Hurrell Froude's death, of Newman's 'cardinal point of time' — the deceptively young and pretty-looking eighteen-year old boy, who was to take the coming decades so largely into his tutelage, was emerging from his schoolboy shell and beginning to support himself by his own efforts. There is evidently no need to think of this last year of boyhood as unhappy, because it was lonely. There had been earlier and great unhappiness. The iron had entered his soul; though its mark would be concealed, it could never be obliterated. But he had perfected his self-reliance without losing his altruism. He was young. And he had suddenly known the incomparable taste of hard-earned success.

[1] L. & L., i, 41: Tollemache, 14 and 32.
[2] The Times, 6th May 1836, quoted in L. & L., i, 41.

2. LEARNING BEFORE LIVING

Jowett's life at St. Paul's seems to have been fairly free from the gross rough-and-tumble which, at that time, marked the great English public schools. It was free, too, from the forcing-house atmosphere soon to be generated by Dr. Arnold at Rugby and to spread by degrees over the public school world. Certainly Dr. Sleath was not the man to encourage either rough-and-tumble or priggery, though he came as High Master to St. Paul's from Rugby where he had been as a boy and an assistant-master. Walter Savage Landor, one of his Rugby pupils, remembered him affectionately as 'the elegant and generous Doctor John Sleath'.

Nor was there at St. Paul's in Jowett's time any sign of the games system which was soon to become dominant not less at St. Paul's than in the boarding schools. Indeed Dr. Edward C. Mack, the American historian of the British public school system, goes out of his way to instance St. Paul's as a particular victim of the 'universal mania' for organized athleticism which began to possess the schools about 1860.[1] This is the more remarkable since Mack, following the rule made by the Public School Commission of 1861, had excluded St. Paul's along with Merchant Taylors, as being day-schools, from the nine ancient foundations which the Commission was set up to examine, and which laid the pattern for the newer foundations.

When Jowett went to St. Paul's the standard of classical scholarship in the school is said to have been below the high level which it afterwards reached. This may partly account for the fact that, although he was a classical scholar and became a professor of Greek, his scholarship was often thought by other scholars to be inferior to their own. Not more than partly: for though he might wrestle and find pleasure in wrestling (like Browning's heroic pedant) with the 'enclitic *de*', the wrestling was only an incident in a more important adventure. Neither scholarship nor learning was, for him, an end to be finally pursued for its own sake.

The education he had at St. Paul's was, of course, almost exclusively classical and followed the traditional public and grammar school lines. In its earlier stages, and especially if it is administered by the wrong kind of pedagogue to unwilling pupils, no discipline can seem more tedious and pointless. It can kill the faculties of backward boys, while it can encourage clever boys in a dangerously easy conceit of their powers.

The notion that a classical discipline should be given to all public and grammar school boys has long since gone. Yet, for those who can

[1] Mack, *Public Schools and British Opinion*, ii, 123.

profit by it — and they are not confined to 'scholars'[1] — it remains an unrivalled instrument of general education. Its value lies in what its enemies conceive to be its great defect — its apparent irrelevance to modern life. For this irrelevance means that the pupil can make no progress at all without a deliberate adjustment of his mind to the languages, ideas and forms not merely of one but of two highly articulate, vanished civilizations. The effort required is severe, since there is little — less and less as time goes on — in his natural environment to help him. An educational system based mainly upon his native language requires no comparable effort on the learner's part; and if it is based upon other modern languages, there is still much in the curriculum which is a part of his mind before he begins conscious study. Moreover, these dead civilizations, which he is being required to understand in their own perfected languages — the one beautifully elastic, the other beautifully precise — lie at the basis of his own civilization and were in many ways at least its equal if not its superior. No other discipline can teach him this lesson. History can only retail it ineffectively at second hand.

But need the educational discipline of intelligent boys be primarily linguistic? Why should science, with its superb disciplines of measurement, experiment and inductive reasoning, and its romantic history of mind winning the mastery over matter, not stimulate the young brain at least to equal, if not to greater, effort? Could not mathematics, with its equally romantic history and its equal seeming irrelevance to everyday existence, provide the ideal gymnastic for the growing mind? Or, if these studies are too impersonal, why should not history, allied with geography and the rudiments of political and economic theory and tinctured by psychology, furnish the coming generation with all it needs to know?

The short answer is that the supreme object of a general education, after a child has acquired the elementary techniques of reading, writing and arithmetic, and before or alongside the acquisition of more highly specialized techniques, is not so much to impart knowledge, either of facts or of methods, as to persuade the pupil into using his own mind. That, at any rate, was Dr. Sleath's idea of education. He did not profess, he openly said, to be a good scholar, but he made his scholars polish one another. The idiom is old-fashioned; the good sense of it perennial. When we consider what kind of men Dr. Sleath's system turned out, and observe how large a part of modern education has come to mean the

---

[1] Kipling's story *Regulus* in *A Diversity of Creatures* brilliantly exemplifies this point. 'You see,' says King triumphantly to Hartopp. 'It sticks. A little of it sticks among the barbarians.'

injection of second-hand knowledge and second-hand theory, in regu-
lated doses, even at the advanced university stage, we may conclude that
Jowett's education, however imperfect he himself subsequently thought
it to have been, was essentially a good education.

Imperfect it certainly was. When Jowett went to St. Paul's he was
thought to be better at mathematics than at classics. It was a pity that
the school neglected this early promise. As for science, St. Paul's knew
little or nothing of it; and Jowett's contemptuous ignorance of science
was his major intellectual weakness. It was a weakness which he came
himself, in the end, to realize — and his realization of this particular
defect is a paradoxical testimony to the soundness of his education. Men
who have been taught to think with their own minds come, in the end, to
judge their own deficiencies.

Tuckwell has a curious little story, which illustrates this late awakening of Jowett's perceptions. He describes how in 1874 he went walking
one afternoon with the Master, on the cliffs of Exmoor:

I picked up and showed him a chunk of old red sandstone at my feet,
flecked with minute white spots, which under my Coddington lens
became lichens exquisite in shape and chasing. I recall his almost childlike
amazement and delight, his regretful confession that to his mind all
natural science was a blank, wisdom at one entrance quite shut out.

Sir Henry Acland, a champion of natural science in mid-Victorian
Oxford, who was Jowett's physician, relates that he and Jowett often
discussed and disagreed upon the progress of science — Acland proud
of its achievements, Jowett deriding them. After his severe illness in
1891 Jowett, being convalescent, saw Acland to the door

and said, standing still, 'The great thing now is attention to Physical
Science.' I said 'Do not swing that pendulum too far. You and Stanley
thought about this 45 years ago. Do not throw up your dear Plato. Get the
Material and the Spiritual both working together at the problem of all
things.' No other word passed.[1]

It was a naive exchange naively reported, but Acland was then 76 and
Jowett 74. Old men who have known each other for more than half their
lives (though Jowett had sometimes written contemptuously about
Acland to Miss Nightingale) do not need to pick words for the approval
of sophisticated readers not yet born. Both the old men were right, each
yielding to the rightness of the other's position. Acland, clumsy as his
phrases were, had the greater rightness in the unpremeditated argument;
for he saw, more clearly than Jowett could, that science is either a mere
amusement of the mind or an improvement in the ancient tool-making,

[1] From an unpublished portion of a memorandum by Sir H. W. Acland.
(J.P.)

weapon-making, disease-fighting crafts of mankind. Both the pure and the applied sciences are admirable modes of activity; but — so Acland tried to say — no scientific achievement, theoretical or practical, can ever take men nearer to the heart of the perennial mystery. On the contrary, the sense of advancing mastery over material forces breeds the frightful illusion that there is no limit to human ability. Not that Acland could foresee the peril in which the world would find itself, not much more than half a century later, through the development of physical science. Nor that Jowett, in his late conversion to the idea that physical science had become 'the great thing', at all meant to deny the supreme place of philosophy in the order of human thought. Had he done so, he would have been denying his own intellectual history.

Philosophers are quite capable of declaring that they have wasted their lives in the pursuit of a mirage. Philosophy herself has been heard proclaiming in the lecture-room, as if she were proud of the power to see through her own pretensions, that she has nothing of her own to say; that all metaphysical statements are meaningless; and that her only remaining function is to expose the abounding fallacies of human reasoning.

Jowett, if he could have lived into our age with all his young wits about him, would certainly not have dismissed logical positivism — or even existentialism — as nonsense because it appeared to make nonsense of everything he had previously thought sensible. He would have studied these modern manifestations of the philosophical temper with fascinated curiosity. For, though his mind was that of a philosopher rather than that of a linguistic scholar or historian, he was never a professional or an originating philosopher. Philosophy, for him, was a nourishing field of study, not a field in which he aimed to be a star performer. He watched the game from the pavilion; he never bowled or batted, except in what might be described as tip-and-run matches between himself and a few pupils or friends or as a commentator in the lecture-room, where he stood up as a professor of Greek not a professor of modern philosophy, in order to make his listeners aware that there had been Greek thinkers before and European thinkers after Socrates, Plato and Aristotle.

I have wished to suggest that Jowett's education, for all its conventionally narrow classical character and indeed by virtue of this character, trained him better to use his mind in his own later exploration of wider horizons, than any other kind of education could have done. Not the least valuable part of it was the way in which it was given to him — Dr. Sleath's way of letting his scholars polish one another. This kind of teaching releases and does not inhibit mental power.

CHAPTER V

'The tree in the midst of the garden'

In the Hebrew fable of man's fall from innocence the forbidden tree 'which is in the midst of the garden' is the tree of the knowledge of good and evil. Adam and Eve disobey their creator's warning; they eat the fruit of the tree and become ashamed of their nakedness. The knowledge of good and evil, which they gain, is knowledge only that the concupiscence, which they had hitherto innocently enjoyed without shame, is shameful.[1] The fruit of the tree is sexual self-consciousness.

Alongside the forbidden tree, also in the midst of the garden, God was said to have planted another tree, the tree of life.[2] This other tree is not mentioned again, until Adam and Eve have been driven out of Eden, when God 'placed a flaming sword, which turned every way, to keep the way of the tree of life'.

The tree of life was borrowed by the Hebrews from Babylonian mythology; the tree of the knowledge of good and evil was their own invention. In the fable of the fall, related in the second chapter of Genesis, the two trees have evidently become one tree. It is this tree which stands in the very centre of the garden ; a symbol for the mysterious generative force at the heart of the living human world, which all societies — not excluding our own — treat with more or less of awe and surround with myth and ritual, according to their diversity of genius and sophistication.

There is not the slightest indication that Jowett ever knew by direct or deliberate experience the quality of sexual enjoyment. The whole character of his life strongly suggests the contrary. He never plucked or tasted the fruit of the tree, though it grew in the midst of his own as of everyman's garden. Yet his mind and career were so evidently influenced, at many points and in many far-reaching ways, by his attitude towards it,

---

[1] It is worth noticing that the A.V. page-heading 'The institution of marriage' (not repeated in the R.V.) seems to refer to the last four verses of Genesis II, which describe the creation of Eve and the absence of shame in her and Adam's nakedness, before the 'fall'.

[2] Genesis I, 9.

that to depict him as if he enjoyed some peculiar immunity from the universal lot would be like leaving the Ghost out of *Hamlet*.

In our modern mythology the tree, however dangerous it may be to eat its fruit unwarily, is nevertheless the originator, rather than the guardian, of human vigour. The extraordinary energy, which activated Jowett's mind and sustained his wide interests, must certainly have been drawn from some very potent and continuing source. It may, perhaps, have derived — to use a familiar modern psychological metaphor — from a perpetual 'sublimation' of the energy which most men release in acts of sex. But what was the attitude, and why and how was it formed, which made this 'sublimation' not only possible but necessary? The pages that follow, and those that later on relate his approach to the idea of marriage and the nature of its defeat,[1] seek diffidently to suggest, rather than to formulate with assurance, the answer to an obscure problem which cannot be simply ignored.

The beginnings of a full answer would lie, no doubt, partly in infancy and early childhood and partly in his innate physical character. Of early influences we know almost nothing, except that he was very piously brought up by an opinionated father and a shy, anxious, preoccupied mother, and that he was specially attached to his sister Emily, who never ceased to adore him, though he ceased to be intimate with her. Of the innate character we know that he was a pretty, girlish-looking boy; that he retained something of this captivating appearance into early middle age, a remnant of it even into old age; and that his voice never 'broke'. We also know that he was intellectually precocious and seriously minded, and that he exhibited, as a young schoolboy, the marks of calm judgment and steady resolution which were the dominant characters in his adult personality.

It must certainly have been at St. Paul's that he became disgustedly aware of the 'facts of life', as these were understood and relished by some of his schoolfellows. The evidence lies open in the letter he wrote to his young cousin, Sidney Irwin, about schoolboy immorality and indecency.[2] The tone of the letter is unmistakably that of a witness who knows from direct observation what he is writing about.

There is nothing surprising about this. It would be surprising if he had gone through his school life without noticing it. It has been argued that sexual immorality came into English schools with the 'regimented manliness of the late Victorian period'.[3] Jowett's letter to Sidney, written in 1860, is enough to show that this theory is untenable. What Dr. Mack

[1] See below, Chapter XIII.   [2] See above, 65.
[3] Mack, *Public Schools and British Opinion*, ii, 126.

calls the 'prudishness of the Victorians' accounts only for the fact that 'their writings are full of veiled accusations the meaning of which cannot be doubted'. They had become self-conscious and reticent about matters which their less prudish fore-runners had taken for granted. Boys were boys, the tree of knowledge equally tempting, before as after the advent of organized games.

What is really surprising, in Jowett's letter to Sidney, is the severity of its language. He was forty-three and had learned to purge his vocabulary of crude and question-begging phrases like 'horribly wicked'. He would have hesitated to use such words of a grown blackguard. Yet he used them, without compunction, of boys whose 'wickedness' was that they tasted the fruit of the forbidden tree before they were out of their 'teens and shared their excitement with other boys. This may be a very undesirable thing to happen. But — 'horribly wicked'? Carefully as Jowett framed his letter, and right as he was to give Sidney a warning of what he might encounter, something out of his own experience, something that he had never confronted with his whole mind, must have dictated this extravagantly harsh expression.

Was it made deliberately harsh in order to frighten Sidney? His second letter to Sidney[1] shows that he was capable of deliberately acting a false part, in order to give weight to his advice. Was he, then, capable of inventing a sin, or of pretending to believe in the special heinousness of a particular kind of sin, in order to frighten a boy? Plainly he felt and meant what he said. The feeling which dictated his unequivocal choice of words (he was scrupulous in his use of words) was strongly rooted in a still hateful area of memory.

Like Sidney, he had gone to school utterly unprepared for this sort of thing. Mentally he was precocious; carnally he was both ignorant and undeveloped. He was 'Miss Jowett', the kind of innocent, serious, clever, high-principled child whom children of earthier quality enjoy shocking by displays of animal knowledge. It had been possible for his friend Arthur Stanley, also given a feminine nick-name (Nancy) by his schoolfellows, to go through Rugby without even perceiving the existence of schoolboy indecency. Dr. Arnold may have had something to do with that, by throwing a protective *aura* round such clever innocents as Stanley, which shielded them from the grosser school world. But Stanley and Jowett were very differently made. Stanley was always an exceptionally unnoticing, Jowett an exceptionally noticing person.[2] If the two could have exchanged schools, and Jowett could have taken Stanley's

---

[1] See above, 65.
[2] This needs qualification. Stanley noticed *objects*, Jowett noticed *people*.

place at Rugby, he would not have failed, as Stanley did, to know what went on outside the limited radius of light and purity.

Whether the innocent young Pauline noticed these things for himself, or whether they were forced upon his unwilling attention, they induced in him a deep and lasting disgust. It was a premature, excessive and irrational disgust, never qualified by any personal knowledge of the thing which caused it. There is a back side to the mind, which the false armour of disgust often fails to cover. Jowett became famous for the adroitness with which he protected himself, while he indulged his curiosity. If this led to social embarrassments, he was their unembarrassed producer, always emerging dryly victorious. Many stories about him illustrate the pleasure which he took in producing this kind of embarrassment among men of the world.

There is, for example, the familiar anecdote of how he sat up with the male members of a country-house party in the smoking-room, and seized the opportunity of flaying an over-bold *raconteur* with the high-pitched comment: 'I think there is more dirt than wit in that story.' He does not cut a pleasing figure in such anecdotes — though they were told for his credit — wishing to be in the shoal, a man among men, yet using his sharp wit to disperse it. The members of the house-party must have endured a subsequent silence of some length and discomfort and have gone to their bedrooms earlier than their wives expected.

Another story — of which an incomplete version is equally familiar — exhibits him to better advantage. It used to be told more or less as follows. At a dinner in the Master's Lodgings, after the ladies had withdrawn, one of his guests embarked upon a Rabelaisian story. The Master cut this short by rising to his feet and saying blandly: 'Shall we continue this conversation in the drawing-room?' The true version is related by A. L. Smith.[1] The offender was Jowett's own most particular friend, Sir Robert Morier, who was 'giving some reminiscences of inner life in St. Petersburg', where he was then Ambassador.

There were several persons present to whom the description *ingenui vultus puer* might have been applied. Taking advantage of the first embarrassed pause among the company, Jowett said with a twinkle in his eye, and in his most dulcet tones, 'Morier, shall we adjourn this conversation to the drawing-room?' As we trooped out, Sir Robert took me by the arm and whispered delightedly, 'devilish clever that of Jowett, devilish good.'

Stories like these illustrate his cunning power of dominating Victorian male society without concealing his extreme distaste for one of its favourite topics. His attitude is not to be described as prudery — the

[1] *Reminiscences of Jowett* by A.L.S., a pamphlet privately reprinted from 'The Blue Book'.

grille through which timid persons peep at pleasures they envy but dare not pursue. Jowett was not that kind of person. He was always curious to know how other men behaved and talked, but he had no concealed, vicarious enjoyment in a *risqué* anecdote. His distaste was real, not dissembled. It was more than a fastidious dislike of ribaldry; its roots were in a deeply laid antipathy to the very idea of carnal knowledge. He was able, in his middle forties, to overcome this aversion sufficiently to contemplate for a very short time the idea of marriage; but what he really desired was the marriage of true minds, not the union of bodies. His extraordinary friendship with Florence Nightingale put an end to this brief and hesitant adventure, and released him for ever from the danger of finding that, even in marriage, he would be unable to endure physical intimacy.[1]

When Jowett went to St. Paul's, he was a pretty and seemingly defenceless child. Nobody could guess that his fragile body was governed by an exceptionally strong and independent mind, very rapidly developing, though still young and ignorant. Nor could anybody guess that one of the main purposes of this independent mind was to ensure its independence and the independence of the body it controlled. Those who remembered him only as an elderly man remembered him as a uniquely formidable man. 'Since Jowett's death' somebody in Oxford once said to A. L. Smith 'there is no one of whom we are all afraid.' He had always been formidable; formidability belongs also to young and defenceless children, if they are determined to be kings of their own castles. But those who remembered him as a young tutor remembered him rather as uniquely charming — not as a deliberate charmer aware of his power to captivate youth, for he no more wished to take captives than to be taken captive, but rather as a young man whose fascination lay largely in his own complete unawareness of it, so that it seemed almost to have been every younger man's own discovery. Something of this charm entered still into the formidability of the old man. An irresistible asset in the young tutor, who nevertheless kept his pupils at something more than arm's length, it may have been the cause of hateful embarrassment to him when he was a young boy.

There was no boy at St. Paul's who took a special liking for Ben, of the kind he could return. None of his friendships began at school. Had it been otherwise, the later development of his character might have been different. But there were boys of gross clay — 'horribly wicked' boys. It would have been only in the nature of things if among the older or bigger boys there were one or two, already versed in the art of seduction, who

[1] See below, 296–313.

eyed the cherubic newcomer hopefully and attempted to despoil him of his innocence. If the attempt was made, it was uncompromisingly repelled. Such a repulse breeds resentment. The would-be seducer seeks an opportunity of getting his own back upon the weakling who has somehow defeated him. School life can be very crude and cruel. Resentment of this kind would best account for the savage, bullying attack made upon Jowett by a 'boy bigger than himself, but of inferior capacity', which has already been mentioned.[1]

The suggestion that his innocence was exposed to assault — whether clumsy or crafty — during his earlier school-days, is of course not capable of proof. It is rather more than a mere guess; for something must have happened, at St. Paul's, to shock him into the attitude of his letter to Sidney some thirty years later — laughable as it is to imagine that he ever did what he advised Sidney to do, 'give a boy a cuff in the eye'. His defences were not of that physical order. And something must have happened, whether at St. Paul's or at some other time and place, to fix him in his aversion from the idea of sexual intercourse between himself and anybody else, whether man or woman. Something must have also happened to produce his excessive dislike for any element of passion in friendships between men; a dislike which led him into extraordinary difficulties over his interpretation of Plato's *Phaedrus* and *Symposium*, the two great dialogues in which Plato discussed the ideal aspect of 'the loves of men' and which Jowett, in spite of himself, admired almost beyond any other masterpiece of writing.[2] There is something, then, to be explained; and a hypothesis which provides a probable, even if an incomplete, explanation is not to be dismissed as a mere guess.

It is in the conduct of his friendships that Jowett's attitude towards love must be discovered. In all but three of his own numerous friendships, both with men and women, he was careful always to avoid the least appearance of sentiment. The three exceptions were the three friendships which between them covered and coloured his whole adult life: with Arthur Stanley, Robert Morier, and Florence Nightingale. Even in these, and even in the friendship with Florence Nightingale, he avoided the language of love.

Stanley was the first. There was certainly, on Jowett's part, a feeling of deep and tender affection for Stanley. Passion would be too strong a term. But their relationship was so easy and natural — or so it seemed to Jowett — and so happily concerned with the things of the mind and the subject-matter of Anglican theology, that the note of affection never asked to be sounded until Stanley's father died. Then, for once, a sudden

[1] See above, 74. [2] See below, 90.

uprush of sympathy prompted Jowett to assume that his friend would wish to have him by his side. The powerful rebuff which he received from Stanley told him that he had presumed too far and confirmed him, for many years, in the belief that friendship must exclude sentiment.[1]

Morier was the second. Of this friendship something more will soon be said. For the moment all that is necessary to say is that it was a relationship which at once contained and concealed passion. Jowett could not help the fact that it was peculiarly delightful to him to enjoy Morier's physical presence; and that this delight was observed by others. He did not know that he wore his heart so openly on his sleeve. He did not deliberately show it even to himself; least of all did he show it to Morier, though Morier probably always knew more about it than Jowett ever allowed himself to know.

There were, so to speak, two chests in Jowett's inner treasury: one always open, perpetually refilled and generously emptied; the other never opened, kept under lock and key, until — as he grew to be an old man — he began to be freed from the idea that he must never allow anybody to see what it contained. Then, at last, he opened it cautiously and released in words of open affection the love he had hidden away — but only from himself — for so many years.

His friendship with Florence Nightingale was a much stranger, more ambiguous, relationship than his simple relationship with Stanley and Morier. It contained his only uninhibited indulgence in the short-lived ecstasy of passion. Yet even in this extraordinary interlude, and at the peak of its peculiar intensity, Jowett never used the language of open love. The passion was 'platonic', perhaps as illusory as every other kind of passion. For two or three years, nevertheless, it was an excitement beyond his power, or wish, to control.

Though this devouring experience belonged on an ideal, sexless plane, Jowett could not have accepted it if his friend had not been a woman. Yet there was no physical passion in it. The quality in Florence Nightingale which fascinated him was not so much her imperious femininity (though that naturally enhanced her attraction) as her possession of an intellect equal to, and not dissimilar from, his own; of a mind to which his mind could open itself without reserve, and which he could trust to reply in the same coinage.

Convention assisted this curious pattern of Jowett's three great friendships. But convention did not dictate it; for it was he, perhaps more than any other single man, who dictated the convention itself. A remarkable letter from Campbell to Abbott, dated 17th September 1896, makes this

[1] See below, 214 *foll.*

very plain. The letter begins with an allusion to some question raised by Abbott.

I seem to have heard Jowett say something of that kind about *In Memoriam*. He had a 'horror naturalis' of sentimental feelings between men ('diabolical' I have heard him call them). This was one reason for his dislike of Conington, whose influence on the elder Nettleship he thought weakening. Nothing is more remarkable than his persistent attachment to J.A.S.,[1] though they differed so profoundly about this. I rather think that in the later note-books there are some entries that show a more lenient view, confessing that he had exaggerated the evil. Of course nothing of all this is biographically available, but it is useful to think of it.[2]

It is evident from the tone of Campbell's letter that Jowett's attitude struck some of his younger contemporaries as abnormal to the point of eccentricity. In the first half of the nineteenth century and even long after its middle point emotional friendship between men, usually coloured by religious enthusiasm, was an accepted commonplace. Nobody thought it 'queer' or reprehensible. Letters and verses are full of it. I have argued elsewhere that it was a not unimportant factor in the Tractarian movement.[3]

Gradually the climate of opinion changed. The change was slow. Writing in the late 'eighties Roundell Palmer, the first Earl of Selborne, dwelt with particular and unashamed delight on the idyllic happiness of his friendship at Oxford in the 'thirties with a religiously minded undergraduate of his own age — Frederic Faber, the future founder of the Brompton Oratory, then a young man of romantic beauty and irresistible charm. It was a virginal, rapturous and mutual love. 'Our affection for each other' wrote the ex-Lord Chancellor, as he neared his eightieth year, after a life filled to the brim with professional success and public honour and domestic happiness, 'became not only strong, but passionate. There is a place for passion, even in friendship; it was so among the Greeks; and the love of Jonathan for David was "wonderful, passing the love of women".'

It is not possible, therefore, to suppose that Jowett, in this respect, merely took the moral tone of his time.

His attitude softened as he entered old age. Writing to an unidentified correspondent (probably a woman) in 1884 he said:[4]

You ask me where in Plato's writings the idea of Platonic love is to be found. In the *Symposium* and *Phaedrus*, two of the most wonderful of human creations. But I should explain that Platonic love in the modern sense does not exist in Plato. Women, as you rightly conjecture, were too little accounted of among the Greeks. The love of which he speaks is the

---

[1] J. A. Symonds. [2] *J.P.*
[3] *Oxford Apostles*, Chapter VI, section 3. [4] *L. & L.*, ii, 269.

mystical love of men for one another, the union of two souls in a single perfect friendship. Whether such a thing is possible, I do not say — or right. But it appears to have been a much stronger feeling than the regard of men for women.[1]

The note of moral distaste is added almost as an afterthought to the note of scepticism; and neither note is sounded with absolute assurance.

The male friend in whom Jowett most delighted was Sir Robert Morier, a man of the world and professional diplomatist, who became British Ambassador at St. Petersburg. A genial young giant, Morier

had come up to Balliol a lax and imperfectly educated fellow, but Jowett, seeing his great natural capacity, took him in the Long Vacation of 1848 and practically 'converted him' to the doctrine of work. This was the turning point in Morier's life, and the warm friendship between them continued until from his own deathbed (in Switzerland) Morier wrote to the Master, who himself was then either dying or dead.

So Palgrave, quoted by Campbell, who goes on to describe how, one day in 1852, he took some work into Jowett's room and how his thirty-five year old tutor 'turned round from stirring the fire — an habitual action with him — with a brighter look than I had ever seen in his face, and said "Morier is coming!" ' In the summer of 1884, a month before his letter about Platonic love, and on the morrow of a reunion dinner at Balliol which Morier had attended 'and Jowett's happiness was complete', he wrote to his friend in terms of almost unprecedented warmth: 'It has been one of the greatest happinesses of my life to have had your friendship. I have learned so much from it too; you must take my meaning, for I cannot express what I feel.'[2]

He sent from his death-bed, nine years later, a very similar message to Florence Nightingale: 'How large a part has your life been of my life. There is only time, I think, for a few words.'

The long-packed ice loosened at the beginning of the last decade. Sex was still the irrelevance he had always willed it to be. But something had happened to make him, in his sixty-eighth year, less sure than he had been that friendship and love are different states and that there was something wrong in Plato's combination of the two. He was past his grand climacteric; all possibility of earthly passion was not so much spent as gone unspent. Affection remained — a steadier fire at which he might still warm his heart, but only if he now stirred it from time to time, as he had been used to stir the fire in his rooms when he was a young tutor.

Had anything in particular happened, beyond the passage of years?

[1] ibid., 269–70.
[2] ibid., ii, 44. The letter begins: 'My dear Morier'—Jowett followed the old custom of avoiding Christian names — and ends 'ever yours gratefully and affectionately, B. Jowett'. But see below, 335.

There is some reason to think that, at about this time, he was obliged to deal with one of those revelations of homosexual behaviour which now and again disturb the assurance of modern society. Among the letters written to Jowett's biographers is one from Mrs. Josephine Butler to Professor Campbell, which there cannot now be any possible reason for censoring.

Mrs. Butler recalled that Jowett had been a frequent evening visitor at her and her husband's house in Oxford in his and their earlier life.

> We neither of us followed his theological teaching, nor bowed down to him as a spiritual authority, as many did. But we both loved to see him, and my husband regarded him with true affection, tho' he thought him in some respects wanting as a *man*. This was the result of circumstances, the absence of family life etc. early in life. I believe he ripened much in later years. At one time, later, there was an outbreak of abnormal immorality among a few of the young men in Oxford.[1] To such he was (I know) the wisest, most prudent and gentlest of counsellors. He was extremely severe and tender at the same time. We had the unhappiness of having to try and guide for a time one of these youths (now dead) and thus I got to know how implicitly such misguided or guilty creatures might confide in him, and seek and follow his advice. In these matters he was a help and blessing to many beyond what it is possible to publish. The line of work for moral purifying, to which I was called 35 years ago, made me acquainted with some of the saddest aspects of human life. I always admired Mr. Jowett's wonderful reticence and refinement coupled with sternness and *swift, decided action* when needful, in cases where moral corruption called for drastic measures. At the same time he never seemed to give any man up as hopeless, or beyond the reach of sympathy and help. It was different as regards unhappy or vicious women. Here his somewhat defective *experience* was a disadvantage. But he was not, as far as I know, called upon to act on that side.

When can this outbreak have happened? Not, surely, before Josephine had become, in her 'line of work for moral purifying', a public figure of the same accepted and heroic order as Florence Nightingale. The starting point of her public career lay in Liverpool and in the year 1866.[2] Within a year or two, stories of her extraordinary behaviour in Liverpool, where she had exhibited herself in defence of common harlots, were circulating throughout English society. Asked by Florence Nightingale how she should reply to a letter she had received from Josephine Butler, Jowett replied (October 17, 1869):

[1] Mrs. Butler evidently meant what is now called homosexuality. That word had not come into use. The first instance cited by the *O.E.D.* is from Havelock Ellis in 1897. Ellis thought it a 'barbarously hybrid word' and disclaimed all responsibility for it.

[2] Tradition has dated her 'call' two years earlier, when her little daughter fell over the banisters and was killed at her feet. It is possible that this dreadful experience seemed to tell her that her duty lay with 'fallen' women. That her 'line of work' began in Liverpool in 1866 is put beyond possible doubt by her grandson's recent book *Portrait of Josephine Butler* (52 and 66).

I would answer Mrs. Butler shortly, referring her to army reports on the subject about which she writes and saying firmly that you regret you have not time to pursue the matter further. And if she writes again I should repeat the answer.

She is thought to do good, but she is very excitable and emotional — of an over-sympathetic temperament, which leads her to take an interest about a class of sinners whom she had better have left to themselves. She is quite sincere and has a touch of genius.

This account of Josephine Butler's crusade does Jowett no credit. There is something offensive in its knowing superiority, its ignorant contempt for the value of her work, its complacent reference to a class of sinners best left to themselves. It is this reference which seems now especially odious. How could he dare to be so absolute? The answer is that he could not dare not to be absolute. At this time of his life, and in the sphere of sex, he was under a compulsion to retreat from any sympathy with behaviour which conflicted with his own.

His judgment of Josephine Butler herself is a different matter. He could hardly have written so, if he had already been associated with her in an attempt to handle an 'outbreak of abnormal immorality among a few of the young men in Oxford'. Almost certainly that experience must have occurred very much later. The Josephine Butler, about whom he wrote with such misplaced assurance in 1869, was the young, impulsive, married woman whom he had supposed himself to know fifteen years earlier.

A prophet is not without honour but in his own country and in his own house — and that goes for prophetesses, too. Jowett may have forgotten walking back to Oxford from a summer picnic after sunset when he was still in his thirties, and finding Josephine, who had started back earlier, sitting by herself on the side of a dry ditch. He sat down beside her, quite unaware that he was interrupting her 'long pleasant silence', and tried to put her at her ease with remarks about cockchafers and frogs. He could not know that he was an unwelcome interloper; that Josephine, at that moment, was her own company and wished for no other. Nor could he have known how he had amused Josephine's fifteen year old sister, Emily, who had driven him out to the picnic in a dog-cart. Asked how they had got on, Emily replied: 'Oh, very well. I asked him questions; and, if he was very long in replying I drove over some bumps on the roadside, and this joggled the answers out of him. It was a pleasure driving dear Mr. Jowett, who held on with fear and trembling. He had such soft baby hands.'[1]

[1] *Portrait of Josephine Butler*, 48–9. Date, according to Mr. A. S. G. Butler, 'exactly a hundred years ago'— not later, therefore, than 1854. Jowett was then thirty-seven, Josephine twenty-six. A pencil jotting in one of Campbell's note

Emily's fresh and fearless young impressions provide an agreeable corrective to the idea of Jowett which was beginning to form itself in the timid minds of male Oxford. It might have been very good for him to know what Emily and Josephine thought but were too polite to say. It might have warned him to distrust the myth already forming about him; and the warning would have been worth the annoyance it would have caused. Soft baby hands, indeed! Was he not on the way to becoming one of the most considerable men in Oxford? What could the appearance of his hands mean to a young girl recklessly driving a dog-cart? He was already a 'formidable' man, though he was willing to sit in a ditch and talk to Josephine about cockchafers and frogs — subjects of which he knew less than nothing. They were light topics suited to the occasion. Perhaps he chose them with the purpose of forestalling Josephine's disconcerting tendency to talk about serious matters quite outside her comprehension. How little he understood of women, and of their power to understand men far better than men understand themselves!

To return to the question of date, raised by Mrs. Butler's letter. It seems clear that the 'outbreak' of which she speaks must have occurred after 1869. Could it have happened while the Butlers were still at Liverpool — that is to say before 1882?

There are several reasons for thinking this very improbable. The distance between Oxford and Liverpool is one. Josephine's absorption in her new 'line of work' is another. In the beginning she was wholly given up to work among and for the harlots of the great sea-port and the girls who were on their way to becoming professional prostitutes. It was this which made her, at first, notorious rather than famous. About 1869 her efforts took the form of a long and strenuous campaign for the repeal of the Contagious Diseases Acts. These Acts 'gave a legal sanction to vice' by placing women living immoral lives under police supervision. Little by little the campaign made headway, as the woman who started it shook public opinion out of its complacency and made converts of public men. Although full repeal of the Acts was not achieved until 1886, the movement for repeal won its decisive battle in April 1883, when the Commons approved a Government resolution to stop the compulsory examination of prostitutes and the use of the police to administer the Acts. Mrs. Butler was in the Ladies' Gallery. 'When, at one in the morning, she came out to a clear London night, she began to realize the beginning of victory at last, saying it felt like a dream.'[1]

books runs: 'His sensitive hands — enjoyed the bracing cold of Askrigg — but must have warm gloves. He never wore kid — nor gloves at all as a rule.'
[1] *ibid.*, 97 and 103.

In the previous year (1882) George Butler had been installed a Canon of Winchester, and the Butlers had come back to live in the south. Four years of relatively peaceful existence lay ahead, for himself and his wife, until the onset of his long, fatal illness in 1886. In no other period of their joint lives can the events described by Josephine in her letter to Campbell find such probable place. These four years coincided almost exactly with the four years during which Jowett was Vice-Chancellor. Only as Vice-Chancellor could he have had any responsibility for anything that happened outside Balliol; and for anything that happened inside Balliol it is impossible to imagine him allowing Josephine Butler or any other outsider to share his responsibility.

Jowett became Vice-Chancellor at the beginning of the Michaelmas term in 1882. Abbott draws particular attention to the intimate character of the entries which he made in his private notebook in the following summer. He had not looked so closely into his own mind since he had been a young man. There is nothing in these entries — revealing as they are, to the point of naivety — to suggest that he had been obliged to meet any specially disturbing challenge. That experience, perhaps, lay just round the corner. Rather, he was strung up by the general stimulus of his new office to a new interest in himself, his mind and character, and in all the old problems of philosophy and learning and religion and morality.

He was not able to keep up this exhausting effort. Towards the end of his term of office he had to write: 'Having only a certain amount of energy, I find it impossible to continue my diary except occasionally and at intervals.' The reserves were running low; old age was suddenly upon him. Four years of hard labour had taken their unavoided toll. If I am right in my conjecture, he had drawn heavily on his failing reserves in order to be the wise and gentle, individual counsellor, as well as the stern disciplinarian, of young men detected in practices which he regarded as utterly vile.

Virtue had gone out of him. Virtue of another kind came in its place. It would be impertinent to make a pretence of imagining what passed in his conscious mind or happened below the threshold of his consciousness. One can but note — as I have already noted — that his attitude towards love and friendship loosened remarkably in the summer of 1884. The change from rigidity to tenderness seems to be related to some specific but unstated cause. May one cause of this change have been an unexpected entry into the minds of a few broken youngsters? Can he have found, there, something not to be dismissed as wholly and horribly wicked, something in which his master Plato had perceived a latent possibility of the highest excellence? Did he, for the first time in his life, begin to doubt the charity and validity of his own, hitherto absolute, moral judgments?

If there was a late change in Jowett's attitude towards love and friendship, it came too late to matter. He had been an unwavering supporter of the dominant moral code, indeed one of its principal begetters. He was also the acknowledged interpreter of Plato to the modern world; had pinned himself to the view that Plato's philosophy of love must be translated from a Greek into an English fashion; that 'the loves of men' had become unintelligible, if not actually wrong; that they must be replaced in the modern world by 'the loves of women'.

This confident and uncompromising reversal of his master's teaching seems to have occasioned no difficulty either for Jowett himself or his readers; and it would have been at least logically tenable, if he had simply substituted what we now call 'heterosexual' for 'homosexual' love. But he was unable to make so simple a correction. For the free homosexual love of the Greeks ('man meets boy') he did not, he could not, substitute the free love of the modern world ('boy meets girl'). He substituted, he had to substitute, 'marriage'. His whole argument, consequently, went astray in the most extraordinary manner.

This is how he begins to pose the problem in his introduction to the *Phaedrus* — the dialogue which, together with the *Symposium*, explores the question 'What is love?' and provides Plato's answer.

To understand him we must make abstraction of morality and of the Greek manner of regarding the relation of the sexes. In this, as in other discussions about love, what Plato says of the loves of men must be transferred to the loves of women, before we can attach any serious meaning to his words. Had he lived in our times he would have made the transposition himself. But seeing in his own age the impossibility of woman being the intellectual helpmate or friend of man (except in the rare instances of a Diotima or an Aspasia), seeing that, even as to personal beauty, her place was taken by young mankind instead of womankind, he tries to work out the problem of love without regard to the distinctions of nature.

Jowett cites two instances, two exceptional women, to support this curious argument — Diotima, the priestess who was said to have taught Socrates, and Aspasia, the mistress of Pericles and one of the world's most famous courtesans. But these instances undo his whole argument, for they show that there were intelligent Greek women fully capable of sharing the thought of Greek men. The place taken in Greek life by what he called 'the loves of men' does not at all require the hypothesis of intellectual inadequacy on the part of Greek women; even if the average young Athenian is supposed to have been an 'intellectual' — as, of course, he was not. Given the separation of the youth of each sex from the other, and the education of boys and young men together in the palaestra or 'gymnasium', where nakedness was *de rigueur* (at least for the young) and where they walked with older men (such as Socrates himself) hanging on their words or baiting them with naive, eager questions — given this, and hot blood, and admiration of male beauty, what is there to explain except the fact that Plato looked for the perfection of love in the life of the *palaestra* and not in that of the family? And that is one of those facts which have to be accepted, rather than explained.

Jowett could not accept it. He had too great a veneration for Plato to believe that Plato could be fundamentally un-Victorian. 'Had he lived in our times he would have made the transposition himself.' He went so far as to say: 'Like the Scriptures Plato admits of endless applications, if we allow for the difference of times and manners.' His master was the victim of pagan time and circumstance. So he sets to work and redrafts the two speeches about love, which Plato puts into the mouth of Socrates in the dialogue named *Phaedrus*.

Consider the framework of the *Phaedrus*. It is a dialogue between Socrates and his young friend Phaedrus. Its ostensible theme is rhetoric — the technical art of speaking on a given topic. The speeches about love are, as it were, introduced as texts for a discussion of rhetorical technique. At the same time, Socrates' second speech is perhaps the most famous of all pronouncements on the theme of human love. So that the dialogue has two themes — rhetoric and love — and the subsidiary theme is that which has made it famous.

The theme of love is introduced in this way. Socrates accompanies Phaedrus on a country walk. Phaedrus has with him a copy of a speech written by Lysias which he reads to Socrates. It is a rhetorical *tour de force* — it takes the line that the man who doesn't fall in love is superior to the man who does. Phaedrus, interested only in its technical quality, thinks it good. Socrates thinks it not so good. He thinks he could do that sort of thing better himself. Urged on by Phaedrus he delivers an extempore ironical speech in dispraise of love. 'As wolves love lambs, so lovers love their loves.' Having thus outdone Lysias, he is tired of the topic. But something has happened in his mind — his 'daemon' has spoken to him. He has not told the truth. And Phaedrus begs for more. So Socrates then makes another speech, this time in praise of love. This second speech is not a swing from one extravagant view to an opposite point of extravagance. It is the expression, at once passionate and serene, poetical and practical, of Plato's (maybe, also Socrates') belief in the power of love to fit human beings for a future life.

The essence of the speech is that the lovers, if they are to reap the best fruit of their love, must abstain from crude mutual pleasure. They may kiss and embrace; but they must stop there. This lesson is first conveyed in plain language, and is then reinforced by the famous simile of the charioteer and his two horses. It is the charioteer's aim to rein in the ill-conditioned horse, to make him lie back with his better trained or nobler companion.

The love which is the subject-matter of all the three discourses (that of Lysias and the two delivered by Socrates) is love between a man and a boy or younger man. This, for Jowett, is reprehensible. How, then, can he bring out what he feels to be the truth and beauty of Socrates' second speech? He cannot simply substitute heterosexual for homosexual love, since that would oblige him to condone the existence of free love between the sexes, and the result would be hardly less objectionable than the pagan habits of the Athenian palaestra. The love of which his 'modern Socrates' would speak must, therefore, be married love. Accordingly he imagines a modern Socrates to make two speeches, the first in cynical dispraise of marriage (not, be it observed, of married love) the second in praise of ideal marriage.

The first of these two 'parodies' (as he modestly calls them) goes well enough; Jowett shows an unexpected gift for 'turning the seamy side outwards'. But the second plunges into an initial absurdity which vitiates it throughout. There are 'two loves, a higher and a lower, holy and un-holy, a love of the mind and a love of the body' and 'this true love of the mind cannot exist between two souls, until they are purified from the grossness of earthly passion'. The purification, it appears, must be achieved *before* marriage; for 'when they have attained to this exalted state, let them marry (something too may be conceded to the animal nature of man): or live together in holy and innocent friendship'. And Jowett goes on to suggest 'the nature of such a union; how after many struggles the true love was found' (but had they not attained to this exalted state already before they married?); and continues in a passage which Abbott singled out for particular admiration. Here it is; and let me not be thought to quote it for the purpose of disparagement.

The poet might describe in eloquent words the nature of such a union; how after many struggles the true love was found; how the two passed their lives together in the service of God and man; how their characters were reflected upon one another, and seemed to grow more like year by year; how they read in one another's eyes the thoughts, wishes, actions of the other; how they saw each other in God; how in a figure they grew wings like doves, and were 'ready to fly away and be at rest'. And lastly, he might tell how, after a time at no long interval, first one and then the other fell asleep, and 'appeared to the unwise' to die, but were reunited in an-other state of being, in which they saw justice and holiness and truth, not according to the imperfect copies of them which are found in this world, but justice absolute in existence absolute, and so of the rest. And they would hold converse not only with each other, but with blessed souls everywhere; and would be employed in the service of God, every soul fulfilling his own nature and character, and would see into the wonders of earth and heaven, and trace the works of creation to their author.

But what is the initial absurdity which, I have ventured to say, vitiates this beautiful passage? It is the assumption that marriage is merely a concession to the animal in man; that the sooner this animal connection is over and done with the better; that ideal intimacy between husband and wife is independent of the physical intimacy in which, surely, it begins and without which it cannot grow. The Greeks knew all this as well as we do. It was a strange error on Jowett's part to present them as careless of any other kind of love except that in which Plato found the occasion for his highest flights.[1] It was a still stranger error to suppose that the ideal married love, of which he writes so movingly, must not have had its roots in physical love — a truth boldly proclaimed in the startling language of the Anglican marriage rite: 'with my body I thee worship'.

How was it that Jowett could commit such an error, and be apparently quite unaware that he had committed it? He was, perhaps, a little carried away by the ease with which he pulled off his first 'parody'; he went on too quickly to the second. But he was obviously much pleased with the second. The passage I have quoted from the second 'parody' bears the unmistakable mark of all writing in which the author has said something he has specially longed to say and has specially enjoyed saying. The partnership of which he so longingly dreams is that between a no longer young married couple. He had seen this kind of serene partnership flowering in the lives of many of his friends. He admired and envied it deeply. There is no more lovely or desirable human relationship. The 'loves of men' are put quite out of competition (if competition is the word to use) by this last fruiting of the 'loves of women'; for it is only in a life-long union that the kind of ideal love which Jowett depicts can come to its long quiet autumnal glow.

It is like the glow of the 'dogwood crimson in October', of the leaf more beautiful before its fall than in its young green tenderness. But in marriage there must be flower as well as leaf. The flower may fail to become fruit-bearing seed; and its failure may not matter. For most married couples it is the love they share for the children their bodies

---

[1] I do not remember to have anywhere seen it noted that the love invoked in the chorus of the *Antigone*, Ἔρως ἀνίκατε μάχαν (O Eros undefeated), is that which sleeps on the cheek of a girl; though Sophocles himself was reputed to be a lover of boys.

have joined to create which raises their first easy love for each other to a higher level. For some, the gradual change from an animal to an ideal level is too difficult; many childless couples make the transition more easily. But none can make it, without having eaten the fruit of the tree in the midst of the garden.

Jowett never tasted that fruit. His picture of the ideal marriage was a delusive dream. The tree stood — as it always has and always will — in the middle of the garden. He had to make believe that it was a tree of no importance.

CHAPTER VI

Young Men at Balliol

1. BALLIOL IN THE EIGHTEEN-THIRTIES

The Balliol that Jowett entered in 1835 had but recently come to the front. A generation earlier Oriel was the live centre of Oxford thought. Six years before Jowett went up, the Provost of Oriel, alarmed at the proselytizing activities of his team of High Church tutors — Newman, Wilberforce and Froude — had refused to continue them in their office. From that moment Oriel began to decline, as Mark Pattison said, 'both in the calibre of the men who obtained fellowships and in the style and tone of the undergraduates'.

It is not altogether easy to understand why Balliol stepped into the vacant position. Oriel owed her temporary pre-eminence to two Provosts of genius — Eveleigh and Copleston. It might seem that Parsons — Master of Balliol from 1798 to 1819 and co-author with Eveleigh of the new University examination statute which inaugurated the system of honour schools — ought to be similarly recognized as the creator of the new Balliol.[1] The explanation does not quite satisfy. In spite of his part in the reform of the University examination system, and in spite of the efficiency with which he remodelled the teaching system inside his own college — raising the sense of tutorial responsibility, instituting an entrance examination, and holding the college 'collections'[2] every term — Balliol did not begin to move into serious competition with Oriel, until he had ceased to be Master. At Oriel, indeed, the splendid Dr. Copleston rejoiced to mock at the 'quackery' of University class-lists. Perhaps the eagerness of Oriel to discover talent ignored by University examiners was one of the reasons for her decline. Certainly the methods introduced by Dr. Parsons at Balliol were designed to secure results measurable in the schools, and did in fact secure them. But Parsons himself seems to have been the kind of man who is better at devising organization than at using it. His life 'was marked by a series of improvements, of institutions

---

[1] See H. W. C. Davis, *Balliol College*, 201–2.
[2] 'Collections': a short college examination usually followed by a *viva-voce*, testing the progress of the undergraduates in their set studies.

reformed, of revenues augmented, of residences restored and embellished'.

This was just the kind of thing which the fellows of Balliol had wanted Parsons for, when they took him — a Wadham, and not a Balliol man — as Master. Though the eighteenth century was not yet quite done with, the nineteenth-century conscience had already begun to work in the college, after a long period of an apathy even more profound than that which is supposed to have prevailed generally in Oxford. But the workings of conscience seem to have been satisfied, for a time, by mechanical reform. The philosopher Sir William Hamilton, during his pupilage at Balliol (1807–10), had as small a respect for the college lecturers as Southey fifteen years earlier, or Adam Smith in the seventeen-forties, when the legendary coma was at its deepest.[1]

In 1813 Parsons became Bishop of Peterborough, though he continued to hold the Mastership until his death six years later. The vicegerent, in the new Bishop's absence, was Dr. Jenkyns, who was elected Master in due course, and who consequently governed Balliol from 1813 to 1854.

Richard Jenkyns, during the latter part of his reign and for long afterwards, was always called 'the Old Master'. The phrase has an affectionate overtone. A mystery in his life-time, he remains a mystery still. 'His intellect' says Davis 'was in no way remarkable; though his will was strong, his personality could hardly be called commanding. In appearance he was neat and insignificant. His formal manners, his mincing speech, his comical gait, and his little white pony formed the subject of many ludicrous legends.' Not himself educated at a public school he nevertheless reckoned a public school education as part of a gentleman's proper equipment. Three public schools stood in his mind at the head of the list — Eton, Rugby and Harrow. It was from these three schools that 'during his tenure of office the majority of the commoners of the college were carefully chosen'. Yet between them and him there was a gulf fixed, which he had no notion how to cross.

Earlier in his career, when he was a tutor, his ignorance of the public-school game landed him into some uncomfortable situations. In 1811 an undergraduate was obliged to beg pardon of the vicegerent and fellows in the chapel, for having borne himself *minus reverentem* towards Jenkyns; in 1812 another undergraduate was admonished for disobedient and contumacious behaviour towards the same personage. To a very slightly earlier date belongs the story of an hilarious party in William Hamilton's rooms. Late in the night a noise was heard outside. The door was

[1] For Hamilton's attack on the collegiate system see below, 190–1 *foll.*

flung open and disclosed a figure kneeling with his ear where the key-hole had been, instantly recognized as Jenkyns. Prompt action was taken.

In a twinkling the spy was clutched by the collar, and suspended over the well of the staircase, until his reiterated cries for mercy made it impossible to keep up the feint of non-recognition. He was then gently restored to *terra firma* amid a chorus of apologies: 'We never dreamed for a moment that it could be you, Sir!'

Another story, also related by Davis to illustrate Jenkyns's lack of *savoir faire*, is too good not to be repeated.

One of Jenkyns' pupils used to describe with much humour how, on a winter morning after Chapel, the Master sent for him and said, with a trace of asperity, 'I hear, Mr. Rogers, that you sing.' The charge was modestly admitted. 'I hear, Mr. Rogers, that you are a good singer.' Mr. Rogers replied that his friends were sometimes pleased to say as much. 'You sing a song called "Jolly Nose", Mr. Rogers!' This, too, was un-deniable. 'Sing it now, Mr. Rogers!'

How was it possible for such a man not only to win the affectionate respect of such a society as Balliol, under his rule, came to be, but to deserve the general judgment that it was he who raised Balliol to the first rank of Oxford colleges?

Jenkyns's superficial oddities belied his abilities. Not himself bookishly clever he was, in Dean Church's phrase, 'an unfailing judge of a clever man, as a jockey might be of a horse'. By his own instincts and beliefs he was a man of the past, always on every small occasion asserting the stan-dards of the past without the faintest appearance of understanding their present irrelevance. Nevertheless on every serious occasion he supported the party of reform within the college. So ignorant was he thought to be of the classical niceties, that his saying about W. G. Ward 'There is a candid ingenuity about the fellow which pleases me' went the rounds of Oxford as a beautiful malapropism. He was thought to have confused 'ingenuousness' with 'ingenuity'. Possibly he meant what he said: 'candid ingenuity' is a witty phrase. There was more in Dr. Jenkyns's queer mind than the little he took pains to exhibit. 'It was sometimes doubted' observed Jowett some fifty years later 'whether he was a wit or not; I myself am strongly of opinion that he was.'

There could be no one so well fitted to form a true judgment of Jen-kyns as the Master *par excellence* of the Balliol that Jenkyns bequeathed to him after a posthumous interval. They were both of them 'characters'; both (in Jowett's phrase about Jenkyns) myths in their own lifetimes. Jowett used his *persona* to enforce what he wanted; Jenkyns could only put across the things he wanted by pretending not to understand them. Here, then, is Jowett on Jenkyns.[1]

I, too, remember 'the Old Master'. To those who did not know him, I hardly know how to give an idea of him. He was short of stature and very neat in appearance; but, like Louis XIV, he gave us the impression of being larger in person than he really was. There was in him a degree of dignity which impressed our imaginations. He was very different from any of the Fellows, and was held in considerable awe by them. He was a gentleman of the old school, a Tory and a Churchman, high and dry, without much literature, but having a good deal of character. He filled a great space in the eyes of the undergraduates. His young men, as he termed them, speaking in an accent which we all remember, were never tired of mimicking his voice, drawing his portrait, and inventing stories about what he said and did. He became a myth during his own lifetime. There was a time when at any party of Balliol he would have been talked about. His sermon on the 'Sin that doth so easily beset us', by which, as he said in emphatic and almost acrid tones, he meant 'the habit of contracting debts', will never be forgotten by those who heard it. Nor indeed have I ever seen a whole congregation dissolved in laughter for several minutes except on that remarkable occasion. Even now, at the distance of more than a generation, it is impossible to think of him without some ludicrous association arising in the mind. The last time that the privilege of electing the College Visitor was exercised, there were some who wished to have the late Bishop of Oxford.[2] But the Old Master objected. He said he did not like having a doctor who would be in the habit of coming in any morning, and feeling your pulse! And indeed where the little finger of the Bishop of Oxford was once admitted, the whole of his eminent person was likely soon to follow. Others proposed the late learned Bishop of St. David's.[3] But our opponents urged that in early life he had been indiscreet in his theological opinions. And the Old Master said (with what ground I cannot pretend to say) that he lived all by himself and killed cats! He was given to remarkable rhetorical exaggerations. There was in him an imaginary dislike to the Pope; and a very real dislike of dogs. He was a considerable actor, and would put on severe looks to terrify freshmen, but he was really kind-hearted and indulgent towards them. He was in a natural state of war with the Fellows and Scholars on the Close Foundation; and many ludicrous stories were told of his behaviour towards them, of his dislike of smoking, and of his enmity to dogs. He knew no University Commissions, but great was his care for the College. He did a great work.

Jenkyns's success followed from the fact that he knew how to choose men and that he backed his choices, even when his apparent opinions and theirs were in conflict. But why should this crusted old tory have had, beneath his oddities, one unwavering purpose — to make Balliol into an institution unlike anything of which he had ever had any personal experience? 'Probably' says Davis 'he had never read a line of Milton's

---

[1] The passage which follows is a telescoped and slightly re-arranged conflation of two accounts written by Jowett: and *Essays on Men and Manners* (see note below, 432) given in *W.G.W. and the O.M.*, 116–17.
[2] Bishop Wilberforce.　　　　　　　　[3] Bishop Thirlwall.

Areopagitica; but his idea of a healthy intellectual society might have been taken directly from that immortal pamphlet.'

Such an attitude of mind seems to indicate not astute opportunism, but essential wisdom. The single measure which did most to establish the supremacy of Balliol was the opening of the scholarships to free competition. This step was taken in 1828. It has been said that the credit for this reform belonged not to Jenkyns but to the then senior tutor, Charles Ogilvie, who ruled the common room; and that the Master himself consented only 'because the tutors were unanimous'. It may well have appeared to be so; but Jowett's recollection that the Old Master was always at war with the 'close' fellows and scholars suggests that his secret mind was on the side of the revolutionaries, and that his public behaviour was a calculated contribution to a game which he wished to see ending as, in fact, it ended. Dr. Jenkyns, one must suspect, (like Jowett) cared nothing what others thought about him and pursued his aims for their own sake, not his.

The renaissance of Balliol, apart from its debt to Parsons and Jenkyns, sprang from the struggle against a paralysing internal disease.

At first a foundation for undergraduates, and not wholly self-governing, Balliol was brought finally into line with other Oxford colleges by Bishop Fox at the beginning of the sixteenth century. Fox's statutes committed the government of the college to the Master and ten fellows; to these were added, in the early seventeenth century, two more fellows by private benefactions. One of these fellowships — the 'Blundell' fellowship — owed its existence to the will of one Peter Blundell, a native of Tiverton in Somerset. The Blundell foundation proved a long curse to Balliol. It provided, at first, for one scholar and one fellow. The scholar must be from Blundell's School and by preference a native of Tiverton. The fellow must have been a Blundell scholar; and every Blundell scholar had the right of succession to a Blundell fellowship and was to remain a scholar until the fellowship became vacant for him.[1] The Master and fellows of the time were unaccountably short-sighted in their negotiations with Peter Blundell's executors, for they went so far as to bind the college to admit any Blundell scholar, who had taken his degree, to the next vacant fellowship, whether or no it was a Blundell fellowship.

The bad consequences of this concession were a great deal more than doubled when, towards the end of the seventeenth century, they agreed to double the number of the Blundell fellows and scholars. It resulted during the eighteenth century that, at one time, half the governing body of the college consisted of 'Tiverton men', and Balliol appeared to be

---

[1] The tenure of the fellowship was 10 years from the M.A. degree.

'fast degenerating into a county college', without the faintest hope of achieving the destiny which, nevertheless, awaited it.

The 'Tiverton men' naturally upheld a policy of extreme isolationism. If there was not a Tiverton man available, when a vacancy occurred among the fellowships, they could be counted upon to support the view that no outsider should be elected. The new fellow must at least be a Balliol scholar or exhibitioner. That distinction, before 1828, did not necessarily mean very much in the way of ability or academic attainment. Not only were the scholarships and exhibitions confined to Balliol undergraduates, but they were not awarded on any adequate test of merit. There was, therefore, as Davis puts it,

no guarantee that the scholar or exhibitioner would have the slightest tincture of ability. Often he had not. Still, the older generation among the fellows would vote for him. When reprimanded by the Visitor for partiality they fell back on the excuse that they could not find it in their consciences to vote for young men from other colleges, who were indeed very clever scholars, but whose moral character might, for aught they knew, be most indifferent.[1]

This 'conscience' *motif* was by no means peculiar to Balliol electors. Small societies everywhere are naturally and rightly anxious to keep their individual shapes and characters; their distrust of intruders must not be airily dismissed as wrong or disingenuous. Much the same *motif* appeared later in the passionate struggle of All Souls, against the first wave of compulsory reform in the late eighteen-fifties, to preserve 'moral' (the reformists called them 'social') considerations as factors which the electors must properly take into account — a struggle in which the weight of argument was far from lying wholly on the side of the reformists.[2] But in Balliol, before the end of the eighteenth century, the Tiverton interest (in some aspects like the Founder's kin interest at All Souls) had become so malignant a growth that any argument which favoured it was an argument asking for defeat in the minds of reasonable men — even, no doubt, of the best Tiverton men.

So it came about that Balliol, instead of being the last ditch of undeserved privilege and a principal target of the 1854 Commissioners, was forced by her own internal absurdities to reform herself and to anticipate — by at least some thirty years — the reforms which her own 'colonizers'

[1] The above account follows Davis. Dr. R. Hunt, however, points out that between 1807 and 1819 nine of the fourteen fellowships on the old foundation were filled by outsiders; and that Jenkyns started 'with an able set of fellows'. Until 1828 the scholars were nominated alternately by the Master and by the fellows. (*Victoria County History: Oxfordshire*, iii, 85.)

[2] This struggle lasted for some years before and after 1860, and is fully documented. The meagre published references are misleading. See below, 202 *foll.*

were later to propagate and pursue in other Oxford colleges and in the University at large.

'By at least some thirty years' — that is to say, if one treats the opening of the Balliol scholarships to general competition in 1828 as the starting moment of Balliol's internal reform. But that was the culminating point of a long internal war, in which the progressive party had won the really decisive victory another thirty years earlier, when Dr. Parsons was elected Master in 1798. For in Parsons the college chose as ruler a man who had been refused a Balliol scholarship in 1779 because he had not been a Balliol undergraduate. Reform in England is often thought to have been begotten by the ghost of the French Revolution on the elderly body of English puritanism. It is worth noting that this generalization cannot be made to apply to Balliol.

In the size of its governing body Balliol was one of the smaller Oxford colleges. There were only twelve fellows in 1836. Only two of the twelve were 'Tiverton men'. The influence of the Old Master, who had ruled the college for nearly a quarter of a century, had worked wonders. The Balliol common room was beginning to feed Oxford and the outer world with men of outstanding capacity. As Jowett came up, George Moberly went from Balliol to be headmaster of Winchester; Charles Ogilvie — soon to be appointed the first Regius Professor of Pastoral Theology — ceased to be a fellow; and young Herman Merivale was on the threshold of a distinguished career in the Colonial and India offices. To fill these vacancies (and another) four very remarkable elections were made in 1834–5. Tait (Arnold's successor at Rugby, and later Bishop of London and Archbishop of Canterbury) and 'Ideal' Ward made the first pair. Robert Scott (part author of the great Greek Lexicon, and subsequently Master of Balliol before Jowett) and Edward Cardwell (the statesman who, at the War Office, invented or sponsored the 'Cardwell system' of overseas military service) made the second pair. Among the recently elected fellows Edward Twistleton had been called to the Bar, and was to spend his life in political service. Senior to all of these, but still in his thirties, was Frederick Oakeley, the chaplain fellow, who was one of Newman's men and 'went over to Rome' in the same year as Newman and Ward.

It was a young common room. Eight of the twelve fellows were in their twenties, and of the others at least two were under thirty-five.[1] This

---

[1] This should not be a matter of surprise. The effect of the reforms made in the 'fifties and 'seventies was to raise, not to lower, the average age of dons. At All Souls, for example, in 1856 (the last year before the reforming Ordinance of 1857) the average age of the forty fellows was thirty-four, and half of them were in their twenties. But for the existence of two or three ancient celibates the

youthfulness had a dangerous as well as hopeful side. For the younger generation was now beginning to circle round the newly formed tractarian vortex, which was about to become the centre of implacable dissensions.

In the Balliol common room, just at the moment when the old internal cause of dispute was dying, this new dissension took a sharper form than anywhere else. If that somewhat inaccurate chronicler, Tom Mozley of Oriel, is to be trusted, the storm was blowing up before the tractarian movement started in 1833.

At a very early date there were causes at work in the whole University, and specially at Balliol, tending to unsettle minds and drive them in one direction or another. Frank Newman was elected Fellow of Balliol in 1826, Oakeley in 1827, Merivale in 1828. The discussions in the common room, where Ogilvie still ruled, were already becoming unpleasantly warm, ending in some of the Fellows almost regularly absenting themselves. Disputants who pull violently in one direction are seldom aware how much they compel their opponents to pull in the other; and though Oakeley did not like controversy his sentimental nature disposed him to resent the violence of logical, or rather mathematical arguments, and seek rest in reaction.[1]

The 'mathematical arguments' were those of Ward, the fat and abounding mathematical tutor, whose pupils commonly felt, as Clough put it, like pieces of paper being sucked irresistibly up a chimney. But Ward was not elected till 1834; and Frank Newman — Cardinal Newman's contemptuous, dissenting brother — resigned his fellowship in 1830, embracing the Plymouth Brotherhood on his way to Unitarianism. In spite of these typical inaccuracies on points of detail, Mozley's picture is true enough. The Balliol fellows were very sharply divided over the new question of questions for the Oxford intelligentsia — what, really, *was* the Church of England? In the eighteen-thirties it would have been evidence of mental anaemia not to treat that question seriously. The colleges were, in historical fact, ecclesiastical foundations. They were still, legally and actually, clerical incubators. Their clerical character and purpose were being challenged by secular changes and were later to be abolished by Parliament. Meanwhile, the very uncertainty of the issue heightened the tension of debate between those who would put Church above State, those who would put State above Church, and those who hoped that things might continue much as they had been since the end of the Stuarts.

average age would have been considerably lower. This was the natural result of the old rule that a man vacated his fellowship on marriage. It is very important to keep this fact in mind; for the usual notion is that Oxford colleges, a hundred or a hundred and fifty years ago, were ruled by old men. The truth is the exact reverse. Youth was at the helm or, at any rate, in the majority.

[1] Mozley, *Reminiscences of Oriel*, ii, 229.

Whatever disputes took place in the Balliol common room, the dons were doing their best by the undergraduates. At the time of Jowett's entry into the college the two chief classical tutors were Tait and Scott. Tait, though the less accomplished scholar of the two, was by far the better teacher. 'Full of life and common sense and Scotch humour,' as Jowett said long afterwards 'he was the first, or one of the first persons who broke down the wall of partition which used to separate undergraduates from their teachers.' His *brusquerie* and quickness of temper, turned off with a joke at just the right moment, made his pupils think of him as a human being.

Many of us had to thank him for piloting us safely through the rocks and shoals of theology. For the new tendency to Catholicism came upon Oxford like a flood, and we needed such a guide as he was to keep us in the straight path of common sense. He did not attempt the higher flights of metaphysical philosophy, yet his lectures were very interesting and useful. He did not read but spoke them; and he knew how to keep the attention of his class alive by questions and sallies of various kinds. . . . They were always plain and clear, though the knots were sometimes cut after the Gordian fashion.[1]

Jowett's appreciation may seem a little cool. But he was deliberately aiming at truth, not panegyric; and though he thought highly of Tait as a tutor, he did not consider him 'a man of great intellectual power'.

If this was true of Tait, it was truer still of Tait's principal colleague, Scott. 'He was very kind to me in early life' Jowett recalled; 'an excellent man, though not liberal or enlightened, and a distinguished scholar, possessing stores of information on a great variety of subjects — too much given to punning, but also a real humorist.'[2] Scott's humour was at its best in those elaborate Greek and Latin jokes, which make fun of their own learning and are unintelligible except to scholars. For the select few this is a very enjoyable and excellent kind of humour; and the few were not so few in Scott's day as they have since become. The Greek hexameters, in which he described the Heads of Houses going to the installation (in 1834) of the Duke of Wellington as Chancellor of the University, 'were long remembered and quoted'. These belonged to his undergraduate youth — two or three years before he began to teach Jowett. But something went wrong with Scott. The humour faded — perhaps under the grinding of the Greek Lexicon — and with it faded also the sense of proportion which belongs as much to scholarship as to humour. The current opinion of his share in that enormous work was recorded in a cruel quatrain:

[1] Jowett, *Sermons Biographical and Miscellaneous*, 180–1.
[2] *W.G.W. and the O.M.*, 115.

Two men wrote a Lexicon, Liddell and Scott;
One half was clever, one half was not.
Give me the answer, boys, quick, to this riddle:
Which was by Scott, and which was by Liddell?

Scott's 'learned and careful lectures' said Jowett's contemporary Escott 'left comparatively little impression on the mind'. They left, no doubt, the deepest impression they were capable of making upon the mind of the young scholar from St. Paul's in whom, Escott continues, 'fonder then of the literature than of the philosophy of Greece, he [Scott] had a pupil after his own heart, whose accurate scholarship he could at once admire and enrich'. Nevertheless, Jowett's words about Scott are not those of a man owing a tribute; had he felt that there was tribute owing, he would have paid it all the more scrupulously because of the bitter estrangement which took place between them, when Scott became Master of Balliol.

Third of the classical tutors in importance (though senior to Tait and Scott) was Oakeley, the chaplain fellow, dreamy, sensitive, musical, and romantically religious — not a man to make an impact on pupils of different temperament. He lectured, not unmemorably, on Lucretius, and was generally responsible for the 'catechetical lecture' in chapel every Sunday evening, on which all the undergraduates were examined during the subsequent week, 'the best of the answers being chosen by the Lecturer and read by their respective writers on the following Sunday in Chapel'. The catechetical lecture is a perfect instance of the division between the Oxford that was and the Oxford that is. It passes the imagination to picture a modern equivalent. But to the young Jowett it would have seemed a natural and right institution, though he may not have thought very highly of the way in which the thing was done. To the rank and file the catechetical lecture was merely a tiresome imposition like the compulsory attendances at chapel services — once every weekday, and twice every Sunday, with Holy Communion once a term.

The daily routine of an Oxford college, only a hundred and twenty or so years ago, differed astoundingly from its routine to-day. The time was past when dinner had been at three o'clock in the afternoon and everybody must not only dress for it in 'swallow-tail coat, knee-breeches, silk stockings and pumps', but also have his hair 'powdered by the College barber, who began his operations on the junior Freshman a couple of hours before dinner, and worked steadily up the list to the Senior Fellow'.[1] But it was not very long past. The poet Southey, in the seven-

---

[1] Davis, *op. cit.*, 187.

teen-nineties, was the first Balliol undergraduate to sport his own long
hair 'curling naturally over his shoulders'. Forty years later, powdering
had gone, hair was shortening and dress not so elaborate; but the time
of dinner had been postponed only by an hour or two and dressing for
the occasion, if not what it had been, was still *de rigueur* and still included
(at any rate at the high table) 'pumps'.

The theory was that the men had read 'without a break' from morning
chapel at eight to dinner at five. Exercise came in the early evening; and
it was at the peculiar hour of six, or later after a wine-party in somebody's
rooms, that the ordinary residents of Oxford might observe 'the twos
and twos going out for their constitutionals'. The undergraduate with
means of his own or a suitable allowance from his father had, of course,
not spent the earlier part of the day in the manner required by theory.
He had spent it hunting, riding, shooting or 'driving tandem'. But these
amusements were not for a poor boy from St. Paul's, who dared not even
attend wine-parties after dinner, since he could not afford to return them
again.

Two quotations may help to fill the picture out. Here is my favourite
Oxford gossip, Tuckwell, writing just before 1900 and nostalgically
recalling

every phase of College life as it exuberated sixty years ago, fast and slow,
tuft and Bible clerk, reading man and lounger, profligacy and debt,
summer term and Commemoration, boat races, wines, University
sermons . . . a life fuller, more varied, more *youthful*, than is proved
to-day by our golden or our gilded juvenility. Stagecoaches, postchaises
. . . meant more fun than first-class carriages and railway novels . . . I am
a fogey, to be sure, and out of date; but, remembering the days when I . . .
was dropped at the Mitre by Jack Adams 'from the box of the Royal
Defiance', the days when Cowley Marsh was a rush-grown common, and
from Magdalen bridge to Iffley there was not a single roadside house, I
feel for those ancient ways and vanished hours what our present youngsters will mayhap feel for their own some ten or twelve lustres hence.[1]

The second quotation comes from Canon Oakeley's reminiscences of
Balliol under Dr. Jenkyns.

It was one of his misfortunes that he was not a good rider, and yet used
to ride a great deal. He was a little man, and he had a little pony; and
everyone knows that a little man with a little pony is not likely to escape a
great deal of playful criticism on the part of tall men who ride tall horses.
Thus, it would sometimes happen that the Master and his pony would fall
in with a party of riders returning from the hunt. The riders would trot
at a quick pace behind the Master and his pony; and the latter, fretted by the
noise behind it, would start off at a gallop, and thus place the Master in

---

[1] *Reminiscences of Oxford*, 199. The context is Tuckwell's praise of an almost
forgotten book, *Tom Brown at Oxford*.

the awkward position of seeming to head a party of his own undergraduates on their return from the hunting field.[1]

Alas, one must feel, for that vanished time when Oxford was the little unspoiled University town to which 'the boy Jowett' travelled from London by coach. In all essentials the town was complete — beautiful, old, rurally isolated yet intimately connected with State and Church. It pulsated with youth. Those who had lived in it remembered it as adorable — even when (like Jowett) they had laboured to change it, or (like Newman) they had cut themselves off from it, or (like Matthew Arnold or Clough) they had been unable to find in it any stable point between the past and the future. It is still there — that Oxford of 1836 — encrusted by an undisciplined variety of self-conscious architectural additions, surrounded by a vast sprawl of houses, loud with incessant traffic, and inundated by a swarming industrial population. Its small, compact and inviolate beauty — this has gone for ever. In 1836 the High Street was the serene symbol of a perfected horse-drawn civilization — the worst that could happen in it was Dr. Jenkyns galloping ahead of his high-spirited undergraduates. Except under a late moon or in the calm early hours of a midsummer morning it has been difficult, for very many years, to perceive that it still remains one of the world's most beautiful streets. Quiet can be restored to it only if it ceases to be a thoroughfare, and is finally relieved from its ancient purpose and modern burden. Its future character and the method of relief remain undecided, as this book goes to be printed. It is not for the writer, torn between two allegiances, to range himself in this controversy. All his aim is to point the contrast between the Oxford that was and the Oxford that is.

When Jowett went up to Balliol, there were only some eighty undergraduates — against the three hundred and more whom the college educates to-day. Even that small number was split into several 'sets'. In the eighteenth century Balliol had contained its full quota of fashionable youth; and Dr. Jenkyns's predilection for Eton and Harrow had not diminished the supply. But the hot young bloods of Eton and Harrow were now matched with the earnest young moralists from Rugby — the only other public school Dr. Jenkyns seems to have recognized.

This potentially explosive mixture was complicated by the Scottish element introduced into the college by the benefactions of Bishop Warner and, more particularly, John Snell of Ayrshire in the second half of the seventeenth century. These benefactions are said to have had the purpose of recruiting Scottish ordinands for the Church of England; and also to have, perhaps, reflected the idea that Balliol had originally

[1] *Oxford Historical Society*, vol. xxii, 342.

been a Scottish foundation. It is true that the college was founded about 1265 by John de Baliol, an ex-Regent of Scotland and father of a King of Scotland, and that after his death his widow Devorguilla devoted herself to completing his foundation. But de Baliol was not a Scot, and though his wife belonged to the Scottish nobility her education and sympathies lay far south of the border. Moreover de Baliol's action was in the nature of a penance imposed upon him by the Prince Bishop of Durham; and its fulfilment was controlled by the Franciscan friars already established in Oxford. There is no trace of any special connection between Balliol and Scotland before it was set up by Warner and Snell.[1]

It became a connection of extraordinary value. Adam Smith, William Hamilton, Archbishop Tait, Edward Caird — these and very many other distinguished men came to Balliol as Snell exhibitioners from Glasgow University. The influx grew as the value of Snell's property increased. In 1872, Davis says, there were no less than ten Snell exhibitions each worth £116 10s. per annum. These capable, industrious, often brilliant northerners came to Oxford, not indeed at an age necessarily much more advanced than that of the ordinary English undergraduate, but as the survivors of an intensive educational struggle which had no English parallel. Their dour resolution reinforced the earnest idealism of the Rugbeians. The double influence so worked in Balliol, with and in conflict with the influences from Eton and Harrow, as to provide the rich and complex soil needed for the full development of Jowett's genius. Moreover Balliol, in spite of its aristocratic connections, no longer gave privileges, such as some other colleges still gave, to noblemen and 'fellow-commoners'. Warfare was on the level.

Escott describes Balliol, at the time when Jowett joined it, as

rather sharply divided into sets, and even at the tables in Hall, open to all, this division was generally observed. But still the borderers in each set were more or less members of the adjoining set, and a man might have friends in other sets than his own. But it was the stirring activity of the College which most struck the new members as they joined it. Of course in this vigorous life the Scholars took the lead. . . .

When the writer of this book was a boy at Rugby, he owed much to the patient teaching of a young master who had been a Balliol scholar. This young master was not thought, by his pupils, to know very much about the world; and he was unlucky in the possession of a slight lisp. The story went that he had said to one of us: 'When I wath at Balliol

---

[1] Davis's account of the foundation of Balliol (*op. cit.*, 7 *foll.*) should not be missed, if the reader wants to know more. The story is fascinating. The *D.N.B.* articles on the de Baliol family add a little.

there were three thetth — the rowing thet, the thporting thet and the reading thet. I belonged to the thporting thet.' We thought this deliciously absurd. Perhaps it was not, after all, quite so absurd as we supposed.

2. A MIND IN THE MAKING

All accounts agree with Tuckwell's pen-picture of the 'little white-haired lad with shrill voice and cherub face' who, in October 1836, exchanged his lodging in the City Road for rooms in Balliol.

Perhaps 'little' was not quite accurate; or perhaps he had not grown to his full height. Certainly he was thought to be under-sized. Campbell, whose description of the slight figure racing about the quadrangle has already been quoted, tries to correct this impression. 'He was really middle-sized, with rather sloping shoulders, and a chest not broad but deep. His boyish countenance, like Milton's, "deceiving the truth that he to manhood was arrived so near", his delicate complexion, high-pitched voice, finely tapering hands, and small well-moulded feet, contributed to strengthen the illusion' of littleness. Yet, as Campbell himself admits, 'the undergraduates of his own time seem to have shared this impression with those who twenty years afterwards loved to talk of "little Benjamin their ruler".'

The epithet 'white-haired' clearly reports an original flaxen colouring, which grew darker as he grew older before his hair whitened again. Richmond's drawing (circa 1859) suggests fair brown with light reflecting tones. The 'cherub face' is beyond doubt; so is the pitch of the voice, though 'shrill' is again probably not the true word. 'Treble' or 'alto' would be nearer. Unkind or resentful critics spoke of it, sometimes, as a 'piping' voice. Others found it delightful 'especially in reading Scripture', and were drawn to Balliol chapel in order to relish 'a richness in its tones, as of a silver bell'.[1]

'Boyish' is also not the right word. Arthur Hobhouse,[2] a year his junior, recalled his 'pretty, girlish looks, quiet voice and gentle shy manner'. Other recurring adjectives are puny, childish, chubby, cherubic. The schoolboy's shabby round jacket and turned-down collar, which he still wore when he came up to Balliol, emphasized his half-fledged look, and with 'his low shoes and white stockings' and 'his brisk tripping almost childish gait' made his appearance very noticeable.

This childish seeming concealed an adult mind. Behind it, as Hobhouse quickly perceived,

[1] L. & L., i, 206. The epithet 'silver' used to be applied also to Newman's preaching voice.
[2] Afterwards Lord Hobhouse, Lord of Appeal.

there lay a robust masculine understanding, which would not accept commonplaces as true or mere authority as a guide. I think most boys of eighteen are apt to repeat without testing what they have been accustomed to hear. . . . Certainly that was the case with me. And then I came into contact with one who, not flippant nor irreverent nor specially fond of paradox, nor specially desirous of victory in a discussion, yet insisted on seeing everything with his own eyes, and refused to utter a proposition until his own judgment was sufficiently in accord with it. I looked upon Jowett as the freshest and most original mind I had come across; and I still think that I have never held converse with anyone who was more thoroughly original, or more careful to say only what he made his own. . . . One of his characteristics which impressed me even then was his calmness when opinions differed; that he did not, as other men are wont, get heated or argue for victory in a wordy war, but contended only when he had something to say which he believed to be true.

Shy and unassuming, the new scholar took his own quiet road. He made very few friends. According to Tom Farrer,[1] two years his junior and his very first pupil, he was 'absolutely devoid of athletic propensities'. He sometimes went sculling; in his second summer term he took part in a sculling sweepstake, at half-a-crown a head, coming in fourteenth out of nineteen. He took his ordinary exercise either in the regular 'constitutional', walking with a friend or acquaintance, or in bathing at Parson's Pleasure. Like Swinburne, he was a natural swimmer and lover of water.

Jowett's reserve about his own feelings was so fixed a habit that he could never conceivably have written his autobiography. But in the manuscript of his short memoir of Lord Sherbrooke ('Bob' Lowe)[2] there is added, in pencil, a passage which, though it was suggested by Sherbrooke's schooldays at Winchester, seems to have had a closer meaning for the writer's own mind.

It is sad to think how sometimes the restless, half inspired boy has been misunderstood by his parents or friends; and afterwards when he has grown up to be an eminent man from this unknown cause working in him he has been 'misunderstood' still. The consciousness of some personal defect may have sunk too deeply into the mind at a time when reason was not strong enough to fight against such impressions. The child too has sorrows for which no one is to blame, and which no one knows but himself.

These words were evidently written, because the old man's mind had gone back to his own lonely boyhood, to the awareness which awoke in him then of something sadly wrong in his circumstances, and later on of something in himself which differentiated him from other boys and men.

[1] T. H. Farrer, afterwards Lord Farrer, barrister, civil servant, vice-chairman of the L.C.C., and economist.

[2] The man who got Gladstone to send Scott to a deanery and so to make way for Jowett's election to the Mastership. See below, 349.

His particular shyness derived, no doubt, largely from this cause. What is so remarkable in Jowett — so remarkable that it bears frequent repetition — is that from the beginning of his maturity he used his conscious mind to overcome not the fact of his difference from others, for that lay beyond his power, but its social consequences. He fought his shyness into submission to his will; and he compelled generation after generation of men and women, of every age and rank, to forget his peculiarities in affectionate respect for the 'robust masculine understanding' which triumphantly belied them.

Such a conquest is not quick or easy. In this kind of warfare there is never any end; and victory is never more than a matter of degree. But by his early twenties Jowett was beginning to consolidate the ground he had gained. His self-mastery was not won by a succession of wrestling bouts with the world, the flesh or the devil. There had been no inner struggle between concupiscence and virtue, such as Newman darkly hints at in his own history.[1] Consolidation, for Jowett, meant the strengthening of reasoned will, the enlargement of understanding, the unhurried tempering of an instrument he would find later opportunities of using.

3. STANLEY

In his first term at Balliol Jowett, who had made no friend at St. Paul's, began what was to be one of his three most important friendships. A senior scholar, Arthur Penrhyn Stanley, took him out for a walk. Stanley came back saying that he had never met with such a disputatious youth. But nobody else (after Dr. Arnold) ever influenced Stanley as Jowett did; and nobody else influenced Jowett's opening mind to the same degree and in the same way as Stanley did. While they were young men together, and even into early middle age, each kept the other's close company for lap after lap of the theological marathon. Outside the desire they shared for a new and liberal interpretation of Christianity their precocious minds ran alert in tandem, with Jowett in the lead.

It will be seen, later on, how Jowett's friendship with Stanley mattered in Jowett's own career. It will be seen, too, how the 'disputatious youth' took risks which Stanley avoided and disapproved; and how Jowett, after a long decade of frustration, emerged as a man of destiny while Stanley's bright genius faded in the deanery of Westminster. Of the two men

[1] 'More like a devil than a wicked boy, at the age of fifteen.' See *Oxford Apostles*, 31 (Pelican edition).

Jowett more than succeeded in justifying, and Stanley ultimately failed to justify, the expectations they began by exciting. Yet Jowett would never have been the man he was, if he had not had Stanley for his early and continuing friend. Their relationship was close and unique. No attempt to describe Jowett would be worth attention if it did not include an attempt to describe Stanley.

The two boys, almost equally gifted, had very different starts in life and very differently patterned characters. Stanley was definitely of the 'upper ten thousand', Jowett definitely of the lower middle class. Jowett's father was a poor man who had failed in business. Stanley's father was one of those younger sons of aristocratic families, for whom — in the heyday of rural English life — a family living provided the perfect early career.

Sometimes, as one dips into Victorian family history, it is difficult to resist the feeling that about the turn of the eighteenth into the nineteenth century and for several decades before and after, in spite of foreign and domestic anxieties, English country life achieved, at any rate in many localities, an almost miraculous social balance. There are arguments in plenty to prove that no such balance existed or ought to have existed, based, as it was, upon a rigid economic differentiation of classes; and it may be that the view from above was not always in agreement with the view from below. Learned works have been written to prove the degradation of the countryside. Imaginative books and poems have been written with the deliberate intention of producing, in sensitive and sophisticated minds, an indignant sense of the dumb misery endured by Hodge.

Nevertheless, Stanley's life began in what at least seemed to be a happy age, when 'rich' and 'poor' were in charitable company together, none too rich and none too poor, the rich giving service to the poor, the poor giving service to the rich. His own family was the embodiment of all that was best in this idyllic scene. His father, Edward Stanley, after Cambridge (where he was sixteenth wrangler in 1802) and a brief continental tour, took orders and was presented by his father to the family rectory of Alderley in 1805. There, in a 'low house with a verandah, forming a wide balcony for the upper storey, where birdcages hung among the roses; its rooms and passages filled with pictures, books and old carved oak furniture', with the church hardly a stone's throw from the lawn, on the edge of Alderley Park, where old Sir John continued to reign, the black-haired wiry young clergyman settled down for the next thirty-three years, until his appointment to be Bishop of Norwich in 1838.

We hear of the Rector (Arthur's father) as a man of great mental and bodily vigour, conscientious, outspoken, liberal in his opinions,

the life and soul not only of his house but of his parish — now galloping through the lanes on his little black horse, with his pockets full of sugar-plums for the children, with words of sympathy for the sick or sad, and of sharp rebuke for the vicious or disorderly; now returning to study eagerly the latest works on history or natural science, or to write a lecture for his parishioners on the birds or plants of the neighbourhood, or to arrange and classify the specimens which he had collected in his rambles.

At Alderley rectory Arthur was born in 1815. He was a delicate child, very different from his vigorous elder brother Owen, 'with nothing of a boy about him except his love of horses and hatred of dolls ... very liable to be spoiled, with simple pretty ways, and a kind of hanging-on, dependent manner that calls out tenderness ... with a strange sense of delicate beauty ... in ecstasies over every new flower' — so his mother described him, alertly responsive to sounds and sights and taking to books as a duck to the water.

Different though the circumstances and characters of the two boys were there was a certain similarity between Arthur Stanley's inheritance and that of Benjamin Jowett. They both belonged to that delicately organized human type, which seems to occur — or, at any rate, to thrive best — in societies where the life of the mind or of the spirit is honoured before that of the body. They both suffered from extreme shyness. In Stanley fits of alarming reserve and inarticulateness alternated with engaging liveliness. The reserve seems to have been particularly marked when he was alone with his quiet, calm, observant, somewhat reticent and dignified mother. The cause of it remained unknown and uncon-quered; it exerted a strange effect upon Stanley's career, preventing him from ever fully justifying his great promise. The thin, compressed, down-drawn lips in the old man's face, as they appear in the frontispiece to Prothero's biography, tell of more than grief and ill-health. They are the lips of a man who has had to jettison part of himself. By comparison Jowett's mouth, in old age, is that of a man who has been able to keep himself intact.

Jowett may have owed this power to his early isolation — an isolation which kept him free from the necessity of coming too soon to a compro-mise with the outer world. Stanley, on the other hand, was obliged to begin that compromise very early, when at the age of nine he was sent to a small preparatory school at Seaforth. He was, or appeared to be, per-fectly happy there; just as he was perfectly happy, after the first begin-nings, later on at Rugby and Balliol. The shyness vanished easily — perhaps a little too easily — when any chance was given him of using his

3. Arthur Penrhyn Stanley
From a painting
by L. C. Dickinson
(*National Portrait Gallery*)

4. Dean Stanley
A photograph, in later life,
by Lock and Whitfield
(*Picture Post Library*)

natural social gifts. By degrees it came to seem that it had been completely conquered.

The conquest, however, was very unlike Jowett's conquest of his shyness. Jowett conceded no ground to the unseen enemy within himself. Stanley made a number of very odd surrenders. His senses lost their acuteness: his ear for music failed, his sight weakened, his powers of taste and smell perished. It may be, as his biographer suggests, that these sensory changes were the result of some latent constitutional defect, which developed after puberty. But this explanation does not cover the singular change in his attitude towards natural scenery. As he grew older he lost all pleasure in 'the beauties of nature', though this pleasure was peculiarly strong in him as an undergraduate.[1] Its place was taken by a morbidly concentrated interest in the historical and literary associations of places and objects. His passion for sight-seeing became fantastically exaggerated. 'The mountains of Greece,' says his biographer, 'the swelling hills of Palestine, thrilled him with inspiration; but the Alps of Switzerland became to him mere "unmeaning masses".' A friend, who accompanied him to Sweden and Norway, remarked that he took infinitely more interest in hunting for the legendary pile or 'stork' that gave its name to Stockholm, than in the most beautiful Norwegian sunset. When, in the year before he died, he revisited the very places described in his journal — the travel-diary in which, as a boy of twelve or thirteen, he had rapturously and exactly recorded with a skill far beyond his years the natural scenery of the Pyrenees — 'he showed no enthusiasm for the Pics and Dents of the mountains; but was distressed beyond measure at being prevented from visiting the scenes of Southey's "Roderic".'

Gifted as Stanley was, his mind had, or made for itself, severer limitations than Jowett's. In spite of the mathematical aptitude that ran in his family, mathematics was an insuperable mystery to him. As an undergraduate he made a deliberate and determined effort to beat this bogey — and failed. 'I have left off mathematics for good' he wrote in 1835; 'I found it quite hopeless.' To the end of his life he remained incapable even of simple arithmetic. This may have been a natural defect; much more probably it was the result of his father's effort to bend his childish mind too soon and too hardly. Resistance to his father's pressure may also have developed that 'kind of hanging-on, dependent manner that calls out tenderness', which his mother noted and which lasted throughout his life. It stood him in such unfailing stead, that he never lacked

[1] He criticized W. G. Ward (quite unjustly) for having 'no taste for the beauties of scenery' and for his 'want of love for physical beauty', and in the same letter confessed his own inability to share Ward's musical interests. (*Life*, i, 169.)

kindness coming to his rescue — at semi-barbarian Rugby, at sophisticated Balliol, at any of the turns of his career. Yet, though it helped him in every trouble that came his way, it was a quality that he had been better without.

It is difficult to sketch such a mind as Stanley's without stressing its weaknesses; for the weaknesses ask to be noticed and over-shadow even his occasional conquests of weakness. An extraordinary example both of his weakness and of his power to defeat it is displayed in the field where he seemed to move with effortless mastery, the field in which, as a youth, he continually gained a sort of pre-ordained distinction — that of classical accomplishment. He went to Rugby, from an insignificant little school in Cheshire, with a reputation already formed. He scored at Rugby all along the line. He won his scholarship at Balliol with phenomenal ease. And yet 'his incapacity to write Latin verse was remarkable'. His aversion from this unavoidable part of his discipline was scarcely less strong than his repugnance for mathematics; it stirred him to repeated outcries and lamentations. Again and again he characterized verse-composition as odious work, as useless and disagreeable, as of all proficiencies the least valuable and the most tedious.

Yet, if Stanley was to crown his academic career, it was absolutely necessary for him to win the University scholarship, founded ten years earlier 'for the promotion of classical learning and taste'; and it was impossible to win the Ireland without displaying a mastery in the esoteric arts of Greek and Latin verse composition. Twice he sat for the examination, and twice he failed. For the third effort he summoned up all his strength and fought down an almost intolerable nausea. 'Words cannot express the delight I shall feel when I wake to-morrow three weeks, with the absolute certainty that I shall never do a Greek or Latin verse again.' To have succeeded after this, as he did, with a performance so brilliant that he was even suspected by the examiners of having had previous access to the first day's papers, seems to be proof of a remarkable mental toughness. But he had overdone himself. His mind, like the body of an over-strained oarsman, had been irreparably injured. He still had it in his power to write his Life of Arnold — a book not now, perhaps, rated so highly as it used to be. But that was his only contribution to English letters, and it was wrung too quickly out of him.

Of Stanley's time at Rugby the tale is too well known to be repeated in detail. How the gentle, appealing, precocious, delicately coloured and dark-haired child, with his high forehead, finely-cut features, sensitive lips, and the inevitable nickname of Nancy, was accepted by the rough school-world of Rugby as if he belonged to a different and higher order of creation; how he rose so rapidly that he was a praepostor when he was only just fourteen, in the sixth form before he was sixteen; how he won every prize that Rugby had to give him, and topped his school career with a Balliol scholarship; how his adoration for Dr. Arnold did not stop short of worship; how Arnold blessed him, twice over, 'in that low-choked voice which you know' at the painful hour of departure; how completely he lacked understanding of the place in which he had spent these five dream-years, so that when *Tom Brown* came out he exclaimed upon it as a revelation opening up 'a world of which though so near me I was utterly ignorant' — all this is to be found in Prothero's admirable biography, along with Stanley's own, often brilliant, letters.

Such was the background of the young scholar whose name is the first to be closely associated with that of Jowett. They were both very ignorant of life; but, while Jowett had seen something of its hard face, Stanley had never seen it do anything but smile — since those very early days, buried deep beneath memory, when the determined Rector of Alderley and his young dignified wife had unknowingly bruised his sensitive mind. Everything since then had combined to protect him from any further wound. He had enjoyed as much success and praise as a boy can; he had travelled abroad, been the intimate boy-friend of a great man, a guest in great cousinly houses; in the spheres of ideal thought, where the lack of factual experience tells only when the thinker has come to full maturity, he was like a young renaissance scholar soaring ahead of his contemporaries and keeping pace, on even pinion, with the somewhat slack beats of his seniors' wings. Greek, Latin, history, theology, poetry — all the books, except those of mathematics and science, seemed to lie open to him. But for the nausea of composing Greek and Latin verses, it was all a little too easy. His superficial range was wide and accomplished. But in whatever direction his mind took wing, it was a direction leading away from the existing human rookery. He built his own version of the rookery in cloud-cuckoo-land, and in it, like a magpie, he stored all the bright and useless facts which he had a passion for collecting.

Like so many other Victorians — almost, but not quite, like Jowett — he found in the rarefied moral code of his age so perfectly devised a protection for his own fastidious repugnances that he never dreamed of questioning it, or of seeking to find rational support for its extremer assumptions. Certainly he never experienced any temptation to transgress it. His biographer says that, as a boy, he shrank 'from the coarseness and vice that stain school-life'. The only questionable part of this statement is the implied suggestion that he knew anything about coarseness and vice. His last sermon in Westminster Abbey, a week before his death, was an exaltation of purity:

purity from all that defiles and stains the soul — filthy thoughts, filthy actions, filthy words — we know what they are without an attempt to describe them . . . of all the obstacles which can intervene between us and an insight into the invisible and the Divine, nothing presents so coarse and thick a veil as the indulgence of the impure passions which lower our nature.

The criticism of Stanley — of all the Stanleys of this world — implied in the use made of this quotation does not necessarily mean that he was wrong in what he said. The mystical perception of God — if that is the true aim of worldly human life — is only to be achieved, as a continuing or frequent state, by mortification of the senses. But Stanley was not a mystic. He did not set out to discipline or to mortify his senses; they merely withered away. The 'purity of heart and life which those who knew him best considered to be the distinguishing quality of his character and career' was not a deliberate conquest of the old Adam. It was a defect, a negative, cutting him off from any comprehension of the animal affirmatives in which human nature is founded. 'Dean Lake used to say' Tuckwell reported 'that Stanley never was a boy; he left school as he entered it, something between girl and man.'

4. AT THE SCHOLARS' TABLE

Jowett's first rooms were 'in what was then called the Grove'. He shared the top floor of his staircase with another freshman, William Vaux, who became a celebrated numismatist and antiquary. Vaux was sociable, and liked entertaining his friends to tea. Among them was Arthur Hobhouse, the future judge and Lord of Appeal, who remembered how Jowett would, occasionally, come across for tea in his neighbour's rooms; and how 'again occasionally, Jowett would make tea for us, or for me alone, in his own territory.'

In this mild manner Jowett had his first lesson in the pleasures of hospitality, which he exercised lavishly in his later life. So poor, however, was he that Hobhouse 'scrupled even to accept his invitations to tea, but his doing so gave B.J. manifest pleasure'.

The two senior scholars were Edward Goulburn — 'a most excellently good man' Stanley called him, afterwards Headmaster of Rugby (where he was a misfit) and Dean of Norwich — and Samuel Waldegrave, afterwards Bishop of Carlisle. They 'made it a point of duty to get hold of the more promising undergraduates so as to prevent their falling into a bad set'. They took immediate possession of young Jowett, for the prayer-meetings and bible-readings they held regularly in their rooms.

At this time theology, and the practice of religion, and the bearing of politics upon the Church and the Universities, were — outside the studies of the schools — the all-absorbing interests of thoughtful young men at Oxford and Cambridge. In those days the countryside swarmed with educated gentlemen in Anglican orders; the great majority of the abler undergraduates were sons of clergymen; the great majority of these were destined themselves for the Church and must — as a matter of course — be ordained if they became fellows of a college.

A little earlier, though prayer-meetings and bible-readings flourished, the excited atmosphere of discussion, with which Oxford and particularly Balliol now hummed, had not come into being. Keble's famous University sermon, the starting point of the tractarian movement, was preached in 1832. The tractarian movement was still in its early stage when Jowett went up in 1836; the 'Newmania' only just beginning. But its dangerous possibilities were already evident to pastoral, evangelical minds. The prayer-meetings and bible-readings took on an additional purpose: that of arming young men, not merely against the world and the flesh and the old familiar devil, but against the newly revived deviltry of 'high' churchmanship.

To the seriously-minded Oxford undergraduate of Jowett's age this ecclesiastical 'civil war' quickly became the paramount issue and remained so for the best part of the next ten years. The end of the Napoleonic wars lay just behind the year of his birth; it had almost exactly the same place in his memory as the end of the first world war had in the memory of an undergraduate coming up to Oxford a century later. But the resemblance between the boy of 1836 and the boy of 1936 stops at this point. Although the earlier war (with its irrelevant companion, the second American war) was followed by economic exhaustion, and although the country was racked from end to end with recurring agitations, the minds of the clever youngsters in 1836, and in the decade or so before and after, were quite innocent of the chaos which afflicted the minds of young men in the corresponding decades of the twentieth century. They found themselves aware of a wholly different chaos — theological, not economic or moral.

Not that these years lacked economic, industrial, social and political disputes, which had no evident relation to theology. On the contrary, they were years of crisis in the English industrial story, marked by violent struggles and by successive trial solutions of tremendous problems, which — temporary as they were — made possible the more or less

orderly development of the growing century. In retrospect this development looks to have been effected by a succession of miracles. Yet all this
mattered little to clerical Oxford and Cambridge. What seemed to matter
most in both the old Universities, and especially in Oxford, was that the
doctrines of the Church of England were being violently debated; that
her hold upon the masses was weakening year by year; and that her
authoritative and privileged position was in jeopardy and nearing overthrow.

A man of Jowett's age in 1836 would scarcely recall the years of distress and confusion which ended in the beginnings of reform. A precocious child, he might have understood his father speaking with horror
of something in the wind called Catholic emancipation. His political
recollections might perhaps have begun with Canning's death and the
Duke of Wellington's premiership in 1827, when he was ten years old.
He might have heard, when he was eleven, that the Duke said (speaking
out of some secret knowledge, which pained and bewildered tory churchmen but left them without any power of resistance) that the Test Acts
had better be repealed, and dissenters be allowed to hold national and
municipal offices. He might remember, with more clearness, the emancipation of Roman Catholics in the following year. Stanley was then thirteen, and (following his father's liberal opinions) a warm supporter of
emancipation. So, of course, was Dr. Arnold who published a pamphlet
'to show that national injustice is a *sin*'. At Oxford Newman and Keble
flung themselves passionately on the other side into the electioneering
battle which followed Peel's resignation of his seat as senior Burgess of
the University, and helped to secure the return of his reactionary
opponent, Sir Robert Inglis, while 'the Oxford dons, the country parsons, and the more old-fashioned squires raged against the King's government and the victor of Waterloo, with the fury of men betrayed'.[1]

As the schoolboy at St. Paul's entered his 'teens the world began to
move faster. He was thirteen when the Liverpool and Manchester Railway was opened and Huskisson killed. Soon after this the huge iron net-
work began spreading rapidly across the country. Hateful as it seemed to
the then backward-looking spirit of Oxford, there must surely have been
some talk of the new mechanical age at the scholars' table in Balliol hall
and in the fellows' common room.

That year, when the English railway system was born, saw the Paris
and Brussels revolutions, which gave impetus to the agitation in England
for political reform. Times were bad, and Cobbett — whom the boy
Jowett had seen at his father's printing office in Bolt Court[2] — was riding

[1] Trevelyan, *British History in the Nineteenth Century*, 221. [2] See above, 73.

the waves. The political unions came into being. That diseased old anachronism, George IV, died. While workmen drilled in the north, and labourers fired ricks in the south, the new Parliament met and Wellington's tory administration gave place to Lord Grey and the whigs.

The one topic of the succeeding two years was electoral 'reform'. There is no need to retell that story. Jowett was passed fifteen when the struggle ended and the Lords capitulated before the threat of a whole-sale creation of peers. Stanley, now a sixth-form boy at Rugby, 'dreamed of the Reform Bill' and got his dream all mixed up with Homer and Latin Verses. 'I think', he wrote home 'that in this Reform Bill there are more for it than against it, so I am much better off than in the Catholic Question, when there were so few on my side.'

In 1833 — Jowett sixteen, Stanley seventeen — slavery was abolished, the first effective Factory Act was passed, and the Irish Church Tem-poralities Act, suppressing ten redundant Irish bishoprics, excited Keble and Newman and their friends to press the Oxford Movement. The spring of the same year saw the publication of Dr. Arnold's optimistic pamphlet on Church Reform, with its hopeful plan of 'reunion all round' — a plan which provoked the leaders of the Oxford Movement to angry ridicule, and stimulated the hero-worshipping Stanley to cry: 'Monstrous that these men should have the amazing inconsistency to attack a man because he is not made after their notion of orthodoxy, or dare to pretend that they care a straw for the Church of God.'

During the next two years, '34 and '35, the whigs crowned their work with the reform of the poor law and the municipal system. But at Oxford these things mattered much less than the topic of 'subscription' to the Articles of the Church of England, then required of all undergraduates. This filled the whole air. In June 1834 the House of Commons passed the second reading of a bill for the admission of dissenters to University degrees. 'The excitement and alarm in Oxford and Cambridge may be conceived.' The bill was thrown out by the Lords; but moved by the advice of the Duke of Wellington, who was Chancellor of the University, the Oxford Heads of Houses proposed to do away with the rule that undergraduates must sign the Articles and to require instead their signa-ture to a general declaration of conformity. A violent war of pamphlets and talk was ended for the time being in May 1835 by the defeat of this mild proposal in Convocation.

The war over subscription was thick about the ears of young Stanley, now a Balliol undergraduate. He was bitterly disappointed at its issue. Reporting the scene in the Sheldonian Theatre, he wrote:

They, the majority, behaved themselves more like schoolboys in rebellion than clergymen employed in defending what they call the last barrier of orthodoxy. There is a song published here of which the burden is *non placet*; the last two lines are beautifully descriptive of the conduct and spirit of the party:

> *This vile Declaration, we'll never embrace it,*
> *We'll die ere we yield—die shouting* Non placet.

When Jowett came up at the end of '36, the echoes of this Oxford battle were still ringing, reinforced by the violent storm over the appointment of the heretical Dr. Hampden as Regius Professor of Divinity. I have told this story at some length in another book, and must confine myself here to saying that it exposed, to fair-minded men, the extremes of misrepresentation, abuse and vindictiveness, to which theological partisanship can go and for which Jowett himself was, later on, to be a target.[1]

In the political world reform was slowing down. However, the year of the Hampden row at Oxford saw the removal of the fourpenny tax on periodicals and the appointment of an Ecclesiastical Commission to inquire into Church revenues — an action (called 'sacrilege' by Pusey) which led to the permanent Ecclesiastical Commission, and to the removal by legislation of many Church abuses. Outside England events were taking place, which were to influence profoundly the careers of some of Jowett's future pupils — the 'Great Trek' of the Boers, the pacification of Canada, the beginnings of organized emigration to Canada, Australia and New Zealand.

The scholars' table at Balliol seems to have found little of interest either in such topics as these or in the new dawn of English letters. It is to be hoped that clever young men at Balliol were not unaware of the *Pickwick Papers*, when the immortal series was running from the April of '36 to the November of '37; and that they were not too much concerned with serious things to relish *Mr. Midshipman Easy*. But the talk at the scholars' table, as reported by Jowett's fellow-scholar, Henry Holden, reflects nothing so lively.

I can well remember his quiet unassuming manner, when the elder and more advanced Scholars led the conversation and sometimes laid down the law for the juniors in Politics or Theology, subjects at that stirring time very warmly discussed in Oxford. This was likely to be the case when such men as Wickens, afterwards Judge, Stanley, Goulburn and Lake, afterwards Deans, Stafford Northcote, afterwards Chancellor of the Exchequer, Arthur Clough the poet,[2] . . . and several other first class B.A. Scholars

---

[1] *Oxford Apostles*, Chap. IX. See also *Life of Dean Stanley*, 154–63. For the sad effect of all this upon Hampden himself see below, 250.

[2] Clough came up the year after Jowett. Perhaps his natural liveliness was quenched by the prevailing solemnity.

were our table companions. We little thought that the retiring unobtrusive young Pauline was about to develop into a Hertford University Scholar in the following spring, and in the year after that, while still an undergraduate, to be elected over the heads of all the senior Balliol Scholars and a score of other first-classmen from other Colleges, to the high distinction of a Balliol fellowship.

Poverty obliged the young Pauline to keep closely to himself and to his books. His future, he knew, must depend entirely upon his own exertions. He was able, now, to rejoin the household in Bath for his vacations; but his dislike of referring in any way to his family circumstances was a barrier to intimacy with other young men. Hobhouse deliberately tried to pump him. 'But beyond the fact that his anchor was for the present cast in Bath, I learned little. He would give a bare answer to a question; and of course I soon abstained from broaching subjects in which he was not communicative.' The habit had been learned long before he came up to Balliol. The school-fellow who was with him when Cobbett opened the door in Bolt Court, after recording the incident some sixty years later, went on to say: 'I rather fancy the domestic relations between the mere and pere [sic] and the family generally were not quite smooth but of that I really know nothing'; and another contemporary gained a strong impression that the relations between father and son were strained.

Among the young Balliol graduates was an observant and charitable Rugbeian named Greenhill, who was studying medicine. Jowett's poverty was evident to the world — his very clothes betrayed it. Equally evident were his devotion to his books and the excellence of his principles. Greenhill put £20 into an envelope and sent it anonymously to the shabby little scholar with a message telling him to use it to pay for extra tuition, so that he could compete with more chance of success for the Hertford Latin Scholarship. 'I gratefully avail myself' wrote Jowett, in a short and dignified letter to his unknown benefactor, 'of your wonderful and unexpected goodness'; and then, in a postscript inspired, no doubt, by some evangelical expressions in Greenhill's covering note: 'May God bless you for your kindness to me. I never thought much about religion till a few days before your letter came, it has left an impression which I trust I shall never forget.'

Nor did he ever forget it. Greenhill revealed his identity, and became Jowett's first correspondent. Their friendship (though it lasted for life) was never really intimate or easy, for Jowett could not continue in the pietistic vein natural to Greenhill, even if his mind had not very soon outgrown that of the older man. He explained this a little awkwardly in a letter written five years later.

One reason, I would just hint, why I don't write to you oftener is that I do not like writing about religion; and it seems so cold and prosy to write to an intimate friend about anything else. I doubt not that there may be many persons to whom religious communion with one another is of great good; for myself, I fear that I have received all the good that I can gain from it. For the future I would rather go on my way alone, and, to avoid self-deceit, trust to God only.

No passage in any of Jowett's letters is more revealing. It was not easy for him to say to Greenhill, that he couldn't bear being messed about. But that was the truth, put with as much delicacy as determination. Only a year after their acquaintance had begun in the way described he had given Greenhill a fairly plain hint that he could not maintain the kind of correspondence expected of him. After apologizing for his failure to write, he went on:

I most sincerely hope that you will not interpret my neglect into un-kindness or ingratitude. You do not like my saying much on the latter head — the obligation to you — which I have never sufficiently felt, and in comparison with which all your other kindness however great is as nothing — I mean your endeavour to keep me in the right way.

But in spite of his refusal to play the part assigned to him, he never allowed himself, as a lesser man might soon have done, to think of Green-hill with anything but gratitude or to escape from friendship with Green-hill and Greenhill's widow; nor, in the innumerable acts of similar generosity which he himself afterwards performed, did he ever seek to establish any unfair hold over the minds of those whom he befriended.

Jowett won the Hertford in 1837, but was disappointed of the Ireland in the following year. The disappointment was but slightly mitigated by carrying off a college prize (£10 worth of books) for English composi-tion. There is, it must be allowed, no evidence of any coldness towards a brilliant son in the fragments of his father's letters which survive from this period; though there is a curiously self-satisfied and patronizing tone in them. Early in 1838 Mr. Jowett wrote from London to his niece Mrs. Irwin in Australia:

Benjamin continues to give us more and more satisfaction. . . . Of his future destiny, if spared, I cannot form an idea. Except on the deepest reflection, I never should wish, as I have often said, any child of mine to think of the Ministry . . . I would wish never to bias.

Some rather pompous amplification of this point followed. The letter continued:

Benjamin has been trying for the Powell prize at Balliol, for English composition. I wondered very much at his venturing, as it was quite out of his line, at least so I should have concluded. . . . Of course we were glad to find his English had been respectable enough to carry him through.

It appears from the same letter that Jowett pretended to his father that he had no expectation of gaining the Ireland. In fact he was deeply chagrined at his failure. His sister Agnes had died in the early spring, and it is possible that the emotional disturbance of this death, probably the first he had known, may have spoiled his chances. The disappointment had a financial side. The Hertford Scholarship was only for one year; it was absolutely necessary that he should make some addition to his income.

The first part of the Long Vacation in 1838 was spent at Bath in 'close employment in reading, and teaching my two brothers', as he told Greenhill in excuse for his silence. 'My elder brother pleases me much better in every way,' he added: 'his mind seems to have undergone a gradual change, quite losing the proud and sceptical spirit which he once showed. The younger one gives me great delight. He had an excellent character from school last quarter.' There was enough in Jowett's pocket for a modest holiday — it must have been the first he ever took. He went at the end of August to Ilfracombe — 'a terrible passage by the steamer, which, although the distance is but 80 miles, lasted two days' — and spent a week or two tramping along the coast. When he went back to Balliol in October, it was without the least foreknowledge of the change in his fortunes which was upon him.

There were four vacant fellowships to be filled after examination in November. Theoretically, the undergraduate scholars of Balliol were eligible — a very unusual privilege. Tradition said that only one undergraduate scholar had ever profited by it, the Old Master himself. Jowett was advised by Scott to sit for the examination. He did so, and was elected to the fourth vacancy. It was lucky for him that Stanley, a few months earlier, had been elected a fellow of University College, having been warned that his unorthodox religious opinions would stand in his way at Balliol. The worthy electors little knew that, in admitting Jowett, they were admitting a far more powerfully unorthodox mind to the college than Stanley's could ever be.

Jowett sat for the examination with great reluctance, and when the result came out he was nowhere to be found. A friend, going out of Balliol, 'ran full tilt against him' in the gateway, and had considerable difficulty in persuading him that he was not being hoaxed. When at last he realized that he had indeed been elected, his excitement broke down his reserve. He jumped into the air 'as high as he could'; was caught and carried round the quadrangle shoulder high by his friends, before he calmed down sufficiently to present himself before the body of the fellows waiting for him in the chapel.

Next morning he wrote to his father: 'You will be amazed and delighted to hear that I have been elected a Fellow of Balliol. . . . Pray write to me by return of post, as your joy at my success is half the joy of having succeeded.' Whatever constraint there had been in the relationship between father and son was forgotten in this thrilling moment. 'A long epistle of Mr. Jowett's to Mrs. Irwin in Australia' confided to her 'what was probably hidden from those more nearly concerned, his exultant pride and delight in the success of his son, and the ambitious dreams which it awakened in him; but also his fear of spiritual dangers which this might involve to Benjamin.'[1]

[1] *L. & L.*, i, 62.

CHAPTER VII

'Remember Now thy Creator'

1. 'ANOTHER WORK OF EDUCATION'

The heart of young men, one would have thought, should leap within them at the feeling that the future is still theirs, that whatever they do day by day is not a toilsome service to receive its penny a day, but shall bring forth fruit abundantly, turning their life from a waste into a fairly cultivated field on which the sun shines and the rains descend, and it brings forth an hundred fold, for it was sown in due season.

This is part of the opening passage of Jowett's earliest printed sermon, dated 'about 1850'.[1] His text was the verse with which the Preacher opens his wonderful poem of old age: *Remember now thy Creator in the days of thy youth, while the evil days come not, nor the years draw nigh, when thou shalt say, I have no pleasure in them.* The lesson was one that he had learned very fully for himself; his way of imparting it to others seems, therefore, worth attention.

He begins by defining the great, the tragic, difference between youth and age — how youth can form the character of age, but does not realize its opportunity, how age knows only too clearly what youth should have done but 'can no longer do it equally'. The saving adverb 'equally' is a word to notice. The door is not closed until the very end of life.

From this beginning he moves to a topic which always fascinated him. What is the future going to be? What will it be for his hearers, for himself, and for the society to which he and they belong? 'If anyone here is living half a century hence it will be in a changed world.' But he does not profess to foresee 'how the course of the great world itself, with its struggles for empire, and prejudices and passions,' will have changed in that or any longer period. The future will take its own unpredictable course. The thought he wishes to impress upon his hearers is that, in relation to the vast process of history, 'each one here present is as nothing and insignificant, I may say, except in the sight of God only.'

The qualification was much more than a clerical *façon de parler.* In a

---

[1] *College Sermons*, 1. Actually this was not a college sermon, but a short address given to his pupils. The tutors used to address their own pupils on the morning before a Communion Sunday.

notebook belonging to a later period of his life (1867), he wrote apropos of Mill on Liberty: 'I should like to write an essay on an opposite principle, which should show that there was no state of society in which an individual might not have sufficient intellectual freedom.' That was a different, a secular and cooler way of expressing the same belief in the supramundane value of human personality.

Speaking now, in his early thirties, he anticipates the change that would come over the minds of his young listeners, as it had already begun to show itself in his own mind. Why is it especially in the days of youth that we are warned to remember our Creator?

Because [he answers] then we have the power to do it; our knowledge of God afterwards is ever tending to be of a different kind — a knowledge without love — in which our reason seems to go beyond our feelings, which does not interweave itself in our nature, and is certainly not, to the same degree, capable of moulding us to His will. Which of us in after-life by taking thought can add one cubit to his stature? One would scarcely venture to say so much as this of our moral growth, and yet it is true also here that we cannot invert the natural order of things. There is a time to serve God as a little child, and a time to serve Him with the understanding also.

Still young when he uttered these words, though the grey was beginning to fleck his 'wavy locks', Jowett had behind him ten or twelve years spent in strenuous self-husbandry and in sharing the fruits of his own 'fairly-cultivated field' with an increasingly large number of friends and disciples. At the beginning of this period he is a shy, poor, obscure solitary; his mind, for all its natural independence, shaped by a severely narrow curriculum. At the end of it he is still shy, and still — by ordinary standards — poor. But he is no longer either obscure or solitary. The circle that was to widen continually outwards from its Balliol centre through the whole range of the national life is already formed and obeying his influence. His mind, released from scholastic tutelage, has set out to explore the world of ideas for itself. The more it has learned of the minds of others, the more it has become itself, using all that it has learned but making its own original judgments.

Nor has this incessant industry interfered with his humanity. If he sometimes feels 'my own want of freshness: my mind seems at times quite dried up partly, I think, from being strained out of proportion to the physical powers,' he is never barren towards his pupils. And if he occasionally wearies of the pursuit of knowledge, and acknowledges 'an unsatisfied desire after a better and higher sort of life, which makes me impatient of the details of theology', this desire, too, never overlaid by his eager concern with the everyday world, was evidence of that homesickness for the city of God without which man is less than man.

His speculativeness did not dim, seemed rather to intensify, his interest in the practical business of life. As the period of which I am about to write drew to an end, his philosophical studies, which had always been amateur rather than professional, relaxed; the philosopher came into the market-place and the gymnasium. He had never been imprisoned in his high lonely tower; he loved and resorted to it, but he did not live in it, though he had a disconcerting habit of going back there in the middle of a conversation. This was an 'idiosyncrasy', he confessed to Stanley 'which makes me at times very unwilling to be among strangers . . . somehow or other I get thinking about matters speculative or otherwise, and, when not perfectly well, they get such a hold that I cannot relax, and one becomes a sort of ἰδιώτης, wrapped in selfish care and out of tune with ordinary life.' To be in tune with the life of the world in which he lived was a primary duty, fulfilled with pleasure.

Lewis Campbell, with his acute biographical instinct, applies to Jowett a passage which Jowett himself wrote into his commentary on the Epistles of St. Paul: 'As he grows older he mixes more and more with others; first with one or two who have great influence in the direction of his mind. At length the world opens upon him; another work of education begins; and he learns to discern more truly the meaning of things and his relation to men in general.'[1]

This other work of education is a work of self-education; at least it is a process in which the mind is not propelled by an externally organized discipline but moves by its own power. The initial choice of direction may have been already determined. If a man's academical training carries — as in Jowett's youth it carried — the necessity of becoming a priest in order to enter its second, intellectually more difficult and more rewarding stage, the priesthood must be the mode of travel, unless the traveller is a rebel. Jowett was no rebel. He mounted the clerical coach as a matter of course, not for motives of self-advancement or with any reserves of conscience. Sitting on the top of it he looked about him. Tracts of country, remote from the turnpike road, could not be visited unless he got down and explored them for himself.

2. THE APPROACH TO RELIGION

Becoming a fellow did not mean that Jowett ceased to be an undergraduate. He still had to sit for Greats and take his degree. The year which passed between his election to a fellowship and his first class in

[1] *Epistles of St. Paul*, 3rd edition, ii, 57.

the Michaelmas term of 1839 was a busy one. Besides his own reading, he was coaching his two younger brothers in the summer before his examination, and had already begun to take private pupils at Oxford.

The man who enjoyed the singular honour of being Jowett's first unofficial pupil was T. H. Farrer, civil servant and economist, who became permanent secretary to the Board of Trade and was raised to the peerage in the year of his old tutor's death. It was a career of the kind which Jowett again and again had more than a hand in making, not by the pulling of strings but by the teasing of latent into actual power. Farrer, who belonged to a 'healthy but not intellectual' set of Eton and Harrow men, was only two years younger than Jowett and at first saw nothing in his coach except the physical peculiarities and the oddity of dress, which made him so noticeable and hid, rather than revealed, 'promise of the power which he afterwards became'. Yet Farrer began soon to be aware of a dynamic mental influence growing in Balliol and somehow associated with the white-stockinged cherub tripping about the quadrangle.

Very long afterwards, in an after-dinner speech, Jowett said of him: 'And then comes my old friend Farrer, of whom I may perhaps say, that something more might have come of him if he had not been my first pupil.' Farrer thought that kind, but untrue. For Jowett had done the one essential thing: he had 'opened a vista which you were to follow up yourself. He had the Socratic art of saying to youthful eagerness, "Are you sure you are right?" but of saying it in such a manner as to develop zeal in the pursuit of truth.'

A man cannot say this sort of thing effectively to others unless he has been saying it to himself. Jowett's critical intelligence had begun to stir. Scott, lecturing on Niebuhr, 'first aroused in my mind doubts about the gospels', and Tait was the originator of his 'desire to read German theology'. So he recorded in one of his notebooks, in 1876. Too much could be made of this early movement towards a critical re-examination of religious beliefs. It was under the powerful brake of tradition and habit; and his cautious north-country temperament would throw nothing away if there was a good reason for keeping it. But the movement had begun and must continue. Escott, one of his contemporaries,[1] remembered breakfasting in young Jowett's rooms and rashly assenting to 'some disparaging remarks upon "Creeds" '. Upon which 'he jumped up and stretching out his hand over the table said "I must shake hands with

---

[1] The Rev. H. Sweet-Escott, who matriculated in the same year as Jowett and became headmaster of Bath. He died in 1910.

you on that". Yet', Escott added honestly, being an orthodox person, 'I believe his idea and mine were far from being the same.'

That was a crude and youthful revelation of the scepticism which made orthodox believers fear and distrust him as a pretender, an infidel in holy orders. Escott ascribed it to his evangelical upbringing. 'He had been used to hear arguments brought forward to establish facts or doctrines, which he thought clearly insufficient and unfair — in short, false. This caused a great revulsion in a truth-loving mind, and gave an impetus to that destructive tendency — which not only men like myself, but such as Tait (with his liberality and affection for Jowett) felt to be extreme.' But, for all that, Escott was convinced 'that he had more devout, loving and reverent feeling toward the Lord Jesus Christ, as a remainder of the lessons and faith of childhood, than his own teaching could produce, or, *as a fact, did produce*, in others.'

There is some truth in Escott's apologetic analysis. But 'destructive tendency' is a stupid phrase, though a phrase often used by men cleverer than Escott. Jowett's mind was essentially constructive. His scepticism was the scepticism of a builder who tests his materials and, if he is obliged to use a rotten stone, uses it where its disintegration will cause the least possible damage, though he would rather be free to discard it altogether. 'The attempt to show the true character of the Pentateuch and the Gospel History' he wrote later in his life 'is very important negatively; but it does nothing towards reconstructing the religious life of the people. These men had not found a substitute for that which they displaced; they will never get hold of the heart of the world. Human life cannot be reconstructed out of negative results.' And again: 'Believe,' he once said, 'believe as much as you can, the more you believe the better.'[1]

There are no notebooks or memoranda surviving from this time of beginnings. But Escott's story about the creeds shows clearly enough how Jowett's mind was moving. That Christianity was fundamentally 'true' he never doubted, though his conception of what that truth might be underwent continual change. The creeds — the human formulations of truth — the dogmas of the churches: these were another matter. All ambitious systems — whether philosophical or theological — were, he came to think, always erroneous when they pretended to be absolute. In this respect his mind and Stanley's had something in common — but no more than partly in common. Jowett's mind was not, like Stanley's, of the sort to trip up over small points. The main question was always the

[1] I owe these very significant quotations to Professor MacEwen's unpublished paper, referred to in my list of authorities. (*J.P.*) See below, 137, footnote.

important question. His objection to a formal creed was not so much that it was difficult for him to subscribe to it himself as that it put needless obstacles in the way of others.

As he grew older he would, I think, have sometimes preferred not to be a clergyman. In his 1867 notebook there is an entertaining discussion on the theme 'Why really great men are never Clergymen'; which begins by saying that 'Swift, who is the only exception, may certainly be said to prove the rule', and contradicts this a little later with the remark that 'the greatest intelligence who since the Reformation has become a Clergyman is Bossuet'. The best chance, he thinks, 'for a great man in a high Ecclesiastical station would be to drop all dogmatic theology — and to fill his mind with great schemes for the regeneration of mankind which he used the Church as the instrument of effecting'. Great men, he suspects, 'don't like to submit to the gêne of a received creed'.

The same notebook contains a shrewd and lively dissertation on 'Cunning'. The age, he says, is too innocent of cunning; an accomplishment requiring more character and self-control than people nowadays possess. 'Whether' he queries 'a union of great cunning and entire disinterestedness is not possible?' He adds: 'The want of courage and force of character makes me deficient in cunning.'[1] From another (undated) notebook, there may be added this curious prayer, following a note on the difficulty of excluding passion from any great effort of the intellect: 'O Lord make me to know what true greatness is and how far I fall short of it and do away in me with every thought of self.'

To those three revealing passages may be joined a fourth, taken again from the 1867 notebook: 'Is it better to work through or against existing institutions?' So runs the heading, and beneath it are these words: 'Every man who assails the opinions of others must have some $\pi o\hat{v}$ $\sigma\tau\hat{\omega}$ [standing point]: either the intensity of his own ideas and his power of communicating them; or some private influence with ministers; or some hold over existing institutions. — He is liable to be charged with dishonesty if he gains influence by holding a position which involves the recognition of certain opinions.'

When Jowett wrote that, he had himself been unjustly made to suffer under such a charge, and he knew well that, before a literally-minded jury, he could make no more successful defence than Socrates before the Areopagus. He never drew his defence out; it was implicit in his writings and his conversation, and is hinted in such occasional jottings as those which have just been quoted. In essence it could be contained in a plea

---

[1] The last word is written 'courage', but this is an obvious slip of the quick pencil.

that he was a man of his time and must make the best of his time. That is how he might most truthfully have put it in his old age. In his earlier period, when his mind was first feeling its way about the complex pattern of human thought and action, he would have put it rather differently. He would have said: I am a member of a Church, and must make the best of my Church.

A Presbyterian (MacEwen),[1] who went up to Balliol in 1870, describes how he soon came

like many Nonconformists to be impressed by the splendid strength and classical decorum of the Church of England, frequented Chapel zealously, and began to inquire if an unconfirmed person could be admitted to Communion. Jowett sent for me one day, and after staring into the fire for an unusually long time, turned his blinking eyes full upon me and said: 'A man is most likely to be useful in the Church in which he has been brought up. Good morning.'

This interpretation of Jowett's mind is supported from the very early notebook dated 1841, the third year of his fellowship and the year before his ordination.[2] Some account of its contents is given in the *Life and Letters*, but Campbell does not give the particular note to which I refer: 'On the respect due to our Mother Church.' It is too long to be repeated in full; what follows is an extract.

It may fairly be doubted whether the regulations of your own church (i.e. as such and except on matters of order and ceremonial) ought to influence your opinions when you have come to years of discretion. . . . If a person does not believe his church to be in error, he will of course receive her teaching; if he does, he will not; in the mean state of mind he will give considerable weight to her authority — more than to other churches (just as to one's mother more than other mothers), but this will not make him immovable. He will consider that his own church is most likely to adapt itself to his wants — that it teaches him a lesson which God must have intended him to learn, that there is a great obligation to remain where he is — but that all this only throws the burden of proof on the other side, and is not to make him inaccessible to arguments on the subject. The strongest point that can be urged in favour of the extreme view is that *almost under any circumstances it is our duty to remain in the Church* — hence we should be very loath to get out of humour with it. . . . In speaking against or departing from our own church, of course *the first thing is to have truth on our side — 2nd to have a direct practical object. If we have these it would surely seem something of the nature of a pious fraud to hold our tongue*.

[1] Alexander Robertson MacEwen was a Snell exhibitioner. He took Jowett's advice and became a minister in his father's Presbyterian church. He was deputy professor of Greek and assistant professor of Latin at Glasgow, and professor of Church History at Edinburgh. He died in 1916.
[2] The series of annual notebooks does not start until 1873, the earlier (and the more interesting) notebooks are disconnected, mostly undated; the notes may occur in a lecture-book, or be mixed up with notes for sermons; and numbers of notebooks seem to have been accidentally or intentionally destroyed. The later notebooks are all of a very small (uniform) size, and the notes are usually laconic. But see below, Chapter XIX.

This passage has to be read in the context of 1841. What Jowett had in the front of his mind, when he wrote it, was the growing attractiveness of Rome to many Oxonians of his generation. For this was the year of Tract 90, and the shocking event of 1845 (Newman's secession from the Anglican to the Roman communion) was casting its long shadow before in Oxford common rooms. But the argument goes far beyond its occasion. The words italicized state a position equally resistant to scepticism and to ultramontanism. I do not believe that Jowett was ever drawn into the tractarian vortex, though in after-life he probably exaggerated the degree of his indifference. Campbell asserts that for a short time he felt the universal spell, and quotes his confession, ten or twelve years later:

I had resolved to read through the Fathers, and if I found Puseyism there I was to become a Puseyite. It is not unlikely that I might have found it, but before I had gone through my task the vacation [Easter, 1844] ended, and on returning to Oxford we found that Ward was to be married! After that the Tractarian impulse subsided, and while some of us took to German Philosophy, others turned to lobsters and champagne.

The confession was not meant to be taken very seriously.

Still, the Newmania was all about him and had to be reckoned with, while he was finding his feet in the slippery theological field. Equally, scepticism of varying kind and degree was already domiciled in Balliol. In the note of 1841 Jowett was defining a *via media* of his own; he was laying down for himself a very important principle — a principle fully consistent with his subsequent career — a principle of loyalty as opposed to a principle of rebellion, so long as loyalty does not mean a lie in the soul. The qualification requires scrupulous use of a very difficult tool. Jowett would certainly not have allowed it to anybody below the level of a clear first class in Greats. He did not allow it to MacEwen. But MacEwen took a second class.

The years before and after 1840 saw the rise and decline of the Oxford Movement. In the preceding chapter I have suggested that the atmosphere of the Balliol common room was growing warm in the early 'thirties. When Jowett entered it the warmth had acquired a very peculiar geniality from the irresistible bonhomie of William George Ward.[1] Hotly though the dispute continued, the disputants had surprisingly remained 'a very united body'.[2] The dispute raged endlessly between the handsome, curly-headed, practically-minded young Scot — 'Belve-

[1] For the information of readers who have not interested themselves in the history of the Oxford Movement, it should be explained that Ward, often called 'Ideal' Ward from the title of his once notorious book *The Ideal of a Christian Church*, seceded to Rome a month or so before Newman, in 1845.

[2] Jowett's phrase, from his account of the fellows reproduced in *W. G. Ward and the Oxford Movement*, 114.

dere' Tait, Anglican Primate-to-be — and the fat, invincible, inextin-
guishable, mathematical lecturer Ward. It gave the common room 'a life
and animation it would not otherwise have had' said James Lonsdale,
one of the four new fellows of Jowett's year, who relished the nightly
contest so amusingly described by Wilfrid Ward in his *Life* of his
father. Tait retreating to the door, bent on having the last word and
slamming it behind him before Ward had time to answer. Tait, thinking
in the vestry of a good retort and coming back in his surplice to deliver
it at Ward, who 'turns it inside out in a moment, and adds, amid the
roars of laughter which follow his reply: "If you hadn't anything better
than that to say it was hardly worth while coming all the way back in
your surplice." ' Ward, plunging into an argument with such violence
that the chair on which he is leaning collapses beneath his weight like
matchwood. Ward, again, with a number of high churchmen present,
declaring that the only thing to be done with Charles I was to cut his
head off.

That Ward influenced Jowett goes without saying. But the influence
was temporary and external. In the long and admirable account of Ward
which the Master of Balliol wrote for his son's use[1] Jowett says that he is
diffident in describing Ward's more serious qualities 'because, being an
outsider, I may not have understood all his motives and feelings, though
he was very willing to impart them'. These last eight words bring Ward
vividly back. But Jowett, though he acknowledges his intellectual obligations to Ward, does not explain what they were.

Campbell suggests that it was to Ward more than to any other man
that he 'owed his first initiation into metaphysical inquiry'. If so, it was
anything but a formal initiation. When Jowett first saw him, Ward was
a disciple of Bentham and Mill; but that was before Jowett became a
fellow. In the course of 1838 Ward definitely joined the Newmanites;
and from that time onwards all the powers of an intellect, which its owner
modestly regarded as 'in some respects almost infinite',[2] were directed
not to any metaphysical end as such, but to the exaltation of Roman and
the confusion of Protestant theology. Of this exciting performance Jowett,
as a young fellow, was a close spectator, often from behind the scenes.

He once took me, on a Sunday evening, in the middle of summer, about
the year 1839, when his change of opinions was still recent, to Mr.
Newman's church at Littlemore, where he was to preach. We drove out
after dinner and walked home. . . . The sermon which he preached was a
printed one of Dr. Arnold's [Ward's idol only a year or two earlier] but
with additions and alterations which, as he said, it would have driven the
author mad to hear. . . . We walked back to Oxford in the twilight, along

---

[1] *W.G.W. the O. and M.*, 447.   [2] *op. cit.*, 36.

the Iffley Road. He was in high spirits, and sang to me songs out of 'Don Giovanni' and other operas.[1]

Experiences of that sort were excellent medicine for Jowett's serious young mind. They put him in the way of understanding that life should not be lived at one pitch or in one key, and taught him to be listener as well as preacher. Did they do much more than that? Did he, at intervals, punctuate Ward's dialectical flights with the prick of common sense? Or was he stirred by them into his first exploration of metaphysics?

It was, I think, rather from his own contemporaries — apart from the lectures of Tait and Scott — that the impulse came, if indeed it came from outside rather than from inside his own mind. From Shairp, for example, another of the Balliol Scots, who had sampled Kant at Glasgow and lent Jowett his copy of the *Metaphysic of Ethic*. After which Jowett 'went stamping about the quadrangle, as if to assure himself that the solid earth was beneath his feet', much as Dr. Johnson supposed himself to refute Bishop Berkeley.

Another contemporary, who helped to widen his horizon, was Benjamin Brodie, afterwards Professor of Chemistry at Oxford. Young Brodie was an avowed non-believer; it may have been against his negatives that Jowett first began to forge his own small but powerful stock of religious positives. Brodie had an engaging personality. He set a great value upon 'chivalry in male friendships' — a phrase which meant that young men did well to be in love with each other. Stanley, in 1836, called him 'a very clever and very good little man indeed; I am sure you would like him; I wish I knew more of him than I do.' He figures as the earliest of Jowett's regular correspondents (except for Greenhill) — earlier even than Stanley himself. The first of Jowett's surviving letters to Brodie is dated 1844, and evidences a close friendship of some years' standing. Towards the end of it he writes:

One word, my dear Brodie, about the matter which really interests us both far more than anything else in the world. I do not want for the future ever to avoid this, so that I hope you will always speak and write quite unreservedly, if you think there is any use in it. I think, certainly, that great good may come of it to both of us. What appears to me to make the greatest gulph between us is not your taking a rationalistic or mythic view of the Bible, or difficulties about miracles, or even prayer, but that you do not leave any place for religion at all, so that although you may hold the being of God as the Author of the Universe, I do not see how you would be worse off morally if Atheism were proved to demonstration. What would you lose but a little poetry which is a very weak motive to holiness of Life? And having shut yourself out from any moral relation to God as an incentive to Duty does this moral Atheism satisfy human nature?

[1] *W.G.W. and the O.M.*, 446.

Not all, or even much, of Jowett's correspondence with Brodie was in this serious vein. There are many flashes of admirable humour. The best of these is a delicious reference to Ward (in 1845), whose marriage had so ridiculously upset his friends. ' "Hildebrand" the married man is here — the Lady is a very nice person. "Entire cycles of Roman doctrines" may soon be expected.'[1] And even in the more serious passages there is a pleasant use of irony. 'I cannot help often thinking about you, and sometimes — it is at least a harmless superstition — remembering you in prayer.'

The accent in these letters shows the young Jowett capable of the best kind of intimacy with somebody who did not share his own wish to experience a direct relationship with God. He is far more comfortable in writing to Brodie than in writing to his evangelical benefactor Greenhill; and more interesting, at this time, than in his letters to Stanley, whose point of view was so near his own. There is no *arrière pensée;* he knows where he is, and where his correspondent is; they understand if they do not agree with each other.

Unhappily, the two friends were unable to sustain this attitude. Jowett's letters to Brodie between September 1845 and April 1848 are not preserved, but the gap is closed by two short letters of the later year. One, undated, is quoted in the *Life and Letters.*

I hope it will not seem to be from any unkindness that I have not seen so much of you as formerly. It grieves me to think how very much we disagree in opinion, but I trust we have still the 'common ground of conscientiousness' of which you once spoke to me. . . . The strongest feeling that I have is that no merely artistic religion or morality has any real truth or usefulness, or can have any hold on the minds of men in general. Do let me urge you to be as serious as you possibly can in considering these things, which, if not aweful realities, are still very aweful when we think of our absolute ignorance about them.

The second letter (not given in the *Life and Letters*) is dated April 18 from Paris and seems to refer to the first. It is signed 'your's very sincerely' instead of the 'your's affectionately' or 'your affectionate friend' which he had formerly used to Brodie and was now beginning to use to Stanley.

You are mistaken if you suppose that my last letter was intended to call for any *profession de foi* from you. Certainly the answer must be given in

---

[1] It is sad to have to explain so good a joke. Ward's engagement, announced immediately after Convocation had deprived him of his degrees, in consequence of his book *The Ideal of a Christian Church*, was generally thought to have stultified his position as a supporter of celibacy in the clergy. A famous passage in that book boasted that 'the whole cycle of Roman doctrine' was gradually possessing numbers of English clergymen.

something else than words or feelings, and there is hardly time to make it before we are off the scene. I should be sorry to cause offence and therefore will only add that you have taken the latter part of my note more personally than it was meant. It is impossible or at least useless to discuss opinions without taking into account their moral tendencies, and if this appears unseemly far better not to discuss them at all.

The Brodie episode has seemed worth relating, because it shows so very clearly the governing factor in Jowett's religious life — his sense of a moral imperative, of an ideal pattern by which every man must seek to make his own character. This ideal pattern, he believed, had been exemplified in the life of Christ; and the one great function, and justification, of an organized Christian Church was to persuade mankind to honour and, in what measure it could, to imitate that pattern. The obligation was absolute. There was no reward except in its fulfilment.

Such was the simple instinctive belief which limited Jowett's first speculations and affected the conscious management of his whole life. If long afterwards it underwent some transformation, that was not through any weakening of his moral sense but through his late discovery of regions where the moral code he had himself helped to forge seemed to be an instrument of self-righteousness rather than of righteousness. 'The truth' runs a jotting in the 1867 notebook 'shall make you free. The intense pleasure and innocence of freedom of thought. The first quality in speculation is to be afraid of nothing' — not even of a clash, he might have added, between free speculation and the moral conventions of society.

Lionel Tollemache, a pupil of Jowett's in the late 'fifties, in his published study of the Master, found it difficult to determine the nature of his attitude towards sin. Comparing Jowett with his singular contemporary Mark Pattison, Tollemache summed up as follows:

As a philosopher, Jowett did not believe in the heinousness of sin; but as a moralist, he did believe in it. Pattison, as a philosopher, did not believe in it; as a moralist, he pretended to believe in it. . . . The philosopher and the moralist in him [Pattison] were in a manner harnessed together by logic; so that he could not, as Jowett could, let his two selves go careering about in opposite directions.

A random note of Jowett's — 'Consciousness of sin = sin' — lends some appearance of colour to Tollemache's facile paradox. There was a real conflict between Jowett's mature mind and his moral sense; but his personality was never split into two contradictory selves. His moral sense remained unshaken, though he came to apprehend something of its limitations. It was an inheritance from which the philosopher could not escape, even if he wished; but which he could learn to regard, in some of its more rigid manifestations, as a social necessity or a private convenience rather than as a divine command.

If this is an unsatisfactory position, it is — for the philosopher who is also a man of affairs and duties — an unavoidable one. No man can accomplish anything without an inner moral drive of some definite kind; he must feel, not merely think, some paramount good. What was Jowett's paramount good? I do not know that he ever asked or answered that question; and I am sure that he would have hedged in replying to it. He would have followed Plato and identified it with 'truth'. If the argument could have been pursued long enough, and Socrates brought to bay, he might have followed the line of thought suggested in the concluding paragraphs of the Introduction to his translation of the Republic. There, after discussing the two ideals 'which never appeared above the horizon in Greek Philosophy' — the future of the human race in this world, and the future of the individual in another[1] — to both of which he allows almost equal power, though he abstains from considering why the future should be supposed to have a value not belonging to the present or the past — he passes to 'a third ideal', embodied in the divine person of Christ, which he struggles to reconcile with

that image which Plato saw dimly in the distance, which, when existing among men, he called, in the language of Homer, 'the likeness of God', the likeness of a nature which in all ages men have felt to be greater and better than themselves, and which, in endless forms, whether derived from Scripture or nature, from the witness of history or from the human heart, regarded as a person or not as a person, with or without parts or passions, existing in space or not in space, is and will always continue to be to mankind the Idea of Good.

If, mustering sufficient courage and being present in his study as he put down his pen with a sigh of satisfaction at this completion of a great task and a beautifully long sentence, one could have said to him: 'Master, just exactly what does that mean?' what would, or could, he have answered? Would he have admitted, to himself if not to his questioner, that in this high-sounding passage he had lost sight of the 'difference between words and things' and was, like Matthew Arnold in his 'something not ourselves which makes for righteousness', having recourse to what Francis Bradley roundly called 'literary claptrap'? Or might he have said that even philosophy must have its rhetoric and that rhetoric cannot have an exact meaning; that the Idea of Good is beyond man's comprehension and can only be spoken of in quasi-rhetorical terms; that the intensity of the moral conflict, which is the most certain fact of

[1] But this is odd; for the life of the soul, after death of the body, is one of Plato's favourite themes.

awakened human experience, is both unbearable and unintelligible if it is only a sham fight rigged by social opinion; and that, however unable we may be to define the ideal good and however differently it may be conceived by different ages and races and individuals, we cannot fail to recognize it in the persons of the great moral and religious leaders of mankind?

In the end, as in the beginning, the languages of philosophy and rhetoric fail along with the language of theology. The felt reality of the moral conflict remains the basis of Jowett's religion. He says this very plainly in a passage which Tollemache quotes from the Introduction to the *Phaedo*: 'We are more certain of our ideas of truth and right than we are of the existence of God, and are led on in the order of thought from one to the other.' And in one of his college sermons, preached in 1888, he speaks of 'the simplicity' of religion. 'The real difficulty', he says, is not in understanding the words of eternal life, or in finding out what they are, or in satisfying ourselves that they are true, 'but we transfer to the reason what is really the infirmity of the will. All men to some extent, under some name or other, know the laws of God and nature, but they do not make them the laws of their own life.'

If Jowett failed to solve the great riddle of moral philosophy, his failure was more valuable than the solutions of system-mongers. A grain of truth won by experience is worth more than a sackful of theory. The final residue was small, but it was pure gold — gold procured by endless washings. He learned to draw a distinction between what might be called 'tabu' morality and true morality, and to understand that the Idea of Good was not necessarily embodied in the rules of Victorian society.

Privately he went a great deal further in this direction than it would have been possible for him to avow publicly. The 1867 notebook contains four pages of bold speculation upon 'Control of the Passions'. These reflections start with the text *It shall be called the way of holiness — the unclean shall not pass over it.*[1]

Look at it in the most human way that you will the whole Scripture contains a conscious effort to raise men above their passions. The world has disregarded purity of life — the Church has disregarded truth, but in Scripture will be found the voice of purity, the voice of truth. A man is not a man who does not control his passions. (But there are great difficulties about this: marriage is deferred generally for 15 or 20 years after the passions are strongest and is sometimes impossible altogether without loss of rank. Then there is the concealment which takes place about vice. We speak as though this was the exception and yet with the Upper and Middle classes at least it is the rule. And we speak as if there was one rule and one guilt for all. Whereas the degrees of temptation may be absolutely different.)

[1] Isaiah xxxv, 8.

He continued, on a fresh page:

Note the subtle admixture of good and evil in the passions. Energy has a great deal to do with strong passions. Ideals of good have a certain connexion with love and lust. There seems also to be a natural feeling of remorse about sins of impurity.... Two things in this matter greatly exaggerated: (1) The ruin of women; this exaggeration originates in the desire which Society rightly has to create a public opinion against immorality. But then Society creates this ruin, for in the case of women who pass undetected (Mrs. S., Lady ——) there appears to be no such ruin. (2) The notion of Sin after Baptism. This is wholly untrue to human nature and is a horrible fiction of priests who want to introduce the terrors of another world into this in order that they may govern the Earth.

He turned the page again.

Error of supposing that a man is wholly bad because his [the word *religious* is scored through] morals are bad. A man may be a drunkard and yet gentle and good and refined; or he may be licentious and yet full of energy and patriotism and character and high principles. The world is rightly cautious of admitting this: because it wants to bring a sort of terrorism to bear upon licentiousness.

The fourth page opens up a still bolder line of thought.

It has been imagined by Sceptics that all the more intense forms of religion are really bastard or illegitimate results of the relations of sexes. Whether this is true or not, it is plain that there is a close connexion between them and an easy transition from one to the other. Hence an important question. The right use or the right regulation of the passions in religion. How to kill the sense or lust and leave the ideal or aspiration? How to direct the warmth and enthusiasm of human nature — the heart to the eternal and invisible? (ἔρως of Plato in the Symposium.) Nobody can know human nature who has not reflected much and long on the effects and illusions and false forms of the passions in himself and others. They are a central point in human nature, which are often supposed to be non-existent because they are unseen and concealed. Curious effect of the passions on the temper in very moral natures.

These glimpses of Jowett's mature, private mind may seem to have taken us a very long way from the young fellow of Balliol who was ordained fifteen years earlier. But the distance travelled is not so great as it looks, at first sight, to have been. Freely as his mind ranged, in search of explanations and reasons, it was tethered to the peg of morality. Belief in a personal God was implanted in him when he was a child. He held fast to it all his life; but in his manhood it seemed to be the consequence, rather than the cause, of his attachment to the idea of good. He became a priest because that was, in his state of life, an office he was naturally destined to fill; because he believed in the social necessity of religious institutions, in the moral content of Christianity, in the logical necessity of a divine sanction for ideals which were inexplicable by mere humanism. To this belief he was constant, and his constancy justified him in remaining a priest, in spite of the fact that the various dogmatisms of the divided Christian churches came to seem man-made stuff, and often man-made nonsense. Though he could bring himself to suspect that tabu and priestcraft had gone to shape the moral code, he not only obeyed the code, accepted and preached it, but used it as the corner-stone of faith.

No Leslie Stephen could have outdone the sarcasms which he allowed himself to make privately upon the Church and its rulers, and upon the current language of belief. He went so far as to describe the term 'God' as 'the greatest equivoque or ambiguous word that exists'; 'the worship of the Bible' as 'a slavery of the mind and therefore worse than any falling down before outward images'; and 'the notion of God in Plato' as 'far higher than in the Old Testament'.[1] But these expressions of intellectual freedom never, in his own mind, invalidated his clerical status.

There was a profound difference between Jowett's approach to religion and that of Newman, who owed — or so he believed — his religious certainties to an emotional *volte face* at the age of fifteen. There was a similar difference between Jowett's approach and that of a man much nearer in character and in mind to himself than Newman, Archbishop Tait, who at the age of ten or twelve suddenly woke up in the midde of the night in a strange house 'with a deep impression on my mind of the reality and nearness of the world unseen, such as, through God's mercy, has never since left me'. Tait's record of this experience, which had stayed in his mind 'with the vividness of having heard a voice from above', was made when he was sixty-eight years old. It was found in his desk after his death, 'written upon a sheet of foolscap, and folded by itself'.[2]

No mystical encouragement of this kind was vouchsafed to Jowett.

3. THE CLERICAL FRONT

The first year of Jowett's life, as a graduate, is almost a blank in his biography. It must have been spent in private study and coaching and in writing the Latin Essay which won the Chancellor's prize early in 1841.

---

[1] These references are all to the 1867 notebook, of which so much use has been made. As for the references to the Church and its rulers, only space forbids me to extract them. But he thinks the 'tyranny' of the Bible preferable to that of the priesthood. It is pertinent to add that, when Tait became Archbishop, Jowett lamented that the last chance had gone of his (Tait's) 'speaking out'. And see below, 214 (letter to Stanley).

[2] *Life of Tait*, i, 37.

Stanley, with whom he had already become intimate, was finding his feet on the alien *terrain* of University College, and giving his whole energy to the 'subscription' scandal.

'Subscription' meant, at this date, subscription to the Articles and Liturgy of the Church of England as required by law of a clergyman at his ordination. Five years earlier it had been a battle-cry in Oxford with a rather different meaning: subscription to the Articles, required by statute of undergraduates before matriculation.

Stanley found it difficult to stomach, in particular, the damnatory clauses of the Athanasian creed. In the course of the examination, to which the candidate for ordination must submit, he was determined to lug his views somehow into one of his answers. Since this was not the kind of question which Dr. Bagot, the Bishop of Oxford, whose well-bred but embarrassed feet Newman longed to kiss,[1] was at all anxious to grapple with — he had had enough trouble with the tractarians to make him feel that earthquakes might start anywhere at any moment — Stanley had some difficulty in achieving his purpose. He laid hold of the only question which gave him any opportunity: 'What are the tenets of the Church on the sufficiency of Scripture?'

The connection was not obvious. But Stanley was equal to a slender occasion. Article VIII would do the trick: 'The three creeds . . . ought thoroughly to be received and believed: for they may be proved by most certain warrants of holy Scripture.' Did this, asked Stanley in his answer, refer 'to the *doctrines* only of the Athanasian Creed or also to the *censures?*' He went on to interpolate a prepared argument to the effect that the obvious meaning of the damnatory clauses was thoroughly objectionable, as the *obiter dicta* of many Anglican divines had agreed; and that the only tolerable interpretation, if the clauses had to be retained, 'would be to understand them as affirming that, though every error concerning the nature of God or man *may* be in itself harmless, yet, if *fully carried out into all its logical and moral consequences*, it will end in the subversion of the Christian faith in him who holds it.'[2]

Stanley drew the special attention of Archdeacon Clarke to his answer, and at a subsequent interview with the Archdeacon, amusingly reported by the candidate to his sister, he was allowed to remain in possession of his 'rather *forced* interpretation' (the Archdeacon's phrase). It certainly

---

[1] See *Oxford Apostles*, 366 (Pelican edition).
[2] *Life of Dean Stanley*, i, 233. The 'damnatory clauses' are: 'Whosoever will be saved; before all things it is necessary that he hold the Catholick Faith. Which Faith except everyone do keep whole and undefiled: without doubt he shall perish everlastingly. . . . And they that have done good shall go into life everlasting: and they that have done evil into everlasting fire. This is the Catholick Faith: which except a man believe faithfully, he cannot be saved.'

was a forced interpretation, and even so it left the 'everlasting fire' burning as vigorously as ever. Nobody was more conscious of the quibble than Stanley himself; to nobody could the falsity of the position, in which he was obliged to stand, be more hateful. Nor was his discomfort eased by the evident fact that the ecclesiastical authorities thought his scruples absurd. However, he swallowed them manfully; and schooled himself to take the commonsense view which he expressed, some twenty years or more later, to a former pupil troubled as he had been.

Your difficulty about the 'damnatory clauses' is, as you must be aware, not new. . . . There are some softening explanations that can be given of them. . . . But the only satisfactory mode of reconciling our minds to these clauses seems to me this: First, the main question for a clergyman to ask himself is, whether he is willing to receive the Prayer Book as a whole. If he is, then any objection to particular portions ought not to weigh with him. . . . But, secondly, you may rest perfectly assured that your view of the clauses is shared by the vast majority of English clergymen. . . . There is, probably, no bishop who would object to receiving you for Ordination because of your scruples on this point.[1]

Meanwhile he joined himself to the agitation, which reached the House of Lords, for a reform of the terms of subscription; and for months his mind was wholly filled with this painful matter. What could be more detestable than to be obliged, for the sake of the general good, to repeat publicly, with whatever private reservations, what he considered to be a presumptuous and frightful lie? Jowett, certainly, must have been one of the friends to whom he spoke about this — he could speak and think about nothing else. The agitation failed; though Stanley's father, now Bishop of Norwich, 'insisted on the heavy burden that was imposed by the existing terms of subscription on tender and scrupulous consciences.' Dr. Blomfield, Bishop of London, made furious mincemeat of such heretical nonsense. And the petitioners, headed by Whately the Archbishop of Dublin, committed the always fatal error of asking for too much. They wanted the Prayer Book itself to be 'rendered consistent with the practice of the clergy and the acknowledged meaning of the Church'. Stanley, child of innocence though he was, knew that this was going too far; he did not even want the Prayer Book, as such, to be altered. The Lords temporal would no more hear of any change in that Book than the House of Commons nearly a hundred years later.

This all ended in May 1840. Stanley, overstrained by the fearful exertions of his prize-laden Oxford career and the subsequent agonies over ordination and subscription, left England for a long ten months of travelling in Germany and Italy and Greece. But he was not done with

[1] *Life and Letters of Dean Stanley*, ii, 16.

'subscription'. In the early spring of 1841 he learned at Rome that things dreadful and exciting had happened at Oxford: Tract 90, and the Letter of the Four Tutors.

In that famous Tract Newman had anonymously published an argument to the effect that the Articles of the Church of England did not mean what Protestants thought them to mean 'and may be subscribed by those who aim at being Catholic in heart and doctrine'. In the equally famous 'Letter of the Four Tutors' Tait, the senior tutor of Balliol, with three other tutors of other colleges had riposted with a public letter to the editor of the *Tracts for the Times* protesting that this would let into University lecture-rooms and into the pulpits of churches 'the most plainly erroneous doctrines and practices of the Church of Rome', and demanding that the name of the author of the Tract (known by everybody to be Newman himself) should be published. A week later the Heads of Houses pronounced against Newman's tract as 'evading the sense of the Thirty-nine Articles' and as inconsistent with the University statutes.

Stanley wrote about all this to Tait, with a mixture of humour and anxiety:

O, my dear Belvedere, what have you been doing? Rome is only in a less state of excitement than Oxford. The Pope has just issued a Bull defending the Decrees of Trent, on the ground that they are not contradictory to the Thirty-nine Articles; and the Cardinals have just sate in conclave on him, and determined that he is against the usages of the Vatican.[1]. . . Seriously, my dear Greis [one of Tait's nicknames], do not draw these articles too tight, or they will strangle more parties than one. . . . One consolation dawns upon me, and that is, that this convulsion will, directly or indirectly, lead to the subversion of the heads and establishment of Professors on their ruins; in what way I have not now time to explain, but I see it clearly in the distance.

'My dear Child,' Tait began his long answer of self-justification — confident that even Stanley, so prone to see good in every man and right on the wrong side of every question, when he read Tract 90 must perceive it to be a most dishonest document — 'Er sieht Mein Kind sehr viel zu Jesuitisch aus, und wie er sieht, so schreibt er.'[2] Dropping into colloquial German was now a fashionable affectation among the cleverer young Balliol dons; their predecessors had had no German to drop into. It was a good way of warning Stanley, without writing at serious English length, that there was more in Tract 90 than had met his eye. 'At the same time,' Tait continued 'this I must say in justice, that I believe this

[1] Rather an obscure jest. Presumably 'the Pope' is Newman, and the 'Cardinals' are the Heads of Houses.
[2] 'He looks, my child, very much too Jesuitical; and as he looks, so he writes.'

appearance of Jesuitry comes, not from dishonesty, but from a natural defect, a strange bent of the genius that loves tortuous paths, perhaps partly because it requires an exercise of ingenuity to get along in them.'[1]

Stanley was not convinced. 'I have read No. 90 and almost all its consequences' he told Hugh Pearson[2] — his and Jowett's contemporary at Balliol and a life-long friend of both — immediately after his return to England. 'The result clearly is, that Roman Catholics may become members of the Church and Universities of England, which I for one cannot deplore.'

This was at the end of May. Stanley was back at Oxford a week or so later. The scene was an amazing one — the battle was fairly (unless the better word is unfairly) joined between the catholic besiegers and the protestant defenders of the Anglican keep, while men like Stanley and Jowett, who wanted the Church to be, if not all things to all men, as much as possible to as many as possible, looked on sadly at the ferocities inseparable even from academic religious warfare. In Balliol, still Stanley's natural home, the scene was yet more amazing. There, side by side in the midst of all the rising bitterness, were Tait, the first protestant spokesman in the war of words; Ward, 'infinitely' more intelligent, the most extreme and audacious of Newman's disciples; the eccentric Old Master torn between his affection for Ward and his horror of Ward's opinions; earnest young evangelicals, like Goulburn and Waldegrave; all these, and others, involved deeply in the war of opinion which then possessed Oxford as no subsequent controversy has ever possessed it, and yet neither abstaining from argument nor divided from friendship by it.

Few episodes in the history of any small society have been so creditable to the men who composed it. The issues which divided the Balliol common room in 1841 may seem unreal to many modern readers. To the men of that time and place they were at least as real and important as any ideological or political issue of the middle twentieth-century. Indeed they were more 'real'. The careers and livelihoods of some of the disputants were immediately involved. There is no martyrdom in modern Oxford for the holder of any opinions. In the Oxford of the eighteen forties voluntary martyrdom was almost a commonplace. A little later, after the romanists had been expelled, the weight of odium was transferred to the new party of broad churchmen — Jowett's party.

First of the deliberate martyrs was Ward. Stanley was agonized for the outcome.

---

[1] *Life of Tait*, i, 95.
[2] Afterwards Canon of Windsor. Jowett preached his funeral sermon in 1882.

Every hour convinces me how great a calamity Ward's is; not so much in itself or as affecting him, but in its remote and probable consequences, striking far and deep at the foundations of the welfare of the University. There is no blame attaching to anyone, except such as attaches to an error of judgment. Tait was the great mover against Ward, and they are still on perfectly good terms with each other.[1]

As for Ward, he had thrown his whole career into the pot without hesitation. He had written two pamphlets in defence of Newman's notorious Tract. His tutorial colleagues, Tait and Woollcombe, had withdrawn 'the invitation they had given him' (for he was a mere lecturer, not a tutor) 'to co-operate with their official care of the undergraduates'. Ward himself had taken the bull by the horns and of his own will resigned his mathematical and logical lectureships into the Master's hands. 'I must,' he said to Dr. Jenkyns 'if your views on these questions are the true ones, be a most dangerous man.' 'Really, Ward,' replied the Old Master in tones of great relief 'this is just like your generosity.'[2] Stanley, in the letter to Pearson quoted above, went on to say:

the Master shed tears in the final interview . . . it is said that he is overheard grumbling to himself, 'I wish Mrs. Jenkyns would take care of the flowers instead of the cabbages'. . . and then in the next breath, 'I wish Mr. Ward would not write such pamphlets'. . . . He [Ward] loses 250 *l* a year by it.

Humanly a comforting episode. To aid the imagination of it, here are two pictures of which the moral need be no further pointed. A note from Ward reaches Stanley as he is re-introducing himself after his continental Odyssey to the University College common room. Stanley rushes into his room and throws himself into Ward's awaiting arms.

Fast and furious conversation advanced, till it was interrupted by the door flying open and a long procession entering — consisting of Tait, Lake, Woollcombe, Waldegrave, Goulburn — which, after I had pressed 'with salutations meet And reverent love to kiss their honour'd feet', passed away, leaving me again alone with Ward, with whom I have a long walk and tea — then a long dialogue with Tait, — lastly with our dear Donkin — and so to bed.

Fifteen years later Tait, become Bishop of London, was in bitter controversy with Temple, his successor as headmaster of Rugby, who had been his pupil at Balliol in those keen-tempered days, over the part taken by Temple and Jowett in *Essays and Reviews*. 'Remember' Tait wrote 'that in Balliol in old times there was many a painful difficulty of the same kind with Oakeley and Ward. It was understood between us

---

[1] *Life of Stanley*, i, 297.   [2] *W.G.W. and the O.M.*, 166.

that private friendship should not be interfered with by the necessity for public acts.'[1]

The other picture belongs to a date rather later than that of Stanley's return to Oxford in 1841. It is the morning of 28th October 1844, the feast of St. Simon and St. Jude; the fellows and undergraduates are assembled in Balliol chapel. Ward is in the last state of disgrace with the Master, who has forbidden him to act as deputy-chaplain. The notorious *Ideal of a Christian Church* has been out for four months, and has shocked Dr. Jenkyns beyond the bounds of decorum. This morning it is Ward's turn of duty, with the Master, at the Communion table; and, at the proper moment, he advances to the proper place and begins to read the epistle. Instantly Dr. Jenkyns darts to the other side of the table and, just as Ward is beginning, commences in his loudest tones: 'The epistle is taken from the first chapter of St. Jude.'

Mr. Ward made no further attempt to continue, and the Master, now thoroughly roused, read *at him* across the Communion table. The words of the Epistle were singularly appropriate to the situation, and the Master, with ominous pauses and looks at the irreverent Puseyite, who had sown sedition in the Church and blasphemed the Heads of Houses, read as follows slowly and emphatically: 'For there are certain men crept in unawares' (pause and look at Mr. Ward), 'who were before of old ordained unto this condemnation' (pause and look), 'ungodly men' (pause and look); — and a little later still more slowly and bitterly he read, 'they speak evil of dignitaries!'[2]

To return to 1841. It was, for Jowett, a year of quiet preparation, in the midst of these excitements and not untouched by them, for his own ordination and for duties coming more quickly upon him than he knew. The first of his surviving private notebooks, neatly filled in pencil, begins with a long entry, dated 20th May, on the burning topic of subscription.

'Are we justified' he asks 'in signing in an ambiguous sense formulas whose ambiguity was designed by their framers? Especially if the intention of the framers is, to say the least, doubtful and there has been no authoritative declaration of their limits? Are there any consequences which can justify us in doing evil that good may come?' For, he notes, 'subscription is a question of honesty and irrespective of religious belief.' He is not quite sure about the ambiguous intention of the framers, which 'seems to have been at any rate a new discovery'. But he is sure that 'the articles are in fact a deception and all who sign them are parties to the

[1] Oakeley, the gentle-mannered but resolute ally of Ward, had left Balliol for the Margaret Chapel in Margaret Street, London, in 1838; he went over to Rome in October 1845. See below, 256 *foll*, for Tait's agony in the year of this correspondence with Temple.
[2] *W.G.W. and the O.M.*, 326.

deception' and a cause of 'scandal to weak consciences'. To 'take them in their obvious sense', as the Bishop of London (Blomfield) thinks he takes them, is impossible, for they 'are at variance with the Baptismal service, the Communion, the Catechism, and Ordination service, at least in their obvious tone'. The only practical hope is 'to get them altered by the same authority which imposed them'.

It is to be noted that the question which had troubled Stanley — to sign or not to sign — does not appear to have troubled Jowett at all. Whatever dishonesty might be thought to be implied by signature is so general and inescapable that it gives him no personal concern. This is fundamental in him. To some it may seem evidence of weakness; to others evidence of strength — a strength which kept itself for a real occasion, and refused to be dispersed in useless friction with an imperfect, but not alterable, environment.

Religious topics, however, fill only a part of the notebook. Page after page is filled with speculations about Political Economy — an unusual study, at that time, for a young classical scholar. Observations upon the ballot — not introduced until 1872 — upon agriculture, upon the way to write an essay, are interspersed with notes upon Aristotle's Ethics, and lists of questions for scholarship and other examinations. A part of the book is occupied with careful records of sights seen and habits observed upon a trip to the continent which he made in the long Vacation.

This continental tour was the first of several, though he never became so assiduous a traveller as Stanley and never got to Rome, let alone Athens. With a friend referred to as J.P.[1] he made his way through Belgium and by the Moselle and the Rhine towards Heidelberg, where he intended to buy some books. Of Heidelberg itself he says nothing; it is possible that the tourists turned back at Mayence. The notes are uninteresting; they contain no adventures and no personalities and are devoted mainly to the architecture of the cathedrals and churches, which he thought generally inferior to those of England, and to descriptions of pictures. He admired Vandyck and Wouverain, was unattracted by Rubens. At Antwerp and Malines he 'saw no one either a drunkard or a bad character'; and at Ghent he was much impressed by the prison, where the 1500 prisoners were allowed to talk when not at work, wore no chains or fetters, pursued their own occupations, were well fed, had religious books in their cells, and earned money in prison, while the prison itself was a source of substantial revenue to the Government.

[1] Presumably J. Pennefather, a young barrister who matriculated at Balliol two years before Jowett. He took silk, but died prematurely in 1855.

And here is a note, which shows how little he had in common with the 'wild nature' school of romantics. 'Great part of the beauty of the Rhine and Mosel as of the English lakes produced by culture. On the steeper crags the vines are planted in layers the rocks having been blown up on purpose — covered with slate to radiate heat.' Of the Rhine itself he notes: 'moving mass of waters, with their rapid current, give [*sic*] an idea of irresistible power.'

Coming back to Oxford after this first visit abroad, he found himself fitting more closely into the life of Balliol and the University. Use was being made by his college of the twenty-four years old recruit to its staff of fellows: the Master might be old, but Balliol liked its dons to be young. Jowett had a hand already in the teaching of the undergraduates. Outside the college he belonged to a club called the Decade. Stanley was a member of this. So were Matthew Arnold and other Balliol men. It was not a Balliol preserve. George Butler, of Trinity and Exeter, in a letter of this same year 1841, describes his delight at being invited by Jowett to join 'such an excellent set, consisting of the picked men of the University', and his liking for Jowett himself, who didn't 'show off to advantage in a roomful of men' but was 'a very agreeable companion'.[1]

There was some physical and mental trouble working itself out in the agreeable companion. It is not unusual for young men to experience lassitude and disillusion in their early and middle twenties. On his twenty-fifth birthday (April 1842) Jowett looked back upon the immediate past and saw that it was 'evil'. He used the word deliberately, in answer to Greenhill's felicitations.

Considering how evil the last two years of my life have been, it is unpleasant to be reminded how old one has grown. In about a week I am going to bury myself in Paris — it is rather a relief to me to get away from people, and I shall build up dreams of steady reading and devotion. . . . I hope the study of the Gk Testament and regularity in diet may bring me into a better state of mind and body. Change of scene does not seem to be of much use, but I mean to go to Paris to be quiet and get away from all agitating subjects.

Serenity is bought at a price. Jowett kept his own counsel to the very end about the price he paid. That a price had to be paid was evident from the fits of depression which afflicted him at intervals, though they never affected his work. 'He was often very depressed' said Miss Nightingale, speaking of his second half of life. It may be guessed that now, in his middle twenties, he was paying for years of overwork and overstrain; for the right to separate himself from his family; for the use

[1] Quoted by Campbell (*L. & L.*, i, 81) from Josephine Butler's *Recollections of George Butler.*

of his mind at the expense of his body; and for the effort of squaring faith with reason.

Whatever silent struggle may have vexed him during the two years between 1840 and 1842, it ended in the decision formally manifested when he was ordained deacon in 1842. The decision itself was not formal or empty, though there is no record whatever of his feelings when the dedicatory vows were made. His letters to Brodie, already quoted, show how Brodie's disbelief helped to point the sincerity of his own belief. The inner choice made, he cheerfully accepted the duties of his clerical office, performing them with a meticulous honesty which might amuse men of light weight. Two years after his ordination he was staying with the Brodies. A medical student a little older than himself, whom he had not met before, was in the house recovering from a serious illness. Fifty years later Sir Henry Acland, Jowett's physician, recalled how

one night when Jowett heard I was sleepless, he came quietly into my room, sat by the bedside, and said in that small voice once heard never to be forgotten 'You are very unwell. I will read to you'; and he read in the same voice the 14th chapter of St. John and said 'I hope you will feel better', and went away. I often, often have thought [of] this during Oxford Controversies.

CHAPTER VIII

The Tutorship

1. THE OCCASION

The year was 1842. Stanley was settling reluctantly into his duties at University college and learning the names and faces of twelve apathetic pupils. Dr. Arnold, newly appointed Regius Professor of Modern History, had been unfolding 'with characteristic delight the treasures of his favourite study' to Oxford audiences of unprecedented size. Newman was at Littlemore with his disciples, essaying a home-made monastic discipline. The tractarian movement, as such, had entered on its dying phase. Sir Robert Peel had brought in his first budget. The lean years were ending, the era of Victorian prosperity was about to begin. As if to mark a pause and upward turn in the affairs of men the English summer was one of unusual beauty; and Dr. Arnold, on the afternoon before his sudden death on June 12, enjoying his ordinary bathe and walk, 'stopped again and again to look up into the unclouded blue'.

There was a corresponding pause in the routine of Jowett's life. For once, he was spending the summer term away from Oxford. In May he was in Paris, reading in 'the library'. In June he was in Bonn with a pupil, hobnobbing with the professors after Tait's example. It was at Bonn that he heard the news of Arnold's death from Tait, little knowing what it meant for him and Balliol. For Tait was senior tutor; and only ten days after Arnold's death he was a candidate for the headmastership of Rugby: an office which Stanley, with his truthful 'consciousness of treacherous deficiencies' had refused to seek for himself in spite of the pressure immediately put upon him to do so.

Tait was persuaded to send in his name — not that much persuasion was needed — by Stanley and Stanley's young friend and recent pupil, William Lake, also an old Rugbeian. To both of these it was rather as if they were nominating a successor to the Almighty. But somebody had got to be the next headmaster of Rugby. 'O my dear Tait,' wrote the sharp-nosed Lake, ever the candid friend, 'I do not envy you if you do get it. . . . However, I really believe you are far the best. My main fears are for your sermons being dull, and your Latin prose, and composition generally, weak.' Tait was appointed to the vacancy on July 28. When he opened Stanley's ensuing letter he did not find in it the congratulations which successful candidates usually receive from their chief supporters. 'My dear Tait, the awful intelligence of your election has just reached me.... I conjure you ... to lay aside every thought for the present except that of repairing your deficiencies.' Fortunately, Tait's sense of humour was subordinate to his sense of responsibility. 'Without incessant prayer' he confided to his diary 'I am lost, and, if I perish, how many souls perish with me.'

Tait's departure meant that a new tutor must be appointed at Balliol. Almost simultaneously a second vacancy was caused by the resignation of the youngest tutor, James Lonsdale, because of ill-health. Lonsdale — son of a famous Bishop of Lichfield — was only a year older than Jowett. They were elected to their fellowships in the same year. Lonsdale was an Etonian, and therefore had a special mark to his credit in the Old Master's mind. He was one of those brilliant young men who never quite fill out their promise. Tuckwell describes him as 'great in estimation rather than in production as a scholar, the tales of his wit and genius ephemeral and for the most part lost'.[1] But Jowett thought him to have been an excellent teacher; and he, for his part, thought so highly of Jowett that, only a few months before he resigned his tutorship, he wrote to his mother: 'You laugh at my pope Jowett, but really I know of nobody so clever.' Lonsdale survived the threat to his health. He lived to the same age as Jowett, dying in 1892. For fifteen years he held the professorship of classical literature at King's College, London.

Whether it was into Lonsdale's shoes that his 'pope Jowett' formally stepped, or into those of Tait, is a question of no consequence. If there had been only one vacancy, William Lake was marked out for it. Not only was he Tait's favourite pupil, but as a Rugbeian he belonged to one of the three public schools favoured by the Old Master. He, too, was a young man, only three months older than Jowett. His career took him later to a prebendary stall at Wells and then to the deanery of Durham. If Tuckwell is to be believed, he was not very highly esteemed by his Balliol juniors. His 'manner was cold, sarcastic, sneering and a certain slyness earned him the nickname of "Serpent".' He was nicknamed 'Puddle'. The 'u' was sometimes replaced by 'i'.

The double defection of Tait and Lonsdale presented the Old Master

---

[1] He quotes Lonsdale's felicitous refusal of an invitation to preach at Eton:

Cur imparem me cingis honoribus
Me, triste lignum, me vetulum, pigro
Sermone, fundentemque tardo
Ore soporiferum papaver?

with a really serious problem. The other remaining tutor was Edward Woollcombe. Woollcombe was a year older than Lake. The son of a Plymouth doctor, a Repton and Oriel man, he was elected to a Balliol fellowship in the *annus mirabilis* of 1838 along with Lonsdale and Lake and Jowett. He was appointed tutor in 1840 and continued so to 1869. For once, it would seem, the old Master's nose had been at fault. Writing to Morier in January 1870 Jowett, by then the power behind the throne, said that he had 'the College better in hand than formerly, having got rid of Woollcombe and, I believe, of Wall'.[1] Woollcombe remained a fellow until 1879, when he was presented to the Balliol living of Tendring. He died in 1880. His name occurs once or twice in the *Life of Archbishop Tait*, as that of a lifelong friend; but he was not the wearer of Tait's mantle, and left little mark upon men's minds.

A sagacious judge of men, the Old Master must have been aware that neither in Woollcombe nor in Lake, despite their academic abilities, their orthodox evangelical opinions and their provenance from more or less respectable public schools (though Repton was not, in his mind, on a par with Rugby or Eton) had he found real tutorial timber.

Moreover, the small body of Balliol tutors had just lost an outstanding auxiliary in W. G. Ward. Ward was not officially a 'tutor'. He was the mathematical 'lecturer'; but he had been invited by Tait 'to accept an equal share of responsibility' with the three formally appointed tutors. In 1841 this invitation was withdrawn, in consequence of his heretical views; and Ward was deprived of his office as mathematical lecturer, though he remained a fellow of Balliol for the next four years and on the best of personal terms with his protestant friends and enemies.

Ward's expulsion from his lectureship and from his quasi-tutorial office was inevitable. But it was the first step to the expulsion of a vital genius from a small society which might easily have been killed — and was severely shaken — by the expulsion. Ward was torrential, cataclysmic, and (almost incidentally) a brilliant mathematical teacher. It was lucky for Balliol that one of its obnoxious Tiverton men unexpectedly filled the sudden gap, and filled it effectively. This was Frederick Temple, who followed Ward as mathematical lecturer at Balliol, followed Tait as headmaster of Rugby, and followed him finally (after Archbishop Longley) in the see of Canterbury. 'Black-haired, smooth-cheeked and ruddy' Temple took his 'double first' in the Easter term of 1842. He

[1] The letter is given in *L. & L.*, i, 440, but the last ten words of this passage are discreetly omitted. I owe my knowledge of them to Dr. R. Hunt. Woollcombe is not even mentioned in Jowett's detailed description of the Balliol common room, as it was in and after 1838, which is to be found in *W. G. Ward and the Oxford Movement* (114-16).

joined the Balliol teaching staff immediately, turning the young trium-
virate into an even younger quadrumvirate.

The appointment of the tutors lay solely with the Old Master. He
is said to have hesitated over the appointment of Jowett and to have
made it with reluctance. There was much to make him hesitate. St.
Paul's was not in his restricted category of gentlemen's schools. And
there was a distinct whiff of unorthodoxy about Jowett's cherubic self-
possession. Not that Dr. Jenkyns could suspect him of romanist leanings.
Was there, however, not a tendency towards rationalism?

Moreover, something was beginning to go wrong with Balliol. Davis
describes the situation thus:

For some years after 1841 the best minds of the College seemed to be
smitten with a kind of paralysis. They had lost their convictions and had
found nothing with which to replace them. . . . With such a disease of the
intellect Jenkyns was quite unable to deal. . . . There was need of a
younger man who had himself felt the crisis, and who had won his own
battle before he was called upon to arm others for it. Such a man the
College found in Jowett . . . and, in spite of his youth, he became almost
immediately the mainstay of the tutorial body.

It does not appear that Dr. Jenkyns, when he appointed Jowett to be
a tutor, at all appreciated the position in this way. It appears, rather,
that he did not trust Jowett and would have preferred to appoint somebody else, if he could have found somebody else to appoint. But Jowett
had an undeniably strong claim. He had been assisting the official tutors
for two years. He was the next man on the roster. He was favoured by
Lake. He was clever and industrious. He was steady. The Old Master
made up his mind to take a risk, and to back the next horse out of the old
stable.

Dr. Jenkyns left no private account of his actions behind him. But
his peculiar character remained on the record — much more convincing,
as an explanation of the way things happened, than Davis's too easy *ex
post facto* generalization sixty years later. It is obvious that Jowett's
appointment as a tutor was due to an accident, which forced Jenkyns to
take a risk he had not wished to take. It cannot possibly be ascribed to a
special awareness, either in Balliol or in the Old Master's unfathomed
mind, of the need to appoint a tutor who had displayed a peculiar power
of resistance to roman attractions.

Campbell says that the hesitation of Dr. Jenkyns to make Jowett a
tutor was due to his youth. But this explanation will not do, any better
than Davis's. If Jowett was only twenty-five, so was Lake. Woollcombe
and Tait were only twenty-four when they were appointed tutors; Lonsdale had been even younger. Jowett must by now have discarded his 'low

shoes and white stockings'. He must have begun to dress himself more suitably, if not yet in the 'black dress coat of fine broad cloth', which was his habitual uniform by 1850, with 'a faultless shirt-front and white neckerchief loosely tied about the upright collar'. But his appearance was still excessively youthful. And Dr. Jenkyns knew very well that appearances mattered. He knew, also, that Balliol needed the very best she could get, if she was to keep her place. It was already slipping. One of her brightest hopes, Arthur Hugh Clough, had missed his first in 1841. Matthew Arnold was to repeat that failure in 1844. With the gentle Oakeley and the robust Ward and 'good old Tait' all gone, was it wise to reinforce Woollcombe and Lake with somebody who, however clever he might be, looked more like a downy schoolboy than a graduate?

Some such thoughts as these must have disturbed the mind of the Old Master. He had the sense and courage to dismiss them.

2. START AND HANDICAP

The undergraduate population in the care of the three tutors and the mathematical lecturer — Woollcombe, Lake, Jowett and Temple — numbered, in 1842, about forty,[1] including some half-dozen scholars and the same number of Snell exhibitioners. The three tutors parcelled out the undergraduates between them for Latin and Greek composition, and lectured, to all or any, each on his more or less special subject or subjects.

During the first two or three years of his tutorship Jowett's lectures made no specially remembered mark. It was not until he began to lecture upon the early Greek philosophers, breaking quite new ground for himself and for Oxford, that his pupils began to be aware of his originality. This happened round about 1845. According to Edwin Palmer[2] these early lectures 'did not close without a mention of Socrates and Plato'. In their maturer form they began with Plato, to whom the first half of the course was mainly devoted, after which the lecturer reverted to Plato's predecessors, from Thales to Socrates. Among the surviving Jowettiana are two notebooks containing a careful draft of these later lectures written out by Mr. T. W. Jackson of Balliol and Worcester, about the year 1860, amplified by a number of pencil notes in Jowett's own hand-

---

[1] It is now (1956) well over three hundred. The number of fellows has increased from twelve to over thirty.
[2] Fellow of Balliol. Archdeacon of Oxford and Canon of Christ Church. Seven years younger than Jowett. Died 1895.

writing. Throughout his life he was continually altering and improving his presentation of this theme.

It is odd, and a pity, that he never worked these lectures up into a book.[1] But as time grew shorter nothing but the best seemed good enough. And so far as his understanding of them went, these pre-Socratic philosophers were inspired dabblers, excited amateurs; the kind of matter to stir the dawning intelligences of young men, the kind of matter which — for some accidental and unknown cause — had helped to quicken his own intellectual curiosity and led him towards his *magnum opus*, the translation and interpretation of Plato.

In the other, the more immediately important part of his work — the direct and personal tuition of individual pupils — he set both to himself and to his pupils, and from the very beginning, a hard standard. The standard he set for himself was never relaxed. When his ascendancy over his fellow-tutors was established — and in half-a-dozen years it was beyond question — his door was open at any hour to any undergraduate who wished to see him, whether properly his own pupil or not. It was not open for purposes of random conversation. But many a young scholar or commoner, in the late hours of the night, made good the deficiencies of his own appointed tutor by taking a copy of Greek or Latin prose or verse to Jowett and receiving an hour of extra-tutorial criticism.[2]

Yet he soon acquired one of the rarest qualities of a good teacher, that of perceiving the limit of a pupil's physical and mental endurance. 'I owe to him' wrote George Brodrick, afterwards Warden of Merton, who went up to Balliol in 1849 and was nominally assigned to another tutor,

what I consider the most valuable piece of practical advice which I ever received — to limit my reading to 5 hours a day, including lectures, but always to read with concentrated attention. He was aware that I had already injured my health by overstudy. . . . I followed this hazardous prescription for some five years with great benefit to myself.[3]

From the start, however, Jowett's relations with his pupils were not of an easy kind. Here is Edwin Palmer, one of his earlier pupils, again in the witness box:

[1] It was still in his mind in 1887: see below, 409. It is too late for it to be done now by anybody else. Modern knowledge of the early Greek philosophers has put Jowett's views out of date; and he was not equipped to estimate their importance in the history of science, as distinct from metaphysics.

[2] One would suppose that this practice of Jowett's must have greatly annoyed his fellow-tutors. If it did so, their annoyance has gone with the wind.

[3] It was certainly hazardous to treat lectures as 'reading'. But, if reading means close and solitary study, a steady average of five hours a day may be as much as most men can profitably manage. Newman says that he read nine hours a day for five months and increased the number from nine to twelve in his last year. He collapsed ignominiously in the schools. Has any research been done on this topic?

To shy men he was positively alarming. I remember myself one occasion on which he invited me to take a walk with him. The number of words exchanged between us during that walk was incredibly small, and I believe that it was a relief when we both regained the College gate. . . . Others less shy than myself may have found less difficulty in understanding him; but I do not think he would ever in those days have been described as a popular Tutor.

The same experience was frequently repeated in different modes and with different reactions by a long succession of pupils. Yet in spite of this frightening taciturnity, even possibly and partly on account of it, he became in a very few years not merely a popular but an idolized tutor. As Brodrick himself concluded, in words of which those who knew W. P. Ker, a much later and more deliberate master of taciturnity, will recognize the seemingly improbable truth, 'at last even his fits of silence came to have a charm of their own, and to give weight to the pithy utterances which succeeded them'.

Jowett's panegyrists put these silences to his credit. He could not, they tell us, bear to take part in a conversation which was not a real conversation. 'Everything he said had an edge on it', or a carefully considered meaning. It is claimed that he had no use for talkers who talked for the sake of talking;[1] and that his silences were golden under the refinery of thought. In some degree this may have been true; especially when others were chattering round him and he was free to lose himself in speculative reveries. But his *tête-à-tête* silences owned a different, a temperamental cause. He was too intelligent to suppose that spoken words must always embody well-shaped thoughts. Colloquial speech has other functions to perform, at least as important as the rehearsal of argument. It is the chief means whereby individual persons come to knowledge of each other; and in that process trivialities have more value than solemnities. It is a method, too, of trial and error, in which raw ideas can be tested out and improved or thrown away. It is also play.

All this was quite clear to the mature Jowett, if not to the young tutor who stood a little on his dignity. Unfortunately, he did not know how to play, how to talk slang, how to help out a boy as shy as himself. Moreover, he hated to expose his ideas until he had worked them out and given them full logical and grammatical expression. This was a really serious handicap. He did his best to overcome it as he grew older, collecting 'jests' in his notebooks, which might be used as small change in conversation. But the temperamental defect was incurable.

It was, perhaps, less irksome before he became famous — or did it,

---

[1] He said of Disraeli: 'I did not like him much; he flattered a great deal, and always talked for the sake of talking.' *Tollemache*, 100.

rather, then become more irksome? But it was always there. He depended on others to draw him out. In congenial company he could expand into benignant gaiety; but many of his distinguished hostesses learned that they must lay their plans with the nicest skill, if the Master was to appear to his and their best advantage. He liked to talk with their children, and would cover up his inability to think of anything to say to them by a continuous humming noise. With a diffident and shy pupil or young man he was helpless, and apt to break his silence with some devastating snub, which seemed cruel and undeserved. Most of his victims learned to remember these occasions with affectionate amusement and to match them with a kind of competitive pride against similar stories told by others. It was much better to have been snubbed by Jowett than simply ignored. The snub was a slowly perfected device of transferring the blame for his own speechlessness to his speechless companion. It was almost a way of saying: 'Since you are so stupidly afraid of me that you won't help me out, I will give you something to make you really uncomfortable.'

Only with naturally good talkers could he forget his disability and give as good as he got, and then better. He liked the company of anybody who would start plenty of hares — his own expression. Differences of age and temperament did not count. A self-confident, conceited youngster like Lionel Tollemache, who enjoyed putting him through his paces and exhibiting showman's skill; an unselfconscious, vital youth, like Morier; a great egoist like Tennyson; an erratic genius like Swinburne — all these and many others, in their different ways and because they took the stage, released the secret spring of that paralysing shyness, which he confessed to himself, at the age of sixty-five, 'has detracted at least one-third from my life'.

Since the intercourse between pupil and tutor, alone together, exists in speech and in a duologue, which must somehow be kept going without any background of small talk to ease occasional stoppages, one might suppose that this defect of Jowett's would have prevented him from becoming a really successful tutor. It certainly prevented him from making the best out of unsympathetic or resistant material. There were always some who could not get on with him — more of these, perhaps, at the defensive start and at the mannered end than in his more elastic middle period. At the beginning he thought it improper to be on familiar terms with his pupils; at the end his deficiencies had hardened into mannerisms which functioned automatically and had so justified themselves by success that nobody would have been pleased if he had discarded them. Without them he would have seemed to be less than himself. They came to be prized almost for their own sake and as symbols of a unique will to extract the last farthing from even a mediocre talent.

3. AIM

Teaching, at a sixth form or University honours level, must surely be the least analysable of arts. Methods vary even more than aims; for each man's method is, in part, the use of his own personality and peculiar to himself. But aims, too, vary in kind as well as in degree.

There is the teacher whose sole concern is to get as many of his pupils as possible over their examination fences. There is the teacher who cares only for pupils likely to repay him with brilliant performance. There is the teacher who spends his greatest effort on the pupils likely to reward him least. Again, there is the teacher who categorizes ability and tries to secure what he thinks to be the best performance within the limited power of each pupil. Opposed to him, there is the teacher who pays little or no attention to the apparent capacities of his pupils, setting before them a standard which he regards as an ultimate not to be lowered even for schoolboys.[1] Then there is the teacher who deliberately influences his pupils in the direction — moral or religious, as well as intellectual — which he himself has taken.

Finally, perhaps, our catalogue should include on the one hand the teacher who is happiest when a pupil born to a tradition of manual labour or craftsmanship escapes into the world of professional knowledge or abstract thought; and the opposite kind of teacher who seeks for all his pupils continuity between their inheritance and their achievement, between the start and the finish of their lives. Between these two ideally contrasted aims lies, for every teacher, the problem of the best practical compromise; the most difficult of all the many problems with which he has to grapple in a changing society.

The really great teacher is not one but all of these different teachers. He pursues all their aims, selecting and combining them into a different whole according to the needs and abilities of each individual pupil. A man who succeeded unfailingly in doing this would be not a man, but a god. Moreover, the greatest of teachers cannot enjoy the peculiar satisfaction of the artist who produces a succession of separate finished works. The teacher's satisfaction is of a different kind and order. One might almost call it statistical, if that did not imply a collection of exactly

[1] Robert Whitelaw, who ruled the XX at Rugby for generations, was such a man. Many besides the present writer must still remember him, in his old age, as an almost savage taskmaster but a teacher of genius, to whom they owe the best of what they are. It is surprising that Whitelaw finds no place in the *D.N.B.*

ascertained results. But the results which can be exactly ascertained are those of least importance: the decisions of examiners, the records of offices and appointments, the lists of public honours and awards. And, as the roll of worldly successes lengthens, the more one is tempted to ask what was sacrificed for it: whether the teacher who built it up was not deflected from his true purpose by an unconscious desire to find, in the after careers of his pupils, something of the satisfaction which the artist finds in the public acceptance of his *œuvre*.

The statistical test scarcely needs to be attempted for Jowett. His success is legendary; and the legend is, for once, even less than the truth. The value of a statistical test (if it were made) would not lie in its proof of something long known to be true; it would lie in the demonstration of something much less well understood — that is, the astonishing variety in the accomplishments of the best Balliol men, during the time when Jowett was a tutor and during and after the time when he was Master of Balliol.

His own conception of his task, of the methods he used and the aims he followed, is best discovered from the first-hand evidence of those whom he taught. There is another kind of evidence to be got by studying the lives of those who profited from his teaching. To assemble and to assess all this evidence would be an exceedingly formidable effort.[1] Boiled down, it would yield a catalogue of names; many of them once famous, some famous still; and some there be who have left no name behind them because they dwelt peaceably in their habitations and did their duty to their neighbours, high and low, the better because they had been pupils of Jowett and had learned from him 'to do the job that's nearest' with whatever ability they had. Even if all these unremembered or barely remembered men were left out, the record would still be very long and very remarkable. It would embrace statesmen, proconsuls, politicians, judges, lawyers, civil servants, clerics, scholars, historians, philosophers, landowners, farmers, poets . . . the list of categories does not know where to stop, short of the exact sciences, and even in the sea of science (where Jowett professed himself to be, and was, an ignorant man) the catch would hold a fish or two of size.

4. OBVERSE AND REVERSE

Jowett's own age and place knew two other teachers of exceptional genius in John Newman and Mark Pattison. They resembled him in their

[1] *Experto crede.* I have tried to make it and have been beaten by the richness and variety of the human material.

possession of the curious magnetic power, which marks all great teachers. In the *Memoirs* which Pattison, the Rector of Lincoln, wrote or dictated on his death-bed, he recalls his conscious discovery of this strange gift. It might, otherwise, have been forgotten; for he deserted teaching in order to follow his own scholastic aim in selfish isolation. Newman, never unaware of his standing in other men's minds, also deserted his pupils in order to follow his own peculiar destiny. Of these three great teachers Jowett alone never gave any sign that he knew himself to have this exceptional power over young men. He, alone, used it to the full. If he knew of it, he kept the knowledge in a cellar of his mind; preferring to believe in the efficacy of the rational arguments which he used with such success that there was no need to suppose the existence of a Joker in the pack. But the Joker is, perhaps, the all-important card, even if it is not deliberately exposed.

The classic account of Jowett as a tutor, in his middle period, is that written by Lewis Campbell. It is a wholly sympathetic, devoted, description of the still young man whom his pupils banded to adore. Campbell went up to Balliol from Glasgow University, as a Snell exhibitioner in 1849, when he was nineteen and Jowett thirty-two.

His criticism in those days stimulated without discouraging. In setting before the mind a lofty ideal, he implied a belief in powers hereafter to be developed, and the belief seemed to create the thing believed in. But the intellectual stimulus was not all. He seemed to divine one's spiritual needs, and by mere contact and the brightness of his presence, to supply them. . . . Even amongst the Balliol undergraduates, however, Jowett was not universally popular. He had no false dignity, but he had an adequate sense of his position, and his native shyness had not worn off. His long silences were felt as an awkward bar to conversation by those who did not understand that he himself was hardly aware of them, as the intervals were filled with active thought. He was apt to disclaim this when taxed with it, and to declare that he was thinking of nothing, but the fact was often proved by the pregnancy of the few words that followed the silence. . . . To interrupt this silent process by starting a fresh topic was often to provoke a snub. This was partly due, as a friend remarks, 'to his absorption in his work, but also to a natural shyness and aversion to the commonplaces of society. As he never made an unmeaning remark himself, he was impatient of unmeaning remarks from others'. . . . Another thing that somewhat hampered his intercourse with younger men was his fastidiousness on the score of language, which he regarded almost as a sacred thing. Hence the abhorrence of slang, which some undergraduates thought a piece of donnishness. . . .

His appearance at this time was still very youthful, but at moments, at least to younger men, his personality was very impressive. The look of great refinement, yet of manly strength, of subtlety, combined with simplicity; his unaffected candour, tempered with reserve, could not fail to attract even when it baffled observation. His soft wavy locks were already touched with grey, beginning to recede from the temples. . . . His full grey eyes spoke of the clearness of the mind within, yet had a dreamy

5. The adored tutor
The Drawing by George Richmond, 1855
(*Balliol*)

wistful look, sometimes increased by a slight twitching of the eyelid. His mouth in repose appeared full and slack, but the expressive lips were under absolute control. He was always clean-shaven except the scanty whiskers, and the small chin seemed hardly to promise the strength of volition which lay concealed within.[1]

Campbell's view of Jowett's silences is not at all the same as that which I have ventured to suggest. But Campbell endured and survived them, and became a very intimate friend, and had a unique right to say what he thought about them. He was not, one would think, a particularly tongue-tied youngster.

Another early pupil speaks of Jowett at thirty-five as

altogether more unlike other people than he became in after years. I despair of conveying to anyone who did not know him then anything like an exact idea of what he was. He left on one a stronger impression of genius at that time of his life than at any other. Moments of musing and abstraction were allied in him with a singular alertness and rapidity of mind, meditative power went hand in hand with keen insight.

This reporter (W. L. Newman)[2] goes on inevitably to describe the characteristic silences, as Jowett sat, poker in hand before the fire, crooning to himself, and how much of this passed away in later life 'not altogether unregretted by some of us'. Mark Pattison could say, with sub-acid humour, of Jowett in his fifties: 'Now there's affability!'

And here is another witness, Warden Brodrick again:

His greatest skill consisted, like that of Socrates, in helping us to learn and think for ourselves. . . . No other tutor, within my experience, has ever approached him in the depth and extent of his pastoral supervision, if I may so call it, of young thinkers, and it may truly be said that in his pupil-room, thirty, forty and fifty years ago, were disciplined many of the minds which are now exercising a wide influence over the nation. On the other hand, I think some injustice is done him when it is assumed that he deliberately instilled theological doubt into his pupils. He was reported, it is true, to be a Rationalist . . . and it was impossible for men reading and speculating under his guidance, on all the subjects cognate to Theology, never to exchange opinions with him on theological subjects. But I have reason to believe that his counsels were by no means wholly on the negative side, and I know that being sounded on such matters by a young man of orthodox education and no special aptitude for philosophy, he declined to be drawn into them, on the express ground that he thought the young man's father would not wish him to be consulted. . . . Even in that early stage of his life he never affected or specially admired an 'unworldly' character. Though no man was less actuated by the lower

[1] The above short extracts are taken from L. & L., i, 200–6. Campbell's account of Jowett's personal appearance goes on to describe his clothes and his indifference to cold, except in his hands. It confirms the truth of Richmond's drawing, though one 'who was not a Jowett-worshipper' said that Jowett was not the 'lady-killer' depicted in the drawing. (L. & L., i, 256.)

[2] Fellow of Balliol from 1854 to his death in 1923. Ancient historian. No relation of Cardinal Newman. See L. & L., i, 216–20.

forms of ambition, he was always disposed to regard worldly success as a test of merit, in a sense against which I rebelled; and, in one of my early conversations with him, he expressed a most earnest hope that his pupils would not, like those of another great teacher, 'make a mess of life'. . . . It may be added that, even in those early days, he exhibited a certain indulgence for the black sheep of the College.[1]

That last characteristic, however unexpected, is recalled by so many of Jowett's pupils and friends that there can be no question of it as fact. It is witness of a humanity in which the taciturn young tutor, with his 'heroic industry' and his powerful will and his detestation of slang, might otherwise seem to have been unnaturally deficient. Scores of hot-blooded 'unsteady' youngsters were steadied, one by one, into a sense of citizenship by a beardless boy who looked like nobody else: who sat 'crooning' in front of his fire, poker in hand; who knew practically nothing of the world from personal experience; who could play no game and cared to pursue no sport; who was, in short, by their natural standards, a 'muff' of the first water.

What made this possible? Intelligence and character, both of a very rare kind. Intelligence of the kind which does not rest short of the attainable maximum, not so much of learning as of understanding. As Brodrick puts it:

Research was not yet invented, and the value of instruction was not measured by the number of hard and undigested nodules of learning committed to a note-book. In this respect Jowett was not pre-eminent, though he was never 'above the duty of preparing us for examinations'.

That preparation was his first, routine, duty. How well he fulfilled it was shown by Balliol's upward movement in the class lists. But all evidence is united on the one great point: that intercourse with Jowett was impossible, intolerable, unless you used your own mind as well as you could. This compulsion worked upon all, whatever their natural level of ability, except upon those whose temperaments clashed too hardly with his.

It was character which gave the final impetus to his teaching. Let Brodrick speak once more:

No-one can dispute Jowett's originality, but I have always believed that it was an originality of character rather than intellect. Not that he was not, in the best sense, an independent thinker, or that, by his free interpretations of ideas derived from others, he did not become a fountain of thought to his pupils. But, after all, the secret of his power and of his success lay in his unswerving devotion to work, as his paramount duty.

One might say that there is nothing original, if everything praiseworthy, in such devotion. That would convict the Warden of Merton

[1] In this extract I have mainly used material which Campbell refrained from printing. (*J.P.*) But see *L. & L.*, i, 202-3.

only of failure to express the inexpressible. Brodrick well knew what he meant; but when he began to explain it — in a letter intended only to suggest a line of thought to Jowett's biographer — he was forced back into something a little less than the truth.

McEwen comes a little nearer:

He had an almost preposterous belief in what men can do by hard work and self-mastery. He had little mercy on those who pleaded incapability. As a teacher and tutor he got hold of men in that way, men like Sir Alexander Grant and Professor Sellar, and persuaded them by sheer force of will to exercise their will so as to do work of which they thought them- selves utterly incapable. I mention Grant and Sellar as locally known [McEwen was speaking at Edinburgh]: but there were hundreds of men whom Jowett convinced of the power of the human will. He himself throughout life showed resolute strength, determined, unflinching, almost autocratic strength. Yet he combined this with the most humble and child-like submissiveness to the will of God. The truth is, gentlemen, belief in God's will and man's will are experimentally two sides of the same doctrine. Witness Augustine.

Jowett's ascendancy was already beginning to be evident by 1846, when he was just under thirty and had been a tutor for barely four years. Amongst his pupils at this time, Campbell says:

there was a little inner circle, whose relation to him, partly because they most needed his support, was peculiarly intimate. Chief among these were William Y. Sellar, Alexander Grant, T. C. Sanders, W. S. Dugdale, F. T. Palgrave, Theodore Walrond, R. B. D. Morier, and H. J. S. Smith. It was within this group that there sprang up what outsiders designated a sort of 'Jowett-worship'. . . . His devotion to his pupils was, at this time, something unique at Oxford; and it was rendered more effective by the singular personal charm which made him irresistible to younger men, and the candour of his judgment, in which he always sought to take in the man as a whole, without regarding minor points of position, conduct, or opinion.

There were discordant notes in the gathering chorus. Jowett was always a man who had enemies, both inside as well as outside his own camp. There were many different reasons: jealousy of his attainments; distrust and even hatred of his opinions; resentment at his success; tem- peramental antipathy; even physical dislike. These motives operated, for the most part, in the minds of colleagues and rivals rather than of undergraduates; turning against him some of his earlier supporters, among them apparently Edward Woollcombe.[1] In the hostile section of undergraduates a rather different set of motives prevailed: dislike of

[1] 'Another old gentleman named Woolcombe [sic] turned himself into a theological flying Dutchman. He solemnly avowed his intention of driving Jowett out of Balliol. What has become of Mr. Woolcombe we are not aware. Mr. Jowett cared nothing for such trifles as these.' From an article in the periodical Life of 6th November 1884. (J.P.)

ridicule and sarcasm; anger at some peremptory rebuke or imperious instruction; envy of the favoured inner circle; inability to tolerate those ghastly silences; the sense of being misunderstood or unappreciated; the contempt of the philistine for the stigmata of the intellectual, of the young male human animal for an older man lacking the aspect of sexual virility.

Two letters written by Almond of Loretto after Jowett's death report this young masculine hostility. Almond went up to Balliol in 1850, one of the Snell exhibitioners; an over-worked but able and physically vigorous young Scot, intensely self-conscious, sentimental and apt for rebellion. He wrote, in the first of these letters:[1]

Woollcombe was my own tutor. Jowett did a lot of work with men who were not his pupils, myself among them. It was all the kinder of him, because he evidently thought me, till perhaps quite the end of my time, an idle and uninteresting person. Once when I took him a rather less vile bit of Prose than usual, encouraged by some faint praise, I ventured to ask whether he thought I would have any chance of a 2nd class at Moderations, if I worked. 'No no!' rubbing his hands. 'You needn't trouble yourself. Stick to your Mathematics.' I remember angrily stamping my foot as I left his room, muttering 'I'll get my *first* to sell you.' The pleasantest moment of my life was when I met Jowett after getting my *first*.

Perhaps it was his idea of the right way to stir me up. If so, he succeeded with a vengeance. . . .

But, to tell the honest truth, all the Dons, more or less, repelled me. Warmth, confidence asked and given, easy and genial and unsarcastic familiarity, would have won me and saved me from many mistakes. They *all* seemed to me lumps of ice. But the one who *did* most for me was Jowett. Oxford, however, was the dreariest time of my life. . . .

Privately I loathed Scott. I admired Jowett and *thanked* him though I could not say I liked him — but the old man Jenkyns stands out in my memory as far the *greatest* man of the three, and the man who really made Balliol head of the schools, and the leading College — far and away — in Oxford *outside the schools*.

As to Jowett's 'religion'. I used to wonder what he believed. I came to the conclusion that he never put a clear and distinct issue to himself or to anyone else on any speculative subject. He was a Platonist all over — and from Plato I never could extract more than one graspable idea, and that was the education of his ideal governors. I doubt if any downright statement — on speculative matters — was ever true or false to Jowett. It was true 'in a sense'. In another generation it would have been true 'in another sense'. . . . Possibly, to use Andrew Lang's simile, he found a *ledge* somewhere, where he could stand without slipping. But he was incapable by nature of taking up a pickaxe and delving out a '*hole*' in which to stand, as Newman did, or Liddon, or Calvin or Luther.

Returning to the subject of the Balliol dons, Almond wrote in a second letter:

[1] They were written early in 1894 to the Rev. W. H. Langhorne, a relative of Jowett on the distaff side, whose brother had been at Balliol with Almond. They do not appear to have been published. (*J.P.*)

I don't think I am or can be fair in my criticism of *dons*. The entire donnish theory is repugnant to my nature. The dullness, the guarded language, the dread of slang and heartiness, in fact everything that is symbolized by the cap and gown. Jowett was no worse than the rest, but I remember his being slightly sarcastic the first time I saw him when if, at least to a boy of 17, he had been *genial* and 'chaffy' he might have won my heart. For I always felt *grateful* for the trouble he took. . . . The fault with me was the artificial standard of manner and intercourse with juniors which is inherent in the race [of dons]. Of course most public schoolmasters are much the same. If I went to Rugby and talked to boys as I do, i.e. just as a man would talk to a boy he met at a country house and got to know him well, I would be thought clean mad. So probably would a College don who talked to men of 18–22 as any other man of 30–40 would talk to them. And why that 'Mr.'? I'd have expected my tutor soon to be calling me by my Christian name and asking me to have a cup of tea and a pipe! But Jowett and Riddell stand out in my memory as splendid men *for dons*: just as Wall and Scott were odious to me, even for dons.

Well — there it is — I know I'm not *fair*. Had I known Jowett at Tummel Bridge,[1] it might have been otherwise. And yet, I never could have fully appreciated a man who was both a Platonist and no sportsman. It is told of him that he wouldn't believe that trout lay with their heads up stream!

And I remember when the Balliol boat lost the headship of the river, that Jowett and one of our eight were naturally unable to understand one another. We had got 6 firsts at Mods. Jowett thought that even boating men would look on this as far more than atoning for being bumped by B.N.C.! Of course the boating men didn't see it well. I can say that, had I got 4 1st classes,[2] I couldn't have held my present position, had it not been for the training I got in the boat which, practically for me, has been the best bit of education I ever had in my life.

But 'baith's best'!

Jowett never had his eyes quite open to this — in my time at least.

Such were the reactions of a man upon whom Jowett seems to have effectively used his only available spur — that of wounding sarcasm. Almond wanted genial *bonhomie* of a kind which was not in Jowett's locker. His conception of the way in which the dons and Jowett ought to have talked to him may be gathered more clearly from the way in which he wrote and spoke to his boys at Loretto, seeking to use boys' language rather than men's, and signing himself 'your affectionate' even 'your loving Head'. His methods at Loretto were his own; they worked, because the genuine love of boyhood which he claimed as his best gift, his warm heart, his striking personality, and his unusual combination of a boyish temperament with a semi-adult brain kept them fresh and real, and prevented them from deteriorating into a mechanical system or, worse, into sheer sentimentalism. Copied by lesser men, they might be a target for mockery, infinitely more vulnerable than the ceremoniousness he so much disliked at Oxford.

[1] Where Jowett at one time used to have his 'reading parties'. See below, 186.

[2] Almond, in fact, got 2 first classes in classical and mathematical moderations, but fell, significantly perhaps, to seconds in both final examinations.

A century has passed since Almond's time at Balliol, and the old Oxford formalism has given way to an informalism which sometimes makes it difficult to distinguish between tutor and pupil. It is questionable whether the change is entirely for the good. If tutor and pupil are drawn together in a natural intimacy, they can — if the elder man chooses — lay formality altogether aside, when they are alone together. Even so, tutor and pupil do this at a certain peril, unless it is well understood between them that authority is waiting to resume her seat on every proper occasion. It is very tempting for the older man to delude himself that he can step down to the level of the younger, especially in a society which tends to think that value lies with the quick eye and supple sinew and lissom mind, and seeks to continue a pleasant illusion of youth into age. Such a descent was impossible to conceive in Almond's time at Balliol. And even the headmaster of Loretto, however winningly he might be or play the boy, remained in his biographer's memory as 'the only man I ever knew who could smite me on a sudden with the inrush of pale fear'.

For a man of Jowett's calibre to affect an artificial intimacy with a pupil which he did not want or feel would have been worse than ridiculous. He worked within a system which presupposed authority, and he believed in it. He was capable of asking a pupil to tea — for it is on record that, having done so, he asked the unhappy youth why he was there and then forgot his presence. Observing him ten minutes or so later on, he said 'Oh, are you here again?', and being reminded of the invitation to take tea said, 'Well, why don't you have it?' This is not an apocryphal event. It is recorded in an unpublished letter which Walter Morrison of Malham Tarn wrote to Jowett's biographers, and it happened to Morrison himself.

Morrison could take this sort of thing and profit by it. Almond could not. And possibly Jowett knew what he was about, both with Morrison and with Almond. On Almond's own admission he was goaded by Jowett into stretching himself to gain a first class in classical moderations. That he failed to get first classes in both of his final examinations is ascribed to ill-health by his biographer. His comments about Plato, and his general inability to apprehend Jowett's religious views (though his own were merely a very crude version of Jowett's) suggest that — at least in Greats — he was placed where he belonged, and that no amount of tea-drinking and pipe-smoking with either Woollcombe or Jowett would have got him any further. Economy of effort is a first essential to a good tutor. Even the Jowetts of this world have no more than twenty-four hours in the day, and must spend their time where the expenditure will be best repaid or least wasted.

Jowett's tutorship lasted for twenty-eight years, until he became Master in 1870. But in a sense it lasted on through the Mastership to the very end. We are told that he kept track of the work and character and friendships of every undergraduate; and that it was impossible to catch his memory at fault over any Balliol man of any generation.[1] Abbott says:

The change was not great. He continued to ask the undergraduates to breakfast or wine, rarely allowing a day to pass without seeing two or three. He thought of them day and night. He won their confidence as he had always done, and those who were in distress turned to him for help and advice. To evil-doers he was a terror; and the countenance with which an offender left his room was sufficient evidence of what had taken place within. Nor did he entirely give up Tutorial work. He took essays from a number of undergraduates once a week at least. He established weekly Tutorial meetings at which he never failed to attend, going through the whole list of undergraduates and satisfying himself by inquiry about the work of every man. . . . And he kept up as Master his old custom of inviting men to spend part of the Long Vacation with him.

Not all the undergraduates, in these later years of the Mastership, would have endorsed Abbott's eulogy. An anonymous Balliol contributor to Macmillan's Magazine (February 1896) rather spitefully recalled the difference between the privileged circle and the unprivileged outsiders.

It was said by the irreverent that if a man were a peer, a profligate, or a pauper the Master would be sure to take him up; and one sees now the reason that underlay such a method of selection; the physician applying himself to those that were sick. But as undergraduates, a good many men could not help resenting the rather odd way in which one man was taken and another left; and they resented still more the extraordinary character of some of the personages who found their way into the College upon grounds that were certainly not connected with either intellect or industry, and who might hope, if they could be induced to do a little work, to look forward to the possible attainment of a third class. In all perhaps one-third of the College thus saw something of the Master in private life; the residue were only directly touched by his influence at three points; in Chapel, at the brief interval in hall at the end of term, known respectively to dons and undergraduates as Collections or Handshaking; and those still more unpleasant quarters of an hour when one was summoned before the Master for some offence whose enormity transcended the judicial powers of the Deans.

The burden of this writer's complaint is that, as Master, Jowett altogether failed to influence 'the average man'. In this charge there is, no doubt, some inevitable truth. But it is brought in such a way as to make one suspect that wounded vanity lay behind it — the kind of vanity which, like Almond's, asks to be taken at its own fancied level and blinds itself to the truth of an uncomfortable sarcasm by affecting to regard it as a bad joke:

[1] During the four years of his Vice-Chancellorship he was forced to relax his standards.

For example, was it particularly inspiring, at the end of a term of hard work ending in a first class in the College examinations, to hear, after a lengthy survey of one's person, as if one was some rare animal: 'Mr. A. is an intelligent young man, is he not, Mr. Y.?' Such an observation upon an occasion so solemn to the student could only strike one as supremely ridiculous.

And Mr. A. goes on to comment upon the painful contrast between the freshman's position at his public-school

which had brought him into close and constant contact with the head-master, with a man, that is to say, who was in five cases out of six of a vigorous and commanding personality, usually of a contagious and generous enthusiasm [and his disillusionment] in the presence of a man whose manner and speech, as well as his appearance and dress, though one does not want to dwell upon personal peculiarities, fell painfully short of any idea the freshman might have formed of the Head of a great college.

The Mr. A's fortunately always spoil their own case.

CHAPTER IX

The Coming Man

I. RISING CURVE

The twelve years from 1842 to 1854 were the happiest in Jowett's life. He was the centre of a widening circle of brilliant and devoted pupils and ex-pupils. Friends multiplied, as well as pupils. He moved from the obscurity of an unknown college tutor into the agreeable kind of fame which attends the coming man. His capacity for work seemed to be unlimited. Every minute of every long day was used to the full. His mental powers expanded, like a steadily rising river which first surrounds and then overwhelms all shoals and barriers. There appeared to be nothing which could ever interrupt its assured, deepening flow.

At the beginning of this period he experienced occasional fits of the deep depression, which visited him throughout his life more often than he allowed his friends to know. He wrote about them to an unnamed correspondent in 1846:

This malady to which we both seem subject, as far as my experience goes, begins with the stomach, extends itself to the head, where it dries up the fountains of the intellect, and is not wholly unconnected with the weather. This, in the language of Hegel, is its reality. But its ideality embraces a higher field: life, death, eternity etc. The misfortune is that the world sees it from the outside, whereas to yourself it generally retains its sublimer aspect from within. But joking apart.... I feel every day what a serious thing it is, and that there is far more truth in its ideal side than in the other. It is a most painful thing to fancy that you have no moral nature, or power of fixing your own character; no stamina that seems as if it could last you through life.... Let us be of good cheer, and trust that when the sky clears we may have life and spirits to enjoy it.

In a few years' time he was to need his own advice, and to find it very hard to follow; and later still, as he felt himself becoming an old man, the enemy returned to plague him. But, as the curve rose steadily from his twenty-fifth to his thirty-seventh year, depression was the opposite of the mood he showed to his friends. Ralph Lingen,[1] two years his junior,

---

[1] Later Lord Lingen. Not a Balliol, but a Trinity, undergraduate, elected to a Balliol fellowship in 1841. A friend of Jowett, Froude and Temple. One of the first great Victorian civil servants.

who 'was constantly seeing him during these years', remembered him as 'light-hearted and gay'; and his wife (the Lingens married in 1852) 'was greatly struck by the "joyousness" of her husband's friend'. Lingen insisted upon the truth of Richmond's charming portrait, done about 1859, 'to which, let me add, his likeness after death returned with striking reality.' Lewis Campbell, confirming Tollemache's story of Jowett enacting the part of a Chinese executioner at a party in the Balliol common room, recalls 'a touch of lightheartedness unlike his bearing in after years'.

This gaiety (which Swinburne also remembered as a characteristic of his 'friend the Master of Balliol'[1]) was natural to his temperament. It did not show itself in unsympathetic company. In the presence of strangers or voluble celebrities he often withdrew into the background. Thus Sir George Trevelyan remembered how 'when the question of Civil Service reform was at its height' (round about 1853) Jowett constantly came to his father's (Sir Charles Trevelyan's) house in Westbourne Terrace, where Macaulay would be also present, 'and used to sit through the evening, as my boyish recollection goes, quite silent'. Henry de Bunsen, son of the Prussian Ambassador Baron von Bunsen[2] (who met Jowett about this time and considered him 'the deepest mind he had met in England') formed the impression that Jowett was 'a man who lived intimately with a few friends, but was shy and retiring in general society'.

Beneath the 'joyousness' and supporting it, as canvas supports paint, was a firmly woven fabric of integrity and independence. An early glimpse of this is provided by Lingen's recollection of a Balliol college meeting in 1844. Plans drawn by Pugin and other architects for rebuilding the college were before the meeting. The Old Master rose and delivered his views 'in a knock-me-down' style. Lingen supposed that this must settle the question. 'His surprise when the youthful Tutor began to speak was equalled by his admiration of the calm, firm and clear manner in which Jowett expressed an opposite opinion.'

It is not recorded what the opinions of the two speakers were, or which prevailed over the other. Presumably the Old Master opposed, and Jowett favoured, rebuilding; and the college decided to do nothing. When Jowett, five years later, took on the duties of the bursarship he carried a building project — the new 'Caesar' building — against the stout resistance of 'that little fellow' (the Old Master) who 'valiantly takes his stand upon his brew-house, which he disputes our right to pull down'.

To be afraid of nobody is good; to be afraid of nothing is better. No

---

[1] See below, 365 foll.　　　　　　　　[2] See below, 236.

curb checked the young tutor's speculative freedom. He had outgrown
the doctrinal naivety of the evangelicals, and had escaped the tractarian
infection. The way was opening for him, in company with Arthur
Stanley, to seek a more liberal interpretation of Christianity and to
express his views without fear of consequences. The day was far distant
when he would write in one of his notebooks: 'If I live I ought to speak
my mind. The inevitable consequence will be that I shall be called an
atheist.' That was after he had become Master of Balliol, and had learned
the humiliating truth that the governor of a castle is its chief prisoner.
For the present he was wonderfully free; and the sense of freedom is
necessary to the kind of 'joyousness' which he manifested to his more
intimate friends.

Other things are also necessary, and were also present. For Jowett it
must have been an exhilarating experience to discover his genius for
teaching, and to prove it through the achievements of his pupils. It
must have been satisfying to find himself a socially acceptable person,
beginning to be of some consequence in the great world. It must have
flattered his vanity that he astonished the fellows of Balliol by his easy
command of practical matters — as when he became bursar and put the
affairs of the college into order after their careless mismanagement by
Ward. But all these things — even his success as the Old Master's dark
horse among the tutors — would not have generated the peculiar 'joyousness' of Mrs. Lingen's description, the dreamy yet alert, wistful yet
assured, radiance of Richmond's sensitive drawing. The hope of liberalizing the Church of England in company with Stanley scarcely supplies
the missing element. It lay, surely, in the delight which he was beginning
to feel in the free use of his finely disciplined, finely muscled, sensitive
and adventurous mind. He was on the road of discovery — for most of
the time all by himself, even when Stanley was close by his side.

2. HEGEL

In 1844 Jowett and Stanley spent part of the summer vacation together
in a visit to Germany, which went beyond Germany to Prague and
Vienna.

Stanley was just recovering from his two years of intensive labour
on *The Life of Thomas Arnold*, which had been published on the last
day of May. His masterpiece was an unstinted offering on love's altar.
Coming so quickly after the strenuous efforts which had already over-
strained his mind, it left him empty and exhausted; never again would he

be able to recover the power of creative writing. But he was not yet twenty-nine; his intellect was still supple and buoyant; fatigue was not lassitude.

Before they set out on their tour[1] Jowett insisted on a 'compact', which allowed him to spend two or three hours every day in study. He carried in his luggage the recently published Greek Lexicon of Liddell and Scott. Stanley dubbed this a 'monster grievance'. It must certainly have been Jowett who dictated their reading on the journey. This was the German text of Kant's *Critique of Pure Reason*, on which the two travellers (as Stanley humorously said) 'supported their wearied minds by alternate reading, analysing and catechizing'.

The choice of the *Kritik der reinen Vernunft* fitted into a plan, which Jowett carried through with the aid of Stanley's letters of introduction — letters which enabled the younger man to pursue his own serious aim, while Stanley either indulged his increasing passion for sightseeing or submitted with reluctant grace to the necessity of meeting this and that celebrated man. It happened that German scholars were assembled at Dresden in a Congress of Philologers. It was at Dresden that the tour is said to have culminated for Jowett and to have 'made an era in his intellectual life'. To Stanley, on the other hand, it was merely 'one of the most uninteresting places' he ever saw.

The plan into which Kant's *Kritik* seemed casually fitted, almost as if it were a piece of light reading, had nothing to do with the Congress of Philologers. The Congress was a piece of uncovenanted luck. Jowett found it very exciting when 'Zumpt's *Latin Grammar*, Thiersch's *Greek Grammar*, Wunder's *Sophocles*, Lachmann's *Greek Testament*, who were formerly supposed to be myths, sprang up into life and reality'. To meet Lachmann was an event in itself; for it was Lachmann's Greek text which Jowett and Stanley used, a few years later, for their commentaries on the Epistles of St. Paul. But the man he had specially wished to meet was Erdmann of Halle, the disciple and the posthumous interpreter of Hegel, in order to consult him upon 'the best manner of approaching' his master's works.

The meeting took place — if Campbell is right — at Dresden. Jowett came back to Oxford determined to conquer this new world of the mind.

Though Hegel had died in 1831, nobody in the Oxford of 1844 — hardly anybody in England, if anybody at all — knew more about him than that he was another, dead, unintelligible German philosopher. There was no English translation of any of his works; no guide to the

---

[1] The tour is described both by Campbell *L. & L.*, i, 89–91, and by Prothero in the *Life of Stanley*, i, 325–31.

nature of his system. Very few men in Oxford had enough German to grapple for themselves with the peculiar obscurities of Hegel's style. Twenty years earlier, before Pusey went to Göttingen to learn the language for his own theological purposes, there were only two men in Oxford believed to know any German; although 'German Introductions to the New Testament, if written in Latin were read.'[1] The use of Latin, as the international language of learning, had enabled Oxford and Cambridge men to discover what German classical and theological scholars were up to. But the great German philosophers from Kant onwards developed their ideas in their native speech.[2] Their idiom was hard to master. 'It is true' writes Muirhead 'that Hegel claimed for himself the intention of attempting "to teach philosophy to speak in German". But when used to denote philosophical ideas ordinary German words and phrases were apt to break down under the weight of the meaning and leave one with nothing.' And even ordinary German was still a barrier which halted English understanding of German writers.

It was no longer quite the barrier it had been when Pusey first went to Germany. At least not in Balliol. Tait had overcome it so well that he was described by Sommer, Licentiate and Docent of Protestant Divinity in the University of Bonn, in a testimonial for Tait's use as a candidate for the headmastership of Rugby written with a nearly perfect command of English, as 'intimately versed in our language, of which he became master partly by the study of our literature, partly by the personal intercourse with Germans'.[3] But Dr. Arnold, when he visited the great Roman historian Niebuhr, had been content that the conversation should be conducted in the English language, which Niebuhr spoke and understood with ease. The familiarity of educated Germans with the language of their insular English guests was, perhaps, a spur to Tait and his pupils. The use of German became almost a Balliol affectation. Things that could have been more naturally said in English were sometimes deliberately said in German, as if it were a kind of superior argot. Jowett himself wrote whole letters in German to Stanley. But there is a great difference between polite usage or understanding of a foreign language and the ability to penetrate into its depths and ascend its heights. The German mind and the German language contain marshes and highlands, which are not easy for Englishmen to traverse or climb.

Yet Jowett, of his own initiative, undertook a frontal assault upon the frowningly difficult fortress of Hegelian metaphysics, wreathed in clouds

---

[1] *Life of Pusey*, i, 72.
[2] Two early metaphysical essays of Kant were written in Latin.
[3] *Life of Archbishop Tait*, i, 72.

of Germanic phrases. What pointed the way to him? Not any formal teaching; for there was no such teaching to be had in England. His pursuit of philosophy was spontaneous; it had the zest of the pioneer, the mountain-climber, the passionate amateur. His instruction was self-given, as when he and Stanley wrestled with the stiff language of Kant's *Kritik*. But how did he know, so certainly, the direction to take? Ideas seem often to travel in the air, without the embodiment of words. One heard the name of Hegel without knowing more than that it was a name of power. A man like Jowett must wish to find out more about him. The wind blowing across the German ocean carried the scent of German philosophical idealism. Only a little inquiry — of the sort that Jowett was good at making — was needed to discover that Hegel's disciple Erdmann, whose *History of Philosophy* was in the process of publication, was the man to consult.

The consequences of the pilgrimage were far-reaching. Though Jowett never became 'an Hegelian' in the sense of accepting the Hegelian system, the influence of Hegel upon his thought was very great, even profound. The immense effort necessary to comprehend the most difficult of all philosophers, without the aid of any English crib or commentary, added a new dimension to his mind. He said himself, forty years later, that he had received a greater stimulus from Hegel than from anyone. He made light of the difficulty, after he had won understanding. The reason why people thought Hegel difficult was, he said, because they would not sit down to a page of Hegel as to a problem in mathematics. He meant that they failed to apply their will to a kind of argument which needed concentrated attention; not, of course, that Hegel's philosophy had a mathematical character.

His intensive study of Hegel did much more than enlarge his own powers of mind; it brought Hegel into Oxford, and subsequently into Cambridge, and caused 'that naturalization of Hegelian thought in England which was so marked a feature of the close of the nineteenth century'.[1] It was from Jowett that T. H. Green and Edward Caird directly learned their Hegelian alphabet. They began a revolution in English philosophy, which was carried to the down-turning point of triumph by a younger generation of philosophers — in Cambridge M'Taggart of Trinity, in Oxford Bosanquet of Balliol and Bradley of Merton (the most gifted of them all) — before the counter-revolutions, first of 'pragmatism' and then of 'logical positivism', drove 'idealism' into the wilderness from which it is scarcely yet beginning to re-emerge.

Campbell wrote of Jowett's visit to Erdmann that 'the posthumous

[1] A. E. Taylor, in his *D.N.B.* article on F. H. Bradley.

influence of Hegel in his own country had already culminated and was beginning to decline'. This was rather a superficial statement. The Hegelian legacy was being bitterly disputed between philosophers of the right and philosophers of the left. 'Amid these controversies' it has been said 'Hegelianism died.'[1] It would be truer to say that it obeyed its own laws, and split into the thesis and antithesis of Hegel's own 'dialectic' — a division which still awaits a synthesis. For the philosophy of Karl Marx, which has affected the history of the world, is but Hegelianism in reverse. It is curious to think that Jowett could have encountered Marx in the reading room of the British Museum, where the latter spent most of his life from 1849 onwards. The Muse of History misses her chances. What a theme for an imaginary conversation in a Bloomsbury eating-house!

Not that Jowett swallowed Hegel whole. The power and sweep, the very difficulty of Hegel's thought fascinated him. 'One must go on' he wrote to Brodie a year after beginning his Hegelian studies 'or perish in the attempt, that is to say, give up Metaphysics altogether. It is impossible to be satisfied with any other system after you have begun with this.' But his admiration was not uncritical. Writing to Stanley after another twelve months, he struggled to utter a criticism he could not quite express. 'Hegel is untrue, I sometimes fancy, not in the sense of being erroneous, but practically, because it is a consciousness of truth, becoming thereby error. It is very difficult to express what I mean, for it is something which does not make me value Hegel the less as a philosophy. The problem of $\dot{a}\lambda\dot{\eta}\theta\epsilon\iota a$ $\pi\rho a\kappa\tau\iota\kappa\dot{\eta}$, Truth idealized and yet in action, he does not seem to me to have solved; the Gospel of St. John does.' The sudden comparison between Hegel and the author of the fourth Gospel is illuminating and very characteristic of the writer.

If he never became an out-and-out Hegelian, he had no hesitation in accepting the doctrine of continuity, the impossibility of defining any idea without bringing in its opposite. He was lecturing his pupils one day on the concept that 'being both is and is not', when one of them was heard to snigger. 'You may laugh, Mr. Dugdale,' said the lecturer 'but you will find it is true.' Not, perhaps, the most obviously effective of his *bons mots*. But it was remembered, which means that it was delivered with conviction and hit its target.

Professor Muirhead, in his searching essay *How Hegel came to England*, seems to have been quite unaware that Jowett fetched Hegel to Oxford twenty years before J. H. Stirling published *The Secret of Hegel* in 1865.

[1] *Chambers's Encyclopaedia*, in the article on Hegel by Edward Caird, as edited by Professor T. M. Knox for the 1950 edition.

Muirhead mentioned Jowett only to quote from a letter written a few years later, in which the Master of Balliol congratulated Stirling on having 'made the general idea of Hegelianism more plain than it has been made before in England'. That was not saying much. Muirhead quoted with approval a contemporary witticism: 'If Mr. Hutchinson Stirling knows the secret of Hegel he has managed to keep it to himself.' Stirling is, nevertheless, the hero of Muirhead's narrative: the leader of those who 'undismayed by the fate that had overtaken Hegelianism in the land of its birth' saw that 'there was nothing really constructive to be looked for from British philosophy, until it had put itself to school in the German Idealist movement', which began with Kant, developed through Fichte and Schelling, and culminated in Hegel. 'There were skirmishers who went before', especially J. F. Ferrier in the eighteen fifties and later. But Ferrier 'did not know when he was beaten', and did not succeed even in understanding what Hegel meant by the Absolute. 'Up to the middle of the fifties it may be said that no intelligible word had been spoken by British writers as to the place and significance of Hegel's work.'

This explains Jowett's strange absence from Muirhead's brilliant and seemingly exhaustive essay. For Muirhead drew entirely upon published literary sources, and Jowett published nothing about Hegel. Though he collaborated with Temple in a translation of Hegel's *Logic*, this was rather mysteriously broken off in 1849, when it was within sight of being finished.[1] The *Life and Letters* should have enabled Muirhead to fill up this gap in his knowledge. But either he had not read the book, or he had not read it with enough attention. It was an unfortunate *lacuna*. It lessens the historical value of Muirhead's essay, which exhibits complete ignorance of Jowett's most productive intellectual adventure. It is only in forgotten places — such as the unsigned article on Edward Caird in the *Dictionary of National Biography* — that one can find any hint of Jowett's singular contribution to the development of British philosophy.[2]

Though Muirhead is ignorant or silent about Jowett, his essay truthfully describes the isolation of British empirical from German idealist philosophy at the time when Jowett visited Erdmann, and startlingly vindicates the claim that, if Jowett wrote nothing himself about philosophy, he was the pioneer who set others on their road. By fertilizing the

[1] See below, 184, and note.
[2] 'Jowett was Caird's tutor, "watchful and exigent", and at that time "eager to direct students to new sources of thought opened by the German philosophy and theology".' The ex-Provost of Oriel, Sir G. N. Clark, preserves a valuable fragment of oral tradition. He remembers having been told by the late Professor J. A. Smith that nobody except himself (Professor Smith) remembered how Hegel first came to Oxford — through Jowett.

minds of such pupils as Green and Caird with the Hegelian seed he had winnowed for himself, he was the putative father of British philosophy in the second half of the nineteenth century and the first decade or so of the twentieth.

The claim could be carried further. Jowett's mind, even during the initial and prolonged fascination, never surrendered itself to Hegel. It had a salty and empirical side. Traces of this healthy empiricism persisted in the minds of pupils whose later pupils enrolled themselves as partisans of revolt. If the young Jowett, who went to see Erdmann in 1844, could have been confronted with (say) Schiller or Wittgenstein or Ayer or Sartre, he would have been at least intrigued by their various re-statements of the sceptical view with which a part of his mind had always been in sympathy. He would not have surrendered to them, any more than he surrendered to Hegel. He might, however, have said that in this criss-cross of thought, one generation of philosophers denying any intelligible sense to the affirmations of their predecessors, the truth of Hegel's 'dialectic' was being beautifully illustrated by those who were most eager to destroy it.

3. PIONEER

In the Michaelmas term of 1844 Jowett was an unsuccessful candidate for the vacant chair of Moral Philosophy. 'It would suit me better than any other Chair.' His candidature was no more than a *ballon d'essai*. It shows how his interest in philosophy was deepening; and how quickly, now, he was coming to the front of the 'under-thirties' in Oxford.

The two sensational events of 1845 in Oxford were the degradation of Ward in February, and Newman's secession to Rome in October. Between them, in the Long Vacation, Jowett and Stanley again travelled in Germany. Stanley's two sisters joined them for a fortnight. Catherine Vaughan remembered, nearly fifty years later, how 'in those days B. J. was the most charming friend and companion it was possible to have: never out of temper, never depressed, never looking weary or discontented — always full of the most interesting subjects of conversation. He was delightful.' She remembered, too, that he and her brother were so deep in the study of Hebrew that they could scarcely be persuaded to observe the scenery. 'We used to exclaim, "Oh, do look! how beautiful!" and they would hastily raise their eyes, cry out "Yes, very fine", and as hastily return to the contemplation of their Grammar.'[1]

---

[1] Jowett gave up the study of Hebrew after a year or two as 'too trying to the eyes'.

In the winter Jowett was ordained priest by the Bishop of Oxford (Samuel Wilberforce). A letter to Stanley amusingly described his interviews with the Bishop and his examining Chaplain. 'Samuel of Oxford is not unpleasing, if you will resign yourself to be semi-humbugged by a semi-humbug. He was very kind, and would do great good if he could but be persuaded to keep off speculative matters.' The Bishop asked, among other questions, in what sense the candidate signed the Articles. 'In Paley's sense.' 'What does Paley say?' 'That it is an absurdity if the Legislature meant to say that you assented to four or five hundred disputed propositions. It only meant that you were an attached member of the Church of England.' The answer satisfied the Bishop.

The nine years which followed were years of wonderful vigour, but they do not lend themselves easily to a connected narrative; two of the themes which belong to this period — Jowett's part in the first stage of University reform, and the birth of his Commentary on the Epistles of St. Paul — cannot be merged in such a narrative. They will be discussed separately.[1]

Looking at these nine years, and considering them as a self-contained period, one cannot but be struck by the extraordinary amount and power of work which they exhibit. Warden Brodrick thought that his 'heroic industry', simply as a tutor, had never been fully appreciated. That was certainly true outside Balliol. If one adds to this professional industry all his other industry at this time of his life, it is difficult to imagine, as it is difficult to convey, the total effort. It was not as if he found it easy to consolidate and retain every advance of his mind. As he confessed to Florence Nightingale, he was always having to start all over again. But that confession was made later on, when he was growing old. For the present, his store of mental and physical energy seemed illimitable. He had one unfailing asset: he was a sound sleeper.

During these nine years his activity was ceaseless and a great deal of it was pioneering activity. He mastered Hegel and translated, with Temple, 'a good deal of the *Logic*'.[2] He read Kant and other German philosophers (including the 'old twaddler' Schelling, whom he met and liked and respected as probably the only German philosopher who knew anything about art). He made a close study of Comte. He read the economists

---

[1] The former in the succeeding section of the present chapter; the latter in the second section of the next chapter.

[2] This was within sight of being finished in January 1849. See his letter to Stanley, *L. & L.*, i, 142. He speaks of it there as 'my' translation without reference to Temple. According to Campbell (i, 129) it had been 'broken off by Temple's being summoned away to practical life' in 1848; but this is evidently not quite correct. The translation was never published, and the MS seems to have disappeared.

of his time, and even lectured upon political economy, though he erroneously supposed that it was a branch of thought which had exhausted
its possibilities. He taught himself some Hebrew. He laid the foundations
of his life-long work on Plato. He took the practical duties of the Balliol
bursarship in his stride; interested himself in the University extension
movement; became one of the University's public examiners, and helped
to recast the Oxford examination system. He worked out his theological
position in a number of unpublished essays; made an intensive comparison of the synoptic Gospels — 'a work of much time with little to show';
planned, with Stanley, a *magnum opus* of New Testament interpretation.
He became the leading champion of University reform and a consultant
over the reform of the civil service (particularly the Indian civil service).
And all this time, and before all of these various interests and activities,
absorbing and exacting as they were, and to each of which he gave his
full mind — before everything else he was the tirelessly devoted teacher
of young men, whose varied pursuits, as more and more of them went
out into the world, he followed with inexhaustible sympathy. To quote
Campbell again:

If he gave them support and strength, they were his 'wings', to use the
quaint phrase of Niebuhr. He read their books in MS; he followed every
step of their success or their discomfiture; he formed close friendships
with their wives and children. With Sellar he renewed his knowledge of
Lucretius and Virgil; with Grant he saw how Aristotle had absorbed the
ideas of Plato and 'stamped them with logic'; with Morier he took a bird's-
eye view of continental politics; from F. T. Palgrave he sought to gather
new impressions of German and Italian art. Something of the same kind
was true also of younger contemporaries, who were not his pupils.

Foremost among these slightly younger contemporaries was the Ralph
Lingen already mentioned.[1] His recollections give a vivid impression of
the Jowett who often stayed with the newly married young couple in
London in and after 1852. Lingen writes of

our frequent anxieties, in which he never shared, whether he would really
catch the ten o'clock train to Oxford, on which he was bent, with his
breakfast to finish, and our servant packing his things. Then, as up to the
end of his life, he always carried with him papers which he had in hand,
and would work at them upstairs and down; and at all spare times.

After the second German tour with Stanley, Jowett's visits to the continent became shorter and fewer. There was too much to be done; too
little time, now, to spend in travelling. He never saw Rome; only once
'went as far as to Florence': but 'an occasional run to Switzerland might
follow the annual visit to his parents at St. Germain's or Fontainebleau.'

[1] See above, 175.

In the spring of 1848, however, after the February revolution in France, he persuaded Stanley, Palgrave and Morier (described by Stanley as 'a Balliol undergraduate of gigantic size, who talks French better than English, is to wear a blouse, and go about disguised in the Clubs') to go with him to Paris, where they mixed with the crowds and gained the sense of being present at a turning point in history. They enjoyed the experience very much; the more so because there had been talk at home of danger, which Jowett seems to have pooh-poohed. But though he was moved by the eloquence of Lacordaire preaching in Notre Dame and by the noble bearing of Lamartine, Jowett observed that revolution has a drab aspect. He said: 'Paris is now *attristée* — the people in the streets remind me of London.'[1]

Back in England, after this short April adventure in '48, Jowett decided that it would profit him better to take his future long vacation holidays in some quiet northern place, where he could sit down to his own work, with some younger man or men to keep him company. In this particular year he went to Oban and took with him the genial young giant, Morier. Next year, again alone with Morier, he went to 'a farm-house at Grange in Borrowdale; but the season was unpropitious' and he lost 'faith in the refreshing qualities of the Lake Country'. After that he went, as a rule, to Scotland; sometimes to Yorkshire or Cumberland; later in life to West Malvern. In Scotland, Tummel Bridge was the scene of very many reading parties. One of the pupils[2] who went with him there, every summer from 1869 to 1872,

never knew Jowett so happy or light-hearted as at Tummel Bridge. He liked the little inn, and comfortable Miss Menzies who kept it, and he was never tired of the hills and the heather, the brawling Tummel and the keen scent of the bog-myrtle. He was still vigorous enough to enjoy a long tramp across the moors with his young companions, the highland air inspired him, and his conversation had an unwonted ease and buoyancy.

These parties came to include men who were not *in statu pupillari*. It was at Tummel Bridge that Swinburne 'in delightful spirits' stayed in the July and August of 1871 and met Browning 'who was staying near by and often joined the party'.

The ease and buoyancy, recovered at Tummel bridge in his early fifties and exhibited to Swinburne there and in other places later on, were the ease and buoyancy which had captivated his first pupils at

---

[1] *Auctoritate* Palgrave. *L. & L.*, i, 133–6. *Life of Stanley*, i, 389–402. Stanley revisited Paris in October of the same year (*Life*, i, 402–6) after the June battle of the barricades. 'If the first visit' writes Prothero 'had given him insight into revolution, the second afforded him insight into a reaction.'
[2] Edwin Harrison. *L. & L.*, 11, 36. Harrison's own brilliant promise was 'foiled' by illness. But he remained one of Jowett's chief friends and admirers.

6. Sir Robert Morier
A photograph in later life
(*Picture Post Library*)

Oxford. The ten years of bitter frustration, from 1854 to about 1864, of which the story will be told in the coming chapters, had made no essential change in him. Disappointment had hurt, even for a time soured him; duties began to press more heavily; his reserves of energy began to fail. But that happens, more or less, to everybody. It is only when the man to whom it happens is an exceptional man, facing the decline of his powers after a long life of incessant intellectual activity, that it becomes a matter of particular interest to learn how the situation is mastered or suffered.

It might be an exaggeration to say that Jowett foresaw the challenge of old age and laid his plans to meet it long in advance. But it is not an exaggeration to say that he began to find his answer to this far off challenge in 1848, when he took Morier to Oban. It looks as if he stumbled upon this answer by accident. Whether his feeling towards Morier was love or mere liking, it certainly at this time took the place of love in his mind. He had taken him to Paris, and shown him off to Stanley — who saw only an agreeable young hulk with a surprising fluency in French. In the next two long vacations he had Morier all to himself. But at the end of 1849 Morier took his degree — a second class — and these pleasant working holidays à deux came to an end.

They remained in Jowett's mind for their own sake, and because they led him to the institution of his Balliol 'reading parties'. When Arthur Stanley died in 1881, Jowett wrote to Morier:

He was the oldest friend I had; we were first acquainted in 1836, and intimate friends from 1838 onward. In 1844 and 1845 we travelled to-gether, and in 1848 I dare say that you remember his coming to visit us at Oban. Let me in passing tell you with what pleasure I remember the time that I spent with you then and the following year. It was the beginning of a custom which has been continued, with the exception of a single year, ever since, and has, I believe, contributed as much as anything to the success of Balliol. The months spent in this way have not been unpleasant, and I think that they have been the most satisfactory in my life. How much I owe to others, and to you, perhaps, more than any one!

Apparently Jowett came to think of the reading party as if it had been his own invention. So, perhaps, it was; in that he hit upon it accidentally for himself and was the first man to make systematic use of it. The whole series of his long vacation parties continued for about forty years: it seems to have ended in 1887 when he found the effort of entertaining friends and pupils at West Malvern too much for him and tried 'the experiment for more than a week of living alone. Do you know it answers very well, and for an invalid is generally best.'[1]

Inventions are seldom the result of one man's inventiveness. In September 1848 (at the time when Jowett was with Morier at Oban) Arthur Clough was writing his 'long-vacation pastoral' *The Bothie of Tober-na-Vuolich*. Romance, rather than reading, is the *motif* of the poem. Philip, the young lover, has to go back to Oxford to read in earnest for his final school before he marries his Highland lass, Elspie, and emigrates to New Zealand. But the *mise-en-scène* is that of a number of undergraduates on a long vacation party in the Highlands, accompanied by

> *the Tutor, the grave man, nicknamed Adam,*
> *White-tied, clerical, silent, with antique square-cut waistcoat,*
> *Formal, unchanged, of black cloth, but with sense and feeling beneath it.*
> *Skilful in Ethics and Logic, in Pindar and Poets unrivalled;*
> Shady *in Latin, said Lindsay, but* topping *in Plays and Aldrich.*

A pre-Jowettian reading-party, therefore; in the middle of which there is a light-hearted revolt against any more pretence of work and Philip proclaims that he is

> *Weary of Ethic and Logic, of Rhetoric yet more weary,*
> *Eager to range over heather unfettered of ghillie and marquis,*
> *I will away with the rest, and bury my dismal classics.*

And when the Tutor asks

> *Where do you mean to go, and whom do you hope to visit?*

he is answered:

> *Kitcat, a Trinity Coach, has a party at Drumnadrochit;*
> *Mainwaring says they will lodge us, and feed us, and give us a lift too:*
> *Only they talk ere long to remove to Glenmorison. Then at*
> *Castleton, high in Braemar, strange home, with his earliest party,*
> *Harrison, fresh from the schools, has James and Jones and Lauder.*
> *Thirdly, a Cambridge man I know, Smith, a senior wrangler*
> *With a mathematical score hangs out at Inverary.*

So the Highlands, before Jowett went north for the first time with Morier, must have entertained very many parties of high-spirited and talkative young men from Cambridge as well as Oxford, under at least the nominal charge of a don, whether he was fresh from the schools or wore an antique square-cut waistcoat.

If it is impossible to credit Jowett with the invention of the reading party, it seems to be true that his parties had a peculiar quality, which is certainly not very evident in Clough's *Bothie*; and that this quality was produced by the fact that he was at their centre, following his own self-set task. Some illustration of what this meant will be given later on.[1]

I do not think it is possible to exaggerate the benefit which Jowett conferred upon Oxford at large, as well as upon Balliol, by the use to which he put this invention of the reading party. It would be obvious, even if he had not said so himself, that this use sprang from his two working holidays alone with Morier. Some spark was needed to complete it. My guess is that Jowett, looking to the future with a dismayed awareness of no more holidays alone with Morier, realized his perpetual need of youth about him. Next year he went back to Oban 'with a party of four'; and it was then that the famous series really began.

He did not, at this time, put his need of youthful society into words. He did so, many years later. About 1875 (perhaps a year or two earlier) he notes:

Beware of the coming on of age, for it will not be defied. A man cannot become young by over-exerting himself. A man of sixty should lead a quiet, open-air life. He should collect the young about him, though he will find probably in them an inclination to disregard his opinion, for he belongs to another generation. And 'old age and youth' etc. . . . .

Later still, about 1880, with 'the old undertones of thought ever vibrating in his mind' (Abbott's phrase) he tells himself:

I must make the best arrangements — get young men and boys around me in the next ten years — neither spend money, nor take pleasure except for the sake of health.

The governing aim was the desire to make the best possible use of his now flagging powers. The context suggests that the 'young men and boys' were to be the instruments of this purpose. But they had another function to perform, though he never openly declared it even to himself. They were not to be mere proselytes, mere engines of influence upon the changing world; they were to recruit his failing strength with their rising strength. He would charge them with his gospel of work; but they would recharge him with their young energies.

4. REFORMER

As one follows the upward curve, one becomes increasingly conscious of following the wake of a pioneer mind, steering its own course. Originality is a word mostly used of 'creative' artists and thinkers. Jowett did not possess this particular kind of originality; but he did possess, to an

[1] See below, esp. 328 *foll.* and 418–9.

unusual degree, the faculty of perceiving and exploring new directions. These directions are now so old and familiar (or so old and out of date) that it is difficult to realize how new they once were. The sense of Jowett's originality, powerful among his own pupils, died gradually away as his life prolonged itself through the twenty-two years of his Mastership into a new academical age, of which he was one of the principal begetters, but which naturally preferred to think it had begotten itself. And though the Oxford of Jowett's old age owed more to him than it ever acknowledged, it was already moving in a direction which he had always especially disliked — the direction of 'useless learning'. His part in the first and all-important stage of reform has consequently tended to be forgotten.

The movement for the reform of the two ancient English Universities is usually said to have begun in 1831, when Sir William Hamilton 'set forth in two remarkable articles in the *Edinburgh Review* the reasons why Oxford, "of all academical institutions at once the most imperfect and the most perfectible", accomplished in his judgment so little when it ought to accomplish so much.'[1]

Hamilton, at this date, was Professor of Civil History at Edinburgh and beginning to earn his reputation as a philosopher of the Scottish 'realist' school. He had gone to Balliol from Glasgow ten years before Jowett was born; and had direct knowledge of the place he was attacking. It is said that, at Oxford, 'the neglect of an eccentric tutor left him to manage his own studies.'[2] His two short visits to Germany in 1817 and 1820 impressed him with the superior learning of German Universities and led him to denounce the English collegiate system, in which he saw nothing good. 'In a series of slashing and inaccurate antitheses the whole system of College education was impeached.' Three years later in a second pair of articles he demanded that the Universities should be opened to non-conformists and rendered capable of providing a 'public education worthy of the name'.[3]

Hamilton's thrusts were delivered with extraordinary violence, along with ludicrous distortions of fact and preposterous accusations of deliberate dishonesty. It was simply not true that the colleges had encroached by design (as he alleged) upon the functions of either of the ancient Universities. As Sir Charles Mallet says:

Historically speaking College teaching only grew up, at first with very little system, because it was needed to supplement the teaching of the

---

[1] Mallet, *A History of the University of Oxford*, iii, 290.
[2] Leslie Stephen's article in the *D.N.B.*
[3] Mallet, *op. cit.*, iii, 291.

older Regents which was failing, and the teaching of the more modern Professors who never completely took the Regents' place.[1]

Again, if the Heads of Houses had sometimes, or even often, collectively shown themselves to be an incompetent governing body, that was no justification for Hamilton's intemperate and ridiculous charge that they had committed a breach of trust 'unparalleled in the annals of any other Christian institution'.

The *Edinburgh* articles had a powerful effect both outside and inside Oxford. They gave the first external impetus to the movement towards University reform, which came of age politically in 1850. But there was another, an internal and much more important, *primum mobile* in the minds of an increasing number of young Oxford men, among whom were Stanley and Jowett. Without an internal motion towards its own reform, it is questionable whether any institution can be profitably reformed from outside. It can be destroyed and something new can be built out of its ruins. But that is not 'reform'.

The collegiate system of Oxford and Cambridge, which Hamilton denounced as rotten, has triumphantly survived. It has become the envy of many other Universities in and outside England. Some have sought — not without success — to graft colleges upon their own central stems. But no artificial process can ever quite reproduce the virtue of a long natural growth which is rooted in a particular soil and habitat and has developed its own peculiar character through centuries of slow or violent change. The two ancient Universities of Oxford and Cambridge are collegiate Universities of a kind which does not exist and cannot be artificially reproduced elsewhere, even in England itself. A limitation of Hamilton's powerful, but literal, mind blinded him to the value of this uniquely English growth; to the idea of a University which was not a University apart from its halls and colleges.

Nevertheless the Oxford which Hamilton attacked seemed to be defenceless against his attack. 'If' says Mallet 'Hamilton enforced his argument with needless acerbity and some dubious history, it is at least clear that he knew more about the origin of Universities than many of those who engaged in the dispute.'[2]

The first wave of University reform waited for some twenty years after the first wave of electoral reform and after Hamilton's onslaughts. When it came, it fortunately did not follow his drastic Scottish-German pre-

[1] The 'Regents' were the Masters of Arts who presided over the formal 'disputations' in which, from mediaeval times up to the end of the eighteenth century, undergraduates had to take part, before they could obtain their degrees. The 'disputations' were replaced by 'examinations'.

[2] Mallet, *op. cit.*, iii, 292.

scription. The professoriate was enlarged and strengthened, the scope of undergraduate studies was widened, but the collegiate and tutorial system was wisely left alone; or, it would be truer to say, it was given a new opportunity to which it proved more than equal.

In his book *The Age of Reform 1815 to 1870* Sir Llewellyn Woodward summarizes the defects of the system as it stood up to 1854:

Oxford was governed by Laudian, Cambridge by Elizabethan, statutes. Internal reform was not easy. The Colleges were independent societies jealous of outside interference; the governing body in each university was composed mainly of heads of houses, elderly and safe men who did not wish for change, and the clerical vote was almost always in a majority in the general assemblies of masters of arts. The College tutors had little part in the direction of university affairs, and, although many of them were able men, they were burdened with large classes of an elementary kind. There was no inducement for them to stay in the university, since they could not hold their fellowships after marriage.[1] The relation between the Colleges and the university were unsatisfactory. The universities were poor; many of the Colleges were rich, and made little contribution to higher studies. The restriction of most fellowships and scholarships to founder's kin or to persons born in particular localities or educated at particular schools led to abuse, and filled the Colleges with idle and useless members.

These were real and serious defects; and there was the additional, and greater, defect of religious exclusiveness. Oxford and Cambridge were strictly preserved for those who were willing to subscribe to the Articles of the Church of England. This exclusiveness lasted until the abolition of religious tests in 1871. But there are two facts, often overlooked, which need to be emphasized, if the picture is to be fairly seen.

The first is that though the University of Oxford was, and is, 'a corporate body, known for centuries by the style or title of *The Chancellor Masters and Scholars of the University of Oxford*' its physical existence soon came to depend, ever more and more, upon its constituent parts, the lodgings or halls and colleges, which house and teach the undergraduates, furnish the University with its examiners and many of its officers, and provide its professors with their academic homes.

Its principal purpose is, and always has been, that of conferring Degrees as a token of proficiency in certain studies, and to that end of prescribing the studies and other conditions requisite to the attainment of each Degree, of examining candidates, and in certain cases of classifying them according to their merits. Further, out of its own endowments, from the dues levied from its members, from trusts devoted to the encouragement and reward of various branches of learning, and from contributions proceeding from the revenues of Colleges, the University provides for the appointment of professors and readers in different departments of know-

---

[1] This particular restriction was not generally relaxed until 1877.

ledge, and awards scholarships and prizes to its members as marks of academic distinction.[1]

The 'principal purpose' remains to-day what it always has been, though the scope of degrees and the character of instruction and examination altered almost past belief in the nineteenth and twentieth centuries. The 'further' purposes have also been enormously extended. The University of to-day is a very different 'body' from what it was in 1850. Its revenues are augmented by large grants of public money. (In Jowett's day the problem was how to deploy 'our wealth' to the best advantage.) Yet its constitution has not profoundly changed. The old 'Hebdomadal Board', composed of Heads of Houses, has become an elected 'Hebdomadal Council'. This Council is the ruling executive: the Cabinet, so to say, of the Vice-Chancellor, though its members are not his nominees. 'The Ancient House of Congregation', as a legislative body, was replaced in 1854 by a new body called 'The Congregation of the University of Oxford'; the effect of this change was to limit the right of voting upon legislative proposals to resident members of the University. This new body may be loosely described as the effective Parliament of the modern University. 'The House of Convocation', to which all Masters of Arts and holders of equivalent degrees belong, whether resident or non-resident (so long as they have 'kept their names on the books' of their respective colleges) is the body which 'in the last resort has supreme control over the action of the University'.[2] But it cannot originate or amend legislation; it can only endorse or reject it. As time goes by, it is becoming a functionless ghost of its once powerful self.

The reforms in the constitution of Oxford University, thus briefly recounted; the increase in the number of its specialized professors and readers and lecturers; the multiplication of faculties and the expansion of the schools; the erection of new University buildings; the growth of its administrative service; even the development of inter-university races and games;[3] all this, with much else, has by degrees seemed to magnify its corporate personality. Yet, even to-day, the Universities of Oxford and Cambridge exist in and by their colleges and halls, and would be nothing without them. It is hardly more of an exaggeration now, than it would have been in 1850, to say that in both places the University is an idea realized, like the Hegelian Absolute, in the behaviour of its phenomenal parts.

[1] *The Historical Register of the University of Oxford* (1900 edition), 9–10.
[2] *ibid.*
[3] The first cricket match against Cambridge was played in 1827; the first boat race was rowed in 1829; but there were no other fixtures until 1855 when the rackets series began. The full scale of contests developed much later.

The second fact to emphasize is that every college was, and is, a small society properly jealous for its independence and particular traditions. This jealousy can be stupid and hurtful; but even at its worst it is a symptom of vitality. Small societies are elements of value not only in the larger society of which they are the quick, immediate parts, but in the great society of the 'nation'. This is better understood to-day than it was in 1850, when there was a very real danger of reform ignorantly destroying the colleges by taking away from them the power to determine their own character and behaviour. Jowett, who saw the necessity for reform more clearly than most men, saw also that the gradual self-reform of small societies is better than change imposed upon them from outside or above.

Curiously enough, the first motion towards reform at Oxford was made by the rulers of the small societies, the Heads of Houses. It was a movement of panic stupidity. In 1839 the Hebdomadal Board invited Convocation 'to institute new Professorships and to require all undergraduates to attend Professorial lectures'. Convocation sensibly negatived this hurried and ill-considered attempt to appease the Hamiltonians. There was a lot to be said for strengthening and enlarging the professoriate. But there was much more to be said against compelling *all* undergraduates to attend professorial lectures and thereby weakening the responsibilities of the college tutors.

After the failure of this proposal an anonymous pamphlet appeared in Oxford, in the winter of 1839, entitled *Hints on the Formation of a Plan for the Safe and Effectual Revival of the Professorial System at Oxford*. This was the joint work of Tait and Stanley. Tait devised it in walks with Stanley at Bonn in the Long Vacation, where the Balliol tutor and his ex-pupil spent three weeks in 'the task of gaining such an insight into the working of a great German University as would give definite shape to the reforms which they hoped to advocate and promote at Oxford'.[1] This, said Stanley, was his only share in the pamphlet: 'except that Tait wrote it with me sitting in the room, hearing, criticizing, and perhaps correcting each sentence; of course in *some* passages my element preponderates.'

Tait was to be a member, and Stanley the secretary, of the Oxford University Commission set up by Parliament eleven years later, from which a whole century of incessant changes has stemmed. Their pamphlet bore almost no relation to the subsequent, actual course of reform. It is true that they advocated the development of the professoriate on the one hand, the maintenance of the tutorial system on the other. But they wished the tutors to be relieved 'from their present vain attempt to fulfil

[1] *Life of Dean Stanley*, i, 220.

the Professorial office in conjunction with their own'. This seems to have meant that they were to give up lecturing; for they would thus be enabled 'to devote much more time to the moral superintendence of their pupils, and the development of their minds by strictly Tutorial lectures, conducted, that is, by the aid of question and answer' — which is not lecturing at all, or even tutoring, but mere school-mastering. The writers assumed that 'of course in the nineteenth century . . . a liberal education necessarily means a religious one'.

The main idea of the pamphlet was 'a fourth year', intervening between the three years' course which ended in the public examination for the B.A. degree and the act of proceeding to that degree. At this time there was only one public examination, divided into two parts: an examination in Greek and Latin (*in Literis Humanioribus*) and an examination in Mathematics (*in Disciplinis Mathematicis et Physicis*). Nothing was proposed, by Tait and Stanley, to be added or changed in this. The new 'fourth year' was to be spent over some special study ending (but only for candidates who had obtained honours in the public examination) with the submission of a special thesis and the passing of a special examination to the satisfaction of the professor or professors, to whose department the subject of the thesis belonged.

The authors of the pamphlet insisted that none of these special subjects — physical science, law, history, theology — should be exclusively studied until the undergraduate had taken 'the present examination in Arts' (i.e. the public examination). They insisted, with particular emphasis, against honours being granted in special examinations

held contemporaneously with the present examination in Arts. The permitting of this, in the case of Physical Science, would make it assume the position of a groundwork in liberal education, for which it is totally unfitted, and it would open the doors for a similar intrusion of *tripos* upon *tripos* in every conceivable department of human knowledge. Such a scheme, fully carried out, must end in the ruin of English education.

Even the institution of new academical honours in these fourth-year subjects was opposed as 'certain to increase among undergraduates an excitement already too great for health and for the calm pursuit of academic studies'.

For the next few years Oxford was filled with the sound and fury of religious controversy. The idea of reform faded temporarily into the background. In the spring of 1845, some six or seven months before Newman's secession to Rome put an end to the 'ecclesiastical ferment', it came to the front again, when a dissenting Member of Parliament (W. D. Christie) pressed for a Royal Commission of Inquiry. Christie was soon in some sort of correspondence with Jowett and Stanley; no doubt he had them in his mind when he said in the following year, during a debate in the House of Commons on the 'education of the people', that he believed 'some of the most eminent and distinguished men in the University would rejoice if such a Commission were issued'.[1]

Early in 1846 Jowett provided Christie with 'an elaborate draft of questions that might be submitted by such a Parliamentary Committee to Heads of Houses and other persons in Oxford'. This document does not seem to have survived. But in November 1847 he wrote a long letter to Roundell Palmer (later to be Lord Chancellor and the first Earl of Selborne) urging him to take up the matter of Oxford University reform and to bring it before the Ministry 'under the idea that you are half an M.P. for the University of Oxford'. This letter is printed in the *Life and Letters*.[2] It sets out Jowett's considered views about University reform, at this date. Also, it shows how he was already trying to get the right man to say or do the right thing in the right place at the right moment — a method of action not to be mis-described as 'wire-pulling'.

'My answer' wrote Lord Selborne fifty years later 'declining to undertake the question as suggested, was mainly grounded upon the impediment arising out of the oaths which I had taken on my election to a Fellowship at Magdalen.' These oaths explicitly bound the President and fellows 'not to seek for or to accept any change in the Founder's Statutes'. Different men had different opinions about the right way of interpreting an anachronistic obligation. Selborne, towards the end of his life, thought that he had felt himself precluded by his oath from voluntary action on his own part to obtain from the Legislature alterations in the statutes of his own college.[3] But what he said to Jowett at the time was quite different. Jowett reported to Lingen:

He does not consider the oath binding himself, but as the terms of it are very explicit he dislikes the scandal it would make. This I mention in confidence. He is quite willing however to present a petition for open Fellowships and Professorships, and to speak in its favour. He is not sanguine at present.

Jowett's letter to Palmer is too long to reproduce fully. He began by speaking for 'Clough, Lake, Lingen, Temple, Stanley, T. Arnold, and others whom you probably do not know'. All of these 'seemed to think, and I heartily agree, that, for many reasons, the subject would be far

---

[1] *L. & L.*, i, 173. Campbell's chapter on University and Civil Service Reform, with the appended letters (172–94), is the *locus classicus* for Jowett's part in this first stage of Oxford reform. A masterly over-all account is given by Sir Charles Mallet in the third volume of his *History of the University of Oxford*, Chapter XXV, 280–353.
[2] *L. & L.*, i, 188–92.
[3] H. A. Wilson, *Magdalen College*, 252.

better in your hands than in those of Gladstone'. The letter continued, after further explaining its occasion:

Perhaps I am assuming too much in supposing that you would favour any movement to assist the Universities from without. Let me ask what chance there is of reform from within. . . . It is nobody's fault — we cannot reform ourselves. To say nothing of the stationary nature of the place — the close Fellows are interested in keeping up close Fellowships. . . . These things are so invidious, that although they are strictly true I am almost ashamed to state them. . . .

There is nothing I less wish than to see Oxford turned into a German or a London University. On the other hand, is it at all probable that we shall be allowed to remain as we are for twenty years longer, the one solitary, exclusive, unnational Corporation — our enormous wealth without any manifest utilitarian purpose; a place, the studies of which belong to the past, and unfortunately seem to have no power of incorporating new branches of knowledge; so exclusive, that it is scarcely capable of opening to the wants of the Church itself? . . .

I do not wish to make a paper constitution for the University. If Parliament interferes, should not the effort be to limit the interference to one or two great and simple points, such as the opening of the Fellowships and providing . . . for their being honestly given away? Second, the establishment of Professorships which might be formed out of extinguished Fellowships (which would, perhaps, if they were thrown open be too numerous) and might be attached as a sort of compensation to the Colleges from which the Fellowships are taken. To which, third, I would add a pet crotchet of my own, to raise the value of the Scholarships . . . from the same source,— to provide the means for many more persons of the middling class to find their way through the University into professions.

I think at present the close Fellowships work very badly, especially in holding out the prospect of a provision for life, which provision is generally not obtained until a man is twenty-seven or twenty-eight, when it would be better for him to leave the University altogether and settle in a parish: to say nothing of the evil of superannuating in Oxford so many men who are not fitted by nature for a student's life.

As to the Professorships there is not at present a single well-endowed one for any of those subjects which form the staple of the University course, except Theology. There is no inducement for any College Tutor to carry on his reading of Aristotle beyond the routine of his lectures, as far as prospects of this sort are concerned. . . . The great evil at Oxford is the narrowness and isolation of one study from another, and of one part of a study from the other. We are so far below the level of the German Ocean that I fear one day we shall be utterly deluged.

Except that 'interference' went further than Jowett desired, all the ideas put forward in this letter were to be implemented much sooner than either its writer or its recipient could foresee. Jowett had no monopoly in them, and claimed none, except for his 'pet crotchet' of increasing the value of scholarships. But nobody else could phrase them so convincingly, with such a shrewd perception of what could be done and what could not be done, of the difference between reform and revolution. His evidence before the Royal Commission of 1850 is described by his biographer as 'not that of a violent reformer'; it was the more valuable and effective for that reason.

The letter to Palmer does not touch at all upon one particular restriction, which was practically abolished by the coming Commissioners — the obligation upon college fellows (other than those practising in the law courts) to take Anglican Orders. Indeed it seems to assume that the obligation would continue. This was not because Jowett approved it — on the contrary, in his evidence before the Royal Commission he argued strongly for its removal. But in 1847 the appointment of a Commission was not in sight, and the idea of lay fellows was too dangerously controversial to be introduced into a letter designed to capture influential support.

It is not altogether easy, now, to understand the readiness of the Commissioners to remove the inducements which enabled the Church to maintain a steady flow of educated men into the priesthood and, when they married and vacated their fellowships, into the pastorate. All the Commissioners were members of the Church of England, and all but one (Dampier) were clergymen. But they were 'liberals' and wonderful optimists. Stanley himself, the principal secretary to the Commission, preaching in the University Church some years later (in 1872, after the final removal of all religious tests) exulted over

the glorious prospect now for the first time revealed to Oxford of becoming not the battlefield of contending religious factions, but the neutral, the sacred ground, where the healing genius of the place and the equal intercourse of blameless and generous youth shall unite the long estrangements of Judah and of Ephraim, of Jerusalem and Samaria.

This was a rhetorical version of the idea which made the reformers believe that religion is strengthened by weakening its institutional supports. The enemies of the Church of England saw no reason to discourage this view: among them Goldwin Smith, Stanley's brilliant and anti-clerical co-secretary.

The Royal Commission came suddenly, almost out of the blue, putting an end to a book which Jowett and Stanley were writing together on University reform. In April 1850 a radical back-bencher — Mr. Heywood — moved for the issue of a Royal Commission to inquire into the state of the Universities. The resolution was strongly opposed by Gladstone and by Roundell Palmer (who had already told Jowett that he favoured reform). To the general surprise Lord John Russell, the Prime Minister, though he refused to accept Mr. Heywood's motion, decided to do exactly what Mr. Heywood asked. The Commission was set up at the end of August, and began work in October. Its report was published in May 1852. By this time Russell had resigned. Lord Derby was in office, at the head of a weak and short-lived tory administration. This was succeeded in December 1852 by Lord Aberdeen's uneasy coalition, which lasted for only two years.

The Commissioners' report could scarcely have been published at a less favourable moment. It looked like falling to the bottom of the political sea and staying there for a decade or a generation. Perhaps some delay would not have been a bad thing; it would at least have given the Universities and colleges time to go as far as they would or could (and they were now moving at an accelerated if uncertain pace) in the direction of self-reform. But something quite unpredictable happened. Gladstone, who was one of the two Oxford University Burgesses and also Chancellor of the Exchequer in Aberdeen's government, changed his mind. He had once passionately held and said 'that the Universities should not be vexed by the interposition of Parliament'.[1] In 1850 his speech denouncing the proposal to set up the Royal Commission, though it failed to achieve its object, seemed even to Stanley (who heard it) 'very powerful; he said, in the most effective manner, anything which could be said against the Commission.'

John Morley's comment on that speech is also worth isolating:

In truth no worse case was ever more strongly argued, and fortunately the speech is to be recorded as the last manifestation, on a high theme and on a broad scale, of that toryism from which this wonderful pilgrim had started on his shining progress.[2]

Gladstone was converted by reading the Commissioners' report, 'one of the ablest productions submitted in his recollection to Parliament'. At first, according to Morley, 'he did not cease urging his friends at Oxford to make use of this golden opportunity for reforming the University from within, and warning them that delay would be dearly purchased.' If Morley is right, the decision to introduce the Bill was a politically motived decision taken by Aberdeen's Cabinet. 'The originators of the Commission were no longer in office, but things had gone too far for the successors to burke what had been done.'[3]

It may possibly have been so; perhaps Gladstone, as Morley suggests, was put in charge of an inevitable Bill, merely because he was member for Oxford. It does not seem likely that it happened quite in that way,

---

[1] In 1835, when he was twenty-six. Mallet, iii, 299.
[2] *Life of Gladstone*, i, 498.
[3] Morley's account of what happened is perfunctory, poorly documented, and, so far as Jowett's conflict with Gladstone is concerned, both prejudiced and inaccurate.

with Gladstone newly at the Exchequer and the international sky rapidly darkening towards the Crimean war. It seems much more probable that Gladstone himself persuaded the Cabinet to allow him to introduce the Bill. Certainly, in the autumn of 1853, he was utterly self-committed. By the middle of December 'he forwarded to Lord John Russell what he called a rude draft, but the rude draft contained the kernel of the plan that was ultimately carried.' His whole heart, he wrote in the following March, was in the Oxford Bill: 'it is my consolation under the pain with which I view the character my office is assuming under the circumstances of war.' His correspondence over the Bill was gigantic. He was in communication with everybody, answering always 'by return of post fully and at length, quite entering into their case, and showing the greatest acquaintance with it'. No other politician was capable of the passionate enthusiasm, the amazing combination of energy and patience and Parliamentary skill needed for the realization of this now over-riding aim. Sir Charles Mallet's succinct account cannot be bettered.

The passage of the Bill was not easy. It was greatly altered if not maimed in Committee. Wisdom, firmness, temper, labour, wrote Jeune afterwards, had been needed to carry it through, and great courage in a University Member whose seat and popularity were at stake. Mr. Gladstone thought the discussions in Parliament often ill-advised. He had to face criticisms that seemed sometimes impatient and unreasonable from thorough-going reformers like Dr. Liddell. He was not impressed on the one hand by Mr. Disraeli's preference for an Oxford left free with all its anomalies and imperfections. He had more sympathy with the Nonconformist claim for admission. But he felt bound not to include that proposal in the Bill. The House of Commons, however, took this matter into its own hands. A clause removing the test at matriculation was carried against the Government by a large majority. Mr. Gladstone found it necessary to meet this feeling, and a compromise was agreed on which abolished tests for matriculation and for the Bachelor's degree. The tests for the Mastership,[1] for a vote in Convocation, and for Fellowships of Colleges survived. All 'governing and teaching functions' at Oxford the Church of England retained — for a few years more. To Dr. Pusey, one of the most urgent and dejected of Mr. Gladstone's correspondents, even this guarded surrender seemed profoundly sad. But Convocation appeared to be divided on the subject. Lord Derby was half-hearted. Not a single Bishop was prepared to fight. 'Everyone seems to be for giving up something,' wrote Pusey to Keble. How different from the great days of 1834![2]

Not the least of Gladstone's correspondents was Jowett, who disagreed profoundly with the Chancellor on a matter of vital importance. The nature of the disagreement is thus strangely described by John Morley:

[1] That is to say for the degree of Master of Arts.
[2] Mallet, iii, 324–5.

The scheme was in essentials Mr. Gladstone's own. Jowett at the earliest stage sent him a comprehensive plan, and soon after, saw Lord John (Jan. 6). 'I must own,' writes the latter to Gladstone, 'I was much struck by the clearness and completeness of his views.' The difference between Jowett's plan and Mr. Gladstone's was on the highly important point of machinery. Jowett who all his life had a weakness for getting and keeping authority into his own hands, or the hands of those whom he could influence, contended that after Parliament had settled principles, Oxford itself could be trusted to settle details far better than a little body of great personages from outside, unacquainted with special wants and special interests. Mr. Gladstone, on the other hand, invented the idea of an executive commission with statutory powers. The two plans were printed and circulated, and the balance of opinion in the cabinet went decisively for Mr. Gladstone's scheme. The discussion between him and Jowett, ranging over the whole field of the Bill, was maintained until its actual publication, in many interviews and much correspondence.[1]

Morley's account of this conflict is at once ill-natured and ignorant. The best that can possibly be said for it is that it was written some years after Jowett's death[2] and exemplifies the way in which the legendary foibles of Jowett's old age were extended backwards in the minds of his juniors and made to colour retrospectively 'the whole of his life'. When Jowett produced the plan which the Cabinet turned down for Gladstone's, he was only thirty-six and a mere college tutor. True, he was beginning to count for something both inside and outside Oxford, but only by virtue of his ability and courage. It was a remarkable achievement to make such an impression with his plan that it reached the Cabinet table; though it is not surprising that Gladstone carried the day with his own colleagues.

Nothing whatever is known about this plan of Jowett's,[3] except what Morley tells us. It was evidently based upon Jowett's principle of self-reform, whereas Gladstone's was based upon the idea of compulsory reform through his ingenious device of an Executive Commission with powers to make new statutes for colleges who failed to re-model their old statutes to the satisfaction of the Executive Commissioners. It may be guessed that this single concession to self-reform was a modification urged on Gladstone by Jowett, after his own plan had been rejected.

Gladstone's invention was used again in the two later reforming Acts of 1876 and 1923. Most people would say that it has worked, on the whole, very well. A few, perhaps, may think that Jowett was plainly right and Gladstone plainly wrong upon a matter of much greater importance than a mere point of 'machinery'. It was at about this time that

---

[1] Morley, *Life of Gladstone*, i, 501.
[2] Morley began his *Life of Gladstone* in 1897 and finished it in 1903.
[3] It is not even mentioned in the *Life and Letters*. Does it still exist, in some forgotten pigeon-hole?

Jowett first expressed the shrewd distrust of Gladstone which he never discarded, though it was Gladstone who (as will be related) opened the way for him to the Mastership of Balliol. In a lively letter which he wrote to Mrs. Greenhill on New Year's Day 1853 he committed himself to a forecast of Gladstone's future:

He will go through one more 'conscientious' betrayal of his friends, one more 'conscientious' resignation of office. What a pity it is that the most religious and in many ways high-principled man in the House of Commons should have got himself with all mankind the character of being the least straightforward!

If the Act of 1854 fell a little short of the Royal Commission's report it came as near to a planned revolution as 'reform' could go. It did not remake Oxford to a foreign pattern; but, as Professor Feiling rightly says, for the future of higher education its provisions were revolutionary.[1]

The notion is to be found, here and there, and often where one would least expect to find it, that the reforms made by and under the Act were timid.[2] That was not the view taken by those who saw in them an executioner's warrant for the death of the society they knew and loved. Nor is it a view which, at least in the present writer's judgment, passes the test of historical knowledge.

5. JOWETT IN ALL SOULS

When the Executive Commissioners sent to All Souls their draft of the Ordinance they proposed to make for that college, one of the fellows, Frederick Lygon (afterwards Earl Beauchamp and a founder of Keble College), wrote neatly on his copy of the draft Ordinance his name and the date (7th March 1857[3]) with the lines

occidit, occidit
spes omnis et fortuna nostri
nominis

The quotation was more than the neat use of a Horatian tag; it expressed a bitter sense of irremediable defeat. Yet Lygon belonged to the coming, not to the departing, generation. He was thirteen years younger than Jowett. The college of which he was a member — All Souls before

[1] Feiling, *A History of England*, 905.
[2] See, for example, Montague Burrows, *Worthies of All Souls*.
[3] The date of the college meeting at which the draft was considered. The lines are from Horace, Book IV, Ode IV.

reform — was, like Balliol, a predominantly youthful body. But its internal composition and character had been changing rapidly. At one time Christ Church had been its chief recruiting ground; Balliol a very rare contributor. In 1844 this familiar pattern began to alter. Between that year and 1857 the intake from Balliol was nearly double the intake from Christ Church. By 1857 the Christ Church contingent had shrunk to fifteen, of whom six were over forty; the Balliol contingent had risen to fourteen, all of them under forty; the average age of the two groups was respectively about forty-one and twenty-eight.

This remarkable change in All Souls was connected with the emergence of Jowett as the driving force in Balliol, which led to the 'colonization' of other colleges by Balliol men, mostly his own former pupils. How far this was deliberate policy on Jowett's part there is no means of knowing. At the beginning of 1854, when he was arguing with Gladstone, it had not gone quite so far in All Souls as in 1857; there were then only nine fellows from Balliol to nineteen from Christ Church. But this was already something like an invasion in force. Jowett must have known very well that the balance of power inside All Souls — one of the three 'stationary' colleges (Merton, All Souls and Christ Church) which he had described in his letter to Roundell Palmer as obstinately resistant to change — was now fast changing in accordance with his own ideas. In the November of 1854 all four of the fellowships offered by All Souls were secured by entrants from Balliol.

Among the Balliol candidates elected in this and the preceding year were three 'all out' reformists. They were Arthur Watson (Harrow schoolmaster), William Fremantle (later to become the radical Dean of Ripon), and Godfrey Lushington (barrister, civil servant, and finally permanent head of the Home Office). This determined trio appealed to the Visitor of All Souls, the Archbishop of Canterbury, in order to enforce their idea of the way in which the examination and election of candidates should be conducted. The war began in 1857 and continued for seven years, ending with an apparently complete victory for the rebels. In the course of it Archbishop Sumner, as Visitor, was compelled, through an action of *mandamus* in the Queen's Bench, sensationally reported as *The Queen v. the Archbishop of Canterbury*, to re-hear the appeal which he had already decided in favour of the Warden and fellows and to decide it in the opposite sense. That happened in 1861.[1]

It can be imagined that these proceedings were very fully reported and were made the occasion for much scandalous publicity. A leading article in a contemporary newspaper, commenting upon the action in the Queen's

[1] See above, 106; also below, 249 and 271.

Bench, affected 'some degree of commiseration towards these high-bred gentlemen, the Warden and Fellows — some of them in holy orders — for the painful position in which they have placed themselves'. There can be no doubt that the appellants deliberately desired the public scandal and used it in addition to the processes of law, in order to fasten upon their college an examination of the narrowest kind, conducted with unintelligent rigidity. They wished, for example, on the one hand entirely to exclude any attempt whatever to gauge the general ability of the candidates; on the other to exclude any test of their classical attainments. In this effort they were not finally successful; though they succeeded for a time in imposing upon the examiners a method of numerical marking which should arithmetically determine the 'order of merit' — a method wholly repugnant to the Oxford mind and long since abandoned. Nor did they succeed in extinguishing the right (and the duty) of the electing fellows to vote for the candidate whom each honestly considered to be the best man.

In effect, therefore, they failed. But they succeeded in exhibiting reformist zeal in its narrowest and most unpleasing form; in destroying for ever the personal character of the relationship between the Visitor and the college; and in holding their college up to public odium, inside and outside Oxford. The success that they achieved — by temporarily limiting the scope and character of the examination to the raw requirements of the newly constituted school of Law and (English) History — was not worthy of the determination they displayed and did not justify the harm they did.

Would Jowett have himself behaved similarly in like circumstances? Would he have wished his young men to behave so, if he had fully understood what they were doing? Campbell, who gives a very brief and shockingly inaccurate account of the affair,[1] says that he was 'keenly interested in this contest, and greatly pleased with the result, which was obtained in 1861'. If this is true — as perhaps it may be — it is a measure of the weakness into which (as we shall see) he allowed himself to fall for a while, after the collapse of his ambition to become Master of Balliol in 1854 and during the years of frustration which followed.

[1] *L. & L.*, i, 271–2. Campbell says that the three appellants 'had been elected Fellows of All Souls under the reformed Statute' but that 'in a year or two an attempt was made to revert to the former system, in which birth and breeding were preferred to learning and ability.' In fact all three were elected under the old statutes; and there was no attempt whatever to 'revert' from a new to an old system.

CHAPTER X

'Hereticus'

1. THE MASTERSHIP MISSED

On 6th March 1854 the Old Master died. His death was one of several events which marked that year in Oxford as a turning point between past and future. There was the death in December in his hundredth year of Dr. Routh, for sixty-three years President of Magdalen and in command of all his faculties to the very end — the last man in Oxford, perhaps in all England, who still wore a formal wig. There was the passage into law of the University reform bill; the setting up of the Executive Commission and its arrival in Oxford. In the month when Dr. Jenkyns died the Crimean war began: of which G. V. Cox, in his diaristic *Recollections of Oxford*, said that its effect was very soon felt by the University

first in the reduced number of Matriculations, and soon after in the departure of many of its actual members for the seat of war. When it is considered that for nearly forty years there had been no field of the kind opened to our English youths, it was no wonder that the excitement and clang of war should be responded to by young men of spirit and enterprise. And so they went, full of health and ardour and cheerful hopes, to waste that strength, exhaust that ardour, and quench those hopes in the protracted miseries of a siege, and to die (as many of them did) in the trenches of Sebastopol.

The coming of the war did not prevent the fellows of Balliol from throwing themselves into the choice of their new Master with the partisanship peculiar to such occasions.

At first Jowett did not think — or did not allow himself to think — that the succession could fall to him. Soon after the Old Master's death he wrote to James Lonsdale, into whose shoes he had stepped as a tutor: 'Perhaps you may be our new Master; who knows? It would be a great happiness to me if you were'[1]. But this modest mood of self-effacement was very short lived. A group of the electors — that is to say of the fellows, some of whom had been his own pupils — put Jowett forward as their candidate.

There were eleven electors, including Jowett himself. The election

---

[1] Quoted by Campbell (*L. & L.*, i, 228) from the *Life of James Lonsdale*.

was made on the first Tuesday in April; only a month passed between the death of the old and the choice of the new Master. The campaign was fought in a very short space of time — not more than two or three weeks. The account of it given by Campbell in the *Life and Letters* is discreetly general and brief.

> It was largely recognized that no College Tutor had worked so well. And it became apparent that, of the residents, he had the strongest chance. This is proved by the fact that his opponents adopted the expedient of bringing up a candidate from the country. Robert Scott . . . was ortho- dox; and the opposition to Jowett, of which the strength was proved by the event, found in him the most likely card to play. Not that the objec- tions taken to Jowett were wholly theological. There were those who resented the firmness of his attitude in College controversies, and did not choose to place him in authority. The parties were nearly balanced, and all depended on one or two waverers, who on general grounds were thought likely to be on Jowett's side. It is not necessary to mention names; but two votes, on which Jowett had counted, went the other way.

Contemporary gossip, as recalled by Tuckwell, gave a somewhat different version:

> The senior Fellows wished for Temple, an equal number of the juniors wished for Jowett rather than for Temple. So at the last moment Temple's supporters threw him over for Scott, securing Riddell's vote.[1]

A third account, evidently apologetic, was given by Dean Lake in a letter to *The Times* soon after Jowett's death. Lake agreed that the elec- tion of Scott depended on a single, transferred, vote. He denied that Jowett's opponents were influenced by his unorthodox opinions 'then very little known'. They thought of him only as a man who created 'friction'. Before the election 'there was very little discussion'.[2]

The reader will make his own choice between, or amalgamation of, these three versions. For Scott himself the consequences were unhappy. Writing at the end of the century Tuckwell dismissed his Mastership with a shrug.

> For elderly men of to-day, the term 'Master of Balliol' conjures up two visions. They think of Jenkyns in the Thirties and Forties, of Jowett in the Seventies and Eighties; they do *not* think of Scott, who came between. Overlaid, enveloped, eclipsed by the two luminaries who 'went behind him and before', he somehow drops out of sight; his reign is an interven- tion, and is remembered only with an effort. . . . For ten years he was a mere obstructive, wielding his numerical ascendancy to crush all Jowett's

---

[1] *Reminiscences of Oxford*, 203. Temple at this time was Principal of Kneller Hall at Twickenham, a training college for workhouse schoolmasters. He had resigned his fellowship in 1848. Riddell was six years younger than Jowett; he died in 1866.

[2] Lake's letter can be read in the *Memorials of W. C. Lake* (Arnold, 1921).

schemes of reform. 'Your Head', said Jowett to a Fellow of another College, 'seems to be an astute person, who works by winning confidence; here we have a bare struggle for power'; and when, in 1865, successive elections to Fellowships had given Jowett a majority, Scott became a cypher in the College. Nor was he influential beyond the walls of Balliol.

A man is not to be condemned because he stands for a high office in opposition to a friend, even if the event proves him unfit to hold it. But it is not possible to excuse Scott's subsequent behaviour. For some years before his unexpected recall to Balliol he had been half-buried, first in a Cornish and then in a Rutlandshire living. Jowett, grateful to him for teaching, had gone out of his way to keep in touch with his former tutor.

He goes to visit Scott in his country parish, and does duty for him when he is 'blind and solitary', relinquishing pleasant plans for this purpose; he stays with him again under altered circumstances, rejoicing in his new prospects, and the children insist on his coming out to walk with them.[1]

And Scott, brought back to Balliol to keep Jowett out of the Mastership, repays this solicitude by jealous hostility.

Upon Jowett the defeat worked no less hardly, and brought out the worst that was in him. 'If I could begin life again it should not be in a College' — so he wrote to Stanley a few months later. Campbell's account of the way he took his disappointment is so self-contradictory that one must suspect it of having been moulded under some external pressure. Overtly it represents Jowett's behaviour in the most favourable light. 'Severely as he felt the blow, it produced on him a very different effect from that which a similar rejection had on Mark Pattison. Instead of paralysing his energies, it roused him to renewed efforts.' But that this was only half — if so much — of the truth, is clear from several less guarded passages.

In the opening of the chapter which goes on to describe 'the Mastership missed' it is significantly said that 'hitherto Jowett's relations to those about him had been almost uniformly friendly. Some may have thought him opinionated, but there is no trace of any actual discord.'[2] This is followed by a description of his particular efforts on behalf of particular friends. Three of these were friends for life — Stanley, Temple, Lingen. But the first names on the list are those of Scott, and of Lake and Wall, two of the senior fellows who opposed his candidature. Davis, in his history of Balliol, no doubt drawing upon the recollections of his older colleagues, confirms that

there was a breach in the friendly relations of the two parties, which only extreme forbearance and self-control upon both sides prevented from damaging the efficiency of the College. At one time a wave of reaction was

feared. The majority passed a decree for compelling the Scholars to subscribe to the doctrines of the Church of England; it was whispered that
Jowett would be driven out of his tutorship.[1]

That happened in the autumn of 1854; luckily, as Campbell says, 'this
attempt to violate the spirit of the new Statute[2] was vetoed by the Visitor,
to Jowett's great relief.'

Davis goes on to give credit to the new Master and his allies for 'the
real generosity and breadth of mind which lay underneath the crust of
fixed opinions'. If this is more than a daub of charitable whitewash, it
makes the resentment, which had taken temporary possession of Jowett's
serene mind, appear all the more unworthy of him. 'The contention was
acute and undisguised.' So Campbell, quoting the bitter remark about 'a
bare struggle of power' in Balliol, which Tuckwell reproduced. But,
Campbell continues, except in college meetings it was very rarely that
'any resentful word escaped him' although 'he knew that he was himself
the subject of perpetual obloquy'.

A picture rather different from those drawn by Campbell and Davis
and Tuckwell is presented by W. L. Newman in the reminiscences which
Campbell incorporated in his volume:[3]

When the disappointment about the Mastership came, some slight
indications of vexation were traceable in his conversation even with an
undergraduate like me, but his work with his pupils continued precisely
as before. It was not, I think, till some time later that he ceased to dine in
Hall and to appear after dinner in Common Room. The exact date at
which this happened I am unable to recollect. I was absent from Oxford
owing to illness from December 1855, to October 1857, and I think that
this change in his ways may have commenced during my absence. I doubt
whether he dined much in Hall after my return to Oxford. We lost much
by his absence, but even without him the Balliol Common Room remained
a notable gathering ... Jowett's withdrawal did not make his relations
with the rest of our body otherwise than amicable. Some of the Fellows
had been his pupils and felt towards him as pupils would. Achilles preferred his tent, but his tent was a hospitable one. .... Our friendship for
him did not interfere in any degree with friendly relations with the rest of
our seniors among the Fellows. On some topics our opinions were not
theirs, but we found them, and the new Head of the College, so genial
and kindly, and some of them so useful as models and advisers, that we
worked together with real pleasure and in complete harmony. The College
prospered well, and Jowett's influence on it grew as one of his pupils after
another was added to the body of Fellows.

What is one to make of Newman's strange suggestion that, in spite of
Jowett's withdrawal from the common life of the college, all was peace
and harmony within and without? Why, if this were so, did he instinc-

---

[1] Davis, *Balliol*, 214. [2] Not actually in force before 1857.
[3] *L. & L.*, i, 257. Newman was a fellow of Balliol from 1854 to his death in
1923, and one of Jowett's strongest supporters when support was most needed

tively use the simile of Achilles in his tent? And why did he then blunt it by substituting 'preferred his tent' to 'sulked in his tent'? How are his rose-coloured recollections to be reconciled with the 'bare struggle for power'? Perhaps, on his return to Oxford after two years of illness, he was living in a convalescent's dream, which veiled disagreeable facts. Or perhaps, as senior fellow of Balliol in 1894, he felt it his diplomatic duty to gloss over the painful division by which his college had been torn in two forty years earlier.

And what lay behind this deliberate withdrawal of Jowett from hall and common room? We should know nothing at all about it, if it were not for Newman and for two or three casual, incidental allusions by Campbell. The first of these allusions connects the withdrawal with the famous occasion when Jowett was required by the Vice-Chancellor to 'sign the Articles'. That happened in December 1855.[1] 'It was shortly after this that he ceased from dining in Hall and attending Common Room.'

A second allusion occurs a few pages later, when Campbell is setting the scene of a dinner given in Balliol hall, in October 1857, to celebrate the opening of the new chapel.[2] Jowett and a minority of the fellows had been strongly opposed to the demolition of the old chapel and to the erection of the new chapel, designed by Butterfield, as a memorial (singularly inappropriate) to Dr. Jenkyns. He could not decently refrain from taking part in the celebrations, and he attended the dinner. Tait, now Bishop of London, had consecrated the new chapel and made a speech at the dinner. In the course of his speech he went out of his way to say of Jowett: 'I was his Tutor in the old days; he was much more worthy to teach me.' Jowett was forced, after a reluctant pause, to rise 'from where he sat'. He said with deep emotion: 'Any one who labours among the young men will reap his reward in an affection far beyond his deserts.' The incident had the quality of unpremeditated drama; for Jowett was not sitting at the high table. 'He sat amongst the undergraduates, about halfway down the room, on the left side of the long central table.'

Campbell has nothing to say about this strange act of self-isolation; he offers no intelligible explanation or defence of it. The withdrawal must have continued for two years at least; Newman's reminiscences suggest that it hardened into a habit continued for many more years. The nearest that Campbell comes to an explanation is to connect it with an event which occurred outside Balliol. The attacks upon Jowett's orthodoxy, which led to the celebrated scene in the Vice-Chancellor's study, were not fomented by his Balliol colleagues. Suspicion of his orthodoxy had

---

[1] See below, 225–6.　　　　　　　　[2] L. & L., i, 247.

probably been the decisive reason for his failure to be elected Master. It is just conceivable that confirmation, in the wider University field, of the reasons which had prevailed with a bare majority of the Balliol electors, delivered a *coup de grâce* and reduced Jowett to so great a depression of spirit that he wished to live alone. But this hardly seems an adequate explanation; and it is certainly not the kind of explanation which a biographer should commit to a short sentence merely stating that the withdrawal from intimacy with his colleagues followed a ridiculous occurrence for which they could not be blamed. There must surely have been some (or more than one) unrecorded particular Balliol event which acted like a catalyzing agent upon the mixture of trouble in Jowett's mind and precipitated this unnatural, uncharacteristic and wrongful decision to live apart.

It is exasperating that, at this one serious point of obviously censurable failure in Jowett's conduct, evidence should vanish and have to be replaced by questions and guesses. Whatever the reason or reasons for his behaviour may have been, the behaviour itself is a regrettable fact which cannot be slurred or ignored. Was it the result of a decision made in pique, and confirmed by habit? Or was the decision made and continued by policy? Or was it made in pique, or in a mood of despair, and continued by policy?

I do not believe that Jowett's isolation owed more to policy than to pique. Isolationism is always wrong. Nobody knew that better than he did. By 'absenting himself from Hall and Common Room' he fell below the standard of behaviour which he preached to others, and himself otherwise always practised. I prefer to think that he succumbed to a weakness in his temperament than that he made a calculated attempt to undermine Scott's position, intended to achieve the sour success of ruling Balliol without becoming Master, and of reducing the Master to a 'cypher'.

It is true that this was what gradually happened, and finally resulted after ten years. But surely it happened in spite of Jowett's self-isolation rather than in consequence of it. If there had been any reasoned opposition to his election as Master in 1870, its most telling argument would have been that he had not played the game after he had missed the Mastership in 1854. And, of course, Jowett could not possibly foresee that he would ever be given a second chance. So far as he could know, in 1854, Scott would be Master of Balliol during all the time that mattered. If, then, he was deliberately playing for power, he was playing for the kind of long-continued concealed power which corrupts those who wield it far more subtly and dangerously than any open or absolute form of power. Other men, in Oxford and elsewhere, have occasionally followed this contemptible ambition. I cannot bring myself to put Jowett among them.

True to his own rule of reticence about himself, he gave no handle to those who would praise or condemn him. His published letters contain only two brief allusions to his defeat, both written very soon after it had happened. He wrote to Palgrave on 7th April:

You and a few others, if you will excuse my saying so, have a ridiculous opinion of what I am and can do, but though I am aware of this, I must always feel deeply grateful for the affection you show. . . . The event of Tuesday, about which you speak so kindly, is a little hard upon me. . . . But while I can keep the regard of my pupils, I shall stay on and do the utmost I can, though I cannot but feel sadly at having lost a position that in this world seemed all I could desire.[1]

On 12th April, in a letter to Stanley, he dismissed the topic abruptly: 'I will not trouble you any more with the hateful subject of the Balliol election.'

Campbell says that long afterwards he wrote 'to a friend who had experienced a similar disappointment. The language then used appeared exaggerated, but revealed what had passed in his own mind many years before.' Campbell also tells us that later in his life — evidently after he had become Master — he said to another friend, 'I should not have been fit for the Mastership then. I did not know enough of the world.'

Perhaps it was good for him to be reminded, after a long run of un-interrupted success, that perpetual success is nobody's birthright; good for the teacher of young men to be himself taught that success is often denied to men for unfair reasons; good for the self-confident young philosopher and divine to discover the intolerant nature of the world to which he was about to deliver his opinions. This was the external world of which he did not yet know enough. But there was an internal world — a world inside himself — which he had not yet learned to master and in which he behaved, for a while, as less than himself.

2. ST. PAUL—AND STANLEY

The immediate effect of missing the Mastership was to drive Jowett back to work upon an enterprise which he and Stanley had long been planning. This was an elaborate edition of St. Paul's Epistles: Greek text, translation, commentary, introductions and ancillary essays. Stanley was to do Corinthians; Jowett Thessalonians, Galatians and

[1] *L. & L.*, i, 277. The dots indicate passages omitted by the editor.

Romans. The other Epistles were to be shared out later; but this never happened.

The plan had a long history. It had really originated with Dr. Arnold who, at the time of his death, 'was endeavouring to set on foot a Rugby edition' of the Epistles of St. Paul under his own superintendence.[1] Stanley talked about this to Jowett. One afternoon the two friends 'caught in a heavy shower of rain and driven to take refuge in a quarry' decided to carry it out together. The idea expanded into the ambitious desire of a complete commentary upon the New Testament — apparently excluding the Book of Revelation. In 1846 Jowett wrote to Stanley:

I have been thinking a good deal about our Opus Magnum . . . I propose to divide it into two portions (a) the Gospels, and (b) the Acts and the Epistles, to be preceded respectively by two long prefaces, the first containing the hypothesis of the Gospels, and a theory of inspiration to be deduced from it; the second to contain the 'subjective mind' of the Apostolic age, *historisch-psychologisch dargestellt*. I think it should also contain essays. . . .[2]

His formulation of this heroic project was easily accepted by Stanley. At least, Stanley's biographer appropriated it, word for word, as Stanley's own; and added that 'the Epistles were to be brought out first; the Gospels were to be delayed till the two friends had paid a visit to Palestine at the end of 1849' — a visit never made.

By 1849 Stanley's commentary on Corinthians was almost ready for the printer. Jowett's commentary on Thessalonians, Galatians and Romans was nowhere near that stage. He was approaching his task in a very much more laborious manner. True to his belief that the only way of understanding the work of any great writer is to acquire an intimate knowledge of it as a whole, he is said to have learned the Greek text of the Epistles by continual reading and re-reading, until he had it by heart — no mean feat. His 'notes' were 'in progress' and his 'theological position was becoming more clearly defined' between 1846 and 1848, when he read Ferdinand Baur's recently published book on the Apostle Paul, and found in the critical and sceptical mind of the Tübingen theologian an independent texture not unlike that of his own mind. 'Baur' he told Stanley 'appears to me the ablest book I ever read on St. Paul's Epistles: a remarkable combination of Philological and Metaphysical power, without the intrusion of Modern Philosophy.' He had begun to think that German philosophy had undone German theology; in the previous year he complained to Stanley of 'the German theologues' that 'all their various harmonies are but faint echoes of Schelling and Hegel'.

[1] Stanley, *Life of Dr. Arnold*, Chapter IV.
[2] *L. & L.*, i, 100–1.

The progress of Jowett's commentary was interrupted by his and Stanley's absorption in the sudden revival of University reform as a live topic. This did not prevent Stanley from all but finishing his part. He was a facile writer — too much so — and he had no difficult theological journey to make. His position was Arnold's — liberal and optimistic and idealistic, yet practical in its acceptance of Christ as the Divine Man. His un-selfconscious charm and ease and good looks, his unique combination of simplicity and ability with a *flair* for the dramatic occasion, the inner restlessness which he satisfied only by incessant travel and repeated changes of occupation (though he usually represented these changes as reluctant concessions to duty) — these characters all united in a growing inclination away from any really difficult effort of thought.

The difference between the two friends was such that it was bound to result, sooner or later, not indeed in breach of friendship but in the collapse of their early delightful intimacy. At the end of 1846 Jowett was happy in the thought that Stanley was 'committed to Oxford, as you say: σύν τε δύ' ἐρχομένω [two going on together] makes one independent at least'. Earlier in the same year Stanley had proposed to him that he should publish some of his theological essays in a volume of Stanley's own sermons and essays on the Apostolical Age:

Having read your MSS and therefore feeling that I have nothing to say further, I have a total incapacity to write anything on the subject. However, the chief point, which, with all deference, I wish to urge on behalf of it, was this. Do not you think that it would be worth while to have an opportunity of giving people some kind of notion of what your views really are?[1]

So Stanley wrote, and Jowett 'scarcely knew what answer to give'. But, though he 'felt most sincerely that it was truly kind of Stanley to give him a chance he might never have again of putting himself "in oculis hominum" he must, however reluctantly, say No'.[2]

Stanley's advice that Jowett should explain his views was not entirely disinterested. It sprang, as he said, from his own embarrassment 'after running my head into the nest by preaching them' — Jowett's views — at second-hand, 'and so giving occasion to various charges which, I think, would be dispelled by their publication'. Jowett wisely declined his friend's proposal: he could scarcely drape his own half-formed opinions over another man's sermons. But he took the advice seriously, and bent all his powers to follow it in the two publications which, as we shall soon see, were to do him very great, immediate, material harm. For the rest of his life 'to speak my mind' was a never fulfilled, yet never discarded, aim.

[1] *Life of Dean Stanley*, i, 387.   [2] *L. & L.*, i, 153.

There is no sign that Stanley was annoyed by Jowett's refusal. But the proposal shows that he was beginning to chafe at the dominating influence which the 'disputatious youth', whom he had kindly taken out for a walk twenty years earlier, had come to exercise over him. Jowett was utterly unaware of this. His letters to Stanley continued as before: uninhibited letters, bubbling with ideas, full of wit and humour, as crisp and fresh to-day as when they were written. He never wrote better; never again so well. A similar sparkling crispness appears in many of his letters to other friends during the 'radiant' period before his repulse in Balliol; it does not wholly disappear even after that repulse. But it is in the letters to Stanley, while he thought of himself and his friend as 'two going on together', that this delightful quality is best and most continuously displayed.

Here is a random example, not of the crisp style but of the unchecked freedom, taken from a letter of 1846:

Considering how little sympathy I have with the clergy, for I never hear a sermon scarcely which does not seem equally divided between truth and falsehood, it seems like a kind of treachery to be one of them. But I really believe that treachery to the clergy is loyalty to the Church, and that if religion is to be saved at all it must be through the laity and statesmen, etc., not through the clergy.

The surviving letters contain many references to the work on which the two friends were engaged. 'I think we ought to do more towards it than we have done in the last two years, if we are to live to see it finished. I wish we could read the New Testament together, to begin with; otherwise there will be no unity in what we write.' Jowett, of course, to Stanley, probably in 1847. Could they not, he suggested, 'work at it together, something in the same fashion that Liddell and Scott did at their Lexicon?' Next year (1848) agreeing that Stanley should not refuse the Chair of Modern History (for which he was an unsuccessful candidate) he says: 'I do not like to urge your standing for it, considering how we are circumstanced with the Commentary, out of which I look for both of us many happy years' work.' In the following January (1849) he has 'to apologize for much seeming indolence about the Commentary' and explains precisely why it has been 'really unavoidable'.

On 6th September 1849 Stanley's father died, in his son's presence, at Brahan Castle near Dingwall. The reader may remember him as the young Rector of Alderley.[1] He had been Bishop of Norwich for the last ten years. Reading of his death in a newspaper, Jowett at once wrote to Stanley a warmly affectionate letter, dropping the use of Stanley's sur-

---

[1] See above, 117.

name and addressing him as 'My dear Arthur'. He asked: 'Would you like me to come to you? If so, I should like to stay in lodgings near you rather than in the same house.'[1]

Stanley's reply a week later (15th September) declined the offer and avoided the Christian name. 'My dear Jowett' he wrote, explaining that he had hoped 'a note from Edinburgh to Myers' would have 'prepared you for the alarm', and that he had written two other letters which Jowett had evidently not received. The letter continued:

Very many thanks for your kind thoughtfulness in proposing to come. No, my dear friend, it was not needed then, and is not now. We are enough in ourselves for ourselves, and hereafter I will not fail to let you know whether you can be of the slightest service to us.

Jowett's answer to this friendly, but unmistakable, rebuff is not preserved. On 1st October Stanley wrote again, from Norwich. He had been offered and had refused the Deanery of Carlisle; he hoped that Jowett, unlike all his other friends, might approve the refusal. But he had something else to say to his friend.

There is one thing which I have often thought of saying to you, and which the closing sentences of your letter invite me to say now. . . . You know that I believe myself to have learned more from you than from anybody else since Arnold's removal; and therefore I hope you will not misunderstand me when I say that I sometimes feel so much oppressed and depressed in talking to you about these things [Oxford and theology] that I seem to have lost all will of my own. Some means must be taken for avoiding this. Perhaps the long interval and separation from all such topics will of themselves produce all the independence which is requisite. Nor do I wish for the slightest change in our relations on the subject. I only mention it that you may understand why it has been that of late years I have not been able to sustain in your presence the same buoyancy of interest that I used to feel in discussing these matters, and also that I may not be for ever having to explain and apologise for following up my own devices, not as best in themselves, but as the best for me. [He added a postscript:] I have been reading your letter again — this is a sad worldly answer to send in reply to it — but I do hope that it may not be in a worldly spirit that I have written.

Jowett's answer must be given in full, for it marks the end of his youthful confidence in the possibility of a male friendship, based upon intellectual sympathy, to supply his emotional need. It marks his recognition of the fact that, in future, he would have to walk by himself. It also marks — rather, it expresses in terms of touching humility — his first shock of understanding how hardly his personality had pressed upon a friend whom he had supposed to be, at least, equal with himself.[2]

[1] *Letters of Dean Stanley*, 134–42, for this and the following letters.
[2] It is also printed, but not fully, in *L. & L.*, i, 166–8.

Balliol: Oct. 23, 1849

My dear Stanley, — A day or two since I received a kind letter from you dated October 1st, *via* ffolliott, who had kept it in hopes of my coming there.

Almost every one here thinks you were right in giving up the Deanery — Lonsdale and Temple most strongly, whose opinions, from my long experience, I am inclined to put more faith in than almost any one's. I ought to except the Dean of Wells from this general 'consensus', who feels the same kind of difficulties that he did on the occasion of Oakeley's resignation of his fellowship.

I could not help feeling pained at the latter part of your very kind letter. I know well how much better and wiser I ought to be at all to be worthy of the high opinion you express. It will always be a motive with me to try and make myself very different from what I am. I think it is true (and I am glad you mentioned it) that we have not had the same mental interest in talking over subjects of theology that we had formerly. They have lost their novelty, I suppose; we know better where we are, having rolled to the bottom together, and being now only able to make a few uphill steps. I acknowledge fully my own want of freshness; my mind seems at times quite dried up — partly, I think, from being strained out of proportion to the physical powers. And at times I have felt an unsatisfied desire after a better and higher sort of life, which makes me impatient of the details of theology. It is from this source only that I can ever look for any 'times of refreshment'. Had I always done rightly, my life would doubtless have been happier and my mind clearer.

I think sometimes we have been a little too intellectual and over-curious in our conversations about theology. We have not found rest and peace in them so much as we might have done. As to the other point you mention, I am quite sure you cannot be too independent. Your supposed want of judgment is a mere delusion, and if it were not, and I were really able to guide you, it is the greatest absurdity for one man to submit his will to another, merely because he has the power of sympathising with him and has greater energy at a particular moment. I think I see, more clearly than formerly, that you and I and all men must take our own line and act accordingly to our own character, with many errors and imperfections and half-views, yet upon the whole, we trust, for good. We must act boldly and feel the world around us, as a swimmer feels the resisting stream. There is no use in desultory excitement, of which perhaps we have had too much. Steady perseverance and judgment are the requisites. And Oxford is as happy and promising a field as any, such as we are, could desire.

I earnestly hope that the friendship which commenced between us many years ago may be a blessing to last us through life. I feel that, if it is to be so, we must both go onward: otherwise the wear and tear of life and the 'having travelled over each other's minds' and a thousand accidents will be sufficient to break it off. I have often felt the inability to converse with you, but never for an instant the least alienation. There is no one who would not think me happy in having such a friend. We will have no more of this semi-egotistical talk: only I want you to know that I will do all I can to remedy the evil, which is chiefly my fault.

Your affectionate friend,

B. Jowett.

Stanley replied at once:

Many thanks for your kind good letter. I am relieved for once to have spoken out my mind, and now let us dismiss the subject. I am sure I shall be happier for having done so; therefore you must forgive me if it at all grieved you. . . . I long to see you, for there is much to say.

This exchange of letters did not put an end to friendship. But the relations between the two men could never again be what they had formerly been. Stanley was right in thinking that the time had come for him to assert himself. Need he have chosen this particular occasion and this particular method? No doubt he felt that Jowett was seeking the occasion of his father's death to make their intimacy too close; that he must at all costs maintain his own privacy. He made up his mind with the sudden ruthlessness of which weak natures are sometimes capable.

Jowett's hurt was severe. He had supposed that Stanley was as devoted to him, as he to Stanley. For the first time in his life he had jumped the conventional barriers, to be met with a deliberate rebuff. No wonder that afterwards he sought to keep himself to himself; to spread his affections widely and not too deeply; not to expect of male friendship what it would not give. We do not know whether his missing letter contained anything which induced Stanley to make his outspoken assertion of independence; but we may be quite sure that it made no complaint of the way in which his first impulsive show of affection had been received. And in his long reply to Stanley's further letter he humbly takes a great deal more than his fair share of blame for the *impasse* which Stanley had declared.

His tenderness towards Stanley never failed. 'I cannot tell you' he wrote to him in July 1854 'how strongly the isolation in which I feel myself here makes me turn to you and Temple and the few true and warm friends of my own standing whom I have elsewhere.' When Stanley's mother died in 1862 Jowett wrote to him as 'My dearest Friend', and begged him to say 'whether there is anything you would like me to do for you'. He continued: 'Write to me for another reason, which is perhaps a selfish one, that life is very dark with me at present.' In the later years of Stanley's life he addressed him habitually as 'My dear Arthur' — using again the familiar opening which he had only once risked in the earlier years when he thought that he stood in Stanley's mind as Stanley stood in his.

After 1849 their paths ran separately, though their correspondence continued. From 1850 to 1852 Stanley was hard at work as Secretary to the Oxford University Commission; in 1851 he became a resident Canon of Canterbury; during the next two years he spent much time travelling in Egypt and Palestine. His life became shadowed by family troubles —

the deaths of his father and his two brothers, the slow conversion of his sister to Roman Catholicism, his mother's increasing claims upon him. It was not until 1856, when he returned to Oxford as Professor of Ecclesiastical History, that he and Jowett were able to meet and talk with something of the old frequency. By that time, Jowett was in need of all the help his friend could give him. And Stanley, liberally and consistently if not always wisely, gave him all the help he could. But it was help from somebody safely on board the ecclesiastical craft to a lonely swimmer in a difficult sea. It was not the help of a fellow swimmer in the same sea. Nor was it the help that friend can give friend, when their minds are completely in tune together.

After the 'hateful' business of the Balliol election, Jowett threw himself into the task of finishing his Pauline commentary. For a week or two in June he went walking with Temple in Derbyshire. 'The Philosopher' Temple reported to Palgrave 'has only two faults: he walks too slow and unevenly, and he prefers tea or even ginger-beer and biscuits to more generous meat and drink.' They talked of this and that, 'sometimes examining the genuineness of the Pastoral Epistles'.

The two commentaries — Jowett's, in two volumes, upon the Thessalonian, Galatian, and Roman Epistles, and Stanley's upon the Corinthian Epistles — were published almost simultaneously by John Murray in June 1855. Except for the date of their appearance, their arrangement and format, and a certain community of outlook, there was almost every possible contrast between them.

The one, says Prothero, speaking first of Stanley,

is essentially historical, the other is metaphysical; the one is 'external, positive, definite to the verge of superficiality', the other 'subjective, negative, profound at the risk of obscurity'; the one multiplies, the other avoids, illustrations; the one delights in detecting unobtrusive resemblances, the other in unmasking false analogies; the one excels in painting historical pictures, the other in portraying the phenomena which individual minds present at different stages of their growth; the one delights in tracing the threads of connection between different ages, the other points the contrasts which divide one epoch from another.[1]

Prothero says that both commentaries 'provoked a storm of acrimonious controversy: that on the Corinthians for the absence of doctrinal statements, that on the Romans for the mode in which such topics as the Atonement were handled'. The word 'storm' is an appropriate metaphor for the reception of Jowett's commentary. It is not at all the right word for the criticism which Stanley's volume deservedly met — especially from J. B. Lightfoot, then a young fellow of Trinity College Cambridge,

[1] *Life of Dean Stanley*, i, 473. The internal quotation marks are Prothero's.

who was already a leading Biblical scholar. Picturesque, inaccurate and superficial, it added little to Pauline studies and less than little to its author's reputation. Though Stanley corrected and revised it for a second edition, published in 1857, he himself realized that 'critical notes were not his vocation'. He wrote no more commentaries.[1]

If Stanley's avoidance of doctrinal questions disappointed the critics, Jowett's treatment of these questions raised a real wind. It was the essay *On Atonement and Satisfaction* in the second volume, which provoked the greatest general anger. In this essay he said plainly what he felt to be morally disgusting in the doctrine of the Atonement, as it was then commonly expounded.

God is represented as angry with us for what we never did; He is ready to inflict a disproportionate punishment on us for what we are; He is satisfied by the sufferings of His Son in our stead. . . . The imperfection of human law is transferred to the Divine. . . . The death of Christ is also explained by the analogy of the ancient rite of sacrifice. He is a victim laid upon the altar to appease the wrath of God. . . . I shall endeavour to show, 1, that these conceptions of the work of Christ have no foundation in Scripture; 2, that their growth may be traced in ecclesiastical history; 3, that the only sacrifice, atonement, or satisfaction, with which the Christian has to do, is a moral and spiritual one; not the pouring out of blood upon the earth, but the living sacrifice 'to do thy will, O God'; in which the believer has part as well as his Lord; about the meaning of which there can be no more question in our day than there was in the first ages.

Other passages are marked by a passionate force which Jowett never afterwards permitted himself to use. Here is one, chosen by Campbell:

No slave's mind was ever reduced so low as to justify the most disproportionate severity inflicted on himself; neither has God so made His creatures that they will lie down and die, even beneath the hand of Him who gave them life.

Such heat of expression, as Campbell says, helps 'to explain the acrimony of the assaults which followed. There was no mistaking what this man meant. He was one to reckon with.' Nor, in analysing what he called 'the perplexities of the doctrine of the Atonement' did the author use the language of appeasement. He described the forms taken by this doctrine as

the growth of above a thousand years; rooted in language, disguised in figures of speech, fortified by logic, they seem almost to have become part of the human mind itself. . . . One cannot but fear whether it be still possible so to teach Christ as not to cast a shadow on the holiness and truth of God.

[1] *ibid.*, i, 474. See, also, Prothero's article on Stanley in the *D.N.B.*

There was, perhaps, a little but not much substance in the familiar criticism, most temperately made by Lightfoot, that

the value of Mr. Jowett's labours is far from consisting in the definite results attained, which are poorer than might have been looked for. The reconstructive process bears no proportion to the destructive. But after every abatement which has to be made on this score, these volumes will still hold their position in the foremost ranks of recent literature for depth and range of thought.

This not unfavourable review appeared in the *Journal of Classical and Sacred Philology* in March 1856. Stanley wrote generously about it to Jowett:

I must say I was pleased, more pleased with the good he said of you than displeased with the evil he said of myself; and in a man of his turn of mind, I think it specially creditable not to have been deterred from saying this much by the popular clamour which has hounded on the Conybeares, Goulburns, or Wilberforces, and has *muzzled* the *North British*, the *Edinburgh*, and the *Times*.

The 'popular clamour' was not quietened by Lightfoot's review. Already, by the end of 1855, it had begun to be vocal in Oxford. Before the storm broke fully upon him, Jowett (in September) was proposing to set to work at once with the next instalment (Ephesians and Colossians). He wrote to Stanley that, with health, he might

get them out by this time next year. When you see Murray will you sound him about it? If he likes, it may be advertised at once as preparing. Are you of the same mind touching the Philippians and Philemon? If you are, I shall be glad; if not I shall try them myself.

Nothing of this plan was ever to be carried out.

Is Jowett's commentary read to-day by anybody — even by Pauline scholars? It is not so much as mentioned in any of the lists of commentaries upon Thessalonians or Galatians or Romans given in *A New Commentary on Holy Scripture*, published in 1928 under the general editorship of Bishop Gore, Henry Goudge and Alfred Guillaume. This seems strange.[1] Had Jowett, then, *nothing* to say which is still worth remembering? At the least, his was the first English Pauline commentary to discard the *textus receptus*, the traditional Greek text as received in the west, and to follow the earlier eastern text, as reconstituted by Lachmann. Since *A New Commentary* avowed itself to be built on the same basis — that is to say on the basis of the eastern text, as further amended by Westcott and Hort[2] — some acknowledgment of Jowett's

[1] The more so, because Stanley finds a place in the list of commentaries upon I Corinthians.

[2] *A New Commentary*, ii, 720. The line of the great editors who adopted the eastern text is there said to have begun with Griesbach of Halle at the end of the eighteenth century, to have been 'continued through the 19th century by Lachmann' of Berlin and to have culminated in Westcott and Hort.

pioneering effort was surely due, even if it were only a reference to the introduction in which he briefly, but convincingly, justified his abandonment of the *textus receptus*.

Not even this small due of courtesy was paid; let alone acknowledgment that Jowett had anything of value to say. Can it be that the cloud of heresy still hangs about Jowett in the minds of Anglican theologians and scholars? Was Lightfoot's judgment that the two volumes would 'hold their position in the foremost ranks of recent literature for depth and range of thought' so shallow a judgment? Have a hundred years put Jowett's essay on the Atonement so out of date that its attitude and arguments can now be blandly forgotten?

3. THE GREEK PROFESSORSHIP

Almost at the moment when Jowett published his Pauline commentary, Dean Gaisford, the Oxford Regius Professor of Greek, died. The appointment of the 'Regius' professors at Oxford and Cambridge lay and lies with the Crown. After considering two or three other possibilities (one of them Scott himself) the Prime Minister, Lord Palmerston, offered the chair to Jowett. The offer seems to have been made either at the end of September or the beginning of October; and the nomination to have been publicly announced early in October 1854.

It looked at first as if this unexpected appointment were a real recompense for missing the Mastership. Congratulations poured in. Jowett feasted upon them, upon the sense of 'the attachment of a great many warm-hearted persons. . . . They make me half believe what the Dean of Wells said to me the other day "You have the sympathy of everybody".'[1] The mood of elation was quickly extinguished. Before the year was out he was saying to a friend, 'I have no pleasure in looking forward to my lectures now.' Nevertheless his professorial lectures on the *Republic* — which he described as 'the greatest uninspired writing' — filled Balliol hall with crowds of undergraduates from various colleges and laid the foundation of his life-time's work on Plato.

The circumstances of the Greek professorship, at this point of time, were very peculiar indeed. It was one of five Oxford Regius chairs founded by King Henry VIII, the others being Divinity, Civil Law,

---

[1] To Mrs. Greenhill (*L. & L.*, i, 252). The Dean was Dr. G. H. S. Johnson. He was 'Johnson the Observer' (he had been Savilian Professor of Astronomy) who had said to somebody, at the time of Scott's election to the Mastership, that though he did not agree with Jowett in opinions, there was no one whom he would sooner have seen Master of Balliol.

Medicine and Hebrew. To each of these the King had attached a stipend of £40 a year, to be provided by the Dean and Chapter of the newly re-founded Westminster Abbey. They prudently avoided responsibility by surrendering back to the King some part of the property with which he had endowed them. Christ Church, whose foundation Henry had taken over himself after Cardinal Wolsey's fall, was then charged with the stipends of the Divinity, Hebrew and Greek professors; the Royal Exchequer was made responsible for the stipends of the other two.

James I and Charles I increased the emoluments of all these pro-fessorial chairs, except the Greek chair, by canonries and sinecures. The chair of Civil Law lagged behind until 1877, when it was attached to All Souls; but James I at least augmented the professor's remuneration by a lay prebend in the Church of Salisbury, subsequently commuted for an annual payment of £100 by the Ecclesiastical Commissioners. Alone of the five Regius Professors the professor of Greek continued to receive no more than King Henry's £40 a year. Whatever the reason for the exception may have been, it had not hitherto mattered. Most of the men who held the office for any length of time had been, or had soon become, comfortably remunerated Canons of Christ Church, or had filled it only as a preliminary to the well rewarded chair of Divinity.

The last professor, Thomas Gaisford, had held the appointment for forty-four years; for most of that long period he had been first a Canon of one cathedral after another and then (for more than half of it) Dean of Christ Church.

Dr. Gaisford never lectured or took classes or demeaned himself to the level of a teacher. He confined himself to textual criticism in his own closet. Some of his work is still said to have been worth while — notably his edition of the *Poetae Graeci Minores* and his recensions of Stobaeus, Herodotus, Sophocles and Suidas. But it was all done for love and out of a good ecclesiastical income, not for £40 a year.[1]

At the time, therefore, when Jowett was appointed Regius Professor, the idea that this particular appointment implied any specific obligations, of the kind which the University had recently begun to expect its other professors to discharge, might have been said not to exist at all, were it not that the older idea of professorships as little more than rewards or honours was dead or dying, and that the Dean and Chapter of Christ Church, in the year before Dean Gaisford's death in 1855, when asked by the Executive Commissioners if they would make some contribution to

[1] In another book I have quoted his celebrated remark on the study of Greek literature 'which not only elevates above the vulgar herd, but leads not infre-quently to positions of considerable emolument'. I cannot resist repeating it here, and adding that it was made from the pulpit of Christ Church.

academical purposes, 'replied that the most proper object of such benevolence on their part was the endowment of the professorship of Greek'.

It is disagreeable for a son of Christ Church to have to record that this virtuous intention was not honoured until the treatment of Professor Jowett became so great a public scandal, that the Chapter could no longer dare to ignore it. For ten years the new professor, who did not consider his title as 'a mere ornament to decorate a specially deserving Tutor', took on himself a burden for which he received practically no pay. Indeed, he received less than no pay, since he gave up the Balliol bursarship, in order to find time for the work which he (not the University or Christ Church) required of himself as professor.

It is generally supposed that the refusal to augment the new professor's salary was entirely Pusey's doing. It is true that Pusey hated Jowett's theological views, which he thought bound to lead to irreligion and to the destruction of the Church. It is also true that Pusey thought it his duty to oppose any method of increasing the professor's stipend, which appeared to condone what he — and many others — considered 'heresy'. But it is not true that he wished to prevent Jowett from receiving a decent reward. On the contrary, he again and again proposed and advocated an increase in the professor's salary, and was again and again defeated; though he sought — and from his point of view not wrongly — that this increase should come from the University and not from a Cathedral Chapter.[1]

Pusey's plan was, in effect, that the appointment of the professor should be transferred from the Crown to the University; and that the University decree, authorizing an increase of salary (to be met not by Christ Church but by the University) should contain a clause which dissociated the University from approval of any opinions which the professor might have uttered or might utter on theological topics. Pusey obtained the agreement both of Mr. Gladstone and of Lord Palmerston to this plan. But Convocation turned it down. In the end, after ten years of miserable tergiversation, the Christ Church Chapter caved in and made the professor's stipend up to £500 out of its own abundant revenue.

The complicated story of this distressful decade is told at length, from two opposing points of view, both by Lewis Campbell and by Pusey's biographers.[2] The account given by Pusey's biographers is a great deal

---

[1] Until the Christ Church Oxford Act of 1867 the management of the college property lay entirely with the Cathedral Chapter. Mallet, *History of the University of Oxford*, iii, 353.
[2] *L. & L.*, i, Chapter X. *Life of Pusey*, iv, Chapter I. Dr. Liddon had died after completing the third volume of Pusey's *Life*. The story of this episode, though very well told, is not Liddon's work.

fuller and more systematic than Campbell's and explains much that Campbell failed to understand. It convincingly clears Pusey from the suspicion of having 'raised a storm' which he tried later to allay, simply in order to obviate 'the increasing odium against his party'. If the fourth volume of Pusey's *Life* had appeared in time to be read by Campbell, the latter must at least have modified some of his expressions. Unfortunately both volumes were published long after the event and in the same year (1897). Campbell's account is probably the better known. It certainly conveys an inaccurate idea of Pusey's attitude. Yet it is true that Pusey's attitude and actions are not always easy to comprehend.

The story is bound up with the suspicions and charges of heresy to which Jowett exposed himself. In looking at these, we shall better understand what happened to him as professor of Greek. But at this point let Pusey's conscientious biographers be heard, rounding off their version of the controversy over the professor's salary. The reader must remember that he is listening to a partisan record, made some sixty years ago, of a controversy ended over thirty years earlier and already dismissed from the memory of all but a few old men.

At this distance of time and under the altered conditions of University life, it is very hard to understand and appreciate the motives which actuated the refusal of a scheme which at first sight may appear as a mere act of justice. The danger for us now in reading the story is lest we should regard the Oxford of 1860 as having already laid aside its old religious character; it must not be forgotten that it was still largely a body bound by the 'Articles of Religion', and that it still contained many who twenty years earlier had suffered greatly at the hands of Liberals for alleged faithlessness to them.[1] The detailed account of this painful controversy is at least a matter of justice to Pusey's memory. There is no incident in his life which is more frequently remembered against him, and hardly one which suffers more from incomplete remembrance.

The Essay on the Atonement, in Jowett's commentary on the Epistle to the Romans, was the point round which the *odium theologicum* first crystallized. We have already taken a glance at it, and seen enough of its purport to understand that it must give deep offence to those, both 'high' and 'low', who interpreted that doctrine in any of the ways which Jowett denounced. We have also seen that his appointment to the Regius professorship followed soon after the publication of the commentary to which this essay was attached. It was the combination of these two events which provoked attack. At the beginning of December 1855 two members of Convocation denounced him formally to the Vice-Chancellor,

---

[1] But this was special pleading indeed! Who were the 'Liberals' from whom the Puseyites had suffered 'twenty years earlier'? The fight, then, was between the orthodox evangelicals and the Tractarians. The liberal party in the Church, at that time, was little more than dog's meat.

on the ground that he had assailed the doctrine of the Atonement, as held by the Church of England.

One of the two complainants was Dr. Macbride, Principal of Magdalen Hall, an oriental scholar of no great distinction and 'a deeply religious layman of evangelical views'.[1] The other was the Rev. C. P. Golightly,[2] one of those apparently sensible men whose minds are ridden by almost insane obsessions. Campbell describes him rather neatly. 'Mr. Golightly, whom some witty Newmanite had re-christened "Agag", was a local clergyman, of Evangelical principles and restless activity, whose *bêtes noires*, of about equal blackness to him, were Newmanism and Germanism.' It was, presumably, Jowett's deference to German scholarship which touched Golightly off. Neither Macbride nor Golightly were men of serious standing. But it is necessary to have it clear that this first attack on Jowett came entirely from the evangelical quarter. Pusey was not in any way responsible for it.

The Vice-Chancellor was Dr. Cotton the Provost of Worcester. He happened to be Pusey's brother-in-law. Pusey, therefore, was placed to know what was in the wind. He wrote a sympathetic, warning letter to Jowett. Jowett sent it on to Stanley with a comment so uncharitable that it illustrates his inflamed state of mind: 'I was very much affected by it at first, but since reading it I have seen too much of the writer to be capable of being affected by what he says.'

Dr. Cotton was a much undersized man with a large nose and an exaggerated sense of his own importance.[3] Little else of him is recoverable. Even in the four volumes of his famous brother-in-law's biography his name is no more than barely mentioned four or five times. He wrote a book on the *Way of Salvation Plainly and Practically Traced*, published a set of *Lectures on the Holy Sacrament*, and 'printed' some funeral sermons. He is now to be remembered only by the ridiculous figure he cut in his interview with Professor Jowett, whom he had summoned to his private study, much as schoolmasters summon boys under suspicion of gross misbehaviour, to re-subscribe the Articles of the Church of England. The interview is thus reported by Campbell:

Jowett appeared in answer to the summons, and Vice-Chancellor Cotton began to address him solemnly on the 'awfulness' of his situation. Jowett cut him short with the words, 'Mr. Vice-Chancellor, I have come to sign

---

[1] Campbell erroneously refers to him as a Doctor of Divinity. He was, in fact, a Doctor of Civil Law — a degree then often taken by Oxford graduates.

[2] I have written at some length about Golightly in another book (*Oxford Apostles*, 370 *foll.*, Pelican edn.). His mind seems to have been really unbalanced. It was 'haunted by painful illusions' before he died. (*D.N.B.*)

[3] He is caricatured in the frontispiece to Tuckwell's *Reminiscences of Oxford*, as the small 'Vice' preceded and followed by tall men.

the Articles.' Dr. Cotton recommenced his harangue, but was again interrupted. Tradition has it that Jowett simply asked for a new pen. He was always very particular, in beginning any writing, to have a quill pen ready made, and was a proficient in the art of mending them.

Jowett's own account, given in a letter to Stanley, is touched with his characteristic power of humorous reportage:

You will have seen in the newspapers that I have taken the meaner part and signed. It seemed to me that I could not do otherwise without giving up my position as a Clergyman.

Scene. Vice-Chancellor's Study

A domestic picture of Dr. and Mrs. C. . . . Enter Hereticus —'I am come to comply with your request.' 'Will you write your name on this sheet of paper and on that?' Done. Vice-Chancellor turns over letters from Golightly and Heurtley,[1] mumbling something in an undertone of voice. But before the words are out, Hereticus says 'Good morning' and escapes. It grieves me to have been put to this sort of schoolboy degradation, and also to think that such things are possible nowadays. I don't intend to write a single word in reply to the attacks on me. Without taking any notice of them, I shall enlarge the Essay on the Atonement in a second edition.

The scene was silly; the sense of humiliation hard to throw off. As to the matter of his summons before the Vice-Chancellor, apart from this letter to Stanley the only allusion preserved is in Jowett's reply to a letter of invitation from the three year old son of a former pupil (William Sellar):

I will come and play at soldiers next summer, but in the winter-time I must do lessons. A little monkey of an old gentleman, who dresses himself in black and has three pokers walk before him, has been teazing me lately, and I should be in a great row if I had not such good friends as Mama, Papa, and Tornie.[2]

For nearly the next five years there was no change in Jowett's position. Stanley — who had come back to Oxford from Canterbury as Professor of Ecclesiastical History and was soon installed as a Canon of Christ Church — tried to bring about an improvement in the Greek professor's remuneration. He did not, perhaps, quite understand all the difficulties; and he was the kind of advocate who often does more harm than good to the cause he would promote. Pusey wrote to Keble, late in 1859, that Stanley's agitation 'is, of course, a personal act of favour to Jowett'.

Pusey himself was in real trouble of mind. He believed Jowett's theological opinions to be heretical. He could not, therefore, directly consent to a simple increase in the professor's stipend at the cost of the University, which he still regarded as a religious institution. That, as he

---

[1] The Lady Margaret Professor of Divinity. See below, 267.
[2] *L. & L.*, 245. 'Tornie' was his three year old correspondent.

said to Keble, would imply 'assent to the principle that the University takes no notice of any heresy or unbelief in its secular teachers'. Moreover, he felt strongly and Keble agreed, that the University ought not, as a matter of general principle, to subsidize the stipend of a professor, over whose appointment it had no control. This second objection to the simple and unguarded proposal, which Stanley advocated, was felt by many others. It cannot be dismissed as either ridiculous or adventitious.

But Pusey — even while fighting this last, and soon to be lost, battle for the ecclesiastical character of Oxford — was a just man. Deeply as he disliked and distrusted Jowett's opinions, he knew that the labourer is worthy of his hire, and that the new professor of Greek was doing an admirable job of work. In 1858 and 1859, and again in 1860, Stanley's proposal 'to endow the Regius professorship of Greek with £300' was defeated in the Hebdomadal Council. 'Some members opposed on the religious ground. Pusey reserved that point, but urged the constitutional difficulty about the relation to the Crown.'[1] Meanwhile he had been pushing on his own plan. This was that the two ill-endowed professorships of Civil Law and Greek should be vested in a Board

in which the Government should have the majority, but the University be represented (after the pattern of the Boards formed by the Oxford Commission), provided the University would endow.[2]

Lord Palmerston agreed to this plan in principle. It was on the point of receiving approval by the Hebdomadal Council in October 1860. The stipend provided by the University, under this scheme, was to be £400 a year; and would probably have been dated from the beginning of the Michaelmas term. It was Stanley who, at this critical moment, upset the apple-cart by giving notice of moving that the chair should be endowed at once with £300 per annum, until it were permanently endowed. Pusey could not but oppose this plan, which,

while it offers to Professor Jowett less than my arrangement would give him, effectually defeats mine. For if the University, without conditions, endows the Chair with £300 per annum, it would have nothing to offer to Lord Palmerston as a ground for vesting the nomination in a Board. The only object of Professor Stanley's motion can be to make the vote one of confidence in Professor Jowett.

Stanley's motion was defeated, and Pusey's approved. But the delay was fatal. It was not until May 1861, that Pusey's plan could be formally submitted to Convocation for approval by the University. Although

[1] *Life of Pusey*, iv, 13. The quotation refers to the first occasion. Pusey's biographers do not say whether he continued to reserve the religious argument in the later debates.

[2] *ibid.*, iv, 13. From Pusey's letter to Bishop Wilberforce, 31st October 1860.

Pusey spoke for it, as well as Stanley, it was defeated by ninety-one to seventy votes.

The defeat of Pusey's proposal is said to have been procured as much by 'liberals', who disliked the idea of giving the University, still predominantly clerical, a voice in future appointments, as by 'orthodox' churchmen, both 'high' and 'low', who regarded Jowett as a heretic. This must be at any rate partly true, since it is stated as a fact both by Campbell and by Pusey's biographers. Pusey himself put the main responsibility upon the 'liberals'; but he was, perhaps, not very willing to acknowledge the decline of his influence with his own friends and followers.

If it is hard for us to understand the passionate theological or ecclesiastical controversies of the middle nineteenth century, it is sometimes even harder to understand the minds of those who favoured 'reform' in principle and yet opposed it in practice. For Pusey's proposal was wholly in line with the reforms already introduced into Oxford and with the reforms yet to come. If its failure was, as he thought, mainly due to 'liberal' opposition, or even if it was partly due to such opposition, one can but marvel at the pettiness of mind which refused to see any virtue in any proposal, although of a progressive and liberal character, put forward by such a man as Pusey. Jowett himself was not free from this inverted form of the *odium theologicum*.

It may, therefore, be true that even if Stanley had not upset the applecart, and if Pusey's plan had been submitted to Convocation in the Michaelmas term of 1860, it would still have suffered the same fate. But the impression one gains from the record is that this would not have been so; that it was the extraordinary storm over *Essays and Reviews* which defeated Pusey's first effort to settle the painful controversy over Jowett's salary; and that this storm was only beginning to matter in the autumn of 1860.

CHAPTER XI

Essays and Reviews: Act One

1. THE INCEPTION

'Let it be said' wrote Bishop Gore, in the article on *The Bible in the Church* with which he prefaced his *New Commentary on Holy Scripture*, 'that to-day the labour of scholars on the Bible is being chiefly devoted to critical questions. It will be found to be so in much of the work contributed to this Commentary. This is inevitable, because our critical science is in great part a new science, and the foundations of exegesis have to be relaid.'

Hardly a reader of these words in 1928 (when the *New Commentary* was published) can have raised his eyebrows. Forty years earlier Dean Bradley, in his eulogistic article on Stanley in the *Encyclopaedia Britannica*,[1] had declared that most of the critical works published in England since Stanley first lectured as a tutor on the Old and New Testaments

have been written more or less in the spirit in which he would have largely sympathized. It may be added that of these there are few which would not have encountered, if not fierce criticism, yet at least grave suspicion, some forty years ago. The combination of a reverent treatment of Holy Scripture with fearless inquiry into all questions connected with its criticism is a new birth in English literature.

It may be doubted whether Stanley was so much the deliverer of this new birth as Bradley went on to claim. But there can be no doubt that even long after the middle of the nineteenth century fierce criticism and grave suspicion were heavy occupational risks for liberally minded English clergymen. Stanley himself succeeded in avoiding them — nobody ever quite knew how. Some instinct always warned him of trouble ahead or round the corner. It was this instinct which told him to have no part in *Essays and Reviews*, when the idea of that fateful volume was first put up to him and again when Jowett tried, in August 1858, to persuade him into it.

The idea was not Jowett's. It was the invention of Henry Bristow Wilson, who had asked him if he would contribute to a volume 'in which

[1] *Enc. Brit.*, 9th edition, 1887.

229

theological subjects should be freely handled in a becoming spirit'. (The phrase is Campbell's, borrowed from the editorial prefix.[1])

Wilson at this date (1858) was a country clergyman — Vicar of Great Staughton in Huntingdonshire. Before he married and was presented to this college living in 1850, he had been a fellow and tutor of St. John's and a man of considerable note in Oxford. He was one of the carefully chosen signatories to the open 'Letter of the Four Tutors', drafted by Tait, which led to the censure of Newman's Tract 90 by the Heads of Houses in 1841. Fourteen years older than Jowett he 'identified himself in theology with the school of which Jowett and Temple became the best-known members'.[2] He had been Rawlinsonian Professor of Anglo-Saxon; he examined, with Jowett, in the schools; and in 1851 he was Bampton Lecturer, taking as his subject 'The Communion of the Saints: an attempt to illustrate the true principles of Christian Union'. He was the son of Harry Bristow Wilson, divine and antiquary, 'a learned adherent of the evangelical school, with more of the scholar than the divine', whose chronicle precedes his own in the Dictionary of National Biography.

The proposal appealed strongly to Jowett, for it offered him an opportunity of publishing an important essay at which he had been at work, off and on, for more than ten years. He first conceived this essay in 1847, when he and Stanley were meditating their ambitious project of a New Testament '*opus magnum*' — the project of which their Pauline commentaries were the small completed fragments. Jowett's essay was to be 'on the critical study of Scripture'. It was to form part of a commentary on the fourth Gospel. Some part of it was written and laid aside. He planned to incorporate it in the second edition of his Pauline commentary, published in 1859, at which he was working in 1857. But 'constant headaches prevented him from finishing it' in time.[3]

Here was the chance to say what he had long wanted to say. He entered warmly into Wilson's idea of a symposium, and undertook to do his best to rope in Stanley. It is evident that he already knew Stanley to be reluctant, from the letter (dated 15th August 1858) which he wrote to his friend:

Wilson wishes me to write to you respecting a volume of Theological Essays which he has already mentioned, the object of which, however, he thinks he has not clearly set before you, trusting to my being at Oxford, etc. . . . The object is to say what we think freely within the limits of the Church of England. A notice will be prefixed that no one is responsible for any notions but his own. It is, however, an essential part of the plan that

[1] See below, 234.
[2] E. Irving Carlyle in the *D.N.B.* article on Wilson.
[3] *L. & L.*, i, 251 and 273.

names shall be given. . . . We do not wish to do anything rash or irritating to the public or the University, but we are determined not to submit to this abominable system of terrorism, which prevents the statement of the plainest facts, and makes true theology or theological education impossible. . . . I do not deny that in the present state of the world the expression of them [Stanley's opinions] is a matter of great nicety and care, but is it possible to do any good by a system of reticence? . . . We shall talk A.D. 1868. I want to point out that the object is not to be attained by any anonymous writing . . . I don't write as often as I once did, but am not the less truly your sincere and affectionate friend.[1]

Stanley's answer to this letter is not given either by his or Jowett's biographers; but both agree that he was against the project. 'Stanley' Campbell says 'disapproved of the policy of such an open alliance, and Jowett, in persevering with it, acted against his friend's advice.' Prothero says that 'Stanley had from the first declined to take any part in the volume' and confirms that 'he strongly objected to the form and scheme of the work. "In a composite publication" he, from the first, recognized "a decided blunder".' That was one ground of disapproval — whether it was valid or not, is evidently a debatable question. Are composite theological publications always à priori 'blunders'?

Stanley's biographer goes on to quote from a letter which he wrote soon after the appearance of *Essays and Reviews:* 'Jowett's essay is decidedly the best — too negative and antagonistic, of course, but wonderfully fertile of thought and really containing no just ground of offence.'

The charge of being negative, of destroying and not building up, was to be brought against Jowett over and over and over again. There was more than one way of answering it.

There was the kind of answer that Stanley himself had just used to Pusey. In an affectionately worded letter explaining the distress with which he viewed Stanley's return from Canterbury to Oxford as Professor of Ecclesiastical History, Pusey had written:

I am sure that, whatever ground your and Professor Jowett's pupils occupy, it will not be yours. It must be onward or backward. I have said to Professor Jowett that I could not hold his faith for an hour. Intellectually it is, I am sure, inconsistent, and although in some way his religious feeling enables him, I suppose, not to push things to their results, with his pupils it must be different. Pupils see the inconsistency, and either follow out theories to their consequence, or give up the theory. But actual unbelief has made frightful inroads already.

Stanley had replied:

I do not doubt that your teaching, which by many is thought so dangerous, and necessarily conducing to results that you would greatly deprecate, is to some amongst us the best stay of their faith. But I am no less sure that the teaching of those whom you dread may be, and is, the best stay of the

[1] *ibid.*, i, 275–6.

faith of others who, if your teaching were the sole alternative, would be driven into utter unbelief.[1]

Another mode of answer is provided by Stanley's phrase 'wonderfully fertile of thought', with which he immediately annuls his apparent acceptance of the facile, current and recurrent criticism. For how can an argument which is 'too negative' be 'wonderfully fertile'? Here is a contradiction of terms, or of meanings, such as a man makes writing a letter and corrects as his pen travels. If Stanley's 'of course' agreed too readily with general criticism of the friend from whose influence he had resolved to free himself, the rest of the sentence more than redresses that mistake.

The fuller answer had to wait a very long time, and has never been explicitly made. It is implied in the extract from Bishop Gore's preface to *A New Commentary on Holy Scripture*, placed at the beginning of this chapter. The critical approach to a new 'interpretation of scripture', which Jowett's clerical contemporaries so angrily denounced, has long since been accepted. Jowett's only mistake was to be a little in advance of his time. No mistake is more immediately visited upon the culprit; or less remembered to his credit afterwards by those who inherit, often without knowing the what and wherefore of their inheritance, the benefit of his rashness.

Fool of God as Stanley half was, he had gone far enough up the ladder of ecclesiastical preferment to be aware, more clearly than Jowett and looking down from his higher perch, of the turmoil in the Anglican sea. He saw his friend, so much wiser and yet comparatively so innocent, about to commit himself blindly to an enterprise in which he could not succeed and from which he would be lucky to escape unhurt.

In this judgment Stanley was both right and wrong. In the short view he was entirely right; in the long view entirely wrong. But Jowett, too, was wrong; and perhaps his mistake was as bad as Stanley's. He plunged, against Stanley's advice not to plunge in that company. And having plunged and spoken his mind, and having suffered for his plunge, he never plunged again. He never, thereafter, 'spoke his mind' upon theological matters.

Wilson's invitation sent him back to the uncompleted essay which had been so long in his mind. Whatever Stanley said to him in the summer of 1858, and whatever doubts he had of his own, he went resolutely to it. In the winter of 1859, when he was staying with the Tennysons in the Isle of Wight, it filled his mind, when he had any time over from being

[1] *Life of Dean Stanley*, i, 508–9. The letters, not dated, were 'probably written in February 1858'.

Tennyson's guest and listener. He went on from Farringford to Milford in Hampshire, where his pupil and friend and future biographer was Vicar. Campbell relates how his guest's mind was full of the essay and its matter, and how he suddenly turned to Mrs. Campbell and asked 'Can the truth do harm?' She replied that it could surely do no harm to tell the truth. To which he answered: 'That is the verdict of the simple mind.' He was already beginning to understand that truth, however ultimately and grandly simple it may be, is not simple for men amongst men.

2. THE BOOK

Essays and Reviews appeared in February 1860 — a demy octavo volume of 434 pages, bound in the subfusc cloth suitable for theological works, and bearing the discreet symbol of a Greek cross at each of the four cover corners. The publishers were John W. Parker and Son. Parker had been superintendent or manager of the Cambridge University Press from 1829 to 1854; but he had built up a successful publishing business of his own in London. His list was strong in philosophy and theology and had a liberal colour; it included, for example, J. S. Mill and F. D. Maurice. Since 1855 he had published two parallel series of annual volumes called *Oxford Essays* and *Cambridge Essays*. These collections were not of a theological kind. But they were guarantees of Parker's standing in the two Universities and of his ability to handle composite books. And the general character of his list showed that his was the right imprint for a forward-looking theological symposium.[1]

'The spring and the summer passed away, and the volume excited but little attention.'[2] Before the storm breaks, let us take a look at the contents of the volume, leaving Jowett's contribution to the place it occupies there — the last.[3]

There were seven Essays, of unequal length and merit. The contributors were all men of standing. Between them they covered almost the whole ground of the then existing controversies between Anglican churchmen, and between religion and science. The book was said to

---

[1] Parker's son died in 1860. Three years later he sold his business, lock stock and barrel, to Longman's — which explains, at least in some degree, the astonishingly catholic nature of that famous imprint in the last third of the century.
[2] *Life of Dean Stanley*, ii, 30.
[3] The following analysis was written before the publication of Professor Basil Willey's *More Nineteenth Century Studies: A Group of Honest Doubters* (1956) and owes nothing to Professor Willey's analysis in his fourth chapter 'Septem Contra Christum', from which it differs in many ways, and at many points.

suffer from lack of editorship. Another view might be that it made its extraordinary impact, just because it was *not* edited. Each contributor wrote as he chose. Three of the Essays (those by Williams, Baden Powell and Goodwin) might, with advantage, have been subjected to some editorial revision. These three Essays, along with Wilson's (which was much too ably constructed to be so revised), were commonly held up as examples of the bad company which Temple and Jowett and Pattison should have known better than to keep. But since, if there were an editor at all, it must have been Wilson, whose own contribution was one of the most startling in the book, it was useless to suppose that editorship could have prevented the wrath to come, without destroying the effect which the book was sensibly intended to make and did, in fact, make. It was not intended to be homogeneous. It was intended to break through an 'abominable system of terrorism', and it broke through that system, though all the available engines of terrorism were turned against it. It broke through the ecclesiastical barrage into the minds both of the laity and the clergy. It became a best-seller for many years, reprinted over and over again.

It was laid to the discredit of the three best known contributors — is better, now, laid to their credit — that they concerned themselves neither with the matter nor with the manner of the other four. Pattison's indifference was part of his acquired character; but Temple and Jowett were differently constituted, and each had much to risk.

Attempt was made to separate responsibility by a brief editorial prefix, in which the mind of Jowett, if not his hand, is very evident.

It will readily be understood that the Authors of the ensuing Essays are responsible for their respective articles only. They have written in entire independence of each other, and without concert or comparison.

The volume, it is hoped, will be received as an attempt to illustrate the advantage derivable to the cause of religious and moral truth, from a free handling, in a becoming spirit, of subjects peculiarly liable to suffer by the repetition of conventional language, and from traditional methods of treatment.

Temple, who had succeeded Tait as headmaster of Rugby, contributed the opening Essay on *The Education of the World*. This was not written for the occasion. It had, in fact, been delivered as a University sermon, and it suffers from the strained and prolonged use of one of those elaborately false analogies which are the recurring bane of pulpit rhetoric. The life of the world is artificially compared to the life of a man. Just as a man's education is divided into three stages — childhood when he is taught by 'Rules', youth when he learns by 'Examples', manhood when he learns, if at all, by 'Principles' — so is the education of the world to be historically divided. 'First comes the Law, then the Son of Man, then the Gift of the Spirit.' In the working out of this rhetorical conceit, which is the pattern of the sermon, Temple made a number of interesting, but also some very dubious, observations. To take a random example, he pretended to see in the Greek and Roman classics 'the image, there only to be seen, of our highest natural powers in their freshest vigour'; never again would be found 'that universal radiance of fresh life which makes even the most commonplace relics of classic days models for our highest art'. This sad rubbish was necessitated by the rhetorical pattern. The Greeks and the Romans were 'children', owning the radiance of childhood, but living under 'teachers and governors' until the world was sufficiently grown-up to learn from the divine example of Christ.

A reader of the essay to-day will find himself continually baffled by this irritating naivety, and will wonder, until he is more than half-way through, why it was chosen (by Jowett himself) to stand in front of the essays which followed. Obviously, it was good to have something from Temple. But what bearing could this forced and foolish interpretation of history have upon 'the free handling, in a becoming spirit, of subjects peculiarly liable to suffer by the repetition of conventional language'? Towards the end of Temple's sermon the reason gradually begins to show. The world has now grown up. 'Men are beginning to take a wider view.' The preacher refers tactfully to physical science, to researches into history, to changes in 'the interpretation of the Bible', even to geology — 'not long ago it [the Bible] would have been held to condemn geology, and there are still many who so interpret it.' The last two or three pages reveal the purpose for which the whole rhetorical structure has been planned — the advocacy of fearless Biblical study. It is, Temple believes,

utterly impossible . . . in the manhood of the world to imagine any other instructor of mankind. And for that reason, every day makes it more and more evident that the thorough study of the Bible, the investigation of what it teaches and what it does not teach, the determination of the degree of authority to be ascribed to the different books, if any degrees are to be admitted, must take the lead of all other studies. . . . If geology proves to us that we must not interpret the first chapters of Genesis literally; if historical investigations shall show us that inspiration, however it may protect the doctrine, yet was not empowered to protect the narrative of the inspired writers from occasional inaccuracy; if careful criticism shall prove that there have been occasionally interpolations and forgeries in that Book, as in many others; the results should still be welcome. . . . The immediate work of our day is the study of the Bible. . . . For we are now men, governed by principles, if governed at all, and cannot rely any longer on the impulses of youth or the discipline of childhood.

In the second Essay Rowland Williams, Vice-Principal and Professor of Hebrew at Lampeter, described by Campbell as 'a man of genius, somewhat dangerously blent with Celtic fire', wrote enthusiastically on *Bunsen's Biblical Researches*.

Baron von Bunsen was a very able and learned German — or, rather, Prussian — diplomat, whose real love was universal history, in which he sought to trace the imprint of God. He had spent thirteen years as Prussian ambassador at the Court of St. James — Queen Victoria herself chose him for the post out of three names submitted to her by the King of Prussia — and made a deep impression on the minds of very many Englishmen, among them Dr. Arnold. When *Essays and Reviews* appeared, he was a dying man; the English translation of his then famous *Gott in Geschichte* (God in History) was in the process of publication. He had other books to his credit, among them a study of Egyptian history and a new translation of the Bible, partially completed in 1860, intended 'for the people', in which he is said to have made some rather startling alterations and rearrangements of the traditional Hebrew text. His attitude towards the Christian verities was not unlike that which Jowett was developing: Christ was real, and Christianity true, but the dogmatic mould into which the Church had poured belief had made belief set too hard.

Dr. Williams's essay, though garnished with his own good Hebraic learning, was hardly more than an extended paean in praise of Bunsen. But he allowed himself to indulge in some dangerously unorthodox expressions of his own. It was (for example) asking for trouble to write : 'Why may not justification by faith have meant the peace of mind, or sense of Divine approval, which comes of trust in a righteous God, rather than a fiction of merit by transfer?' The idea of 'merit by transfer' may or may not be a fiction; but for most Christians it is still the sheet-anchor of their faith; and many, even of those who think it a fiction, recognize the truth it embodies and say in their hearts 'Nothing in my hand I bring.'

The third Essay was written by Baden Powell, a fellow of the Royal Society and Savilian Professor of Geometry at Oxford. It was wrongly titled *On the Study of the Evidences of Christianity*. A more accurate title would have been *On the Evidential Value of Miracles*. It is an exasperatingly long-winded affair, abounding in italics which emphasize the writer's inability to clarify his thought, to extract what is to the point and to exclude what is not, and to express the result in readable language. Stanley found the argument unintelligible; and so it is — or nearly so — through long stretches of clumsy dissertation. The author's own summary indicates its purpose, and something also of the involved presentation.

To conclude, an alleged miracle can only be regarded in one of two ways; — either (1) abstractedly as a physical event, and therefore to be investigated by reason and physical evidence, and referred to physical causes, possibly to *known* causes, but at all events to some higher cause or law, if at present unknown; it then ceases to be supernatural, yet still might be appealed to in support of religious truth, especially as referring to the state of knowledge and apprehension of the parties addressed in past ages; or (2) as connected with religious doctrine, regarded in a sacred light, asserted on the authority of inspiration. In this case it ceases to be capable of investigation by reason, or to own its dominion; it is accepted on religious grounds, and can appeal only to the principle and influence of faith.

The general drift of the essay was unmistakable. Baden Powell, a clerical scientist, rejected the miraculous 'evidences' of Christianity. And he had some shrewd things to say, though he could never get them effectively off his pen. Were miracles 'necessary' in order to convince unbelievers? Or were they not really 'miracles' but happenings capable of scientific explanation? Such inconsistent defences of miraculous narratives offer a beautiful opportunity of attack to a skilful controversialist. But Baden Powell was not a skilful controversialist. Again and again he loses the attention and sympathy of his reader in the host of laborious qualifications with which he thinks himself compelled to surround every statement. He never succeeds in baring the heart of any position. He incurred the odium of orthodox, without deserving the gratitude of liberal, churchmen. He was marked down, with Williams and Wilson, for ecclesiastical prosecution. But he died before that could happen. In the offensively presumptuous language used of him by Jowett's Oxford prosecutors, 'after denying Miracles' he had been 'removed to a higher tribunal'.

The fourth Essay, *Séances Historiques de Genève — The National Church*, calls for longer comment. Many people found it the most shocking and disturbing thing in the whole book. It was written by Henry Bristow Wilson, in whose mind the idea of *Essays and Reviews* was conceived. It was the longest of all the essays, except Jowett's; it occupied the central position; it was ably written and fearlessly argued; and it set out a view of what the Church of England, considered as a National Church, ought to be, which made the term 'broad church' seem by comparison mild and orthodox.

As the cumbrous title of the essay suggests, it is not a simple piece of writing, and not easy to summarize. It needs to be read, and it repays careful reading, even after more than a hundred years. What follows is a very inadequate attempt to convey its character and meaning.

A 'series of addresses by distinguished persons holding Evangelical sentiments' had been recently staged in Geneva. These addresses had, in themselves, very little to do with Wilson's main theme. Perhaps he hoped that by bringing Geneva so prominently into the title he would conciliate low church readers; if so, his stratagem failed. But the reference to the Séances Historiques de Genève was by no means pointless. An almost accidental altercation between two of the Genevan lecturers had provided him with a concept, and with a word for it, which he used to introduce his own argument for a much wider tolerance of divergent views than the Church of England had ever entertained.

According to one of the Genevan lecturers, Count de Gasparin, the Emperor Constantine, by inaugurating the union between the State and the Christian Church, had introduced the false and pagan principle of 'multitudinisme'.[1] Another Genevan lecturer, M. Bungener, warmly replied to de Gasparin. 'Le multitudinisme' he said 'est une force qui peut, comme toute force, être mal dirigée, mal exploitée, mais qui peut aussi l'être au profit de la vérité, de la piété, de la vie. . . . Elle a été, elle est, elle restera notre mère à tous.'

Wilson sided with Bungener. He took 'le multitudinisme' as a word of valuable meaning; introduced it into English as 'multitudinism'; and applied the concept, of which it was the intended label, to the Church of England. He assumed that everybody would know what 'multitudinism' meant. But nobody knew what it meant. And Wilson, having used it to get his essay started, never stopped to explain it. His idea of its meaning has to be gathered out of his argument.

The word has not taken root in English — perhaps not even in French. It is all the more important that it should be properly understood — that is, understood in the sense in which Wilson used it, and not in a quite different sense which he never intended. Unfortunately the word has been defined by the Oxford English Dictionary in such a way as to make complete nonsense of Wilson's concept. The Oxford Dictionary definition is: 'the principle according to which the interests of multitudes are placed before those of individuals, *esp.* in religion'. At first sight this definition looks beautifully clear. But the more it is studied, the less clear it becomes, until finally all shred of meaning vanishes. What 'especially in religion' are 'the interests of multitudes' as opposed to, or preferred before, 'those of individuals'?

If one goes back to Wilson's essay, it is quickly evident that, whatever he meant by 'multitudinism', he meant nothing at all like this. Far from

---

[1] I do not know whether de Gasparin invented this word, or used an old word in a new sense. It is not given in Mansion's French Dictionary.

imagining the salvation of souls in the mass, of multitudes before persons, he insisted, as strongly as anybody possibly could, that each individual soul has unique importance. On the concluding page of his essay he writes:

The Christian Church can only tend on those who are committed to its care, to the verge of that abyss which parts this world from the world unseen. Some few of those fostered by her are now ripe for entering on a higher career: the many are but rudimentary spirits — germinal souls. What shall become of them? If we look abroad in the world and regard the neutral character of the multitude, we are at a loss to apply to them, either the promises, or the denunciations of revelation. . . . The Roman Church has imagined a *limbus infantium*. We must rather entertain a hope that there shall be found, after the great adjudication, receptacles suitable for those who shall be infants, not as to years of terrestrial, but as to spiritual development — nurseries as it were and seed-grounds, where the undeveloped may grow up under new conditions — the stunted may become strong, and the perverted be restored.

This is not the language of a man who prefers 'the interests of multitudes' before 'those of individuals'. His hope may seem naive to some, heretical to others; but nobody can say that it looks to any other end than the ultimate salvation of individuals. Its only departure from orthodoxy is its trust that God will care for the single souls which make up the 'neutral multitude', when they are called to account after the death of the body.

It was because he held this charitable view, that Wilson was prosecuted, not only along with Williams for denying the inspiration of Holy Scripture, but especially for denying what his prosecutors asserted to be an essential doctrine of the Church of England — the doctrine that wicked men are irretrievably damned and will be punished for ever.

In the hundred years since Wilson wrote his essay we have gone, perhaps, too far in repudiating the idea that punishment is essentially retributive; that men should pay, with pain, for wrongdoing; that unless punishment remains punishment, it cannot bear the humane purposes we would put upon it. We think, now, of the punishments that human law inflicts as justifiable only by their power of preventing other men from criminal acts — by their 'deterrent' effect; and as occasions for psychological experiments upon men under forcible restraint — the 'reformatory' aspect of punishment. A generation committed to this benevolent conception of penology must find it impossible to understand the horror which Wilson's belief in an untiring and everlasting divine mercy caused to great numbers of pious and kindly Christians.

It is necessary to remember that the idea of sinfulness, as not only the natural state of unregenerate man but a deliberate attachment to evil and betrayal of good, and therefore deserving of utterly final punishment, was still dominant in the religious world, to which Wilson belonged, whether Anglican or Nonconformist. Secular thought had already revolted against it, to the point of jettisoning the very concept of 'sin'. It is nearly true to say that only in one part of the English religious world — that newly growing or re-growing part of the Church of England which was beginning to be called its 'broad' part,[1] — some few men were coming to think that the concept of sin needed to be re-examined; and that the idea of God's eternal wrath with human failures, or with the doomed human partisans of satanic resistance,[2] had become not so much horrible as silly; and that, if the formularies of the Church required intelligent men to accept it, that would mean the end of the Church in no very long time.[3]

Fortunately for the Church of England it was held, on appeal, that her formularies did not require assent to this belief. It may be thought that Wilson, therefore, did a service to his Church — though his recklessness frightened Stanley and other liberal but timid churchmen — by raising this particular issue of eternal damnation, at that particular point of time.

But eternal damnation was not the main or even a primary topic of Wilson's essay. It was a side-topic, erected into a main issue by the fanatical mood of his prosecutors. His main theme was the national character of the Church of England. How far had she truly maintained that character? What had she done to forfeit it? What chances remained to her of justifying it, and of retrieving or redressing her past mistakes?

A truly national church, Wilson argued, *must* be a 'multitudinist' church. He did not mean that men, if saved at all, must be saved *en masse;* that the 'neutral multitude' had, as we might say, an irresistible card vote for admission to the kingdom of heaven. He meant that a national church ceases to be a national church if it takes up a dogmatic position which is repudiated by a great part of the nation, by the 'multitude'. Nothing could be more painfully clear, in the middle of the nine-

---

[1] 'Broad' is, of course, merely a translation into common English of 'latitudinarian' — a term with eighteenth-century associations, often used by such men as Pusey and Wilberforce as almost synonymous with 'atheistical'.

[2] Belief in eternal damnation implied that the war between God and Satan was a mock war, of which the issue had always been determined. *Paradise Lost,* for all its imaginative and musical magnificence, fails in its epic character because Lucifer starts as a beaten rebel without the least chance of recovery, and the reader is expected to know this and to approve it before the poem begins. An epic of hopeless rebellion is conceivable; but not when the poet himself detests his hero.

[3] I am writing about the Church of England, not about the Roman Church, whose apologists will possibly say that their Church has never been committed to so crude a doctrine.

teenth century, than that the Church of England had long ceased to be, by this criterion, a national church. The huge process of dissent had created other, new, *soi-disants* Christian churches, with multitudes of members. This process had, in itself, gone far to destroy the Church of England's claim to be *de facto* as well as *de jure* the 'Church of England'. Her possession of this arrogant title; her uniquely privileged part in the constitution of the kingdom; her monopoly of ancient religious buildings and endowments; all these things, surely, imposed upon her the obligation of seeking to be, in truth and not merely in name and privilege, a body to which the great majority of English Christians would willingly accord the name of the Church of England.

Wilson contrasted the schisms, which had almost destroyed the claim of the Church of England to be what her name asserted her to be, with the solidarity of the pagan pre-Christian churches. This, it may be thought, was the weakest link in his argument. But it was not a link; it was an approach. 'Look!' he said, in effect. 'Even the pagan churches did better than we. At least they understood, as we seem not to understand, the several needs of their various races and cultures, each for a religious institution which holds all its citizens together.'

His conception of a 'national' church is open to very obvious criticisms. The answer to nearly all these criticisms is that Wilson was posing a particular question, about a particular church owning a title which (by his argument) it did not merit. The Church of England did not possess the 'multitudinist' character which should belong to a national church. He thought that, by an effort, she might acquire or recover that character; meanwhile, she was what he called an 'individual' church — a church committed to this and that peculiarity of doctrine, and aiming at the inclusion of the relatively few rather than at the inclusion of the relatively many.

This was — it still is and is likely to remain — an extremely difficult question. No little courage was needed for an Anglican priest to formulate it in 1860. To-day, when the Church of England is deliberately risking the loss of some of her members to the Church of Rome by an effort to recover communion with dissent, Wilson's remarkable essay is once more highly topical. But in 1860 he, and the few Anglican clergymen who thought as he did, were thinking less of re-union with the nonconformist churches (though there is very much in his essay which bears upon this topic) than of the dangerous possibility that, as time went on, fewer and fewer intelligent Englishmen would find Christianity, in any form at all, a creed possible for them to accept.

Wilson's essay infuriated most of his fellow clergymen. His argument was bitterly received and grossly misrepresented. The misrepresentation possibly explains the Oxford Dictionary's error of definition; for the Dictionary supports itself by a quotation from one of the many counter-blasts to *Essays and Reviews*,[1] which merely exhibits misunderstanding: 'Whether primitive Christianity ... was "multitudinistic" ... or whe-ther it was "exclusive" and sought access to the individual conscience of the few.'

Even Stanley — but he had always disapproved of getting 'seven men, without real agreement of view, to combine as if they had' — was harsh in his judgment of Wilson's essay. He wrote privately to the editor of the *Edinburgh Review*, after singling out Temple's and Pattison's and Jowett's essays and coming down to the others, that Wilson's

the ablest of the four, has committed the unpardonable rashness of throwing out statements, without a grain of proof, which can have no other object than to terrify and irritate, and which have no connection with the main argument of his Essay.

Tait wrote, in a private memorandum:

I deeply deplore, and indeed execrate, the spirit of much of *Essays and Reviews*. I have lately read over again with the utmost care Wilson's and Williams' essays before writing my memorandum for the judgement of their cases before the Privy Council ... I do not wonder at the outcry and alarm, but what are bishops appointed for except to direct the clergy in times of alarm? I pray that I may never fall into the snare of following rather than leading the clergy of my diocese.

If such men as Tait and, even, Stanley were unable to see in Wilson's essay anything which at least needed to be said, whatever the conse-quences might be, the leaders of the two opposing parties, Pusey and Wilberforce, treated it as a symptom of mental confusion needing no specific answer, except by way of prosecution.

Pusey, for example, writing to the *Guardian*[2] sought to treat 'the un-happy *Essays and Reviews*' as 'an undigested heap of errors' incapable and undeserving of 'a systematic answer'. He made no attempt to meet any of the intelligible and sensible propositions advanced by the Essayists. He listed a number of the 'undigested errors'; and among them he alluded to Wilson's assertion that

under the terms of the sixth Article one may accept literally, or allegori-cally, or as parable, or poetry, or legend, the story of a serpent tempter, of an ass speaking with man's voice, of an arresting of the earth's motion, of a reversal of its motion, of waters standing in a solid heap, of witches, and a variety of apparitions ... the primeval institution of the Sabbath, the universality of the deluge, the confusion of tongues, the corporal

[1] W. J. Irons, *Replies to Essays and Reviews*.
[2] *Life of E. B. Pusey*, iv, 40–2.

taking up of Elijah into Heaven, the nature of angels, the reality of demoniacal possession, the personality of Satan, and the miraculous particulars of many events.

For Pusey held that all these stories were simply and factually true, and that, without belief in this sort of fable, Christianity must fall to pieces.

The fifth Essay *On the Mosaic Cosmogony* was written by Charles Goodwin, a remarkable Cambridge all-rounder. He was the only lay contributor; and was, therefore, not liable to any ecclesiastical pains and penalties. It is said that this 'plain-spoken' essay widened his reputation. But he wasted his effort in tilting at windmills, and did not succeed in breaking down the barrier which had suddenly grown between the new science and orthodox religion. Geology was the first organized body of knowledge to menace belief in the Biblical story of creation. If the geologists were right, it was impossible to maintain this belief, however ingeniously the Biblical story might be interpreted. It is distressing to watch Pusey's childish attempts to cope with this problem. While he realized that, if this defence of his fundamentalist position were breached, a large part of his ground would have to be abandoned, he clung to the hope that the geologists were all wrong and that their theories belonged to a realm of pure fancy, incapable of proof.

Goodwin's chief title to fame was that of an Egyptologist. He was also 'in early life a fair Hebraist, botanist, and geologist, an accomplished Anglo-Saxon and a good German scholar'. He was forty-three when *Essays and Reviews* was published. Later, he was satisfied to be a judge in Shanghai and, then, Yokohama.

His essay easily — perhaps a shade too easily — overthrew Buckland's crude attempt to reconcile Genesis and Geology by assuming that each 'day' of creation really meant 'an age or immense geological period'. What, he asked, became 'of the evening and morning of which each day is said to have consisted?' Were there supposed to have been enormous intervals of total darkness? 'Such an ordeal would have completely destroyed the whole vegetable creation.' He had even less difficulty in overturning a later attempt made by the pious geologist, Hugh Miller, to meet this type of objection.

The story of creation was, he said, a simple Hebrew myth: for ages it

satisfied the wants of man, and formed a sufficient basis for theological teaching, and if modern research now shows it to be physically untenable, our respect for the narrative which has played so important a part in the culture of our race need be in nowise diminished. . . . [It is] a human utterance, which it has pleased Providence to use in a special way for the education of mankind.

Goodwin's essay could not expose him to prosecution, since he was a layman. Nor would it have been possible to prove him at fault, since that would have meant a frontal attack upon geological science. His essay was not marred by rash and intemperate theological expressions. The simple fact was that there was no possible answer to it. But the arguments men cannot answer are those which excite their deepest resentment. And the essay took the form not of an original argument but of a polemical and sometimes sarcastic reply to the ridiculous theories of Buckland and Miller. This may have been difficult for him to avoid. It was not the less unfortunate. It stoked a fire which needed no stoking; and stoked it in a specially provocative way.

The sixth Essay was Mark Pattison's. Nothing that Pattison ever wrote was devoid of deliberate meaning or based on assailable data. He discreetly called his article *Tendencies of Religious Thought in England, 1688–1750*. In spite of the inoffensive title, the studied impartiality, the careful adherence to the historical theme, he knew exactly how to barb his shaft without danger to himself. His examination of this rationalizing period in English religious thought ended with a paragraph, in his best ironical manner, which would exasperate an enemy and yet give him nothing to lay hold of.[1]

Such appears to be the past history of the Theory of Belief in the Church of England. Whoever would take the religious literature of the present day as a whole, and endeavour to make out clearly on what basis Revelation is supposed by it to rest, whether on Authority, on the Inward Light, Reason, self-evidencing Scripture, or on the combination of the four, or some of them, and in what proportions, would probably find that he had undertaken a perplexing but not altogether profitless inquiry.

Jowett's own Essay, the last in the volume, *On the Interpretation of Scripture* was on a plane above all the other six contributions. In essence it was a plea for the use of reason, as more important even than profound or exact scholarship, in the interpretation of scripture. The plea is closely argued for a hundred pages. The writer succeeds in following up every branch and byway without losing sight of his main theme. No page is superfluous. Almost every page contains memorable sentences of pith and moment. All hangs together in a sustained argument which deserves to be remembered for its own sake as a masterpiece of cool, but not cold, English writing upon a hot and explosive topic.

Few educated men to-day would dream of contesting the argument. Practically everything that Jowett said has long ago been conceded even

---

[1] Professor Willey gives, I think, too much of his space to Pattison's essay, which he places 'in a class apart from all the other essays'. I put Jowett's essay, alone, in that separate class; and find Pattison's essay relatively uninteresting.

by those who have inherited the various theological standpoints of his bitterest contemporary enemies. Nevertheless it remains one of those few topical masterpieces as easy and profitable to read after a hundred years as when they were first written. No matter what advances in the art of interpreting the scriptures have been made since Jowett's time, or how the various parties in the various churches have accommodated themselves to these advances, or where they all variously stand to-day, Jowett's essay has the lasting quality of a classic statement.

If a summary is needed, it is best given in his own words.

Of what has been said, this is the sum: — That Scripture, like other books, has one meaning, which is to be gathered from itself without reference to the adaptations of Fathers or Divines; and without regard to *à priori* notions about its nature and origin. It is to be interpreted like other books, with attention to the character of its authors, and the prevailing state of civilization and knowledge, with allowance for peculiarities of style and language, and modes of thought and figures of speech. Yet not without a sense that as we read there grows upon us the witness of God in the world, anticipating in a rude and primitive age the truth that was to be, shining more and more unto the perfect day in the life of Christ, which again is reflected from different points of view in the teaching of His Apostles.

To that general, reverently phrased, account, given by Jowett himself of the argument he had developed with convincing clarity of detail, may be added a few sentences from the passage near the end of his essay, in which he warns the reader (whom he naturally supposes to be 'about to become a clergyman') that he 'may possibly not be the person who is called upon to make such inquiries'. The theologian, he says,

as well as the philosopher has need of 'dry light', of light 'unmingled with any tincture of the affections',[1] the more so as his conclusions are oftener liable to be disordered by them. He who is of another temperament may find another work to do, which is in some respects a higher one. Unlike philosophy, the Gospel has an ideal life to offer, not to a few only, but to all. There is one word of caution, however, to be given to those who reverence inquiry; it is that they cannot retain the right to condemn inquirers.

3. THE ARCHBISHOP'S LETTER

Such, in bare outline, were the contents of the book which was to raise the greatest religious storm of the century. The *furore* was not — as it would be now, if it could be imagined to happen again — confined

[1] These are Jowett's own quotation marks. The expression 'dry light' comes from Bacon's essay on Friendship: 'Heraclitus saith in one of his Aenigmaes: Dry Light is ever the best.' I do not know the source of the second quotation, but others will.

to ecclesiastical circles. As the clerical agitation grew, *Essays and Reviews* became a more and more popular book. When eleven editions had been sold, Jowett said 'We have had enough of this volume: let us turn to something else.'[1] But that was not the view of the general public, which was beginning to discover an intelligent interest in matters it had for a long time been content to leave to professionals. The success of the book was of course promoted by the violence of the clerical outcry against it; but it showed that a great many people were on the side of the Essayists. Two eminent exceptions deserve to be noted. In January 1862 Wilberforce rode with Carlyle and complacently recorded in his diary: 'Carlyle against the essayists on dishonesty ground and atheistic.'[2] And eight years later Matthew Arnold (of all men!) said something of the same kind to Temple.[3]

The extraordinary course of the events, public and private, which followed the publication of *Essays and Reviews*, must be a part of any book about Jowett; for it affected him directly, and also indirectly through his friends and through the air of controversy which he had to breathe for very many years. The story is now so little remembered that it needs to be told with enough detail to make it come alive. It is strange that the whole episode should have been so generally dismissed as *vieux jeu* — an old affair not worth the trouble of digging up. For it is the key to one of the cupboards, in which our own recent history has been pushed away out of sight. Also, the story of it is dramatically exciting.

The reaction to *Essays and Reviews* developed slowly. Its sudden emergence into peak-height, and the swift growth of the peak into a peak over-topping all others, were the result of two opposed forces.

The spring and summer passed away, and the volume had excited but little attention. The appearance of an article in the 'Westminster Review' followed, first, by the autumn Charge of Bishop Wilberforce, and then by his article in the Quarterly Review at the beginning of 1861, gave the signal for a wild and panic-stricken agitation. Addresses, memorials, and remonstrances against the mischievous tendencies of the book poured in upon the Archbishops and Bishops . . . and the Archbishops were entreated to take action against the Essayists, who were described as traitors to their sacred calling, and as guilty of moral dishonesty.[4]

The article in the *Westminster and Foreign Quarterly Review*, written by Frederick Harrison, which is said to have thus sprung the mine, had an anti-clerical purpose. The Review was 'the organ of the Positivist school, whose reputed aim was to reconstruct society upon the ruins of existing systems; and the liberalizing of Christianity plainly did not fall

[1] *L. & L.*, i, 299.   [2] *Life of Bishop Wilberforce*, iii, 8.
[3] See below, 314.   [4] *Life of Dean Stanley*, ii, 30–1.

in with such a project.' The article was headed 'Neo-Christianity'; it
'caricatured' the position of the Essayists 'as one of hopeless inconsistency'.[1]

The aim, Campbell thought, was 'to push these writers over the precipice'. It was, I fancy, subtler and more ambitious than that. Here was a
chance to provoke the main body of earnest churchmen — whether high
or low — into such a display of reactionary intolerance that the influence
of the church among educated people would be permanently impaired.
As Campbell himself says, 'the clergy, who had hardly recovered from
the Darwinian scare, were in the mood to think, "If this gives offence in
such a quarter, how bad it must be!" '

The *Westminster* article appeared on 1st October. By itself it might
not have attracted notice. But the Bishop of Oxford, the outstanding
prelate of the time, by his denunciation of *Essays and Reviews* whipped
alarm into frenzy. His article in the January issue of the *Quarterly Review*
(which, in competition with the *Edinburgh Review*, still exercised a very
powerful influence upon educated minds) was vehemently out-spoken.
'We hold' he wrote 'that the attempt of the essayists to combine their
advocacy of such doctrines with the retention of the status and emolument of Church of England clergymen is simply moral dishonesty.' The
article was unsigned; but everybody knew who had written it. 'The
subtle influence of Bishop Wilberforce was easily detected, at once
depreciating the literary merit of the volume, and emphasizing both its
dangerous tendency and the position of the clerical contributors.' So
Campbell; who thought it characteristic of Wilberforce that he should
use his knowledge of Jowett's tribulations in Balliol and as professor of
Greek, to find in his Essay 'a certain sense of disappointment and concealed bitterness'.

Immediately after the appearance of Wilberforce's attack, Stanley
was asked to write an article for the *Edinburgh Review*. He accepted the
invitation. 'No doubt' he wrote to the editor 'the "Edinburgh" ought
to steer a middle course between the bottomless Charybdis of the
"Westminster" and the barking Scylla of the "Quarterly".' He saw no
difficulty 'in finding such a position'. His article appeared in April.
'Powerfully written, and full both of "swing" and "sting" ', it was not a
defence of *Essays and Reviews* (a project he had always disapproved) but
an attack 'upon the injustice with which the writers had been treated'
and upon the inconsistency of many of those who had 'taken the lead in
condemning the volume'. It was thought by Stanley and his mother that
this article prevented him from 'ever being a Bishop'. Certainly, it

[1] *L. & L.*, i, 292.

landed him in trouble 'for months, and even years, to come'. But it had no effect whatever upon the march of events, which had already begun and could not be halted by a 'fiery' article in the *Edinburgh* 'steering a middle course'.[1]

On 1st February there was a meeting of Bishops at Lambeth — one of the private meetings held from time to time, at which questions of policy were informally discussed. What passed on these occasions was supposed to be treated as entirely confidential. No record of any kind was kept; not even a rough minute-book.[2] In the ordinary course, therefore, these meetings cannot have resulted in decisions which had to be definitely implemented. Nevertheless a decision was certainly taken at this particular meeting, though no one except the Bishop of Oxford seems to have been quite sure what it was. Two laconic entries in his diary tell us what happened.

February 1. — (Cuddesdon.) Up early for the train. Wrote sermon all the way up. Saw Gladstone. Then to meeting of Bishops; long discussion on *Essays and Reviews*. Came down to Fulham with Bishops of London, Rochester, Carlisle. At night very much tired.

February 2. — (Fulham.) At the entreaty of Bishops, drew up an answer to addresses, which they all adopted, and we sent it out. Then to London, and I set to work on sermon for to-morrow, and down to Oxford by 3 train. Dined at Oriel Gaudy; small party; no college enthusiasm; quite understand its decline. Provost good, but far too cold for the post.[3]

The 'answer' drawn up by Wilberforce was the letter which Archbishop Sumner signed and which was dated from Lambeth ten days later. 'We sent it out' can mean only that copies of Wilberforce's draft were made and sent by post to *all* the Bishops for their approval, including those who had not been at the Lambeth meeting.[4] The Bishops, who entreated him to write the answer and who 'all' adopted it, can have been only those who had spent the night with him at Fulham. The composition of the answer may have been left to them, as a sort of subcommittee, by the general wish of the Bishops present at the Lambeth meeting. But it must have been evident that the task would be willingly shouldered by the Bishop of Oxford. It would seem that his draft was almost universally accepted. At any rate his biographer reproduces the Archbishop's letter as 'the Bishop's composition'.[5]

[1] *Life of Dean Stanley*, ii, 33–4, 40–1.
[2] *Life of Archbishop Tait*, i, 283 footnote.
[3] *Life of Bishop Wilberforce*, iii, 2 and 4. The note about Oriel, though interesting in itself, is relevant only because it completes the picture of two important but over-crowded days.
[4] See below, 252 second footnote.
[5] Wilberforce's draft may have contained one word which had to be corrected: 'their' instead of 'these' at the beginning of the second paragraph. At least this seems to be a likely explanation of the 'misprint' in the text of the letter as it was published, without authority, by *The Times*. See below, 252 and 255.

Is it usual for the Primate of All England to sign an important letter, entirely written for him by somebody else, which seeks to convey the impression that it is all his own work? One hopes not; for that would be the negation of honesty where, if anywhere, honesty claims to belong. It is true that Archbishop Sumner was an old and failing man. His spirit had been broken some fourteen months earlier by allegations against his integrity, eloquently made in the Court of Queen's Bench by a rising young barrister named Coleridge. Coleridge, at the conclusion of the hearing (the case was legally entitled *The Queen v. the Archbishop of Canterbury*) apologized for the language he had used. He could easily afford to apologize; for he had won his game and publicly humiliated the Archbishop, and it was nothing to him that the Archbishop should, thereafter, give his personal office over to others. Indeed, in Coleridge's reformist mind, that was the way for such offices to go.[1]

The Archbishop fell into his fatal illness in May 1861 — three months or so after the Lambeth meeting, at which he presided and spoke very sensibly. He died next year, aged eighty-two, but he was not, in February 1861, an ill man — not at least a man so ill that he must be used, if at all, as a rubber stamp. Yet that was how he was used; and he consented meekly. What is shocking is not the old man's humble surrender, but the facile assumption of all the Bishops, without (it seems) one single dissentient, that it was honest to put out a letter, bearing his signature but not written by him, as if it were his own composition. Even Tait saw nothing dishonest in this pretence. It has been through the too easy growth of 'statesmanlike' dishonesty that our own world has begun to founder. Cant displaces truth. It is frightening to perceive this annihilating process at work in Lambeth a hundred years ago; and to perceive that nobody concerned in it saw anything whatever to be ashamed of.

Wilberforce speaks of 'an answer to addresses'. In narrow fact it was an answer to one particular address 'emanating from a rural deanery in Dorsetshire'; though, by implication, it was an answer to all the addresses. The choice of this Dorsetshire address must have been made at the Lambeth meeting; and the reason is not far to seek. It was discreetly worded; it named no book and no person.

Besides the two entries in his diary, Wilberforce's papers included a rough note of what he thought to have been said by the chief speakers

---

[1] The 'office' was not that of Archbishop, but of the Visitor of All Souls; but the Visitor was the Archbishop, and Sumner's confidence in his capacity to use his own judgment in either office was fatally wounded. So was the confidence of his advisers, and of the Bishops, and of the college of which he was Visitor. See above, 203–4 *foll.* and below, 271.

at the Lambeth meeting. Tait's biographers were severe on Reginald Wilberforce for publishing this note in his *Life* of his father, and they denied the accuracy of the Bishop's recollections.[1]

Wilberforce can hardly have been mistaken over the two questions round which the debate turned. Should the Bishops issue a 'declaration of doctrine'? Should they prosecute? The sense of the meeting was against a declaration partly, as the Bishop of Oxford succinctly put it, 'because by such action Bishops would originate'; and partly, as the Bishop of St. David's (Thirlwall, perhaps the most intelligent man on the bench) shrewdly pointed out, because 'a mere Declaration by the Bishops, unless followed by action, would be an admission "that we had no means of repressing prolate heresy"; he strongly deprecated any discussion in Convocation'.

The idea of prosecution was not, it seems, unconditionally favoured by anybody except — *mirabile dictu* — Bishop Hampden of Hereford, who thought 'that this was a question between Infidelity and Christianity, and that we ought to prosecute: a question of Christianity or no Christianity'. Those present who recalled Hampden's once notorious Bampton Lectures, and the accusations of free-thinking infidelity under which he had formerly suffered, must have felt some embarrassment to hear Satan thus rebuke sin.[2] There was a general desire to prosecute; but also a fear (as the event proved, a well-founded fear) that prosecution might fail. The Bishop of Winchester (Archbishop Sumner's younger brother) hemmed and hawed: 'how are we to stop after a declaration? our present position is very difficult, it would then be worse — there are difficulties on both sides — inclined to take legal advice. Agreed with the Bishop of Oxford.'

Nearly half Wilberforce's note is taken up with Tait's contributions to the debate.

The Bishop of London: 'The difficulty is that we have two sets of people to consider. (1) Those likely to be injured by the book; and (2) those who are not. For the first, the only way is to let everyone who can answer them [the essayists] show their shallowness and further point out the great doctrines which all the essayists undervalue. For the second, that we ought to think of the effect on others.' Two of the essayists were dear friends of his. Of the essays he considered Pattison's unobjectionable, and as to Temple's he defied any man to extract anything heretical from it. Jowett's essay, he said, could only be answered by bringing out the doctrines which he neglects. He expressed himself strongly in favour of a

---

[1] *Life of Bishop Wilberforce*, iii, 2–4. *Life of Archbishop Tait*, i, 283 footnote.
[2] See *Oxford Apostles*, Chapter ix, § 3. It is sad to observe that Hampden, turned Bishop, was concerned only to obliterate his record, to the point of advocating the punishment of men who used their minds honestly, as he had once used his own.

Declaration of doctrine, in which he was supported by the Archbishop. . . .
He did not agree with the argument that it was a reflection on the Church
of England that her Articles did not meet every form of evil. He thought
that false doctrine must be endured.

If this summary did not do justice to what Tait thought he had said —
and certainly the argument it reproduces is neither lucid nor consistent
— it supports the account given by his biographer, that

he seems from the first to have taken the line to which he adhered to the
end, drawing a marked distinction between the different essays, while he
joined in his brethren's censure of the rash and harmful character of the
volume regarded as a whole.

Already, at the Lambeth meeting on 1st February, Tait perceived, if
he did not yet fully understand, the extraordinary difficulty of his
position. This difficulty was to be increased, to the point almost of agony,
by the publication of the Archbishop's letter which Wilberforce drafted
under Tait's roof at Fulham on 2nd February. Tait could not but approve
the draft. Whether he liked or disliked, trusted or distrusted, the Bishop
of Oxford, he was a man of fundamentally simple piety and faith; the
premises upon which he relied were those which Wilberforce, also, took
for granted. Moreover, he was the younger man — not so much younger
in years as younger in episcopal experience. For Wilberforce, though
only six years older, had been Bishop of Oxford for more than fifteen
years; and Tait had been Bishop of London for barely six years. Again,
Tait had behind him an experience of a kind Wilberforce had never even
remotely touched — that of a Balliol tutor — in which he had shared and
encouraged the speculative freedom of his young colleagues and pupils.
This experience had been too soon cut short and blunted by the headmastership of Rugby. Finally, he lacked Wilberforce's magnetic personal force, his rapidity of thought and mastery of argumentative speech.
The two days of 1st and 2nd February, and especially the morning of the
second day, when Wilberforce took complete charge of the situation,
must have been hard for Tait to live through. There was worse to come.

It had been intended that the Archbishop's letter should be published,
authoritatively, together with the Dorsetshire address selected for particular reply. Before this happened, *The Times* (and perhaps some other
newspapers) published the text of the letter without the address. The
effect of this unauthorized publication was completely to annul the discreet purpose of choosing the Dorsetshire address as the address to be
answered. The letter was at once taken by everybody to refer to *Essays
and Reviews* as a book; to convey a judgment upon *all* the Essayists. A
curious mistake in the first line of the third paragraph (where 'their' was

printed instead of 'these') was universally thought to emphasize this intention. It is anybody's guess how this unfortunate mistake came to be made.

Here is the text of the address and of the letter.

The address

We wish to make known to your Grace and to all the Bishops the alarm we feel at some late indications of the spread of rationalistic and semi-infidel doctrines among the beneficed clergy of this realm. We allude especially to the denial of the atoning efficacy of the Death and Passion of our Blessed Saviour Jesus Christ, both God and Man, for us men and for our salvation, and to the denial also of a Divine Inspiration, peculiar to themselves alone, of the Canonical Scriptures of the Old and New Testament.

We would earnestly beseech your Grace and your Lordships, as faithful stewards over the House of God, to discourage by all means in your power the spread of speculations which would rob our countrymen, more especially the poor and unlearned, of their only sure stay and comfort for time and for eternity. And to this end we would more especially and most earnestly beseech you, in your Ordinations, to 'lay hands suddenly on no man' till you have convinced yourselves (as far as human precaution can secure it) that each Deacon who in reply to the question, 'Do you unfeignedly believe all the Canonical Scriptures of the Old and New Testament?' answers 'I do believe them', *speaks the truth* as in the sight of God.

The reply

To the Rev. H. B. Williams   Lambeth, February 12, 1861

Reverend Sir,—I have taken the opportunity of meeting many of my Episcopal brethren in London to lay your address before them.

They unanimously agree with me in expressing the pain it has given them that any clergyman of our Church should have published such opinions as those concerning which you have addressed us.

We cannot understand how these[1] opinions can be held consistently with many of the fundamental doctrines with which they appear to us essentially at variance.

Whether the language in which these views are expressed is such as to make the publication an act which could be visited in the Ecclesiastical Courts or to justify the Synodical condemnation of the book which contains them is still under our gravest consideration. But our main hope is our reliance on the blessing of God, in the continued and increasing earnestness with which we trust that we and the clergy of our several dioceses may be enabled to teach and preach that good deposit of sound doctrine which our Church teaches in its fulness, and which we pray that she may, by God's grace, ever set forth as the uncorrupted Gospel of our Lord Jesus Christ. — I remain, reverend Sir, your faithful servant,

J. B. Cantuar.

I am authorized to append the following names. [Here follow the names of the Archbishop of York and twenty-four Bishops.][2]

[1] The word 'these' was printed as 'their', when the letter was published in *The Times*.

[2] According to the *Life of Bishop Wilberforce*, iii, 2, the Archbishops of Canterbury and York and 17 Bishops were present at the Lambeth meeting. The

252

4. TAIT IN TROUBLE

The unauthorized publication of the Archbishop's letter, on 16th February, raised the excitement of the educated public to a new plane. To the great majority of churchmen the terms of the letter and the names of the signatories seemed to promise that the Bishops were determined to root out the weed of rationalism. To the minority, who believed that the Church must either allow her ministers to use the tools of science and criticism or herself 'die from the top' downwards, the letter delivered a frightening shock.

What — wondered Stanley and others of Tait's old Balliol friends and pupils — could possibly have persuaded the Bishop of London to join himself with this reactionary pronouncement, except that he had become a Bishop and lost his former sense of words and meanings? They knew nothing of Tait's crude, indestructible, religious fundamentalism — he had kept it secret from them, while he was their tutor, he had kept it secret to himself. They had thought of him as a man of intellectual power; his behaviour, in this crisis, seemed to them utterly incomprehensible. Indeed, it is not easy to understand it now; except by putting oneself imaginatively into Tait's position, as an ex-headmaster at school again in the art of episcopal diplomacy — not yet an expert like Wilberforce, but thinking himself on the way to becoming so.

Stanley and Jowett and Temple had all been, separately, at Fulham since the public agitation against *Essays and Reviews* had begun. Jowett was there for two days, only two or three weeks before the mustering of Bishops. He came away from his visit without the least suspicion of what was in the wind or in Tait's mind. Temple, meeting him soon afterwards, asked how the visit had gone. He answered: 'Tait was very kind, and on the whole gave me the impression that he agreed with me.' Temple himself had received a very similar impression a few days earlier.

The Bishop had confided to his diary a quite opposite idea about Jowett. He felt

an obscurity over what he believes of the centre of Christianity . . . the Central Figure of the Lord Jesus, the central doctrine of the efficacy of His Sacrifice — in fact St. Paul's Christianity — is this distinctly recognized by the writers of his school? I have urged both on him and Temple who has also been with me, that they are bound to state for their own sakes and

signatures appended to the letter included, therefore, the signatures of no fewer than 7 Bishops who had not been present. Of the 26 Bishops who, in 1861, occupied the episcopal sees of the two Provinces of Canterbury and York, only the Bishops of Worcester and Sodor and Man failed to endorse the Archbishop's letter.

for the sakes of those whom they are likely to influence what is the *positive* Christianity, which they hold. It is a poor thing to be pulling down. Let them build up. Lord, fix my own heart and soul on the great Christian Verities.

When the Archbishop's letter appeared Jowett followed his rule of silence. He said nothing in public and little to his friends. Veiling his inner distress, he adopted a jocular attitude. He wrote to Stanley, explaining why he had decided not to send to Tait a letter of protest written out in 'fair calligraphic hand (beautiful writing, and the term which you added about the Formularies of the Church of England quite admirable)'. It was going to be a long contest:

I am afraid in my case as long as life; and there will be other opportunities of showing that I am not cowed by this apparition of the twenty-five Bishops; in the meantime it is of great importance to speak evil of no one and to irritate no one.

He had begun to learn the most valuable of the lessons life had to teach him, and he to teach his pupils: *aequam memento rebus in arduis servare mentem*, calling humour in to prevent serenity from becoming too self-conscious and pompous and thus destroying itself. He was learning to maintain his personality against the slings and arrows of outrageous fortune better than by the childish resentment which nevertheless still continued to affect his behaviour in Balliol.

His letter to Stanley continued:

Whether this plan is successful or not, depends partly on the manner in which it is carried out, and this on health and other matters over which I have no control. When I look at the matter seriously and not comically, as I do sometimes with you and Mrs. Vaughan — who is positively deserting me in my misfortunes, no doubt for good and wise reasons, (when I am burnt in the Churchyard at Doncaster, the Vicar preaching a sermon on the occasion, I expect her to give me breakfast) — I believe the motto should be, 'in quietness and confidence shall be your strength'. Therefore I shall cease to trouble you and Mrs. Stanley any more on the subject.[1]

Concerning Tait's action in signing the Archbishop's letter Jowett is reported to have said only: 'It is natural in him but it ruins confidence.' But Stanley and Temple were furiously angry. Each told the Bishop of London what he thought in a series of hotly outspoken letters. Some account of this extraordinary correspondence is necessary, if one is to understand the nature of the controversy which occasioned it. Though Jowett took no open part in that controversy, it conditioned the rest of his life.

[1] *L. & L.*, i, 346–7. Mrs. Stanley, of course, was Stanley's mother. Stanley was not yet married to Lady Augusta Bruce. Mrs. Vaughan was Stanley's youngest sister; her husband had just become Vicar of Doncaster.

'I do not know' wrote Stanley to Tait on 16th February 'when I have been more startled than in seeing your name appended to the document which this morning appeared in *The Times*.' Tait had given him clearly to understand that he 'saw nothing seriously to condemn in Jowett's Essay and hardly anything in Temple's' and that 'no measure could be taken by the Bishops except a general recommendation to preach the truth more actively'. Stanley had treated the latter statement as confidential. But the former he had repeated 'in various places'. Tait's subscription to the Archbishop's letter directly contradicted both assurances. 'How can I explain this? What can I say in your defence?'[1]

Tait's answer began by resting itself upon the 'typographical error' in the Archbishop's letter, as given in *The Times*, which — he thought — materially altered its tone. 'The word "their" is substituted for "these". This shall be publicly corrected.' If the letter were so corrected, it would be seen that there was no contradiction.

No allusion . . . is made to any individual writer, and it is open for each to show that he is not responsible for what the others have written, or for the general system which the public has put together from comparing the seven essays. Trust me that I have done in this matter what is best, and what was absolutely necessary.

Stanley replied that 'the typographical correction makes grammar, where before there was none, but unfortunately makes the sense . . . worse than before'. (Did it?) He was grieved that Tait had not 'been able to remove the contradiction between your acquittal of three of the Essayists[2] to me in private and the sweeping censure of them in public'. He could not understand 'any popular panic justifying such a course'. An attempt was being made to drive such men as Temple, Jowett and Pattison out of the Church of England; and Tait had lent himself to this. For the present, 'we had better have no more communication on this subject'. To this suggestion Tait agreed, still 'perfectly confident of the rightness and wisdom of what has been done', still maintaining that he had not been guilty of any inconsistency. He was due to stay with Stanley towards the end of March. 'By that time I almost expect that you will be of my mind in the matter: but if not, we can agree to differ.'

He added, in a postscript, that Stanley was 'quite at liberty to repeat what I have said respecting Temple's, Pattison's and Jowett's Essays. . . . Would that their Essays were freed from the company of Powell, Williams, and Wilson.' This was the line of counter-attack most likely to

[1] The whole of the correspondence is given in the *Life of Archbishop Tait*, i, chapter XII.
[2] The third essayist was Mark Pattison, not mentioned in Stanley's first letter, but mentioned in Tait's reply, as also not subject to the condemnation implied in the Archbishop's letter.

discomfit Stanley, who had always thought the plan of *Essays and Reviews* ill advised.

No sooner had this correspondence with Stanley ended, at least for the time being, than Tait found himself engaged in a very much longer and infinitely more painful correspondence with Temple. Although he maintained, as uncompromisingly to Temple as to Stanley, that the Bishops had acted rightly, and indeed always continued to say so in public, his diary suggests that he was beginning to suffer some private doubt. On 24th February he noted: 'Anxiety as to the judgment of the Bishops on *Essays and Reviews*. Fear of misunderstandings with old friends.' On 3rd March: 'This week has been one of great trial. Temple's letters respecting the declaration of the Bishops have greatly pained me.' On 7th March: 'How difficult is my position. ————'s letter speaks the truth. "For once," he says, "I have no desire to be a Bishop." . . . O Lord, grant me wisdom to help, even in spite of themselves, those whom I so greatly regard.'[1]

It was all very well to fear 'misunderstandings'. But three of his old friends had all come away from Fulham, after separate visits, with exactly the same 'misunderstandings' of what he had said to them and the same inability to reconcile what he had said with his action in endorsing the Archbishop's letter.

Temple wrote bitterly:

If you do not wish to alienate your friends, do not treat them as you have treated me. Do not, if one of them seem to you to have done a foolish, or even a wrong thing, ask him to your house, speak of the subject kindly, condemn in such a tone as to imply no severe reprobation; and then, in deference to a popular clamour, join in an act of unexampled severity. . . . What you did had not the intention, but it had all the effect, of treachery. You will not keep friends if you compel them to feel that in every crisis of life they must be on their guard against trusting you.

Tait replied that this was not just; that he had 'endeavoured to act with a full remembrance of all that has passed between us'; and that 'it is the misery of an official position that if a man is determined that his private friendships and his public acts shall never appear to come into collision, he must give up his private friendships'. To which Temple answered furiously: 'The greatest kindness you can now do me is to forget till all this is over that any friendship ever existed between us. That will at any rate save me from such mischief as your speech in Convocation yesterday [28th February] is certain to do me.'

The Bishop of St. David's wise warning had failed. The issue *had* been raised and discussed in Convocation, and Tait had walked his tight

---

[1] *Life of Archbishop Tait*, ii, 307.

rope, swaying precariously. In his speech he had referred to his long private friendship with Dr. Temple, and had said that while he disliked Temple's essay it was 'totally different in character from other passages which occur in this volume', and that he could not understand why the author should not publicly 'declare that he does not approve of various things which are to be found in this unfortunate book'.

Tait was provoked by Temple's angry rejoinder into hitting back. He ended his reply with a sharp reference to Temple's 'somewhat arrogant over-estimate of the infallibility' of his own opinion. Whereupon Temple, though still maintaining his criticism of Tait's behaviour and his version of what Tait had said to him at Fulham, wrote back in a humbler spirit:

I am very sorry if I have been arrogant. I was not conscious of it. I cannot honestly say that I am conscious of it now. But a man smarting under a sense of having been unfairly treated by a friend is not a fair judge of his own temper. At any rate, I am honestly grateful to you for telling me. That at least is straightforward and friendly. I will try to be on my guard against the fault. I owe you very much: more than I can ever repay. . . . Forgive me if I have written hotly.

It was not surprising that he should have written hotly. Tait's endorsement of the Archbishop's letter had put Temple into a position of extraordinary trouble at Rugby — trouble which Tait seems simply not to have foreseen. For here was the ex-headmaster, now Bishop of London, lending his name (so everybody thought) to a public, official, episcopal censure of his own successor.

Alarm spread rapidly among masters and parents. A few days after the appearance of the Archbishop's letter in *The Times* one of the Rugby masters wrote privately to the Bishop of London begging that the address should be published as well as the answer to it, since

no one can say exactly who or what has been censured. Most of us think that Dr. Temple's essay is not included in the general censure. I am one of the few who hope that your lordships have only agreed in condemning certain specified opinions not maintained by Dr. Temple.[1]

The Bishop replied that the address was to be found in the 'last *Guardian*'; and that it contained 'no allusion to Dr. Temple, nor to any opinion which his essay, as I understand it, maintains'.

On the day of this reply (23rd February) the headmaster addressed his assistant masters. The Bishop's solicitous Rugby informant sent him a private report of this address. What the headmaster had said 'showed, in the opinion of the writer, how deeply he was distressed by much that the volume contained, and how conscious he was of the pain which it had caused to parents of the Rugby boys'. Tait very foolishly accepted

[1] These two sentences plainly contradict each other.

this piece of reportage at its face value. He at once wrote a long and unwise letter to Temple, urging him once more to dissociate himself publicly from his fellow Essayists. Temple was adamantine: 'I can only say that nothing on earth will induce me to do what you propose. I do not judge for others, but in me it would be base and untrue.' This was the letter in which he asked Tait to forget 'that any friendship ever existed between us'.

Temple knew that some well-meaning busybody on his staff was misinforming the Bishop. He wrote again, in order to make his standpoint as clear as he possibly could:

I was quite aware that in speaking to the masters I ran a considerable risk of being misrepresented by half-statements of what I said. But I thought their relation to me made openness their due in spite of the risk. Such a half-statement, however, as I feared, seems to have reached you. For I do not think that whoever told you of what I said can have told you that my last words to the masters were: 'You will see that if any public statement of my disapproval of the other writers in the volume is made, I shall probably find it my duty to contradict it.' I think you could neither have been told this, nor what, you can see from its tenor, preceded it.

To this Tait, at the end of a last letter mainly intended to justify his, as against Temple's, recollection of what he had said at Fulham a few weeks earlier, shortly replied: 'I had no information of the closing words of your address to the masters. I should add that I do not now see that they are wise or right.'

Besides addressing his assistant masters, Temple spoke to the boys. He was obliged, also, to justify himself to the School's Trustees, by whom he had been appointed. Tait, writing to Stanley in July, knew — or thought that he knew — all about these occasions:

Temple has found no impossibility in separating himself from the extreme section of the Essayists by his semi-public declarations to the masters, boys, and trustees. It is much to be regretted that he should have imagined for himself any impossibility in saying publicly what he has said semi-publicly.

For some months it seemed that Temple would be forced to resign. So violent was the clerical odium and so long-lasting that, when Mr. Gladstone advised the Queen to nominate him for the Bishopric of Exeter in 1869, there was actually talk of refusing the *congé d'élire*,[1] and 'the Bishops, for the most part, shrank from joining in the consecration'. Archbishop Tait was ill and absent from the ceremony. There were last-minute protests, and a very long delay while the crowded congregation

---

[1] The election was, in fact, disputed. It was carried by 13 votes to 6, four members of the Chapter being absent. *Memoirs of Archbishop Temple*, i, 291.

sat, wondering what had gone wrong, before these protests were disposed of. The darkness in the Abbey was

beyond all precedent. It was difficult, even with all the lights in the Abbey, to discern one person from another; and so, in the language of a High Church newspaper, 'on that darkest day in the whole year [21st December] was perpetrated the darkest crime which had been perpetrated in the English Church.'[1]

The portents were false. The new Bishop conciliated his clergy by withdrawing his contribution to *Essays and Reviews*, in spite of his former determination to do nothing of the kind. His career resumed its extraordinary parallel with Tait's when he went to Fulham from Exeter in 1885 and to Canterbury from Fulham in 1896. He went one better than Tait. He fathered another Archbishop of Canterbury.

The news of Temple's precarious position at Rugby caused great alarm to the up and coming generation of intelligent clergymen. Campbell recorded that

men like Dr. Vaughan (the present Dean of Llandaff), Dr. Lightfoot (afterwards Bishop of Durham), and Dr. Westcott (the present Bishop of Durham), agreed with Stanley in regarding such a result as a national calamity, as well as in deprecating the violent and sweeping charges with which the Essayists were assailed.

Dr. Lightfoot feared a division

into two well-defined and extreme parties, the one consisting of irrational champions of so-called orthodoxy, the other of men who, under the pressure of opposition, will be driven into a position of reckless scepticism.

Dr. Westcott pointed out, what was 'acknowledged by all, that men of high intellectual culture have for some years shrunk from taking Orders'. If free criticism were banished from theology, 'if our ministers, as a class, should fall below the laity in sacred learning', the result would be 'a serious calamity'.

Jowett himself, writing to Dean Elliot, had said much the same:

Do you know that Convocation, at the instigation of Dr. Jelf, are going to consider and perhaps censure the book called *Essays and Reviews*? How injurious to Convocation, to what is termed orthodoxy, to every one except the writers of the book and their friends! . . . At present the book is a sort of bugbear among the Bishops and Clergy, showing, I venture to think, that some inquiries of the sort were needed, if the evidences of religion are to have anything but a conventional value. In a few years there will be no religion in Oxford among intellectual young men, unless religion is shown to be consistent with criticism. I wish the Bishops were alive to the great and increasing evil of the want of ability among young clergymen.

How did Tait stand in relation to all this? 'Many years ago' Temple reminded him 'you urged us from the University pulpit to undertake

[1] *Life of Dean Stanley*, ii, 371–2.

the critical study of the Bible. You said that it was a dangerous study, but indispensable.' Such a study, Temple said, 'imperatively demands freedom for its condition. To tell a man to study, and yet bid him, under heavy penalties, come to the same conclusions with those who have not studied, is to mock him.' Admittedly, Temple wrote,

toleration must have limits or the Church would fall to pieces. But the student has a right to claim, *first*, that those limits should be known beforehand, and contained in formularies within his reach; not locked up in the breasts of certain of his brethren; *secondly*, that his having transgressed them should be decided after fair, open trial by men practised in such decisions. Instead of that what do we see? A set of men publish a book containing the results of their study and thought, which, rightly or wrongly, they believe to be within the limits traced out by the formularies. Suddenly, without any warning to them that they are on their trial, without any proof that they have really transgressed the limits prescribed, the whole Bench of Bishops join in inflicting a severe censure, and insinuating that they are dishonest men. . . . You complain that young men of ability will not take orders. How can you expect it when this is what befalls whoever does not think just as you do? . . . I for one joined in writing this book in the hope of breaking through that mischievous reticence which, go where I would, I perpetually found destroying the truthfulness of religion.

Tait's defence against this passionate protest was strangely beside the point:

It is in vain to say, as you do, that such a declaration as that of the Bishops makes the exhortation to Biblical studies a mockery. You grant that there must be limits to the freedom of the conclusions at which clergymen arrive, and which they teach. Suppose a man unfortunately to arrive at the opinion, as the result of his Biblical studies, that there is no God, and that the Bible is from the beginning to the end a lie. Am I to allow him to teach this as a clergyman of the Church of England? Or if I condemn the result of his studies, am I to be said to discourage all study? Is not this a *reductio ad absurdum*?

Indeed it was a reduction to absurdity; but the absurdity was imported into the argument by Tait himself.

Sharp as these exchanges were, to the point of bitterness, they did not destroy the warmth of Tait's feelings towards his two friends or of their feelings towards him. Within twelve months he was writing to his 'dearest Stanley' and signing himself 'yours ever affectionately'. Some three years after his correspondence with Temple, in which both men had said more than enough to kill any ordinary friendship for ever, he stayed in the School House at Rugby. Sitting in the bedroom where his children had been born and where he had lain 'for so many weeks in helpless sickness', he prayed in his diary:

O Lord, bless the work here. Bless Temple in his vigorous honest course. Deepen every religious impression of his teaching. Last night he addressed the communicants in Chapel with great earnestness and plainness.

According to Abbott the friendship between Tait and Jowett was 'never broken in spite of their wide difference in religious opinions'. That was perhaps something of an overstatement; if not actually broken, the friendship was interrupted and strained to the breaking point. But just before the Archbishop's death in 1882 Jowett went to see him, and set down afterwards the gist of what passed between them. 'I know' said the dying man 'that what you wrote was only written out of a love of the truth. May the spirit of God grow and increase in you . . . God bless you, my dear friend.' Jowett answered that he would never forget those last words.

This human warmth over-rode the faults which, at the time of *Essays and Reviews*, seemed to Tait's three Balliol friends to have undone the man in the prelate. They were the more distressed by his apparent repudiation of their search for truth, because it was to his mental vigour that they owed no small part of their own. They felt that he had gone back on himself as well as on them.

5. THE BOOK BEFORE CONVOCATION

While Tait and Temple were still locked in angry argument, the agitation against *Essays and Reviews* moved into the stage anticipated by Jowett. The book became the subject of debate in the Lower and Upper Houses of Convocation.

Although the Bishop of London had stood firmly by the Archbishop's letter and his own part in that letter, and always continued to do so, it was impossible that he could be altogether deaf to Stanley's and Temple's protests or blind to the consequences, if the fundamentalists should achieve their object of driving the Essayists, or some of them, out of the Church of England. That must lead both to dishonest conformity within the Church and to its increasing isolation from contemporary thought.

These were possibilities which a man of Tait's intellectual calibre could hardly fail to perceive. He was then just beginning to grasp the elements of ecclesiastical statecraft. He never quite learned that most difficult of human arts. Few men are capable of doing so and of retaining faith in God and men. Nevertheless he saw, clearly enough, that the agitation against *Essays and Reviews* was getting out of hand. He did his utmost, now, to restrain it. But he had already made his fatal error. If he had refused to put his signature to the Archbishop's letter, he would have stood in a position of strength, when Convocation came to debate *Essays and Reviews*. As it was, he stood in a position of weakness. In spite of his courage and eloquence, what he said went — or so it seemed — for less than nothing.

The question came first before the Lower House on February 26, when 'some of the speakers gave expression' to their wrath or their alarm 'in language of the wildest kind'. Archdeacon Denison, for example, spoke of 'the young, who are tainted and corrupted and thrust almost to Hell by the action of this Book'. In the Upper House, on 28th February, after the Bishop of Oxford had spoken with his usual vehemence, the Bishop of London tried to separate Temple's and Jowett's essays from the others. He clung to his hope that these two writers would publicly disavow their fellow-essayists; he considered it 'their bounden duty' to do so. He thought the book, as a whole, was 'likely to do great and grievous harm'; he hoped 'even against hope' that 'these individuals might return, however far they may have gone astray'; but, he said, 'I for one shall not permit myself to doubt of their honesty, and I shall not trouble myself about their consistency.'

This lame defence of the two essayists with whom, he said, 'I have been, and am at this moment, the intimate personal friend', did no good to anybody, least of all to Tait himself. It infuriated Temple; it did not restore Jowett's ruined confidence; it made no impression upon the Bishops; it earned him the distrust of the clerical rank-and-file; it drew down upon him the vindictive calumny of the clerical press. It was said that he had 'compromised and even vilified the faith he was appointed to maintain', had 'sacrificed truth to friendship, and linked himself without shame to the heresiarchs of the Church'. As an essay in statesmanship his speech illustrates the extreme difficulty of recovering ground after an initially false or unwise step. But great and real courage was needed to make it.

When Convocation met again in March

the whole subject was re-opened, and after warm debate the Bishops resolved, by eight votes to four, that a Committee of the Lower House should examine the book and report whether there were sufficient grounds for a 'synodical judgment' upon it. Bishop Tait opposed this step with all his might.

It seems odd that so few Bishops attended to decide such an important matter.[1] Can the explanation be that the absentees did not take much account of the Convocation of Canterbury, whose recently revived powers were due to the restless energy of Bishop Wilberforce? Or was it that most of them took the result of the debate for granted and preferred

---

[1] At this date there were 20 Bishops in the Province of Canterbury, 7 in the Province of York, besides the two Archbishops.

to stay in their dioceses, rather than make a long and unnecessary journey?

Tait's line of opposition was that 'a grave and weighty document has already gone forth to the whole country, and in my judgment it has as much authority as any document bearing upon the subject is ever likely to have'. The clergy were not 'likely to be much misled by the book'; and in his intercourse with the laity he did 'not find that there is such high and reverent regard for Convocation as is, no doubt, to be desired'. He pointed out that the more fuss was made about *Essays and Reviews*, the better the book sold. 'Even the protest we Bishops have already made has had the effect of causing this book to be much more generally read than if we had let it alone.' He told the story of a Pope, who was asked to recommend a certain book and replied that he could not do that, but would do it a better service by condemning it.

This change of tone suggests that Tait was beginning to discover the serious nature of the mistake which he and his fellow Bishops had made on 1st February. But his arguments carried no weight. The committee was appointed; and in June 1861 the Lower House (by 31 to 8) resolved 'that there are sufficient grounds for proceeding to a synodical judgment upon the Book entitled *Essays and Reviews*'. The resolution was transmitted to the Upper House. The Bishops, however, preferred to wait for the present and see what would happen to two of the essayists, who were about to be prosecuted in the Court of Arches.

CHAPTER XII

Essays and Reviews: Act Two

1. WILLIAMS AND WILSON PROSECUTED

The chosen victims were Professor Rowland Williams, who had written on *Bunsen's Biblical Researches*, and Mr. Henry Bristow Wilson, who had written on *The National Church*.

Williams was a Welshman, Vice-Principal and Professor of Hebrew at Lampeter; but he held the living of Broad Chalke near Salisbury, and was prosecuted by his diocesan, Bishop Hamilton, who had 'with deep feeling explained his reasons for admitting Williams into his diocese' to his fellow Bishops at Lambeth.

Wilson was Vicar of Great Staughton in Huntingdonshire, and was also under episcopal jurisdiction. But his prosecutor was a 'private clergyman', a Mr. Fendall. It is said that the real instigator of the prosecution was John Burgon, the future Dean of Chichester, at this time 'devoting himself to literary work' in Oxford and apparently without an English cure. 'A high churchman of the old school, he was as opposed to ritualism as to rationalism, and every form of liberalism he abhorred.'[1]

The choice of Williams and Wilson as the targets of attack seems to have been determined simply by the fact that they were the only Essayists who, being incumbents of 'presentative' livings, could be prosecuted in this way. Of the other Essayists, Temple, as headmaster of Rugby and Chaplain in Ordinary to the Queen 'was subject to other than ecclesiastical or academical discipline'; Baden Powell had died and was 'removed to a higher tribunal'; Goodwin was a layman; Mark Pattison held a 'donative' living 'not subject to episcopal institutions'; and neither he nor Jowett, as resident Masters of the University, could be prosecuted elsewhere than in the Vice-Chancellor's Court at Oxford.[2]

The cases against Williams and Wilson were opened simultaneously before the Dean of Arches, Dr. Stephen Lushington, in December 1861. Each was accused of denying the inspiration of Holy Scripture; Wilson

---

[1] *D.N.B.*
[2] *L. & L.*, i, 310 footnote. *Life of E. B. Pusey*, iv, 29. *D.N.B.* (Pattison). 'Donative' benefices were abolished, as such, in 1898.

was further accused of denying the doctrine of Eternal Punishment. There were many other charges; but these were the principal 'articles of indictment'. The hearing, continued in January, took ten days. The defendants were represented by Counsel. In June 1862 Dr. Lushington delivered an 'interlocutory' judgment; but it was not until December, a year after the opening of the two cases, that he gave his final judgment. He held that the main charges had been proved and sentenced each of the defendants to a year's suspension, with payment of the costs, which must have been far from inconsiderable. They appealed to the Privy Council. Their appeal was heard in June 1863 — the hearing took eight days — and on 8th February 1864 the Judicial Committee of the Council over-turned the judgment of the Dean of Arches.

That was the time-sequence. It had, as will soon be seen, an important bearing on the prosecution brought separately against Jowett. But at this point the reader may like to know what happened to the two men who bore the first brunt of the attack.

Wilson, who was the older by some fourteen years, long outlived Williams; indeed he lived to be eighty-five. But his health was 'broken by the anxieties of his position'. He never recovered from the strain, left his Huntingdonshire vicarage, and died unmarried amongst the fuchsias of Lee in 1888. It was a pathetic, long drawn out, anti-climax. But Pusey may have thought it altogether too mild a punishment for a man who 'identified himself in theology' with the school of his heretical juniors.

Williams died prematurely at the age of fifty-two, less than six years after his acquittal by the Privy Council. He was an ebullient Welshman 'of short stature, with a large head and massive brow, features of the Celtic type, deep-set dark blue eyes and brown hair'. While the trial was in progress he printed *Hints to my Counsel in the Court of Arches*, and 'on his deathbed directed that copies should be sent to libraries in England and Wales'. Though Dr. Lushington's interlocutory judgment, dismissing most of the charges, evidently foreshadowed an adverse judgment upon the remainder, Williams was not in the least set back by it. 'Whatever freedom I have claimed' he wrote 'is judicially conceived as permissible by the Church of England. If we gain nothing more, I feel this day that I have not lived in vain; my Master has done a work by me which will abide.' But he, also, paid a heavy price. 'Of a finely strung, sensitive, and nervous temperament, he felt too deeply the controversies and misunderstandings with which his life was beset, and, conscious of integrity, suffered much from insinuations to the contrary.' In the summer of 1862 he was forced by the odium, into which his name had been brought, to resign his office and his chair of Hebrew at Lampeter, to his own great grief and to the equally great misfortune of St. David's College.[1]

2. THE PROSECUTION OF JOWETT

Meanwhile a different piece of ecclesiastical machinery was being set in motion at Oxford against Jowett. The prime mover there was Pusey, influenced by his friend, Bishop Hamilton of Salisbury. The decision to prosecute was stimulated by the interlocutory judgment of the Dean of Arches in June 1862; but Pusey had had it in his mind much earlier in the year. He wrote about it to Keble on 4th February.[2]

It is far from easy to understand or to justify the workings of Pusey's mind on this particular occasion. On the one hand, he was trying hard to find a way of securing that Jowett should be decently paid for the work he was doing as professor of Greek, so long as that did not imply University approval of the professor's religious opinions. On the other, the storm over *Essays and Reviews* obviously provided an atmosphere favourable to a prosecution of Jowett for heresy. There was no ideal inconsistency in simultaneously seeking both these objects; though there was, surely, an astounding absence of practical wisdom. But, if Pusey's biographers correctly described the 'conviction' expressed in his letter to Keble (the letter of 4th February, referred to above) it is impossible to present his motives as altogether above suspicion.

In the circumstances Pusey thought there was nothing to be done but directly to challenge the orthodoxy of the Professor. *If that were to succeed, the idea of an increased emolument would for the present be withdrawn*: if it failed, he could not imagine that there could be any reasonable ground for continued opposition on the part of even the most conservative of his friends.[3]

It is abundantly clear that he hoped, and was given good reasons for hoping, that it would succeed.

Pusey spent part of the Long Vacation of 1862 in collecting incriminatory passages from Jowett's Commentary and Essay. In September a case was submitted to Dr. Phillimore, the Queen's Advocate. In October Phillimore gave his opinion. He advised that Jowett's Essay on the Atonement 'did contradict the doctrine contained in the Articles and the Liturgy, and set up another and a different doctrine'; that the Essay

---

[1] See Mrs. Rowland Williams's sympathetic memoir in the *D.N.B.* She also edited his *Life and Letters*; but I have not seen that book.
[2] *Life of E. B. Pusey*, iv, 23. The letter is not given or quoted.
[3] *ibid.*, iv, 22–3. The italics are mine.

on the Interpretation of Scripture certainly contradicted 'the doctrine of the Church of England as contained in her formularies' according to the recent interlocutory judgment of the Dean of Arches; and that it 'plainly contradicted' the Eighth Article on the Three Creeds. He further advised that an action would lie in the Vice-Chancellor's Court; and that, if the Vice-Chancellor refused to hear it, he could be compelled to do so by a writ of *mandamus* obtained in the High Court.

Pusey then set to work to find two other prosecutors. This did not prove easy. 'It is the old story,' he wrote to Keble in November ' "who is to bell the cat?" Here in Oxford, we seem to be so familiar with our evils as to acquiesce in them, sleeping in the snow, which is death.' However, a few days later, he captured Charles Ogilvie, the first Regius Professor of Pastoral Theology, a Canon of Christ Church and a former fellow of Balliol. It might be supposed that Ogilvie, enjoying the handsome emoluments of an unexacting chair and canonry as well as the stipend of a comfortable living (Ross in Herefordshire), would have felt some impropriety in joining himself to the prosecution of another Regius Professor, who worked a great deal harder for a purely nominal remuneration, enjoyed no plurality of offices and was the outstanding figure in Ogilvie's own former college. If he had any qualms of this sort, he subdued them.

Pusey captured the third prosecutor during the Christmas vacation — Charles Abel Heurtley, the Lady Margaret Professor of Divinity. This was a considerable triumph. Heurtley was a strong churchman, but not at all of Pusey's party. The direct descendant of a Huguenot named Charles Abel Hertelen, he was 'a staunch Protestant' and an evangelical. He and Pusey were very far indeed from theological agreement. Moreover, in the language of Dean Strong,[1] he was 'learned, courteous, retiring, reading and thinking much, but writing little'. With 'extreme reluctance and distress' he gave in to Pusey's argument that

nothing but absolute sense of duty could make me [Pusey] move in this sad case. . . . There has been no time in the history of the Church when its teachers would have been allowed to deny such truth as Professor Jowett has denied. . . . But after all, prosecution is not persecution.[2]

Pusey was much pleased with that last phrase.

Proceedings were formally opened in the Vice-Chancellor's Court before the Assessor (appointed by the Vice-Chancellor for this purpose) Mr. Mountague Bernard. Bernard is remembered better as an international than as an ecclesiastical lawyer. Perhaps that helps to explain his masterly management of a potentially very dangerous affair.

[1] Dean of Christ Church, and author of the article on Heurtley in the *D.N.B.*
[2] *Life of E. B. Pusey*, iv, 26–7.

Notice of what was about to happen reached Jowett at the beginning of February 1863. It 'made no difference in his outward bearing' but he was, nevertheless, plainly more than a little frightened. He wrote at once to Stanley (3rd February) asking if he would

talk the matter over with Bowen.[1]... Pattison counsels submission. But submission appears to imply that the limits of the Church of England in the University are acknowledged to be narrowed, and gives up all the legal difficulties. Will you get two copies of the Church Discipline Act? Do you think I should put the matter in the hands of Stephen?[2] Will you call on Murray and warn him not to give any assistance in proving the publication? — he cannot be compelled. I am sorry to give you trouble. But I need the help of friends and feel the value of such a friend as you. I must get you, when you return, to stir up the Dean[3] and Jackson[4] and everybody to help. It is the isolation in which they have left me which makes the attack possible. ....P.S. Can A.C.T. be got to do anything in the matter?[5]

The 'monition' was issued in the Vice-Chancellor's Court in the following week. An element of farce was provided by this archaic document, in which the Chancellor formally

commanded the Yeoman Bedell of Law to cite the Rev. Benjamin Jowett to appear before our Vice-Chancellor or his Assessor ... to answer to certain articles to be administered and objected to him by virtue of our office concerning the reformation and correction of his manners and excesses, but more especially for infringing the Statutes and privileges of the University by having published ... a certain book entitled *The Epistles of St. Paul* etc. etc.: also in a book called *Essays and Reviews* a certain article ... entitled 'On the interpretation of Scripture'; and by having in such book and such article ... advisedly promulgated ... certain erroneous and strange doctrines ... contrary to and inconsistent with the doctrines of the Church of England. ...[6]

On 13th February the case was formally opened before Mr. Mountague Bernard. It was adjourned for a week at the request of Jowett's counsel (technically his 'proctor') Mr. Pottinger, who 'announced his intention of entering a protest against the jurisdiction of the Court, and of taking every possible objection to the citation as to matter and form'.[7]

The fact, and the nature and gravity, of the prosecution were now public property. Next day *The Times* carried a leading article, which scathingly condemned the prosecution and questioned the competency of the Court. It spoke, for example, of the Vice-Chancellor's jurisdiction

[1] Charles Bowen, Fellow of Balliol 1857–62. Later a Judge of the Queen's Bench, Visitor of Balliol, and a Lord of Appeal. He had resigned from the staff of the *Saturday Review* in protest against that paper's attacks on *Essays and Reviews*.
[2] James Stephen, counsel for Rowland Williams.
[3] The Dean of Christ Church, Henry Liddell.
[4] John Jackson, Bishop of Lincoln and later of London, and Visitor of Balliol.
[5] *L. & L.*, i, 311–12.　　　　　[6] *ibid.*, i, 311, footnote.
[7] *Life of E. B. Pusey*, iv, 27.

as a 'rusty engine of intolerance'; it went on to say that the question arose whether Balliol and the cause of education in Oxford were 'to be sacrificed to the *odium theologicum* of a few infatuated dignitaries'; and it ended with an expression of pity for

Dr. Pusey and his co-prosecutors, for they know not what they do, but we trust, for the sake of interests far higher than they seem to discern, that the deadly blow which they are now aiming at the peace of the Church of England will not be suffered to take effect.

This was certainly hard language; but few would now agree with Pusey's biographers that it 'really begged the whole question at issue'. On the contrary it stated, in plain terms, the folly of trying to use an antiquated quasi-legal procedure in order to prevent Oxford clergymen from using their minds. This, in the view of *The Times*, was the real question at issue.

Pusey then made a characteristic mistake. He wrote a long reply, which appeared in *The Times* the day before the proceedings in the Vice-Chancellor's Court were resumed. The *gravamen* of his letter was that nothing could be 'more demoralizing than that clergymen should profess their belief in great fundamental truths, and assert the contrary'. He accused Jowett of doing precisely this, and elaborated the accusation. Professor Jowett's teaching was 'part of a larger whole — a systematic attempt to revolutionize the Church of England'. He ended by saying that he might have said much more, if the subject were not now before the Court, but that he held it to be his 'duty to abstain from saying anything except as to the abstract principle'.[1] It may be thought that the 'abstract principle' could not possibly be stated at that point of time without particular corollaries; and that it was both impolitic and improper for Pusey to try to justify in public his appeal to what he called in his letter 'the majesty of Justice', while the prosecution he had promoted was not only *sub judice* but still unheard.

The case was resumed on 20th February. Mr. Pottinger challenged the jurisdiction of the Court. The Assessor 'refused to admit' that he had no jurisdiction. He thought it 'doubtful' whether he had jurisdiction; but, if he had, it was 'a jurisdiction which the Statutes do not imperatively bind me to exercise upon this citation'. He rejected Mr. Pottinger's protest. 'But' he said 'I shall refuse to order Mr. Jowett to appear, and shall refuse to admit articles on the part of the promoters.' He added that the promoters (the prosecutors) were of course at liberty to appeal.

Immediately after this unexpected dismissal of the suit Jowett went for a walk with his solicitor, Frederick Farrer. Farrer recalled that 'he

[1] *ibid.*, iv, 28–9, where the letter is given in full.

was very low at the decision. I remember him saying, "You don't know Pusey; he has the tenacity of a bull-dog." '

But the bull-dog was forced to let go. The prosecution had been launched in the belief that, if the Vice-Chancellor should refuse to hear the case, he could be compelled to do so by a writ of *mandamus* issued in the Court of Queen's Bench. That had been part of the opinion given by the Queen's Advocate, Dr. Phillimore. But now Phillimore and John Duke Coleridge, in a joint opinion, while they considered that the Assessor's decision was 'incorrect, inconsistent, and without precedent', advised that the judges of the Queen's Bench 'would probably be very reluctant to interfere in a matter which was one of academical opinion'.[1] On 8th May the three 'promoters' notified the Vice-Chancellor that 'they did not intend to carry the suit any further'.

The Vice-Chancellor sent a copy of their letter to Jowett, who 'lost no time in forwarding it to his mother'. He had recovered his confidence some weeks earlier. 'I think I have escaped from my adversaries' he wrote 'to a trusted' but unnamed friend on 15th March. 'Lawyers seem to think that there is so little chance of their obtaining the *mandamus* that I should doubt whether they will make the attempt.' Nevertheless, he had been frightened, though he told Palgrave that he thought he was not deceiving himself in saying that he didn't mind about the 'persecution'; and that 'annoyances in College, which I sometimes receive, trouble me more'. But that was on 22nd March, when he was sure that Pusey was beaten.[2] And he never again 'spoke his mind' in public on theological matters.

What would have happened if Mountague Bernard had not refused to hear the suit? He might, I suppose, have found Jowett innocent of the charges. But the attack was formidably mounted and would have been relentlessly argued. The 'rusty engine of intolerance', once put in motion, could not go into reverse, and might be compelled by its own archaic limitations to deliver a verdict against the accused professor. Even if the verdict had finally gone in Jowett's favour, the trial must have fanned to even greater heights the flames of a religious agitation, which was already damaging the national prestige of the Church of England. And Oxford itself had had its belly too full, too long, of theological wind. Aware of all this, the Vice-Chancellor's Assessor boldly took what we have learned to call evasive action.

Bernard had been one of Roundell Palmer's young men, an academi-

---

[1] *Life of E. B. Pusey*, iv, 30. Campbell (*L. & L.*, i, 313) suggests that the reason for the adverse opinion lay in the existence of a University Statute which required the prosecutors to appeal, if at all, to the House of Congregation.
[2] *L. & L.*, i, 313.

cal lawyer not an advocate. He was interested in Church affairs — he was one of the founders of the *Guardian* and is said to have edited it for a while. At the time of Jowett's prosecution he was the standing 'assessor or judge' in the Vice-Chancellor's Court. In that office he was 'instrumental in assimilating its procedure, which had previously been that of the civilians, to the practice of the courts of common law'. In less technical language, he disliked the *enclave* of medieval, ecclesiastically framed law inside the system of English law, and did his best to break it up. It was certainly fortunate for Jowett that the Vice-Chancellor's Assessor was a lawyer of this kind.

It was also fortunate for Jowett that his adversaries consulted Coleridge. Left to himself Phillimore might well have held to his original opinion and advised them to try their luck in the Queen's Bench. Whether they succeeded or failed, the action would have been reported at full length in the great newspapers; and things would have been said in open Court which might have stirred the old guard, still in a majority at Balliol, into a really determined effort to rid the college of the heretic in their midst.

At first sight it seems very odd that Coleridge was asked to assist Phillimore in a second opinion. He was a liberal both in politics and Church affairs, a reformist, a 'march of mind' man, and only at his best when he found himself in full sympathy with his clients.

Solicitors usually know a good deal about the characters of eminent barristers. Pusey's solicitors must have known that Coleridge could not be sympathetic with Pusey's prosecution of Jowett. Why, then, was he brought in? The reason must have been that three years earlier he had scored a celebrated success by persuading Chief Justice Cockburn and two other judges of the Queen's Bench that there were grounds for issuing a writ of *mandamus*, requiring the Archbishop of Canterbury to hear the appeal — which he, poor man, supposed himself to have already heard — addressed to him as Visitor of All Souls by three junior fellows of that college.[1] The writ was not, in fact, issued. But that was only because the Archbishop was 'turned round' in the course of the hearing; and his turning round was the direct result of Coleridge's impassioned eloquence. This action was the talk of the day; and in the legal world Coleridge at once became the *mandamus* expert. To essay another action of this class, especially an action having its origin in Oxford, without consulting him, would have seemed foolish to any solicitor.

It is not at all improbable that Pusey's solicitors may have been, themselves, afraid for the action that Pusey wanted to institute in the Queen's

[1] See above, 203–4 and 249.

Bench. They may have deliberately brought Coleridge in, as the expert advocate who must obviously be consulted, hoping that he would advise against it — as he did.

Though Coleridge was a junior contemporary of Jowett's at Balliol and the two men must have often met and been well acquainted, there is no trace whatever of any friendship between them. This is the more surprising because they shared much the same liberal and reformist outlook, and Jowett is said to have been particularly delighted with the result of Coleridge's success in *The Queen v. The Archbishop of Canterbury*. Yet Coleridge's advice not to apply for a writ of *mandamus*, which meant dropping the prosecution, may well have saved Jowett for the Mastership of Balliol.

3. 'HELL DISMISSED WITH COSTS'

A month after this flat collapse of Pusey's elaborate attempt to prosecute Jowett, the appeals of Williams and Wilson against their conviction in the Court of Arches came before a Judicial Committee of the Privy Council. The Committee consisted of seven members: the Lord Chancellor (Lord Westbury) presiding, three Law Lords, the two Archbishops and the Bishop of London. Judgment was not delivered until nearly eight months later, on 8th February 1864. The Judicial Committee upheld the appeals of both clergymen. The two Archbishops dissented from the judgment, so far as it dismissed the charge of denying the inspiration of Holy Scripture. The Bishop of London (Tait) agreed with the Law Lords in dismissing this charge. All the members of the Judicial Committee agreed in dismissing the charge of denying the doctrine of the Church of England about eternal damnation.

The judgment meant very different things to different people. To Stanley it seemed (mistakenly) that it would end the panic about *Essays and Reviews* 'by establishing the legality of the two great doctrines for which the prophets have contended against the whole bench of bishops'.[1] It is not easy to imagine what Stanley meant by the 'two great doctrines', which he supposed to have been established. Two great doctrines were alleged to have been *denied*; the judgment said either that they had not been denied or that they were not legally established doctrines of the Church of England. But it is certainly true that Stanley saw in the judgment 'a charter of intellectual freedom within the walls of the Establishment', though these were not his own words. The learned writer who

[1] *Life of Dean Stanley*, ii, 158.

used them plainly thought Stanley's understanding of the Privy Council's judgment very defective.[1]

From Jowett the judgment evoked no comment, except that writing to Mrs. Tennyson he blamed it as the 'cause of the result' — meaning, in the context of his domestic letter, that it had set back the prospect of his being decently paid as professor of Greek. 'If so,' he added 'there is ample compensation.' He had, by this time, come to realize that his hope of bringing reason into contemporary Anglican theology had no more to do with legal and ecclesiastical judgments, than his hope of being paid an honest wage. He shrugged his shoulders and went back to his work.

To Pusey the Privy Council's judgment did not come as a shock, only because he had somehow learned, well beforehand, what it would be. He had written 'a series of long and earnest letters' to the Bishop of London 'pointing out the evil consequences that must follow should the essayists be acquitted'. It would be 'an end of all faith in each other, of all trust in man, if our hearts do not believe what in their plain meaning our tongues profess'. How could the highest Court of Appeal allow 'our clergy to take the word "everlasting" in a sense contrary to its known English meaning'?[2]

When the judgment was given and published, Pusey wrote at once to Bishop Hamilton of Salisbury. He could stomach the acquittal of Williams on the charge of denying the inspiration of Holy Scripture: for 'he had been acquitted by his words being taken in a sound sense. If he accepts the acquittal, he virtually withdraws what he said.' (It is difficult to refrain, here, from substituting an exclamation mark for the full point.) But as for Mr. Wilson, and 'in regard to that awful doctrine of the Eternity of Punishment' the judgment was 'most demoralizing'. It 'teaches people dishonesty on the largest scale'. To Bishop Wilberforce he wrote, three days later:

One can hardly think of anything for the hidden blasphemy of that Judgment which declares that to be uncertain which our Lord taught, and for the loss of the countless souls which it will involve, if not repudiated by the Church. For nothing, I suppose, keeps men from any sin except the love of God or the fear of Hell.

Stanley and Pusey were equally wrong in their interpretations of the judgment. The Judicial Committee was not — at least the legal members of it were certain that it was not — empowered to assert or to interpret the doctrines of the Church of England. Nor was it concerned with the liberal tendencies or pernicious consequences of *Essays and Reviews*. All that it had to do was to decide whether the particular passages selected

---

[1] J. B. Atlay in his *Lives of the Victorian Chancellors* (1908), ii, 263.
[2] *Life of Archbishop Tait*, i, 318.

for prosecution did in fact conflict with the Articles and Formularies of the Church. The legal members were unanimous, and Tait's logical mind had to go with them, that there was no clear conflict.

It is true that William Thomson, the Archbishop of York, also had a logical mind. In his early twenties, before he was ordained, he had published his *Outlines of the Laws of Thought*, a book which earned him a considerable and lasting reputation as a logician. Moreover, he was — or had been — a man of liberal mind. As a tutor of Queen's he was a prominent advocate of University reform, associating himself 'with Benjamin Jowett and the newer school of broad churchmen'.[1] Such a man, one might suppose, would be bound to acknowledge the force of the arguments which dictated the Judicial Committee's decision. He could not resist them, any more than his brother of Canterbury, when they were applied to the charge that Wilson had denied the doctrine of eternal punishment; since that doctrine was not proved to have been unequivocally stated in the Articles and Formularies of the Church. Yet he, with Archbishop Longley, held out against the acquittal of both Williams and Wilson on the charge of denying the inspiration of the Bible. It may have been that he felt a necessity of making some stand to satisfy the demands of the clergy. More probably, it was because he had himself taken immediate offence from *Essays and Reviews*, severing himself from his 'broad church' friends, and editing a volume of counter essays called *Aids to Faith*.

Archbishop Longley, Sumner's recent successor at Lambeth and Thomson's own predecessor at York, though 'a man of learning, of cultivated intellect, of courteous manners, and an even temper', and very handsome to see, had no such distinctive qualities. He sought to avoid storms, not to ride them. Although he regarded himself as a liberal in politics, he opposed every measure of reform, whether in the University or in the Church. His anonymous biographer says that he 'won public confidence' — whether in consequence or in despite of all this.[2] But the phrase means little more than that he won some confidence from the high church party without forfeiting that of the low church party, to which he himself belonged.

The confidence, which Archbishop Longley thus precariously enjoyed from the two opposing wings of the Church, was temporarily much shaken by his assent to the acquittal of Wilson on the charge of having denied eternal punishment.

The judgment of the Privy Council on this point was particularly clear and definite.

[1] *D.N.B.*   [2] *ibid.*

We are not required, or at liberty, to express any opinion upon the mysterious question of the eternity of future punishment, further than to say that we do not find in the Formularies to which this article [i.e. accusation] refers any such distinct declaration of our Church upon the subject as to require us to condemn as penal the expression of hope by a clergyman that even the ultimate pardon of the wicked who are condemned in the day of judgment may be consistent with the will of Almighty God.

The two Archbishops were unable to dissent from that unexceptionable statement. Perhaps Longley might have done so, if he had been the only Archbishop on the Committee. But he could hardly separate himself from the Archbishop of York; and Thomson, even if he had been able to find a logical flaw in this part of the judgment, could hardly forget that he had written and published an essay on *Crime and its Excuses*.[1]

Although the two Archbishops separated themselves from the Judicial Committee's dismissal of the charge that Wilson and Williams had denied the inspiration of the scriptures, their attitude over eternal punishment was generally felt, by the clerical rank and file and their lay supporters, to have been most unsatisfactory. The high church leaders and statesmen were particularly vehement. Bishop Phillpotts of Exeter — an uncompromising high churchman of the older school and an untiring controversialist — together with Keble and Pusey pressed Archbishop Longley hard. They persuaded him to issue a statement, described as a 'private assurance' but published in the *Guardian*. It was dated 4th March, 1864, and headed 'Lambeth Palace'.

I wish it to be generally understood that, in assenting to the reversal of the Judgment of Dr. Lushington on the subject of Eternal Punishment in the case of Mr. Wilson, I did so solely on technical grounds; in so much as the charge against him on this point was so worded that I did not think it could be borne out by the facts.
The Eternity of Punishment rests, according to my mind, exactly on the same ground as the Eternity of Blessedness; they must both stand or fall together; and the Church of England, as I maintain, holds both doctrines clearly and decidedly.

It is not easy to imagine how the Archbishop reconciled this remarkable statement with the terms of the judgment to which he had assented. But at least it affirmed his belief in endless misery as the corollary of endless blessedness — the doctrine to which nine-tenths of the clergy fervently clung.

The attitude of intelligent laymen towards this doctrine was wittily expressed in the famous contemporary mock epitaph on Richard

---

[1] This essay was a contribution to the series of *Oxford Essays*, published by Parker, the publisher of *Essays and Reviews*. It appeared in 1855, when Thomson was in his 'broad church' period.

Bethell, Lord Westbury. The epitaph was written, of course, while its subject was very much alive and just before his fall from power in 1865. If it reflects the dislike which he positively enjoyed exciting, it also reflects admiration. The sarcasm of the second half of the epitaph was directed not against Westbury, but against a more vulnerable, if more venerable, target.

RICHARD, BARON WESTBURY

Lord High Chancellor of England.
He was an eminent Christian,
An energetic and merciful statesman,
And a still more eminent and merciful Judge.
During his three years' tenure of office
He abolished the ancient method of conveying land,
The time-honoured institution of the Insolvents' Court
And
The Eternity of Punishment.
Towards the close of his earthly career
In the Judicial Committee of the Privy Council
He dismissed Hell with costs,
And took away from orthodox members of the Church of
England
Their last hope of everlasting damnation.[1]

4. THE PUSEY-WILBERFORCE AXIS

Pusey was quick to see that he must look for new allies. Soon after the acquittal of Wilson and Williams he asked his brother-in-law Dr. Cotton 'to stir up the *Record*' — a religious weekly periodical with a large low church circulation. For, he said to Keble, 'we have no organ, now that the *Guardian* is liberalised'.

His strategic object was to unite low and high against liberal or broad churchmen. As his biographers said:

He had long anticipated the coming of a time when the pressure of the common enemy of unbelief would draw into one band all who love their Lord as their Redeemer and their God, and the Bible as being indeed the very Word of God. He laid great stress on the wide practical evil and loss of souls that would result from any seeming doubt about everlasting Punishment. His special wish was that in some way or other there should be a general reaffirmation of belief in that subject.

The *Record* played up eagerly. It printed Pusey's long and earnest letters. It denounced the decision of the Judicial Committee. In parti-

[1] J. B. Atlay, *Lives of the Victorian Chancellors*, ii, 264. Mr. Atlay says that the epitaph was 'commonly attributed to Sir Philip Rose, though the most pungent line in it is said to have been endorsed on his brief by one of the counsel (Charles Bowen) *currente calamo*'. It was, obviously, a composite joke of the Junior Bar.

cular, it violently attacked the Bishop of London. The lay lords on the Committee might have been 'misled by their inexperience in theology. . . . But they are able to shield themselves behind the authority of an Ecclesiastical judge, a Ruler in the Church, one of those whose "lips should keep knowledge" '. It described the course taken by the Bishop of London as

disastrous to his own reputation. It has awakened mingled shame and indignation, not only among the dignitaries and clergy of the Church, but, we may add, the laity, always excepting the minority of the clergy who may be called latitudinarians, and that section of the laity who may be termed freethinkers.

Pusey and Keble ceased to read the *Guardian*, or 'to use it, as before, as a medium of communication with their friends'.

An attempt on Pusey's part to stir up Gladstone was less successful. The Chancellor of the Exchequer 'acknowledged the unsatisfactory nature both of the Court and of its decisions', but he 'did not, to Pusey's great disappointment, hold out any hope of effectual assistance'. He did, indeed, write an expostulatory letter to the Bishop of London. Tait replied that his distinguished correspondent, if he had been a member of the Court, could scarcely himself have come to any other decision; and he pointed out the folly of prosecutions, which sought to find a non-existent legal justification for condemning 'by implication, if not directly, the acknowledged and publicly recognised sentiments of very many who were most sincerely attached to the Church and had shaped all their teachings by its articles'. It does not appear that Gladstone returned to the attack.

Pusey's failure to rope in Gladstone was balanced by 'the complete establishment of the most friendly relations with Bishop Wilberforce'. The first step in this powerful alliance of opposites was taken when the Bishop of Oxford sent to Pusey, on 21st February 1864, two documents drawn up by two clergymen in his diocese, the Rev. W. R. Fremantle (afterwards Dean of Ripon) and the Rev. J. R. Woodford (afterwards Bishop of Ely). One was a proposed Declaration of belief in 'the Divine authority of the Canonical Scriptures as being the Word of God, and in the certainty of the Everlasting Punishment of the wicked'; the other was a proposed memorial to the Queen praying for a Commission to inquire into the constitution and practice of the Judicial Committee of the Privy Council.

Pusey came down against the second proposal: 'after a year's delay they would only obtain an unsatisfactory answer, and by that time people's energies would have cooled down.' Wilberforce reluctantly agreed to drop the second and to concentrate on the first document. 'What I am most anxious about for the present is that you should do your utmost to weld together for this purpose the two great sections of the Church, High and Low.'

The Rev. W. R. Fremantle, Rector of Claydon, who thus assisted Pusey and the Bishop of Oxford, must not be confused with his better remembered clerical nephew, W. H. Fremantle. But the relation and the contrast between the two strikingly illustrate the change which was already beginning to come over the Church, in spite of all that Pusey and Wilberforce could do. The uncle was a man 'of strong evangelical views and character'. The nephew was a disciple of Jowett, and one of the three young rebels at All Souls, whose headstrong behaviour so much gratified his former tutor. While acting as curate to his uncle at Claydon he wrote an essay for a University prize denouncing the doctrine 'that Christ was punished instead of us'. His uncle persuaded him not to send it in, but could not persuade him to alter his view. He 'resented the clamour raised against *Essays and Reviews*'; and 'valued especially' the essays by Jowett and Pattison, 'but most of all the essay by the editor, Mr. Wilson'. He heard the judgment of the Judicial Committee pronounced; was 'convinced that it was just' and thankful that 'liberty of thought has prevailed'. For a few years he was Bishop Tait's resident chaplain. He succeeded his uncle as Dean of Ripon.[1]

A 'representative' committee was at once set up in Oxford to draft the proposed Declaration so as 'to exclude evasion without going beyond the Formularies of the Church of England'. There were difficulties in meeting the views of various sticklers for the inclusion of this and the omission of that. But the committee worked very fast: so fast that by the beginning of March copies of an agreed document were being sent out to the clergy for signature. It was eventually presented to the Archbishop on 12th July, signed by (it is variously said) eleven or twelve thousand or more 'presbyters and deacons in holy orders of the Church of England and Ireland'. The signatories held it their bounden duty to affirm that their Church,

in common with the whole Catholic Church, maintains without reserve or qualification the inspiration and Divine authority of the whole canonical Scriptures, as not only containing, but being, the Word of God, and further teaches, in the words of our blessed Lord, that the 'punishment' of the 'cursed' equally with the 'life' of the 'righteous' is 'everlasting'.

Meanwhile the order of battle was taking clear shape. Three particular events helped to determine the alignment of parties and persons.

[1] *Recollections of Dean Fremantle.*

278

First, the refusal by Pusey and Keble and Liddon of Dean Stanley's invitations to preach in Westminster Abbey. Second, a long argument between Pusey and F. D. Maurice in *The Times*. It will be worth while to say a little more about these two events. The third can be quickly described and is best taken before the other two.

The two Archbishops felt that they could not wait, until the signatures to the Pusey-Wilberforce Declaration had been collected, to put themselves right with the mass of the clergy. Each issued a Pastoral letter — Canterbury in March, York in April. Archbishop Longley's letter reiterated his conviction that 'the Church has no more sure warrant for belief in the eternal happiness of the saved than it has for belief in the eternal suffering of the lost'. He explained once more that he had been obliged to concur in the acquittal of Mr. Wilson for technical reasons. He does not seem to have well understood what these reasons were. For in his earlier statement he had blamed the wording of the *charge* — 'it was so worded that I did not think it could be borne out by the facts.' Now, he put the whole blame on 'the obscurity of Mr. Wilson's *language*'. Archbishop Thomson's letter is said to have been 'to the same effect'.[1]

Pusey's refusal of Stanley's invitation to preach in the Abbey — along with the similar refusals of Keble and Liddon — illustrates the hopelessness, in that day and time, of Stanley's optimistic attempt to reconcile broad and high churchmen. He failed, also, in his apparently more successful first attempt to find common ground with low churchmen.

What he thought to be for the life of Christianity both ecclesiastical parties held to be for its death. Much that they regarded as vital seemed to him to be trivial, if not deadly. Time only widened the breach.

Time, that is to say, measured by Stanley's own remaining fifteen or sixteen years of life. No doubt the breach between what might be described as rational Christianity and what has come to be called fundamentalism,[2] is no less difficult to bridge now than it was in Stanley's day. But the sphere of pure fundamentalism has greatly contracted. If it had not done so, it is probable that the Church of England would have sunk to the level of an unrepresentative and over-privileged sect. Perhaps, then,

---

[1] *Life of E. B. Pusey*, iv, 62–6. *Life of Dean Stanley*, ii, 159–73.

[2] Various shades of meaning have been put upon the word 'fundamentalism'. I understand it myself to mean unqualified belief in the literal truth of the Old and New Testaments, coupled with unqualified belief in the doctrines of vicarious sacrifice and eternal damnation. Fundamentalism is usually thought to be a low church character; but if Pusey and Keble were not fundamentalists, I do not know what the word can be supposed to mean. I have used it here to denote that 'common ground' which a high churchman like Pusey shared with evangelical subscribers to the *Record* and with Bishop Wilberforce, but could not find with such men as Stanley or even Temple, let alone Jowett or Maurice.

Stanley's optimism was not quite so vain as it looked, in his own lifetime, to have been.

Stanley was installed as Dean of Westminster on 9th January 1864. The 'ancient instrument' used in the ceremony told him that he was set there 'for the enlargement of the Christian Church'. The phrase struck him with great force. It inspired him to invite 'representatives both of the High Church and Evangelical parties' to preach in the Abbey. The leading low churchmen accepted his invitation; but Keble, Pusey and Liddon all declined.[1]

Pusey, obeying his nature, took a fortnight or so to make up his mind. At last he wrote: 'I dare not. . . . The essence of your scheme seems to me to be to exhibit as one those whose differences I believe to be vital.' He had already said, in his first letter, that he believed

the present to be a struggle for the life or death of the Church of England, and what you believe to be for life I believe to be for death; and you think the same reciprocally of me.

Stanley, arguing in vain against this rock-like antagonism, tactlessly confessed himself to have been 'startled and pained by your letter of adhesion to a newspaper . . . of so scandalous a character as the *Record*'. Pusey replied that he 'wrote to the *Record* because I wanted to unite with the party who take it in, and to whom I had access through it . . . I must, and do, join heart and soul with those who oppose this tide of Rationalism.' In the same letter he said:

You appeal to me kindly in the name of 'our common Christianity'. Alas! I do not know what the common Christianity of myself and Professor Jowett is. I do not know what single truth we hold in common, except that somehow Jesus came from God, which the Mahommedans believe too. I do not think that Professor Jowett believes our Lord to have been Very God, or God the Holy Ghost to be a Personal Being. The doctrine of the Atonement, as he states it, is something wholly unmeaning.

Answering this, Stanley expressed his surprise that Pusey

should scruple about preaching in the same Church with the Archbishop and myself, and not scruple about making an ally (without a word of justification) of a newspaper which notoriously violates the first principles of truth and charity every week.

The retort stung Pusey's sensitive conscience to the quick. He was always being torn in two between the truth as he saw it and his calculated use of worldly and suspect devices to defend and propound it. He turned to Keble and Bishop Hamilton for advice. Keble, too, was much perplexed, though quite sure that he himself would refuse the invitation, if it came to him — as it did. At last he wrote back that he thought Pusey 'having

[1] *Life of Dean Stanley*, ii, 159.

such countenance as that of Archbishop Longley' might 'say "yes" without scandal'. Bishop Hamilton, quicker off the mark, had urged Pusey to say no; and Pusey had done so, without waiting for Keble's slow answer.

A day or two after Pusey's final refusal of Stanley's invitation a letter from F. D. Maurice[1] appeared in *The Times*, criticizing as 'ambiguous' the wording of the 'Oxford Declaration'. Maurice was passionate and eloquent, but not a master of exactitudes — he is reported to have described himself as 'a muddy mystic'. For such a man to accuse Pusey of 'ambiguity' was a rash action. Pusey fell upon him and drove him off the field. Maurice, not knowing when he was beaten, returned to the attack and was again driven off the field. But Pusey never knew when to stop. He ended his second letter thus:

Mr. Wilson, in reinforcing his own opinions by an extract from a Rotterdam pastor who denies eternity of punishment as inconsistent with the attributes of God, shows the depth and breadth of the questions at issue. We do not believe in the same God. God Whom we adore in His awful and inscrutable justice and holiness, these writers affirm to be cruel. The God whom they acknowledge we believe to be the creature of their own minds, not the God Who has revealed Himself to man.

Many readers of *The Times* must have withdrawn their first judgment of Pusey as the 'knock-out' champion in the religious ring, when they read this denunciation of those who attributed to God an infinite compassion for all his creatures. It was an open declaration of uncompromising war, made incidentally in a newspaper letter which had begun by promising to avoid 'theological controversy'.

If Maurice had possessed any art of polemical writing, he would have now had Pusey at his mercy. He never even saw the obvious *riposte*. He was roused into an anger which dictated an illogical, irrelevant, passionate and perhaps, therefore, more effective reply. Writing in the heat of anger he brought into his argument the already notorious instance of Jowett's ill-treatment. The Declaration, he said,

means 'Young clergymen, poor curates, poor incumbents, sign, or we will turn the whole force of religious public feeling against you. Sign or we will starve you! Look at the Greek Professor! You see we can take that vengeance on those whom we do not like. You see that we are willing to take it, and that no consideration of faithful and devoted services will hinder us.' This is what is called signing 'for the love of God'. I accept Mr. Pusey's statement, tremendous as it is. I say that the God whom we are adjured to love, under these penalties, is not the God of whom I have read in the 'Canonical Scriptures', not the God who declares that He abhors robbery for burnt offering.

[1] The Rev. Frederic Denison Maurice (1805–72), the founder of 'Christian Socialism'. The correspondence in *The Times* is reproduced in full in the *Life of E. B. Pusey*, iv, 57–62. It is fascinating to read.

In so far as it related to Jowett, this charge came too near the truth to be easily answered. Pusey, in his reply, ignored the reference to 'the Greek Professor' and insisted that the Declaration was not in any sense a test or an instrument of oppression. Again, he had the best of the argument; and again he threw away the advantage he had won in the minds of readers not already in his own way of thinking, by his closing paragraph:

Mr. Maurice excepts against our 'asking other clergymen to join us for the love of God'. This arises from our opposite convictions. What else could they do who feared lest people should be encouraged to disbelieve the Bible and Hell and that they were in risk of losing their faith and their souls?

The Greek professor kept his own silence. He had escaped from the attempt to prosecute him; but the storm which Pusey was now engaged in promoting defeated Pusey's own repeated attempt to end the scandal of the £40 a year. Once more, Pusey introduced a University statute, which would make the professor's remuneration up to £400 'on the understanding that the University shall be held to have pronounced no judgment upon his writings, in so far as they touch the Catholic Faith'. Keble had originally suggested some such formula; Stanley accepted it; Jowett 'seems to have hoped that it would succeed'. The statute, having passed Congregation came before Convocation on 8th March 1864. It was defeated by 467 to 395 votes. The country clergy could sign the 'Oxford Declaration'; but they could not see why a heretical professor should be decently paid. Even Pusey's own allies in the University were puzzled to understand the differences between the behaviour of his right hand and his left.

Jowett's disappointment was sharpened by a cruel absurdity. The result of the voting was, at first, wrongly interpreted by the Proctors, so that the statute was thought to have been passed.[1] 'Liddell ran with the false news to Jowett, who took it very quietly.' He took its reversal no less quietly. His published letters contain (I think) only two references to it. The briefer of these is in a letter to Mrs. Tennyson. He was grieved that 'so kind a friend as you should be disappointed. I believe the Judgment [Lord Westbury's] was the cause of the result; if so, there is ample compensation.'[2] The other, longer, reference occurs in a letter of March 1864 to Lady Stanley of Alderley, whom he had first met in 1861 and in whom he found one of his most sympathetic and intelligent women

---

[1] *L. & L.*, i, 315. The first announcement caused 'a burst of cheering from the undergraduates and friends of Professor Jowett' which 'continued for some few minutes'. The correction 'was received with loud cheers from the opponents of the Statute, and violent hissing from the undergraduate gallery'.

[2] *ibid.*, i, 326.

friends. The passage shows what was happening in his mind at the very time when Pusey was exhibiting *his* mind to the readers of *The Times*.

I shall try to avoid being 'snuffed out'. But I suppose that life (which through a combination of unfortunate accidents has been rather against me) must be a battle, and no battle can be won without a battle. I believe the Judgment of the Privy Council was the cause of the defeat [of Pusey's proposed statute]. I wonder what the end of all this will be. It sometimes seems as if no educated man, woman or child would have any more belief, if religion is to be identified with the union of Dr. Pusey with the *Record*.[1]

Later in the year — after the synodical condemnation of *Essays and Reviews* — he wrote to Stanley, apropos of a debate in the Lords concerning the capacity of Convocation to pass judgment on books, a letter which also illustrates the general tendency of his thought:

I was sorry to see Tait's speech in the House of Lords, cautious in a certain way, yet so utterly unconscious of the real state of matters. What is Truth against an *esprit de corps*? The Bishops think that they are fighting a few clergymen who must be put down. They are really fighting against Criticism, against the Law or at least the Spirit of the Law, against the Conscience and moral perceptions of mankind; things which I believe to be invincible even when arrayed against that figment of theologians, the Catholic Church. The Bishop of Oxford certainly puts clergymen in an awkward position by bringing them back to the letter of their obligation. Does he consider in what a much more awkward position he puts himself and the Church by wholly, without a rag to cover him, giving up the very pretence of truth of fact?

It would be wrong to suppose that the agitation against *Essays and Reviews* was wholly clerical. In the middle of March 'a deputation waited on the two Archbishops at Lambeth Palace to present an address signed, it was said, by 137,000 lay members of the Church of England, who desired to thank the primates for the course they had pursued'. The signatories were a small percentage of a large and docile flock. And monster addresses and petitions, which purport to represent a massive solidarity of opinion, seldom reflect more than the pertinacity of their organizers. But arithmetical numbers are always impressive. The delivery of this address, four months in advance of the clerically-signed 'Oxford Declaration', comforted the rulers of the Church with a deceptive assurance that the faithful laity was behind them, to the last articulate sheep.

5. SYNODICAL CONDEMNATION

When the Convocation of Canterbury met in April 1864, Bishop Wilberforce moved that:

[1] *ibid.*, i, 366. Lady Stanley was not, of course, Dean Stanley's wife, Lady Augusta Stanley; but the wife of Lord Stanley, who was the Dean's first cousin.

in as much as the suit before the Privy Council was now concluded, the consideration of the subject, which had been for three years discontinued, pending the judicial decision, should now be resumed, and a committee appointed to report upon the volume as a whole.[1]

In the debate which followed Bishop Thirlwall of St. David's, not the least distinguished of English episcopal scholars,[2] ridiculed the mass value of the signatures then being procured for the Oxford Declaration:

Am I to suppose that the framers of this declaration believe that the youngest 'literate' — or illiterate, they often mean nearly the same thing — who has been last admitted into Deacon's Orders is competent to express an opinion upon the subject which has occupied some of the ablest and most intellectual minds for the last two years? . . . If Dr. Pusey is not able to satisfy us with his authority on such a question, will the name of this young deacon do anything towards it? Will any number of men signing it? If they are the names of persons of equal learning, equally competent to judge on such a very difficult question, I admit they will, but otherwise I cannot consider these names, whatever be their numbers — they are said to have exceeded 12,000 — I cannot consider them in the light of so many ciphers, which add to the value of the figures they follow; but I consider them in the light of a row of figures preceded by a decimal point, so that however far the series may be prolonged, it never can rise to the value of a single unit.[3]

Archbishop Tait's biography tells us that

not a little indignation was aroused by this somewhat contemptuous estimate of the solemn declaration of the clergy [and] by the Bishop of London's angry denunciation — no milder word is possible — of the form of the condemnatory 'schedule' drawn up by Archdeacon Denison's committee three years before and now resuscitated by Bishop Wilberforce.

Tait himself let himself go in the debate. He deeply regretted

that such a paper should ever have seen the light of day. If the book entitled *Essays and Reviews* is likely to do harm to the Christian faith [this paper][4] is a document which, I undertake to say, would be received with contempt and ridicule by every impartial person who understands what the subject is which has been brought before us. Of all the foolish publications which it has been the misfortune of these controversies to call out, if there be one which, more than another, is likely to injure the Christian faith, it is this.

[1] *Life of Archbishop Tait*, i, 319–20.
[2] His great work was his *History of Greece*. He was a remarkable man in every way, and not least for the fact that he learned to preach in Welsh, after becoming Bishop of St. David's. He was buried in Westminster Abbey, in the same grave with Grote.
[3] *Life of Archbishop Tait*, i, 320, quoting from the *Chronicle of Convocation* for 21st April 1864 — presumably a short-hand report of an extempore speech, not put into literary form.
[4] Viz. Archdeacon Denison's 'schedule'. I have not seen this document, and reproduce Tait's comments upon it for their own sake. For the text of the schedule the reference is to the *Chronicle of Convocation*, 18th June 1861, 673–87.

He suggested that the proper place for it was 'the flames'.

Tait's eloquence and Thirlwall's sarcasms very nearly carried the day. But Wilberforce 'spoke with equal warmth for the other side' — and Wilberforce in debate was an advocate of great power. The voting was level. The President used his casting vote in favour of Wilberforce's motion. The new committee was set up, and went to work with a will.

The committee reported, some two months later, to the effect that *Essays and Reviews* — the book as a whole, not two or three essays in it — should be synodically condemned. Towards the end of June it was so condemned 'by a large majority in both Houses' as 'containing teaching contrary to the doctrine received by the United Church of England and Ireland in common with the whole Catholic Church of Christ'. The majority in the Upper House was that of 8 votes to 2. In the Lower House the majority was that of 39 votes to 19. The full membership of the Upper House, at this time, was 21 — the Archbishop of Canterbury and the Bishops of his province (the province of York being, of course, excluded); of the Lower House 145. The attendance in both Houses seems to have been remarkably inadequate to the occasion.

Only once in the past three centuries had Convocation passed — or, rather, been on the brink of passing — such a sentence upon a book. That was in 1717, when the Lower House unanimously ordered a report to be presented to the Upper House condemning Bishop Hoadly's latitudinarian tract *A Preservative against the Principles and Practices of the Non-Jurors both in Church and State*, together with a sermon preached before George I and printed by the King's command. The immediate result was that the Convocation of Canterbury was indefinitely prorogued by royal writs until Parliament was dissolved. Both Convocations (Canterbury and York) remained, in the absence of the royal license, practically in abeyance for early a century and a half. It was not until 1852 that the Convocation of Canterbury was resuscitated, largely through the efforts of Bishop Wilberforce; the Convocation of York came back to life four years later.

As to the later history, a third House of Laymen was added to the Convocation of Canterbury in 1886, to that of York in 1892. It was not until 1896 that the two Convocations began occasionally to sit together; and not until 1904 that all three houses of both Convocations 'requested the archbishops to call them together as a Representative Church Council'. They so met in that year; but the Council had no power to deal with matters of doctrine. It proved 'a singularly conservative body; its first act was to approve a Licensing Bill of the Conservative government against the opinion of a majority of the bishops'.[1] In 1919 Parliament, by the so-called Enabling Act, set up the present National Assembly of the Church of England, which has replaced the Representative Church Council. This statutory Assembly, with its three Houses of Bishops Clergy and Laymen, has become, so far as its subordination to Parliament allows, the governing authority of the Church and exercises powers wider than those belonging to the Convocations of Canterbury and York, though these historic bodies still exist and meet and transact their provincial business.[2]

All this future development was quite invisible in 1864. And here was the Convocation of Canterbury, recently suffered to meet again, once more playing dangerously with fire. So, at least, it seemed to him 'whom men call Baron Houghton, but the gods call Dicky Milnes'.[3] Milnes was a minor poet, a friend of Tennyson, a patron of letters, a politician, a 'socialite' who 'knew everyone of note and was present at almost every great gathering'. He was one of those who contrive to be remembered, long after they have died, as persons who had been important when they were alive; though, when one asks why they are so remembered, the answers add up to little more than nothing. It was Lord Houghton who raised the question in the House of Lords, on 15th July 1864, whether the Convocation of Canterbury had the power to pass a synodical judgment on a book. 'As a patron of literature he affected to scent a return to the restriction upon unlicensed printing and the institution of an Index Expurgatorius.'

The Lord Chancellor, Lord Westbury, seized the opportunity offered to him. In one of his most rudely sarcastic speeches he jeered at Convocation. There were, he said, three possible ways of handling that body:

The first is, while they are harmlessly busy, to take no notice of their proceedings. The second is, when they seem likely to get into mischief, to prorogue them and put a stop to their proceedings. The third, when they have done something clearly beyond their powers, is to bring them to the bar of justice for punishment.

Those who had participated in the so-called synodical judgment had, he said, certainly exposed themselves to a *praemunire*.[4] But there was no

---

[1] Wakeman, *Introduction to the History of the Church of England*, 11th edition, 503.
[2] A clear and concise account of the government of the Church is to be found in Dr. Cecilia Ady's *The English Church* (1940). See especially Chapter II on the Councils of the Church.
[3] J. B. Atlay, *The Victorian Chancellors*, ii, 265. I do not know who was the author of the *bon mot*.
[4] The technical name of a writ issued against persons accused of asserting or maintaining papal jurisdiction in England. Westbury's threat was an empty one.

need to treat the matter so seriously. The judgment was meaningless and worthless. It was no more than

> a series of well-lubricated terms, a sentence so oily and saponaceous that no one could grasp it. Like an eel, it slips through your fingers and is simply nothing.

The allusion to Wilberforce's nick-name of Soapy Sam was not missed by his hearers.

The Lords listened disapprovingly to the Chancellor's contemptuous harangue. They had always disliked him and his insolent way of addressing them. On this occasion Westbury delivered himself into the hands of his most particular enemy, Bishop Wilberforce. They had already met in battle, head on, when Westbury defeated Wilberforce's Bill 'for constituting bishoprics in heathen countries without the license of the Crown', but had roused Wilberforce's stinging eloquence. The day after that debate

> Lord Chelmsford, who had himself experienced quite recently a *mauvais quart d'heure* at the hands of the Chancellor, saw the Bishop in Cockspur Street and said to him, 'I should think this morning Westbury feels the same sensations mentally that an Eton boy would bodily after an interview with Keate.'[1]

If the Lord Chancellor thought that he had revenged himself, now, for that earlier lambasting, he soon discovered his mistake. The Bishop of Oxford 'retorted in a scathing speech, delivered at white heat, and while opinions differed as to its Episcopal character, he was universally felt to have come off victor in the combat'.[2]

A year later Lord Westbury was forced to resign, by a scandal over an abuse of his official patronage.[3] As he left the Queen's presence at Windsor, after surrendering the Great Seal, he encountered Bishop Wilberforce. The two men were not on speaking terms; they passed each other without a word. 'Later on' Wilberforce recorded in his diary 'I met him on the broad staircase looking quite *down* as he wandered alone into the town.'

And here, the reader will perhaps feel, is a suitable place at which to end this long account of the agitation caused by *Essays and Reviews*, with Wilberforce and Pusey in the ascendant, the liberal church party in danger of annihilation, Jowett consuming his own smoke, and the Lord Chancellor, the architect of the judgment which had seemed to Stanley like 'a

---

[1] Atlay, *op. cit.*, ii, 262–3.
[2] *Life of Archbishop Tait*, i, 323. Mr. Atlay also describes Wilberforce as 'in a white heat of indignation'. Mr. Reginald Wilberforce, on the other hand, speaks of his father's reply as 'a calm and dignified rebuke'.
[3] The blame seems to have belonged rather to his wastrel son Richard, who became the second Lord Westbury.

charter of intellectual freedom within the walls of the Establishment', fallen from greatness.

'What is wanted' wrote Tait in a private memorandum during the height of the storm, trying to reconcile his own painfully conflicting views, 'is a deeply religious liberal party, and almost all who might have formed it have, in the alarm, deserted. . . . The great evil is that the liberals are deficient in religion, and the religious are deficient in liberality. Let us pray for an outpouring of the very Spirit of Truth.'

One is irresistibly reminded of Elizabeth Wordsworth's immortal jingle:

> If only the good were the clever,
> If only the clever were good,
> The world would be better than ever
> We thought that it possibly could.
> But, alas, it is seldom or never
> That either behave as they should;
> For the good are so harsh to the clever,
> The clever so rude to the good.

CHAPTER XIII

Private Worlds[1]

1. A MISTAKE ABOUT THE PAST

It is time to pick up again the thread of Jowett's family history, which had so little visible connection with his public career. In fact there was a very deep and very painful connection. The curious utterance on the part of his adoring sister Emily, which has provided the heading used above,[2] would be enough to suggest that this was so, if there were nothing in the fragmentary record to bear it out. But the record, if it does not quite explain what Emily meant, leaves no doubt that there was a never-resolved conflict in her brother's inmost mind between his family affections and his duty to himself. It is a sad, uncomfortable, even tragic story. The beginning part of it has already been told. Here are the middle and the end.

Though Balliol and his pupils and friends and the part he came to play in the world mattered more to Jowett than his own flesh and blood — so much more that he divided his life into two different compartments and allowed less and less room for family affections, even to a point of seeming cruelty — nevertheless the ties of birth and brotherhood remained for him, as for most men, ties of peculiar feeling. Behind the hard isolation of his schooldays lay poignant recollections of the nursery life from which he had been exiled. We do not often hear him speak of his mother, brothers and sisters. There is a troubled note in his voice, when he does so — a note of wistfulness amounting to pain. Successive acts of fate had cut him off from the intimacies of a settled home. And in the family itself — where, except by his father, he was treated rather as a visiting god than as an ordinary son and brother — each once budding promise shrivelled and died, till nothing was left but might-have-beens. Of his brother William, who died in India in 1850, he wrote to his friend ffolliott with a particular accent of love and admiration recalling

---

[1] The evidence used in this chapter, apart from the little published in the *Life and Letters* and from Jowett's letters to Florence Nightingale, comes from the Jowett Papers.
[2] See below, 293.

his cheerful happy ways amid the trials he had to undergo in his early life. . . . I never knew in a young fellow a greater union of manliness and gentleness and good sense. I hoped when he came back in two years' time to introduce him to my friends: therefore let me talk of him to you now, as it pleases me to do so, if it does not bore you.[1]

In the summer after his election to a Balliol fellowship his youngest sister, Ellen, died at Tenby in his presence. This event shook him cruelly. He wrote about it at length to his benefactor Greenhill in a stilted yet moving letter:

Although I never saw death before, I do not think it can be often seen in so dreadful a form. . . . When I remember her form and disposition, such as I never saw united in anyone else, I feel persuaded that I can never again be so happy as I was before. . . . Out of a family of nine there are now only five remaining.

The next younger sister, Agnes, had died two years earlier. Francis and Isabella had died in infancy. There remained only Benjamin himself; his two younger brothers Alfred and William, his sister Emily, and a third brother, Frederick, who had been injured as a baby and was mentally deficient. He died in 1850 — the year of William's death.

The hopes of the family, after Benjamin, lay in Alfred and William and Emily. The father was committing himself utterly to his metrical translation of the psalms — an occupation which, if it kept him happily busy, extinguished whatever chance he still had of even partially supporting his wife and children. That burden fell wholly upon his eldest son, until William and Alfred began, for a little while, to relieve it.

William and Alfred, whom their brother was coaching at Bath in the summer of Ellen's death, were educated at the Bath Grammar School. They seem to have done well there. William was invited in 1838 by Major Irwin (his first cousin by marriage) to go out to Australia. Mr. Jowett sat firmly and unfortunately on this suggestion. He wrote to Mrs. Irwin, his wife's niece:

I hope his kind offer has not unsettled William, but really I feel some alarm about it, as his friendly offer has reached his ears and he is all agog to become a colonist, dear fellow. I want him to keep steadily to his books, he did exceedingly well last half-year; but we allowed him to go to Haverfordwest in the Midsummer holidays and he now shows a seafaring turn, which we never dreamed of. Still he is tractable, and I hope this mania will pass off. . . .

A little later Lord Ashley settled the question of both William's and Alfred's careers. William went to India as an ensign in 1842. 'I think it is a nice prospect for him' his brother at Balliol approved. And so it

[1] *L. & L.*, i, 144.

looked to be, for he was officially reported to be a young officer of great promise 'conspicuous by his study of the hindoostanee', with 'a good knowledge of military tactics'. But he died eight years later, two months short of his twenty-fifth birthday. After his death (Frederick died in the same year) poor Mrs. Jowett had none left to her except her husband, with whom the 'Psalmody Versification' had 'now become a complete monomania', Benjamin at Balliol, her daughter Emily, and her 'dearest Alfred'. But Alfred was in India, too, and had been there since 1846, as a surgeon. Emily, to her father's horror and her mother's grief, had become a Roman Catholic. And Benjamin, assiduous as he was in removing financial worries (and both William and Alfred had begun to take what share they could in that duty)

is such a great fag at College, we seldom hear from him, for he says though he thinks of us often when he is so tired, he can not settle his mind to write, so you must not wonder if he does so to you. I can truly assure you it does not arise from forgetfulness or want of affection.

Thus Isabella wrote to Alfred, who took the remaining place in her heart after William's death. Another eight years — without, apparently, any thought of leave in anybody's mind — and Alfred followed after William, dying at the end of the Indian Mutiny.

Meanwhile the domicile of Mr. and Mrs. Jowett and their pathetic slave Emily had shifted many times: from Bath to Blackheath, while William was being got ready for his cadetship and Alfred entered on his medical studies; then to Teignmouth; then, when Alfred had gone east, to Paris and from Paris for a time to Bonn. To Paris 'by the advice of Benjamin'. Living was cheaper in France, but Benjamin's plan may have owed something to the fact that he had nothing whatever in common with his father — or, indeed, now with his mother. It was easier to visit his parents occasionally in Paris or at St. Germain's than to be expected perpetually to break his busy routine by running down to some such place as Teignmouth or Tenby. But to Tenby (where Ellen had died) they returned in 1856.

Not long after this Mr. Jowett somehow contrived to publish his metrical translation of the Psalms. The return of his father was very irksome to Benjamin. The old man was full of his psalms; the young man full of his commentary on the Epistles of St. Paul. The one a waste of labour on an obsessive hobby, for which the fortunes and happiness of others had been uselessly sacrificed; the other a bold, pioneering work, achieved without the interruption of other duties — a work which had excited orthodox criticism and was being strenuously revised for the second edition. Moreover the years immediately after 1854 were years, for the younger Jowett, of bitter disappointment and disillusion, when life 'seemed dark and miserable'.

A New Metrical Translation of the Book of Psalms appeared anonymously in 1857. In April of that year Emily wrote unhappily to her brother Alfred:

The last few months we have had a renewal of our old anxieties on this account as it regards the publishing of the P's, which we fear though done anonymously will through the risk that they should become known injure and annoy another. I had always looked upon them as a harmless amusement, that would be never ending . . . only this I ask if you can say a word for dear B. say it, for it is indeed a hard case.

The old man was not to be deterred; and Emily's sensitive fears on her brother's account were needless. But Benjamin was quite unable to play up to his father, who wrote acidly to Alfred in October:

Benj. has just spent five days with us; but he has been so taciturn that I think that every thing he has said might have been said perhaps in 5 minutes. He is certainly much occupied, but this need not prevent him from unbending a little. I had, for my portion, one brief question on business, and the monosyllabic 'no' in answer to a question. I am happy to say that he appears to be carefully revising his work which certainly needed it.

Next year Alfred died, and in the year after that old Mr. Jowett's ineffective career came to its end. His son wrote of him to Stanley, with charitable piety:

He was one of the best men I ever knew, perfectly guileless and childlike, and would have been one of the happiest, if life could have been spent only in doing kindnesses to others. Though possessed of considerable ability and very great activity of mind, he was entirely ignorant of the world and of business, in some respects like a child throughout life.

Mrs. Jowett went to Torquay after her husband's death, and she lived there with Emily for ten years, a frail and charming old lady, watching from a distance the astonishing rise of her eldest son into the great world, with pride but not with much understanding. 'She was not a clever person' he confided to Florence Nightingale, writing on the day of her death, 'but she had great power of appreciation and the strongest affection I have ever known, not only to her own family but to every one whom she knew.' She had never understood him, or perhaps been at ease with him, since he had been parted from her as a young boy. Upon him that separation, following the earlier circumstances of his childhood, his father's overbearing discipline, his mother's preoccupation with her younger children, had inflicted an utterly incurable wound. If his people were not at ease with him, he was not at ease with them.

7. 'Old Mr. Jowett'
An amateur photograph taken in France
(*Balliol*)

8. 'Such a great fag at College'
Young Mr. Jowett
A photograph by
Hills and Saunders
(*Balliol*)

This constraint came most poignantly between Emily and himself. She wrote very sadly about this to Alfred in 1857:

There is no use in lamenting over things we cannot change and especially as persons grow older, tho I can understand fully dear B's feeling about them. He never writes to me now. But I know he is under some strange mistake which for a while blinds him as to the past: though in his *own* way he gives us all proof of his remembrance. So that I cease now to look for or even offer sympathy as I once could. Would that I could have made him happier.

'Some strange mistake which for a while blinds him as to the past?' It is impossible to know fully what Emily meant by this enigmatic phrase, though one can see how it fits with the recoverable facts. Only it was not so much a mistake of reasoning as a maladjustment of feeling, which no amount of deliberate effort could possibly correct. Whether Emily understood this or not, she laid no blame upon her brother. On the outside of an envelope containing one of his brief letters to his mother, she wrote:

> Do not smile at me that I boast him off
> For thou shalt find '*he*' will outstrip all praise
> And make it halt behind '*him*'.

This letter was one that he wrote in 1863 — one in which he made an almost unaccustomed effort of tenderness.

My dear Mother, I write a line to say how very sorry I am to hear that you have been ill. I hope you are better, and that you mean to remain with us many years. I shall always feel as long as I live deeply grateful to you for your care for us. I hope you will think of me always as your affectionate son B. Jowett. I am in the midst of my lectures at present. But I can come at any time and see you, if you would like me to come. I shall be down at Xmas.

'My dear Mother, I send a cheque on the other side for £50. . . . With love to Emily Ever yours affy B. Jowett.' Such was the usual formula. A few laconic details of his movements; an occasional description, hurriedly written, of a great house where he happened to be staying; a reference, barely intelligible, to some reform at Balliol for which he was responsible; an excuse for not writing oftener; an adjuration to have a fire in her bedroom: things like these were the substance of his letters, which seldom (if ever) ran to more than a very few lines. Obviously written against the grain, they conspicuously lack the note of eager interest in his correspondents' doings which his ordinary letters exhibit. A common enough characteristic of sons' letters to their mothers. But in Jowett, with his peculiar power and habit of projecting himself into the lives of others, it is a symptom of an emotional estrangement which he not only could not overcome, but made no real attempt to overcome. It is as if he had said to himself: 'I have my duties as a son and a brother, and these I will scrupulously perform. But I will not pretend to feelings I have lost.'

And yet, when his mother died, her appearance seemed to follow him about — so he told Florence Nightingale. And to Morier, at the same time, he wrote: 'I seem to see her constantly.' The feelings, to which he would not pretend, had never really died in him. The refusal to pretend was in itself a pretence which he had been forced, without knowing what he was doing, to set up in his boyhood. If you feel yourself deserted, you must fall back upon yourself and pretend that you are better out of the nest than in it. The self-protective pretence soon hardens into a shell which no inner movement of the spirit can break. Was not this the 'mistake' which Emily's intuition divined in her brother?

His mother's death in 1869 shook a composure which he became more than ever resolved to maintain. Continuing his letter to Miss Nightingale, he wrote:

More and more for myself I see two or three things which this late trouble rather tends to impress on me. First, that I must be absorbed in my work and use all means towards this (not neglecting health) and shut out all trivial thoughts and personal feelings of all sorts. Secondly, that I must aim at perfect calmness. . . . Thirdly that I must try to act more simply and on a larger scale, not tiring myself with mere drudgery, or shrinking into a coterie, or caring only for the affection of admiring friends.

Isabella died in her sleep on a Sunday morning after having been ill for ten days. Her son had been informed of her illness, but the reports suggested that it was not serious, and he did not cancel or shorten a visit to Florence Nightingale's parents at Embley in Hampshire, where Florence herself was staying. When the urgent summons came he hurried to Torquay. But it was too late. His mother had died before he reached the house. He refused to blame himself and with equal determination refused to let Miss Nightingale blame herself. 'You did not really prevent my seeing my dear mother again' he assured her. 'But we were deceived about her state and did not calculate on the danger of illness at her age. I intended to have gone on from Embley, if the report had not been favourable.' And he added, with a peremptoriness meant, perhaps, to silence his own misgivings: 'Do not think any more of this.'

Emily lived on for some years at Torquay. It was her brother's decision. She had good friends there. She would really not be happy in Oxford — as he carefully explained to Miss Nightingale — for his spare time was all taken up by people coming in to talk with him. Nor, when he became Master in the year after his mother's death, did he ask her to preside in the Master's lodging. She was not 'efficient in the business of life'. Moreover, she was a Roman Catholic.

These were powerful, even decisive, reasons. They prevented him from examining his mind more deeply. For the truth was that he was still a victim of the strange mistake which blinded him to the past. In all but the essential outward obligations he had broken with that past, at first unconsciously and then deliberately; and for too many years now he had lived his own life in his own way, removed from uncomfortable intimacies even with the sister to whom he was beyond either praise or blame.

Emily was allowed to stay with him at Balliol 'more than once' during the remaining thirteen years of her life. Those visits must have been attended for her with painful difficulties, with a distressing sense of her unfitness to share her brother's great position, underlined by the contrast between her tongue-tied state and the assurance of Miss Martha Knight, her brother's confidential and formidable housekeeper. She had always been as afraid of Benjamin as she was devoted to him — unable to 'do herself justice even in playing the piano before him'.[1] He would tell her that she was not playing well, ignorant of the cause. She was unable to explain it, unable to do herself justice in his presence. She soon forgot, if she had ever known, the art of breaking his silences. But he had not been distant from her when they shut themselves together as children.

'In the hours of gloom and misunderstanding she loved to dwell on the earlier days of free and joyous intercourse, which could never be recalled.'[2] All her life had been spent in a self-abnegation which he might respect in theory but abominated in practice. How could she even begin to take the smallest part, now, in his brilliantly rational existence? It was happier for her, and happier for him, that she should stay at Torquay, playing the piano to herself and receiving, at regular intervals, those orders for £50, which must be properly endorsed before they were convertible into cash, 'on the other side' of those brief punctilious letters beginning 'My dear Sister' and ending with 'Believe me Ever yours B. Jowett'.

Two years before she died, Emily had a stroke. Her cousins, the Irwins, came to her rescue — and, incidentally, to her brother's rescue — and took her into their house at Clifton. This debt, too, he repaid faithfully and fully in his own coin.[3] When the first seizure came she

---

[1] *ibid.*, i, 25. She 'kept up her accomplishment in music.'
[2] *ibid.*, i, 26.
[3] I mean, by his generous, yet aloof, treatment of Guy and Sidney Irwin.

wrote on a piece of paper the words 'Make not my will to be thine, but thy will to be mine, O God' and caused this to be sent to her brother. So he told Lady Airlie, adding a comment curiously similar to that which he had made to Dr. Greenhill on the death of his sister Ellen more than forty years earlier: 'There were once nine of us and now there are only two.' The identity of phrasing is extraordinarily significant. One by one the others had dropped off; and he, the eldest of them all, the one fledgling who had been tossed into the air to fly by himself, he had been the only one to achieve anything; he would be the only one left alive; and after him there would be nobody. There was a kind of rightness in that. But there was also — coming painfully to the surface of his mind, as each successive blow of the axe fell or threatened, and always present in the abysses of memory — a cruel contrast between the full golden age of the nursery and the empty failure of the many sickrooms.

On the day of Emily's death, in December 1882, he wrote pitifully:

She was a saint in private life, who never thought of herself. All her days were devoted to my father and mother, and she made life possible and easy for them. For though intelligent and educated people they were unable to take care of themselves.[1]

When the funeral was over he went to see the one friend who might have been more to him than a friend, Miss Elliot, a daughter of the Dean of Bristol. Alone with her, he broke down and cried helplessly, so that he would not see her father.[2] He was beginning to be an old man now — though still only in his middle sixties — and, one might have thought, past the bitterness of unavailing regret. Perhaps, as he wept in Miss Elliot's drawing room, he was expiating a twofold mistake — a mistake about the past and a mistake about the future. He had failed to be a son and a brother, and he had failed to become a husband and father. All that he had done was to become Master of Balliol and Vice-Chancellor of Oxford University — and to prefer a paper friendship with one woman to marriage with another.

2. THE UNMARRIED MAN

'So you wish me to marry' Jowett wrote to Stanley in March 1865, after Christ Church had raised his professional stipend to £500.

I don't wonder at this when I see and rejoice to see how happy and successful the experiment has been in your case. But I have come to the conclusion that I am better as I am now. I could not marry without giving

---

[1] *L. & L.*, ii, 237.　　　　　　[2] See below, 302.

up Balliol, on which my life has been spent, and probably signing the XXXIX Articles over again, or having to make a statement of opinions to a Bishop, if I took a living or could get a Deanery or Canonry: and I am obliged always to deduct about £400 a year from my income (this is a matter which I never mention and do not you mention; it has continued nearly twenty-five years — I never like to speak or to think of it). The position at Balliol is a painful one, but I get more used to it, and I think the influence and usefulness, if I may say so, are greater or, certainly, not less. My chief desire is to make the most of the years that remain. I am glad of this additional £460 a year because it will enable me to do a great deal more than I do at present in the Professorship in the way of composition and additional lectures, and also leave more leisure for permanent work.

Life has had a good deal of painfulness to me (not this matter of the Professorship, or the attacks of people in the newspapers). But I always feel that I have had a wonderful compensation in the devotion and attachment of friends and pupils. 'No one has better friends' (don't you think so?), and among them I reckon you and Lady Augusta.[1]

Stanley's 'experiment' was little more than a year old. He had married Lady Augusta Bruce at the end of 1863. It was a happy marriage. His wife filled the aching void created by his mother's death in 1862; and she gave him the unstinted woman's love without which he (unlike Jowett) felt himself not so much alone as lost. He was never the same man again after his wife's death in 1876. Not long before his own death in 1881, he wrote movingly to a widowed friend:

Alas! what can we say to each other? When I was speaking to my dear Augusta, she said, in the midst of her sufferings, which were then very severe, 'I have nothing left but this crushed and miserable body.' I said to her, 'Yes, you have something besides. There is your undying love.' She looked me very steadily in the face, and answered with all her strength, 'That is my identity.'

Nevertheless, Stanley's marriage was thought by some of those who knew him well to have diverted him from his true career. 'Among his friends at Oxford the prevailing feeling was one of almost unmixed dismay.'[2] Jowett's description of it as an 'experiment' (a strange word to use about the marriage of an old friend) reflects this opinion.

Lady Augusta Bruce was an intimate friend of the Prince and Princess of Wales; it was natural that she should wish her husband to obtain high preferment. The immediate consequences were his appointment as Dean of Westminster, and his resignation of the chair of Ecclesiastical History at Oxford. Stanley himself was very unhappy over this. He told his *fiancée* that he 'dreaded the plunge' and relied on her to be his 'wings'. When he had been formally installed, 'I confess that I felt no elation, nothing but depression, at the prospect before me. It seemed to me as if

---

[1] *L. & L.*, i, 374. [2] *Life of Dean Stanley*, ii, 142.

I were going down into the sepulchre.'[1] And it was true that, as Dean of Westminster, Stanley said goodbye to the hopes of him which Jowett and his Oxford friends still tried to keep alive.

Writing to congratulate Stanley upon his approaching marriage, Jowett had wished him

> every blessing and joy in your marriage. I think you are quite right and wise in marrying. And I am sure you could not have made a better choice. . . . I rejoice at your marriage. I saw the lady once, and I thought she was frank and good and wise, and very unlike my imperfect notions of people who live at Court, in being the most natural person in the world.

Under these sugar coatings lay the Jowettian pill of what he called 'crabbed and unasked for counsel'. He advised Stanley to look at Genesis xxiv, 67. This is the verse which says: 'And Isaac brought her into his mother Sarah's tent, and took Rebekah, and she became his wife; and he loved her: and Isaac was comforted after his mother's death.' A bold thing to say to a friend marrying a wife to replace a mother. He went on:

> I hardly like to tell you that I regret the other step [the leaving of Oxford for Westminster] as much as I rejoice in this. I believe you could be of more use to the Court at Oxford than in London, and of much more use to the Church. The London clergy cannot be influenced like young men at Oxford; your time would be wasted in meetings and business. Your influence upon society depends a good deal on your having another sphere which enables you to withdraw from it. For a very slight addition to possible influence in London, you give up the eminent success which you have had at Oxford. You will be thought to have withdrawn from the Liberal cause at Oxford, and to have accepted a great preferment at a time when you have begun a war against the majority.
>
> My view is, that you should continue to fight the battle here, and, when your opinions have made more way, four or five years hence, *cum consensu omnium*, you should be made a bishop, to fight the same battle in another place. I cannot think that, if this were properly represented to the Queen, she, or any other true friend of yours, could wish you to accept the Deanery of Westminster.

The advice was thrown away. Stanley had got what he needed, a wife who found herself — her very 'identity' — in devotion to him and to his interest as she understood it. He had always had to lean upon somebody — Dr. Arnold, his mother, for a while Jowett. Now he leaned upon his Rebekah. She knew so clearly what he should do; she was his 'wings'; her devotion warmed him, her determination possessed him. She took charge of his life from the beginning of each day, preparing his 'frugal breakfast' with her own hands.[2] Some thought that she 'came

---

[1] *ibid.*, ii, 142. Nevertheless the ceremony moved him deeply. See above, 280.
[2] *ibid.*, ii, 491. Various women, including his sister Mary, 'took it in turns' to look after him after his wife's death. 'On them devolved the duties which Lady Augusta had so lovingly performed. . . . His frugal breakfast was prepared

between him and intimacy'; among them Miss Elliot and Matthew Arnold.

All this is far from irrelevant to Jowett's private history. His attitude towards Stanley's marriage is the nearest we can get to any indication, in his own words, of his attitude towards marriage as an adventure which he might himself undertake. The practical reasons he showed to Stanley against such an adventure for himself were good enough. But they were not his real reasons. It was true that he had lost his chance of being elected to the one fellowship which permitted marriage, under the 1857 Ordinance for Balliol. The fellow so privileged had to be a University professor or lecturer. Henry Wall, who was professor of Logic and had resigned his old fellowship, was re-elected to the new one at a special meeting on 27th June 1862. Jowett was one of the five fellows present. Had he also made an application similar to Wall's, which had been turned down? The record does not say. Certainly he felt resentment. Perhaps, as Dr. Richard Hunt has suggested to me, Wall stole a march on him.

In 1865, therefore, and for the next five years, marriage was impossible for Jowett unless he left Balliol. But he no longer wished to marry; and he had to say something, which would not go too deep and would seem to make tolerable and cheerful sense, in answer to Stanley's eager propagandism. Is it possible to know how far he went towards the idea of marriage, and to discover — or at least to make a sensible guess of — the reasons which led him to abandon it?

3. 'M.E.'

The first volume of the *Life and Letters*, which ends with Jowett's election as Master of Balliol in 1870, avoids both these questions. Not that Campbell wanted to avoid them. He was compelled to avoid them by the small group of younger men who assumed editorial control over his part of the biography and felt that Jowett's earlier life should be discreetly presented as a long preparation for the great climax of the Mastership. It was their censorship which principally prevented Campbell from saying much that he wished to say; in particular — though here he had to respect difficulties created by the fact that the two women concerned were still living — from relating what he knew, or had discovered, about Jowett's approach to the idea of marriage and his recession from it.

as Lady Augusta had prepared it, and his *Times* taken from him and read aloud, lest, absorbed in its contents, he should altogether omit the meal.' And so on, throughout the day.

The published text of Campbell's volume nevertheless contains many allusions and letters which, if read in the light of the document I am about to reproduce, mean more than they have hitherto appeared to mean. It would be tiresome to trace and explain all these survivals of what Campbell originally wanted to say. Here are a few instances, for the benefit of those who may wish to look them up. Jowett's several letters to Dean Elliot and his daughter take on a new significance. So does 'Mrs. Cradock's Rose-garden' (i, 267). So does the passage (i, 308) describing Jowett's resentment of the fact that another fellow had been allowed to marry, and he not: 'My College want to get rid of me which is rather hard.' This is linked to 'a piece of gossip' casually retailed in a letter of Matthew Arnold's, in November 1862.

The suppressed story survives in a notebook of Campbell's. The note-book itself is a cheap little affair, with a shiny black cover on which Campbell pasted a square-cut piece of paper bearing the initials 'M. E.' The first twenty-three pages had been used for miscellaneous personal memoranda, before Campbell started to jot down in pencil some fragmentary and disconnected recollections of 'B. J.' These recollections occupy the next thirteen pages. They were obviously made very soon after Jowett's death. Then, under the date of 7th January 1894, the note-book is put to the special purpose which caused it to be labelled 'M. E.' The only possible way of using this evidence is to reproduce it as it was written.

The initials stood for Margaret Elliot, the elder daughter of Gilbert Elliot, Dean of Bristol. Elliot was a Cambridge man. He was born in 1800, a member of a distinguished Scottish family. His grandfather was the third baronet to bear the title of Sir Gilbert Elliot. His uncle succeeded to the baronetcy and became the first Earl of Minto. His father was a Governor of Madras and a Privy Councillor. Dean Elliot married twice. His first wife was a Williamina Brydon, whom he married in 1825. She died in 1853. There were two surviving daughters, Margaret and her younger sister Emma.[1] The Dean married again in 1863. His second wife was a widow, who bore him no children. These dates are not irrelevant; for they show that Jowett's acquaintance with the family began after the death of the first Mrs. Elliot and ripened before the Dean's second marriage. Margaret died unmarried in 1901. Her sister Emma married, in 1862, a Mr. Montague Blackett, who died in 1866; there were no children. Emma (the delicate beauty) lived far longer than Margaret. She was listed as still alive in the 1925 edition of Burke's *Peerage*.

[1] A tablet in Bristol Cathedral, dedicated to the memory of their mother, also records a son Gilbert who was lost at sea, and a daughter Mary who died at the age of thirteen.

Dean Elliot is not given a place in the *Dictionary of National Biography* alongside the other Gilbert Elliots who were baronets or earls. Yet he seems to have been reckoned as a man of character by his younger contemporaries. Jowett, certainly, so regarded him. The letters to Dean Elliot, included in Campbell's volume, bring that out very clearly. It is obvious enough that Jowett began this correspondence thinking that he might ask the Dean's daughter to marry him. He never did so. But he found in her father a congenial spirit. Long after the once current rumour that he was courting Miss Elliot had been generally forgotten, Abbott wrote of the Dean's death in 1891 that 'Jowett had lost a friend, whose support and sympathy had been extended to him at a time when he was very greatly in need of them'.

Here is a full and (as nearly as I can be sure) an exact transcription of Campbell's long note.

Sunday — Jany 7th 1894.

M.E. has important letters from B.J. to herself and to the Dean of Bristol ('60–'62). She had met him occasionally between '54–'59 but her first real acquaintance was in 'Bunny's' (Mrs. Cradock's)[1] garden at Brasenose in '60. Her sister Emma was the *beauty*, and when stories thrown into a hat were read out Emma's was taken for best by all but L. Stanley[2] and B.J. Her own came last and was read by her in the garden. L.S. and B.J. found her out. B.J. borrowed it from Mrs. Cradock, and made Mathew Knight[3] copy it. Then flowers were plucked and Emma gave them round. M.E. complained 'No one has given me a rose'; and Jowett gave her his. Some banter followed and a poem on the subject with drawings representing E. disconsolate and B.J. *empressé* offering his rose to M. was found pinned to a gooseberry bush next day. (Who wrote these lines — L.S.?) B.J. heard of this, and was not pleased. But when E. was ordered abroad, and they all went, he asked leave to correspond and wrote long and (for him) effusive letters.

When they returned, he was invited to the Deanery[4] — but before going, gave his Essay for the Dean (not wishing to appear in false colours). The Dean sent a message back, 'I have been talking Jowettism all my life without knowing it. Pray let him come.' They talked. The Dean said I dare say he is a good friend, but not much as an acquaintance?

In his letters he constantly referred to the prospects of his salary. And when the plan for it (which he only partially approved but said it would be Quixotic to oppose it) was defeated in '61, he seems to have applied to the College for leave to marry on his Fellowship (and Tutorship). About this time, her sister being engaged, the rumours of M.'s engagement reached

[1] Dr. Cradock was Principal of Brasenose. Mrs. Cradock 'loved to bring young people together'. *L. & L.*, i, 267.

[2] The Hon. Edward Lyulph Stanley, a young cousin of Arthur Stanley's, and at this time a pupil of Jowett's at Balliol. He was a fellow of Balliol from 1862 to 1869. In 1903 he succeeded his brother as Lord Stanley of Alderley, and in 1909 to the title of Lord Sheffield. He died in 1925.

[3] The studious young son of Jowett's college servant, who later became his secretary, and was the brother of Martha Knight who became his housekeeper. See below, 417 *foll.*

[4] The Deanery at Bristol.

him and he pressed for an interview with Mrs. Cradock, to make sure
that it was not so. When Wall gained the permission against him,[1] he
wrote to M. saying that his circumstances were entirely altered and he
could no longer correspond with friends in the same way and it was
evident his College wanted to get rid of him, and after this the correspondence dropped. When her father married again (her sister being
married) he wrote her 'a curious letter' full of advice as to what she should
do.

Some years afterwards, his sister died at Clifton and he went to the
funeral. He paid M. a visit and poured out his grief (he had left the
lonely grave in the Church Yard) and felt all alone. He wept — and would
not see the Dean. When the Dean died, B. J. wrote a letter full of kindness,
and after this he had no reserve with her — was most kind about her
father's MSS. and paid her a long visit in July 1893.

In 1860–2 she said that childhood is not the happiest time. He said, 'I
think so too.' When she said in some theological discussion that confusion arose because truth was sacrificed to charity, he said 'I am afraid
you are right'.[2]

She was ill, after her sister's marriage — and was reading the last letter,
when Dr. Symonds called to see her about 9 p.m. He was concerned at her
state and came next morning and said, 'I have found the solution my son
writes that Jowett has failed in obtaining leave to marry.'

'While Stanley is here I shall not have to fear to meet my enemies in
the gate.'[3]

M. E. first met Stanley too at Mrs. Cradock's. She had *enthused* over
Arnold's life and it was a great day when she met his biographer. They
went to look for Arnold's Rock in Bagley Wood — A. P. S. could not find it
but Cradock did. They met again at Boulogne when he was returning
from Palestine with a long black beard. Dean Elliot did not recognize him
but she did, and they had a walk on the windy beach. (They were storm-
staid.) He was talking eagerly when he fell over a hawser. But he got up
and talked on as if there had been no interruption.

B. J. 'The inexorable' — This was Stanley's soubriquet for him, when
on their foreign tour he insisted on their compact of giving an hour a day
to study.

Was this the explanation of his never returning to the broken

[1] This appears to mean that Wall and Jowett simultaneously applied for leave
to marry and that Wall's application was granted and Jowett's refused. Wall
remained a fellow until 1870, when he took the Balliol living of Huntspill. He
was a year junior to Jowett as a fellow and had not been an undergraduate at
Balliol. Campbell may have felt that he hadn't got his facts quite right; for he
put a note on the opposite page 'N.B. Ask Newman and Bowen'.

[2] Campbell first wrote 'charity should not go before truth', then crossed these
words through and substituted 'confusion arose because truth was sacrificed to
charity'. I suspect that the first version was nearer to Miss Elliot's *ipsissima verba*.
The page reporting these two not very remarkable conversational exchanges was
scribbled in great haste. At the bottom of it, after Jowett's 'I am afraid you are
right', Campbell added a comment so indecipherable that I cannot confidently
transcribe it. However, here is the best I can do: '3 people have made that for
instance — Stanley, Charity. Gladstone, humility. Temple, candour.' The
illegible part is the middle, which I have rendered 'made that for instance'.

[3] This seems to be a quotation from Jowett, used as a text on which to hang
Miss Elliot's following slight reminiscences of Stanley. I do not omit these since
I feel that this part of Campbell's note-book must be given entire. Moreover, as
will soon become clear, Miss Elliot's relations with the Stanley family led her
into an antagonistic attitude towards Florence Nightingale.

intercourse? Why could he not have married in '64? Was it that when ill-used by his colleagues, he resolved to devote himself to the College, and having made this resolution, kept it? (Or was it that at 47 his habits were too fixed, or that by this time he was a religious leader and thought it would weaken his influence? Or had some Platonic friendship (F. N.) come between?)

Up to this point the notes are written with a rapid, but legible pencil. A second series of notes, neatly and deliberately written in ink, begins a new page. The inked notes add a little more information about Margaret's 'story' and about the poem found in Mrs. Cradock's garden; but their point lies mainly in Miss Elliot's old-maidish gossip about people she had intimately known. It looks as if Campbell sought and had another talk with her. The gossip was first-hand gossip; it will be seen to have some bearing upon the relationship between Miss Elliot herself and Jowett; and it is at least an interesting new foot-note to the lives of Jowett and some of this friends.

M. E. (See Phaedrus — introd. and sermon or lecture at Edinburgh.[1])
Among the stories dropped into 'Bunny's' basket were Augustus Hare's and Lyulph Stanley's.
At a ball shortly afterwards C. Bowen[2] said he had heard of M. E.'s 'Jowett liked it'. Froude[3] then unknown to her asked to see it. It had been lent to Miss Cobbe. She showed it to J. who took it away in his pocket — then wrote to M. E. It ultimately appeared in Fraser.[4]
Lady S. of Alderley was obliged to listen to the story — *because it was Bunny's birthday* — and Lady S. wanted sadly to be introduced to B. J. who was Lyulph's Tutor.[5]
In the garden at Brasenoze [sic] Emma had plucked flowers for everyone except her sister. B. J. presented his flower to M. E. This led to some raillery — as the flower had been presented to him by the other sister who was much admired.
Some verses were written on the occasion by Lyulph Stanley with an illustration by Sir C. Wood (Lord Halifax).
B. J. at Bunny's liked joining in the evening hymn and confessed his love for music.
He assented to two things 'I would not be a child again' and 'good music is the greatest pleasure in life'. At the dean's he said after visiting Miss Carpenter's school 'We have been flirting with the Unitarians to-day. I wonder they come so near us, and not come all the way' — (M. E. thought that he came very near them.) 1862. (E. C. M.[6] said (in 1864?) 'He is still of an age when men are expected to marry'.)

[1] I have not confidently identified this Edinburgh lecture. Nor do I know for certain what Campbell meant by the reference to the introduction to the *Phaedrus*. But see above, 96 *foll.*, and below, 432 Note.
[2] At this time a young fellow of Balliol.   [3] J. A. Froude, the historian.
[4] *Fraser's Magazine?*
[5] Lady Stanley of Alderley was Lyulph's mother. I suppose that she had to sit on her anxiety to meet Jowett, in respect for her hostess. But I don't quite understand the point of the italics (which, of course, merely reproduce Campbell's underlining).
[6] Margaret Elliot's sister Emma.

The quarrel between F. N. and M. Stanley occurred in this way. When F. N. was already at Scutari, M. S.[1] spoke to Sidney Herbert who said they wanted more nurses. M. S. went out with introductions on a troop-ship and on arriving off Scutari sent her credentials ashore. F. N. simply replied that none were wanted, and M. S. lay off shore for two days and never landed. Ultimately she went to Therapia. 'It was not kindly done.'

M. S. told M. E. that her first impulse towards Rome came from F. N.'s conversation and correspondence. (This as Mrs. A. H. Clough told me was soon after her father's death.) Both had resolved to take no decisive step till after the Crimea. When they came out F. N. made no change, M. S. did.

The 'fret and fume' of which A. P. S. wrote were caused by Lady A.[2] who came between him and intimacy. M. S.[3] was given to understand (e.g.) that she must not come to lunch without letting them know. M. E. and Mat Arnold sympathized about this. After Lady A.'s death Mat said with a wafture of his hand 'Most interesting, to see the Myth growing!'

M. S. rejoiced when A. P. S. left Oxford 'that dreadful place that makes people so cynical'.

M. E. still has the flowers gathered in Bagley Wood when Cradock found Dr. Arnold's rock, for which A. P. Stanley searched in vain.

Temple was staying at the Deanery[4] when he wrote his *recantation*[5] (the Bishoprick was secure but he could not bear the *feelings* of the clergy.) He did not tell Stanley who saw the letter first in *The Times*. M. E. who was also staying there never saw anyone look so terribly aghast.

He[6] spoke of an aunt as the most selfless person he ever knew.

Campbell's notes end at this point. They assume (though they do not explicitly state or prove) that in 1860 and for a year or so afterwards Jowett was deliberately courting Miss Elliot. The several long letters he wrote to her and to her father during this time certainly bear out this view. So does the abrupt stoppage of the published correspondence.

Six of Jowett's letters to Dean Elliot were published, all in the first volume of the *Life and Letters*. The first was written in October 1860, the last in March 1863. Five letters to Miss Elliot are published in the same volume; another nine in the supplementary volume of *Letters*. The first letter is dated January 1861; it begins with an enthusiastic reference to a pamphlet on *Destitute Incurables in Workhouses* which 'appears to be written by some one who bears your name. I thought it extremely well

---

[1] Mary Stanley, Arthur's sister.
[2] Lady Augusta Stanley, Arthur's wife.
[3] 'M.S.' or 'M.E.'? Campbell's written S and E are identical, except that the bottom of the one usually turns a little to the left, of the other a little to the right. The letter here has a barely perceptible kick to the right, which makes it look more like E than S. Why should Margaret Elliot have expected to lunch with the Stanleys 'without letting them know'? I think that Campbell meant to write 'M.S.' But I may, of course, be wrong.
[4] The Deanery at Westminster.
[5] The 'recantation' was Temple's withdrawal of his essay from future reprints of *Essays and Reviews*, on the occasion of his becoming a Bishop — an act which Jowett, for one, thought a sad piece of episcopal humbug.
[6] Temple? More probably Jowett.

done, very touching and simple, and really practical and businesslike.' It was, in fact, written by his Miss Elliot in collaboration with Miss Cobbe;[1] as Jowett probably knew, for he adds that 'like Miss Cobbe I hate Philanthropists'. The last letter is dated June 1862. It is no less friendly and conversational than all the other letters written during the short period — only eighteen months — covered by the published correspondence. But is there, perhaps, a warning note in the first sentence of the last letter as printed? Dots indicate the omission of opening matter; the printed letter then begins by saying: 'You greatly undervalue Plato, who is a most faithful friend to me — too faithful for indeed I can't get rid of him. . . .'

These fourteen letters are very well worth reading. They can be easily discovered from the indexes to the *Life and Letters* and the *Letters*. The whole series establishes the fact that for some eighteen months Margaret Elliot occupied a specially privileged place in Jowett's mind. He admits her to everything he is thinking or feeling about this and that — about, for example, the non-existence of an 'abyss of Theology'; about the 'ridiculous position of a Head of a House'; about Tennyson's shyness and painful need of sympathy ('I shouldn't tell it to you if I did not think *you* would comprehend it'); about the Bishop of London ('very weak'); about 'my poor friend Clough' who would 'have been a great genius . . . if he had not been overworked'.

It may have been with the object of covering up the significance of the relationship between Jowett and Miss Elliot that so many of his letters to her were published in the *Letters* and not in the *Life*, and separated there under different headings. A little trouble is needed, therefore, to read the series in sequence. But the trouble is self-rewarding.

We should know nothing of these letters if Campbell had not been given them by Miss Elliot after Jowett's death. If there were any affectionate passages, they have been suppressed. But there is no reason to suppose that he did more than write to her, at somewhat unusual length and with an appearance of easy freedom, about the things that then mattered between intelligent friends. There is a delicate overtone of solicitude — as if he were saying to himself 'Will she be interested? I will write as if I were sure that she is, and I won't put it too forbiddingly.' And in the letters to Dean Elliot there is unquestionably a touch — light, but sustained — of the manner, at once intimate and deferential, which a man of Jowett's age and quality would naturally adopt towards a

[1] Frances Power Cobbe (1822–1904), the Irish philanthropist and religious writer and journalist.

dignitary who might become his father-in-law. Subtle care was used in both series of letters, and the note in each series is different from the note in the other.

It is possible that there may have been other letters belonging to this period — if Campbell's account is accurate, there was at least one such letter not surrendered for publication. It is also possible that the correspondence was not so completely interrupted as the published series suggests. Jowett was once more writing to Miss Elliot in 1890: 'I am touched to hear that your father wishes to be remembered by me. He certainly will not fall out of my recollection while I live.' And when the Dean died in 1891, the Master of Balliol wrote to the daughter:

He is at rest and you are alone. You gave up everything to him . . . I hope you will not think that your occupation in this world is gone. . . . It seems to me that the later years of life are after all the most valuable, because we have experience and are more disengaged from the world. . . .

And a week later:

I am glad to hear that you are leaving Bristol and going to London. I hope that I may have the pleasure of sometimes coming to see you at the old place. . . . It pleases me to hear that you are not giving up life, but bravely beginning it again. . . .[1]

'The old place'? And what did he mean by saying that she had given up 'everything' for her father? That could have happened only after her stepmother's death in 1866, by which time she must have discovered that Jowett was not for her, if for any woman. Had he persuaded himself, as life went on, that 'everything' included the marriage which he had had in his own mind but never proposed? It may have been so. Conscience makes cowards of us all. It is so much more comfortable for an old man to feel that responsibility for the emptiness of somebody else's life does not lie with him, but with a father who has claimed her selfless devotion.

4. 'F.N.'

What was it, then, that sent him into reverse — into a position which was, for some time, dangerously similar to that of his 'poor friend' Clough, killed by overwork? Campbell splits this question into four. Was it, he asks first, that 'when ill-used by his colleagues, he resolved to devote himself to the college, and having made this resolution, kept it' in his 'inexorable' way? Or was it that his 'habits' were too fixed? Or that marriage 'would weaken his influence' as a 'religious leader'?

[1] *L. & L.*, ii, 381, 397–9.

This third notion can be eliminated. It is nonsensical. The first two may contain something. 'B. J. the inexorable' did not easily change his mind, once it was made up. And his bachelor habits *were* becoming fixed, at the age of forty-seven; though they burst and overflowed into an abounding hospitality, when he became Master.

If Campbell's first two questions notched the target, the fourth — more tentatively loosed — found the gold. 'Or' he asked 'had some Platonic friendship (F. N.) come between?'

Miss Nightingale did much more than come between Jowett and Miss Elliot. For some years she eclipsed her and every other friend he had, male or female, with the one exception of Robert Morier, who was in every imaginable way her complete opposite. 'It has been one of the greatest happinesses of my life to have had your friendship' he wrote to Morier in 1884; 'I have learned so much from it too; you must take my meaning, for I cannot express what I feel.' As he was dying, eight or nine years later — Morier dying at the same time in Switzerland — he dictated his last letter to Miss Nightingale: 'How large a part has your life been of my life. There is only time I think for a few words.' The sentiment in the two letters is unmistakably the same; the brevity of expression startlingly similar.

The close likeness in his feelings for his oldest and dearest man friend and his greatest woman friend — the one a genial masculine extrovert, taking the rough with the smooth as a man of the world should, the other a driving genius of a woman, at once egoist and altruist, worker and hypochondriac, tyrant of others and slave of purpose, equally restless in her fight against administrative folly and in her search for mystical union with God — this close likeness in Jowett's feelings for two such utterly different persons of opposite sexes indicates an ambivalency of temperament which could not have been satisfied in wedlock. It was fortunate both for himself and for Miss Elliot that he had not asked her to marry him before Miss Nightingale's star rose, suddenly, into the zenith of his sky.

The *Life and Letters* is completely silent about Florence Nightingale. Not even the bare fact of friendship between her and Jowett is disclosed, let alone its extraordinary character. There are two or three allusions, which only a privately informed reader could have perceived to refer to her; some of his letters to her are included (by Miss Nightingale's direction) but without any clue to the identity of his correspondent. Her name is nowhere mentioned. This total silence is a very serious defect in the biography; it makes Jowett appear like a man empty of passion, at the very time when passion was simultaneously invigorating and exhausting him. His biographers are not to be blamed; they had to obey Miss Nightingale's imperious wish.

It was about the beginning of 1861 that Jowett began to correspond with Miss Nightingale; but it was not until October 1862 that he actually met her. This was when he went to her house, at her request, to administer the Sacrament to her in her room. It was the first of many such visits. There were often other people present at the ceremony — Miss Nightingale's parents or intimate friends.

From this date also began his frequent visits — usually many times a year — to Miss Nightingale herself; indeed he was seldom, if ever, in London without spending an afternoon with her.[1]

He became a friend of her family's; and when, at last, she was persuaded to spend part of her time in the country at Lea Hurst or at Embley (her father's two houses) he was often staying under the same roof.

There was, consequently, nothing in the least secret about the fact of their friendship, though its inner character baffled most observers — not least those who belonged to the Nightingale family. Only Lewis Campbell, by the tentative query in his 'M. E.' note-book, reveals the clue. He was unable to follow it up himself; it is the starting point of the speculations developed in the next chapter.[2]

Miss Nightingale's refusal to allow her name to be used by Jowett's biographers, even though she allowed them to use long extracts from his letters, was not wise. Among those — and they were many — who knew very well that she had counted in his life as nobody else of her sex ever counted, the silence of the biography upon so notorious a fact could not fail to encourage doubt of its trustworthiness. The uninformed public was left in complete ignorance even of the fact that Jowett knew Miss Nightingale. It was this ignorance which made it possible for Lytton Strachey to present the fact almost as if it were his own discovery, and to distort the presentation of it in his own peculiar way, in the essay upon Florence Nightingale which is (nevertheless) nearer to the truth than the essays upon his other three *Eminent Victorians*.[3]

Strachey's explosive best-seller (published in May 1918) made an extraordinary impact upon an English public very ready, at that date, to despise the men and women whom it had been brought up to revere. Nothing in it was new, except the ironical style and the 'debunking' zest, exactly suited to the generation which had just experienced the first World War and seen all its Victorian or post-Victorian notions toppled

---

[1] Sir Edward Cook, *The Life of Florence Nightingale*, ii, 96, 162–3.
[2] Below, 332 *foll.*
[3] The others were Cardinal Manning, Dr. Arnold and General Gordon.

9. Florence Nightingale
A photograph, taken for Queen Victoria, after her return from the Crimea in 1856
(*Picture Post Library*)

into Flanders mud. The overthrow of idols, by a writer who seemed to know all their hinder parts, gratified an instinct for revenge upon the past. Strachey laid his great abilities out to gratify that instinct, and to gratify at the same time his own itch for a sense of superiority over the past which, nevertheless, had produced him and his reading public. It is impossible, now, to write seriously about the Victorians without coming up against Strachey at every turn; and, at every turn, what one encounters is a clever distortion of historical truth so as to turn tradition inside out and make of it an entanglement from which the intelligent man must be assisted by any means, fair or foul, to escape.

For his essay about Florence Nightingale Strachey did no serious research. He lists nine books in the 'bibliography' at the end of the essay. One of these is the *Life and Letters of Benjamin Jowett* — a book from which, if he read it, he retained nothing of value. But he does list, as the first of his authorities, Sir Edward Cook's *Life of Florence Nightingale*. From this book he dug what suited his purpose, ignoring or mis-reporting what did not.

Mrs. Woodham-Smith's later study of Florence Nightingale has corrected Strachey's gross errors of drawing; and it contains a far more sympathetic and understanding sketch of Jowett, as a person in Miss Nightingale's life, than Strachey's absurd and incidental caricature. It adds, also, new material of great value to the detailed account of that life given by Sir Edward Cook. Yet Strachey's misrepresentations have an obstinately persisting quality, which even Mrs. Woodham-Smith's brilliant power of evocation has not entirely defeated. Moreover Jowett is, necessarily, no more than a character in her extraordinary heroine's life. He is not, as he is in this book, the central figure.

The story of the strange friendship between Jowett and Miss Nightingale was not made public until Sir Edward Cook's two volumes appeared in 1914. The year of publication was unfortunate; the book just 'missed the bus'. It was possible, therefore, for Strachey, only four years later, to build his essay upon Cook and to present as his own discovery the picture of Miss Nightingale as a ruthless, tyrannical exploitress of male (and female) worshippers. The picture was not untrue. But it was shamelessly plagiarized, and shamelessly distorted in the act of plagiarization.

The origin and the development of the intimacy between Jowett and Miss Nightingale were first told by Cook, with all the detail one needs to know. He had access to, and made use of, the whole series of Jowett's letters to Miss Nightingale. This correspondence will, I hope, soon be fully published. Meanwhile there is enough, published or published about it, to go upon.

Strachey, in his essay, drew a supercilious and misleading picture of the relationship between the two correspondents; rounding off his account of it with the one irritable phrase which Florence ever used about Jowett (she was not sparing in her use of such phrases about other people) during a momentary coolness, as if that was what it had all amounted to in the end. 'He comes and talks to me' she said 'as if I were some one else.' Not, be it noted, 'as if I were a public meeting' — Queen Victoria's celebrated complaint about Mr. Gladstone; but somehow, such is Strachey's malicious art, it seems to be the same kind of complaint and to have the same sort of deadly truth. In fact it was a very different kind of complaint; and the truth it contained was truth about herself, rather than truth about Jowett; it was a confession of the wilfulness which he alone had the courage to rebuke and the power to subdue.

Strachey's caricature has stayed in the minds of those who remember the two clever paragraphs, which were all that he gave to the relationship between Miss Nightingale and Mr. Jowett — whom he described as 'her spiritual adviser' and as 'the Master of Balliol', though he was not Master of Balliol during the first eight (and more important) years of their friendship or, in any professional sense, her 'spiritual adviser'.

He discussed with her in a series of enormous letters the problems of religion and philosophy; he criticized her writings on those subjects with the sympathy of a cleric who was also a man of the world; and he even ventured to attempt at times to instil into her rebellious nature some of his own peculiar suavity. . . . Their relations became intimate. 'The spirit of the twenty-third psalm and the spirit of the nineteenth psalm should be united in our lives' Mr. Jowett said. Eventually, she asked him to do her a singular favour. Would he, knowing what he did of her religious views, come to London and administer to her the Holy Sacrament? He did not hesitate, and afterwards declared that he would always regard the occasion as a solemn event in his life. He was devoted to her; though the precise nature of his feelings towards her never transpired.

And then:

as time went on . . . the acrimony of her nature asserted itself . . . she was exhausted, she was annoyed, by his conversation. Her tongue, one day, could not refrain from shooting out at him.

We are left with the impression that suavity was finally dissolved in gall. The impression was deliberately contrived, and is entirely untrue. It was created by the simplest of the techniques of misrepresentation, by treating an incident as a principal event, so that a momentary, irritable utterance is made to mean the disintegration and to exclude the renewal of love.

A more complex and offensive twist is given to the truth by Strachey's rendering of Jowett's visit to administer the Holy Sacrament to Miss

Nightingale. The whole passage is false in tone; the subtle inflections of the abbreviated story convey a carefully wrong and derisory picture of the request and of the response, of the circumstances in which the request was made, and of what the request and the response meant, severally, to the two persons concerned. It is even introduced by a mis-statement. 'Eventually'? What could Strachey have intended his readers to understand from this word, except that there had been a considerable length of time, during which the friendship between Florence Nightingale and her spiritual adviser 'the Master of Balliol' had gradually developed to a point when she was moved to ask, and he to confer, a priestly service which Strachey invites his readers to treat as ridiculous.

In fact, this visit (in October 1862) was the first he made; the occasion of their first meeting. They had corresponded for some two years; but this was the point after which their correspondence became the correspondence of friends who have met face to face. Jowett did what he was asked to do, and what it was his professional duty to do. 'I shall be very glad' he wrote simply 'to give you the Sacrament. I am sure that many other clergymen would be equally glad.'

Jowett did not play a large part — less than two pages — in Strachey's essay; and the effect of the essay was to reduce his stature in the minds of those who read it. He was long dead and gone. A legend subsisted, but nobody cared whether it was true or false. Then, in 1950, Mrs. Woodham-Smith suddenly captured the whole reading world with her biography of *Florence Nightingale* — a book which, like Sir Edward Cook's, gave Jowett something like his due place in the life of a very extraordinary woman.

If Jowett has thus been again taken fairly into Miss Nightingale's career, her place in his life has never been explained. Yet Jowett was also a remarkable person; his true magnitude was not less than hers. The momentary clash between them, which Strachey used for his own unscrupulous purpose, really illustrates the equal power of the two personalities. Jowett not only kept his own magnitude but held Miss Nightingale up against the feminine weakness which she was too apt to assume as a cover for lapses in her masculine will.

Mrs. Woodham-Smith's description of this unique friendship is accompanied by a quick and sensitive *vignette* of Jowett. If there is anything to criticize in this *vignette*, it is that Jowett is inevitably depicted as a man in Florence Nightingale's life — as one of her many admirers, even if the only one whom she acknowledged to be her equal. Of Florence as a woman — as *the* woman — in Jowett's life it is difficult for anybody to write. Jowett always kept his own counsel. Strachey's remark, that the precise nature of Jowett's feelings towards Miss Nightingale never transpired, though he used the *cliché* deliberately with his tongue in his cheek, happens to be true.

Mrs. Woodham-Smith says that 'affection became devotion, and it was known to their friends that Jowett was pressing her to marry him. She refused, but their friendship was unaltered'.[1] There is no doubt of the devotion. But we are free to doubt the alleged proposal of marriage. There is no written evidence of it; the story rests only upon a persistent belief in Miss Nightingale's family. Everything is possible in this peculiar world. It might be rash to affirm, with absolute assurance, that Jowett never suggested marriage to Miss Nightingale. But it seems far more probable that Miss Nightingale's relatives put their own construction upon an intimacy outside their understanding and that Campbell was right in his imagination of it as a 'Platonic' friendship. It reached down into the heart of reason, for him and for her. But marriage? Intimacy of bodies? Even a conventional appearance of intimacy, in the management of a house?

It is much more difficult to suppose that Jowett ever thought of proposing marriage to this extraordinary woman than to suppose that she ever wanted him to do so. Miss Nightingale was far from being indifferent to her gift of fascination over both men and women; she liked the sense of that power too much, to the extent of exaggerating it in her own mind. She even enjoyed saying no; it is not at all inconceivable that she may have hoped to say no even to her 'darling Jowett'; not even inconceivable that she supposed herself to have done so. But it is surely inconceivable that Jowett can have seriously wished to marry her. If one begins to imagine the practical difficulties of such a marriage, they are enough — in themselves — to make the imagination highly ridiculous. Jowett, shrewdly aware of the world in which he had to live, could never have thought of introducing into it a tamed version of Florence Nightingale, raised from her bed to follow and assist him in his career. The bare notion is absurd, and would have seemed at least as much so to him as to anybody else.

Let us take it, simply, that Jowett found in Florence Nightingale a mind not unlike his own — the only mind of that order he had ever encountered. From the first full moment of encounter she became the one woman in his life, and she remained so to his last breath. He never desired her as a woman, nor did she ever desire him as a man. But, when he had met and known her, every other fancy left his mind — except his equal, but unexacting, devotion to Robert Morier.

[1] *Florence Nightingale*, 352.

Very many years after this extraordinary disturbance of his emotional life, the Master of Balliol became an elderly victim of a very attractive and pertinacious young woman, given to asking unexpected questions and nailing down answers and fixing eminent people in odd positions. Margot Tennant set herself to fascinate Jowett. (A number of his letters to her, very charming letters, are to be found in the *Life and Letters*.) She asked him if he had ever been in love. 'Yes, my dear,' he answered 'I was once very much in love.' After a moment or two, Margot asked him what the lady was like. 'Very violent, my dear, very violent.'[1]

Was Jowett, perhaps, enjoying the old man's privilege of pulling a young woman's leg? Or had he really been 'in love' with Florence Nightingale? Who can say? And who can say what love is or means?

The one thing clear is that in 1862 Florence Nightingale drove Margaret Elliot out of Jowett's mind. It was an unequal contest. Miss Nightingale, one supposes, was sublimely unaware that there was a contest at all. Miss Elliot must have come to know that she had been eclipsed by a woman whom she already disliked on Mary Stanley's account; but she kept to herself whatever bitterness she felt. If Jowett experienced any twinges of conscience he kept them also to himself.

His intimacy with Florence Nightingale was bought at a very high price. It even affected his behaviour towards his young men; and it compelled him to abandon all idea of a normal marriage. At the time, he paid the price willingly. Later on he understood how high it had been. 'The great want of life' he confided to a note-book of 1880 'can never be supplied, and I must do without it.' He was then sixty-three. Towards the end of his life he wrote again, in one of his last note-books: 'There is one happiness which I have never had.'[2]

---

[1] I owe my first knowledge of this story to Mrs. Woodham-Smith. It is told, also, by Lady Oxford herself in her Memoirs.

[2] *L. & L.*, i, 309. Campbell says, there, that the 'reasons for this are expressed in his letter to Dean Stanley of 10th March 1865': the letter reproduced above, 296. It is, of course, my argument that this letter refrained from giving the true reason.

CHAPTER XIV

Tides at the Ebb

1. COLENSO

The fog of unreason, in which the Church of England wrapped herself against the infidel Essayists and Reviewers, was slow to dissipate. It stayed thickest in country parishes; but visibility long continued to be poor round many a low-lying deanery and episcopal palace. Lay travellers were liable to lose their sense of direction when they left the familiar highways. Even Matthew Arnold, the apostle of sweetness and light, who 'threw over the whole cargo of orthodox doctrine with a cheerful completeness which staggered the compromisers',[1] was found amongst the Philistines. Writing to his mother from the Athenaeum in February 1870, he told her:

> I met Temple here a day or two ago, looking very well in his new dress. I told him I approved of his withdrawal of his Essay, which the Liberals, who turn religion into mere politics, are so angry with him for; he seemed pleased. I told him also that I thought the *Essays and Reviews* could not be described throughout as 'a free handling, in *a becoming spirit*, of religious matters', and he said he quite agreed with me. . . . He is a fine character.[2]

Yet the fog was thinning wherever men were free to use their minds and willing to use their freedom. In spite of the alliance between Wilberforce and Pusey it was perceptibly clearing in Oxford. In Balliol the clearance was almost rapid. By 1866 more than half the fellows were of Jowett's party.

Mere passage of time does nothing to a fog. Something must happen, some change of weather, some movement of the air. There was certainly no lack of movement in the air of the eighteen-sixties. Perhaps no other decade of the nineteenth century so well exhibits the kaleidoscopic character of that secular *renaissance* which we inadequately label as the Victorian Age. It was impossible that this general stir of mind, this gathering impatience with anachronisms which pretended to be above all criticism, should not affect a 'national' Church.

[1] Oliver Elton, *A Survey of English Literature 1830–1880*, i, 275.
[2] *Letters of Matthew Arnold*, edited by G. W. E. Russell, ii, 32.

314

The necessity, for the Church of England, of discovering common ground with the new and critically minded succession of young men, was a governing idea in Jowett's mind. It was also the point of Wilson's remarkable contribution to *Essays and Reviews* and the cause of the especial hatred with which that contribution was received. It is not fair or reasonable to blame 'priesthoods' for their slowness in responding to secular pressure. It is almost the first function of priesthoods to resist secular pressure. They exist in order to safeguard the community against superstition on the one hand, unbelief on the other; at least, that is why they can command general support even in sophisticated societies. But a danger point is reached when the difference between belief and the criticism of belief yawns so wide that it becomes impossible for the priesthood to retain more than the bored attention of educated congregations. At that point the danger exists, that such congregations will eventually melt away.

This point had been reached by the Church of England long before *Essays and Reviews* was published. The purpose of that publication was to bring an existing, but concealed, trouble into the open. It achieved its purpose, and thereby did an incalculable service both to the Church and to English society. If *Essays and Reviews*, or some similarly execrated book, had not been published, the Church of England might soon have altogether lost the last chance of justifying her proud title.

Beside the secular surge — critical and scientific and social — which was so marked a feature of the Victorian Age, there were waves of great violence inside the Church itself. The first of these major waves was the Oxford Movement. That was a purely internal movement; in so far as it was caused by external and secular events, it was a protest against them — against the Whig threat to the Church in Ireland, against the so-called 'march of mind'. The whole aim of its leaders was to glorify the Church and to assert its independence of secular pressures. It divided the Church into two violently antagonistic parties, each concerned to promote its own interpretation of doctrine, and each equally indifferent or hostile to the growth of ideas which could not be reconciled with either evangelical or tractarian fundamentalism.

This result of the Oxford Movement — quite apart from the stimulus and nourishment it gave to the Roman Catholics — seemed to be very dangerous. Between the upper and the nether millstones of 'high' and 'low' dogmatism, it looked as if every grain of living thought must be ground to dead powder. But, first, the very opposition between the two parties and, then, their unnatural alliance against 'infidelity' encouraged the development of a third party, which was nick-named Broad Church, on the analogy of Low and High.[1] As the Oxford Dictionary says, the name 'is not used in the same manner' (i.e. the analogy is unreal). The broad churchmen never constituted an organized party. It is 'a designation popularly applied to members of the Church of England who take its formularies and doctrines in a broad or liberal sense and hold that the Church should be comprehensive and tolerant'.

When the title was coined in the middle of the century, the number of the broad churchmen was small and few of them occupied positions of influence. They were hardly more than a smattering of individuals who reflected in their own various ways the spirit of the new age. Just because they did not constitute an organized party with an agreed policy, and were united only by hatred of terrorism and by the conviction that the Church could not afford to silence truth, they became the medium through which she gradually regained contact with the modern world. This was anything but a spontaneous or comfortable process; and it needed the repeated stimulus of shock.

The first great shock was the publication of *Essays and Reviews*. The book was meant to shake orthodox complacency; but nobody foresaw how violently hostile the clerical reaction would be. It seemed, for a long time, that it had defeated its own purpose; that it had put back the hands of the clock. It is possible, now, to see that this was not so. The opinions which the book expressed had a cumulative effect, especially upon the minds of younger men, until at length they became such commonplace stuff, that the excitement they had once caused became no more than an embarrassing memory, easily forgotten.

A second shock followed very quickly upon the first. This was the extraordinary affair of Bishop Colenso. Though this was an episode in which Jowett made no direct personal appearance, it is as much a part of his history as *Essays and Reviews*. Like the story of that book, it is now so inaccurately remembered that it asks to be retold.

Like the first shock it revealed the growth inside the Church of opinions which the great majority of churchmen regarded as utterly heretical. This time, however, they were the opinions of a single man, not of a group, and that man a consecrated Bishop. Again like the first shock, it showed a dangerous division between Church and State. But this time the division was of a far more serious kind. On the first occasion the Church merely failed to uphold the conviction of Wilson and Williams before the court of final appeal; and it then pronounced a 'synodical'

---

[1] 'According to the Master of Balliol (Prof. Jowett) the term was first proposed in conversation, in his hearing, by the late A. H. Clough.' *O.E.D.*, which cites Stanley's use of it in 1850, in an article on the Gorham controversy.

judgment, of no lasting or even immediate doctrinal validity, against the whole book in which their essays had appeared. On the second occasion it endorsed and, as far as it could do so, supported an outrageously illegal action of the Bishop in charge of the ecclesiastical province of South Africa — Bishop Gray of Capetown. There was a head-on collision between Church and State. This, in itself, was enough to disturb all but the extremer, or more ignorant, churchmen.

What made matters still worse was the fact that Bishop Gray's action was not only illegal but presumptuous. He took it on himself to exercise powers which he knew that he did not legally possess — powers which even the Archbishops of Canterbury had long forgotten to use, if they were ever theirs to use. By so doing he forced the English episcopate into a position where it must either support or repudiate him. Since the great majority of the English clergy (except for such broad churchmen as were, at that time, ordained clergymen) agreed with Bishop Gray that Bishop Colenso was a heretic, it was difficult for English ecclesiastical authority to rebuke and disown Gray. Yet discipline required this rebuke. If a stronger man than Longley had then occupied the seat of Augustine, he would not have allowed the Church of England to tie herself to Bishop Gray's flaming chariot wheels. For Archbishop Longley well knew that the Bishop of Capetown was in the wrong. It was said that he lay awake, night after night, dreading to find another tempestuous letter from Gray on his breakfast table next morning.

John Colenso[1] was a Cornishman, the son of a mineral agent employed by the Duchy of Cornwall. His father tried to improve his circumstances by engaging in 'some mining operations' on his own account. He failed, and his son grew up in grinding poverty. The boy was one of those gifted and determined creatures who struggle out of every adversity, and for whom fate is always preparing a new blow. At seventeen he was an usher in a private school at Dartmouth, working a fifteen-hour day. It was his longing to enter the ministry of the Church of England. Some relatives lent him some money, which he afterwards repaid in full. He became a sizar of St. John's College, Cambridge, where his life was 'hard to severity'. In 1836 he was second wrangler and Smith's prizeman, and was elected to a fellowship of his college. In 1839 Longley (who was to be Archbishop of Canterbury, when the Colenso storm burst more than twenty years later) appointed him to a mathematical mastership at Harrow. Longley was succeeded by Wordsworth

---

[1] The biographical details which follow are taken from the article in the *D.N.B.* by Sir G. W. Cox, who also wrote the *Life* of Colenso. Cox was Colenso's devoted disciple and champion; but there is no challenge of his accuracy in matters of fact.

as headmaster. The school went into a temporary decline. Colenso's boarding house was destroyed by fire. Heavily in debt, he went back to St. John's as a tutor. During this time he wrote two books, on algebra and arithmetic, which 'raised his reputation to the highest pitch'. In 1846 he married and was presented to a St. John's living in Norfolk, Forncett St. Mary. There he lived and worked happily for seven years, taking in pupils. And then, in 1853, he was appointed to be Bishop of Natal — a newly created colonial diocese, carved out of the original See of Capetown. He was still a young man — just short of forty.

Hitherto Colenso had not seriously departed from the narrow way of evangelical orthodoxy. A volume of sermons, dedicated to his friend F. D. Maurice, which was published about the time of his consecration, had, however, come under fire from the *Record*. According to his biographer, it 'showed at the least that he could not rest contented with some notions generally associated with the theological school in which he had been trained'. The breeze subsided. The new Bishop was a man with a question-mark against his name in the *Record's* scandal file; but that did not mean much. Neither the *Record* nor Colenso himself could foresee what would happen to him in Natal — a mathematically minded youngish man, with a passion for truth, no pastoral experience except for seven years in a rural Norfolk vicarage, and a good prospect of future high preferment.

What happened, and was the cause of all that happened later, was that he discovered in himself a natural sympathy with the Zulu mind. He learned the Zulu speech and taught young Zulus to help him in producing

a grammar of the Zulu language (1859), a Zulu-English dictionary (1861), selections and reading-books in Zulu, manuals of instruction for the natives in the English language in geography, history, astronomy and other subjects, with translations of Genesis, Exodus, Samuel, and of the whole of the New Testament (1876). In the printing of these books a great part of the work was done by a Zulu lad whom he took as a young savage from his kraal, with some others who were given to him by their fathers for education during a period of five years only. To these poor lads the bishop was emphatically Sobantu, the 'father of the people'; but as he was their teacher and guide, so in turn he was stimulated by their questions to the most momentous inquiries.[1]

During the earlier years Bishop Colenso and his 'metropolitan' Bishop Gray were intimate friends. Colenso had been Gray's own choice for the new See of Natal. At first it seemed to the Bishop of Capetown that he had backed a winner. But after a time he began to have uncomfortable doubts. Colenso's theological opinions were taking a very unorthodox turn. In October 1861 he published a *Commentary on the Epistle to the*

[1] Sir George Cox in the *D.N.B.*

Romans, which confirmed Gray's worst fears. From that moment friendship ceased, and Colenso became, in Gray's passionately literal and tenacious mind, the arch enemy of true religion.

Others of Colenso's friends were distressed. In the words of his own biographer, the book

struck at the roots of what is commonly called the sacramental system. The Epistle to the Romans, in his opinion, dealt the death-blow to all notions of covenant and privilege. It asserted that the benefits received from and through Christ were received for all the world, and that the divine work was a work for the extinction of sin, not merely for its punishment. He allowed that on this point his eyes had been opened to see that all theories of partial satisfaction implied, not the conquest of evil, but a compromise with it; and having been brought to this conviction, he expressed it with absolute fearlessness. He was now translating the book of Genesis, for human beings [Zulus] with the docility of a child, but with the reasoning powers of mature age, and he was met at every step by the point-blank question 'Is all that true?' 'My heart', he says, 'answered, in the words of the Prophet, Shall a man speak lies in the name of the Lord? I dared not do so.' Those questions had set him free. Critics in England found satisfaction in relating how 'the newly appointed bishop went to convert and was converted himself'. The bishop went on with his scrutiny of the Pentateuch.[1]

For the moment nothing in particular happened. There was 'a loud outcry', drowned in England by the excitement over *Essays and Reviews*. But Tait, 'in common with others in responsible positions, was gravely anxious'. He wrote to Colenso's brother-in-law, Bishop M'Dougall of Labuan, and received a most disturbing reply. Colenso had already sent M'Dougall the first part of his new book. M'Dougall wrote:

It is an attack upon the Pentateuch, denying its inspiration, or that it was written by Moses. . . . His mathematical notions and Western [*sic*] mode of viewing things have plainly led him astray. He says, in short, that he can believe a miracle, but cannot believe in a bad sum and false arithmetical statements; and so he falls foul of the Book of Numbers especially . . . poor dear Colenso . . . I love him much as a brother and a friend. I know him to be a noble, brave-hearted, loving man, but I can in no way agree with him in theology. . . . Poor J. W. N. [J. W. Natal], he is much in my thoughts. I hope his coming to England may dispel the fogs Natal seems to have generated in his mind. If he had been here in my place, instead of in Natal, he would not have had the time for encouraging these doubts and mists, and perhaps intercourse with Eastern people would have been a good corrective.[2]

The first three volumes of *The Pentateuch Examined* appeared late in 1862 and in the following year.[3] And now the fat was really in the fire. Gray, exasperated by the inactivity or the helplessness of the English

[1] Sir George Cox, *D.N.B.*
[2] *Life of Archbishop Tait*, i, 334–5.
[3] Nothing stopped Colenso. The seventh, and last, volume was published in 1879.

319

ecclesiastical authorities, resolved to take action himself against Colenso. Exercising the authority he wrongly supposed himself to possess (though, as will be seen, he must have known that the Privy Council had already declared otherwise) as the metropolitan Bishop over the South African province, to whom Colenso had taken an oath of 'due obedience', he procured a prosecution of Colenso for heresy before himself in Capetown.

The 'trial' was held in November 1863. Colenso refused to appear; he protested, by deputy, that the Bishop of Capetown had no such jurisdiction over him. Gray rejected the protest, and on 16th December 'deposed' Colenso from his Bishopric, unless he should, within four months, fully retract his opinions. Colenso appealed to the Queen in Council. In March 1865 his appeal was upheld. But upon his return to Durban in November, Bishop Gray

pronounced a solemn sentence of 'the greater excommunication', and required it to be publicly read and 'promulged' in the Cathedral of the Diocese of Natal. This document declared John William Colenso 'separated from the communion of the Church of Christ' and 'to be taken of the whole multitude of the faithful as a heathen and a publican'.

Well might Keble, wholly sympathetic to Bishop Gray, speak admiringly of his language as 'like a fragment of the fourth century recovered for the use of the nineteenth'.[1]

The Bishop of Capetown did not possess the authority he claimed. When the original See of Capetown was divided into three (Capetown, Grahamstown and Natal) he was re-appointed Bishop of Capetown in 1853 under new Letters Patent which purported to give him 'metropolitan' jurisdiction over the two new Sees. But, when the Cape Parliament was set up in 1850, 'the Crown ceased to have the power of conferring by Letters Patent any such coercive jurisdiction, ecclesiastical or civil, within the Colony.'[2] This was the purely legal ground which the Privy Council took in annulling Gray's attempt to depose Colenso; and which it had already taken in annulling an earlier attempt by Gray to punish a junior clergyman in his own diocese, a Mr. Long who refused to attend two of his Bishop's 'synods', by depriving him of his cure of souls.

But, suppose that Gray's Letters Patent had been fully valid. Would they, then, have conferred upon him the right of deposing Colenso, and

[1] Keble was actually referring to the Bishop of Capetown's 'fiery' charge, delivered in Colenso's own Cathedral in May, 1864; not to the later sentence of excommunication. This was the charge in which Gray told his hearers that 'your late Bishop, led captive of the Evil One, has parted with the Truth of God'.
[2] *Life of Archbishop Tait*, i, 333.

the right of excommunicating him? Ecclesiastical law is a great mystery; when it becomes entangled with the complexities of English law, the mystery deepens to the point when almost any interpretation begins to seem imaginable. But it is surely impossible to think that the Crown ever intended to put a colonial Bishop into the position of an absolute spiritual ruler. Tait did not think so. He wrote to Archbishop Longley:

I will never believe that it was the intention of the letters patent, or whatever it is that clothes the Bishop of Capetown with authority, to make him so irresponsible that there should be no earthly appeal from his decision.[1]

This letter was written in May 1863, before the pretentious make-believe of Colenso's 'trial' in Capetown at the end of that year, and a month before the Privy Council's decision upon Mr. Long's appeal. That decision settled the legal issue raised, later, by Colenso's appeal; for it established the fact that the Letters Patent were invalid, in so far as they purported to give Gray any 'coercive jurisdiction'. This fact was, of course, known to everybody before Gray 'tried' and 'deposed' Colenso.

In 1866 the whole scandal was at its highest point, with Colenso resolutely using his own Cathedral and performing his duties as Bishop, and Gray behaving as if Colenso did not exist and responsibility for the diocese of Natal had fallen back on him. The powerful Societies for the Propagation of the Gospel and the Promotion of Christian Knowledge were doing their best to reduce Colenso to submission by transferring their missionary grants to the Bishop of Capetown, and by threatening Colenso's loyal clergy with penury, if they did not renounce their allegiance to him. The Colonial Bishoprics Fund also tried to starve Colenso out. Gladstone, one of the trustees, wrote to Miss Burdett Coutts:

We, founding ourselves on the judgment, say there is no See of Natal in the sense of the founders of the fund, and therefore, of course, no bishop of such a See.[2]

But this piece of casuistry did not commend itself to the Master of the Rolls, Lord Romilly. The trustees of the fund were compelled to give Colenso his due.

At this point it occurred to Tait that it might be helpful to find out what colonial churchmen really thought — for speaker after speaker, in Parliament and elsewhere, had simply assumed that the whole of the colonial Church sided with Bishop Gray. He addressed a questionnaire to 'all the Colonial Bishops, Deans, and Archdeacons of the Anglican Communion'. This questionnaire excited Bishop Gray to great anger. But it was 'only from South Africa that the Bishop [Tait] received other

[1] *ibid.*, i, 349.   [2] Morley's *Life of Gladstone*, ii, 168.

than friendly replies' and it was from Bishop Gray's own diocese that there came the strongest, and the most intelligent, criticism of his behaviour. This letter said:

We are fully persuaded that it is most desirable, as a means of keeping up the unity of the Church, that all her Bishops in the Colonies, without exception, should receive mission from, and take the oath of Canonical obedience to, the See of Canterbury. If the claim put forward by the Bishop of Capetown, to have his decisions as Metropolitan regarded as final, be allowed, — if, in other words, as he affirms, there is no appeal to any court on earth from a judgment which he may pronounce as Metropolitan, it is evident that the Suffragan Bishops of the Province are in far worse position than the humblest Priest in pre-Reformation times: he at least had an appeal to the Roman Pontiff, whilst they are subject without appeal to the sentence, however arbitrary, of the Metropolitan.[1]

Colenso stayed in his see until his death in 1883, preaching to crowded congregations. 'The dean held other services at a different hour.' And in 1869 Gray took the extraordinary step of consecrating at Capetown a rival 'Bishop of Maritzburg' without the Queen's mandate. This was made financially possible by the S.P.G. and the S.P.C.K.[2] In his last years Colenso raised fresh trouble for himself by his courageous defence of a Zulu chief who had been sentenced to transportation for life. He went to England 'and returned with something like redress for the prisoner'. This cost him the sympathy of the European colonists and put him in conflict with the Governor of the Cape, Sir Bartle Frere. But the battle with Gray had ended when the Bishop of Capetown died in 1872.

The Church of England had been shaken to her very foundations by their quarrel; long-standing friendships had been violently broken; all sorts of people had supposed that an issue of supreme importance was being fought, and either won or lost. What remains of it now? At first sight, nothing more than the dim memory of a scandal, from which all meaning has departed, except in the minds of Colenso's spiritual children, some of whose descendants in South Africa still obstinately maintain their own independent existence, isolated equally from the Church of England at home and the province of the Church in South Africa.

But something more than this resulted. One can best see what it was by asking the question: what was Colenso's peculiar offence? Did his teaching differ, in any notable way, from that of the Essayists and Reviewers? Did it differ essentially from the teaching of Jowett, in his Essay on the Atonement and his Essay on the Interpretation of Scripture? The answer must be that there was no essential difference. Colenso's criticism originated in the naive questions put to him by his Zulu converts, Jowett's in the self-questioning of a sophisticated society. Colenso's

[1] *Life of Tait*, i, 373–4.   [2] *D.N.B.* Articles on Gray and Macrorie.

answers were shaped by the mathematical cast of his mind, Jowett's by the linguistic and metaphysical cast of *his* mind. But the general direction of both men's answers was the same; and is the direction which has long since come to govern modern Protestant scholarship, whatever peculiar mistakes about particular matters these and other pioneer critics may be said to have made.

It was an easy gibe against Colenso that he reduced theology to simple arithmetic. The gibe was easy to counter. If 'inspired' writings use bad arithmetic, then their inspiration is faulty; and if it is faulty in one field, where the fault is measurable and demonstrable, then it cannot be simply taken for granted in any other field.

What Jowett thought of Colenso's *Commentary on the Epistle to the Romans* is not in the record. Of his *Pentateuch* — of the first volume — he wrote to Stanley in 1862:

I think the tone is a good deal mistaken. But don't be hurt or pained by it. You work in one way, he in another. I perhaps in a third way. All good persons should agree in heartily sympathizing with the effort to state the facts of Scripture exactly as they are. Then you really seem like Athanasius against the whole Christian world, past and present.[1]

Was that a half-hearted identification of his own with Colenso's position? It seemed to begin so, but — 'like Athanasius'? Jowett was the cautious Oxonian, who had learned to keep his wick low; Colenso the enthusiastic missionary, who wished to light up darkness. But Jowett knew well that he and Colenso were travellers on the same road. His 'whole sympathy was with Colenso'. After Colenso's death he wrote:

He has made an epoch in criticism by his straightforwardness. No one now talks of verbal inspiration. He was attacked bitterly, but the recollection of the attacks has passed away; the effect of his writings, though they are no longer read, is permanent.[2]

Jowett's opinion is Colenso's true epitaph. Nobody would dream, now, of supposing that he got to the bottom either of the Books of Moses or of the Epistle to the Romans. But he got some way down. Like Jowett, he tried to understand his texts honestly, instead of merely accepting what other people had repeated about them. Like Jowett, he believed in God and in Christ, but not in conventional statements about God and Christ. Like Jowett, he suffered persecution. But the persecution he suffered was far more severe than the brief persecution suffered by Jowett. He lived and died under it. Jowett sailed on into a serene sea lit by a slowly descending and kindly sun. The Master of Balliol was not a Colenso. He knew just too much of persecution to risk more of it; just

---

[1] *L. & L.*, i, 301. [2] *ibid.*, ii, 65.

too little to understand that, if he took that risk, he might cap Colenso and be remembered as more than a great tutor, and a translator of Plato, and a Master of Balliol. If Jowett could have had a touch of Colenso's rashness added to his caution, there would be no need to argue whether he was, or was not, a great man.

2. THEOLOGY OR PLATO?

Soon after the defeat in Convocation, on 8th March 1864, of Pusey's proposed statute, which would have raised Jowett's professional stipend to £400,[1] Lord Westbury introduced a Bill in the House of Lords 'for the better endowment of the Regius Professor of Greek in the University of Oxford'. This was to be done by attaching to the chair the next vacant Canonry or Prebend in the gift of the Lord Chancellor. The proposal went clean against the grain of all sensible opinion. It would have made the appointment of a lay professor impracticable; yet it would have used an ecclesiastical endowment for a lay purpose. Jowett himself thought it unwise.[2] The Bill was rightly defeated in Committee, on 14th May.

There seemed to be an end to all hope that the problem of the professor's salary would ever be solved. Jowett accepted the situation calmly, as he had accepted the false report of the voting carried to him before the defeat of Pusey's proposal was known. 'I see nothing' he wrote to Stanley on 15th March 'to lament in the business of last Tuesday, except the noise and the bustle.' To another friend, in July, he wrote: 'I get on well except as to personal interests; and those, I feel, are really lost in higher ones. I have in the thought of my old pupils . . . a great deal to make me happy.'

He spent the summer vacation this year first at Askrigg in Wensley-dale, and then at Pitlochry, with the usual party of young men. Lewis Campbell also stayed for a while at Askrigg. He and one of the under-graduate members of the reading party have left unusually detailed descriptions of Jowett's behaviour this summer.[3] Using these two different view-points, helped by his correspondence and by the new fragments of knowledge concerning his private life, and remembering his history in the preceding years, one ought to be able to construct something like a three-dimensional picture of Jowett at this 'darkest hour before the dawn'.

[1] See above, 282.
[2] In a letter to Stanley, referred to but not quoted, in L. & L., i, 316.
[3] L. & L., i, 333–7.

His dominant working purpose in this summer of 1864 was Plato. He had been eager, three years earlier, to finish off the *Republic*, 'to get rid of Plato and return to Theology', and he took leave of absence for the summer term in 1861 'with this object in view'. Campbell thought that the object had been defeated only by a difficulty of time; and that 'the projected works on Theology' merely receded, because Plato could not be so quickly dismissed.

It was not quite so simple a matter. Jowett still talked in 1864 of theology as waiting for him round the corner. He wrote to Stanley in July from Askrigg saying that he had 'some thoughts, if there is anything left of me from the Plato, of coming to town for eight or ten Sundays next year' in order to preach some sermons on theological topics, which might be published 'in a small volume'. And Campbell says that 'the reception of his sermons in London, about 1864 [*sic*], led him to think more favourably' of a friend's advice, given a good many years earlier, to make sermons 'the vehicle of his theological views'; and that with this object 'in the summer of 1865 he wrote a whole volume of theological notes'.

Nothing came out of all this. A preacher without a pulpit, he could not easily find in sermons a means of giving 'form and substance to those positive views of religious truth which he regarded as essential and permanent'. Catechetical lectures had replaced sermons in Balliol; even if Jowett were now trusted to deliver these, he did not do so. He had not stood in the University pulpit since 1851.[1] His voice was 'occasionally heard in out-of-the-way parts in London'; and some of these London sermons made a deep impression upon some of their hearers. 'He looks at me as I never knew any preacher do' wrote Frances Cobbe in her *Autobiography*. But Campbell himself says that 'although the sermons generally contained some expression of liberal opinion, their main tenor was hortatory — "idealizing life" '.

Plato was encroaching more and more on his mind, as well as on his time. Already in 1864 his notes on the *Republic* were expanding into a much more ambitious book. Next year the full concept of his *magnum opus* first took shape — the analysis and translation of *all* the Platonic dialogues. In Plato he found what was to be a lifelong escape from exposition of his theological ideas — from the task to which he had once longed to dedicate himself. What was the use of writing for a hostile, ignorant, powerfully prejudiced clerical public? The reception of his two outspoken essays *On Atonement and Satisfaction* and *On the Interpretation of Scripture* had forced him to realize that most of what he thought

[1] This exclusion ended in November 1871. *Ibid.*, ii, 27.

was not only anathema to the great majority of clergymen, but would be repudiated even by such men as Tait or Temple. The bitterness of being rejected by his own college, the prosecutions of Wilson and Williams, the attempt to put him on trial before the Vice-Chancellor, the fate of Colenso, the miserable level of debates in Convocation, the stupidity of the more stupid Bishops, the intellectual cowardice of the abler Bishops — all this, on top of the humiliation and injustice meted out to him as a hard-working professor, had taught him to hold his tongue before a generation which seemed incapable of understanding anything he might think seriously worth saying in the field of theological discourse. There were other and more effective ways of using his abilities.

This change of purpose must have been developing for at least a year or two before 1864. It was clinched, as his position changed from that of an outcast to that of a ruler — even though, for a few years, the ruler stood behind the throne. Campbell has to end his picture of 'theological designs, which grew from year to year' by the significant admission that 'to have given the world a new speculative shock before his practical efforts had taken a firm hold, might have checked the rising prosperity of Balliol'.[1]

It is true that Jowett went on privately proposing to himself plan after ambitious theological plan. At one time it had been, together with Stanley, a Commentary upon the whole of the New Testament. 'On this' — as Campbell says, though he reduces it to a Commentary on the Gospels — 'there gradually supervened the vision, which never left him, of a Life of Christ, and also the conception, which sometimes competed with this, of a short treatise upon moral ideas.' But nothing of all this was ever done, or even attempted, after *Essays and Reviews*. It was a kind of day-dreaming hopefully recorded, now and again, in the casual notebooks of a man, who knew that his energies were fully committed and that there was no room or power for more. By degrees, he found in Plato the other half of his life-work.

Listen, now, to Campbell describing how Jowett spent the summer vacation of 1864. He had been 'revising his notes to the *Republic*'. As he did so, it

occurred to him that a complete analysis of the *Dialogues* would form a suitable 'Prolegomena' to his book. The analysis, as he conceived it, was to be a sort of condensed translation, in which nothing essential should be omitted, and even the force of connecting particles should be preserved. All was to be in perfect English, and the labour spent on such a work was naturally great. When I was with him at Askrigg, in the summer of 1864, he was struggling with the analysis of the *Parmenides* and the other

[1] *ibid.*, i, 382–3.

dialectical dialogues. His taste in language was becoming more and more fastidious. At this time he was resolved to turn every sentence so as to exclude the colourless pronoun '*it*'. I troubled him with the remark that 'which' was not much better, and one or the other was inevitable. After this he became more tolerant of 'it', but still objected to it, except in the impersonal verb. Finding the commentary sometimes tedious, he used to say, 'I am longing to get at the more general treatment of the subject.'

An interesting glimpse of the meticulous craftsman at work. Such a labour over so apparently small a matter! But the Greeks, like the Romans, had no word for 'it'; and Jowett was irritated by the necessity of loading his analyses with the lifeless pronouns which uninflected languages like English are obliged to use.

Campbell's account of Jowett's aim as a translator alludes also to the different, the reverse, difficulty of rendering the Greek 'particles'. Classical Greek abounds with particles, tiny little words of two or three letters which add *nuances* of meaning to phrases and sentences — *nuances* often so subtle and various that grammarians can spend their lives in trying to classify them. Plato's dialogues, written in conversational form, abound with these gleaming imps of Greek speech. The heavy-footed English translator can find no corresponding terms in his own language. He is forced to tackle his problem by so casting his English sentences as to convey to a contemporary English reader the Greek meaning as the translator understands it. This necessitates paraphrase, rather than direct translation.

The weakness of the paraphrase is not only that it inevitably loses the simplicity and elasticity and verve of the original Greek, but that it tends to introduce ideas or suggestions of ideas, which are familiar to the English reader but were unknown to the Greek writer. There is no possible escape from this weakness, unless the reader of the translation has enough Greek to be able to compare the translation with the original. It must be remembered that almost all Jowett's contemporaries and most of his juniors had enough Greek to be able to do that. Nevertheless, he took enormous pains to make a translation which might be understood by readers utterly ignorant of Greek. The value of such a translation must not only vary with the verbal skill of the translator and his power to render Greek ideas in the language of his own time; it must also change, as times change, as the character of the translator's own language changes, and as the world, once receptive of his translation, comes to find it out-of-date. This applies both to 'analysis' and 'translation'.

Jowett followed the paraphrastic method. His translations of the Platonic Dialogues have begun, now, to seem a little stiff and old-fashioned; to reflect, rather too obviously, Victorian modes of thought.

But there is no likelihood of their being generally superseded for a very long time to come. The contemporary element in them is easily detected and (if the reader is alert) easily discounted. It may be said, even, that it adds to their attractiveness. We know where we are, when we read them. But not the least of the reasons, why Jowett's translations of Plato into English will continue to provide most English readers, whether they have some or no Greek, with the best means of approaching and understanding Plato, lies in the all but infinite labour of the translator, both at the microscopic and at the macroscopic ends of the scale.

The product of a day's work at Askrigg was said by Campbell to have been 'four pages of fresh writing and rather more of revision'. The day was at least an eight-hour, probably a nine-hour day, for six days in the week. From about ten in the morning to about four in the afternoon, without any break; then from nine in the evening to midnight. There was letter-writing 'at odd times, mostly, I suspect, after the day's task was done'. Sunday was also a day of work, though the hours were reduced. This was the work pattern of Jowett's holiday time. As one of his pupils said, he worked harder and longer with his mind than most workmen with their hands.

In working with him [Campbell recalled] one was astonished at the number of ways which occurred to him for turning a particular phrase. If, holding firmly by the Greek, I objected to an expression, another was produced, and then another and another, until Greek and English appeared to coincide. But perhaps the one last hit upon would be afterwards discarded, as not harmonizing with the rhythm or colour of the whole. This protracted labour was almost finished, when a casual remark of Pattison's (I think) convinced him that the analysis could never be complete, and that the *Republic*, at all events, must be translated in full. As he proceeded with this in 1865, he formed the resolution of translating the whole of Plato.

3. ALOOFNESS AT ASKRIGG

The make-up of the party at Askrigg is worth looking at. It included R. A. H. Mitchell, captain of the Oxford cricket eleven for three successive years — described by Canon Sanday as 'the greatest Oxford cricketer of the century' and as a man 'of commanding build and stature, as well as commanding in every other way'.[1] He had taken a second class in Mods, and was now reading for Greats, in which he also took a second. He became a master at Eton. R. A. Duncan, soon to succeed his father as Earl of Camperdown, was also one of the party, though he had recently

---

[1] *Memoirs of Sir William Anson*, edited by Hensley Henson, 45.

taken his degree after first classes in both Mods and Greats. Another young man at Askrigg was the Earl of Kerry, who had just finished his first year and was to take second classes in Mods and Greats. He succeeded his father as Marquess of Lansdowne, before he took his degree. Duncan, Mitchell and Kerry were all Etonians and congenial spirits. Apart from Jowett and Campbell, the party was completed by John Purves, one of Balliol's brilliant importations from Glasgow. Purves was the oldest of the young men — a year older than Duncan — but he was still an undergraduate. He was a winner of first classes and University scholarships and became a fellow of Balliol. At Askrigg he was thought by the Etonian contingent to be 'helping the Master with his work'.[1]

It was the sort of party Jowett collected together year after year: a 'commanding' young cricketer, whom he obliged to work hard for an honours degree; a Scottish nobleman, who repaid his tuition by a first class degree and a life of quiet public service; an Irish nobleman, also persuaded to work for an honours degree, who subsequently filled a long succession of the highest and most onerous offices of State: and a clever hard-working Scot, educated in Glasgow.

Mitchell's recollections of the Askrigg party confirm the pattern of Jowett's day; but they introduce a quite unexpected impression of remoteness — an impression strengthened, though not caused, by his inability to remember his tutor except as 'the Master', though the Mastership was still six years away. After recalling that 'we had only two regular meals in the day' and 'I don't think the Master ever supplemented these meals, though we did, as you will not be slow to understand', and that 'the Master never thought anything about his food, and was content with the simplest diet', Mitchell continues:

At that time his whole thought seemed to be engrossed in his Plato, and he was not so ready to talk as he was in his later years. He worked entirely in his own room. I have never seen him at work, but he used to begin immediately after breakfast and work on till dinner at four o'clock. He then went for a walk, and on coming in retired again and worked, I believe, till about twelve o'clock.

Breakfast was rather a tiresome affair; because Jowett 'was not an early riser, seldom appearing before ten, but he would not allow breakfast to be ordered later than nine'. The whole party moved off, subsequently, to Pitlochry, where Jowett

proposed that any one who was five minutes late for breakfast should be fined the sum of one shilling. The first morning he appeared quite punctually, the second he was a little late, the next he said that, as he was late,

---

[1] Purves died in 1889 before he was fifty. He published *Selections from Plato* in 1883; his translation of the *Iliad* was published after his death.

he thought he would take his shilling's worth. After that, he found that ten o'clock suited him better than nine. However, at the end of the time he insisted on paying a shilling a day to the common expenses.

This is small change, but so much in Jowett's characteristic currency that it is worth keeping. In the next paragraph Mitchell resumes his serious description of Jowett's behaviour to the young men.

His example of hard work and simplicity was of great value to us, and made hard work all the easier at a time when it was very essential for me to be kept to my books. He did not profess or attempt to coach us regularly, but he was anxious that we should ask him questions, and he took great trouble in explaining difficulties and making his answers clear. Knowing that he was working so hard himself, I think we were reluctant to burden him with too many questions, ever ready though he was to help us. What I found most valuable was his sympathy and encouragement; he led one to suppose that one could do well, provided there was hard work. . . . I do not think that we found it easy to converse with him; his interests and thoughts were very far removed from those of the ordinary undergraduate, or the small-talk of life; but he had a quiet sympathy for all that with one's pursuits, with a word of warning against spending too much time upon them.

Mitchell could not resist correcting this austere portrait by recalling that he had been the subject of a shilling bet made by Jowett with Dr. Cradock, Principal of Brasenose, that Mitchell would score at least forty runs in a match between Balliol and Christ Church. Jowett went to see the match and won his bet.

Yet at Askrigg and at Pitlochry he was markedly more aloof from his young companions than he had been in earlier years or showed himself to be later on at similar reading-parties. Mitchell and his friends put this aloofness down to the fact that he was working so hard at his Plato. In a way they were right. Plato had come between him and them. But there was a deeper cause of which they knew nothing — an inner private preoccupation, even an obsession, which made the high-spirited chatter of young men seem empty of meaning. Only Plato had anything to say to him, worth his serious listening, while he was passing through the delight and agony of an experience unlike any other.

4. MISS NIGHTINGALE AT ASKRIGG

Was this deeper cause only the cumulative result of his frustrations during the past ten years? Had he come to feel so much at odds with the world and his time and his college, that he withdrew into himself and into Plato? It is true that his determination to consume his own smoke had meant also a lessening of his once radiantly joyous energy. He had retreated from his colleagues into his tent. But he had not sulked there. On the contrary, he entertained freely in it; and whatever he felt towards his colleagues, he was still finding his consolations among his pupils and friends.

In the early 'sixties, after the right to marry was lost to him, his manner stiffened unmistakably. 'Even his younger colleagues after this perceived that he was more reserved in his dealings with them than formerly. They were aware of a coolness which they could not account for.'[1] But this coolness had been reserved for 'colleagues'. He may never have known which of them had supported Wall's application against — or by way of forestalling — his own. It is certain that he would never have asked; and more than likely that his new frostiness made the topic unapproachable by others. His younger colleagues were members of the governing body; they shared the responsibility for its decisions; he displayed towards them the 'coolness' of a man who has been rebuffed by a decision which, for all he knew, they might have supported. All this had nothing whatever to do with Miss Nightingale, whom he had not then met. He did not know what it was to be so passionately interested in somebody, that all other people became shadows. He wanted to marry, and he thought that Margaret Elliot would be a nice woman to marry. But nothing can be clearer, than that he had not 'fallen in love' with her. He was approaching the idea of marriage as a good state to enjoy, but without the impulse of passion. His resentment at being thus shut off from marriage was no more than the natural resentment of a man kept in a celibate cage when he wants to be given freedom to marry without being deprived of his job.

Whatever cause he had, or supposed himself to have, for coolness towards his 'colleagues' he had no cause for any change in his behaviour towards his pupils or friends. His letters to his friends, though they sometimes alluded to his troubles, showed no trace of any coolness. At least up to the end of 1862, to a lessening degree in 1863, they were as free and gay and sympathetic as ever. After that, for a year or so, they seem to have been less frequent (or less worth publishing) and to have lacked most of the old familiar sparkle.

He could not have doubted where he stood in his friends' minds. For at the beginning of 1862 he was astonished to receive from Lingen the news that they had raised £2000, which they wished him to accept as a partial contribution to the arrears of the salary he ought to have been receiving as a professor. He refused to take the gift. 'Though I wish to see an endowment provided for the Chair, I ought not to receive money

[1] L. & L., i, 308–9.

from those on whom I have no claim.' So he wrote to Lingen, at the end of January 1862, in a letter which illustrates the difficulty he always felt in expressing his deepest feelings:

Will you give my best thanks to the subscribers, and assure them that the possession of the list of their names gives me a satisfaction far greater than the pecuniary advantage which they designed for me?

To 'a private friend abroad' he wrote in his natural and best manner:

You saw in the Italian papers about the poor *indotato* Professor. What do you think has happened to him since? His friends collected a subscription of £2000 to pay his salary for the last five years (Earl Russell, Lord Lansdowne, and various old Whigs and lovers of religious liberty were among the subscribers.) It is a great pity that though he loves money, which he believes to be the source of every good, he could not make up his mind to accept it. . . . It does not do, and is not consistent with the dignity of a human being, to have received about £20 from everybody you meet at dinner. Yet he is very sensible that it is a great thing to have such friends.[1]

The characteristic style of Jowett's private correspondence (very well illustrated by the letter just quoted) continued at least up to the end of 1862. What little sparkle is to be found in the few published letters of 1863 occurs in his letters to Mrs. Tennyson. (It was to her that he usually wrote; seldom to the Bard himself.) But there is only one real Jowettian sparkle even in the letters to Mrs. Tennyson. This came out of him in a letter, dated 21st December 1863, when it looked as if Pusey's proposed statute for the endowment of the Greek chair would go through. 'I mean to do a great deal more mischief now that they are going to give me some money.' He was, just at this moment of time, looking and speaking like a man on the top of the world. After Stanley's sermon on 'great opportunities', with which the new Dean of Westminster bade farewell to Oxford on 29th November 1863, Edward Caird said to Jowett:

'Who will sing us battle-songs any more?' 'We must carry on the fight though', said he, looking as pertinacious and as saintly-wicked as usual.[2]

There is a well-known reference to Florence Nightingale in Jowett's essay on the Interpretation of Scripture.[3] It comes in the passage where he says, in effect, that Christ's precepts of behaviour are not to be interpreted too literally in a society very different from that of the Jews at the beginning of the Christian era. He quotes with approval Lessing's paradox: 'the Christian religion has been tried for eighteen centuries; the

---

[1] *ibid.*, i, 306–7. The 'friend abroad' may have been Lewis Campbell himself.
[2] *ibid.*, i, 333. The quotation is from a letter of Caird to John Nichol, a fellow Balliol-Scotsman, who had just become Professor of English Literature at Glasgow.
[3] *Essays and Reviews*, 363.

religion of Christ remains to be tried.' And he goes on to suggest, by a series of not wholly imaginary instances, the manner in which the religion of Christ was most truly followed in his own time by individual persons, whether rich or poor, high or low. The last of these instances was inspired by the fame of 'the lady with the lamp'. It runs:

And there may be some tender and delicate woman among us, who feels that she has a divine vocation to fulfil the most repulsive offices towards the dying inmates of a hospital, or the soldier perishing in a foreign land.

When Jowett paid this rhetorical and rather sentimental tribute to Miss Nightingale, he knew nothing of her, except by report.

At the end of 1859 Miss Nightingale began to have what she liked to call her 'stuff' set up by a printer. It made an enormous book, in three volumes 'comprising in all 829 large octavo pages', entitled *Suggestions for Thought*.[1] It seems to have contained everything that she thought about everything. The first and third volumes were 'a philosophical exposition of her creed'; their theme, according to Sir Edward Cook, was 'Law, as the basis of a new Theology'. The second volume was devoted to 'Practical Deductions', and was 'a criticism of the religious and social life of her day'. The criticism was 'scathing and full of touches of her characteristically caustic humour'.

The whole book was violently alive, brimming with ideas, many of them almost revolutionary. But it was very ill organized and far too long and much of it was written with an excess of anger, which (Jowett told her) would defeat her purpose. The authoress had not the patience to work over it, though Jowett did his utmost to persuade her to do so. But his careful and understanding criticisms prevailed over the advice given to her by others, especially by J. S. Mill, that she ought to publish the book as it stood. It was never published. A few copies were struck off and sent to various friends for their criticism and advice. This was the cause of Jowett's introduction to the real Miss Nightingale, whom he had ignorantly idealized in *Essays and Reviews*.

Part of the 'stuff' — presumably the proofs of the first volume — was lent by Arthur Clough to Jowett at some undetermined date — certainly after *Essays and Reviews* was in the press; and almost certainly some time after the publication of that book in February 1860. Clough kept back the name of the author.

Jowett was more than intrigued by what he read. He was excited and exhilarated. He told Clough that it seemed to him as if he had received

---

[1] Cook, *Life of Florence Nightingale*, i, 470. What follows depends almost entirely on Cook: especially i, 470–85 and ii, 96–103. I have not myself seen any part of the 'stuff'.

the impress of a new mind. According to Sir Edward Cook, Clough then revealed who the author was and asked Jowett to write to her. Mrs. Woodham-Smith says that Jowett first wrote to Clough a letter of criticism 'for your friend'. On 22nd July 1860, he wrote again, this time to Miss Nightingale directly — the first of 'the many hundreds of letters' he wrote to her during the rest of his life.

The correspondence was at first entirely concerned with Miss Nightingale's *Suggestions for Thought*. Jowett carefully annotated all three volumes. It was absolutely necessary, he told her, that they should be revised according to a clear plan: but, he said,

I should be very sorry if the greater part of this book did not in some form see the light. I have been greatly struck by reading it, and I am sure it would similarly affect others. Many sparks will blaze up in people's minds from it.

Miss Nightingale treasured the annotated copy and listened to his advice, but she could not or would not face the labour of revision.[1]

She, too, had received the impress of a new mind. 'I do so like Mr. Jowett' she recorded at an early stage of their long correspondence; and he, about the same time, wrote to her: 'I reckon you (if I may do so) among unseen friends.' The 'stuff' was now no longer the sole theme of their letters. 'She was already (1862) giving to him most of her intimate confidence'; and he was responding. 'Presently' says Sir Edward Cook, rather prosaically, 'they met; the friendship ripened, and remained firm to the end.' Mrs. Woodham-Smith is very much nearer the mark when she writes that 'affection became devotion'. Both accounts indicate that there was a period — not exactly defined or dated — during which Jowett's feeling grew to its peak of intensity. After that peak had been reached, both the law of nature and Jowett's own character required a levelling off. Sir Edward Cook says only that their friendship 'remained firm to the end'; Mrs. Woodham-Smith that it was 'unaltered' even after she had refused to marry him — if we can bring ourselves to believe that he ever asked her to do so.

The period during which Jowett's affection grew to its peak, after his meeting with Miss Nightingale in October 1862, cannot have been very long — not more than a year or so. How long did it stay at the point of its highest intensity? Again, not for a very long time. Certainly his published letters from 1865 to 1870 indicate a welcome revival of his eager

---

[1] Early in 1862, 'in some testamentary instructions' she desired that the 'stuff' should be revised 'according to the hints of Mr. Jowett and Mr. Mill, but without altering the spirit according to their principles with which I entirely disagree'. In 1865 she asked Jowett to edit it for her. But he would not do so; it needed much more than mere editing. Cook, *Life of Florence Nightingale*, i, 477.

interest in other friends. There is, for example, a long and peculiarly warm letter to Morier written in January 1866, beginning 'My dear Old Fellow'; in the course of which he says

Will you give my kindest regards and love to your wife and child? Two things I wonder at: (1) Why you retain your old undergraduate affection for me. (2) Why your wife is not jealous.

It seems, therefore, not improbable that his devotion was growing rapidly during 1863, that it reached its obsessive height in 1864, and that it then subsided into a steadier feeling which no longer claimed almost the whole of his private mind. But he was still obedient to her advice — or, at least, he pretended to be so. In June 1866 he promised her that he would 'never work after twelve for the future'. He went on to say: 'I am quite well in health, but I am aware that my mind is tired.'

If this is a true account of his one near approach to passion — it is desirable to avoid the word 'surrender' — it provides an explanation of his aloofness at Askrigg in the summer of 1864. Miss Nightingale was beginning to exhaust him, then, as she had exhausted all her earlier admirers. She had already killed Herbert and Clough. If Jowett had been a lesser man, she would have killed him too. But he was her equal — even her superior — not a man she could wear to death. Nevertheless, for a time, even he was in danger.

Plato was almost an escape from danger into worse danger. When he shut himself up in his room at Askrigg, his young men thought that Plato was its only other inhabitant. They were wrong. Florence Nightingale was there. He was not always working at his Plato; he was talking to her far into the night, long after the time when they supposed him to have gone to bed; writing and writing and writing 'enormous' letters, which must have taken hours to put on paper. One of these, dated from Askrigg in July, was thought by Miss Nightingale to be 'one of the most beautiful, if not the most beautiful, of the whole collection'. She particularly marked those passages in it which told her that 'a sense of the identity of their own action with the will of God', so strong 'as to exclude every other feeling', would give those who could acquire that sense 'infinite rest and almost infinite power'; and that he did not see 'why active life might not become a sort of passive life too, passive in the hands of God and in the fulfilment of the laws of nature. I sometimes fancy that there are possibilities of character much greater than have been realized. . . .'

He was telling her, in effect, that for all her incessant practical aims she was that kind of person; that he, too, in her company and holding fast to Plato as his other guide, could be passive as well as active; and that, between them, they could explore unrealized 'possibilities of character'.

5. 'AN INFERIOR CLERK'

Campbell begins his last chapter, covering the five years before the Mastership, with a felicitous quotation from a letter which Jowett wrote to Mrs. Tennyson in 1861: 'Prosperity is the blessing of the Old Testament, adversity of the New. Still that Old Testament blessing would do a great deal of good to some of us.' At last, in 1865, after a long spell of grim weather, the sky suddenly began to clear. Prosperity set in. For the remaining twenty-eight years of his life the Old Testament blessing descended with ever greater abundance upon his whitening head.

The darkest hour is that before the dawn. Towards the end of 1864 and at the beginning of 1865 Jowett's hitherto confident lamp was burning very low. He wrote to Florence Nightingale from Pitlochry in September — he would not have so confessed his loss of self-confidence to anybody else:

People sometimes say to me, 'Ah, you don't mind raising a blister occasionally, but won't you tell us what you think?' If you won't think me very egotistical I will tell you why I have as yet been able to do so little on these subjects. First of all because I know that it is very doubtful whether I could in any degree succeed in working them out, and I certainly could not succeed without entire health and rest, and a good deal of reading and thought. But then at present I have the translation and edition of Plato on hand, and besides this, my pupils; — this last is a perfectly unlimited field, and when I see men passing through College or in the University, to whose course I might have given a twist in the right way, if only I had time or energy, I feel very much the responsibility of this. And the result is that I cannot possibly add a third object to the two which I have already.

He could not very well add that it was a whole-time job, in itself, to be a pen-friend of Miss Nightingale's. But he could tell her, as his sense of humour began to moderate his passion, that she had had it in her power to make what she liked of him. 'Do not suppose' (he wrote to her in August 1865) 'that I don't feel and understand' what she might have done with Lord Herbert, if he had lived. And then, between brackets, as if he were saying something merely humorous: 'And you might have made me Dean of Christ Church: the only preferment that I would like to have, and I would have reformed the University and bullied the Canons.'

This jesting imagination of himself as Dean of Christ Church shows a recovery from the depth of depression which he had touched in January

1865. He wrote to Miss Nightingale in that month, from Torquay where his mother and sister were living. He had just ended a visit to the Tennysons at Freshwater. The poet was in great need of a subject. Could she think of one? 'I have given him one — the "Grandmother", which has answered, and have been urging *Galileo* upon him, but he is not inclined to this. He has been amusing himself with translating passages of Homer.' One gets the impression that Tennyson had been rather fretful, the visit less rewarding than usual, and Jowett himself not so fertile of ideas as he would have liked to be. This, perhaps, may have accounted for the mood of self-analysis in which the letter opens. Certainly the climate of Torquay was not to blame. 'I like this place,' he wrote after his mother's death there in 1869 'at which I always do more and with less exertion than anywhere else.'

Here is the opening paragraph — the greater part of the letter is a discussion of religious ideas, which does not suggest any diminution of his powers but is not relevant to his state of mind at this time. It begins almost jauntily; but the tone passes quickly through bitterness into something not far removed from despair.

I see that you think I am hungering after the fleshpots of Egypt. But indeed that is not the case. I have long been aware that this head is so oddly constructed that, if mitres were to rain from heaven as thick as hail, not one of them would fit it: also I agree with Lord Melbourne. 'My dear fellow, would you wear such a dress as that for £10,000 a year?' Deaneries have more to be said for them. But not having quite forgiven 'Anglicanus'[1] for deserting me, I am not going to give up the young life of Oxford (so full of hope) for the dead men's bones of a Cathedral town. Still I have difficulties; the greatest of them all is perhaps Balliol College, which is to me 'the War Office', in which I am only an inferior clerk, having to force along the inefficiency of others, and this will probably continue all my life. Also, though I am aware of the great opportunity which has been given me at Oxford, and truly thankful to have such an opportunity, I feel often very uncertain whether I can use this, owing to my being tired in mind. Though I have the will, and am really not afraid, yet I believe that I never had the intellectual power which was needed for the task. But I am not going to trouble you with any more such reflections. You know Carlyle's saying, 'Consume your own smoke', which perhaps has the advantage of increasing the internal heat.

'Only an inferior clerk'? It was a rather feeble punning allusion, not meant to be taken too seriously, suggested by his comparison of Balliol to the War Office, with which Miss Nightingale was for ever struggling. He was a clerk in Holy Orders; and there were clerks of another kind in the War Office. All the same, it was a wilful misrepresentation of the truth. Miss Nightingale was partly responsible for this. She disliked

---

[1] Stanley's *non de plume*.

mealy-mouthed language and encouraged Jowett to let himself go.[1] On the whole, this was good for him. Writing to her, he learned to let off steam and to reduce the pressure of that 'internal heat'. But it was not good for him to exaggerate the opposition he had to meet in Balliol. He knew — he must have known — that the boot would very soon be on the other leg.

It was not like him to falsify facts in this way. He did so because he really was very near to a point of exhaustion and unaware that the whole face of fortune was about to change.

[1] Cook, *Life of Florence Nightingale*, ii, 99. 'I gather from one of his letters that she may have reminded him of Dr. Johnson's love of a good hater, for Mr. Jowett promises to try and satisfy her a little better in that respect in the future. And, as far as it was in him to do so, he seems to have kept his word. . . . There are passages about "rascals" and "rogue Elephants" and "beasts", which are almost as downright as was Miss Nightingale herself in this sort.'

CHAPTER XV

The Turn of the Wheel

1. £500 A YEAR

In the autumn of 1864 yet another attempt was made to end the scandal of the Greek professorship. On 31st October a proposal, sponsored by the Vice-Chancellor, Dr. J. P. Lightfoot, Rector of Exeter,[1] came before the Hebdomadal Council. It was on the same lines as the statute defeated in Convocation on 8th March. The stipend was to be raised to £450, at the cost of the University, 'with the guarding clause *modo nec Academia scripta eius, quae ad fidem Catholicam pertinent, comprobasse teneatur, neque rectae fidei Professorum horum incuriosa esse censeatur.*'[2]

In spite of 'the intense strain of ecclesiastical feeling at the moment', after the synodical condemnation of *Essays and Reviews*, and the 'widespread alarm and distrust about the teaching with which Professor Jowett's name was associated'; in spite of Archdeacon Denison's public and frantic denunciation of 'this act of Edward Bouverie Pusey' as the supreme example of principle sacrificed to expediency; in spite of Wilberforce's private warning in 'one of his most urgent letters' that the proposal aimed 'a very deadly blow at the truth of God'; in spite, even, of Keble's doubts and fears, Pusey did his utmost to persuade Council to endorse the proposed statute. It was thrown out by a majority of one.

Pusey wrote to Keble:

I read to the Council a statement of the Archbishop of Canterbury: 'I trust that the Jowett affair will be settled before Parliament meets again. It is most important that it should be so. Indeed I feel so strongly about it, that if it comes on again, the Archbishop of York and I shall come to vote for the measure', but it had no effect . . . I have ringing in my ears, *Quos Deus vult perdere, dementat prius.*[3]

The effort to reconcile the two halves of Pusey's extraordinary mind is

---

[1] Not to be confused with Dr. J. B. Lightfoot, the Cambridge biblical scholar (later Bishop of Durham) who had praised Jowett's commentary.

[2] 'provided that the Academy [University] be neither held to have approved those of his writings which pertain to the Catholic faith, nor judged to be indifferent to the correctness of the faith of these Professors.'

[3] *Life of E. B. Pusey*, iv, 34–6.

often baffling; but it is impossible not to admire his courage and his common sense.

The Hebdomadal Council was sufficiently shaken to set up a committee, of which Pusey was made a member, 'to inquire into and report upon the endowment of the Professorship'. The committee met, almost at once, and agreed to recommend to Council the resumption of Pusey's proposals. What would have happened to this recommendation, nobody can say; for the affair suddenly took an entirely new turn, and the Hebdomadal Council thankfully surrendered its place in the limelight to the Dean and Chapter of Christ Church.

Some time in October, Edward Freeman, the historian, who will re-appear later in this book as Arthur Evans's father-in-law and one of Jowett's bitterest enemies,[1] wrote a letter to the *Daily News* about the Greek chair at Oxford and the responsibility for increasing the stipend attached to it. His letter — which he re-published as a pamphlet — stirred educated men to indignation. The scandal of the Greek professor's wage had spread beyond Oxford. Public opinion, as it became aware of the facts, found them equally incomprehensible and insufferable. An obvious and gross injustice had been going on for ten years, and clerical Oxford was apparently content that it should go on indefinitely. The Queen herself was indignantly on Jowett's side. She said to Tennyson at Osborne, in May 1863, that 'Oxford had used him shamefully'.[2] Freeman's letter placed the responsibility for increasing the professor's stipend where it plainly lay — with Christ Church.

At this date Freeman, who became Regius Professor of Modern History at Oxford twenty years later in succession to Stubbs, was living the dedicated life of a scholar with considerable private means in his Somersetshire country house. He had not yet published his *History of the Norman Conquest*, and had been an unsuccessful candidate for two Oxford professorships. But his reputation was growing; what he asserted to be historical truth could not be simply ignored.

Freeman's argument severely shook, but did not yet quite shatter, the complacency of the Cathedral Chapter. He said:

Whenever money stipends have to be paid to officers of any kind . . . there is always some class of people receiving a less proportion of the corporate income than the founder meant them to receive. . . . The old Bishops who founded the elder Cathedrals, more wise in their generation, guarded against this evil by giving so many officers separate estates. But when a Chapter has to pay certain payments, though after three centuries it is very

[1] See below, 387 *foll.*
[2] *L. & L.*, i, 342. Mrs. Tennyson repeated the Queen's remark to Jowett, who repeated it to his mother. It is not recorded either by Hallam or by Charles Tennyson.

plain that the £40 ought to be increased to £400, there is no particular year in which it is plain that £40 should be increased to £45 or £45 to £50. Had King Harry, instead of granting estates to Christ Church, granted them to the University, the Professor would now have his proper income.

There was a gap in Freeman's argument; no undeniable proof had been produced that any lands, specifically charged to provide a stipend for the Greek chair, had been conveyed to Christ Church. The Chapter, therefore, although its income had multiplied itself many times since it had been made responsible for the professor's salary, still refused to admit that it had any duty beyond the payment of £40 a year.

If, said Dean Liddon on 18th November, in a formal statement on behalf of his Chapter — with whose majority view he privately disagreed, wishing himself to accept Freeman's argument without more ado — if it could be shown

that the Chapter held lands specifically granted for the purpose of paying the Professor . . . he would immediately propose to the Chapter to augment the stipend now paid to the Professor according to a fair estimate of the value of money.

The members of the Chapter seem to have thought that they had taken up a position historically and legally unassailable. Many years before, in Dean Gaisford's time, Pusey had asked whoever in Christ Church was then supposed to know that sort of thing, 'about it, but could learn nothing.'[1] He assumed, not unnaturally, that there was nothing to learn. But the members of the Chapter were as ignorant of its history as they were foolish in their attachment to a purely technical point. Their answer to Freeman's pamphlet was a confident challenge to their critics: 'Prove our duty to us, and we will do it.' The challenge was taken up by Charles Elton, a young historical lawyer, a former Balliol man and now a fellow of Queen's. He found no great difficulty in showing that the lands originally granted to the Chapter of Westminster Abbey, for the support of the Greek as well as the Divinity and Hebrew professors, had been re-granted to Christ Church for the same purposes, when Westminster asked to be relieved of them. He published his proof in a letter to The Times on 16th January 1865.

It might be supposed that, the technical gap in Freeman's argument having been thus filled by Elton, Christ Church would now immediately fulfil the undertaking given on its behalf by the Dean. But no. Though the historical facts were as Elton had shown, and as Christ Church should have known, them to be, did they impose a legal obligation on the Chapter? Two very eminent lawyers (Roundell Palmer and Cairns)

[1] Life of E. B. Pusey, iv, 37.

thought not. Their opinion, whether good or bad, enabled the Chapter to put some face of free-will upon its act of final surrender. On 17th February the Dean informed the Vice-Chancellor that Christ Church had decided to raise the professor's salary to £500. Perhaps the extra £100 (for the usual estimate of the proper salary had been £400) was intended to compensate the professor for the years during which he had received next to nothing. It is at least agreeable to think that, when Christ Church at last recognized her obligations, she was moved to do a little more than had been expected of her.

Soon after this decision an amusing mock-mathematical pamphlet was published in Oxford, called *The New Method of Evaluation as applied to Π*. It carried, as a motto, the nursery lines: 'Little Jack Horner sat in a corner eating his Christmas pie.' Everybody knew, of course, that the author was the witty, queerish, mathematical lecturer of Christ Church, the Rev. Charles Dodgson, not yet famous as Lewis Carroll.[1] The fact that Dodgson was a Christ Church don added malicious fire to his deceptively quiet squib.

The problem of evaluating π, which has engaged the attention of mathematicians from the earliest ages, had, down to our own time, been considered as purely arithmetical. It was reserved for this generation to discover that it is in reality a dynamical problem; and the true value of π which appeared an *ignis fatuus* to our forefathers, has been at last obtained under pressure. The following are the main elements of the problem: Let U = the University, G = Greek, and P = Professor. Then GP = Greek Professor; let this be reduced to its lowest terms, and call the result $\mathcal{J}$. Also let W = the work done, T = *The Times* [newspaper], p = the given payment, π = the payment according to T, and S = the sum required; so that $\pi = S$. The problem is to obtain a value for π which shall be commensurable with W.

With mocking ingenuity the satirist described the failure of all previous methods to settle this intractable problem. At last, under repeated pressure EAF (where F is 'a Force acting equally in all directions and varying directly as T' and A = Able and E = Enlightened) the final result is obtained:

$\pi = S = 500.00000$. The result differs considerably from the anticipated value, namely 400.00000: still there can be no doubt that the process has been correctly performed, and that the learned world may be congratulated on the final settlement of this most difficult problem.[2]

Jowett took the sudden change in his circumstances quietly. But he

---

[1] *Adventures in Wonderland* came out later in the same year, 1865.
[2] The pamphlet is reprinted in the Nonesuch one-volume edition of *The Complete Works of Lewis Carroll*, 1123–9. The joke depends, of course, on the fact that π (or *pi*), the ratio of the circumference of a circle to its diameter, cannot be arithmetically stated with exact precision. Its value is usually given to five decimal points; and Dodgson's squib makes agreeable use of five decimal noughts.

did not even try to be fair to Pusey. The fact, he inaccurately told Mrs. Tennyson, was that

Dr. Pusey, who first raised the opposition, has got his party into a scrape, and therefore to get them out again has made Christ Church fulfil their obligation . . . I am neither grateful nor ungrateful. You must not look a gift horse in the mouth. I was rather glad that you did not write to congratulate. Having more money I hope to get more done for the undergraduates.

To another (unnamed) friend he wrote:

This is the last you will ever hear of this matter. I am greatly indebted to some of my young friends, who without my knowledge hunted this matter out and assailed the Dean and Chapter in the newspapers.

To another (also unnamed) friend:

I am glad that the world will cease to hear any longer about the Greek Professorship . . . . I place the support and sympathy I have received far above the money.

If he was a great deal less than fair to Pusey, it must be admitted that Pusey's handling of the whole affair had been such as to invite cynical misunderstanding. His biographers were right in saying that there was no incident in his life which was more frequently remembered against him, and hardly one which suffered more from incomplete remembrance. But it was a serious fault in Jowett that he was incapable of entering into the mind of his arch-opponent; and it is a serious fault in Campbell's story that he merely follows Jowett's lead, as when he says that 'Dr. Pusey found that it is easier to raise a storm than allay it'.

As to the money. Jowett was perfectly sincere and unaffected in his attitude. He is reported to have said to more than one friend that it had come too late to matter to him personally, though it might have been otherwise a few years earlier. This was taken by Campbell to mean that if it had come to him sooner he might have married. In that case Margaret Elliot would have become Mrs. Jowett. But by 1865 Miss Elliot had been swept into a corner; and there was no marrying or giving in marriage on the ideal plane, where Miss Nightingale and he were now strenuously intimate.

So the money was of no particular domestic value to him. He had enough without it both for his own needs, and for the support of his mother and sister. Yet it was a large sum — several times larger than it looks, now, to have been. Income tax was negligible; super-tax and sur-tax had not been invented; and the pound itself could buy many times

[1] *L. & L.*, i, 308.

over what it can buy now. £500 a year was not an income or an incre-ment to be despised.[1]

It seems that he used the money for the general purpose hinted in his letter to Mrs. Tennyson: 'to get more done for the undergraduates'. The phrase concealed a special, private, aim. What he really meant, but naturally would not say, was: 'to help *needy* undergraduates'. He never forgot the financial help given to him by Greenhill, when he was an undergraduate and desperately poor; and now that he had more than enough money for his own needs he used the excess for charitable pur-poses, of which he never said anything to anybody.

'It was now' says Campbell 'that he began those liberal gifts to younger men, which were so often repeated in later years.' His generosity 'had no limit'. But it was never paraded. Nobody ever more strictly interpreted the command: 'Let not thy left hand know what thy right hand doeth.' His gifts were usually so made that nobody except the reci-pients could know of them. But here is an instance, accidentally dis-covered by Campbell, of a timely present made to a young (unmarried) graduate, apparently of another college, who was taking private pupils. Jowett learned that he was not doing very well and could not afford to go to Germany in the vacation. A few days later he 'sent for' the young man and gave him an envelope 'with the words, "I hope you will go to Ger-many: good bye" '.[2]

Of his more substantial gifts no record exists, or could exist. But of his lesser acts of generosity there are many stories. One of the best concerns a bicycle. An undergraduate at one of his vacation parties had been ill. Jowett decided that he must have bicycle exercise. Nothing would do but the very best bicycle that money could buy; and it must be on the spot immediately. A telegram was sent to a London dealer, and the bicycle arrived forthwith by passenger train.

2. DESTINY

The end of the long wrangle over his professorial stipend marked the end of Jowett's struggles and humiliations. It also marked — though he did not realize this at the time — the beginning of the end of his private

---

[1] It would be interesting to know what his income was, and how it was made up, at this and at earlier and later dates; but I cannot even offer a guess. Living in Balliol would have cost very little; but he could afford to entertain 'in his tent', and to travel as he pleased.

[2] *L. & L.*, i, 376. Campbell took this story from the New York *Nation*, where it appeared in 1893 over the initials W. Y. A. The Balliol Register knows of no Balliol man with these initials.

freedom. The mental fatigue, which he confessed to Miss Nightingale, was no more than a passing symptom. If he had cared to snap his fingers at the fickle goddess called Fortune, who had suddenly decided to make amends for her unkind behaviour — if he had pocketed his first £500 and gone away on a long sabbatical holiday and left his young men to get along for a while as well as they could without him — the old intellectual and moral fascinations would very soon have reasserted themselves. His mind would have gone back, with fresh vigour, to its favourite hunting-ground, the border country between theology and philosophy.

But this was not what the goddess — whose better name seems to be Destiny — intended. Secure, now, of her purpose she set to work with a will. All impediments to her *protégé's* freedom could now be safely removed; the more quickly the better. She intended him to be Master of Balliol. It would not do for him to go directly into such an office from the position of 'an inferior clerk'. On the other hand, he must not be allowed to spoil her plan by speaking his mind too freely on dangerous topics. She took him with a rush through the next five years, reminding him occasionally, with the aid of Miss Nightingale, that he was not so young as he had been and must cut down his vacation hours of strenuous work. This was risky; for, whenever he spent less time gruelling over detail, the sense of mental fatigue disappeared and the old speculative energy began to return.

He came very near to spoiling her plan, just before she got him into the Mastership, by agreeing to contribute two long articles to a second series of *Essays and Reviews*; one on the Principles of the Reformation, and one on the Reign of Law (a subject probably derived from Miss Nightingale's *Suggestions for Thought*). He was working eagerly at this task in 1870, and was very full of it. One may reasonably regret that he never wrote either of these essays, and that the whole project came to nothing. Campbell thinks that this was because Wilson had a stroke; though he adds that

Jowett himself may well have hesitated, after his appointment to the Mastership, to risk another storm while his honours, in which Balliol was involved, were 'in their newest gloss'.[1]

There was no time to be lost. The goddess had been a little over confident. One is tempted to imagine a scene on Olympus, in which Zeus reluctantly yields to her demands, consigns Scott with haste to the Deanery of Rochester, and prepares a double thunderbolt for the unfortunate Wilson and the Rev. Charles Voysey, whose recent condemna-

[1] *ibid.*, i, 404–5. See also Jowett's letters to Caird in January and February *ibid.*, i, 441–5).

tion by the Chancellor's Court in the Diocese of York was dangerously stirring Jowett's rebellious sympathies.[1]

In 1865 these alarming symptoms were five years away in the future. What Jowett then needed, and received, was evidence of a real change in his fortunes. No sooner had Christ Church increased his stipend to £500, than he suddenly became a Yorkshire landowner. The curious story of this inheritance has been told in an earlier chapter.[2] He went north to inspect his property — it lay at Birstwith and Telliscliffe in the forest of Knaresborough — and met a friend on this journey, to whom he said: 'I am going to look after my estate; you did not know I was a landed proprietor!'

Two swift and sudden turns of the wheel had made Jowett a man of property enjoying a substantial income. Later in the year, the goddess flicked the wheel again. It was hardly even a flick. All that happened was the automatic fulfilment of a little arrangement she had made in the previous year, when Courtenay Ilbert was elected to a fellowship at Balliol. In those days a new fellow had to undergo a 'probationary' year before he was admitted as a full fellow and became a member of the governing body with a vote. The end of Ilbert's probation 'turned the scale in favour of the promotion of liberal measures in College meetings'.

It is odd that Jowett seems to have shut his eyes to what was happening until it had actually happened. When he described himself to Miss Nightingale as only 'an inferior clerk' he was already the unofficial leader of a confident and growing minority which needed only a single additional adherent to become a majority. Perhaps he deliberately exaggerated his difficulties in order to make Miss Nightingale feel that they resembled hers. Perhaps his withdrawal from the common room and the high table had weakened his understanding of his colleagues; so that he doubted the sincerity of some who supported him, whenever they differed from him upon any particular occasion. Perhaps he was so little of a party man that he did not think of himself at all as the leader of an

---

[1] Voysey's condemnation in York happened in 1869. He appealed to the Privy Council, but was condemned by the Judicial Committee in 1871. Tait, as Archbishop of Canterbury, was a member of the Committee and approved the judgment. Jowett, though he contributed publicly to a fund raised for Voysey's defence, saw that he was bound to be convicted and advised him to 'resign'. Voysey had gone so far as to say — or was alleged to have said — that the worship of Christ was 'idolatry and inconsistent with the worship of the true God'. After his conviction he founded 'the Theistic Church', and preached to sympathetic congregations in Swallow Street, Piccadilly, for nearly thirty years. He died in 1912. See *L. & L.*, i, 402–4 (where two letters from Jowett to Voysey are to be found); *Life of Archbishop Tait*, ii, 88–90; *D.N.B.*, third supplement, published in 1927.

[2] See above, 48; also *L. & L.*, i, 375. Campbell has not got his facts quite right.

opposition, but only as a reasonable man, condemned to be thwarted for the rest of his life by unreasonable men.

The explanation may lie not in one but in all three of these guesses. But by about 1866 he was beginning to realize that he could now usually carry the college with him. His plan for using part of the Balliol revenues in support of a scheme of University extension was approved 'without a division'; and a Balliol 'hall' was established, under T. H. Green. This was a first experiment: 'a small scheme', as he explained to a friend, for 'men to lodge out and pay no College fees, receiving education gratuitously'. He had long believed that something on these lines must be done, if the University was to fulfil in the national life the kind of 'charitable' purpose for which the colleges had been originally founded.

He wrote to another friend:

At present not a tenth or a twentieth part of the ability of the country comes to the University. This scheme is intended to draw from a new class, and with this object I should propose that the subjects of examination be not confined to Latin and Greek, but embrace physical science, mathematics, etc. The great difficulty in working it out is the present state of the Grammar schools.

If any of my readers still thinks of Jowett as a tuft-hunter, perhaps this quotation may persuade him to think again.

In the following years the movement for University extension made much headway both in Parliament and in Oxford. Balliol, at Jowett's instigation, was foremost in taking advantage of the repeal of an ancient University statute, which required that every 'scholar' must dwell in a 'hall'. This repeal enabled Balliol to remit 'terminal charges to out-College students' and to award, every year, six £40 exhibitions to candidates 'elected after an examination in general subjects as well as in Latin and Greek'. The successful candidates were freed from the payment of any tutorial fees.

The history of University extension lies outside the scope of this book. The few facts, given above, are simply lifted from Campbell's account of Jowett's first real success in putting Balliol upon the road which he wished her to follow. He wrote exultantly to his mother, with an unaccustomed buoyancy and freedom:

Oxford, or rather Balliol, is much pleasanter than formerly. I have no longer any difficulty in carrying out my views, from the Fellows; and I believe that we shall succeed in making it a really great place of education.

He was particularly pleased with the new Balliol building, completed in 1868. He thought it really beautiful — the best thing that has been done in Oxford in this way. . . . You will be glad to hear also that I carried a plan for poor students.

Apart from building (not, perhaps, quite so beautifully as he supposed) and establishing a Balliol 'hall', and carrying through various internal reforms or changes and, as always, caring for his young men, Jowett was now mainly occupied in bringing his work on Plato's Dialogues towards the point of first publication. The translation was actually published in February 1871 — a few months after he became Master. 'By the election to the Mastership' says Abbott, very truly, 'and the publication of his Plato, Jowett's work in life became fixed. Henceforth the practical power was developed at the expense of the speculative.' Destiny had her way. The two theological essays, planned for the new series of *Essays and Reviews*, remained unwritten.

CHAPTER XVI

The Mastership

1. THE WAY IT HAPPENED

It was in December 1869, when he was fifty-two years old, that Jowett first saw what might be coming to him. He paid a

delightful visit to Mr. Lowe who is a devoted friend to me. He said that he had been told by Gladstone to ask whether he could do anything for me. I told him that I did not intend to leave Oxford, and therefore that the only thing that could be done for me would be to make Scott a Dean or a Bishop. Mr. Lowe thought that this would be done and set about the matter with great zeal. But I do not expect this, nor much care.[1]

Robert Lowe (later Lord Sherbrooke) — Bob Lowe to everybody who knew him, except those who suffered from his sarcasms — had been Gladstone's Chancellor of the Exchequer for a year and was at the height of his political career.

Jowett had been staying, early in October, at Camperdown House near Dundee. His host was the young Earl of Camperdown who, as Robert Duncan, had been one of the Askrigg reading party only five years before. Camperdown was one of Jowett's abler pupils. He was great-grandson of the famous Admiral Duncan whose brilliant defeat of the Dutch off Camperdown in 1797 restored the morale of the British navy after the mutinies. He had succeeded in 1867 to the earldom earned by his great-grandfather's victory, and to the ownership of some 14,000 acres in Forfar and Perth, with a rent-roll of nearly £12,000 a year.

A political career seemed to be opening before him. At the time of Jowett's visit to Camperdown House, he was a mere Lord-in-Waiting; but next year (1870), when he was still under thirty, he became Civil Lord of the Admiralty in Gladstone's first administration. For whatever reason, he abandoned politics after Gladstone's resignation in 1874 and contented himself with his own and local Scottish affairs. He wrote a book about his great-grandfather and died unmarried in 1918. But it was through young Camperdown's early political ambitions that Jowett found himself for several days in the intimate company of the Prime Minister.

[1] *L. & L.*, i, 408–9. The letter is dated from Torquay, December 26.

If this had not happened, in all probability Jowett would never have become Master of Balliol. It cannot be described as a purely accidental meeting; for it is evident that the young Earl of Camperdown deliberately contrived it, and it is possible that Lowe may have put the idea into Camperdown's mind. Jowett, Campbell says,

had looked forward with great eagerness to this visit, and his host reports that he had never seen him so absorbed in anyone. They talked incessantly for hours in the library and about the grounds. Jowett was very much provoked one morning when Gladstone had insisted on rising early and going to hear an Episcopal preacher at Perth.

It does not seem that Jowett's desire of meeting Gladstone arose from any motive of self-interest. He had met Gladstone before — Campbell says that 'they had breakfasted together in London' — and he was eager to discover what went on inside that powerful but, to him, peculiar and unsatisfactory mind. Far from seeking to flatter the Prime Minister, he engaged him in a direct and prolonged battle of argument, principally over the Irish question.[1]

On his way back to Oxford Jowett stopped for a night or two at St. Andrews with Professor Campbell. He was brim full of Gladstone. 'It was the first time that any one of such great simplicity had been in so exalted a position.' But he thought it perilous that anyone 'so powerful and so unsound' should be where he was and preparing what he was preparing. Gladstone had turned a deaf ear to Jowett's argument 'that the moral excuses for political crime ought not to make a statesman less firm in repressing it'.

From St. Andrews Jowett returned to Balliol, and then went on to the Nightingales at Embley. While he was at Embley his mother was taken ill. She died at Torquay, before he reached her bedside, on October 16th.[2] He stayed at Torquay with his sister for a month; went back to Balliol for three or four weeks; and then, after his 'delightful visit' to Bob Lowe at Caterham, rejoined his sister at Torquay for Christmas.

The conversations at Camperdown House had made a deep mark on the Prime Minister's mind. He had entirely failed to bring Jowett round to his way of thinking, and Jowett had equally failed to shake him. But in Jowett he had seen a man to respect and admire, a man to be advanced. If Bob Lowe was not dissembling a little, when he said later that Gladstone had asked him to find out what Jowett would like to have done for him, one would suspect that what Gladstone had in his mind for Jowett was merely ecclesiastical preferment. But the initiative may have been Lowe's. The Chancellor may have taken advantage of the impression

---

[1] *ibid.*, i, 406.   [2] See above, 294.

made on the Prime Minister by Jowett to suggest that something else might be done for him, and to obtain authority to sound him out.

Lowe had been one of Jowett's warmest admirers for some years. He had come to appreciate Jowett's unique quality, when he was Vice-President of the Committee of Council on Education from 1859 to 1864. He was not a Balliol man; but he was an Oxford (University college) man, of the generation just before that of Stanley and Jowett. His sympathies were like theirs — liberal and reformist — though he was a leading opponent of the Reform Bill introduced by the Liberals in 1866, and of the Reform Act passed by the Conservatives in 1867. And he knew — as Gladstone had no habit of knowing — what was happening in Oxford and, particularly, in Balliol.

Jowett affected not to care whether Lowe's 'zeal' would come to anything. But his behaviour, when he suddenly heard of Scott's appointment to the Deanery of Rochester, gave him away. He was staying in a country house, when the news was given to him. He was seen to lean his head against the mantelpiece and was heard to pray aloud: 'O spare me a little, that I may recover strength, before I go hence, and be no more seen.' He wrote soon afterwards to Emily that this would make him Master of Balliol, and that it was Lowe's doing. He had found 'great goodwill in Oxford about the proposal'. He considered it 'the second piece of good luck' he had had in his life; his election to a Balliol fellowship 'thirty-two years ago' was the first. 'I wish our dear mother had been alive to hear this news.'[1]

He was right about the luck. If Camperdown had not happened, just at this point of time, to be in Gladstone's view as a likely young man for responsible office, then the meeting at Camperdown House between Jowett and the Prime Minister would not have occurred.

2. OUTLINE

The battle of Sedan was fought on 1st September 1870. The French Emperor and his army capitulated next day. A republic was proclaimed in Paris on 4th September; the Empress Eugénie took refuge in England; on 20th September the siege of Paris began.

The election of Scott's successor at Balliol was made on 7th September. In comparison with the news from France, it was a very small domestic event; moreover, the result of the election was 'a foregone conclusion . . . no other choice was possible' than that of Jowett.

[1] *L. & L.*, i, 409.

Yet the papers found time to say a few words about Balliol and Jowett. Everyone was asking: What use would he make of his new position? Would he cast aside all restraint, and reform the College after his own heart — or what was thought to be after his own heart? . . . What would become of the Chapel services: would they too be reformed on the new lines? Every one felt that changes were at hand. . . .

So Abbott begins the second volume of the *Life and Letters*, exciting an expectation which his long 'story of the Mastership' curiously disappoints. There were no spectacular changes; there was no autocratically contrived revolution. Those who expected that kind of thing had an altogether false idea of Jowett as a thwarted revolutionary. He was, indeed, determined to make some small, long overdue, domestic changes. The limited nature of these is indicated by an extract from a letter written in October 1870 by Edwin Harrison 'one of Jowett's intimate friends, who was then an undergraduate at Balliol'.

I had a walk with 'the Reverend The Master of Balliol' the other day. He is in a reforming mood — has passed a sumptuary law restricting each man to one guest at dinner weekly, has abolished the long grace-duet after meat, and substituted a short grace-solo before it, and now meditates a grand revolution in Balliol cookery — opprobrium of our race. The head-cook died at the end of last Term, full of iniquities, so there is a chance of better things.[1]

It was in this kind of 'reforming mood' that Jowett entered into the possession of the small kingdom he was to rule for nearly a quarter of a century — determined to do away with a long and cumbrous ritualistic interruption in the middle of a meal; to substitute good cooking for bad cooking and careful for lazy administration. His attention to cookery is particularly notable. He was, of course, primarily concerned to make sure that the undergraduates were well fed; but he was also concerned for the standard of the dinner served at the high table, and for the standard of the meals, cooked in the college kitchen, which were served to his own guests in the Master's Lodge.

Excellent as these 'reforms' were, and true to Jowett's nature, they cannot be said to add up to anything very startling. And it cannot be said that there was anything startling about Jowett's Mastership, except that Balliol went on from strength to strength. That Jowett was the man finally responsible for that extraordinary progress is not to be doubted. But the way in which he procured it cannot be illustrated from any series of dramatic acts performed by the Master.

So little does the chronicle of events begin, now, to matter, that Abbott, though he had filled a volume of some five hundred pages with 'the story of the Mastership', found almost nothing to say about it in the

[1] *ibid.*, ii, 4.

10. The new Master of Balliol
The drawing by Désiré Laugée, at Oxford, June 1871
(*Balliol*)

long article on Jowett which he contributed a little later to the first supplement of the *Dictionary of National Biography*. His account of the last twenty-three years, if one leaves out of the reckoning what he says about Jowett's literary work (mainly the *Plato*), is less than a tenth part of the whole article; and almost half of it concerns Jowett's Vice-Chancellorship and his educational interests outside Oxford.

A fresh study of his achievements during these years, both inside and outside Oxford, very much needs to be written. That would be a book for students of academic history, rather than for the general reader. There is need, too, for a detailed study of the relations which developed between the Master and his tutors: a fascinating topic which only a Balliol man could dare to handle. Meanwhile, Abbott's authoritative account holds the field; and his own outline, written for the *Dictionary of National Biography*, gives the essential facts in the shortest possible compass. It seems better frankly to reproduce, rather than feebly to imitate it.

By his election to the mastership (7 Sept. 1870) Jowett attained the position which he most coveted. He now enjoyed more leisure than hitherto, and he had as much power as the head of a house could have. For some years after his election he was much occupied with the enlargement of the college. A new hall was built (1877) and the old one transformed into a library for the use of the undergraduates. Later on a hope, formed many years before, was realised, and a field for cricket and football was secured for the college. To this, as to everything connected with Balliol, Jowett gave liberally from his private purse, and finally he built at his own expense a house for a tutor adjacent to the field.

Jowett's interests in education were not confined to Oxford. The University College of Bristol owed much to him, he strongly supported the claims of secondary education and university extension, and at the time of his death he was busy with a scheme for bringing the university and the secondary schools together. When it was arranged in 1874–5 that the age of the candidates for the Indian civil service should be fixed at seventeen to nineteen, and that successful candidates should pass two years of probation at a university, Jowett made arrangements to receive a number of candidates at Balliol College, and helped in establishing a school of oriental languages. In the university commission of 1877–81 he was of course greatly interested. He had not much sympathy with research, beyond certain limits, and on the other hand he urged strongly the claims of secondary education in the large towns, a movement in which he thought it would be wise for the university to take a part. The better organisation of the teaching of the non-collegiate students was strongly pressed, and, above all, the retention to a large extent of prize fellowships, on which Jowett placed great value. . . .[1]

From 1882 to 1886 he was vice-chancellor and carried into the administration of the office the restless energy which was one of the most marked characteristics of his nature. He was able to do something for the non-collegiate students, and, in a different line, for the drainage of the Thames

[1] The passage omitted here concerns Plato.

Valley, in conjunction with Dean Liddell — though but a small part of their schemes was realized — and a memorial of his work remains in the name 'Vice-Chancellor's Cut',[1] which was given to the new outlet made for the Cherwell into the Isis. He also did much for the recognition and and elevation of dramatic representations at Oxford. . . .[2] In the same liberal spirit he encouraged music in his own college, inviting John Farmer from Harrow to superintend, and giving an organ for the hall. This was the beginning of the Sunday concerts at Balliol. Another subject to which he gave much thought and care was the university press. . . .[3]

The strain of the vice-chancellorship was more than Jowett's health could bear. In 1887 he fell ill, and though he recovered a considerable degree of health, he was quite unequal to the tasks he laid upon himself. . . .[4]

In 1891 Jowett had a very serious illness, which returned upon him in 1893. Towards the end of September in this year he left Oxford on a visit to Professor Campbell in London. Thence he went to Headley Park . . . where he died on 1 Oct.

Such were the events of Jowett's Mastership as summarized by his biographer. They do not seem to make very much of a story. Why, then, is he so persistently remembered as the great Master of Balliol? Is that merely one of the curious tricks played upon posterity by earlier, contemporary, opinion? Or did his greatness, if he was indeed a great man, lie elsewhere than in his use of the office for which he is chiefly remembered — in his mind, perhaps, or in his personality, or in his Plato? Or did it lie, at any rate so far as Balliol was concerned, in some continuous educative power not to be discovered by any list of achievements?

H. W. C. Davis in his history of *Balliol College* comes nearer than Abbott to answering these questions. This is how, writing as a very young man, at about the same time as Abbott and in the shadow of the reaction which almost immediately followed Jowett's death, Davis described the nature of his gift to Balliol, before and after he became Master:[5]

After 1864 the deadlock came to an end. A single election turned the scale in Jowett's favour. Thenceforth to the day of his death there was no question of his supremacy. His ideal was now thoroughly formed, and so, too, was the method through which he thought it could be realised. When, six years later, he was at length elected to the Mastership (1870) he could afford to leave routine work in the hands of younger men. He never neglected the duty, to which he was bound by the Statutes, of partici-

---

[1] More commonly called the 'New Cut'— at least in my time.
[2] Some instances are omitted here, including Sir Henry Irving's lecture at Oxford, when the actor stayed at the Master's Lodge. See below 388 for Professor Freeman's vehement diatribe against Jowett for his encouragement of the drama at Oxford.
[3] The omitted passage concerns Aristotle.
[4] A long omitted passage concerns Plato.
[5] Davis's book was published in 1899; the *D.N.B.* Supplement (containing Abbott's dry summary of the Mastership) in 1901. See also above, 42.

pating in the tutorial work. He took the keenest interest in the weekly conclaves, instituted by himself, in which the work and conduct of every individual undergraduate were passed in review. The sensations with which the freshmen carried their first essay to his study are vividly remembered by those who entered the College so late as 1890. But then, and indeed for some time before then, the ordeal had become more of an inspection than a lesson. Rebuke or praise was given in a few emphatic words; suggestions and explanations came but rarely. The consciousness that he distinguished good work from bad at a glance was an immense incentive. His verdict was accepted as irreversible. But it was no longer his part to show how the work should be done, any more than it is the duty of a general to drill the rank and file.

The machine which he had made continued to work with unabated vigour. And enough has now been said to show why it could influence and develop minds of the most various casts. The matter of Jowett's curriculum was mainly the philosophy and the literature of ancient Greece; the spirit of it was critical; the aim proposed was to excite the love of truth and to stimulate sound methods of reflection. Hence he taught some to analyse the theory of art, others to be metaphysicians, others to explore the thoughts and the springs of action of the past; while of others again he made debaters and statesmen. . . . He had something to teach everyone; and no man ever had a more devoted band of followers.

Davis went on to answer the old criticism that Jowett's teaching was too negative. He supplied two answers. In the first he was on the firmest possible ground:

He held that the only results of value are those which a man reaches for himself. Truth cannot be seen with the eye of another; the most that a teacher can do is to indicate the road which leads to the vision. He had his own beliefs and held them fast; but he knew that no good would come of dictating them into note-books. Perhaps he put this view of the case too strongly; but the truth involved in his position has been more or less recognized by all great educators from the days of Socrates downward.

In his second answer Davis involved himself in a very dubious theory — a theory related to the aim of specialized teaching and specialized research so much disliked by Jowett, which had reared its head in Balliol long before his death. Jowett's 'exaggeration' of his dislike for this academic aim was to be explained, so Davis thought, by the nature of 'the raw material on which he had to work in the years when his theory was forming'. The youthful historian of Balliol went on to develop this theory in a passage of astounding but fascinating naivety:

The freshman of the thirties and forties, to whatever cause we may ascribe the fact, was a more mature being than his counterpart of to-day.[1] He was, perhaps, not so fine a scholar, nor even so erudite, but, if any faith may be placed in memoirs and biographies, he had more ideas on things in general. The fear was, less that he would be left without a creed, than that

[1] Davis was writing at the end of the eighteen-nineties. What, one wonders, would he have found to alter in this passage, if he had lived into the nineteen-fifties?

he would come to man's estate with a jumble of strong but mutually inconsistent convictions. Even scepticism in him was the outcome of fire and fury. The work of a tutor in that age was much more to clarify ideas than to impart them. Jowett was accustomed to say, towards the end of his life, that he missed in the rising generation the enthusiasm which had characterised his own contemporaries.[1] The time for revising his method to suit new conditions had long since passed. But fortunately that method was, for some years before and after his accession to the Mastership, supplemented, and in a measure counteracted, by the rival methods of Arnold Toynbee and T. H. Green.

3. THE HEART OF THE MATTER

'Rival methods'? Only if it is agreed that the work of a tutor is to 'impart' ideas rather than to 'clarify' them.

Certainly Toynbee, using (as Davis says) 'enthusiasm of a kind which was almost foreign to the Master's nature', raised a passion like his own in his pupils. But was that really a work of education? Was it not, rather, proselytism? Is it not reasonable to think that Jowett's cooler perception of the need to reduce 'the estrangement of class from class' — an aim which he steadily pursued, but never to the point of denying virtue in class distinctions — was a better base for a tutor to work from than enthusiasm? He distrusted emotional approaches to any problem; and most of all he distrusted them in education. Preaching, he might have said, is not teaching; and teaching ought never to become preaching.

Green, as Davis himself says, was 'above all things a system-builder, and, for that reason, the magnetic influence which he exercised . . . caused Jowett some hours of uneasiness'. For Jowett had long learned to distrust philosophical systems, as much as he distrusted enthusiasm. Between Green and himself 'there was the greatest affection possible'; but he could not bear to see Green's pupils compelled to absorb their tutor's home-spun system, before they were equipped to criticize it. Green

very wisely and generously gave way. For a year ot two before he became Professor of Moral Philosophy he took but a small share in the teaching of the College.[2]

The clash between the idea that it is right for a tutor to make disciples out of his pupils, and the idea that this is an abuse of his position, is a recurring clash in universities. In many subjects, especially those of a

---

[1] But, surely, that is the commonplace attitude of ageing men? The enthusiasms of one generation are boredom to another; and the young know better than to expose their enthusiasms to unsympathetic elders.

[2] *L. & L.*, ii, 192–3.

scientific or technical nature, it does not immediately appear to exist — though it is at least conceivable that a student may suffer severely from being persuaded into a false scientific or technical theory by a teacher overbent upon imparting it. The fields in which the clash is most obviously visible vary from time to time and age to age according to the topics which are most engaging public controversy. They may be religious, or philosophical, or social, or political, or economic, or historical, or even 'scientific'. Whatever the field, the question is always the same question: the general question of the tutor's right to instil his own views into the minds of pupils who are not yet capable of critical resistance.

In Oxford, this general question had been raised in a peculiarly sharp and particular way at Oriel in 1830, when Newman and his fellow-tutors were dismissed from their tutorial offices by Provost Hawkins, because they were planning to introduce their own brand of religious doctrine into the minds of the young men committed to their care. Unhappy as the effect of this dismissal was in many different ways — not least upon Hawkins himself — and hard as the cost of it was to Oriel, the Provost's decision was plainly right, and its rightness was generally upheld in Oxford.[1] It is not fair to young men that they should be prematurely persuaded by the private enthusiasms of older men, before they have learned how to make their own judgments, into opinions which may fix or mark them for life.

Provost Hawkins was concerned to stop a particular kind of religious propagandism. Jowett had proposed to himself, and had followed in his own tutorship, a wider principle than that of Hawkins: that tutors ought to refrain from *any* kind of proselytism, that the true aim of the teacher is to make his pupil think for himself, not to make him think what his teacher thinks. After he became Master, some of the Balliol tutors found this principle altogether unsatisfying. Green and Toynbee, especially, discarded it.[2] They did not hesitate to use every opportunity of framing and fixing the mind of any worthwhile young man who swam into their tutorial nets. Teach him to think for himself? Teach him, rather, to think the right way, *my* way.

Thus, even while Jowett was in the full tide of his Mastership and long before he became an old man, there was already a strong movement away from his governing principle. The tutors wished not only to estab-

---

[1] See *Oxford Apostles*, Chapter VII, section 1, 'War in Oriel'.
[2] T. H. Green was born in 1836, and was nearly twenty years younger than Jowett. Arnold Toynbee was born as late as 1852, and was nearly thirty-five years younger than Jowett. Toynbee was a 'disciple' of Green. Both men died young: Green in 1882, Toynbee in 1883.

lish themselves as authorities in their various fields of learning, but to be privileged advocates of their own private solutions.

The opposition — one of aim, rather than of method — is very clear; and it is illustrated by Davis's curious misdescription of Jowett as a man who 'taught' his pupils to become this and that and the other. All that he taught any of them was the simple duty of stretching their own minds; and the method he used was the very simple method of persuading them to work hard for an honours degree, instead of idling.

As his influence strengthened and lengthened, the contribution of Balliol to the national life became increasingly pre-eminent. It was, in fact, an all-round contribution; but, naturally, the Balliol *quota* of famous public servants seemed to top the bill. When, for example, Curzon went to Balliol in 1878, it was 'the obvious setting'. By the late 'seventies Balliol, dominated by Jowett, had become 'a famous nursery of public men'. Curzon himself, and a little earlier Milner, were perhaps the greatest of her proconsuls. But neither Milner nor Curzon, let alone the lesser men who went out from Balliol into Whitehall or India or Africa or elsewhere, had been 'taught' by Jowett to do what they did — any more than Asquith or Grey were taught by him to be statesmen, Bowen or Loreburn to be lawyers, Gore or Lang to be ecclesiastics, Morier or Spring-Rice to be diplomats, Tout to be a historian, Caird to be a philosopher, Swinburne to be a poet, and so on *ad libitum*.

It would be very stupid to think of Jowett as a kind of super-crammer of candidates for public service. It would be equally stupid to suppose that public service, in the popular sense of the phrase, was the sole or even the chief occupation of the men whom his Balliol sent out into the world. If one roughly analyses the memorable Balliol output from 1840 to 1893, the 'public men' — the civil servants, the diplomats, the politicians, the statesmen, the proconsuls, the judges and the law-lords — scarcely make up a quarter of it, if so much. The other three quarters were scholars, historians, philosophers, teachers, men of letters, journalists, working lawyers and barristers, clergymen, landowners, and men who enriched the national life in less easily classifiable ways. The quality which made Balliol men so pre-eminent, in so many different ways and callings, was not the result of specialized teaching. It was the result of accepting Jowett's simple gospel of hard, honest, brainwork. This needs to be said with emphasis.

The natural fruits of ability and hard work are careers distinguished above those of ordinary folk. Perhaps Jowett, as he grew older, tended to reckon each distinguished career as one more item in the statistical record of Balliol successes. Perhaps maintenance of the flow seemed to become an object in itself; the machine to be more important than the goods it delivered. I do not, myself, think that this was so; but that was how it looked to his detractors in other Oxford colleges, where the ever-mounting prestige of Balliol bred envy and not a little gall. As I see it, the heart of the matter lay in the living tradition of strenuous work which he succeeded in communicating to generations of Balliol undergraduates and supported by his own ceaseless example.

Many of these undergraduates, but for Jowett, would have idled through their critical three or four years at Oxford. How did he contrive to persuade them into doing what they had never intended to do? A clue is given by his advice to one rich young idler. 'You are a fool' he said to Walter Morrison. 'You must be sick of idling. It is too late for you to do much. But the class matters nothing. What does matter is the sense of power which comes from steady working.'[1]

'The sense of *power*'?

What did he mean by that phrase, which hit Morrison so hard that it changed his whole life? Not mere power over the lives of others; money and position could provide that. Nor, even, power to stimulate the minds of other people. That was Jowett's own form of power; not communicable by teaching or example. What he meant, and what Morrison knew him to mean, was power over self; power in a man to control and direct his own life, instead of drifting on the currents of fortune and self-indulgence. It was a cunning lure, skilfully used.

One is tempted, at times, to ask whether it might not have been better for Jowett and for the world of reason, if he had been forced out of Balliol in the early 'sixties and made to 'speak his mind'. But this sort of imagination is foolish. Things have been as they have been. There is no point in guessing what they might have been, if other things had not been what, in fact, they were. If this seems too dreary and unadventurous an attitude towards the course of history, one can make the more hopeful and adventurous assumption that the finger of God enters into human affairs.

It seems, at least, to have entered into Jowett's life; and to have entered into it very early. For Jowett's desire to make his young men succeed undoubtedly took its emotive impulse from his determined hatred of failure. He would have not much approved of Bernard Shaw. But he would have wholly approved of Shaw's notorious paradox: 'The greatest of evils and the worst of crimes is poverty.' He would have thought it a plain truism, not a paradox at all.

---

[1] See above, 172.

CHAPTER XVII

Friendly Witnesses

1. MILNER

Success, then, lay in the power over self acquired by work; not in the acquisition of money or of authority or of the power which money and authority give. A man must have or earn enough money to keep himself and his dependents and to fulfil the duties of his station — money counted, for those proper purposes, in the definition of success. Positions of authority and influence? Yes, these counted and counted heavily, but not for their own sake. They were worse than valueless, if they were sought only to feed a man's vanity. No aim could be more contemptible, unless it were lust after power for the sake of power — a motive which Jowett would have thought not so much contemptible as insane, if he had ever troubled to think about it at all. Authority was an objective, to be temperately pursued, only if the man who pursued it honestly believed that, given the opportunity, he would be able to do something for the general good.

By a fortunate accident two significant letters, written to Jowett at the middle point of his Mastership, escaped Miss Knight's bonfire. They happen to illustrate, in a very remarkable way, the nature of his influence upon younger men and the need which they felt of justifying themselves to him, as the Master of Balliol, not to a mere tutor. They have never been published; and since they illuminate not only Jowett's standing in the minds of his two young correspondents but the turning point in the career of one of Balliol's most illustrious sons, it seems desirable to reproduce them in full.[1]

The first letter is from Alfred Milner, explaining and justifying his decision to abandon the Bar. The second, from his friend Philip Lyttelton Gell, is a testimonial to the honesty of Milner's letter, and to the anxiety with which both friends desired Jowett's approval of Milner's

---

[1] I found these two letters among the Jowett Papers — my only find of this sort — and am grateful for permission to publish them here. In a broadcast talk about Jowett in 1947 I quoted a few fragmentary sentences from Milner's letter.

momentous, but apparently reckless, decision to change his course. Both letters were written on the same day, 2nd February 1882.

Gell was then just short of thirty, Milner just short of twenty-eight, Jowett nearing sixty-five. Gell went up to Balliol in 1872, Milner a year later. Neither of them, therefore, had been tutored by Jowett — a point to be stressed, since the letters show the nature of the influence he exerted as Master over grown men who had never had him for their tutor.

At the time when these letters were written, Gell was learning something about publishing in the firm of Cassell and Galpin. Next year, he was appointed Secretary to the Delegates of the Oxford University Press. Milner, after an impressive career as an undergraduate — a scholar of Balliol, first classes in Mods and Greats, the Hertford and Craven scholarships, and the presidency of the Oxford Union — had been elected to a fellowship at New College. He was called to the Bar in 1881, the year before he wrote the letter reproduced below.

Milner had no money except what he had managed to earn or save. He was the son of a Lancastrian physician with (so the son said) 'twice my brains' but (as Basil Williams says) 'with interests too varied to make him a success in his chosen profession', practising sometimes in Germany — for his mother was a German — sometimes in England.[1] Like so many of the great Victorians — like Jowett himself — young Milner grew up under the harsh goad of poverty. His letter to Jowett shows that he did not allow this goad to dictate the pattern of his life. There can be no doubt that, if he had continued at the Bar, he would have risen to the most lucrative heights of his profession; or that his name would have been added to the roll of great English lawyers. He made up his mind about his career upon idealistic, not financial or even (so far as he could possibly then know) practical considerations. This idealism was an essential part of his character. It had been stimulated, especially, by Arnold Toynbee, whose 'enthusiasm for social equality' (Milner's own words) had deeply impressed him. He was one of the founders, and to the end of his life a principal supporter, of Toynbee Hall — the famous University settlement in East London, named after his closest friend.

It seems, therefore, to have been Toynbee's influence rather than Jowett's, which prevailed in Milner's mind when he decided to abandon the Bar. Jowett's natural advice to him would, no doubt, have been to stick to the Law and not to go drifting into unknown, uncharted seas. Milner, whose mind was as realistic as it was idealistic, knew quite well

[1] *D.N.B.* Supplement, 1922–40.

what Jowett's advice would be; and that it would be very difficult to disregard. He made up his mind for himself, before Jowett could change it. But, having made up his mind, he wrote to Jowett a letter which reveals much both about Milner himself and about the man before whom, as before nobody else, he must justify his decision.

54 Claverton Street, S.W.[1]
Feb. 2nd '82.

Dear Mr. Jowett.

Thank you very much for sending Mr. Romdili's letter. It is of course a great satisfaction to find that my small service to Lord Dysart should be so generously appreciated, or rather over-appreciated. I will, as you wish, make any reasonable sacrifice for Lord Dysart. He certainly begins to treat me with considerable confidence and my only fear is that he may in time rely too much on my opinion. I do not think, however, that we ought to count upon the continuation of his present humour, for he is certainly erratic, not to say fickle. But I really like him and I am sorry for him, and between liking and pity I think I may be trusted to do all I can for his interest. There is the making of a good man in him, but he is physically very weak, so weak in fact that I fear both mind and character must suffer with the body.[2]

Now for myself. First let me thank you with all my heart for your incessant and valuable help of and thought for me. I really feel greatly touched by your constant kindness. In the next place I hope it will not be a great disappointment to you, when I say that I have given up all thought of making a career at the Bar. What I feel, and the feeling is decisive, is that I had rather be a poor obscure man all my life, doing the work I care for very much, than a well-to-do and possibly distinguished man doing work I scarcely care for at all. I cannot reconcile myself to the thought of living with my head in one pursuit and my heart in another. And I feel very strongly that I cannot do two things. Versatility is not my gift. If I were to stick to the Bar I should become absorbed in it, so absorbed that I could not work at any thing else, but never, I am quite certain, so absorbed that I should not regret the work I had left behind me. The only subject I am deeply interested in, is literature, especially political literature, and politics. Nobody knows, except myself, how strong that interest is, and I hardly knew [it] till I was brought face to face with the prospect of relinquishing it. And that *was* the prospect. I am not turning away from the Bar in disgust at not succeeding. What alarms me is the likelihood of succeeding, of being entirely taken up with legal work, as I know I soon should be, if I stuck to it. It was this prospect which finally clinched my wavering resolution.

You will ask me what I mean to do. Frankly speaking, I have as yet no idea. I have various openings, but I am quite determined not to commit

[1] The address was that of a cousin, named Malcolm. Milner 'boarded' with the Malcolms as a boy and again when he left Oxford in 1879.

[2] This Lord Dysart must have been the ninth Earl of Dysart, born in 1859, who succeeded his grandfather in 1878. In spite of his physical weakness as a young man, he lived to be seventy-six. I know nothing about the circumstances of Milner's association with him. It is obvious that Jowett had interested himself in the young Earl. The connecting link may have been the Hon. Lionel Arthur Tollemache, who was a scholar of Balliol in 1856 and a pupil of Jowett, and who wrote a good little book about him. The family name of the Dysarts was Tollemache; Lionel Tollemache's own branch was descended from the fourth Earl.

myself to any new career till I have looked about me. I am rising eight and twenty and cannot afford to waste time. But just to look around me for a little, while making up some leeway in my favourite studies, will not be waste of time but the best way to prevent such waste in the future. I have some advantages; improved, if not robust, health; excellent friends, many of whom I owe to you; and a sufficient supply of money. I can afford to wait, provided I continue learning — both from books and men. My friends, who have shown themselves willing to help me in the career they thought best for me, will after a little while be equally willing to do so on my new road, little as they may at first approve my striking into it. I should for instance at some future time be very glad of a Private Secretaryship to a really eminent politician. I believe I could do him efficient service. But such places of course are rare and none may ever come in my way.

For the immediate future I shall be only too glad to have no duties beyond the light ones I have at present undertaken. But of course if a good opportunity offered I should feel bound to seize it.

There are two things more I want to say for fear you should think me light-headed. The first is, I am not dazzled by the prospect of a great political career. A man without money, and at this rate I shall never have money, can scarcely hope to get into Parliament. But I am quite convinced from what I have seen myself that there are many useful careers outside Parliament, any one of which I personally should prefer even to great success at the Bar. Secondly, you must not think that I want to escape hard work. My only idea is hard work, provided my heart is in it. And with so many things in the world which I could do with zest, I cannot reconcile myself to a business which I should indeed pursue with energy, if once in it, but never with real satisfaction. So I think it better never to begin it. I have been called a year but have as yet had no work of my own, and if a brief were sent to me to-morrow I should unhesitatingly return it. I have read Law honestly. No one can reasonably blame me for stopping now. But if I were to go further and then turn back or to go on half-heartedly, it would be a failure.

In conclusion I can only once more offer you my warmest thanks. If I live, I mean to do you some credit yet. Will you forgive the length of this letter? To such a friend as you I felt that I owed a full explanation. Believe me

Yours very sincerely

Alfred Milner

What I am saying to you I have as yet only said to my most intimate friends. For many reasons I should prefer that ordinary acquaintances should think of me, for the present, as merely one of the herd of briefless barristers. But on no condition would I take a brief.

According to Basil Williams, the change of direction in Milner's life was the result of the fact that he was not getting enough work. 'Briefs were scarce, and he turned to journalism as a means of livelihood, working on the old *Pall Mall Gazette*, first under John Morley and in 1883 as assistant editor to William Thomas Stead.'[1] But Milner's own letter proves that scarcity of briefs was not the cause of the change. He

<hr>

[1] *D.N.B.*

had simply not found his vocation. Gell's letter confirms this; and it adds, in confidence to Jowett, some penetrating comments upon his friend's character.

La Belle Sauvage,
E.C.
Feb. 2nd /82

My dear Master,

I have been having lately much talk with Milner about his plans in life — a subject upon which I know well you are just now as anxious as myself; and as he is writing in answer to your letter and will probably be himself in Oxford on Sunday, I venture as his oldest and nearest friend to write you a few lines upon the matter, believing that it may be as much in your power as I know it is in your will to serve him in what may be a turning point in his life.

In the first place I would say that I do not think he is wrong in giving up the bar. It is a step that has been impending from the first. He has no taste for it. The farther he has gone the more repugnant to him has become the idea of that engrossment in purely legal work which a successful career would involve. He has said to me long ago that the one thing which he dreaded more than failure at the Bar was success — such success as has devoured the lives of Bowen and others. The interest of Law to him has never been different to what he would take in a new puzzle or a point of scholarship. It has never absorbed him, and never would; yet he is a man who never does anything well until he is absorbed — and will be always dilettante until he has work which does absorb him. What he craves and what alone will hold him are strong human interests. I think nobody in the world except myself dreams what resolute and unremitting labour, and what sacrifices of time attention and opportunity he makes when that cord is touched. It is indeed the unreality to him of all besides that makes him appear dilettante and irregular in what people have decided he *should* be working at: but all the time he remains a strenuous and active man, only that his energies are flowing away in hidden — and not always fruitless channels.

Consequently I have been gaining a growing conviction that the only barrier which would economize, accumulate and direct his energies is fixed work in which his heart can take hold. Offer him this, and you make a man of him forthwith. But he will find this neither at the Bar nor at the University — only in one of two positions — on the staff of a journal or in political life — using the latter word in a sense far wider than parliamentary life.

The former however — journalism — does not present that fixity and regularity of duties which, I feel, might order life so valuably to himself and his future. His work upon the *Pall Mall* is admirable — it was he who blew the first note from the Liberal camp upon the Jewish question — and Morley values his help exceedingly. But it is only help that Milner gives — not regular work, and the future in that direction is far from offering the needful conditions.

It is this which brings me to the point of this long letter — which is that Milner's friends would, I am firmly convinced, serve him best by saddling him with definite work of a political character. As secretary to a Royal Commission, or to a leading Politician, or to some political association, he would render most loyal and helpful service. It is true these paths lead no further; but I feel myself (in all confidence) that his future

364

depends upon securing in the *immediate* future some *routine* of employment which will relieve him perforce of the hundred minor obligations which now fritter away his energies, and recall him to the quickly fading habit of doing one thing well. His home circumstances and troubles are such that his time will always be frittered at, until the responsibilities he undertakes there, are dominated or supplanted by responsibilities yet more commanding.

His knowledge of foreign politics is unusual — the Pall Mall will testify to it. He should be Dilke's or Granville's secretary. Work out of England for a time would be good.

There is a secret also which I feel I should tell you — as it is a factor in the problem. A friend has guaranteed his expenses if he will stand for Parliament at the next election, and has already lodged £1000 for this purpose and no other. I have told no one but you and Dalhousie of this.

> With kindest regards,
> Yours very sincerely,
> P. L. Gell.

These two letters, together, give a unique picture of Jowett's standing in the minds of younger Balliol men, now growing towards their life work, at this middle point of his Mastership. Were they written with the object of soliciting his practical help? Gell certainly wrote with that object. Milner seems to have been much more concerned to have Jowett's approval of his decision, than to obtain his help in finding what he wanted. He did, in fact, find exactly what he wanted when, in 1884, George Goschen took him on as his private secretary. What part, if any, Jowett had in procuring this appointment, I do not know. Perhaps none at all. The survival of these two letters does, however, seem to indicate that Milner's future was a problem with which Jowett continued to concern himself. They survived only because he had not placed them with the letters which Martha Knight destroyed. He must have had some particular reason for putting them apart.

2. SWINBURNE

It would be difficult to imagine two men of seemingly more opposite temperaments than Swinburne and Jowett; two men less likely to discover common ground. One can see easily enough how Swinburne — who went up to Balliol in 1856 and departed, more or less under a cloud, three years later without taking his degree — seemed to Jowett a problem child of genius; how Jowett 'never ceased to follow Swinburne's career'; and how, during the poet's dangerous passage from youth to middle age, he successfully used his utmost skill to save his life and sanity. It is less easy to explain the peculiar relationship — one of close intellectual sympathy and strong personal affection — which grew up between the two men, and to which Swinburne bore his own remarkable testimony after Jowett's death.

What could be more improbable than that 'the reverend the Master of Balliol' not suffered but relished the impertinences of the author of *Poems and Ballads*? Or that the poet himself found the society of the Master more continually to his taste than that of any other man he knew? Yet so it was. The difference of age was not so very great — a mere twenty years, just the right difference for Jowett if the younger man was of the sort to disregard it. And Swinburne, even in Jowett's company, never put any restraint upon his bubbling tongue.

The oddity of Jowett's regard for Swinburne is pointed by his curious dislike of Shelley — the English poet with whom Swinburne has been usually thought to have some affinity. A letter which the Master wrote to Margot Tennant in 1887 illustrates this persistent contempt:

Why do you read such books as Godwin's *Political Justice*, which is crude and old-fashioned? If you want to study such things, read Plato's *Republic*, and Sir Thomas More's *Utopia*, and Milton's *Areopagitica*. It is a great principle in all serious reading to stick to the works of great writers. Do you really know Shakespeare well, who is a hundred times greater than Shelley or Keats? By the way, I went to see the Shelleys not long since. I was shown his books and the drowned Aeschylus which he had in his pocket when he was drowned. I think that they had better have left him where the late Mrs. Shelley left him, for it is impossible to convert him into a decent or honourable man.

Sir Edmund Gosse in his *Life of Algernon Charles Swinburne* has much to say about this strange friendship. He tells us, for instance, that it was Jowett who thought of canalizing the poet's 'intellectual high spirits' by 'concentrating his energies on the Republican movement in Italy'. He describes how Jowett went to the London house of Mr. George Howard, later the Earl of Carlisle, with some others, including Mazzini who was then an exile in England, in order to discuss 'what could be done *with* and *for* Algernon'. Mazzini 'consented to take intellectual charge of him'. The issue of this typically Jowettian contrivance, three years later, was *Songs before Sunrise* (1871).[1]

There are many amusing and revealing touches in Gosse's description of Jowett's attitude towards the oddest of Balliol's children. Some of the best came from Ingram Bywater, who succeeded Jowett (but not until

[1] Gosse, *Algernon Charles Swinburne*, 165–7. Abbott (*L. & L.*, ii, 10–11) misdates this meeting to 1871, and completely ignores its purpose. He finds it of interest only because Jowett made some notes of Mazzini's conversation. Is it possible that Jowett met Mazzini twice? Abbott's account, however, is that of a *first* meeting. He reproduces George Howard's vivid sketch of Mazzini and Jowett in conversation, Mazzini gesticulating with a cigarette, Jowett listening attentively and holding in his left hand a small fan to shield his face from the fire.

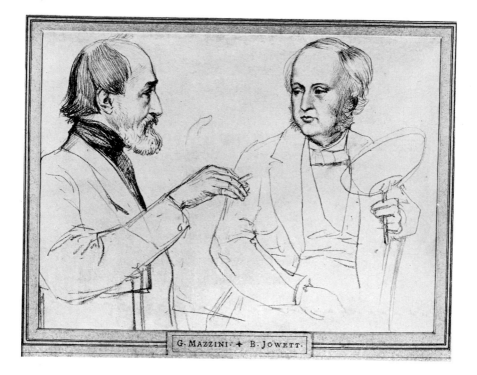

11. Mazzini talking, Jowett listening
A sketch by the Hon. G. Howard, 1868
(*Balliol*)

Jowett was dead) in the chair of Greek. Bywater told Gosse how he had once been entertaining the poet in Exeter College when 'Jowett swooped down on Swinburne, and carried him off like an indignant nurse, with a glare at Bywater as he did so'. And there is the delicious story, also provided by Bywater, of Swinburne faulting one of Jowett's translations. 'Another howler, Master!' And of the Master's meek reply, 'Thank you, Algernon, thank you!' This sounds as if it must have been *ben trovato*. But Bywater 'was present at some of the meetings which led to the second edition of Jowett's *Plato*'; and Swinburne himself 'used with pride to tell how, when once staying at Balliol, the Master asked him to go over his first version of the *Symposium* of Plato with the Greek text, and see if anything seemed to him to need correction'. He diffidently suggested, after a while, that a particular sentence might, perhaps, be differently construed. 'Mr. Jowett turned and looked at him with surprised and widened eyes: and said after a minute or so, "Of course that is the meaning. You would be a good scholar if you were to study." '[1]

Other anecdotes stem from Swinburne's behaviour at the reading-parties which Jowett continued after he had become Master. One of the best relates how the poet stayed in bed all one morning at Tummel Bridge in order to cut the opening scene of *Bothwell*, which the Master had said the day before was far too long. He produced the revised version 'triumphantly at luncheon, when Jowett dryly observed that it was three lines longer than it was before'. Another, almost better and equally well-attested, story describes how, at one of the later West Malvern reading-parties, the poet threw himself on the floor in front of Jowett with the immortal words: 'Master, I feel I have never thanked you enough for cutting four thousand lines out of *Bothwell*'; at which Jowett 'laughed and said, "Oh! I don't know, I don't know! I daresay I was quite wrong!" ' And there are glimpses of Swinburne in moods of inimitable gaiety, as when at Tummel Bridge he was 'the life and the soul of the party, enlivening the evenings with paradoxes and hyperboles and recitations of Mrs. Gamp'.[2]

These fragmentary recollections, apocryphal or not, give brightness to the picture of Jowett as well as to that of Swinburne. They are taken up into Gosse's careful judgment of what the Master did for the poet. Writing of Swinburne's 'middle years' Gosse says:

In this comparative isolation the friendship of Jowett was of the highest value to him. During these years, which were frequently painful, the great Master of Balliol preserved an influence that was serenely beneficial over

[1] This story is told by Swinburne himself in his *Recollections of Professor Jowett*, as well as by Gosse.
[2] *D.N.B.* (article by Gosse). Confirmed by Harrison (*L. & L.*, ii, 34).

the most wayward and the most brilliant of his old pupils. Visits to Oxford, protracted sojournings in Cornwall, at Holmwood,[1] and — through successive autumns — in Scotland, long walks and long talks in which all came out that was best in the oddly-assorted couple, these more than anything carried Swinburne across the reefs of a dangerous and critical time. Jowett displayed a wonderful tact in dealing with his guest, cajoling, calming, interesting him and even submitting his own translations to his disciple's judgment.

The only better tribute to Jowett's altruistic catholicity and wisdom was that written by Swinburne himself from his seclusion at Putney under the care of Watts-Dunton, when all but intellectual passion was spent and gone. His *Recollections of Professor Jowett* are to be found in the *Studies of Prose and Poetry*, published in 1894. They have a certain slightness of content rather unsuited to the pontifical tone which the utterances from Putney tended to assume. But they are obviously based upon genuine admiration; and the slightness was just what was needed to correct the solemnity of the obituary notices. Moreover, the picture of Jowett which they convey is the only picture drawn of him by a man of genius.

Swinburne begins with a conventional apology for offering 'the modest reminiscences of one to whom the Master of Balliol was officially a stranger, and Mr. Jowett was an honoured and valued friend'. But his reminiscences quickly come alive:

For my own part, I always think of him as he was wont to show himself in the open air during the course of a long walk and a long talk, intermittent and informal and discursive and irregular to the last and most desirable degree. The perfect freedom, the quaint and positive independence, of his views on character and his outlook on letters would have given interest to the conversation of a far less distinguished man.

He goes on to recall some of Jowett's judgments concerning a number of English writers. One of these is peculiarly interesting:

Tennyson, Browning and Carlyle were all still among us when I once happened to ask him whom he thought the first of living English writers. He hesitated for a minute or so, and then replied, 'If Dickens were alive I shouldn't hesitate.' As it was, he gave of course the first place to Tennyson, and admitted that he must reluctantly give the second to Carlyle.

That was a surprising judgment; for Jowett disliked and distrusted Carlyle — whom Swinburne himself called a 'perverse and sinister and splendid genius' — at least as much as Carlyle disliked and distrusted Jowett. On some later occasion he told Swinburne that 'no writer had done so much harm to young men as the preacher of tyranny and the

[1] Holmwood, or Holm Wood, was a house near Henley, which Admiral Swinburne, the poet's father, took on lease. It had belonged, curiously enough, to Maria Josepha, a former Lady Stanley of Alderley, the friend of Gibbon.

apologist of cruelty'. Yet, walking and talking with Swinburne, he put Carlyle into the second place of living English writers. It must be supposed that he was giving Carlyle credit for his stylistic impact — intolerable now, but irresistible then — and passing no judgment upon his message. The message, he said to Swinburne in a later walk, seemed to him abominable.

Much of these walking conversations was 'literary' conversation. But other matters kept breaking in upon Swinburne's memory. In his placid Putney retreat the poet of passion recalled Jowett's asceticism. He could still not quite agree with it, but he respected it and he perceived something of the peculiar sensibility which created this protective crust.

Upon self-indulgence and sensuality he may have been inclined to pass sentence in a tone or spirit so austere as to prove, had other evidence been wanting, how perfectly and how naturally Spartan was his own devotion to a purely and exclusively intellectual and moral line of life and scheme of thought. And yet he had for the most affected of sensualists and the most pretentious of profligates a sort of tender or admiring weakness . . . which does not as usual admit of the obvious explanation that he was himself a writer of bad verses. The one point on which I can understand or imagine that he should ever have felt himself in touch with Byron was about the very last that might have been expected from a studious and philosophic man of books and cloisters.

I never knew a man of better nerve: and I have known Richard Burton. The physical energy with which he would press up a hill-side or a mountain-side — Malvern or Schehallion — was very agreeable and admirable to witness: but twice at least during a week's winter excursion in Cornwall I knew, and had reason to know, what it was to feel nervous: for he would follow along the broken rampart of a ruined castle, and stand without any touch of support at the edge of a magnificent precipice, as though he had been a younger man bred up from boyhood to the scaling of cliffs and the breasting of breakers.

His love of nature, I should say, was temperate but genuine; certainly genuine, but decidedly temperate. The unique and incomparable sublimity of loveliness which distinguishes the serpentine rocks and cliffs and slopes and platforms of Kynance Cove from any other possible presentation of an earthly paradise could not and did not fail to excite his admiring notice: but I doubt if he recognized that there could be nothing like it in the world. At Tintagel, and again at St. Michael's Mount, I noticed that his energetic perseverance in the rough and steep ascent was more remarkable, and to himself apparently more pleasurable, than his enjoyment of the glorious outlook so sturdily and so hardily attained.

After an excursus concerned with Jowett's resemblance, in this and other ways, to Dr. Johnson, with the fact that Jowett's favourite Shakespearean play was *The Merry Wives of Windsor*, and with Jowett's project for a Children's Bible, Swinburne settled back to complete his portrait. It troubled him much that Jowett was a kind of superior schoolmaster; and this led him to liberate his own special hatreds by a sudden outburst of the ferocious invective in which he had always excelled:

Even in Mr. Jowett the Master of Balliol would occasionally, though rarely, break out and rise to the surface 'when there was no need of such vanity'. But these slips or descents from the natural man into the professional pedagogue were admirably rare: and even if it cannot be confidently affirmed that his bright and brave intelligence was always wholly unaffected by the foggy damp of Oxonian atmosphere, it is certainly undeniable that the affection was never so serious as to make it possible for the most malignant imbecile to compare or to confound him with such morally and spiritually typical and unmistakable apes of the Dead Sea as Mark Pattison, or such renascent blossoms of the Italian renascence as the Platonic amorist of blue-breeched gondoliers who is now in Aretino's bosom. The cult of the calamus, as expounded by Mr. Addington Symonds to his fellow-calamites, would have found no acceptance or tolerance with the translator of Plato.[1]

Extravagant as it is, the outburst does help to point, by contrast, the qualities in Jowett which, for Swinburne, saved him from pedagoguery: his conception of scholarship as a tool, not as an end in itself, and his dislike of fine writing for writing's sake. But the violence of the invective is really shocking; Mark Pattison had been dead nine years, J. A. Symonds some six or seven months. For the moment the Putney recluse had slipped back into the past; the objects of his hatred were once more alive in his passionate and unrelenting mind.

So, also, his walks and talks with Jowett, twenty years gone, came as vividly to his memory as if they had happened yesterday. The opinions uttered on these occasions were, it would seem and as one would expect, mostly Swinburne's. But much of Jowett comes through the egotistical reporting: his literary conservatism; his masterly knowledge of Shakespeare (though he 'disclaimed the honour of being what he really sometimes seemed to be, a living concordance to Shakespeare'); his ignorance of Dante; his odd contempt for Euripides (which Swinburne shared to the extent of calling Euripides 'the clumsiest of botchers that ever floundered through his work as a dramatist'); his somewhat cool appreciation of Browning; his admiration of Dr. Johnson (admitting 'with a smile of satisfaction that he was or that he might be' a living concordance to Boswell[2]). If one allows for Swinburne's interest in himself — and that is easy to do — treating him rather as one treats an

[1] *Calamus* means, literally, a reed-pen; and *calamite* must be supposed to mean a user of a pen. But Swinburne evidently meant the reader to think of the word *catamite*.

[2] 'And year after year did he renew the promise to fulfil his project and redeem his engagement to undertake the vindication of Boswell as genius and as man.' But Jowett lived long before the discovery and publication of Boswell's private papers. He would, I imagine, have had considerably to revise his idea of the kind of man Boswell was.

interviewer of genius whose questions take up more room than the answers, his portrait nevertheless gives us much of Jowett that can be found nowhere else.

Here is the concluding passage, which begins with a picture of the romantic Poet talking plain sense to the prosaic Master.

Few men, I should say, whose line of life lay so far apart from a naturalist's or a poet's, can ever have loved nature and poetry better; after the temperate though very real and serious fashion which I have already tried to define or to indicate; but his perception or recollection of the influences of nature upon poetry in particular instances was hardly always accurate. We were returning from a walk across and above the magnificent valley of the Spey, when I remarked on the likeness or kinship of the scenery about us to the poetry of Wordsworth, and he rejoined that he could not associate Wordsworth's poetry with a country which had no lakes in it; forgetting how little of water and how much of mountain or hillside there is in that poet's habitual and representative landscape: so little of lakes and so much of the hill-tops that but for a senseless nickname we might hardly remember that his life had been spent beside the waters on which some of his finest verses commemorate the perennially happy results of his skating as a boy.

Of the average academic or collegiate one is inclined to think that, in Rossetti's accurate phrase, 'he dies not — never having lived — but ceases': of Mr. Jowett it is almost impossible at first to think as dead. I, at any rate, never found it harder, if so hard, to realize the death of any one. There was about him a simple and spontaneous force of fresh and various vitality, of happy and natural and wellnigh sleepless energy, which seemed not so much to defy extinction as to deride it. 'He laboured, so must we', says Ben Jonson of Plato in a noble little book which I had the pleasure of introducing to Mr. Jowett's appreciative acquaintance; and assuredly no man ever lived closer up to that standard of active and studious life than the translator of Plato. But this living energy, this natural force of will and action, was coloured and suffused and trans-figured by so rare a quality of goodness, of kindness, of simple and noble amiability, that the intellectual side of his nature is neither the first nor the last side on which the loving and mourning memory of any one ever admitted to his friendship can feel inclined or be expected to dwell.

Swinburne was unaware that his friendship with the Master of Balliol flowered on the very stock of pedagoguery. There was an ulterior motive behind the invitation to Tummel Bridge and the walks and talks there and elsewhere: the motive that 'something must be done *with* and *for* Algernon'. But Jowett's sure instinct told him that the only hope lay in meeting Algernon on Algernon's own ground, as equal with equal. His hortatory weapons must be left hanging in the tutorial cupboard.

Swinburne would have had a little experience of these weapons when he was an undergraduate, though his tutor was wise enough to make the least possible use of them. Just before his visit to Tummel Bridge in 1871 he wrote to Frederick Locker that he was well enough to go 'on my promised visit to the Master of Balliol — (who would have told me so

10 years ago when I was rusticated and all but expelled?)'. Before long the poet was speaking proudly of 'my friend, and former tutor Mr. Jowett, the Oxford Professor of Greek and Master of the leading College there'.[1]

It was Jowett's most astonishing achievement, for Swinburne never, to the end of his life, forgave Oxford for his 'total and scandalous failure' as an undergraduate.[2] Moreover, he was a voluble master of his ground — that is to say, almost the whole field of post-renaissance European letters — and had little use for a companion, however reverend and classically equipped, who could not keep pace with him. Jowett managed to keep pace so well that Swinburne, recalling their conversations after his distinguished friend's death, even recalled some of his friend's remarks in the process of recalling his own.

The pedagogic aim would have failed if there had been no inner sympathy, which bridged not so much the difference of age, as the differences of temperament, circumstance and genius. One cannot define this kind of mutual understanding. There was a rebel inside Jowett; there was a scholar inside Swinburne; and each of them was set apart from the ordinary run of men. Perhaps these facts point towards the curious harmony which enabled Jowett not only to win Swinburne's confidence and devotion, but to be — and not merely to play the part of being — his friend.

[1] *Letters of Algernon Charles Swinburne*, i, 101 and 144.
[2] *Life of A. C. S.*, 64, 213.

CHAPTER XVIII

The Gentle Art of Making Enemies

I. THE 'TOUCH OF IRON'

Yet neither Milner nor Swinburne, nor Abbott in his 'story of the Mastership', nor all of them together, enable us to see the Master of Balliol as a whole man. If it were possible to make a final analysis, it might be agreed that Swinburne's phrase 'simple and noble amiability' went to the root of his character. But it did not seem so to his opponents or enemies, or even always so to his friends. Nor did Jowett see himself as an amiable man. He would not have been at all pleased to imagine an obituary which praised him for 'simple' amiability, however 'noble'. That, he might have wryly reflected, was what came of trying to save genius from destroying itself.

Campbell, who knew Jowett much longer and more shrewdly than Abbott and did not love him less, is at pains not to conceal his less amiable side, as it developed after the repulse from the Mastership and during his years in the wilderness. At the beginning of an acute and candid character-sketch of Jowett, at about the age of fifty, he observes that he was always

reviewing his own life and bent on beginning anew from within. To one who asked, 'Can a man improve himself after forty?' he replied, 'I am long past forty, and I mean to improve myself pretty considerably, I can tell you!'

He uses this very Jowettian utterance to support his opinion that Jowett's 'seemingly abstract observations were really autobiographical'.

He continues:

The trials to which he had been subjected, and the effort involved in acting as if they were not, had given to his mental constitution the touch of iron. *To be independent of all persons*, never to worry, to listen more to what his enemies said of him than to his friends, to find a *modus vivendi* with everybody, and above all 'never quarrel', were among the rules he laid down for himself. He perceived that he had resented some things too keenly, and that his opinions of persons and their acts had been too much influenced by his own feelings; also that he had been too free and open in criticizing persons to one another.

373

To this passage Campbell appends an important footnote:

What did his enemies say? I may be permitted here to quote an *advocatus diaboli* who shall be nameless: 'With a singleness of mind which is more than merely Christian, he has an element of bitterness, which nothing but his solitary character can have prevented him from struggling against and which makes it notoriously difficult for most of his *equals in age* to get on with him. With all his goodness he is a tyrant and careless of giving pain, or rather can't help giving it.'

Again, writing of Jowett's attitude to his friends, Campbell insists that it was often hard for them to live up to.

A friendship, once established, meant for him that his friend should have no rest while any fault remained unreproved, any defect uncorrected. And if that friend's position in life were such as to give opportunities for influence or distinction, Jowett was never weary of inciting to fresh exertions, nor would desist from the attempt because of advancing age, although he was well aware that 'miracles are only wrought upon the young'.

The 'irrepressible Mentor' might retire for a space, as in his correspondence with Stanley — and 'perhaps there never was an equal friendship more complete than that between him and Stanley' — but never finally retired.

Hence it resulted that a letter of consolation from him, as a friend remarks, 'was not only the greatest comfort, but seemed to have the effect of making one pull oneself together'.

In Balliol itself the achievement of his dearest ambition soon began to seem to Jowett a hollow success. Let Campbell come again into the witness-box. Though he is speaking immediately of the three years before Jowett succeeded to the Mastership, what he says is equally true of the early Mastership, as Jowett's own confession to Florence Nightingale will be seen to prove. But here, first, is Campbell:

From 1867 onwards Jowett held the College in his hand, and he was practically Master. Still his ends could not be effected without a certain amount of friction. His views were steadily opposed by a small but compact minority; nor were his followers in Balliol the sort of persons who could be absolutely reckoned on to vote mechanically in his favour. They were men of active intellects and independent minds, who shared his liberal principles, but did not therefore accept his *fiat* on every practical question. The continual need of persuasion and management grew more and more distasteful to him; it was the one crook in his lot; and it may be that the painfulness of the position in part accounted for what seemed to his younger colleagues the undue vehemence with which he sometimes pressed his advantages. Long-pent-up forces are impetuous when they find an outlet, and impetuosity, although mostly held under firm control, and often unsuspected, was one of his native characteristics.

12. 'The touch of iron'
The painting by G. F. Watts, dated 1889
(*Balliol*)

It did not take long for the new Master to discover the impediments to what Green had described in advance as a '*régime* of strong personal government'. The first exhilaration of finding himself in control of the college he had done so much to fashion very soon began to wane. In February 1872, when he had been Master for less than eighteen months, he wrote to Florence Nightingale:

I feel more difficulty about the College than I used to do. All the mechanical part is pretty well in order; the dinners are good, and the College servants are well in hand. But I feel that men's characters are not easily trained or formed, and I have not so much opportunity of influencing them as I had when I was only a Tutor. I can avoid some of the mistakes of Dr. Arnold, but I can't do what he did. I must go on hoping that I may some day accomplish more; at present the external measure of success is beyond the real success.

That was a truthful, objective judgment. He did, in the end, 'accomplish more'. But he had first to learn that in becoming Master he had ceased to be a tutor; and that he must now trust others to do what he had hitherto done himself. This was the first condition of making his Mastership a success. Of all lessons it was the hardest. It was a cruel disillusionment to find that his new position cut him off from the power of directly influencing the young Balliol intake. It was a disappointment, too, that even in the general government of the college he was not always able to have his way. It was another disappointment to discover that he was more than ever debarred from 'speaking his mind' upon religious and theological matters.

Had he not foreseen and discounted these inevitable consequences? No doubt, in a way, he had done so. But there is a world of difference between the anticipation of drawbacks to a greatly desired office and the realization of the drawbacks once the ambition has been fulfilled. And Jowett 'married to Balliol' had no private life in which he could find comfort or refreshment — no wife, no children, no hobby except Plato, no *confidante* except Florence Nightingale. He had to face and conquer a sense of frustration all the more painful because it was the result of his being what he had ardently wished to become. The struggle was silent. The mask of serenity — only it was more than a mask, for it expressed his inner, undefeated will — was seldom, if ever, allowed to fall. But the 'touch of iron' hardened.

By the middle of the 'seventies the struggle was over, or as nearly over as it could be before the onset of old age. There was a compromise visible in the outward appearance well described by the first of the enemies, whose evidence will now be called.

2. DR. JENKINSON

The first hostile witness is W. H. Mallock, whose view of Jowett is conveyed in *The New Republic* — that witty and still wonderfully readable imagination of 'culture, faith, and philosophy in an English country house', where a party of celebrated people is assembled and given what their host describes as a 'menu' of conversational topics for the weekend. The date is half-way through the eighteen-seventies.

Among the principal guests, disguised by other names, are Jowett (Dr. Jenkinson), Huxley (Mr. Storks), Tyndall (Professor Stockton), Ruskin (Mr. Herbert), Matthew Arnold (Mr. Luke), Walter Pater (Mr. Rose), Carlyle (Donald Gordon), Mrs. Mark Pattison (Lady Grace). Some of the caricatures are insipid, but the best are so good that they compete with, rather than mimic, the originals. 'Mr. Rose' said a contemporary reviewer 'is worth gold, and so too is Mr. Luke; while there are touches in the Jenkinson-Jowett that are, in their way, as neat as anything of the sort in modern letters.'

Mallock went up to Balliol in 1869, won the Newdigate, but did not distinguish himself in the schools. He went down in 1874. Jowett 'thought little of him, regarding him as a mere dilettante'. Mallock, for his part, despised the temper of Jowett's religious liberalism; the *New Republic* was, it has been said, written to 'demonstrate the impossible position of undogmatic belief'. He died in 1923. 'On his death-bed he accepted the ministrations of the Roman Catholic Church.'[1]

His portrayal of Jowett is, therefore, anything but sympathetic. Indeed, it was very maliciously intended. Yet a recurring and perplexing note of respect somehow queers the intention.

Take, for example, Mallock's principal *tour de force* — the Sunday sermon delivered by Dr. Jenkinson on the stage of his host's private theatre. Every farcical device is used to ensure that Jenkinson shall appear ridiculous. He has 'read the service' from the stalls of the theatre 'in a simple, earnest voice' inaudible to most of his unwilling, half atheistic, congregation; and to the sad confusion of pious Lady Ambrose, who has tried to follow the service in her prayer-book. The reason for her confusion 'was not far to seek. The Doctor was opening the proceedings' with a 'passage from the Koran, which he had once designed to use in Westminster Abbey as the text of a missionary sermon'. This was followed by 'the Confession, the Absolution, and a number of other selections from the English morning service, omitting,

[1] A. Cochrane, article on Mallock in the *D.N.B.*

however, the Creed' and concluding 'with a short prayer of St. Francis Xavier's'.

Then, Dr. Jenkinson, grateful for being told in time that he could not be heard from his position in the stalls, readily consented to deliver his sermon from the stage:

> In a few moments the curtain was observed to twitch and tremble; two or three abortive pulls were evidently being made; and at last Faust and the young witch rapidly rolled up, and discovered first the feet and legs, and then the entire person of Doctor Jenkinson, standing in the middle of a gorge in the Indian Caucasus — the remains of a presentation of *Prometheus Bound* which had taken place last February.

Having got Jenkinson into this ludicrous situation, Mallock at once undoes the effect by a vivid little picture of Jowett:

> The Doctor was not a man to be abashed by incongruities. He looked about him for a moment: he slightly raised his eyebrows, and then, without the least discomposure, and in a clear incisive voice, began. . . .

The sermon which follows is meant to be a parody, a *reductio ad absurdum* of Jowett's 'undogmatic belief'. But the parody does not come off. It is not so much a parody as a rather flat statement of the common ground between all 'seekers after God'. It is not sufficiently absurd to justify the farcical setting. Mallock himself must have realized this and felt that some extra spice was necessary. For he makes Jenkinson end his sermon with

> certain memorable words spoken by Christ himself, though unfortunately not to be found in the Gospels, but preserved to us by Clement of Alexandria. 'The Lord', Clement tells us, 'being asked when His kingdom should come, said, When two shall be one, and that which is without as that which is within, and the male with the female — neither male nor female.'

This was hitting below the belt. The covert allusion to Jowett's lack of masculine characteristics was in the nastiest possible taste; and the suggestion that ambiguity of sex was the basis of his religious opinions was a contemptible resort to the meanest kind of controversial weapon.

But Mallock had no fighting scruples. When he introduced Dr. Jenkinson to the readers of *The New Republic* he flavoured the introduction with a peculiarly unpleasing innuendo. Nevertheless, the introduction, like the episode of the sermon, does give a vivid picture of Jowett's external appearance, as it looked to a clever young man who disliked him, at the point of transition from middle age to the beginning of old age. The senile aspect is, of course, over stressed.

The stage must be set. *The New Republic* begins with the arrival of

377

Robert Leslie, an old friend of his host, Otho Laurence.[1] Leslie is the last and least of the guests to arrive. He is quickly briefed by Laurence over a few of his fellow-guests, particularly Jenkinson:

Then we have Dr. Jenkinson, the great Broad-church divine who thinks that Christianity is not dead, but changed by himself and his followers in the twinkling of an eye.

To which Leslie replies that he has met Dr. Jenkinson, just before he went abroad, 'at a great dinner given by Baron Isaacs, in honour of his horse having won the Derby'. The reader is to take Dr. Jenkinson as a worldly-minded ecclesiastic, owning no real religious or other principles, cultivating the society of a wealthy Jew — in short, an impostor on the make.

Then Leslie, having changed for dinner, joins the company in the drawing room. His eye is at once caught by a handsome woman with a charming voice, who is talking with a tall distinguished-looking young man.[2] Hovering on the edge of their *tête-à-tête* is a third person 'dropping in a word or two at intervals', whom Leslie recognizes as

the celebrated Dr. Jenkinson — still full of vigour, though his hair was silvery — the sharp and restless sparkle of whose eyes, strangely joined with the most benevolent of smiles, Leslie remembered to have noticed at Baron Isaacs' festival.

Approached at this moment by his host, with further information about the members of the house-party, Leslie says: 'Dr. Jenkinson is the only one I know and, naturally enough, he forgets me.'

Twice, therefore, in the first fourteen pages we are given what might be called the Baron Isaacs *motif*; a little enlarged the second time by the suggestion that Dr. Jenkinson is the kind of snob who forgets young acquaintances. But this *motif* is afterwards completely dropped. Why, then, was it used at all? Simply to create prejudice, to persuade the reader that Dr. Jenkinson, for all his silvery hair and sharp eyes and benevolent smile, is a moral as well as an intellectual humbug. All the mechanical tricks in Mallock's box are afterwards used in turn, whenever Dr. Jenkinson is given a speaking part, to reinforce this impression of fundamental dishonesty. Yet they fail to do so. There is something in Dr. Jenkinson which contradicts his creator's obviously venomous purpose.

The reason for Mallock's failure to achieve his purpose — nearly as

[1] Leslie was said to be a 'Mr. Hardinge'. But there were several Mr. Hardinges. None of them seems quite to fit. And who was 'Laurence'? Can he have been a wishful self-projection of Mallock himself? If so, Leslie might be a projection of W. M. Hardinge, novelist and poet, who was his younger contemporary at Balliol?

[2] They are 'Lady Ambrose' and 'Lord Allen'; I do not know whom they were intended to represent.

he comes to doing so — is curiously simple. Dr. Jenkinson is too *like* his prototype. In drawing him Mallock had to be at pains to make him, in his appearance and his manner of conversation and preaching, an outwardly convincing replica of Jowett. Because of Mallock's accuracy in drawing this superficial likeness of a man he detested and wished to ridicule, enough of the real man is given to make the caricature evidently false.

The prototype, whose external image is so vividly described by Mallock, certainly had the power of exciting enmity. In his dealings with people whom he distrusted, or whom he thought old enough to know better than to behave as they did, Jowett was apt to be ruthless. If that meant giving pain, then he was careless of the pain; grown men should not be sentimental about pain. It was never his *object* to inflict pain; and he was capable of a gentleness towards suffering beyond the usual power of men — 'kindness itself — as tender and solicitous as a woman' said Edwin Harrison, whom he nursed through a serious illness at West Malvern.[1] What he detested was the attitude which erects pain, whether of body or mind, into the stature of an irresistible enemy.

3. ROSE *v.* JENKINSON

Neither Jowett nor his biographers took any notice of Dr. Jenkinson. Walter Pater, on the other hand, was deeply hurt by Mr. Rose. In the study of Pater, which he contributed to the English Men of Letters series, Arthur Benson rightly protested against the falsity and bad taste of Mallock's 'disagreeable innuendoes'. But Benson did not protest against the antagonism between Rose and Jenkinson which is one of *The New Republic*'s deliberate *motifs*. ' "All this is very poor stuff — *very* poor stuff," murmured Dr. Jenkinson, whose face had become gradually the very picture of crossness' as he listened to Mr. Rose languidly monopolizing the conversation at the dinner-table.

Far from protesting, Benson gave his own account of this antagonism. It does not correspond with Mallock's. But it is peculiarly interesting, since it is founded upon contemporary gossip and conveys an opinion of Jowett which is nowhere else quite so plainly exhibited.[2] It provides a valuable link between Mallock's view and the yet more hostile view which will be reproduced in the next part of the present chapter.

Edmund Gosse, in the *Dictionary of National Biography*, tells us that

[1] *L. & L.*, ii, 70.
[2] A. C. Benson, *Walter Pater*, 54–8.

Pater was 'coached' by Jowett, who prophesied that he 'would come to great eminence'.[1] Gosse adds that

some years afterwards there was an estrangement between Jowett and Pater, but this was removed in the last year of the life of each, and the master of Balliol was among those who congratulated Pater most cordially on his *Plato and Platonism*.

Benson repeats this story, without adding anything to it, and then continues:

It has even been said that Jowett took up a line of definite opposition to Pater, and used his influence to prevent his obtaining University work and appointments. It is not impossible that this was the case.

No evidence whatever is given — or, so far as I know, has ever been given — to support this disagreeable statement. Benson uses it merely as a peg on which to hang his own interpretation of Jowett's character.

Jowett, in spite of his genius, in spite of his liberality of view and his deliberate tolerance, was undoubtedly an opportunist. He was not exactly guided by the trend of public opinion, but he took care not to back men or measures unless he would be likely to have the support of a strong section of the community, or at least conceived it possible that his line would eventually be endorsed by public opinion. Thus his religious position was based not on the fact that he wished to be in opposition to popular orthodoxy, but that he followed an enlightened line, with a belief that, in the long-run, the best intelligence of the country would adopt similar views. That this is not an over-statement is clear from Jowett's *Life*, where he is revealed as a far more liberal, even destructive critic of popular religion than he allowed to appear in either his writings or public utterances.

Cloudiness of thought pervades this seemingly perspicuous judgment. For Benson wrote *currente calamo*, two hours every afternoon; he seldom stopped to read critically what had run off his pen. The passage is valuable, nevertheless. It is evidence of what a number of people in Cambridge, not to speak of Oxford, thought and said about Jowett: that he was an opportunist, as well as an unscrupulous enemy. It helps to fill out the emptiness of Dr. Jenkinson. And Benson's instinct takes him at once to the ground which Mallock had unsuccessfully tried to exploit — the 'religious' ground.

What would this have had to do with the 'estrangement' between Jowett and Pater? One might suppose, ignorantly, nothing. And Benson, with his inconsequent pen, all but drops the topic in his next paragraph.

Probably Jowett either identified Pater with the advanced aesthetic school, or supposed that at all events his teaching was adapted to

[1] Pater of course, was not one of Jowett's Balliol pupils. He was up at Queen's from 1858 to 1862; he became a fellow of Brasenose in 1865.

strengthen a species of Hedonism, or modern Paganism, which was alien to the spirit of the age. Or possibly he was alarmed at the mental and moral attitude with which Pater was publicly credited, owing in considerable measure to the appearance of the *New Republic* — in which he himself was pilloried as the representative of advanced religious liberalism — and thought that on public grounds he must combat the accredited leaders of a movement which was certainly unfashionable, and which was regarded with suspicion by men of practical minds. Whatever his motives were, he certainly meant to make it plain that he did not desire to see the supposed exponents of the aesthetic philosophy holding office in the University.

What was 'not impossible' on page 54 has become 'certainly' on page 55 of Benson's essay. Yet not a single shred of evidence has been given. The reader still knows nothing at all about the nature of what Gosse called the 'estrangement', and Benson the 'misunderstanding', between the older and the younger man; and nothing about the steps which Jowett is 'said' to have taken to block Pater's advancement. What Benson gives are 'probablys' and 'possiblys', turned at once into certainties. Satisfied with these, he rebukes the Master of Balliol:

One feels that Jowett, with his talent for frank remonstrance, had better have employed direct rather than indirect methods; but the fact remains that he not only disliked the tendency of Pater's thought, but endeavoured, by means that are invariably ineffectual, to subvert his influence.

Gossip has now not only become a report of fact but has acquired a still more sinister look. Jowett was not only determined to shut Pater out of University appointments; he was attempting, albeit ineffectually, 'to subvert his influence'.

Benson then comes to his idea of what Pater thought about Jowett. He quotes nothing that Pater said or wrote; cites no authority. We have simply to take what he says, without any means of knowing how much of it was Pater and how much of it was Benson.

It is not difficult to arrive at Pater's view of Jowett; he regarded his qualities, both administrative and mental, with a considerable degree of admiration. He half envied and was half amused by the skilful way in which Jowett contrived, taught by adversity and opposition, to harmonize advanced religious views with popular conceptions, and to subordinate philosophical speculation to practical effectiveness. He considered him an excellent specimen of the best kind of virtuous sophist.

After Jowett's death, and just before his own, Pater wrote in a letter to Campbell some recollections of the young Balliol tutor who

seemed to have taken the measure not merely of all opinions, but of all possible ones, and to have put the last refinements on literary expression. The charm of that was enhanced by a certain mystery about his own philosophic and other opinions.

Benson cites this letter as if it confirmed his report of Pater's view. One has to look for the confirmation in the empty spaces between the lines.

Benson himself seems to have become aware, in the very act of transcribing it, that this letter failed to bear out what he had just written. For he continues:

At the same time Pater had no sort of inner sympathy with Jowett's position as a priest of the Anglican Church, considering the opinions on the subject of Christian doctrine which he held, or which Pater believed him to hold. There is practically no doubt that in the review of *Robert Elsmere* which Pater contributed to the *Guardian*, he had Jowett in his mind in the following passage: 'Of course, a man such as Robert Elsmere came to be ought not to be a clergyman of the Anglican Church. The priest is still, and will, we think, remain, one of the necessary types of humanity; and he is untrue to his type, unless, with whatever inevitable doubts in this doubting age, he feels, on the whole, the preponderance in it of those influences which make for faith. . . . We have little patience with those liberal clergy who dwell on nothing else than the difficulties of faith and the propriety of concession to the opposite force.'

Except that it was Pater who wrote it, there is nothing formidable in this criticism of the 'broad churchmen'. It dealt unfairly with them; if it was aimed at Jowett, it mis-stated Jowett's position. Far from 'dwelling on nothing else than the difficulties of faith' Jowett sought to reconcile faith with reason. He was, in consequence, always under the easy accusation of being a 'negative' or a 'destructive' thinker from those who thought that faith, though above reason, was in danger from it. This charge had lain against him ever since his attempt to discuss the doctrine of the Atonement in rational language. But what was Pater, that he should so resurrect it in 1888, when *Robert Elsmere* was published? If any man ever put himself into an equivocal position, surely Pater did so, in his review of Mrs. Humphry Ward's novel.

In this review Pater wrote as if he were himself an orthodox believer. But his position was, to say the least, not less ambiguous — indeed it was much more ambiguous — than that of the 'liberal clergy' whom he denounced. A hint that he was not unaware of this ambiguity is, perhaps, given by his surprising use of the *cliché*: 'We have little patience with. . . .' That kind of phrase was abhorrent to Pater's 'jewelled' style. He used it because, as *clichés* do, it covered a gap in his own thinking; or, at least, a gap in the disclosure of his own thinking to the readers of *The Guardian*.

Pater's own religious views are matter for guess-work. The utmost that Benson could find to say was that 'he came both to feel and to express a deep and sincere sympathy with the Christian point of view'.[1] He went, quite often, to church services. Mallock, in *The New Republic*, made some not wholly unfair fun of this, in one of the speeches he put into the languid mouth of Mr. Rose:

I every now and then when I am in the weary mood for it, attend the services of our English Ritualists, and I admire their churches very much indeed. In some places the whole thing is really managed with surprising skill. The dim religious twilight, fragrant with the smoke of incense; the tangled roofs . . . ; the tapers, the high altar, and the strange intonation of the priests, all produce a curious old-world effect, and seem to unite one with things that have been long dead. Indeed, it all seems to me far more a part of the past than the services of the Catholics.

That is Mallock, the precocious young satirist, ridiculing Pater. Yet, with allowance for the touch of exaggeration, Pater might well be supposed to have said that sort of thing. For he, like Rose, enjoyed the savour of ritual, even if he had lost belief in the literal truth of the 'sacred story' behind it. Had he, in fact, lost this belief? That is a question to which he never gave an open answer. He was in two minds about it. He did not know what he believed, or whether he believed in anything except the power of a limited and finished beauty to touch his senses and command a temporary surrender.

His attitude towards the priesthood, in the *Robert Elsmere* review, reveals a wish for unambiguous but vicarious surrender. The priest must be the complete slave of his church; if he has any doubts he must banish them; if he cannot do so, and continues to be a priest, he is a dishonest man. Just so he might have written if, in a previous incarnation, he had taken the side (say) of the orthodox Egyptian priesthood against the heretic Pharaoh Akhnaten. His attitude towards the Anglican priesthood of his own day was that of a man fascinated by the trappings of a religion in which he had ceased to have any real belief.

It is seldom remembered that Keble 'walked and talked much with' Pater when Pater was a boy 'and encouraged him in his religious aspirations'; that Pater's first design was to be a clergyman, his second to be a Unitarian minister — a notion which he seems not to have finally discarded until he was half-way through his twenties. Criticizing *Robert Elsmere*, he was really applauding himself for his own courage and independence. At the same time he took a whack at Jowett along with everybody else who had not found it possible to run, as easily as he did, both with the hounds and the hare.

Unperturbed by any idea that Pater's view, as expressed in his critique of *Robert Elsmere*, might be open to criticism, Benson continued his equable way:

[1] *Walter Pater*, 199.

The truth is that the two temperaments were radically opposed, though they had certain philosophical interests in common. At bottom Jowett was a man of the world, and valued effectiveness above most qualifications; while Pater set no particular value upon administrative energy. Jowett was indifferent to art, except in so far as it ministered to agreeable social intercourse;[1] with Pater art provided what were the deepest and most sacred experiences of his life. Not until Pater became a growing power in the literary and artistic world, not until it became clear that he had no practical sympathy with the exponents of a bastard aestheticism, did Jowett recognize the fame of his former pupil; and as the respect of Jowett, when conceded to persons with whom he did not agree, may be recognized as having a certain value of barometrical indication, as reflecting the opinion of the world in a species of enlightened mirror, we may consider that Jowett's expressed admiration of *Plato and Platonism* was a belated admission that Pater had indubitably attained to the eminence which the Professor of Greek had long before prophesied for him.

4. 'TRADESCANT'S ARK'

Humbug, snob, opportunist, success-monger — it is a pretty enough catalogue of meannesses, with more than a hint of something meaner still in the allegation that Jowett did all he could to thwart Pater's Oxford career. But the unpleasing view of Jowett, thus distilled from Mallock and Benson, nevertheless falls short of the more virulent view which one must believe to have been entertained by not a few of his Oxford contemporaries.

The posthumous gossip of Oxford common rooms, thirty or forty years after his death, usually pointed by some maliciously-toned though never quite authenticated anecdote, reflected something of that ancient hostility. To one young listener, at least, at the beginning of the nineteen-twenties, when Oxford gossip was peculiarly thrown back upon the past, it seemed that only a smouldering fire of something very like hatred could account for the acrid, still lingering smoke. Yet when, many years later, he became concerned to know something of the truth about Jowett, he could find no convincing contemporary proof of the enmity which that faded, malicious gossip had seemed to presuppose.

It was not until 1943, fifty years after Jowett's death, that the gap was authoritatively filled by the publication of Dr. Joan Evans's fascinating book *Time and Chance: the story of Arthur Evans and his forebears*. In Chapter XV of that book Dr. Evans, from a series of contemporary and uninhibited letters exchanged between her famous half-brother, his

---

[1] If music is art, this is simply untrue. I think it is also untrue, even if music is excluded; though Jowett's appreciation of visual art was certainly not that of an art-critic or a professed aesthete (in the best sense of that abused word).

father-in-law Edward Freeman, and his friend Charles Drury Fortnum, vividly describes the clash in 1884 (eight years before Dr. Evans herself was born) between Evans and Jowett over the Old Ashmolean.

The peculiar interest of this story is that it is uncompromisingly black and white. Not a single redeeming quality is conceded to Jowett. There must have been another side to the story — there are two sides to every story — and something of the case for the defence will be suggested in the following pages. But the charges brought against Jowett, whether they were just or unjust, certainly illustrate his mastery of the gentle art of making enemies and his complete indifference to the effect upon his personal reputation of exercising this dangerous gift.

Sir Arthur Evans, excavator of Knossos and discoverer of the Minoan civilization, died in July 1941. He was in his ninety-first year. In 'Youlbury', the large house he had built on Boars Hill above Oxford, lay an enormous mass — 'a lifetime's accumulation' — of letters and papers. The house was requisitioned immediately after his death. The papers 'had to be sorted and cleared in haste'. It was a wonderful feat on the part of his distinguished half-sister, that using these papers as her chief material she wrote *Time and Chance* within eighteen months of his death.[1] Her achievement is the more astonishing because, as she herself says, her 'first preoccupation was with the records of the excavation of Knossos, and the material for the unpublished volumes of *Scripta Minoa*'.

Time and Chance is a rare masterpiece in the peculiarly difficult *genre* of family biography. It is no matter for criticism that, in the chapter on the Old Ashmolean, the angry opinions of young Evans and his correspondents are not corrected by a balanced editorial judgment. Those immediate opinions are exactly what most need to be, and so seldom are, preserved and published. It is not the least of the merits of *Time and Chance* that the characters speak for themselves in their own words.

In January 1883 Arthur Evans and his wife settled in Oxford. He was then thirty-one; the eldest son of the famous antiquary Sir John Evans by his father's first marriage to Harriet Dickinson, who belonged to the great paper-making family. Sir John was a generous father and himself a rich man. Arthur, as David Hogarth told him roundly many years later, had 'never been at a loss for money', and was never able to understand the need of most archaeologists to be economical in their work. His own taste, not shared by Hogarth, for elaborate and costly reconstructions — which he nevertheless wished the public to assist by subscription —

---

[1] The preface to *Time and Chance* is dated 1942.

reflected this financial carelessness.[1] Ultimately, under his maternal grandfather's Will, he inherited a share of the substantial Dickinson fortune. Lifelong familiarity with wealth explains his recurring inability to understand the necessity of prudence on the part of others, and perhaps points to the hidden cause of his quarrel with Jowett.

After taking a first class Oxford degree in History Arthur spent the best part of eight years travelling in the Balkans. His main interests were political. He was a stormy traveller, whose passionate partisanship sometimes embarrassed the Foreign Office. At one time he was Balkan correspondent to the *Manchester Guardian*. Like his father he was a born antiquary and collector; and he indulged this bent during his Balkan travels, whenever there was an opportunity to do so. As yet, however, his political interests came first; his antiquarian or archaeological pursuits were hardly more than the hobby of a very gifted and well-provided young man. They were not directed to any specific end or confined to any period. Something in him — something which perhaps marks the true antiquary as distinct from the archaeologist — drove him off the beaten tracks. He was a deliberate rebel against 'classical antiquity', and against the Oxford concentration of interest upon the articulate, sophisticated civilizations of classical Greece and Rome.

Some time in 1875 Evans — a forceful, pugnacious, very short-sighted but very observant young man of twenty-four — met the already celebrated English historian Edward Freeman at Cattaro. Freeman was nearly thirty years older than Evans; but the two men were thenceforward fast friends. What brought them together so closely, in the first place, was probably their common hatred of 'the Ottoman rule in Europe'.[2] But Freeman confessed his envy of the younger man's minutely observant, though short-sighted eye:

How you notice everything: things about fiddles and pots, which I should never think of, and things about noses and eyes which I always wish to notice, but don't know how. The more things that are noticed the better.

Thereafter Freeman was 'one of Evans's most fervent supporters in England'; and when, in 1884, he succeeded Stubbs in the Oxford Chair of Modern History, whatever influence he had in Oxford was certainly used on Evans's behalf. Meanwhile Evans had become his son-in-law, marrying his daughter Margaret in 1878.

---

[1] *Time and Chance*, 341. I shall not give every reference to *Time and Chance* for every quotation made in the following pages. The book must be read for its own sake. Much of the story can also be found in Mr. Leonard Cottrell's *The Bull of Minos*, republished in a paper-backed edition by Pan Books.

[2] *D.N.B.* article on Freeman. For Freeman's earlier part in Jowett's history see above, 340.

Evans took Freeman captive. He, not Freeman, was the dominating partner in their triangular relationship. But he liked and admired his father-in-law. Their relationship is vividly depicted by Dr. Joan Evans:

The short legged, long bearded, steely little historian could not fail to appeal to Arthur Evans, because there was something noble and generous about him. His pugnacity in lost causes, his disinterested devotion to the principles of liberty, and his historic sense of the origin of things, stirred like chords in Arthur Evans.

In January 1883 the Evanses settled at Oxford, in 'the upper part of 32 Broad Street', after their escape from Ragusa, where Arthur had been arrested and imprisoned. Arthur 'was trying to find a niche for himself in Oxford', though he was also planning 'to make a first visit to Macedonia and Greece in the spring'. Only one 'niche' seemed then to be in prospect. This was the new Lincoln chair of Classical Art and Archaeology, one of six new chairs established by the Oxford Commissioners of 1877. There was argument over the Lincoln college statutes, so that the professorship was not actually constituted until 1884; the first appointment not made until 1885. But the Commissioners had already determined the scope and duties of the professor, the first manner of his remuneration (by a fellowship at Lincoln), and the composition of the board of electors. When Evans came back to Oxford everybody knew all this and knew, also, that an election would soon be made.

It seems strange that anybody should have supposed him to be a possible candidate. He was barely thirty; he had no professional standing; his status was that of an amateur; he despised the very idea of 'classical' archaeology. What he needed was a 'niche', not a chair. Dr. Joan Evans says that 'history does not relate if Arthur actually stood for the Professorship'. It would be surprising to discover that he did do so; for by that time he had found his 'niche' in the Keepership of the Ashmolean. Moreover he knew that the new chair would be, for him, quite the wrong kind of job. Nevertheless he wrote about it seriously to his father-in-law. His letter and Freeman's reply to it reveal the deep dislike of Jowett, and of everything for which Jowett stood, which both of them already shared before the new Keeper of the Ashmolean found himself at loggerheads with the Vice-Chancellor.

Evans wrote in March 1883:

By the way there is going to be established a Professorship of 'Classical' Archaeology, and I have been strongly advised to stand. I do not think I shall, unless I see any real prospect of getting it: and to say the truth I see very little. To begin with, it is to be called the Professorship of 'Classical Archaeology', and I understand that the Electors, including Jowett and

Newton of the Brit. Mus.[1] (who prevented my getting the Archaeological Travelling Studentship of old) regard 'archaeology' as ending with the Christian Era.[2] Anyhow to confine a Professorship of Archaeology to classical times seems to me as reasonable as to create a Chair of 'Insular Geography' or 'Mesozoic Geology'. Further it appears that a knowledge of Semitic or Egyptian antiquities is to be admitted: anything in short Oriental, but Europe, except the Europe of a favoured period and a very limited area (for I take it that neither Gaul, Britain or Illyricum were ever 'classical' in Jowett's sense) is to be rigorously excluded!

Freeman answered with a savage exaggeration of Evans's hostility to the Vice-Chancellor:

Delendus est Jowett. Every ass knoweth his master's crib, and they do it for what they call *Greats*. Of course all those people will make a stand against you, just because you know more than they do and go beyond their wretched narrow circle. They are the obscurantists and answer exactly to the *Trojans* of the sixteenth century.[3] As men fought then for the *knowledge* of Greek and the Jowetts of that day opposed them, so we fight for the *use* of Greek, for the proper place of Greek in the history of the world, and the Jowetts of this day — the cribmongers — oppose us. But I think you should stand, if only for a protest. . . . Of course they will have some narrow Balliol fool, suspending all sound learning at the end of his crooked nose, to represent self-satisfied ignorance against you, but I would go in just to tell them a thing or two. . . .

One would like to think that Freeman's splenetic language was provoked by the gout, from which he often suffered. But detestation of Oxford in general, and of Jowett in particular, was becoming an obsession with him. His appointment next year (1884) to the Regius Professorship of Modern History

did not add to his happiness . . . he disliked many of the changes which had been effected at Oxford of late years, was annoyed at being powerless to direct the school of which he was nominally the head, and was disappointed at the general neglect of his lectures by the undergraduates.[4]

In 1887 he wrote two articles on 'Oxford after Forty Years' for the *Contemporary Review*. 'The criticisms in these papers seem sometimes a little captious' is the gently adverse comment of Sir Charles Mallet. He 'had hardly a good word to say for the Commission of 1877' and 'complained that the Professors had been treated like ushers'.[5] As for Jowett:

Professor Freeman returning to Oxford after forty years, and finding much to criticize in its Schools, its buildings, its methods, its ideals, in the 'direct glorification of idleness, the amazing importance attached to mere amusements', reserved his sharpest censure for the 'portentous rage for play-acting', which 'the chief resident officer of the University' seemed to

[1] Keeper of Greek and Roman antiquities.
[2] '*Ending* with the Christian Era' must, of course, mean '*ending with the beginning* of the Christian Era'.
[3] A nickname for the Latinists who fought against the Greek revival.
'*D.N.B.*   [5] Mallet, *History of University of Oxford*, iii, 347 *n*.

sanction and approve. But [Mallet dryly adds] public opinion was not long in endorsing the Vice-Chancellor's common sense.[1]

It seems all but certain that Evans cannot have finally followed his father-in-law's advice. The election of the first professor was not made till 1885. In the previous summer Evans had found an infinitely more congenial and convenient 'niche' in the Keepership of the Ashmolean Museum, which became vacant by the death in January of the last of the old 'Kimeliarchs', John Henry Parker, the Oxford bookseller-publisher and antiquary. Parker had enjoyed the Keepership for its own sake, and also because it gave him a quasi-academic status in Oxford. In 1869 he endowed it 'with a sum yielding £250 a year';[2] he was nominated Keeper by a University statute in 1870.

In September 1883 Evans came back again to Oxford from his tour of Greece and Macedonia. Parker, now old and ill, 'was thought to show signs of retiring, and Arthur wished to succeed him'. Financially, the net value of the Keepership was little enough. But this was not, for Evans, a matter of any serious importance. On Parker's death he applied for the post; and on 17th June 1884 he was appointed Keeper *nemine contradicente* by the board of Visitors of which the Vice-Chancellor was chairman.

Nobody has ever accused Jowett of being a careless chairman. On the contrary, his enemies took it for granted that he worked tirelessly for his own purposes in this sort of business. At the very least, then, he must be credited with the deliberate approval of Evans's appointment; though this was not remembered in his favour by Evans and his friends. Moreover, the future of the Ashmolean was a matter in the very forefront of his mind.

In the summer of 1882, before he entered upon the office of Vice-Chancellor, he drew up a summary list of seventeen numbered items — things he deliberately planned to get done. This list was found among his papers after his death, and was reproduced by Abbott in the second volume of the *Life and Letters*. Abbott says of it:

As was always the case in his agenda, Jowett has here set down far more than there was any hope of his accomplishing. But he did accomplish a great deal, and if in some points he fell short of his programme, in others, as in his plans for the Non-Collegiates and the Clarendon Press, he went beyond it.

[1] Mallet, *op. cit.*, iii, 464.
[2] *D.N.B.* Dr. Evans in *Time and Chance* (266) says nothing of £250 a year; only that Parker 'founded a lectureship in the Science of Antiquities of £100 a year to be held by the Keeper, who had to pay the assistant and the boy out of it.' Was this additional to the £250? A basic stipend of about £75 a year had been provided by Dr. John Rawlinson of St. John's College in the seventeenth century.

Here is the list:

Agenda, 1882–1886, *during my Vice-Chancellorship*

1. Indian Institute.
2. Archaeological Museum at the Ashmolean.
3. Museum of Greek Antiquities and Art.
4. Cricket for the University.
5. Swimming Baths.
6. Repairs of St. Mary's Church.
7. Physiological Laboratory.
8. Rearrangement of the Bodleian.
9. Planting of Broad Street.
10. Furnishing of the Schools.
11. Purchase of ground and bridge over the Cherwell.
12. The river to be improved.
13. Establishment of a Philological School.
14. Improvement of Commemoration.
15. Performance of Shakespeare or of Greek plays in the Theatre at Oxford.
16. The creation of a Medical School at Oxford.
17. To fill St. Mary's with stained glass.

The heading of the list, the numbering and ordering of the items, the economy of wording, all indicate that it was a summary of tentative but considered priorities. There is no need to insist that this was so. If the list is taken to be no more than a succession of casual jottings set down at random, the earlier items were obviously those which came first into the writer's mind. Whichever way it is regarded, it proves that Jowett was very much concerned for the future of the Ashmolean as an *archaeological* museum, quite separate from, and placed before, his plan for a museum of *Greek* antiquities and art.

The high place of these two items in the list is, at first sight, surprising. It seems to contradict his view, recorded by Abbott, that archaeology was too uncertain a study to be taken very seriously.[1] Even in the field of 'classical archaeology' — or, rather, in that part of it which belonged to his own Greek studies — he was at pains to insist that the light given by archaeology, though 'real', was not 'considerable'. The detailed essay, seventy pages long, on Inscriptions of the Age of Thucydides, which opens the second volume of his *Thucydides,* shows that he was well abreast of the work done at that date (1881) by German, French, English and Greek scholars. In the concluding paragraph of this essay he indicates, in language touched with condescending rhetoric, the value and the limits of the contribution which such studies can make to

[1] *L. & L.*, ii, 145; where Abbott describes how Jowett pulled to pieces, in an after-dinner conversation, the supposition that Schliemann had discovered the body of Agamemnon himself at Mycenae.

the better understanding of a dead, but fully articulate civilization. (It is no matter that he had never himself trod Greek soil.)

To be busy on Greek soil, under the light of the blue heaven, amid the scenes of ancient glory, in reading inscriptions, or putting together fragments of stone or marble, has a charm of another kind than that which is to be found in the language of ancient authors. Yet even to appreciate truly the value of such remains, it is to the higher study of the mind of Hellas and of her great men that we must return, finding some little pleasure by the way (like that of looking at an autograph) in deciphering the handwriting of her children amid the dust of her ruins.[1]

If this was his opinion in 1881, why did he put an archaeological museum at the Ashmolean and a museum of Greek antiquities, in that order, at the top of his agenda in 1882? The answer seems to be that he did not treat the Vice-Chancellorship as an opportunity for merely promoting his own ideas. Whatever he might himself think about the value of archaeological studies, in comparison with the study of the great classical writers, these newer studies had come to stay. The chair of Classical Archaeology must be supported by a well-provided museum. That was self-evident; but it involved the whole, very difficult question of the future of the Old Ashmolean museum.[2]

The Ashmolean building was erected by Oxford University in 1683 to receive the 'Tradescant' collections presented by Elias Ashmole. It stands close to Wren's Sheldonian Theatre, finished fourteen years earlier. Whether its architect Wood, an Oxford stone-cutter, worked alone or had any help from Wren, it holds its own in the group of remarkable buildings clustered round the Bodleian Library.[3]

The housing of Ashmole's collections was never the sole purpose of this building. The inscription over the north door said *Museum Ashmoleanum Schola Naturalis Historiae Officina Chymica*. As time went on, the inscription became illegible; but the needs of the University pressed more and more hardly upon the museum. As Dr. Joan Evans says:

The institution of examinations had created needs which had been met by taking over the original Tradescant gallery, stripping it of its panelling and cases, and packing away its portraits of benefactors into a loft at the top of the Old Clarendon buildings.

Parts of the collections were removed: the coins to the Bodleian, the natural history specimens to the new (natural science) University

---

[1] *Thucydides*, ii, lxxviii.
[2] It is to be noted that Jowett's memorandum says nothing about Roman antiquities. Can 'Greek' have been shorthand for 'Graeco-Roman'?
[3] In Appendix A of vol. iii of his *History of the University of Oxford* Sir Charles Mallet demolished the notion that Wren was the architect of the Ashmolean Building.

Museum in Park Road; the anthropological specimens were promised to the same destination. The MSS of Anthony Wood and others were transferred to the Bodleian in 1860.

The origin of the Ashmolean collections lay in 'Tradescant's Ark'. This was a house and garden in Lambeth, where John Tradescant established a museum and physic garden round about 1630. Tradescant was a travelling naturalist, who became gardener to Charles I. He collected foreign plants which he introduced into England — for example, the lilac. He had, also, the magpie instinct of the antiquary. The 'Tradescantium Museum' housed an astonishing medley: 'birds, quadrupeds, fish, shells, insects, minerals, fruits, war instruments, habits, utensils, coins, and medals'. His son, of the same name and kidney, compiled a detailed catalogue of its contents. 'The wonderful variety and incongruous juxtaposition of the objects make the catalogue very amusing reading.'[1] The collection included a complete stuffed dodo. The head and a foot of this specimen are — or were — preserved in the University Museum.

Elias Ashmole successfully asserted his claim to the ownership of the Tradescant collections, under a deed of gift alleged to have been executed by the younger Tradescant two or three years before his death in 1662. In 1661 Tradescant had made a will, leaving his 'Closet of Rarities' to his wife for her life and then 'to the Universities of Oxford or Cambridge, to which of them shee shall think fitt at her decease'. Ashmole claimed that Tradescant had already given the 'Closet of Rarities' to him. He contested the will, won his case, and removed the rarities into his own possession. Tradescant's widow drowned herself in her own pond three or four years later. The story has an unpleasant smell, which becomes stronger as one looks at the outline of Ashmole's career.

Ashmole, once described as 'the greatest virtuoso and curioso that ever was known or read of in England before his time', looks now rather to have been the kind of astute man who climbs over other people's shoulders and comes out of troubled times with a reputation he has done little to earn. Like Dr. Johnson, he was a Lichfield boy. His father was a saddler; his mother was a relation or connection of James Pagitt, a Baron of the Exchequer. Pagitt helped him to become a solicitor 'with an indifferent good practice'. He advanced himself a little by a first, prudent marriage. After his first wife's death, by an extraordinary dis-

---

[1] Sir William Flower, in his *Essays on Museums* (1898), quoted in the *D.N.B.* article on the younger Tradescant. It hardly needs to be said that the full history of the Ashmolean is much more complex and interesting than this brief sketch can suggest.

play of pertinacity he overcame the reluctance of 'the Lady Main-waring' — a woman twenty years older than he was — to take him for husband. He related cynically in his diary that he enjoyed her estate, 'though not her company for altogether'. After her death he married again 'a much younger lady, the daughter of his friend the herald Dug-dale'. His intellectual interests exhibited the same sort of worldly shrewdness. When it was useful to be an alchemist, he was an alchemist. If astrology mattered, he was an astrologer. If antiquities were in fashion, he was the great curioso. Alchemy was 'quietly dropped'. Astrology faded into the background. The curioso finally took the stage.

His *magnum opus* was a work on the *Institution Laws and Ceremonies of the Garter*. Richard Garnett, set to say the best that could be said of him in the *Dictionary of National Biography*, calls this work 'a noble example of antiquarian zeal and research'. But Garnett, in the same article, had already felt himself obliged to say that 'the Ashmolean Museum, though really formed by Tradescant, has secured for its donor a celebrity which he could not have obtained for his writings'. And the biographer of the younger Tradescant, in the same *Dictionary*, quotes — with evident approval — the blunt remark of Richard Pulteney, the celebrated eighteenth-century botanist, that 'the name of John Tradescant was unjustly sunk in that of Ashmole'.

Having become the legal owner of the Tradescant collections, Ash-mole offered them to Oxford, on the condition that the University should house them at its own expense. By this arrangement he got rid of all responsibility for their upkeep and assured himself of an immortality which, spurious from the beginning, was undeservedly perpetuated when his name was attached to the modern Ashmolean museum.

So much for Ashmole — more, perhaps, than is strictly relevant. Stripped of the coins and the zoological specimens, and excluded from the original Tradescant gallery, the once famous 'closet of rarities' languished, a forlorn remnant of seventeenth-century inquisitiveness and acquisitiveness, in a part of the old Ashmolean building. Some additions had been casually made to it from time to time:

specimens of birds, beasts and fishes; relics of the South Sea Islands brought back from Captain Cook's Voyages; the Alfred Jewel, given by a graduate; and a certain number of Anglo-Saxon, Egyptian and Etruscan objects, of the most disparate kinds, collected by members of the Univer-sity. The Keepers were usually non-resident, and the assistant keepers, who did the work, rather ignorant and very ill-paid.[1]

Yet there was still a potential value in the Museum. Its random curiosities could become the useful nucleus of a more systematic, more

[1] *Time and Chance*, 265.

ambitious, archaeological museum. There were many people troubled by the neglect into which the Tradescant collections had fallen. The idea floated in the air of Victorian Oxford that something ought to be done. The Rev. Greville Chester wrote a pamphlet about the *Present and Future of the Archaeological Collections of the University of Oxford* in 1881, which may have influenced Jowett when he drew up his own *agenda*.[1]

Jowett became Vice-Chancellor in the Michaelmas term of 1882. He was still new in his office when, at the end of 1882, Charles Drury Fortnum approached him, through Greville Chester,

with a generous offer: the loan and eventual bequest of his collection of antique and Renaissance works of art. The Vice-Chancellor, however, was less than luke-warm; he preferred to have the Tradescant gallery used as an examination hall. In the best Oxford manner he raised difficult points, such as who was to pay for the cases to hold the objects and how the matter was to be put to Convocation. 'You see, Mr. Fortnum,' he piped, 'we don't want to force your hand!' Finally, he succeeded in stifling the offer; but it seemed as though any Keeper of the Ashmolean appointed at this juncture might have an unusual opportunity for developing the Museum could he renew and enlist Fortnum's interest in it as a home for his collection.[2]

The derogatory tone of this account, drawn from a letter of Evans to his father, is not justified by the line which Jowett is said to have taken. The Vice-Chancellor was obliged to raise the essential question of cost, before encouraging Fortnum to commit himself too far. Had he not done so, at the very beginning, he might have opened the door to an endless series of misunderstandings. Like many another generous bene-factor, Fortnum was slow to recognize the necessity of enabling the University to receive his gift. His negotiations with the University were not completed until 1892, six years after Jowett ceased to be Vice-Chancellor. 'During his lifetime and by his will' he contributed a large number of works of art to the Ashmolean collections, and also gave a large amount of property for the endowment of the Museum, and the augmentation of the Keeper's stipend.'[3] The University, for its part, bore the cost of extending the Galleries in Beaumont Street, which had been opened in 1845. To this enlarged building, which ranks among the world's great museums, the contents of the Old Ashmolean were even-tually removed in 1897, the year before Fortnum's death, and four years after Jowett's death.

---

[1] *ibid.*, 466, where Chester's very comprehensive suggestions are summarized. Dr. Evans says that he was 'a member of the University who had been employed on the excavations of the Palestine Exploration Fund'. He was a Balliol man compelled by ill-health to winter abroad for many years, chiefly in Egypt, Syria and Palestine. (Dawson, *Who was Who in Egyptology*, 1951.)
[2] *ibid.*, 267. [3] *Oxford Historical Register* (1900).

The entire credit for all this is commonly given to Sir Arthur Evans — as the man who saved Fortnum for Oxford, after Jowett had tried hard to stop Fortnum from doing anything. There can be no doubt that, but for Evans, the New Ashmolean would be a much less comprehensive and less well-endowed institution than it is, even apart from his own contributions. But others played their useful parts, among them Percy Gardner, professor of that Classical Archaeology which so offended Evans. And Jowett, though no words were strong enough for the detestation in which Evans and Fortnum and Freeman held him, ought at least to be credited with, and not supposed to be discredited by, his plain speaking to Fortnum in 1882; though his manner ruffled Fortnum's feathers and his high-pitched voice irritated Fortnum's ears.

The official Minutes of the Old Ashmolean, during the years of Jowett's Vice-Chancellorship (1882–6), make no mention at all of Fortnum or of his offered gift. They are so scanty as to invite the supposition that a great deal, including matters of importance, must have been left out. Fortnum's name does not even appear in the Minutes until 1891. The story of Jowett's opposition is still a firm tradition in the Department of Antiquities, where one would expect — if anywhere — to find some awareness of the attitude indicated in his 1882 *agenda*. There is a large box of correspondence in the Ashmolean, thought to be correspondence between Evans and Fortnum — perhaps the correspondence which passed through Dr. Joan Evans's hands or a part of it — but nobody has yet worked through this material.[1]

Since this is so, and since there is nothing at all about Fortnum or Evans or the Ashmolean in Jowett's *Life and Letters*, except the reference to 'an archaeological museum at the Ashmolean' in his 1882 *agenda*, the only evidence at present available lies in the excerpts from Evans's correspondence given in *Time and Chance*. Naturally these do not, could not, give an unprejudiced account of what happened. But they distil the quintessence of the feeling — part fear, part contempt, part antipathy and part sheer miscomprehension — which the Vice-Chancellor managed to create in the minds of some of his contemporaries.

He seems to have cared nothing at all about it. When he came into collision with Evans he was nearing seventy. His physical energy was failing. He channelled it, as best he could, into directions where he could see it to be useful. It was something to husband, not to waste in

[1] The statements in this paragraph are based upon information kindly supplied to me by the present Senior Assistant Keeper, Mr. Ian Robertson.

dispute with unpersuadable young men. And Evans, whom he had himself backed as Keeper of the Ashmolean, was a peculiarly unpersuadable young man, demanding more than Jowett thought to be practicable. There was not enough time, not enough energy, left to spend upon matters which would eventually settle themselves. The Vice-Chancellor felt, not without cause, that he was being rushed; was curt when he was expected to be sympathetic; seemed to be obstructive when he was expected to be compliant. If he failed in tact and understanding, so did his importunator. But Evans was neither a tactful nor an understanding man; and he started from an already formed dislike of Jowett as a narrow classicist, which Freeman had done his utmost to encourage.

The new Vice-Chancellor was batting on a very difficult wicket. He had little money to play with; and he had to carry Council and Convocation with him. Whatever he might wish to do was conditioned by the things he was *obliged* to do. One of his first problems was to provide the new chair of Classical Archaeology (set up by the Parliamentary Commissioners) with an adequately equipped museum. Fortnum's sudden offer of his collections, which ranged over an enormously wide field and were not particularly rich in 'classical' pieces, was (it seems) not accompanied by any offer to bear or even to share the cost of housing them. Jowett asked some reasonable, practical, financial questions; and Fortnum retired indignant.

In the summer of 1884 Arthur Evans, newly appointed Keeper of the Ashmolean, was 'full of plans for setting my new house in order'. He wanted, particularly, to get back 'the coins at present hidden away in the Bodleian . . . but there seems to be a superstition here in favour of Boards and Delegates which I do not understand'. He did not understand, Dr. Evans here comments, 'the *vis inertiae* which would postpone the creation of a coin room for fifty years'. Fortnum — who was a friend, or at any rate an acquaintance, of Sir John Evans, Arthur's father — 'was soon in touch with him and showing a strong wish to exhibit his collection'. By August 'they were in correspondence about the cases for the collection' — the 'difficult point' which Jowett had raised 'in the best Oxford manner' two years earlier. In this month Evans wrote to Fortnum:

I am happy to say that the University has now thoroughly committed itself to the plan of collecting under one roof its scattered Archaeological Collections. And there is one point in which I go with you heart and soul: the absurdity of separating off as 'Classical' the remains of a few privileged centuries. Freeman's advent here, I am glad to think, will be a crushing blow to the narrow 'Classical' School.

By the beginning of September Evans, having consulted nobody, had worked out 'plans for the new rooms at the Ashmolean'. On 4th September he

took them, together with those for the new heating apparatus, for Jowett's inspection. The V. C. was however in no hurry to look at them as he was just about to leave Oxford for a month. I asked him if I should leave them with him, but he declined. I then proposed to call a month hence, but he said he should prefer the beginning of term. So there are plenty of prospects of delay. He also said that he didn't think the University would be able to set the Ashmolean in order at present, 'there was so much to spend on the new Professors'! So you see there is some prospect of obstruction.

This was said in a letter to his wife, Margaret. Alice, one of his younger sisters,

represented the views of those who knew him best when she wrote to Margaret a few days later: 'You don't expect me to condole with the Keeper on his prospective difficulties with Jowett? I should congratulate him on a fight, if not on a 'grievance'. I can see him snuffing up the tainted breeze and pawing like a war horse already in his note.

At about this time Evans wrote to Fortnum:

If we had simply to do with the University, in Convocation or Congregation, I feel confident that all would be granted. Unfortunately, however, all proposals have to pass that close body the Hebdomadal Council, and still more unfortunately Jowett is the only one of the Visitors of the Museum who happens to be on Council. It is hopeless to expect such a man to sympathize with archaeology. He is besides a master of intrigue.... As soon as Stubbs has resigned his Regius Professorship, Freeman will be one of my Visitors — a very favourable circumstance![1]

On 2nd November 1884 Evans gave his inaugural lecture as Keeper, on the subject of 'The Ashmolean Museum as a Home of Archaeology in Oxford'. The lecture is rather fully summarized in *Time and Chance*, and was evidently a calculated performance. After praising the new science of 'what has been called Prae-historic Archaeology, but which in truth was never more Historic, in widening the horizon of our Past', saying that 'the unwritten History of Mankind precedes the written, the lore of monuments precedes the lore of books' — a statement of the kind which confuses two utterly different things by the use of an ambiguous verb ('precedes') — he displayed unexpected tact by turning to the praise of classical archaeology. Science, he said,

has recovered some at least of the monuments that men deemed irrevocably lost. By the patient collection of first-hand materials, the pure gold of Hellenic workmanship has at last been cleansed and purged from

[1] Dr. Evans does not give the date of this letter, but — from the context — it appears to have been written in September or October 1884.

its later alloy. We no longer see the image of the Hellenic genius darkly, as in a Roman mirror, but stand face to face with its undimmed glory. . . .

Surely this was language designed to please Jowett! He went on to say that the University had no more than 'the tolerable nucleus of a collection' of Hellenic antiquities, a collection at present 'unworthy of a great University'.

With most of this Jowett could hardly wish to disagree; for he had (apparently unknown to Evans) already planned for a museum of Greek antiquities and art. He was probably present at the lecture, as Vice-Chancellor and as Chairman of the Board of Visitors which had appointed Evans. But the intended effect on the Vice-Chancellor of the lecturer's *excursus* in favour of classical archaeology was likely to be ruined by the theatrical gesture with which Evans, at this point, 'exhibited' some terracotta figures he had himself acquired, 'and then and there presented them to the Museum'. Jowett was not the man to be favourably impressed by this sort of thing, even if he had been taken in by the lecturer's attempt to persuade his audience that he was not against 'classical archaeology'. Nor would he have failed to see that Evans had no perception whatever of the difference between 'monuments' and 'books', whether in their own nature or as educational instruments.

As Evans went on to expound his ideas for the future of the Ashmolean, Jowett must have seen, clearly enough, what was coming — and that it was coming too quickly and too powerfully for him to control or direct it. If it may be imagined that, when he went back to his study, he took out his 1882 *agenda* and looked at it, a little ruefully. It may be imagined also that he scored out the second and third items. Evans was going to look after them; there was no need for him to bother about them any more. His own function, now, was simply that of a man in a short-term responsible position, with a foot on the brake.

In the concluding part of his lecture Evans — quite unaware of what might be passing in the Vice-Chancellor's mind — insisted that 'those, and they are I am convinced an increasing number, who look to the Ashmolean as a future home for Archaeological research and teaching, will require something more' — something more than 'a mere repository of curiosities'. And then came an allusion to Fortnum, which perhaps the Vice-Chancellor alone fully understood. The lecturer

darkly showed forth the glories of an anonymous collection — Fortnum's — which *might* come to the University if it gave him all the improvements he asked for, and passed to a good fighting peroration.[1]

[1] The name of Fortnum seems to have been inserted here by Dr. Evans, to explain what the collection was to which Arthur Evans referred as 'anonymous'.

It is something, he said,

in a University where whole periods, and these not the least important, are divorced from our History School, in a country where knowledge is stereotyped in the interests of conventionalism, and centralized in the interests of cram, that we should have one Institution at least which, as the home of Archaeology in its widest extent, should be a refuge for neglected studies and forgotten arts. Such, and no other, is the place I would claim for the Ashmolean Museum.

On 12th November — ten days after Evans's lecture — Fortnum wrote to the Vice-Chancellor

giving an account of the refusal of his former offer of his collections. Once more he offered them on loan, with a promise of an ultimate bequest, provided that the University would do its part and consider the creation of a central museum of Art and archaeology in Oxford under the Keeper of the Ashmolean.

Dr. Evans tells us that Evans, at this time, put the capital cost of satisfying Fortnum's conditions at £2,000, and the annual cost at a minimum of £250. (The ultimate cost must have been very much greater.) Evans 'had great hopes' of the Visitors; but he foresaw difficulty with the University. And, of course, there was the wicked old Vice-Chancellor to reckon with. The events of the next ten days have to be told in Evans's words; for there is no other record of them. He wrote to Fortnum on 21st November 1884:

When I saw the Vice-Chancellor two days since he had 'not had time to read' my Report,[1] but he glanced through it in my presence, and, as one scheme after another began to unfold itself, grew visibly warm, and at last turned round on me and told me that it was quite impossible for me to think of getting such a sum out of the University. 'Most improbable contingency' was his reference to yourself.

This was not promising. However, by dint of private negotiations with other Visitors of the Museum, I got them to arrange an hour for looking at the plans etc. relating to my Scheme, in the Keeper's Room at the Museum, at 3 p.m. on Wednesday. Sayce, who was ready to stand by me, was leaving for Egypt on Thursday, and thought that Jowett would postpone a meeting of the Visitors for months; and to secure his presence [i.e. Sayce's presence] I had to get a meeting together at once. I then wrote to the Vice-Chancellor and told him that I had arranged for the other Visitors to look at my plans privately in my room and 'that it might perhaps suit his convenience and facilitate the dispatch of business' if he summoned them *officially* for that hour, which of course I had no right to do. The V. C., seeing that the Visitors were likely to constitute a quorum, whether he summoned them or not, made a virtue of necessity and adopted my proposal.

[1] It is not quite clear whether this was the scheme for the enlargement of the Old Ashmolean, which he had taken to Jowett on 4th September, or a draft of his first annual Report. Since he brought away the former from his interview with Jowett in September, it would seem that the 'Report' mentioned in this letter was a later, official, document which no doubt incorporated the earlier scheme.

When he came, he almost refused to recognize me. However, he soon discovered that he was in a minority of one and with his usual adroitness in such situations, became wonderfully amenable. The final result was that the Visitors adopted my Report unanimously and commissioned the V. C. to lay it before Council.

This is a first and signal triumph! But with such a *rusé* old University politician to deal with as Jowett, the battle is never won till you hold in your hands the fruits of Victory. Great pressure will have to be put on Council from without to get them to act.

From this moment Jowett vanishes from *Time and Chance*, except for a reference to his succession in the Vice-Chancellorship by Dr. Bellamy 'who did not share his predecessor's distrust of the arts'. Evans celebrated his triumph by a party in the Tradescant gallery 'from which he had succeeded in driving Examiners and Candidates' — it is not said *how* he succeeded. In February 1885 Council passed a grant of £1,050, which Convocation immediately confirmed, for a strong room, heating apparatus, and a first instalment of cases to house Fortnum's treasures.

If Jowett had in fact been defeated, he took his defeat with grace and did his best to ease the way for Evans, who wearied very quickly of University business and spent little time in Oxford.

The lame and inarticulate Assistant, Edward Evans, was left in charge; he soon fell into the habit of replying to all enquirers: 'The Keeper, Sir, is somewhere in Bohemia.'[1]

Yet, if Evans's letter to Fortnum was truthful, it was he, not less than Jowett, who deserved to be called a 'master of intrigue'.

Anybody who understands the kind of men that Jowett and Evans were cannot fail to suspect that both the battle and the victory were products of Evans's forceful imagination. He had to seem to himself to be winning a fight. Jowett was his windmill. What Jowett thought of the whole affair is nowhere recorded. It has to be guessed. The most probable guess is that he shrugged his shoulders and left it to Evans to get on with the job of doing what he had, himself, designed to do. He would not have given a moment's thought to the posthumous figure he might be made to cut in Evans's correspondence.

So far as Jowett was concerned, the story is finished. So far as Evans and Fortnum and the University were concerned, it has barely begun. The rest of it is outlined in *Time and Chance*; and the outline is admirably filled out by Dr. Evans's excerpts from her half-brother's correspondence. Fortnum becomes an exasperating egoist, always finding it difficult to make up his mind and speaking of his collections in affected language as his 'children', his 'babies', his 'dolls'. They must, he warned Evans in language difficult to tolerate, be

[1] *Time and Chance*, 276.

13. Sir Henry Acland, Jowett and the President of Trinity
A surprise photograph taken by H. W. Taunt in 1892
(*Oxford City Library*)

worthily lodged, not shabby cheap make-shift things. . . . But first catch your hare! Then the alteration of the building; then the hot water; then the cleaning down and making tidy to receive the cases — then *may* come the things to put into them, probably beginning with antiquities of pottery and bronze, then the ceramic series, the Majolica, then the Renaissance bronzes, and so to sculpture, as space and *will* permitted. I tell you this as the scheme that at present disturbs my brain from the more sensible course of keeping my dolls for my own enjoyment.

This letter, written in December 1884, ended with a kind of threat: 'If *you* cannot move the powers . . . they will assuredly *have no further opportunity from me.*' The powers were moved to make the grant of £1,050 mentioned above.

By 1886, when Jowett was followed by Bellamy, 'the Bodleian was disgorging the bronze plaques and figurines that had been transferred to it from the Ashmolean, and more and more cases were coming in from Fortnum and Stanmore'. By the spring of 1888 'the major part of the Fortnum Collections had reached Oxford'. They 'made a fine show in the Tradescant Gallery'. But the Old Ashmolean was now so full of things that it could hold no more. Evans and Fortnum, together, perceived that a new effort must be made. The result was the creation of the New Ashmolean Museum, by the enlargement of the University Galleries in Beaumont Street.

Jowett had no part in that effort, either of opposition or of approval. He was a dying man. If he thought about it at all, he would have said to himself that it was a good solution of problems which had vexed him unnecessarily some years earlier; and that he had been wise to let Evans gang his ain gait. He would not have cared at all, lest his attitude might be misrepresented fifty years later. 'The way to get things done' he once said 'is not to mind who gets the credit for doing them.' He might have added, as a rider, that the man who gets things done must not mind being wrongfully accused as the man who tried to prevent them from being done.

CHAPTER XIX

'Vita Mea'

As time went on Jowett gradually became less exacting in the standards he set to others, but he never relaxed those which he had set up, once for all, to himself. Describing him as he was in his seventies, Abbott singles out this uncommon persistence. To the last he wished to make the most of life, improving not others only, but himself.

The notion of perpetual self-improvement may be illusory. Who knows? It is at least a noble illusion. At best, it may be the heroic stimulus of a life so lived as to affect, through the lives of others, the very pattern of an age. Such a life was Jowett's. Not that he was alone among the Victorians in discovering, as it seemed for himself and by himself, the categorical imperative which Christ illustrated in the parable of the talents. Some took the imperative to be a divine command. Others interpreted it as the pressure of some superior social or racial aim upon the individual conscience. But the notion of deliberate self-improvement — as a purpose to be pursued by the individual, whether or no it served the distinct purpose of social improvement — was omnipresent in the air of the nineteenth century. No man held to it more firmly than Jowett, and few worked so persistently to realize it for himself or communicated it to so many other persons.

Two opposing strands of thought — or, rather, of feeling charged with thought — recur in his notebooks with increasing frequency during the years of the Mastership. Both of these strands — one dark and despondent, the other bright and resolute — had run through his whole adult life. But after 1870 they seem to become, more and more obviously, the warp and woof of his mind. *'Vita mea'* was often the recurrent heading which he put before these private attempts to weigh his own character.

The honesty and continuity of this curiously objective self-appraisal, in which hope and despair alternate but hope prevails over despair, can be conveyed only by bringing together some of the salient passages. The excerpts which follow are those which seem to be especially illuminating. They are all to be found in the second volume of the *Life and Letters*, where long extracts from the notebooks are inserted, from time to time, in the chronological narrative. The date of the extracts is not always exactly discoverable; and there are many more passages, of great interest, besides those here reproduced.[1]

Let me begin with a passage, apparently written in 1873, which expresses neither despondency nor hope. It concerns 'Memory in Later Life'; I choose it because the sense of having an imperfect memory was a perpetual and agonizing thorn in Jowett's mind. Yet here he is, writing about it in a perfectly matter-of-fact way:

At fifty-five you fail to remember things — words, pictures, persons — after six months' or a year's interval. Yet the circle of objects which you recognize is ever becoming wider, and this power of recognition is a great gift if cultivated. There is the greatest value in 'forgotten knowledge'. Instead of the stores of memory oppressing you, with a little trouble you can recall all that is useful or necessary. Use a younger person's memory as yours gets older and your own reason, and in this way the last twenty years of life may be the most productive. — Memory is greatly disturbed by efforts of thought or feeling. Repose is the natural state of memory. Thoughts should not be allowed to jostle one another.

Nothing could be more simply said.

But the last sentence indicates a disturbance in the writer's mind. Thoughts *were* jostling one another. In the very next paragraph, with no more than the paragraph break, he continues:

Newman, Manning, Gladstone would call me an infidel. Are they quite certain that they are not more infidel than I am, and more materialist? They believe in the Church only and an ecclesiastical organization. I try to believe in God and in the presence and possibility of God everywhere.

A little later, in the same series of notes, he condemns himself for failing to face the music. I have often alluded to a part of this confessional passage. Here it is in full. The heading of it is 'Speaking out'.

The difference between one man and another is not so much in his power of thought as in his demonstrativeness and willingness to give expression to his thought. Thus it is a great fault to keep one's thoughts to oneself instead of expressing them. If I live I ought to speak my mind. The inevitable consequences will be that I shall be called atheist. The world will be the harder upon me because it supposes that I shall be frightened. Terrorism is always practised when it is supposed to be effectual. It will be said that I had not the courage to speak out while anything could be lost. Now in advanced years, when there is nothing to be hoped for, I say out my mind. But this is *not true*.

He goes on to warn himself that 'a man of sixty should lead a quiet open-air life', should 'collect the young about him' and 'set other men to work'; and to prescribe a pattern of approach to the old age, which he perceives already to be drawing near.

[1] See, particularly, the series of notes written in 1886, (*L. & L.*, ii, 310–14) on 'Criticism and Dogma' 'Changes in Religion' 'The New Christianity' and 'The Two Great Forms of Religion'.

The prison walls were closing in. But the reason which had prevented — and still prevented — him from 'speaking out' did not really lie in age or weakness, or in cowardice or in lack of 'demonstrativeness'. It lay in the fact that he had ceased to be a private person. He was the Master of Balliol, and his first duty was towards Balliol. He had lost the liberty of speech enjoyed by private men, who can suffer the whole consequences of their words or actions in their own lives.

The note of this frustration vibrated for a little in his mind, though he never finally wrote the reason for it down on paper, and seems not to have spoken of it to anybody. Then it died away. On his fifty-ninth birthday, 15th April 1876, he wrote into his notebook one of his most confident and hopeful entries:

I cannot say vixi, for I feel as if I were only just beginning and had not half completed what I have intended. If I live twenty years more I will, Dei gratia, accomplish a great work for Oxford and for philosophy in England. Activity, temperance, no enmities, self-denial, saving eyes, never over-work. . . . To arrange my own life in the best possible way, that I may be able to arrange other people's. Is it possible . . . for age to retain the force of youth?

The answer to that question is, alas, no. Age can have a force of its own, but it cannot have the force of youth. A little later Jowett, only a year or two past sixty, is saying to himself, in the tabular form which he sometimes used for sorting out his private problems, as if to give his answers or resolutions a look of finality:

(a) Must be more alone, and get above phases of mind which come upon me in bad weather or when I am alone.

(b) To rely on no one but myself, and to rely on myself. All through life I have had a false sensitiveness and egotism.

(c) I seem to have had great power in thinking and dealing privately with persons, but no power in public or society.

It had been in a happier mood, just before his sixtieth birthday, that he wrote enthusiastically to Morier about the new buildings at Balliol. There had been

a solemn inauguration. . . . I wish you had been there. . . . Everybody appeared to have been greatly pleased. And I was pleased, and hope it will be the beginning of a new life to the College.

But new life is not generated by new buildings. The fallacy of supposing that buildings can do, what flesh and blood and brains are unable to do, is as old as civilization itself. Nobody, one would have supposed, was more aware of it than Jowett. Was he not taking refuge, in these visible demonstrations of his power to 'improve' the physical aspect of Balliol, from the disappointment of discovering that he no longer had any pupils of his own to improve? If so, he was under a double illusion. The buildings were not what he thought them to be. But the young men were coming along very well indeed, though no longer under his personal tuition.

By 1880, when he had been ten years Master and was approaching the very height of his reputation as head of his college, a sense of ultimate failure began to possess his private mind. 'Despondency and Bereavement' is the title given by Abbott to the chapter which deals with the years 1880–2. It opens with a moving entry, made by Jowett in one of his notebooks, when he was sixty-three.

Age is the chief cause of my despondency. I fear that I shall not be able to accomplish all that I desire. I must economise time and health, and get my work done. I must commune with myself about this, but speak to no one. In weakness I must be passive and go to sleep, and seize only favourable moments. To look at Wordsworth's poem — 'Greater silence, greater dignity; moving slowly to death'; of that I would wish to carry the impression always. My life has been such a waste of vanity and egotism, that I must make the most of the remaining fifteen years.[1] I desire nothing, and can have no further disappointments, except the non-completion of my work. This I go to fulfil. Working and resting, diet, place of abode, must always be directed to this end. *Aetatis* sixty-three I feel very old. I must do the utmost for my friends by kindness and correspondence. The great want of life can never be supplied, and I must do without it.[2]

A year or two later his confidence is still at the lowest point of the ebbing tide, though his aim has recovered something of its younger spring.

I am growing old, too old to undertake a great work. Yet I must and do resolve to devote all my serious thoughts to it. I grow more ambitious every year. All my time, money, thoughts, I would like to devote to gaining influence of the best kind; and an increasing influence yearly. I must make the best arrangements — get young men and boys around me in the next ten years — neither spend money nor take pleasure except for the sake of health. I seem to be not so strong as formerly, and yet to have escaped from maladies of which I had the beginning ten years ago. I ought to get rid of shyness, which has detracted at least one-third from my life.

Morning and evening prayers are almost impossible to me. Church is difficult. But I desire more and more never to let a day pass without some idea or aspiration arising in my mind. And this appears to be retained. I am always thinking of death and of God and of the improvement of human nature, though sometimes interrupted by false and petty conceits of self.

This was not the kind of diary kept by a Dr. Jenkinson, for the purposes of posthumous publicity. It was painful self-examination of the closest and most honest kind. Yet, as Abbott says, 'even to his intimate

---

[1] Actually, thirteen. Not a bad forecast.
[2] *L. & L.*, ii, 174–5. The 'great want' was, of course, a wife.

friends he showed little of the self-criticizing despondent mood.'
Abbott quotes Edwin Harrison, writing from Balliol in October 1881:

The Master is looking older, but I see no other change in him. He still
walks briskly and his mind is as fresh and active as ever. He has bravely
got Thucydides off his hands, and is already busy with a translation of the
Politics of Aristotle. He says he only works four or five hours a day; which
shows either that the Master does not know how to count, or that he
reckons as play many things which other men take to be hard work.

In fact Jowett had begun a little to relax, not indeed his aim but his
approach to his aim. Matthew Knight (of whom more will be said) was
now easing the mechanical burden of his work. In August 1881 Jowett
wrote to Lady Abercromby:

This vacation I am living the life of a free man and a gentleman, reading,
not writing, which is slavery and drudgery (though the slavery must begin
shortly). I have even time to write to a friend without feeling weary.

Yet something of creative power was beginning to go. In a letter to
an unnamed friend (not Florence Nightingale), written on 1st January
1882, he makes the revealing remark that he has 'lost the power of
dreaming almost entirely'.[1] This point of mental fatigue — the point at
which the mind, even in sleep, loses freedom to escape — was reached
before he took on the exhausting office of the Vice-Chancellorship.

It is a curious relic of our ancestral respect for old men that the most
important and onerous public offices are so often filled by men who are
really too old to take the strain — men near or past the normal age of
retirement. This was certainly true of Jowett. He was an outstandingly
good Vice-Chancellor; but the effort of filling the office broke and helped
to kill him.

Nevertheless he enjoyed the work and the distinction of the Vice-
Chancellorship. It was a powerful stimulant, calling up energies which
had seemed to be nearly exhausted. The return of power did not,
however, quell the impulse of self-criticism. Rather, it intensified his
habitual feeling that he fell far short of the man he ought to be. Here is
his own long description of the faults which troubled him most at this
time, and also of such redeeming features as he dared to discover in
himself, set down in 1883, more than half-way through the first of his
four years as Vice-Chancellor. Many of the sentences contained in it
have been used at earlier points of the present book. Again, it seems
right to reproduce them here in their full context.

The Actual Analysis of the Mind

April 19. — If I ask myself what takes place in my own mind, I am at a
loss.

[1] *ibid.*, ii, 207.

I can only reply: 'A good deal of semi-conscious dreamy fancy, in which I go capriciously from one notion to another.' Some passing vanity or semi-sensuality is constantly interrupting me in prayer, or in any other serious thought. What I do is done by sparks and flashes, and not by steady thought. I put down these sparks and let them run into one another.

My mind is paralyzed by a rude unsympathetic person, and greatly quickened by intelligent sympathy. I know that this is a weakness; it makes me dependent on other persons; it prevents me from being ever ready because before I can collect myself I must resist the pain which is given by a rude remark.

Half a dozen times since I began to write this page my mind has run about in all sorts of directions.

Prayer

May 9. Nothing makes me more conscious of poverty and shallowness of character than the difficulty in praying or attending to prayer.

Any thoughts about self, sometimes thoughts of evil, day-dreams, love fancies, easily find an abode in the mind. But the thought of God and of right and truth will not stay there, except with a very few persons. I fail to understand my own nature in this particular. There is nothing which at a distance I seem to desire more than the knowledge of God, the idea, the universal; and yet for two minutes I cannot keep my mind upon them. But I read a great work of fiction, and can hardly take my mind from it. If I had any real love of God, would not my mind dwell upon Him, like the believer in Wesley's Hymns?

Vita Mea

May 13. My own experience of life suggests such enormous waste. Had I been taught well in my youth, had I had guidance, had I not wasted my memory, had I had any noble idea better than success in life, I seem as if I might have attained to real greatness.

My feeling is one of intense gratitude to Providence for having brought me this far on my way without any great shipwreck or mistake. I have a great position. May every hour of this day and every pound I have to spend be given to God.

There are many things to be done in the way of improving society and study at Oxford. I will carry on this work as long as I live, and on my deathbed I will carry it on still, remembering the words which A. C. T. said to me.[1]

I must try to revive religion if possible in Oxford, and to concentrate my thoughts.

May 16. I find that a new position, e.g. the headship of a College, or the Vice-Chancellorship, does really change the character a good deal. To myself I seem to have got rid of my old sensitiveness and want of punctuality. I have no idea except that of fulfilling my duty to the University, and of devoting the remaining years to the service of God. It appears that I have very much changed during the last year, and I pray God that I may go on to perfection.[2]

Pensées

May 19. Is it possible to feel inspired by the 'great power of God'; to live altogether above human thoughts and opinions, out of self, meditating

[1] See above, 261.
[2] Unsympathetic readers must understand this phrase, before they mock it. Jowett was not hoping for unqualified perfection 'here below'.

on the means and ways of perfection; to live altogether for others and for the highest, not for gain or honour or self-satisfaction? Is it possible to attain a divine force? I hardly know. Sometimes I feel as if old things had passed away and all things had become new. Then again, I relapse, through some weakness. I eat or drink too much, and do not retain thorough self-command or self-respect. Yet upon the whole I certainly make progress. I have no quarrels or sensitiveness; or at any rate I get rid of them as fast as I can: and I am afraid of nobody. I have far greater enjoyment of solitude and of my own thoughts.

Work

June 15. I wish my last years to be employed in original work, which may help men and women to live better and to be happier.

In three years I think it possible that I may finish —

> The *Politics*
> The *Republic* and the new edition of Plato
> The *History of Greek Philosophy*
> *Thucydides* ed. 2

I shall then devote the rest of my days to sermon writing and moral philosophy, the Life of Christ, a commentary on the New Testament Scripture.

Could I write as well as Renan?[1]

Use has been made, at various earlier points in this book, of some sentences taken from these remarkable jottings. They bear repetition in their full context and in the sequence of Jowett's repeated attempts to understand himself. One feature must strike anybody who reads this particular series of confessional passages. They begin in a key of almost despairing self-criticism; but the key gradually changes. It becomes almost what Browning's Abt Vogler called 'the C Major of this life', though dissonances and doubts are still audible in the recovered self-confidence.

The confidence was evidently the result of Jowett's pleasure in discovering, at the age of sixty-five, a satisfying field for the exercise of his great administrative abilities. The Mastership of Balliol had not given him any comparable compensation for the sacrifice of his supreme tutorial gift. In a letter written to a long-standing friend, Professor John Nichol of Glasgow, who had been one of his earlier pupils — the letter is dated December 1883 — he displays the mood of acceptance which his success in the Vice-Chancellorship was engendering:

I am not an optimist, but I wish to take the world as it is, and do the best I can. I thankfully acknowledge that my outward circumstances during the last thirteen years have been very happy, and that therefore I ought to do all I can for others.

In that innermost part of the mind where true happiness lies, he was not quite so happy as he declared to Nichol. He was not content with

[1] See above, 31.

what he had done for Balliol in the past when he was a mere tutor, or with what he was doing for Balliol in the present almost by the mere fact that he, and nobody else, was Master. The Vice-Chancellorship was only a four-years long flash in the pan. He had failed, also, to fulfil the promises of his Pauline commentary and his essay on the Interpretation of Scripture. He had not even finished off Plato: his old servant, Knight, had not been far wrong in shaking his head and saying 'that translation, Sir, will be the death of him'. Yet, regardless of his failure to implement his repeated resolutions (such as that, quoted above, which he wrote down on 15th June 1883) and of his failing health, he thought — or tried to convince himself — that there was still time to carry out the astonishing plan of work which he proposed to himself on his seventieth birthday, 15th April 1887, when he was clear of the Vice-Chancellorship but still buoyed up by the stimulus it had given him.

Scheme of Life. Aetatis 70.

Eight years of work

1 year, *Politics, Republic, Dialogues* of Plato.
2 years, Moral Philosophy.
2 years, Life of Christ.
1 year, Sermons.
2 years, Greek Philosophy: Thales to Socrates.

All of this plan that he was able to carry out was to finish the revision of his Plato; and that took him four years instead of one. 'The hopes' as Abbott says 'soon began to fade away.' The serious nature of the illness which attacked him in 1887 was slow to declare itself. In April, when he drew up this plan of work, he was trying to persuade himself and everybody else that he was simply suffering from the effects of a cold. But already, in February, at the end of a peculiarly charming letter to Margot Tennant he had hinted how it really was with him.

I have nothing so interesting as your hunting to talk about. Do you think that there will be hunting in the next world? Virgil says so! I am not a rider at all; but only a broken-down horse who tries in vain to run a race. I sometimes think of giving it all up, and getting rid of this contradiction of sciences. But before I have settled the question I expect that it will have settled itself for me.

He fell back, at last, upon his devotion to Balliol. 'The College is my real happiness and business; and probably the only business which I can carry on for eight years more. The rest are *nugae* or impossibilities.' It did not really matter, now, very much what he did. While he was alive and in possession of his faculties, nobody else could be Master of Balliol; that was a position he could never abandon or be allowed by others to abandon. For the rest, in a spirit of calm acquiescence, he confided to himself that his eight-years plan was an old man's evening dream.

Nevertheless, working as and when he had the strength to do so, he succeeded in finishing off Plato. 'If he could not work for an hour, he worked for half-an-hour, and if that was found too great a strain, he rested and contented himself with a quarter of an hour.' The revised edition of the translation of the *Republic* was published in 1888. In 1892 the 'third edition' of the *Dialogues of Plato* at last made its public appearance. As Abbott says, 'he had at least the happiness of seeing his great work issued in a form which satisfied him'.

The fact that physical weakness now prevented him from doing more than this — it is astonishing that he was able to do so much — did not release him from the sense that he must never let the management of character slip from his control. Abbott remarks that

a curious result of his illness was an increased degree of self-criticism. Among his memoranda I find: 'After every visitor, to consider whether I can charge myself with weakness, vanity, irrelevance, egotism'; and in another passage he resolves to 'keep his mind on the adverse side of things'. For though he was a resolute enemy of depression, whether in himself or in others, Jowett's view of life was that of a man who was conscious of his own weakness and dependence on a higher power.

After 1887, during the last five years of his life, the strenuous effort of self-analysis and self-criticism died away — or, if it was continued, it was continued in thoughts not confided to paper. During these last five years he seems to have deliberately economized his energies for the now more fruitful purpose of following younger men's lives. His letters are abundant, understanding, warm with sympathy, less taken up with the duty of hard advice. When people went to see him — even when he was 'very ill' — they found him much readier to talk, much easier to talk to. It is in the letters of this last period, rather than in his private notes, that the mellowed mind of the slowly dying man is most nearly to be touched — when he had passed the point of caring about his own achievement but was nowhere near the point of ceasing to care about the achievements, or to grieve for the misfortunes, of his friends. The evidence of these letters can be given only by the letters themselves — they are there, or enough of them, in the second volume of the *Life and Letters*. But one particular instance of this increasing sympathy with the difficulties of younger men, not contained in his letters, seems to be worth recall.

The witness is Edward Seymour, a young clergyman forty or more years junior to Jowett, who took a second class in Mods; became curate

of Tamworth, and rector of a Nottinghamshire living, and died unmarried two years before Jowett himself.

Why should Abbott have thought it worth while to dig up Seymour's
rather commonplace testimony? Well, the Seymours were a Balliol
family. But Seymour's testimony, commonplace in itself, is far from
commonplace if it is put into the perspective of Jowett's last years. He
went to see Jowett in September 1888, and was admitted into the
Master's bedroom.

Had quite a touching interview with Mr. Jowett at Merevale. . . . It was
some years since I had seen him, and it was astonishing how accurately he
remembered all connected with me — especially the gloomy time I had
halfway through my Oxford course. He expressed the greatest pleasure in
seeing me; his sympathy was real, not forced. I had not before realized
what a warm, pathetic personality his was. Hitherto we had been master
and pupil; now we were genial friends.

Seymour was at a point of religious doubt and difficulty, and broached
his trouble without the least consideration for the Master's state of
health.

He at once said how sorry he should be to see me leave the Church; any
wise bishop would tell me to stay. . . . An altogether delightful interview
because so unexpected in its character. I came away infected with something of the calm, serene atmosphere of philosophy in which his spirit
seems to move.

Seymour visited Jowett again at Balliol in December of the same time.
What, on this visit, especially struck him was the Master's pleasure at an
undergraduate concert in the hall, presided over by John Farmer (for
whom Jowett had built at his own expense an organ, designed by Willis,
at a cost of about £2000). Jowett made a happy little speech after the
concert, which much moved Seymour. On the way back to the lodge
he took Seymour's arm 'on which he pressed heavily; [he] has been in
very poor health, I understand, and [is] only just beginning to regain his
ordinary spirits and habits of life.' Nevertheless Seymour, having already
dined with the Master and been taken to the concert, remorselessly
stayed on. 'We now had some talk about my affairs.'

It matters less to know exactly what Jowett had to say to a young
clergyman, troubled about Christian evidences, than to know that at
this late time in his own life he could spend a whole long and exhausting
evening upon the effort of assisting a not brilliantly intelligent or
considerate guest towards a point of decision which mattered only to
the guest. However, Seymour — if not aware of the strain he was putting upon his host — did imperfectly record something quite remarkable

said by Jowett. He remembered — or thought that he remembered — Jowett to have observed that

holiness has its sources elsewhere than in history. The true use of authority is this: it is due to one wiser than oneself and to an expert. All else is a mere matter of conduct. . . .

The report is exasperatingly imperfect. Jowett must have said, or have meant to say, more than this. For what did he mean by 'holiness'? The whole of religious argument finally turns upon this single mysterious word. It may be a word of supreme value or a word of hocuspocus. Just at the moment when Jowett seemed to be on the point of telling Seymour what he thought 'holiness' to be, either he failed to complete his sentence or Seymour failed to understand what was being said.

During these last years the alternating moods of self-criticism and despondency were replaced by a graceful acceptance of old age, in spite of — possibly even in consequence of — the fact that illness put a stop to further planning. For years he had looked forward to old age, much in the spirit of Browning's 'Grow old along with me, the best is yet to be, the last of life for which the first is made.' But he had never thought of it as a period in which he might be unable to work.

In 1880, Abbott tells us, he 'was still as convinced as ever that the last years of life were the best'. He thought of them as

not a period of inactivity and decay, of mournful retrospect and idle regrets; not even the quiet repose of one whose toil is ended, but a season of fruitful labour and mental ripeness, in which to bring home the sheaves, to set the house in order, to finish the work which is given us to do — that was old age as Jowett wished to live it.

He did not foresee how hardly his infirmities would press upon him, so that he would only with very great difficulty bring home a very few of the sheaves he hoped to harvest. Yet, when the time came for him to accept inactivity and bodily, though never mental, decay, he made his acceptance with grace, with the beautiful serenity which seals the lives of men who have tried to make the very utmost of their talents, and have been prevented from exceeding the limits of human performance only by premature subjection to mortality.

For Jowett died prematurely, at the age of seventy-six. His mind was at its best, his temperament had found its level. It was the body that failed, not through senescence but before a series of pulmonary and cardiac onslaughts which might, at least conceivably, have been prevented or postponed by better medical advice — and by a less reckless and prolonged earlier exploitation of his physical resources. How far the effect of this exploitation could have been lessened, if Acland had known what doctors know now and had been able to persuade his patient to obey his orders, is anybody's guess. It is also anybody's guess whether Jowett, if he had been minded to obey his doctor's orders, would have done so much as he did. Men of his sort take the risk of mortality without suffering it to stand between them and their work.

Beneath the affectionate mockery of Balliol undergraduates in whose

lighter moments it was 'dear old Jowler' whose sayings they repeated 'with a difference' fixing all kinds of absurd stories upon him, which were handed down from generation to generation

there lay

a veneration such as few men have inspired. He was like no other person; one whose 'life retaught what life should be', a saint without asceticism, moving in a world of truth and purity and wisdom; and in a world of strength, too, for with him sympathy did not spell weakness.

So Abbott, whose description of the old man convincingly reinforces Campbell's more vivid report of the adored young tutor.

Abbott found it

much to be regretted that he never wrote the works which he contemplated on morals and religion. Had he given to these subjects the time and the labour which he devoted to translating and commenting on Greek authors he would have left a deeper impression on his age.

But tasks come in their own order of urgency. Jowett, dying, at least knew that he had met them in that order and dealt with them faithfully.

CHAPTER XX

'Such Fruit as Men Reap from Spent Hours and Wear'[1]

Long before he became Master, Jowett had been recklessly over-working. His health was beginning to trouble his friends at least as early as 1858, when he was only forty. He went walking at that time in the Lake country with George Brodrick, who recalled that

> even then he could not trust his heart for mountain climbing; and in walking from Langdale to Lodore he paused so often and advanced so slowly up the steep ascent of Rossett Gill as to make it impossible to reach our destination before dark.

Campbell adds a confirmatory sentence from the *Life of J. A. Symonds*: 'Toiling up Constitution Hill from the Cathedral [at Bristol] he said, "Our young legs don't mind this, do they?" puffing all the time.'[2]

During the next ten years he became alarmed for himself. Fits of physical and nervous exhaustion, headaches, eye-fatigue, a throat affection which 'threatened to become chronic' — such symptoms as these probably distressed him less than the 'powerlessness of brain, want of sustained thought, and imperfect memory', of which he complained to a medical friend as early as 1861.[3] Campbell says that his 'recuperative powers enabled him to rally from brief intervals of exhaustion and depression'. Warnings of this sort come to most men in middle life; but for a man of great and incessant cerebral activity, as Jowett was, they seem to menace the whole purpose of existence. By the time of his fiftieth birthday he realized

> the necessity of husbanding his physical powers in order to make the most of life. He tried certain experiments in diet, and for a time even attempted total abstinence.[4]

He gave in, also, to Miss Nightingale's peremptory and very sensible advice that he must reduce his hours of work. He promised her not 'to

[1] The heading of this last chapter is a line from Althaea's speech to Meleager between the second and third choruses of *Atalanta in Calydon*.
[2] *L. & L.*, i, 394.
[3] Dr. Symonds of Clifton, the father of J. A. Symonds. *L. & L.*, i, 395.
[4] *L. & L.*, i, 395. But the motive of his temporary 'total abstinence' was 'to help one of his dependents by his example'.

work hard, but only three hours a day, and never more than an hour at a time, or after eleven o'clock at night'.[1]

At least, he seemed to give in. But there were many concealed limitations to the promise. Writing letters wasn't 'work'; nor was reading: nor walking and talking with Swinburne or another; nor — in the sense of his promise to Florence Nightingale — were his term-time duties, even if they extended into vacation-time. All that the promise really meant was that he wouldn't spend more than three solid hours a day over his never-ending *Plato*. He seems to have kept this promise only by the aid of casuistry. Instead of sitting up after midnight, he got up earlier and worked 'for an hour or more every morning before breakfast'.

'Little time is lost through ill-health,' he had once told Lionel Tollemache 'though much is lost through idleness.'[2] He detested his own enforced 'idleness' and kept it so well within bounds that nobody but himself believed in it. He was of Seneca's opinion that health depends largely upon a man's own will: *pars sanitatis velle sanari fuit*. For a time, however, this prescription, which he had been fond of dispensing to others, seemed to have lost its efficacy for himself. The will to be well had begun to need external reinforcement.

Two such reinforcements were on their way: his election to the Mastership in 1870 and his succession to the Vice-Chancellorship in 1882. To each of these challenges his mind responded with its whole energy; and his body obeyed his mind. In spite of the discouragements and disappointments which attended the early years of the Mastership, the stimulus it gave to him was such that his physical weaknesses seem, for a while, to have been practically forgotten. How else could he have managed to keep more or less abreast of Swinburne's sylph-like passages up Tintagel or the steep sides of the Malvern Hills?

The recuperative powers, which the attainment of the Mastership — and later on the Vice-Chancellorship — called into play, would not have sufficed of themselves to see him through the rest of his life. He needed the assistance of somebody who was more than a merely capable secretary; and in 1867 he found this assistance where perhaps no other man would have thought of looking for it, in the young son of his servant Knight — a precocious lad of fourteen. He 'hit upon another plan for easing his labours' — that is, beside reducing his own hours of work. He decided to employ this lad 'in transcribing the notes to the *Republic*, and in other ways as an amanuensis'. A written page covered with scrawled corrections was given to the boy to copy out fairly; the fair copy, so

---

[1] *ibid.*, i, 396. The date of this promise was March 1867.
[2] Tollemache, *Benjamin Jowett*, 1. Date between 1856 and 1860.

covered with further corrections that it was barely legible, was again given to him; and so on to the point, one might suppose, of young young Matthew Knight's rebellion. But Matthew did not rebel, and did not wish to rebel; for he owed it to his master that he had the capacity to serve him.

Long before he hit upon this plan, Jowett had taken a hand in the boy's education,

making him repeat the Latin Grammar and lines of Virgil at odd times (for example, while his dinner, brought from the kitchen half an hour before, was lying still untouched within the fender.) Under Jowett's supervision Matthew had learned to write a beautiful hand, and had, as Jowett once said to me [Campbell] before the boy, 'a good sprag memory'.[1]

Writing to Florence Nightingale in June 1867, Jowett told her that he liked to think of himself 'as beginning and not ending'; and he went on at once to describe Matthew:

My boy, who is extremely clever, has been reading St. Theresa's life in the English. 'Don't you think, sir, that she was religiously mad?' 'Well, not a very bad kind of madness.' 'Are not all persons mad who take sincerely to a monastic life?' He is only fourteen, and he seems to me to be always reading and thinking about what he reads.

Campbell says that the 'amanuensis became, as a matter of course, a favoured pupil'. He became much more than that. He grew, one might almost say, to be Jowett's younger self.

Matthew would have been about seventeen when Jowett became Master at the age of fifty-three. His father and the whole Knight family moved with Jowett into the Master's lodge. The father now became the Master's butler and general factotum. With the aid of Mrs. Knight and his daughter Martha, he looked after the house. Meals were supplied by the college kitchen — a system which enabled Jowett to indulge his habit of adding to the number of his guests without warning his household. The story has more than once been told of the guest who heard Knight groan, as he surrendered his hat and coat, and asked sympathetically if anything was wrong. 'Nothing, Sir, only that the Master said there would be twelve to dinner, and you are the eighteenth to come so far.'

The older Knight became something of a figure in Oxford, Jowett's round-faced, cheerful, welcoming *major domo*. The two children, Martha and Matthew, became more than their father and mother; Matthew as Jowett's secretary, Martha as his confidential housekeeper, held in some

---

[1] A good instance of Jowett's meaningful use of Shakespearean allusions. *Merry Wives of Windsor*, iv, i, 84: 'He is a good sprag memory' rather than a 'scholler'. The word is said by the *O.E.D.* to be a variant of *sprack*, meaning 'brisk, active, alert, smart'.

awe even by the younger fellows of Balliol.[1] The world is full of Martha Knights; old men nearing death are putty in their hands. But Matthew Knights are few and far between. Not that Martha is to be thought of as seeking her own personal advantage. She may, perhaps, have been a little jealous of her brother and have tried to fill something of his place in Jowett's mind. For a time she even acted as Jowett's secretary, when Matthew fell ill in 1878. 'His place as secretary was taken in part by his sister, who wrote letters for Jowett and kept his correspondence in order.' He left her the same legacy, £2000, as he left to Matthew.

The boy's fresh, active unformed mind was the kindest gift the gods could have possibly given to Jowett, a *tabula rasa* on which to inscribe his own wisdom. He put all that he had into the delightful task of completing Matthew's education. How he did this was told by Matthew himself, after his master's death; how well he succeeded is evident enough from the informed yet unaffected simplicity of Matthew's style.

He would occasionally ask me to write essays for him, but he taught me *more Socratico*, by conversation. We talked of everything under the sun, and he endeavoured to arouse my interest in the most varied topics. The educational process was the more effective because he expected me to understand all of which he spoke, and so compelled me to use my mind to the utmost of my power.

If there was a selfish purpose on the teacher's part — a conscious intention of training the pupil to relieve the teacher — the pupil neither perceived nor resisted it. It would be absurd to suppose that Jowett, having 'hit upon' the idea of using young Matthew as his amanuensis, excluded this idea altogether from the 'educational process'. But it is perfectly clear that there was no distortion or mis-direction. The boy's ranging intelligence was compelled only by the attraction which such a mind as Jowett's could not fail to exert upon an alert young intelligence brought daily and hourly into close companionship with it. Matthew's mind moved into a planetary orbit round Jowett's sun; and became the companion of Jowett's journey towards the undiscoverable end of human existence. All that the pupil knew was that his master taught him by treating him as an equal.

Though Matthew grew up to be, in a sense, Jowett's willing and intelligent slave — taking over all the drudgery which Jowett had hitherto mostly done for himself — he was far more than that. For him, there was nobody in the world to compare with Jowett; for Jowett, there was nobody in the world capable of such service as Matthew's. The

[1] *Auctoritate* Mr. Cyril Bailey, who — reading the first draft of the earlier part of this book — commented that he and his contemporaries never thought of her as having a Christian name.

Master and his secretary became two halves of a whole person. *Animae dimidium meae* would not have been too strong a tribute for either to pay to the other; though Matthew would have thought that it grossly over-stated his share in Jowett, and Jowett (if Matthew had died before he did) might have said that it understated his debt to Matthew.

The young amanuensis, as a matter of course, was a member of the vacation reading-parties. He was accepted by Jowett's pupils and ex-pupils as one of themselves. If there was any distinction between him and them, the distinction was in his favour, not in theirs; for it was his privilege to be devoting himself to his and their Master. They did not think of him, nor did he think or need to think of himself, as a hired hand, the son of a college servant.

There is an account of the West Malvern reading-parties, written by Matthew at Abbott's request, in the *Life and Letters*. It is rather long; but it gives so vivid a picture of Jowett, and implies so much of Matthew's own modesty and ability, that it must be reproduced here without any abbreviation.[1]

The Master was often seen at his best during these little parties at Malvern. He had a stock of stories to which he was constantly adding, and which he told with the greatest enjoyment. I remember Mr. B. relating a Scotch story at table of a minister who seeing one of his congregation asleep brought him up with a pause, and then holding out a finger said solemnly, 'There'll be no sleeping in hell, John;' to which the offender retorted, 'Aye, but it'll no be for the lack of ministers.' Jowett was very much amused with this, and after a little time said, 'Now, B., let us have have another story, equally good and equally wicked with the last.' In Scotch stories indeed he took an especial delight, and always came back from Scotland with a new store.

Sometimes, however, he would be *distrait* and weary, and sit silent at the head of the table, leaving us to our own devices and only interposing an occasional remark when something caught his ear. Once when we were talking among ourselves about the Middle Ages, and at last I happened to say that 'it would be interesting to know more about the real character of the people', he roused himself at this, and observed in his quick way. 'Oh, much like ourselves, I expect, only dirtier in their habits.'

But in general he treated us in the Socratic manner, and often contrived to elicit from us a good deal more than was ever in us. Like Dr. Johnson, he would argue a question contrary to his own convictions, either in a dialectical spirit or in order to put our opinions to the test. He attached great importance to good conversation, and would sometimes say, half apologetically, 'I wish that I had had some one to point out my mistakes when I was your age.'

At times his rebukes were of what Boswell would call an 'overwhelming character'. Once, for instance, when on his way to Clifton, I accompanied him as far as Tewkesbury. The quaint old-world town seemed asleep in the summer sunshine, and after we had walked about some time, I rashly ventured to say, 'I believe that there are more dogs than people in the

---

[1] *L. & L.*, ii, 147–8. I have taken the liberty of breaking it up into paragraphs.

streets this morning.' He instantly awoke from his reverie and replied, 'If you have nothing more sensible to observe, you had better be silent altogether.'

He rarely failed to go to the village church on Sunday mornings, or sometimes, for a change, to the Priory Church at Great Malvern, and he was pleased if we accompanied him, although he did not mention the subject. He once gave me a characteristic piece of advice: 'Always read the best poets, and keep up a habit of regular attendance at church.'

The gods, having made this great gift to Jowett, cruelly withdrew it. In 1878 Matthew 'fell very seriously ill of lung disease, and became quite incapable of work'. Jowett sent him to stay at Torquay with Emily; and next year 'when he had somewhat recovered' to Davos. 'But it was a long time before he could undertake any active work, and indeed he never quite returned to his old duties.' Martha Knight did what she could to help the Master out; and there was a clever young boy in the library who took on the task of copyist. How long this makeshift arrangement lasted, it is impossible to know; for Abbott's narrative, so far as Matthew is concerned, is fragmentary and unsystematic. But it would seem that Matthew must have recovered his health sufficiently to go back to the more important part of his work by 1882, when Jowett became Vice-Chancellor; for it was not until 1886, the year in which he ceased to be Vice-Chancellor, that the boy in the library became his 'secretary in literary matters'. Soon after Matthew's illness declared itself, Jowett also lost the services of Matthew's father, whose health broke down in 1880 and whose departure from his house he felt 'as the loss of a friend'.

Matthew outlived his master by only two years. He died on 24th September 1895. He must then have been about forty-one; and the last seventeen years of his short life had been a losing struggle with consumption. There is no memorial of him that I know of, except for the scattered references which are brought together here and Jowett's own published acknowledgments.

In the preface to the 1892 edition of the *Dialogues of Plato* Jowett wrote:

In this, the Third Edition, I am under very great obligations to Mr. Matthew Knight, who has not only favoured me with valuable suggestions throughout the work, but has largely extended the Index (from 61 to 175 pages) and translated the *Eryxias* and second *Alcibiades*.

In his Will Jowett expressed to Matthew 'grateful recognition of his valuable services to me and the many happy hours we have passed together'. Without these services and that companionship it seems certain that Jowett's work on Plato could not have reached its final form.

Matthew Knight's place was taken in 1886 by a young man of nineteen, whose education had also been of Jowett's contriving. 'I get on pretty well' he wrote after Matthew's first collapse in 1878; 'the youth in the Library helps me in matters purely mechanical (he is very punctual and good, if only he wrote a better hand).' The youth in the library was a boy of eleven, Frank Fletcher, another of Jowett's characteristic discoveries. For 'he never let slip an opportunity of giving a poor and deserving lad a good education'. Fletcher was such a lad; he and another boy were brought into the library by Jowett as assistants, and given the prospect of going through the University course later on 'along with their occupation'. So, in the very year when he became the Master's secretary 'in literary matters' Fletcher matriculated at Balliol. He won the Gaisford Prize for Greek Verse, played in the Oxfordshire cricket and football teams, took an honours degree and eventually became Professor of Classics at Exeter. He retired in 1933, after a long and distinguished career, and died early in 1956, in his ninetieth year.

Fletcher, like Knight, repaid his benefactor with able and devoted service; and he, too, was mentioned in Jowett's Will and in the preface to the third edition of the *Dialogues*, where Jowett bracketed him with Matthew Knight as 'my secretary, who has assisted me chiefly in Vols. iii, iv and v'.

The reduction of working time in the vacations, the development of Matthew Knight into a pupil-secretary, the stimulus of the Mastership — all these things enabled Jowett to overcome his anxieties about health and to go on actively working, even after Matthew Knight's illness, until his succession to the Vice-Chancellorship gave the second great stimulus to his internal powers. Matthew's illness had, indeed, set him back. 'His dream of finishing his translations vanished' Abbott says *sub anno* 1878, and quotes him as writing: 'I am going to print Thucydides; poor Knight's illness makes me give up the *Politics* for the present.'

He had a rather curious reason for his interest in Aristotle's *Politics*, which must have seriously interfered with his main work on Plato. 'I find it' he said 'a satisfactory work, because it is the summing up of so much desultory reading. But for difficulty I believe that no book equals it.' His translation of the *Politics* was not, however, wholly pushed into a pigeon-hole. Volume I, containing the Introduction and Translation, and the first part of Volume II, containing the Notes, were published in 1885. The second part of Volume II was never completed. This was to contain a series of essays, so clearly imagined by Jowett that he actually gave a detailed list of them in his preface to Volume I, saying that they would be published shortly and would complete that volume. His language almost suggests that they had already been written.

In this preface, too, Jowett showed how well he was aware of Matthew Knight's unusual quality. The translator (for that is how he speaks of himself)

has also to express his gratitude to his friend and secretary, Mr. Matthew Knight, for the excellent Indices he has prepared both of the Text and Notes, and for many valuable suggestions which occur in different parts of the book. He wishes that Mr. Knight could be induced to bestow on some work of his own the knowledge and thought which he devotes to the work of another.

Alas, Matthew Knight had spent all that the gods would allow him to spend, upon 'the work of another'. He had taken up again, for a short time, his life's single purpose — the service of his incomparable friend and teacher. But by 1886 there was no possibility of continuing in that service. He must die by slow degrees, and follow his master as soon as might be into the world of Plato's imagining.

Jowett held out bravely against physical decay. He never experienced a real illness before 1887. In that year, having lost Matthew and having drawn upon his own reserves of energy during the four years of his Vice-Chancellorship to the point of exhaustion, he fell, for the first time, seriously ill. It was the kind of prolonged *malaise* which goes on and on and defies (at least, it defied Acland's) diagnosis. It was nothing. It was a common cold. It was the after-effect of a common cold. But it persisted; and Jowett began, at last, to perceive that he could not hope to escape, very much longer or by any means, the ordinary fate of men. The illness which afflicted him in this year seems to have been a pulmonary disease, not the cardiac disease which killed him five years later. But the body was running down towards its final stop.

He recovered for a while. In 1891 Azrael struck again. This second visitation was to the heart. In the summer of that year he suffered what he described to Lady Wemyss, excusing himself for not making his annual visit to Scotland, as

a slight attack of the heart — not dangerous, I think, but it requires rest and care. It is a good warning to me. Did you ever hear the story of a man who asked his physician whether he was not dangerously ill? 'No, sir; but you are dangerously old.' So I too have come to the creaky places of life.

It was a humorous approach to the inevitable end, which he continued gallantly to resist — the end of activity, of useful cerebration. He recovered and went about his business again; he saw the third edition of his *Plato* through the press, after writing a new preface for it; and he took up his ordinary duties as Master of Balliol. But the spring of this recovery lacked the strength to maintain itself.

And most of his friends were dead or dying, or suffering disasters equal to death. The catalogue of these losses in his last year or two of life was heavy enough, let alone all similar losses in preceding years. Morier lost his son in June 1892; his friend's agony pierced Jowett, as if it were his own. Bob Lowe — Lord Sherbrooke — who had got Jowett to be Master of Balliol, died in July. Young Nettleship, one of Balliol's most 'beloved' tutors, died in a snowstorm on Mont Blanc in August. Jowett felt this blow all the more bitterly because he knew that he had never quite recognized Nettleship's value. In October, Tennyson died, Jowett's friend of very many years. This was not so unexpected as the death of the new Duke of Bedford, early in 1893. The Duke of Bedford? It may be asked, with a lift of the eyebrows, why this should so much matter. But the Duke, not then a Duke, had been one of Jowett's most responsive aristocratic pupils — not academically brilliant, for he took only a third class in Modern History. But his 'humorous and pathetic character'[1] had greatly appealed to Jowett. The Master was saddened by his death; as he was always saddened by premature deaths. A little later in the same summer, J. A. Symonds died in Rome.

The familiar stars were being put out in his sky, one after another. His own life's work was finished — its limits had been made clear to him some years before these last serious threatenings. But his mind was still vigorously alive, its purpose still active. It dwelt now, increasingly, on small things — such as the flowers to be cultivated in the college garden. Some time in 1892, in the year before his death, Morier came to visit him in Abbott's Headington cottage for a day 'which both remembered as one of the happiest of their lives', though Jowett was 'far from well, and a friend tells me [Abbott] that when she called at the house the ambassador came himself on tiptoe to the door, whispering "He is asleep".'

Next year, his seventy-sixth, death began to throw the unmistakable shadow. Long before, Jowett had asked a medical friend for guidance in the conduct of his old age. He was told two things, both of which greatly pleased and comforted him. First, that old men ought to cultivate the society of very young people 'of both sexes'. Second, that the brain — unless it is itself physically diseased — outlasts the body; it dies only because the body dies. There was no weakening of Jowett's intelligence up to the last conscious moment before his death. As he lay dying in October 1893, his friend Morier — whom he had loved longer and more

[1] 'Pathetic' in the sense, no doubt, of 'sympathetic'.

steadily than he had loved anybody else, even Florence Nightingale — lay dying at Montreux. It is pleasant to imagine that their released spirits crossed the river together, with laughter over that happy coincidence. Miss Nightingale had another seventeen years of earthly life to endure; Matthew Knight only two.

For some years before the end those who knew Jowett intimately came to discover a new kind of beauty in him. It was a muted repetition, in a minor key, of the young beauty which had won the adoration of his first 'worshippers' — a beauty of spirit, rather than of body, though Richmond's drawing of Jowett is the drawing of a beautiful, young, expressive face. There was no physical beauty of that sort in the old man — though it was said to have returned to his face after his death. But there was the beauty which belongs to 'the sweet wise death of old men honourable'.

To his friends he became, if possible, dearer than ever in those last years. 'Lenit albescens animum capillus,' one said of him, who had known him in his youth — 'Grey hairs bring gentle moods.' Age and failing health caused him to lean more on others, and his heart was touched to its depths by the kindness which it received. The children of old friends were now grown up, and looked on him with reverence and love which he repaid with an almost parental care. It was his desire to help them in every way; he entered fully into their joys and sorrows, and sought to pilot them through the troubles of life by his own experience.

Abbott lacks Campbell's lighter touch. What he says hangs a little too solemnly, a little too heavily on the ear, like a tolling bell or an obituary notice. I wish that I knew how to disperse this funereal tone. Abbott tried to break it by using the familiar Horatian tag: *lenit albescens animum capillus*.[1] But he omitted to complete the quotation; it continues *litium et rixae cupidos protervae*, meaning that the spirit, softening with the whitening hair, had once been greedy for battles and wanton strife. Horace was talking about himself; and there have been few men to whom Horace's self-description applied less than Jowett. Yet, perhaps, the Latin tag fitted him tolerably well. If he had not been greedy for strife, he had suffered much from it; and, as his hair whitened, all sense of resentment had utterly left him.

Azrael struck, for the third and last time, on 23rd September 1893. There could be no recovery from this attack — it seems to have been the renewal of a coronary thrombosis which had nearly killed him in 1891. There was no prolonged agony between the onset of illness and death. He died, very peacefully, after a short week of restlessness and pain, on the first day of October — a beautiful autumn afternoon.

[1] The right reading is *animos* not *animum* — in the plural, not the singular. It doesn't really matter. The meaning is 'whitening hair gentles the mind'.

It is never possible for any child of man, however wise he may think himself to be, to understand death until it comes to him. All we who are yet alive can learn about death, as the last experience of individual man, has to be gained from observation. How do men die? How do they behave in the face of death when they have to lie and wait for it? How does their behaviour, then, conform with their past, more or less confident, behaviour? Does mind remain in control? Or does it lose control and slip into fear or sentimentality?

I will not attempt to answer these or any other of the similar questions, which begin to seem important to most of us only as we begin ourselves to approach within sight of our own ending. There are several accounts of Jowett's approach to the hour of death. They all essentially agree. He knew well what was coming. He was not afraid; he was still himself — urging Martha Knight, for example, to make the best use of her life after he was gone. The description which strikes me most deeply is that of Lady Sophia Palmer, who went to see him with her father Lord Selborne (Roundell Palmer) five days before his death. At first the meeting was a little cloudy; the dying man had some difficulty in bringing himself back to his visitors' world.

Suddenly the Master raised himself and said, with a sudden glow of vigour and brightness which I shall never forget, 'I bless God for my life, I bless God for my life;' and then, falling back on the pillow, he murmured, again and again, as if we were not there, 'I bless God for my life.' Father thought him wandering and weaker, and that we ought to go, and he knelt by the bedside, and took the Master's hand, which lay on the coverlet, and reverently kissed it. Then Mr. Jowett looked up to him and said (curiously almost word for word what my father said), 'Mine has been a happy life, I bless God for my life.'

On the Sunday when he died, Mrs. Green (the widow of T. H. Green) was with him. Her account is such as to bring tears to the eyes and comfort to the mind. Let it end this story, and let its simplicity resolve all the long argument.

I shall always remember the beautiful Sunday afternoon when he passed away. He was looking so ill and suffering those last days, and when the last peace had come all the beauty and grandeur came back and he lay asleep so that it was a joy to behold. The windows were wide open to the country, and Sir Robert and Lady Wright brought heather and wild flowers and laid them round his bed. Later, the moon shone in and lit up his beautiful marble face and the shining white hair. There seemed to be a blending of the dignity and wisdom of old age and of the simplicity and radiant freshness of youth.

14. The 'old man honourable'
A photograph by H. H. H. Cameron in 1893
(*Balliol*)

APPENDIX I

'Abbott and Campbell'

The official biography was published by John Murray in two long demy 8vo volumes in 1897. The preface is dated 7th January. The task of collecting material and letters, and of composition, had therefore been completed in barely three years from the date of Jowett's death (1st October 1893). Much of the book, if not all of it, was in type long before the preface was written.

The full title is *The Life and letters/of/Benjamin Jowett, M.A./Master of Balliol College, Oxford.* The title page of each volume carries the names of the two authors, Evelyn Abbott, M.A., LL.D., and Lewis Campbell, M.A., LL.D., in that order.

Each volume contains seven illustrations. Four of these are portraits. The frontispiece to the first volume is Richmond's drawing, done in 1855; that to the second volume is Lady Abercromby's water-colour portrait done in 1892. The second volume also reproduces a lively pencil sketch of Mazzini and Jowett in conversation in 1868, done by George Howard, and a photograph taken by H. H. H. Cameron in 1893. The other illustrations are drawings of Balliol and Tummel Bridge, and facsimiles of Jowett's hand-writing. An appendix lists three other known portraits (not reproduced); a drawing by Laugée, dated 1871; an oil painting by G. F. Watts; and a pastel by Cavaliere N. M. Ross. Three photographs are also mentioned: one taken by Valery in 1886; and two taken by Cameron in 1893, of which one is the photograph reproduced in Volume II.

In 1899 a supplementary volume was published entitled *Letters/of/ Benjamin Jowett, M.A./Master of Balliol College, Oxford.* These are 'arranged and edited' by Abbott and Campbell. The title fails to indicate that the volume contains a short, but valuable, concluding section of 'Notes and Sayings'. The letters are grouped by topics — not always very well grouped — and many of them lack the quick, personal, interest which belongs to most of the letters printed in the two earlier volumes. They are mostly letters written about public topics. The volume has, as frontispiece, the drawing by Laugée mentioned above. This third volume is very much shorter than either of the two volumes of

The Life and Letters — 262 pages (including index) compared with the 446 pages of the first volume, and the 499 pages (including index) of the second. It is made to look the same length, only because it is 'bulked out' by the use of thicker paper.

John Murray's advertisement at the end of the third volume announces a reprint of *The Life and Letters*, price 32s. for the two volumes. It quotes a rather ineffective commendation from the *Standard*:

A most agreeable impression of his own personal character is left upon us by this biography, one to make those who read it realize what a privilege it was to be intimate with him, and to account for the almost religious respect with which he was regarded by successive generations of Balliol men.

Tuckwell, my own favourite guide to nineteenth-century Oxford, thought very highly indeed of *The Life and Letters*. He speaks of it as 'a book which for my own part I never open without extracting from it gold unalloyed'. The book is, certainly, a rich mine. But it cannot be described as a good biography. It would have been very difficult even for a single biographer to present Jowett's life in a true perspective, so soon after his death and in the intellectual and moral atmosphere of the closing century. Stanley had a far easier problem after Arnold's death. R. E. Prothero said in a letter to William Markby (one of Jowett's executors) criticizing Campbell's volume: 'Stanley's biography of Arnold is a work of genius, such as no writer of the present day could, I believe, accomplish.'

This (unpublished) letter of Prothero's was written in June 1896, from 50 Albemarle Street, where he was then acting as literary adviser to the third John Murray. It was in answer to an enquiry from Markby 'on the subject of Jowett's Life', and it began by saying that 'John Murray, whom I have just consulted, is very strongly of my opinion'. It concerned only the first, Campbell's, volume.

The general effect is very flat. Jowett does not stand out with any clearness or definiteness of outline. I think this is partially owing to the number of persons who cross and recross the stage. It is also partly due to the practice of concluding each chapter with a batch of correspondence. In this practice the author is, of course, following the practice of Stanley in his *Life of Arnold*. But Stanley's vivid, picturesque style created an impression, which outlasts the interpolated letters and carries the reader on into the next chapter of continuous narrative. In less skilful hands the practice is a dangerous one.

Prothero suggested two remedies:

(1) to strengthen the narrative and work it up into something brighter and more attractive (2) to throw the letters together at the end.

After some criticisms of detail and further reference to Stanley's *Life of Arnold* Prothero concluded:

Of course I am writing to you with the intention that you should make such use of this letter as you think useful: but naturally it is not for the eye of Mr. Lewis Campbell.

It seems entirely clear, from the concluding sentence and also from the fact that the letter was preserved by Abbott, that Prothero's criticisms were directed against the first volume (written exclusively by Campbell) which was already in the 'slip' proof stage: that is to say, in galley form, but divided into pages. This stage had been reached by May 1896, so far as Campbell's volume was concerned. I do not know how, at that date, Abbott's volume stood. It seems to have been less well advanced; for Campbell, writing to Abbott on 14th July 1896, says: 'it has been a great pleasure to me to see the opening chapters of vol. 2.'

I wish to say that I think very poorly of Prothero's comments and suggestions. The selection and arrangement of the letters, chapter by chapter, seems to me to have been a good and necessary plan; it was followed by Abbott as well as by Campbell. I disagree strongly with the criticism that Jowett (in Campbell's volume) doesn't 'stand out'. Nevertheless, Prothero's letter appears to have reflected the general view of all concerned that Campbell hadn't measured up to the job. They were of a later generation than Campbell. He, alone, had known his hero as a young man and was curious, as they were not, about his boyhood and adolescence, his early manhood and middle life. For me, the younger Jowett is a more interesting figure than the Master. I find Campbell's volume rich in matter of which nobody but he then perceived the importance. Even so, he was obliged to leave unsaid a great deal that he wanted to say, and had actually written out. Some of the enforced deletions were, I suppose, necessitated by delicacy towards Margaret Elliot and some were dictated by Florence Nightingale. He could make no more than a vague and unintelligible allusion to Jowett's idea of marriage. And he had to fight hard to be allowed to retain his account of Jowett's religious opinions at the time of his ordination.

Who were the 'they', in a position to exercise this restraint? In his Will Jowett named as his executors Courtenay Ilbert, Sir William James Farrer and Sir William Markby; giving them the ultimate decision, if any difference of opinion should arise about any of the provisions of his Will. He left the 'perpetual copyright' of his writings to Balliol, directing that they should be 'republished from time to time'. The income thence accruing was to be 'applied in the first place to the improvement or correction of them' and then for the benefit of the study of Greek literature or the advancement of learning. The college was to appoint Mr. C. P. Ilbert, Mr. Justice Wright, Professor Lewis Campbell, Mr. Hardie 'or other suitable persons' to carry out these instructions. A month before his death he added a codicil, in which he appointed 'Professor Lewis Campbell, Mr. Evelyn Abbott and Mr. Lyttleton Gell my Literary Executors' and gave them 'entire control over my papers and other writings excepting so far as provision is made for them by the terms of my Will'.

Campbell, therefore, stood under the Will in an exceptionally strong position. He was the only person mentioned both in the Will and the Codicil. He was senior to all the other persons named, except Farrer, and the only one who had been a pupil of Jowett when his tutor was still under forty. Moreover Campbell had remained on intimate, easy and affectionate terms with Jowett all his life. At the time of Jowett's death he had just retired from the chair of Greek at St. Andrews, which he had held for all but thirty years; he was sixty-three, brim-full of imagination and energy (he lived to be seventy-eight), and a distinguished man in his own right.

All this makes his subordination to Abbott difficult to understand. It is true enough that, after sixty, men often begin to lose confidence in their own powers and to defer, with a sort of inverted reverence, to the unabated confidence of their juniors. There is no overt sign of this in Campbell's correspondence with Abbott, or in his own approach to the extraordinarily difficult task he had undertaken. His letters to Abbott, during their difficult partnership, never convey any touchiness or resentment. One or two of them exhibit a really remarkable understanding of their common task. There is a very interesting letter in which he draws a contrast between the kind of biography upon which he and Abbott were engaged, and what he terms the *éloge*, the considered, judicious, well-proportioned, but *short* biography, which cannot be undertaken until a sufficient length of time has passed.

Yet Campbell was firmly relegated to a subordinate place. It seems that Ilbert and Markby, along with Abbott and Gell, must have agreed with Murray and Prothero, that he had made rather a mess of the first volume. At any rate, when *The Life and Letters* was published, Abbott's name appeared on the title-page of both volumes before that of Campbell — though Campbell was the senior, and had written the whole of the first volume. And the first volume, Campbell's own sole work, carried a preface written and signed solely by Abbott. Nobody seems ever to have observed how extremely odd, not to say improper, this was. To me, as a publisher, it was clear and immediate evidence that the collaboration had not been happy, and that Campbell had been deliberately pushed off the stage at some late point in the preparation of the two volumes. Prothero's letter to Markby, which I discovered later, confirmed this rather obvious inference.

The opening sentences of Abbott's preface, printed at the beginning of Campbell's volume, while they contradict Prothero's particular criticism over the use of letters, make it quite plain that Campbell had been reduced to inferior status. They reveal also (as I think) the main fault of the biography considered as a whole — that is, the division of Jowett's life into two separate volumes, written by two different men. This is what Abbott says; and what he says seems to me to open from an utterly wrong angle.

Professor Jowett's life naturally falls into two sections — the period before the Mastership, and the Mastership. The first of these volumes contains the first period, and is the work of Professor Campbell; in the second, I have written the story of the Mastership; and I am responsible for the whole. The plan followed in both volumes is of course the same. A few letters have been worked into the narrative; others, far too numerous to be used in such a manner, but of a personal character, have been appended to the chapters according to their dates, and thus form as it were illustrations of the text, giving in Jowett's own words his thoughts and feelings at the time.

Campbell's letters to Abbott upon the aims of their joint undertaking, written while it was in progress, exhibit (as I have said) no trace of resentment. There is no sharpness of tone or breach of friendliness. It is an entirely one-sided correspondence; for Abbott, when he deposited Campbell's letters in one of Jowett's deed boxes, either retained or destroyed his own. The absence of replies helps to deepen the impression of a fundamental lack of sympathy between the two men. The impression grows, as one reads Campbell's letters, of an older man becoming gradually and rather pathetically aware that he had been assigned what the younger generation supposed to be the less important part in the collaboration, and that his own idea of the way in which even this lesser part should be written was in conflict with theirs.

Here is one example. Abbott and Caird (Jowett's successor in the Mastership), had, apparently, criticized Campbell's narrative on the ground that it lacked 'connexion'. Campbell replied, with considerable force: 'Connexion in a biography is not the same thing as in a reasoned treatise.' In a later letter (written from Milan, in April 1896) he said, more humbly: 'I will try to study "connexion", but things "do come abruptly" in a human life!' In the same letter, he refused to succumb to the myth of an unchanging Jowett. Jowett's career, he said, cannot be treated as if he were *qualis ab incepto*. His tenacious persistence went along with a continual process of growth and re-adaptation. And notions long since dead and buried gain an interest in the retrospect from the 'living will' which penetrated them when they were present things. That when he was Stanley's junior, and comparatively unknown, *he* was the steadier and more active influence in all that they did together, is to my mind a very characteristic point.

In this passage, it seems to me that Campbell shows a grasp of the biographer's aim, which Abbott and 'they' failed to share.

The criticism about want of 'connexion' had been particularly applied to the chapter (iv) in which Campbell sought to describe Jowett's religious views at the time of his ordination; and here he more or less held his own against the cautious objections of Caird and Abbott, though he set to work at once to recast what he had written.

I am sure that neither of you wish that any essential fact should be disguised. And the state of his mind on religious questions at the time of Ordination does seem an essential fact, on which the notebook of 1841 and the correspondence of 1838, 1839 threw unexpected light. Nor is it unessential to the biography that in the early years he had difficulties which he overcame and even trials of an inward sort which he 'crushed' upon the threshold of the 'mind'. And my own inclination would be to present the facts both outward and inward as they arise without setting up a signpost pointing to the change which followed. But, as you indicate, one must consider the imagination, or want of imagination, of the average reader; and I will try to meet this.

These few and brief quotations from Campbell's letters to Abbott may help to show why the resulting two-volume biography, for all the immense mass of detailed information it contains and for all the skilled labour spent upon it, has never taken rank as a satisfying, consistent, interpretation of its baffling hero — and can even less take such rank now, when we know what it was obliged to omit.

The two collaborators were of different age, mind and temperament. Campbell went to Balliol in 1849, when Jowett was thirty-two and (as boxers say) in his 'pride'; Abbott in 1862, when that wonderful bloom was gone. Campbell had remained on far more intimate terms with Jowett than Abbott ever was; he belonged, almost, to Jowett's youth. He was a distinguished Hellenist, and so was his collaborator; but there the similarity ended. Campbell was highly strung, passionately interested in drama, imaginative, capable of rapid (and even shocking) inaccuracies but also of brilliant intuitive insight. Abbott was a man of solid indomitable will and resolute exactitude.

Their histories differed significantly. Campbell, on taking his degree, stayed in Oxford as a fellow of Queen's, and was ordained. After five years in a Hampshire vicarage (where he no doubt expounded 'the liberal theology which he had learned from Jowett') he succeeded Sellar as professor of Greek at St. Andrews. This was in 1863. In 1893 he resigned his chair and built a house at Alassio, where he died — still mentally alert and active — in 1908. He was Gifford Lecturer in 1894 and 1895. His letters to Abbott are mostly written from St. Andrews or Dundee or Headington or Kensington; and it is evident that he spent most of his time in the United Kingdom, while he was writing his part of Jowett's life — a free, active, happily married man in his early sixties, with a *pied à terre* in Italy and nothing to do but what he wanted to do. And, since Jowett's strange personality had been the dominant, creative, force in his life, there was nothing he so much wished to do as to repay and explain this debt. His eager exploration of Jowett's otherwise utterly unknown family background — cut down to a few pages in the *Life* but fully preserved in the Jowett Papers — has extraordinary value. Without it, Jowett is an inexplicable person. With it, he becomes explicable. Abbott could never have undertaken this kind of enquiry; and would never have thought it worth while.

Abbott's career was in a different, more heroic, key. He was one of those all-rounders whom Fate tries and fails to destroy. As a young man of twenty-five, with the worlds of scholarship and athleticism equally at his feet, he

fell in a hurdle race and injured his spine. Unhappily, he was so unaccustomed to illness that he did not recognize the serious nature of the accident, and continued his exertions, both at his books and at cricket, as if nothing had occurred.

He became 'hopelessly paralysed in the lower limbs'; and for the rest of his life 'never put foot to the ground'. He met this physical disaster with the most determined courage and cheerfulness; first taking private pupils, and then teaching at Clifton. In 1874 Jowett brought him back to Balliol, as fellow and tutor. He died in 1901.

The differences between the two men illuminate the weaknesses of a book which, nevertheless, contains 'gold unalloyed': Campbell released but devoted, Abbott devoted but not released. Behind Abbott were ranged 'they' — the authoritative men, most of whom had never known Jowett until he had become the undisputed ruler of Balliol, whether *de facto* or *de jure*. The Life to be written was to be the Life of the Master. But Campbell wished to discover the origins and tell the story of the young man whom he remembered as 'they' did not. Whatever its faults — and they are many, but by no means all of them are Campbell's — his volume has a dynamic quality. Jowett grows. In Abbott's half of the *Life* Jowett is a static figure in a great position. It is to Campbell, not to

Abbott, that one must turn to understand Jowett; and Campbell's own idiosyncrasies — his dislike of artificially contrived 'connexion', his instinctive enthusiasms and recollections, the natural looseness of his style, even his very inaccuracies (easily discoverable) — if these seemed vices to his publisher and to his publisher's reader and to his collaborator and to the critical Executors and Literary Executors of Jowett's Will and to the rulers of the new Balliol, for us (at least for me) they are virtues. They give us truth, instead of a balanced panegyric constructed to the requirements of a too quickly assumed perspective.

NOTE

An intriguing mystery attaches to the little book *Essays on Men and Manners*, mentioned above (104 footnote) and listed below (441). Edited by Gell, it contains four addresses given by Jowett (the first at Edinburgh) on the character of Socrates, his trial and death, Boswell and Johnson, and Johnson's own writings and character. A fifth section, 'Friends and Contemporaries', is made up of extracts culled from Jowett's Balliol speeches and sermons. I drew on this to report Jowett's description of the old Master (above, 104).

The B.M. Catalogue does not know of this or of any similar book. Nor (Mr. Quinn tells me) does the English Catalogue of Books. Nor do its intended publishers (John Murray). It seems to exist only in a proof-state. Balliol has a number of paper-bound, crown 8vo, imperfect copies. They bear Murray's imprint and a publication date (1895). A gap in the pagination suggests that eight pages had been dropped between the fourth and fifth sections. Two of the footnotes contain blank spaces for the insertion of dates.

The *Life and Letters* (ii, 479), published in 1897, does not mention this book. It does list, as in preparation, '*Lectures and Addresses*; cr. 8vo; edited by P. Lyttelton Gell'. Mr. Quinn suggests, and I agree, that the reference is to the book proofed for publication in 1895 and still unpublished in 1897. The change of title may, perhaps, indicate some intended change of structure.

My own inference is that Gell ran into much the same trouble with the Executors as Campbell did; and that 'they' considered these occasional pieces unworthy of the monument to be erected. A letter of Gell's, which I have recently seen at Balliol, shows that he was afraid of being charged with misusing his position as a Literary Executor for his own profit.

APPENDIX II

Books and Documents

(*N.B.* Those items, which the author has not seen, but which are included in the following lists for the sake of an approach to completeness, are enclosed in square brackets. When more than one edition is named, the edition first named is that possessed and used by the writer.)

A. JOWETT'S PUBLISHED WORKS

(This list does not purport to be a complete bibliography. It does, however, include all the publications ascribed to him in the British Museum or Balliol Libraries.)

[1. *De Etruscorum Cultu moribus et legibus eorumque apud Romanos vestigiis: oratio in Theatro Sheldoniano habita, die Junii* 15, 1841. Oxon., 1841.]

[2. The Indian Civil Service. A Report to the Rt. Hon. Sir C. Wood by T. B. Macaulay and others. The 'others' include Jowett. London, 1855.]

3. *The Epistles of St. Paul to the Thessalonians, Galatians, Romans.* With critical notes and dissertations. 2 vols. Second, revised, edition. Murray, 1859. (First edition 1855; third edition, edited and condensed by Professor Campbell, 1894.)

4. *On the Interpretation of Scripture.* This is the 7th essay in 'Essays and Reviews'. Parker, 1860. (Jowett's essay was incorporated in the third edition of his 'Epistles of St. Paul'. It was frequently reprinted in 'Essays and Reviews' and was used in the posthumous collections of Jowett's theological writings edited by Campbell.)

5. *The Dialogues of Plato* translated into English with analyses and introductions. 5 vols. Third edition, revised and corrected throughout, with marginal analyses and an index of subjects and proper names. Clarendon Press, 1892. (First edition in 4 vols. 1871; second edition in 5 vols. 1875.)

6. *The Republic of Plato* translated into English with introduction, analysis, marginal analysis, and index. Third edition, revised and corrected throughout. Clarendon Press, 1888. (This was a separate

issue; the two former editions were contained in the first and second editions of the Dialogues. The third edition was incorporated, without further change, in vol. iii of the third and final edition of the Dialogues.)

7. *Lord Lytton: the man and the author.* A very short 'discourse delivered in Westminster Abbey' used as a preface to 'a carefully written biography by M. Marsden'. Farrah, 1873. (A penny pamphlet.)

[8. *The School and Children's Bible* prepared under the supervision of the Rev. William Rogers. Longman, 1873. Revised edition 1874. Reprinted in 1886. The idea of this book originated with Rogers but 'the selection was practically made by Jowett' (*L. & L.*, ii, 36.) Not recognized as Jowett's in the British Museum Catalogue.]

[9. *Suggestions for University Reform*, 1874. Reproduced by Campbell in his *On the nationalisation of the old English universities*. London, 1901.]

10. *Thucydides* translated into English with introduction, marginal analysis, notes, and indices. Vol. i containing the text; vol. ii containing the notes, to which are added an essay on contemporary inscriptions and other brief dissertations. Clarendon Press, 1881.

11. A short memoir of Arnold Toynbee prefixed to Toynbee's posthumous *Lectures on the Industrial Revolution in England*. London, 1884. (2nd edition 1887.)

[12. A preface to a volume of Greek *Selections from the Dialogues of Plato* edited by Jowett and Purves. Clarendon Press, 1883. This preface was used again for a volume of English *Selections from Plato* edited by Jowett and Matthew Knight. Clarendon Press, 1894.]

13. *The Politics of Aristotle* translated into English with introduction, marginal analysis, essays, notes and indices. Vol. i containing the introduction and translation; vol. ii part i containing the notes. Clarendon Press, 1885. (Vol. ii part ii, intended to contain the essays, was never published.)

14. *Recollections of Professor Smith*. A short memoir prefixed to vol. i of H. J. S. Smith's *Collected Mathematical Papers*. Clarendon Press, 1894.

15. *College Sermons* edited by the Hon. and Very Rev. W. H. Fremantle, Dean of Ripon. Murray, 1895. (In the codicil to his Will, a month before he died, Jowett said: 'I am doubtful if my sermons or unfinished papers should be published at all.' He left this to the discretion of his Literary Executors — Campbell, Abbott and Gell.)

16. *Sermons Biographical and Miscellaneous* edited by Fremantle. Murray, 1899.

17. *Sermons on Faith and Doctrine* edited by Fremantle. Murray, 1901.

18. *Select Passages from the Theological Writings of Benjamin Jowett* edited by Lewis Campbell. Murray, 1902. The only previously unpublished material in this book consists of a few 'MS fragments'. Two further posthumous volumes, edited by Campbell, were *Theological Essays* (Frowde 1906) and *Scripture and Truth* (Frowde 1907); but they contain no matter not already published.

B. BIOGRAPHIES AND BIOGRAPHICAL ESSAYS

1. *Benjamin Jowett etc.: His Life and Work. With Reminiscences and Memorials by Pupils and Friends. Westminster Extra*, No. 4, October 1893. An illustrated newspaper supplement of remarkable quality.

[2. *Benjamin Jowett*. A Sermon preached in Balliol Chapel on Sunday November 12 1893 by William Rogers M.A. Rector of Bishopsgate. Spottiswoode, 1893. Balliol Library.]

[3. *Some Personal Recollections of the Master of Balliol* by William M. Hardinge. Temple Bar, October 1894. Balliol Library.]

4. *Recollections of Professor Jowett*. By Algernon Charles Swinburne. Included in *Studies in Prose and Poetry*, Chatto, 1894.

5. *Benjamin Jowett, Master of Balliol*. By the Hon. Lionel A. Tollemache. Second edition, Arnold, 1895. (Originally published in the Journal of Education, May 1895; expanded in book form.)

6. *Professor Jowett*. By Edward Caird, Balliol College, Oxford. An off-print from the International Journal of Ethics, October 1897.

7. *The Life and Letters of Benjamin Jowett, M.A. Master of Balliol College, Oxford*. By Evelyn Abbott and Lewis Campbell. Vol. i, by Campbell, 1817–1870; vol. ii by Abbott, 1870–1893. Murray, 1897. (See Appendix I.)

8. *Letters of Benjamin Jowett, M.A. Master of Balliol College, Oxford*. Arranged and edited by Evelyn Abbott and Lewis Campbell. Murray, 1899. Described by Abbott as 'merely a supplement to the *Life and Letters*'. Arranged 'into sections, according to the subjects treated in them', viz. Church Reform, Educational, European Politics, Letters on India, Miscellaneous Notes and Sayings. The last section consists of *obiter dicta*. The letters are well annotated.

9. *Jowett's Life*. By Leslie Stephen. Included in the 2nd vol. of

435

Stephen's *Studies of a Biographer*, Duckworth, 1898. (Reissued in 1910 and reprinted in the same year; my copy is that of the 1910 reprint. Written as a review of the *Life and Letters*.)

10. *Life of Jowett*. By the Rev. Professor A. R. MacEwen. The Balliol College Register refers to this as if it had been published. I know it only as a typescript preserved in the Jowett Papers. No date.

11. Article on Benjamin Jowett in the *Dictionary of National Biography*, first supplement, vol. iii, by Evelyn Abbott. Smith, Elder, 1901.

12. Article on Benjamin Jowett in the *Encyclopaedia Britannica*, tenth edition, vol. xxix, by Lewis Campbell. 'The Times', 1902. The best summary account.

13. *Jowett of Balliol*. By R. Bruce Boswell. London, 1902. A very short, but well informed, appreciation in a 'miniature series' of similar short appreciations of eminent men. [I have not seen the Balliol Library copy; which is dated 1903 and described as belonging to a series called 'Makers of modern Britain'.]

14. *Reminiscences of Jowett*. By A. L. S. Privately circulated from *The Blue Book*. Arden Press, Letchworth. No date.

C. SECONDARY PUBLISHED SOURCES, BOOKS OF REFERENCE, ETC.

(These are legion. The following list names most of the books specifically used or consulted by the writer, and is divided into three categories. The order of mention is very roughly adjusted to the sequence of the argument or story unfolded in the present volume. The books which have contributed most to its structure are marked with an asterisk.)

(i) HISTORIES, BOOKS OF REFERENCE AND COMMENTARIES

*1. *The Dictionary of National Biography* and its Supplements. Smith Elder and the Oxford University Press.

*2. *The Balliol College Register*. Edited by Sir Ivo Elliott. Second edition, 1833–1933. Oxford, 1934. Printed for private circulation. (The indispensable guide.)

*3. *Balliol College*. By H. W. Carless Davis. (In the series of 'College Histories'.) Robinson, 1899.

4. *The University of Oxford*. Oxford University Press, 1954. (This is vol. iii of the Victorian History of the County of Oxford. It contains an article on the history of Balliol by R. W. Hunt.)

*5. *A History of the University of Oxford*. By Charles Mallet. Vol. iii, Modern Oxford. Methuen, 1927.

6. *The Historical Register of the University of Oxford.* Clarendon Press, 1900.

7. *Public Schools and British Opinion.* By Edward C. Mack. Vol. i, 1780–1860. Methuen, 1938. Vol. ii, since 1860. Columbia University Press, 1941.

8. *The Age of Reform* 1815–1870. By E. L. Woodward. Clarendon Press, third corrected reprint, 1946. (First published in 1938.)

9. *British History in the Nineteenth Century.* By G. M. Trevelyan. Longman, 1922.

10. *Annals of English Literature* 1475–1925. Clarendon Press, 1835.

11. *A Survey of English Literature* 1830–1880. By Oliver Elton. 2 vols. Arnold, 1920.

12. *A New Commentary on Holy Scripture.* Edited by Charles Gore and others. 2 vols. S.P.C.K., 1928, reprinted 1929.

13. *The English Church and how it works.* By Cecilia M. Ady. Faber, 1940.

14. *The Great Landowners of Great Britain and Ireland.* By John Bateman. New edition. Harrison, 1879.

15. Burke's *Peerage* and *Landed Gentry* (the 1925 and 1937 editions, respectively) which have enabled me to close some minor gaps.

(ii) BIOGRAPHIES, LETTERS AND REMINISCENCES

16. *Life of Thomas Arnold.* By Arthur Penrhyn Stanley. Popular edition, with a preface by Sir Joshua Fitch. Murray, 1904. (First published in 1844.)

*17. *Reminiscences of Oxford.* By the Rev. W. Tuckwell. Cassell, 1901.

18. *James Leigh Strachan-Davidson* Master of Balliol. A memoir by J. W. Mackail. Clarendon Press, 1925.

19. *Arthur Lionel Smith* Master of Balliol (1916–1924). A biography and some reminiscences by his wife. Murray, 1928.

20. *Memoir of Thomas Hill Green.* By R. L. Nettleship. Longman, 1906.

21. *Lord Bowen.* A biographical sketch. By Sir Henry Stewart Cunningham. Murray, 1897.

22. *Memories of Sir William Markby.* By his wife. Clarendon Press, 1917.

23. *A Memoir of the Right Hon. Sir William Anson.* Edited by Herbert Hensley Henson. Clarendon Press, 1920.

24. *Almond of Loretto.* Being the life and a selection from the letters of Hely Hutchinson Almond. By R. J. Mackenzie. Constable, 1905.

25. *Memorials.* Part I Family and Personal. By Roundell Palmer, Earl of Selborne. Privately printed. Edinburgh, 1889.

*26. *William George Ward and the Oxford Movement.* By Wilfrid Ward. Second edition. Macmillan, 1890.

27. *Memoirs.* By Mark Pattison. Macmillan, 1885.

28. *Reminiscences Chiefly of Oriel College and the Oxford Movement.* By the Rev. T. Mozley. 2 vols. Longman, 1882.

29. *Recollections of Oxford.* By G. V. Cox. Macmillan, 1868.

*30. *The Life and Correspondence of Arthur Penrhyn Stanley D.D.* By Rowland Prothero. 2 vols. Murray, 1893.

*31. *Letters and Verses of Arthur Penrhyn Stanley D.D.* Edited by Rowland Prothero. Murray, 1895.

*32. *Life of Archibald Campbell Tait,* Archbishop of Canterbury. By Randall Davidson, Bishop of Rochester, and Canon Benham. 2 vols. Third edition, Macmillan, 1891. (First and second editions 1891.)

*33. *Life of Edward Bouverie Pusey.* Vol iv (1860–1882) by the Rev. J. O. Johnston and Canon W. C. E. Newbolt. Longman, 1897.
(Canon Liddon figures on the title-page as the principal author; but he died before the 4th volume was written.)

34. *Memoirs of Archbishop Temple.* By seven friends, edited by Archdeacon Sandford. 2 vols. Macmillan, 1906.

*35. *The Life of the Right Reverend Samuel Wilberforce D.D.* With selections from his diaries and correspondence. 3 vols. Vol. i by Canon Ashwell. Murray, 1880. Vol. ii by Reginald G. Wilberforce. Second edition. Murray, 1881. Vol. iii by the same. Murray, 1882.

*36. *Portrait of Josephine Butler.* By A. S. G. Butler. Faber, 1954.

37. *The Life of William Ewart Gladstone.* By John Morley. 3 vols. Macmillan, 1903.

38. *Recollections of Dean Fremantle* chiefly by himself. Edited by the Master of the Temple. Cassell, 1921.

*39. *The Victorian Chancellors.* By J. B. Atlay. 2 vols. Smith Elder, 1906. (The second volume, containing the essay on Lord Westbury.)

40. *The Life of Richard Lord Westbury.* By Thomas Arthur Nash. 2 vols. Bentley, 1888.

41. *Letters of Matthew Arnold 1848–1888.* Collected and arranged by George W. E. Russell. 2 vols. Macmillan, 1901.

42. *Alfred Lord Tennyson.* A memoir by his son. Macmillan, 1899.

43. *Alfred Tennyson.* By his grandson, Charles Tennyson. Macmillan, 1949.

*44. *The Life of Algernon Charles Swinburne*. By Edmund Gosse. Macmillan, 1917.

45. *The Letters of Algernon Charles Swinburne*. Edited by Edmund Gosse and T. J. Wise. 2 vols. Heinemann, 1918.

*46. *The Life of Florence Nightingale*. By Sir Edward Cook. 2 vols. Macmillan, 1914.

*47. *Florence Nightingale, 1820–1910*. By Cecil Woodham-Smith. Constable, 1950.

*48. *Florence Nightingale* by Lytton Strachey. In 'Eminent Victorians'. Chatto, 1918.

49. *The Autobiography of Margot Asquith*. 2 vols. Penguin Books, 1936. (First published in 1920.)

*50. *Walter Pater*. By A. C. Benson. 'English Men of Letters.' Macmillan, 1906.

*51. *Time and Chance*. The story of Arthur Evans and his forebears. By Joan Evans. Longman, 1943.

52. *Memories and Reflections 1852–1927*. By the Earl of Oxford and Asquith. 2 vols. Cassell, 1928.

53. *Memoirs*. By the Right Hon. Viscount Samuel. Cresset Press, 1945.

(iii) MISCELLANEOUS

54. *The New Method of Evaluation as applied to Π*. Anonymous. Included in 'The Complete Works of Lewis Carroll', Nonesuch Press edition. (Originally published in Oxford in 1865.)

*55. *The New Republic or Culture, Faith, and Philosophy in an English Country House*. By W. H. Mallock. A new edition. Chatto, 1878.

56. *Immanuel Kant in England 1793–1838*. By René Wellek. Princeton University Press, 1931.

57. *How Hegel came to England*. By J. H. Muirhead. ('Mind', vol. xxxvi, October, 1927.)

58. *The English Philosophers*. By Leslie Paul. Faber, 1953.

59. *More Nineteenth Century Studies: A Group of Honest Doubters*. By Professor Basil Willey. Chatto, 1956.

60. *The Poems of Arthur Hugh Clough*. Clarendon Press, 1951.

D. JOWETT'S LETTERS AND NOTEBOOKS

1. *The Letters to Florence Nightingale*. With the exception of a few letters, deposited by Sir Edward Cook's advice in the British Museum, the long series of holograph letters from 1862 to 1893, bound in 8

volumes, is in the Balliol College Library. Some of them were printed or quoted in the *Life and Letters* and some in Sir Edward Cook's *Life of Florence Nightingale*. The complete series, edited by Mr. J. N. Bryson, Fellow and Librarian of Balliol, is being prepared for publication. (See Preface.)

2. *Other Letters*. These are mostly to be found in the *Life and Letters* and the *Letters*. Some letters to Stanley, not used by Abbott and Campbell, are in the *Life of Dean Stanley*. No doubt there are many letters in private ownership which have not been printed. (I have been given a copy of one which surprisingly urged Lady Verney to write a life of her sister, Miss Nightingale.) The Jowett Papers (see below) include copies of letters to his mother and sister and to his cousin Sidney Irwin. The originals of these letters have been recently discovered at Balliol.

3. *Notebooks*. The private notebooks are preserved at Balliol among the Jowett Papers. (See footnote to p. 137.) The Papers also contain several lecture notebooks; the most important are notes for, and a transcript of, his lectures upon the Pre-Socratic Philosophers. (See p. 161.)

4. *The Jowett Papers*. Except for the aforesaid letters and notebooks, and for such matter as contributions to memoirs of distinguished Balliol men, these papers contain nothing — or practically nothing — written by Jowett. (See below under E.)

E. THE JOWETT PAPERS

Besides the material, mentioned above under D. 2 and 3, these contain a mass of what has to be described as biographical *débris*. But some of this *débris* consists of unused, or of only partially used, matter and is of very great biographical value: particularly the information collected by Lewis Campbell concerning Jowett's family history, Campbell's letters to Abbott, Campbell's 'M.E.' notebook, and Milner's and Gell's letters. (See Preface.)

For what it may be worth I append a short list showing the arrangement of the material, as it was when I returned it to Balliol.

GENERAL DISPOSITION OF JOWETT PAPERS

Black Tin Boxes

   A. Quarto notebooks, containing notes for lectures.

   B. Ditto (pre-Socratics, Plato).

      Unbound ditto (Homer, Thucydides).

C. Miscellaneous lecture and reading notes; notes for speeches; a number of small notebooks on particular subjects.

D. Notes for sermons; sermons; speech-notes.
Some miscellaneous notebooks.

E. Letters, notes and short memoirs of some biographical interest.

F. Letters copied for use by Abbott and Campbell.
Four A. & C. folders, for which no room in Wooden Box.

Wooden Box
1. Large letter case, containing Campbell's letters to Abbott.
2. Smaller ditto, containing family letters (concerning Jowett and Langhorne families).
3. Box of relics.
4. Mass of A. & C. material (mainly Campbell's galley proofs).

Brown Tin Box
The Jowett-Nightingale letters.
The personal notebooks.

N.B. — Campbell's 'M.E.' notebook and another small notebook were sent back later, and were not put by me into any of these eight boxes.

ADDENDA TO LIST A

(The following three items are in the Balliol Library)

[19. *Statements of Christian Doctrine and Practice* extracted from the published writings of the Rev. Benjamin Jowett. Oxford, Parker, 1861.]

[20. *Essays and Reviews* by the late Henry H. Lancaster. With a prefatory notice by the Rev. B. Jowett. Edinburgh, Edmonston and Douglas, 1876.]

21. *Essays on Men and Manners* by the late Benjamin Jowett [etc.] edited by Philip Lyttelton Gell. Murray, 1895. See the *Note* on p. 432.

5. A new edition of *The Dialogues of Plato*, re-edited by D. J. Allan and H. E. Dale, was published in 4 vols. by the Clarendon Press in 1953.

APPENDIX III

Jowett Family Outline

(The black lettering indicates the Master of Balliol's two lines of descent.
R = Rector)

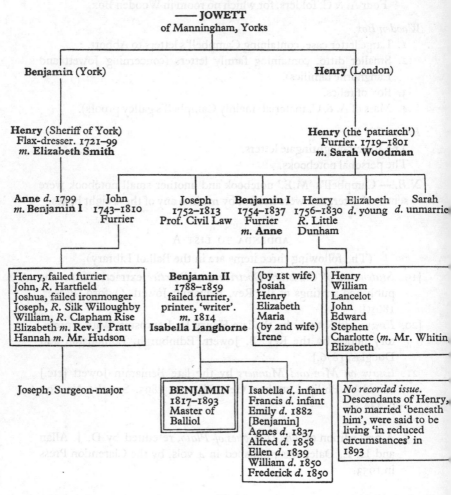

—— JOWETT
of Manningham, Yorks

Benjamin (York)

Henry (London)

Henry (Sheriff of York)
Flax-dresser. 1721–99
m. Elizabeth Smith

Henry (the 'patriarch')
Furrier. 1719–1801
m. Sarah Woodman

Anne d. 1799
m. Benjamin I

John
1743–1810
Furrier

Joseph
1752–1813
Prof. Civil Law

Benjamin I
1754–1837
Furrier
m. Anne

Henry
1756–1830
R. Little
Dunham

Elizabeth
d. young

Sarah
d. unmarried

Henry, failed furrier
John, R. Hartfield
Joshua, failed ironmonger
Joseph, R. Silk Willoughby
William, R. Clapham Rise
Elizabeth m. Rev. J. Pratt
Hannah m. Mr. Hudson

Benjamin II
1788–1859
failed furrier,
printer, 'writer'.
m. 1814
Isabella Langhorne

(by 1st wife)
Josiah
Henry
Elizabeth
Maria
(by 2nd wife)
Irene

Henry
William
Lancelot
John
Edward
Stephen
Charlotte (m. Mr. Whiting)
Elizabeth

Joseph, Surgeon-major

BENJAMIN
1817–1893
Master of
Balliol

Isabella d. infant
Francis d. infant
Emily d. 1882
[Benjamin]
Agnes d. 1837
Alfred d. 1858
Ellen d. 1839
William d. 1850
Frederick d. 1850

No recorded issue.
Descendants of Henry,
who married 'beneath
him', were said to be
living 'in reduced
circumstances' in
1893

No known issue

No issue

No known issue

442

Langhorne Family Outline

(The black lettering indicates the Master of Balliol's apparent line of descent.
R = Rector; V = Vicar.)

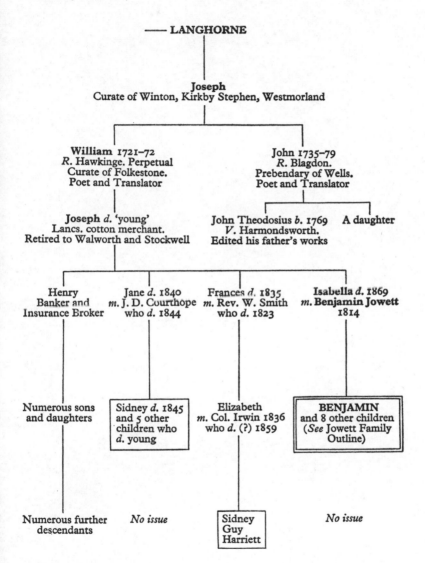

—— **LANGHORNE**

Joseph
Curate of Winton, Kirkby Stephen, Westmorland

William 1721–72
R. Hawkinge. Perpetual
Curate of Folkestone.
Poet and Translator

John 1735–79
R. Blagdon.
Prebendary of Wells.
Poet and Translator

Joseph d. 'young'
Lancs. cotton merchant.
Retired to Walworth and Stockwell

John Theodosius b. 1769
V. Harmondsworth.
Edited his father's works

A daughter

Henry
Banker and
Insurance Broker

Jane d. 1840
m. J. D. Courthope
who d. 1844

Frances d. 1835
m. Rev. W. Smith
who d. 1823

Isabella d. 1869
m. **Benjamin Jowett**
1814

Numerous sons
and daughters

Sidney d. 1845
and 5 other
children who
d. young

Elizabeth
m. Col. Irwin 1836
who d. (?) 1859

BENJAMIN
and 8 other children
(*See* Jowett Family
Outline)

Numerous further
descendants

No issue

Sidney
Guy
Harriett

No issue

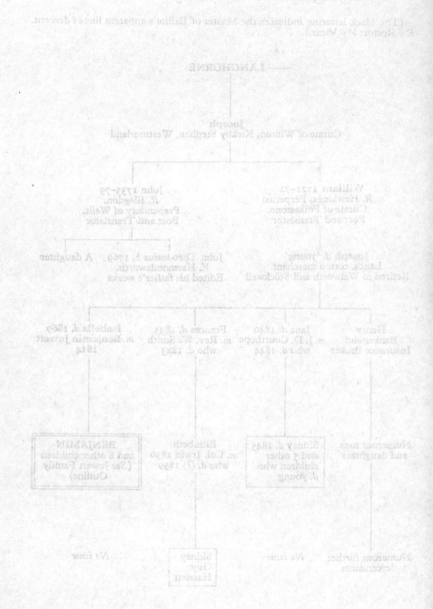

Index

448

449